Business and Economic Ethics

Business and Economic Ethics

The Ethics of Economic Systems

Arthur Rich

With an Introduction by Georges Enderle

PEETERS
LEUVEN – PARIS – DUDLEY, MA
2006

Library of Congress Cataloging-in-Publication Data

Rich, Arthur, 1910-
[Wirtschaftsethik. English]
Business and economic ethics : the ethics of economic systems / Arthur Rich with an introduction by Georges Enderle -- 4th ed.
p. cm.
Includes bibliographical references.
ISBN 90-429-1439-4 (alk. paper)
1. Christian ethics. 2. Economics--Moral and ethical aspects. I. Enderle, Georges. II. Title

BJ1253.R4613 2004
241'.64--dc22

2004041194

ISBN-10 90-429-1439-4
ISBN-13 9789042914391
D. 2004/0602/46

TABLE OF CONTENTS
VOLUME I: Foundations from a Theological Perspective

Foreword 5

Foreword to the Fourth Edition 7

I. Preliminary Questions 9

1. The Bi-Dimensionality of the Fundamental Ethical Question 11
2. Directions of Research and Main Schools of Thought in Ethics 17
   - 2.1 Directions of Research 17
     - 2.1.1 Descriptive Ethics 17
     - 2.1.2 Normative Ethics 19
     - 2.1.3 Metaethics 19
   - 2.2 Main Schools of Thought in Normative Ethics in their Internal Problematic 21
     - 2.2.1 Empiricist Ethics 21
     - 2.2.2 Norm or Principle Ethics 23
     - 2.2.3 Casuistic Ethics 25
     - 2.2.4 Situation Ethics 27
     - 2.2.5 The Ethics of Conviction 30
     - 2.2.6 The Ethics of Responsibility 31
   - 2.3 Preliminary Summary 34
3. Basic Aspects and Main Fields of the Ethical 37
   - 3.1 The Relationship Field of Ethics 37
     - 3.1.1 The First Basic Relationship: I-Self (The Individual Aspect) 38
     - 3.1.2 The Second Basic Relationship: I-Thou (The Personal Aspect) 38
     - 3.1.3 The Third Basic Relationship: I/We-It (The Ecological Aspect) 42
   - 3.2 The Basic Relationships in their Institutional Mediation 45

3.2.1 The Institutionalizing Effect in the I/We-It Relationship . . . 46
3.2.2 The Institutionalizing Effect in the I-Thou Relationship . . . 48
3.2.3 The Institutionalizing Effect in the I-Self Relationship . . . 50
3.3 The Main Aspects of Ethical Responsibility and their Integration in Social Ethics . . . 52
3.3.1 Individual Ethics . . . 53
3.3.2 Personal Ethics . . . 55
3.3.3 Environmental Ethics . . . 57
3.3.4 Social Ethics . . . 59
3.4 Business and Economic Ethics as a Special Case of Social Ethics . . . 61

II. Foundational Considerations . . . 63

4. Social Ethics in the Context of the Social Sciences . . . 65
4.1 The Relationship to the Social Sciences . . . 65
4.2 Economic Rationality and Human Justice . . . 70
4.3 The Problem of the Normative in the Social Sciences . . 76
4.3.1 The Natural Law Approach . . . 77
4.3.2 The Approach of Critical Theory . . . 80
4.3.3 The Approach of Critical Rationalism . . . 83
4.3.4 The Approach of Gerhard Weisser's Normative Social Science . . . 88
4.3.5 Conclusions . . . 93
4.4 Methodological Consequences . . . 95
5. Humanity originating from Faith, Hope, and Love . . . 99
5.1 The Horizon of General Human Experience Rooted in Faith, Hope, and Love . . . 99
5.2 The Experience of Evil . . . 102
5.3 The Experience of the Totally Other . . . 109
5.4 The Specifically Christian in the Humanity originating from Faith, Hope, and Love . . . 116
5.5 The Specifically Christian and the Generally Human in the Humanity originating from Faith, Hope, and Love . 121
6. The Theological Approach . . . 125
6.1 The Eschatological Dimension of the Humanity originating from Faith, Hope, and Love . . . 125

6.2 The Absolute and the Relative in the Problem Field of Theological Ethics 129
6.2.1 The Transcendental-Eschatological Approach (The Early Karl Barth) 130
6.2.2 The Creation-Theological Approach (Emil Brunner) 138
6.2.3 The Christological Approach (The Late Karl Barth) 147
6.2.4 The Historical-Theological Approach (Theology of Revolution or Liberation) 154
6.2.5 The Existential-Eschatological Approach (The New Way) 159
6.3 The Three Levels of Social-Ethical Argumentation . . . 167
7. Criteria of the Humanly Just and their Orientation towards Social Justice 169
7.1 The Basis of the Humanly Just 169
7.2 Explication of the Criteria of Human Justice 170
7.2.1 The Criterion of Creatureliness 170
7.2.2 The Criterion of Critical Distance 176
7.2.3 The Criterion of Relative Reception 178
7.2.4 The Criterion of Relationality 181
7.2.5 The Criterion of Fellow-Humanness 189
7.2.6 The Criterion of Fellow-Creatureliness 191
7.2.7 The Criterion of Participation 193
7.3 Human Justice Originating from Faith, Hope, and Love and Social Justice 198
7.3.1 The Criteria of Human Justice as Conditions of Social Justice 198
7.3.2 Social Justice as a Permanent Duty of the Hoping Love of Faith 199
7.3.3 John Rawls' Theory of Justice from the Perspective of the Criterial Requirements of Human Justice from Faith, Hope, and Love 204
7.3.4 Guidelines for Social Justice 214
8. Social-Ethical Maxims 221
8.1 The Formal Aspect of Maxims 221
8.2 The Principal Steps in the Formation of Maxims 223
8.2.1 Demonstration of the Problem 223
8.2.2 Examining Existing or Postulated Concepts of Analysis 224
8.2.3 Norm-Critical Clarifications 224
8.2.4 Determination of the Guidelines 225

8.2.5 Critical Examination 226
8.3 The Maxims' Claim to Validity 227
8.4 On Dealing with Biblical Maxims 232
8.5 The Distinctive Characteristic of Christian Social Ethics . 240

Bibliography 243

TABLE OF CONTENTS
VOLUME II: Market Economy, Planned Economy, and Global Economy from the Perspective of Social Ethics

Foreword 267

1. The Question of Meaning in the Economy 269
   1.1 The Ethical Dimension of the Question of Meaning in the Economy 269
   1.2 The Question of Meaning in the Economy as the Question of Human Justice in the Economy 273
   1.3 The Criteria of the Humanity Originating from Faith, Hope, and Love as Guidelines for Clarifying the Question of Meaning in the Economy 275
      1.3.1 The Fundamental Purpose of the Economy 275
      1.3.2 The Humane Purpose of the Economy 277
      1.3.3 The Social Purpose of the Economy 282
      1.3.4 The Ecological Purpose of the Economy 286
      1.3.5 The Relationality of the Purposes 290
      1.3.6 The Question of Meaning in the Economy within the Area of Tension between the Relative and the Absolute 295
2. Aspects and Perspectives of the Modern Industrial Economy 299
   2.1 What is the Economy? 299
   2.2 Industry and Industrialization 301
   2.3 The Process of Industrial Rationalization 305
      2.3.1 Rationalization as a Basic Phenomenon of the Economy 305
      2.3.2 Product-Oriented Division of Labor 306
      2.3.3 Production-Oriented Division of Labor 308
         2.3.3.1 Production-Oriented Division of Labor under the Conditions of Mechanically-Aided Rationalization 308

2.3.3.2 Production-Oriented Division of Labor under the Conditions of Electronically-Aided Rationalization . . . 314
2.3.3.3 Specific Effects and Possibilities in the Field of Production . . . 318
2.3.4 Socially and Economically Relevant Consequences of the Process of Industrial Rationalization for Human Persons . . . 326
2.4 The Factors of Production . . . 329
2.4.1 On the Taxonomy of Terminology . . . 329
2.4.2 An Overview of the Factors of Production . . . 331
2.4.2.1 The Factor of Land, or Nature . . . 331
2.4.2.2 The Factor of Labor . . . 333
2.4.2.3 The Factor of Capital . . . 337
2.4.3 The Question of Determining the Relationship between "Capital" and "Labor" . . . 340
2.5 Economic Subjects . . . 342
2.5.1 Producers . . . 342
2.5.2 Consumers . . . 348
2.5.3 The State . . . 351
2.6 Industrial Economy as the Economy of Markets . . . 355
2.6.1 The Concept and Morphology of the Market . . . 355
2.6.2 The Multiplicity and Borderless Expansion of Markets . . . 358
2.6.3 Multinationalization . . . 361
2.7 Economic Growth . . . 371
2.7.1 The Magnitude and Stimuli of Economic Growth . 371
2.7.2 Industrial Capitalism . . . 377
2.7.3 Quantitative and Qualitative Economic Growth . 380
2.8 The Double Face of the Industrial Economy . . . 384
3. An Analysis of the Principal Problems in Business and Economic Ethics . . . 389
3.1 Fundamental Questions of Economic Order . . . 389
3.2 Ethical Implications of the Three Fundamental Questions 390
3.2.1 Ethical Implications of the First Fundamental Question (What and how much should be produced?) 390
3.2.2 Ethical Implications of the Second Fundamental Question (How should goods and services be produced?) . . . 392

3.2.3 Ethical Implications of the Third Fundamental Question (For whom should goods and services be produced?) . 394
3.3 Principal Ethical Problems in View of the Question of Ordering the Economy 397
3.3.1 The Fundamental Problem 397
3.3.2 The Problem of Efficiency 398
3.3.3 The Problem of Human Justice in the Economy . 399
3.3.4 Human Justice from the Perspective of Fellow-Humanness 400
3.3.5 Human Justice from the Perspective of Participation 401
3.3.5.1 Participative Cooperation 402
3.3.5.2 Participative Distribution 404
3.3.5.3 A Participative Global Economy 416
3.3.6 Human Justice from the Perspective of Fellow-Creatureliness 420
3.3.6.1 Stabilization of Population 421
3.3.6.2 Stabilization of Demands 423
3.3.6.3 Stabilization of the Environment 424
3.3.7 Human Justice from the Perspective of Relationality 427
3.3.7.1 Relationality of the Basic Values 427
3.3.7.2 The Relationality of Human Justice and Economic Rationality 429
4. Basic Economic Systems 435
4.1 Preliminaries 435
4.1.1 Transition 435
4.1.2 "Economic System" and "Economic Order": Demarcation of Terminology 435
4.1.3 Theories of Economic Systems 436
4.2 The Basic System of the Market Economy 439
4.2.1 On the Concept of the Market Economy 439
4.2.2 The Coordination System of the Market Economy (Order through Competition) 441
4.2.2.1 The Basic Principle 441
4.2.2.2 The Economic Subject or Planner 441
4.2.2.3 Market-Economic Coordination 442
4.2.2.4 The Actually Existing Market Economy . 446
4.2.2.5 The Coordination Dilemma 452
4.2.3 The Limitations of the Market Economy 455
4.2.4 Relativization of the Market Economy 461

4.3 The Basic System of the Centrally Planned Economy . . 463
4.3.1 Terminology 463
4.3.2 Beginnings and First New Approaches of the Theory of Central Planning in Marxism-Leninism 463
4.3.3 The Coordination System of the Centrally Planned Economy (Order through Central Planning) . . . 469
4.3.3.1 The Basic Principle 469
4.3.3.2 State Collective Property and Central Planning 470
4.3.3.3 State Economy and Power Monopoly of the Communist Party 472
4.3.3.4 Economic Subject and Planner 473
4.3.3.5 Problems of Coordinating in the Centrally Planned Economy 474
4.3.4 The Limits of the Centrally Planned Economy . . 483
4.3.5 Relativization of the Centrally Planned System . 486
5. Evaluation and Decision Maxims for the System Question in the Economy 489
5.1 On the Concept of Maxims 489
5.2 Basic Considerations for Finding Maxims 490
5.2.1 Basic Considerations from the Perspective of Human Justice 490
5.2.1.1 Self-Interest and Common Good 491
5.2.1.2 Adam Smith's Concept of the Market Economy 492
5.2.1.3 Basic Conditions of the Reception of the System 496
5.2.2 Basis Considerations from the Perspective of Economic Rationality 498
5.2.2.1 The Question of the Convergence of the Decentralized Market System and the Centralized Planning System 498
5.2.2.2 Delimitation of the Relativization Principle of the Convergence Thesis 503
5.2.2.3 Fundamental Possibilities of Combining Market and Plan 505
5.2.2.4 Market Modification of the Planned Economy 506
5.2.2.5 The Plan-Modified Market Economy . . . 513
5.3 Maxims 520

6. Maxims for Evaluation and Decision-Making Regarding the Question of Order in Economic Systems 525
6.1 Preliminary Remarks 525
6.2 Categories of Order within the Market-Economy 526
6.2.1 The Capitalist Market Economy 526
6.2.2. The Social Market Economy 536
6.2.3 The Democratic Market Economy (The Swedish Model) 545
6.2.4 The Socialist Market Economy 554
6.2.4.1 The Western Type of the Socialist Market Economy 554
6.2.4.2 The Eastern Version of the Socialist Market Economy 559
6.2.5 Humanly Reformed Market Economy (Ota Šik's Human Economic Democracy) 565
6.2.5.1 Macro-Economic Plan of Distribution . . 566
6.2.5.2 Democratic Planning Decisions 568
6.2.5.3 Šik's Ownership Reform (Collaberative Companies) 570
6.2.5.4 Problems 575
6.2.6 The Ecologically Regulated Market Economy . . 579
6.2.6.1 The Fundamental Problem 579
6.2.6.2 The Ecology-Oriented Economy 581
6.2.6.3 Elements of an Ecology-Oriented Regulatory System of the Market Economy 583
6.2.6.4 Unanswered Questions 587
6.3 Some Basic Ideas about Finding Maxims Regarding the Problem of Order in the Economy 589
6.3.1 Some Basic Thoughts on the Aspect of Economic Rationality 590
6.3.2 Some Basic Reflections on What is Humanly Just . 594
6.3.2.1 Principal Issues 594
6.3.2.2 Weighing the Options 598
6.4. Maxims 612
7. The Global Economic Outlook 619
7.1 Preliminary Remarks 619
7.2 Global Challenges for the Market Economy 620
7.3 Basic Conditions for Participative Cooperation in the Global Economy 625
7.3.1 Participative Debt Redemption 625

7.3.2 Participative Market Order 631
7.3.3. Requirements for Developing Countries 633
7.3.3.1 Requirements with Regard to the Economic Efficiency of an Economic System 633
7.3.3.2 Requirements in View of the Social Efficiency of an Economic System 634
7.3.3.3 Requirements in View of the Ecological Efficiency of an Economic System 635
7.3.3.4 Order-Political Requirements 636
7.4 Global Economic Market Regulation: A Problem in Need of Solution 637
7.5 Maxims 641
8. Epilogue 645

Bibliography 653

INTRODUCTION TO ARTHUR RICH'S *BUSINESS AND ECONOMIC ETHICS*

Georges Enderle

After the fall of the Berlin wall and shortly before his death, Arthur Rich, in his self-critical and self-effacing way, asked me if his second volume of *Business and Economic Ethics* hadn't appeared too late. Despite serious ailment, he had worked very hard during his entire retirement age to complete his 650-page work. But then, the triumph of capitalism seemed to have answered the question of the ethics of economic systems once and for all. The answer I gave him at that time, that it wasn't too late indeed, has been confirmed and even more validated today, given the dramatic and continued socio-economic changes in many countries and at the global level as well. In the following I would like to emphasize several concerns elaborated in depth by Rich, but widely neglected by mainstream business ethics: the mediation of ethical reasoning and economic rationality, the contribution of Christian theology to business ethics, his focus on the ethics of economic systems and orders, and his development of maxims or guidelines for advancing the market economy at the national and global levels to become more just in human and environmental terms.

The mediation of ethical reasoning and economic rationality

In contrast to the early 1990s, business ethics and "corporate social responsibility" have become fashionable in the United States, in Europe, and in other parts of the world, not the least provoked by numerous business scandals. However, this appears to be a mixed blessing. Extensive rhetoric and quick-fix solutions often gloss over deeper-rooted problems. Business ethics seems to be an easy thing for business people: Just do the right thing and apply some basic moral principles to business! With the implicit pretension that ethical reasoning based on philosophical and theological traditions is irrelevant in today's business climate, a very simple notion of ethics and responsibility is invoked. To cut through these superficialities, Rich offers a concise and comprehensive understanding of ethics that can provide a firm basis to overcome the widespread moral confusion (see pages 9-62).

On the other hand, business ethics also seems to be an easy thing for those who have a rather rudimentary notion of business, often disconnected from economics. The terms of business and economics are left vague and may reflect a common split between business and economics, which, by the way, causes many difficulties in translating the term "business ethics" into other languages. In this view, ethics comes from "outside," and the field of application (i.e., the "inside") is irrelevant as long as the ethical values and principles are clearly stated and well argued for. In contrast, for Rich, a thorough understanding of business and economics is indispensable precisely from the applied-ethical point of view. He, therefore, extensively scrutinizes the field of application, in particular on pages 299-386 and 433-486.

Rich's systematic investigation of both the ethical and the economic dimension is already an exceptional scholarly achievement. But he does even more. Instead of falling into the trap of a "two-world" approach that separates the ethical from the economic, he succeeds in mediating both dimensions (which could be called a "two-legged" approach; see Enderle 2003). He establishes the fundamental proposition, valid at the level of maxims or guidelines for action, and develops it throughout his work:

"That which is not economically rational cannot really be humanly just; and that which contradicts human justice cannot really be economically rational." (pp. 74-75)

Hence the mediation consists of the interaction between two equally important viewpoints: the ethical or the humanly just and the economically rational, that is, in Rich's German terminology, "das Menschengerechte" and "das Sachgemässe." While the first term, meaning "to do justice to humanity," is straightforward, the second term has no precise equivalent in English. Literally, it says "in accordance with the matter." It means what is "objectively" required, based on theoretical knowledge and/or practical expertise of the field of the application of ethics. Given the context of business and economic ethics, we then usually translate "das Sachgemässe"with "the economically rational." (As for further translation issues, see the remarks below.)

The mediation of the ethical and the economic seems to be a very general and abstract notion. However, Rich consequently relates it to core concepts such as market, competition, economic efficiency, work, profit, property, economic growth, distribution, welfare, economic rationality, economic meaning, and economic orders. For instance, predatory competition is both ethically and economically wrong; economic efficiency must include total efficiency of the economy, nationally and globally; economic growth has to be environmentally sustainable; and economic orders need to be evaluated and judged according to both ethical and economic criteria. Rich develops the guidelines for action, or, as he calls them, the maxims for normative judgment and decision, "within, not outside, the economic contexts and their own logic" (p. 432). They constitute norms, the nature of which is prescriptive and explicative as well, and they have only a relative degree of certainty. At the level of maxims, business and economic ethics clearly comes from "within."

The contribution of Christian theology to business and economic ethics

What Christian theology can contribute to business and economic ethics is a controversial matter. Not only are there many different theologies under the Christian "umbrella," but, in most societies, they also have to face a pluralistic and secular environment. So, how can Christians come to grips with these challenges? If Christian ethical principles and values are dogmatically assumed and imposed, non-Christians cannot understand and reasonably embrace them. If, on the other extreme, one adopts a relativistic ethics, Christians are not able to accept such a position. And keeping silent on these matters is not a solution either since it contradicts intellectual honesty and is hardly feasible in the global context, in which Islam and other world religions cannot be silenced anymore.

In my view, Rich offers a well-grounded and sophisticated model to address these challenges convincingly. His theological perspective is based on the Christian experience of "faith, hope, and love," from which "humanity" originates. Although Rich does not speak of three divine virtues through which, according to Catholic theology, God's grace is essentially effective, the experience base is the same and can be shared by most Christian theologies. It is then interesting how

Rich relates this Christian experience to "the general human horizon of faith, hope, and love" (see pages 99-124). Similar to Karl Rahner's fundamental-theological approach (see *Hearer of the Word*, New York 1994), non-Christians also have an elementary understanding of faith, hope, and love. In the horizon of general human experience, faith, hope, and love are basic categories of human existence. From them originates humanity accessible to Christians and non-Christians alike. This humanity is challenged by the experience of the evil in personal and structural terms and of the totally other. What is specifically Christian does not lie in the substance of humanity, but in its deep rootedness in the event of Christ.

After a differentiated examination of several prominent Protestant theologies and the development of his own existential-eschatological approach, Rich then sets out to specify "humanity originating from faith, hope, and love" by elaborating seven criteria of human justice: creatureliness, critical distance, relative reception, relationality, fellow-humanness, fellow-creatureliness, and participation. They are norms of a purely prescriptive kind and express, with a definite experience-certitude, what must in principle be valid ethically, formally comparable with "basic matters of concern" or "fundamental value judgments." These criteria contain the normative foundation which permeates Rich's work in substantive and methodological respects. In particular, coming from "outside" of business and economics, they provide the normative input to the elaboration of the maxims for evaluation and decision making. Some of these maxims will be discussed below.

In sum, Rich's foundations of business and economic ethics from his Christian theological perspective are neither dogmatic nor relativistic. Based on careful theological and philosophical reasoning, they present firm normative-ethical guidance in a pluralistic and secular society. While strongly emphasizing the importance of reason for ethics in a "Catholic" fashion, he also stresses, in a "Protestant" manner, the reality of personal and structural evil and the transcending experience of the totally other. His discussion of Biblical maxims (on pages 232-240) reflects a deep familiarity with the Scriptures and aptly illustrates the meaning and relevance of maxims in general. Without exaggeration, Rich's dealing with theological, philosophical, and ethical issues can also serve as a model for scholarly work in business and economic ethics from other religious perspectives.

The focus on the ethics of economic systems and orders

As ethical issues in business and economics are widely discussed in public and in many business ethics textbooks, they focus on the ethical responsibilities of individual actors and business organizations, while the economic system in which they operate is taken for granted and not addressed in an explicit way. Such a limited view might be understandable as long as one is only interested in problems within a well-established business environment. After all, one does not have to see a mechanic if the car functions properly.

However, when business transcends the usual environment and goes global, it would be naive and also very costly to assume that the economic system in the foreign country is the same or of no concern. Despite globalization, there are considerable differences in how the economic system works between the United States, Europe, Japan, economies in transition, and developing countries. As a prominent example, take the People's Republic of China that claims to be a "socialist market economy with Chinese characteristics." To really understand the ethical challenges of business, one has no choice but to address the ethics of economic systems. Of course, this is particularly difficult in a process of transition (like in China or the global economy), in which one has, so to speak, to reconstruct a locomotive of a train that is in motion.

In his pioneering work Rich provides sophisticated analytical tools and sound ethical reasoning for dealing with the ethics of economic systems. To my knowledge, such a systematic and thorough approach is truly unique and hasn't been undertaken in the last fifty years. It grew out of a constellation of historical circumstances, two of which are especially relevant for our context. The first is a lesson the Christian churches in Germany learned from their ethical failures during the Nazi regime. Individual ethics, as strong as it may be, can never stem the flood of systemic forces. Therefore, systemic ethics or "social ethics" which pertains to the structures of social institutions must be addressed directly and extensively, as Rich does in his business and economic ethics conceived as a special case of social ethics. (It goes without saying that it has to be complemented by the ethics of organizational actors, including companies, parties, and churches, as well as individual ethics.) The second historical fact relates to the co-existence of two opposing economic systems in the same country of Germany over 40 years: the Social Market Economy and the Centrally-Planned Socialist Economy. This "competition" was on the mind of many observers in continental Europe and lead to widespread discussions about the ethical quality of economic systems. Against this backdrop, Rich developed his own approach to business and economic ethics, first in writings such as *Co-Determination in Industry* (1973) and the article "Factual Constraints and the Structural Evil in the Economy" (1982) and then systematically in this monograph of 1984/1990. His focus on systemic ethics is a reminder against the current overestimation of individual and organizational ethics and his distinction between (basic) economic systems and (more concrete) economic orders helps clarify the often vague and misleading rhetoric of "capitalism" and encourages "competition" among different economic orders.

Maxims for evaluation and decision making

As indicated above, maxims constitute norms, the nature of which is prescriptive and explicative as well. They are determined by the seven criteria of human justice on the one hand and by economic rationality or what is "objectively" required on the basis of theoretical knowledge and practical expertise in business and economics on the other hand. Unlike the criteria which have experience-certitude, the maxims are only of a relative degree of certainty and thus changeable in accordance with the ethical criteria and economic rationality. Rich developed a number of maxims regarding the system question in the economy (see pages 518-521), the option of the economic order (see pages 610-616) and the global economic market regulation (see pages 639-642). But, given the limited scope of this introduction, only a few maxims can be mentioned here.

With regard to the basic, constitutive economic system, both the market economy and the centrally planned economy can be accepted only relatively from the standpoint of the humanity originating from faith, hope, and love. For the first system does not account sufficiently for the general interests while the second system is deficient with respect to individual interests. Moreover, since the centrally planned economy, in contrast to the market system, cannot really be relativized, the order-political option turns out in favor of the market economy as the basic system. However, this option does not yet amount to a decision for one of the order forms of the market economy that actually exists or is in the process of becoming. Rather, alternative order possibilities on the basis of the market principle are to be examined.

Regarding the order form of the market economy, an institutionalized regulatory device is needed that permits legitimate individual interests the necessary amount of free play that benefits economic efficiency, but also regulates them in a manner that primarily emphasizes general interests. The standpoint of humanity in the defined sense entails that the subsidiary regulatory system orients itself towards the criteria of the humanly just and the meaningful purposes of the economy, which are consistent with these criteria and specified in a number of goals for the market economy. In light of these normative requirements, a reform of the traditional market economy is necessary. While the "capitalist" or libertarian form of the market economy has to be rejected, the social market economy is acceptable, but needs continuous, on-going development in terms of humanization of working conditions and environmental regulations. This allows for various possible options.

With respect to the global economy, Rich recognizes the emerging web of complex interdependencies that makes international cooperation among individual national economies indispensable. However, drastic economic imbalances between "the North and the South" exist, which, as experience shows, cannot be corrected by the market economy left on its own. Therefore, the confrontational structure of international economic relations needs to be changed to an equitable and participatory structure by regulatory and enforceable measures. This means the creation of general conditions that will enable developing countries to eventually catch up with the competition from their industrialized counterparts. Although Rich wrote his global economic outlook in the late 1980s, his sharp observations and clear normative demands have proved even more relevant today. Debt relief for developing countries, fair prices of raw materials, removal of protectionist trade barriers in industrialized countries, sustainable environmental policies, and the living rights of the poorest of the poor remain with increasing urgency on the global agenda for the years to come.

Concluding remarks on the difficulties, advantages, and importance of this translation

The translation of Arthur Rich's masterpiece *Business and Economic Ethics* into English was a major undertaking which took many more years than we had expected at its inception in 1993. The length of 650-plus pages, the terminologies of philosophy, theology, economics, business, and other social sciences, and the often complicated written style with occasional old-fashioned vocabulary compounded the difficulties common to any translation. In addition to this came the time-consuming verification of the publicized English translations of authors such as Aristotle, Karl Barth, Emil Brunner, Martin Buber, Friedrich Engels, Immanuel Kant, W. I. Lenin, Konrad Lorenz, Karl Marx, Joseph Schumpeter, Gerhard von Rad, and Max Weber. A number of key German terms were particularly difficult to translate: *das Menschengerechte* (the humanly just), *das Sachgemässe* (what is "objectively" required on the basis of theoretical knowledge and practical expertise of, say, business and economics), *die Wirtschaftsethik* and *wirtschaftsethisch* (the ethics of the economic sphere of life, of business and economics), *Humanität aus Glaube, Hoffnung und Liebe* (humanity originating from or rooted in faith, hope, and love), *der allgemeinmenschliche Erfahrungshorizont* (the horizon of general human experience), *Geschöpflichkeit* (creatureliness), *Mitmenschlichkeit* (fellow-humanness), *Mitgeschöpflichkeit* (fellow-creatureliness), *Ich-Du/Ihr* (I-Though as one-one or one-many relationships), *Zuspruch* and *Anspruch* (comfort and demand of the kingdom of God), *Zukunft* and *Zu-kunft* (future and advent), *schützenswerte Güter* (intrinsic goods), *Aufhebung* in the Hegelian sense (sublation), Max Weber's term *Gesinnungsethik* (ethics of conviction), *sozialer Ausgleich* (social balance), *liberal* (sometimes liberal, sometimes libertarian), *Erwerbseigentum* (business ownership), and *Erwerbskapital* (capital stock).

However, translating is not only a painstaking and tedious process, required for the sake of accuracy in thinking and writing and expected out of fidelity to the author. It is also fascinating and creative, considerably deepening the understanding of the text by exposing it to two different worlds of language and culture. It would be greatly rewarding if, as in the case of Kant's writings, Rich's *Business and Economic Ethics* turned out to be even more readable in English than in German. In any event, the door to Rich's masterpiece is now open to the English-speaking world. In my view, it is an important step of internationalizing business ethics. For sure, Rich's work has not arrived too late; its time has only come.

To conclude, I would like to express my gratitude to all those who contributed, in different ways, to open this door. First of all, my thanks go to Mrs. Elisabeth Rich-Schneider, the wife of the late

Arthur Rich, their family, Siegfried Karg, the Emil-Brunner Foundation, and the Church Councils of the Cantons of Schaffhausen and Zurich for their moral and financial support over all the years. I especially thank David W. Lutz who translated the lion's share of this work with long-lasting dedication, sensitivity and accuracy and Albert Wimmer who readily stepped in to complete the translation. I am also very grateful to Peeters Publishers in Leuven, Belgium, for the careful layout and printing and the continuous support. May this ground breaking work help us to better understand and fulfill our ethical responsibilities in economic life.

Reference

Enderle, Georges. "Business Ethics." In: Bunnin, N., Tsui-James, E. P. (eds.) *The Blackwell Companion to Philosophy*. Second edition. Oxford: Blackwell Publishers, 2003, pp. 531-551.

ARTHUR RICH,
BUSINESS AND ECONOMIC ETHICS

VOLUME I:
Foundations from a Theological Perspective

Translated by David W. Lutz
in Collaboration with Georges Enderle

To Heinz-Dietrich Wendland,
Trailblazer, Colleague, and Friend

FOREWORD

The objective of this book is to lay the foundation of business and economic ethics from a theological perspective. The original intention was to unite both the principal theoretical reflections and their concretization in a single volume by dealing with the problem of the economic order. But as the difficulty of the project caused the text to lengthen, it proved advisable to publish separately the theological foundation of economic ethics as it appeared in the development of my own approach to social ethics. Meanwhile, the continuation of the entire work will follow as quickly as possible.

Heinz-Dietrich Wendland has recently reminded us that "in the Protestant social tradition, and in theological social ethics concerned with economic ethics, there exists a giant hole." In fact, the first and thus far only theory of Protestant business and economic ethics in the German-speaking region, that of Georg Wünsch, dates from 1927. An advance in this area was therefore overdue. It would certainly be arrogant to suggest that my attempt could already close the aforementioned hole. That cannot possibly be accomplished today by a single person.

What I will attempt is a contribution to the clarification of the theological and economic foundations of a theory of Protestant business and economic ethics that is relevant to the present situation. Thus, in both this volume and the projected sequel, one will not find a summary of information in the foreground, but rather the foundation of ethically informed competence of judgment. What criteria for judgments and decisions in situations relevant to business and economic ethics can meet both the standards of human justice rooted in faith, hope, and love and those of economic rationality?

I am fully aware of the difficulty of this project. I am encouraged to undertake it, however, by the echo that my earlier work in the area of social ethics found, as well as by the response that my lecture notes on the fundamental questions of business and economic ethics received. I am also motivated, pressed from different directions, to present in some unity my social-ethical approach, which has developed gradually through long work with important particular questions, and to test its usefulness for tackling central problems of business and economic ethics. The latter, of course, will not be possible until the second volume.

The individual sections begin, as a rule, with a suggestion of works that can supplement or critically continue the section. The selection, which had to be kept within limits, was not easy and, because it was definitely subjective, could have turned out differently.

At this point, I would like to thank those who made possible the writing and publication of this book. In the first place, I am thinking of the many interlocutors in the theological, ecclesial, social-scientific, and last but not least business and economic camps, who have helped me very much through stimulation, instruction, and critique. I am also grateful for the spontaneous and helpful assistance of Ina Praetorius with the proofreading. I am especially obliged to my part-time assistant Siegfried Karg, B.D./Th.M. His conscientious, precise, and painstaking collaboration was very helpful to me above all in obtaining literature, formatting the text, checking quotations, and producing the indices. The project was made possible by the generous financial support of the Swiss National Science Foundation. Furthermore, the Association of Higher Education in the Canton of Zürich assisted with a substantial contribution to the printing costs of this book. A well-deserved thanks is expressed to both of these institutions.

Zürich, August 1984 *Arthur Rich*

FOREWORD TO THE FOURTH EDITION

The first volume of this work operates at the level of principles. It presents a theologically grounded approach to reaching ethical judgments and decisions that relates the normative to the economically rational and can serve as the foundation of a substantive dialogue between ethics and economics. The fact that this endeavor received enough attention — not only in theology and economics, but also with a broader audience — that a fourth edition is already possible, fills the author with joy and thankfulness.

Critics have noted on various occasions that concrete ethical problems are discussed only peripherally in this book, and thus remain in the region of abstract principles and, consequently, that of the non-obligatory. In the meantime, the second volume appeared, with the objective of concretizing the approach and the practical testing of it with the help of the coordination problem in economics. It seeks to provide evidence that with controversial, fundamental, economic questions the stringent, real-world humanity originating from faith, hope, and love can achieve normative judgment and decision maxims that accept responsibility for the claims of both human justice and economic rationality, and that avoid absolute, doctrinaire assertions just as they avoid unprincipled, relativistic permissiveness. The two volumes thus belong together and can be best understood as a unit.

Zürich, Autumn 1990 *Arthur Rich*

I. PRELIMINARY QUESTIONS

1. THE BI-DIMENSIONALITY OF THE FUNDAMENTAL ETHICAL QUESTION

The term "ethics" is derived from the Greek word "*ethos*."[1] It originally meant "usual seat," then the place where one lives and thus is at home. From that the abstract use of "*ethos*" in the sense of "habit," "convention," "tradition," and finally "custom" can be understood. In this way, "*ethos*" acquired the meaning of morally appropriate conduct that conforms to what has become the norm or law in one's own home and region of life through habit, tradition, and convention. In fact, ethics always has something to do with that,[2] but not merely with that.

The Greek word "*ethos*" was given early on — for the first time with Socrates — a totally different meaning: instead of habitual conduct, it came to mean that which I *should do* based on my reasoned insight and thus in accordance with my convictions.[3] "*Ethos*" in the sense of custom and convention is a traditional and thus socially inherited norm-good, which can condition human conduct similarly to the way biologically determined instincts and behavioral mechanisms condition the behavior of animals.[4] "Ethos" in the sense of "you shall," and this means, succinctly, in the sense of a categorical

[1] Strictly speaking, this word occurs in two forms. In addition to ἔθος, there is the synonymous ἦθος, which is distinguished only by the lengthening of the first vowel.

[2] According to Aristotle, "moral virtue comes about as a result of habit, whence also its name ἠθικός is one that is formed by a slight variation from the word habit ἔθος or ἦθος" (*Nicomachean Ethics*, II, 1, 1103a, trans. W. D. Ross, in Richard McKeon, ed., *The Basic Works of Aristotle*, New York, 1941, p. 952).

[3] An aftereffect of this Socratic differentiation is the Aristotelian distinction between "dianoetical" (intellectual) and "ethical" (moral) virtues (*Nicomachean Ethics*, I, 13, 1103a).

[4] See Konrad Lorenz, *On Aggression*, trans. Marjorie K. Wilson, New York, 1966, especially pp. 109-38 ("Behavioral Analogies to Morality") and pp. 165-219 ("The Bond"). As the upshot of his research, Lorenz writes that we can speak of "the social behavior patterns of higher animals which are analogous with those of man" (p. 219).

imperative, however, is of a totally different kind. This is ultimately about a demand to which one does not become accustomed by growing up in society, which seeks instead to call one out from the customary and, in contrast to merely conventional "law," seeks to challenge one to a new manner of conduct. When that happens, ethos is opposed to ethos, that which *I should do* to that which *one does*, conscience to convention. And this leads inevitably to a crisis of morals, of morals as the quintessence of customs and conventions, as the code of conventional values. Indeed, this leads to a crisis of morals, not from immorality, but from morality. More precisely, this leads to a crisis from ethics, for which the ethical is not something given once and for all, in which one can accustom oneself in a conformist way, but is instead a charge that demands, absolutely demands, and thus compels one to ask in a nonconformist manner, above and beyond prevailing customs and prevailing laws, about the good and the right, here and now. The ethical question makes itself known only in questions that are distressed in this way, because they lead to inner unrest. This is about a question that human persons, at least alert and attentive persons, can never avoid, no matter how much they attempt to safeguard themselves from its grasp, whether by morality or by immorality.[5]

The ethical question in its true nature is thus a question about the *good* and the *right*, which is more than morals, customs, and civic legality. In other words, it turns out to be a question about absolute demand, as opposed to merely limited demands, as they are articulated in morality, custom, and law. Wherever the ethical question breaks through in its absoluteness, this opposition is also present. This opposition of morality and legality is probably best known with Kant.[6] Also Pascal's aphorism, "True morality has no time for morality,"[7] makes the same point as Jesus' saying: "If your righteousness is not greater than that of the Scribes and Pharisees, you will not

[5] Emil Brunner persuasively addresses the impossibility of evading the question of the good: *The Divine Imperative*, trans. Olive Wyon, Philadelphia, 1947, pp. 17-20.

[6] Immanuel Kant, *The Metaphysical Elements of Justice; Part I of The Metaphysics of Morals*, trans. John Ladd, New York, 1985, p. 19: "The mere agreement or disagreement of an action with the law, without regard to the incentive of the action, is called *legality;* but, when the Idea of duty arising from the law is at the same time the incentive of the action, then the agreement is called the *morality* of the action."

[7] Pascal, Blaise, *Pensées*, Frg. 4, trans. A. J. Krailsheimer, Harmondsworth, 1966, p. 212.

enter the Kingdom of God."[8] In all of these passages, ethos is opposed to ethos, the ethos of the absolute against the ethos of the merely qualified, the true law against the law that gained acceptance historically and that can, as mere legality, become unjust or conceal injustice. This ethos is essentially dangerous, because it is revolutionary. It is no coincidence that Socrates, the first person really to raise the fundamental ethical question, was suspected by his countrymen of being a subversive and finally was sentenced to death by the cup of poison.

The basic ethical question is, however, a dangerous question not only because it can lead, by virtue of its tendency to nonconformism, those who really take it seriously into difficulty, especially political difficulty. It is also a dangerous question because it can easily lead astray unclear minds into sheer contempt for morality, custom, right, etc. and thus, in extremis, can evoke a nihilism of values or laws. Socrates also saw this other danger in the basic ethical question. Plato showed this in his short but important dialogue *Crito*.[9]

In that dialogue Socrates argues with his friend Crito, who wishes to save the philosopher, who has been sentenced to death by his judges in the exercise of their legal authority, by persuading him to save himself by fleeing illegally from imprisonment. Although Socrates sees injustice in his conviction, he, contrary to all expectation, does not want to get involved in this comfortable escape. And why not? Because he cannot unhesitatingly play off his ethos of reason or conscience, and thus the higher right, against the legal-right and its legitimate implementer. For that would mean ruining the laws as the legal basis of a political community of citizens in a state, concretely in the city-state of Athens, and thus leaving it to the mercy of chaotic anarchy. "Who would like to live in a city without laws?" he asks in reply. He means by that: we cannot do without laws, in which the justice and the morals currently in force are objectified. That would be possible only if everyone let themselves be led by free pieces of the ethics of reason, of the demand of the absolutely just. Because this prerequisite is never in existence, however, laws are necessary and may not simply be ignored, even if they cannot at all continue to exist before the demand of the absolute, and thus give cause

[8] Matthew 5,20.

[9] Plato, "Crito," trans. Hugh Tredennick, in Edith Hamilton and Huntington Cairns, eds., *The Collected Dialogues of Plato*, New York, 1961, pp. 27-39.

for ethical conflicts. If one believed otherwise, the always-necessary critique, just rehearsed by Socrates, of the conventional tradition-good of moral, justice, and law would have to descend into social-political destruction. Therefore, the Athenian philosopher tells his friend and student Crito: "A destroyer of laws might very well be supposed to have a destructive influence upon young and foolish human beings."[10] And with that a wider dimension comes into view, which may not be ignored in defining the basic ethical question, and thus what ethics really means.

The basic ethical question was characterized just now as the question about the good or the just, which is more than morals, more than customary law, and more than civic legality. Now, however, it must be understood above and beyond that, as has already been encountered with Socrates, as the question to what extent this good and right that is always merely qualified also has meaning for the obligated person who understand himself to be obligated by ethos in its absoluteness. In other words, discussion of the fundamental ethical question is not only concerned with the critique of the relative before the demand of the absolute; it is also about holding onto the law of the relative during genuine interactions with the absolute, without trivializing or completely hiding the difference between the relative and the absolute.[11] The basic ethical question is consequently two-dimensional, not merely one-dimensional. In other words, when it is concrete, it is always a question to which there is no definite, straightforward, and conflict-harmonizing answer, with which one could come to rest.

Anyone who, touched by the demand of the absolute, has ever stood before a difficult ethical decision and has not avoided it, either moralistically or anti-moralistically, knows the secret unrest that overcomes one precisely when one responsibly faces the question of the genuine good and just. In borderline cases, what Nikolai Gogol groaned in agonizing pain may also not be avoided: "Sadness overcomes my soul, because I am not able to see the good in the good." I myself know of conscientious objectors, who were driven to their actions by the most inner urgings, without thereby simply having a "good conscience," but instead suffering from having to violate the

[10] *Ibid.*, 53a-c.

[11] Zwingli deserves credit for having seen this problem clearly and for reflecting upon it with theological precision. See the discussion on pp. 227-30.

legal order of their country and thus unable to see the good in the good that this legal order, according to its social function, also seeks. Ethics, understood as conscious and reflective interaction with the basic ethical question, does not lead to a soothed conscience. It instead maintains the conscience in restlessness and continually urges it to ask, above and beyond "morals," "right," and "law," about the true good and just, without thoughtlessly and frivolously disregarding the good in morals and law, to which the ethos of ethics always also refers. And in that ultimately can be found the reason conscientious ethics can never be presented as a finished, self-contained, and conclusive system of values, able to offer the finished prescription for action. It is and remains a task that never ends, a question that one cannot pacify with any definitive answer, and that therefore reminds us that we must urgently accept responsibility for the good, for which we wish to be accountable in the conflict-filled society of today.

2. DIRECTIONS OF RESEARCH AND MAIN SCHOOLS OF THOUGHT IN ETHICS

2.1 Directions of Research

Depending upon what one is interested in discovering, three different fundamental schools of research in ethics can be distinguished: *descriptive ethics, normative ethics,* and *metaethics*. Descriptive ethics is concerned with the ethical as empirical fact, normative ethics with the ethical as obligatory, and metaethics with philosophical clarification of the presuppositions of ethical judgments. If these research directions of ethics are presented only briefly here — the same goes for the main schools of thought — this is done simply to call attention to certain problems that are tackled for the project of definition.

2.1.1 *Descriptive Ethics*

The objective of descriptive ethics or the science of morality is to describe the ethical as precisely as possible in its various culturally dependent expressions and with its related instructions for action. Because it restricts itself to this, it functions as a strictly empirical discipline. It is concerned with ascertaining descriptively what ethically "is," more precisely, what counts as "moral" or "unmoral" for certain ethnic groups, nations, and cultures or social groups, levels, and classes, etc., and what consequences this has in cultural contexts. It is also concerned with showing which factors are involved in changes of moral concepts, or which biological, psychological, and sociological basic conditions underlie certain processes of actions. Through this primary research interest, descriptive ethics coincides closely with *ethology* as the science that deals with the customs and habits of a people, on the one hand, and with the behavior of animals, on the other hand. Since this is true, its method corresponds to a great extent with that of the natural sciences. And this is the reason many people are willing to grant truth-content only to this direction of ethical research. But this is based upon positivistic prejudice, with its reduction of the real to causally explainable "facts." It is, of course, not disputed that descriptive ethics has truth-content. It is epistemologically significant when one is concerned with ascertaining the biological, sociological, psychological, and cultural-historical conditions of existing ethical behavior, especially of existing ethical behavior in the sense of customs, habits, legality, etc. These conditions certainly exist, and any theory of ethics that tries to ignore them will become blind to reality. For this reason, descriptive ethics belongs indispensably to the complete discipline of ethics.

Descriptive ethics becomes problematic, however, when it attempts to understand the relative nature of existing ethical behavior deterministically, above and beyond that which is descriptive and determinable, analogously to mechanistic behavior-processes. In that case, there is no room for ethics understood as the demand of the absolute, as ethical obligation, which presupposes freedom of decision. This ethics is also reality, however, and indeed, reality that can be experienced. Again and again people understand themselves to be challenged to break out of the habitual, the conditioned, that "which one does," and to dare the unusual, and thus to revolutionize previous behavior and to set previously non-customary standards. One thinks of Francis of Assisi, who, as a member of a rich family, showed his solidarity with the poor of his day; of Elisabeth of Thuringia, who, as a princess, cared for the sick, for whom no one else cared; of Heinrich Pestalozzi, who, while still an adolescent, opposed a corrupt governor from the nobility of his home city, thereby putting his civic future at risk; and also of Karl Marx and Friedrich Engels, who, contrary to their own class in society, became advocates of the proletariat. The same goes for many others, who have no name, but like their famous companions, followed the voice of the uncustomary. They all behaved inconsistently with the familial, social, and cultural requirements under which they had been raised. These are also "facts," facts that can be ascertained in a thoroughly descriptive manner, but that can never be explained deterministically, no matter how refined a social-cultural or biological theory one uses. This is about another dimension, the dimension of the truly ethical or normatively-obligatory, which eludes every casual method of clarification in the sense of deterministic schemes. Normative ethics is rooted in this basic experience.

2.1.2 *Normative Ethics*

Normative ethics is understood here, in contrast to descriptive ethics, as the research direction that, instead of addressing the phenomenon of ethics from the viewpoint of how human conduct actually is manifested, evaluates it according to *how human persons should act*. The normative always refers to what should be, not to what is. It points out that which is authoritative, guiding, obligatory, and consequently, valid and binding. In other words, it does not state why a person acts one way and not another, but rather why one should act one way and not another. Of course norms also show motives or grounds of conduct that determine action, but not in a causal-deterministic way, rather in a *final* way that sets goals for actions and obligates towards them. And, of course, they can also secondarily become mere habits, "second nature," as it was once called, elements of the "super-ego," as we are now in the habit of saying. As such they then have, for the most part unconsciously, a compelling and in this respect causing character. Norms of the conscious or reflective life, which has been awakened from a vague "one must" to a bright "I shall," are, however, of a completely different, final kind. They establish goals that do not compel the acting person, but expect something of him that one can deliberately and willfully violate. Because this is about the ethical at its true core, any form of ethics that does not fail itself is always encountered in the mode of the normative, though without ultimately becoming absorbed in it. In so far as that is the case, all ethics has a normative structure, not just normative ethics. For no theory of ethics can avoid asking about the basis and the knowledge of the normative as the motive of ethically responsible action. Depending upon how this fundamental question is answered, different basic forms of normative ethics arise. They must be brought more closely into view in their inner problematic. But first a hint of metaethics is necessary.

2.1.3 *Metaethics*

Metaethics — the word is a new linguistic entity — is a research direction that has arisen recently, primarily in the Anglo-American linguistic area, and that can be characterized in analogy to so-called metatheory. While the formulation of theory is about the conception of a system that consistently follows its immanent presuppositions, without calling them into question, metatheory is about the critical analysis of a system and its immanent conditions. Metaethics has an analogous function. While normative ethics starts out from the obligatory, in order then to reach definite consequences of actions as consistently as possible, whether with inclusion or exclusion of the social-historical context, metaethics is primarily concerned with critical analysis of and reflection on language, which can have as its goal the semantic meaning of basic moral concepts like "should," "good," "right," etc., but also the formal-logical correctness or incorrectness of ethical judgments in general. A sharp demarcation from the two previously mentioned research directions, especially from normative ethics, is thus impossible. There are, on the contrary, many areas of overlap. In brief, it can be said that metaethics, in contrast to normative directions of research, has nothing to do with establishing fundamental moral principles or specific objectives of actions. It restricts itself to analyzing the logical structure of ethical concepts and propositions, which is why metaethics is also called *analytic ethics*. It must still be noted that in the area of normative ethics, thinking first of all of Kant and Aristotle, there already exist problems of language that have a specifically metaethical character.

It can be added that there are various schools of thought within the domain of metaethics, of which noncognitivism and cognitivism deserve special attention in view of this discussion. *Noncognitivism* challenges the possibility of scientific-objective knowledge in the sphere of the moral, thereby presupposing the theory of logical positivism, whose criteria of truth are based upon logical-mathematical proof or verification by observation and experiment. *Cognitivism*, on the other hand, maintains the in-principle cognizability of the moral. It is not a unified approach, but is itself split into naturalism and intuitionism.

The naturalist variant of cognitivism is closely related to descriptive ethics, in that it equates particular empirical predicates, for instance "useful," with normative determinations, for instance "good," and thus reinterprets the descriptive as prescriptive. This way of equating concepts with each other rests in turn, in the opinion of intuitionists, on a "naturalistic fallacy,"[1] which is inadmissible. They maintain, in contrast, that foundational ethical concepts and judgments are non-derivative, because they are self-evident and in

[1] See note 5 below.

this respect accessible, if not to empirical-scientific discovery, nevertheless to intuitive discovery with its own kind of certainty. But this raises the question whether there are adequate criteria to make possible a distinction between true and false feelings or intuitions.

From what has been said it is clear that metaethics, with its critical reflection and analysis of normative ethics that remains in the sphere of the formal and logical, can never replace the latter. If it seemed for some time that metaethics wanted to push normative ethics into the background, many of its prominent advocates, such as William K. Frankena, have recently ascertained "a return to normative ethics."[2] Ethical thought, if it wishes to avoid remaining in the realm of the formal, abstract, and ultimately non-obligatory, which would mean the elimination of real ethics, cannot avoid the question of the normative and its concrete determinability. And that is why normative ethics retains its central importance.

2.2 Main Schools of Thought in Normative Ethics in their Internal Problematic

The concept of normative ethics, as has already been intimated above, will intentionally be understood very broadly here. It includes all ethical approaches that reflect in any way the basis and knowledge of that which should be done, even if they do not formulate strong norms with definite content. At this point only the most significant schools of thought in normative ethics will be presented, and only briefly.

2.2.1 *Empiricist Ethics*

If one understands the concept of normative ethics in the intended breadth, it also includes the *empiricist founding of morals*. To be sure, this classification may at first appear contradictory, because there exists a close relationship between empiricist and descriptive ethics. What connects the two, almost to the point of indistinguishability, is the common empirical basis. Empiricist ethics also wishes, according

[2] Norbert Hoerster, Foreword to William K. Frankena, *Analytische Ethik: Eine Einführung*, Munich, 1972 (German translation of *Ethics*, Englewood Cliffs, 1963), p. 14.

to its basic intention, to be empirical science, and thus to determine the moral descriptively as a being or actually existing thing, as so-called "moral statistics"[3] does in a classical way. Nevertheless, it goes completely above and beyond the purely descriptive, by elevating a particular, empirically describable and as a rule statistically verifiable behavior, for instance that one normally pursues one's economic utility, to the level of an ethical value, and giving it normative power. This means, in plain language, the *normativeness of the factual*.

It is difficult to deny that in everyday experience certain basic attitudes and ways of conduct are frequently justified ethically by reference to the actual behavior of a large number of persons. That has been and is especially common in the area of business and economics. Because human persons seek their own economic utility as a rule, classical economics spoke bluntly of "*homo oeconomicus*." They meant by that not only that human persons as a rule pursue their economic utility in their economic behavior, whether as producers or as consumers, but that they also should pursue it, because doing so would be economically rational. In addition, it cannot be overlooked that there are, especially again in the area of business and economics, conditions or facts — "factual constraints," as one likes to say today — on which the setting of normative objectives and their realizability are dependent. In view above all of this fact, one cannot deny the empiricist way of examination and judgment its relative right.

That notwithstanding, empiricist ethics is based upon a fundamental logical mistake. No "ought," and thus no ethical norm, can be derived logically from the factual as "is." If experience shows — to remain with the above example — that we generally seek our own advantage in our economic behavior, one can probably draw the conclusion that we behave self-interestedly for the most part, but not that we *should* behave self-interestedly.[4] Since the time of metaethicist

[3] Moral-statistical methods are used in, for example, the Kinsey Reports (Alfred C. Kinsey, *et al.*, *Sexual Behavior in the Human Male*, Philadelphia, 1948 and *Sexual Behavior in the Human Female*, Philadelphia, 1953).

[4] See Henner Kleinewefers, "Rationalität und ökonomisches Normalverhalten," Pub. No. 7 of the Institute of Economics and Social Sciences of the University of Fribourg, 1981, p. 11. He asserts with justification that the term "economic" or "rational" behavior suggests exclusiveness and thus recommends speaking "of 'average economic behavior' in the sense of the average behavior of empirically observable agents."

G. E. Moore, such a conclusion has correctly been called a "naturalistic fallacy."[5] Whenever descriptive is-statements are translated into normative ought-statements, hidden values are always already involved. Not only is "*homo oeconomicus*" concerned about his personal utility, he also acts, according to the judgment of the empiricist, "rationally," that is, as one should act, because he owes it to himself to act "reasonably." The economic-utility way of thinking, which is close to economic egoism, is thus understood here *a priori*, though not openly, as a normative value. In this way empiricist ethics proves to be a secret variety of norm ethics.

2.2.2 *Norm or Principle Ethics*

Norm ethics is understood as the approach that sees the normative as established in certain principles that tend towards absoluteness, and that lead to absolutely valid norms or precepts or prohibitions. In so far as such norms can be reduced to a single moral principle — there can be several of them, only in that case they must converge — a normative system emerges that is coherent in itself, and that ideally is independent of empirical knowledge and situations, and is also timeless, and consequently universally valid. For this reason, norm ethics and normative ethics are often equated, which however in my opinion contains an understanding of the normative that is too narrow.

Thus norm or principle ethics, in contrast to the empiricist grounding of ethics, does not see in the norms any values that are related to experience because they are oriented towards the actual behavior of persons in their predetermined cultures and time periods, but instead precepts whose validity is indubitably certain, whether or not they are followed. Thus, for instance, the *demand of truthfulness* is a norm of indisputable validity, although experientially there is hardly anyone who has never in his life lied and although concrete cases are possible in which doctrinaire truthfulness necessarily causes harm. In this way, the norms receive the character of a kind of in principle "law," which one can indeed culpably violate, but can never render invalid.

Depending upon the establishment or choice of the highest moral principles, various types of norm ethics emerge. The highest moral

[5] Since the publication of G. E. Moore's *Principia Ethica* in 1903, moving improperly from descriptive "is" statements to normative "ought" statements (for example, from "x is useful" to "you should do x") has been called the "naturalistic fallacy."

principles can be interpreted in terms of natural law as rules of a timeless order, based in the ahistorical nature of human persons and world, can be interpreted philosophically-psychologically as an inner imperative perceptible through reason or conscience, or finally can be interpreted theologically as revealed commands of God. Thus we have *natural law, philosophical-psychological,* and *theological* norm ethics.

If one sees the principle of universal utility or welfare as the highest principle of human behavior, then *utilitarian* norm ethics follows. This type of norm ethics has a tendency towards altruism. If the utility principle is individualized, then of course the altruistic tendency is transformed into an egoistic one, which however can also be justified in utilitarian terms. In contrast, there is the *deontological* type of norm ethics. According to it, neither the general nor the individual welfare, but the (autonomous) *moral law,* understood as the absolute commandment of duty, becomes the highest, behavior-determining moral principle, as it is encountered most purely in Kant. All of these types of norm ethics, however one interprets them, have in common that their basic norms intentionally have the obligation of inviolable moral laws. The characteristic sign of every kind of norm ethics, consequently, is *ethical lawfulness.*

The inner law of norm ethics, provided that it does not just preach pure self-interest, will be to know how to make the ethical clear as an "ought," which must orient itself towards in principle imperatives that make demands on human persons absolutely. Consequently, it is the decided opponent of empirical pragmatism, which, shunning the fundamental, insinuates ideologizing blindness to everything stated in principle, in order only all too easily to descend into ethical indifference, for which the comfortable attitude of compromise is characteristic. All in all, norm ethics, especially in its deontological form, formulates the seriousness of the ethical demand.

Just as much as that must be emphasized, the other side is also true: Absolute ethical demands seldom do justice to the complexity of reality and often enough lead in concrete situations to hopeless apories. One could think, for instance, of a doctor who is called to the hospital because of dire complications with a birth and finds himself placed before the tragic choice of sacrificing either the life of the child to save the mother or the life of the mother to save the child. How should the strict norm ethicist, for whom the command "Thou shalt not kill!" has absolute validity, decide? The legal norm says nothing and can say nothing about this. It only forbids killing. But the doctor in this situation will kill in any case, however he acts. And if he did nothing, in order apparently to escape from the dilemma, he would really kill, because in that case two human lives would perish. Cases like this or similar borderline cases arise time and again. Because of an economic recession, a business manager is confronted by the necessity of dismissing a part of the workforce, in the interest of the firm, as well as in his own. If he does it, the social welfare of a minority of the employees will undoubtedly suffer. If he does not, the social welfare of the entire workforce will be endangered. Either way, according to a strict norm-ethical standard, there is an action contrary to the moral principle of the common good. From all of that it is evident that rigorously implemented norm ethics can no more be the last word than can an empiricist ethics that leads into pure pragmatism, which would choose here the lesser evil, if not the path of least resistance. Ethics, which understands the dimension of the absolute in the "ought," will understand itself constantly to be obligated by an absolute demand in its endeavor to find the normative. It can, however, never refrain from the concrete situation in real life, in which both individual and social human existence take place. This is related to the fact that norm ethics often has a striking tendency to casuistry and, therefore, to its own self-relativization.

2.2.3 *Casuistic Ethics*

"Casuistry" is understood to mean, first of all, a methodical procedure that applies universal norms, whether of moral or of civil law, to particular cases (*casus*). With respect to norm ethics, this means dismantling the validity of a moral norm into binding instructions for the individual, concretely encountered case. Such a procedure is factually inevitable, for its part, because universal norm-ethical precepts, as has already been shown, cannot provide unambiguous instructions for action, especially in borderline cases with their unavoidable conflicts of conscience or clashes of duty, but instead leave those who are responsible for decisions ultimately with no guidance.

Casuistic ethics undertakes establishing the validity of a norm for the particular and thus concretely intended case. If it happens, as in the two cases cited above, that one and the same norm leads to the dilemma of having to choose between two intrinsic goods (the life of the mother and the life of the child, the social welfare of a minority and the social welfare of the majority), there is necessarily a choice between conflicting goods with the goal of finding criteria for responsible prioritization regarding the controversial goods. If, to return to the obstetrician's value conflict, the weighing of goods turns out in favor of the child's life, then, if it cannot otherwise be saved, the sacrifice of the mother is ethically permissible.[6] In the opposite case, killing the child to save the mother's life is morally justified.[7] Either way — if one understands the command "Thou shalt not kill" as a strict, absolute demand, permitting no exceptions — a relativization of what is absolutely valid takes place.

Demonstrating its inherent relativization of norms that, according to their nature, raise a claim to universal validity does not, of course, discredit the casuistic way of arguing. It must on the contrary be judged, according to its own purpose, as a respectable attempt to show the ethical to its best advantage as conscientiously as possible in its absolute obligatory character in the realm of the relative, and thus in the complex reality of life, human beings, and society. It follows that absolute norms, removed from reality and therefore remaining abstract, cannot at all be treated as equivalent to the demand of the absolute or, in theological terms, the actual will of God. Casuistic ethics, with its well-founded tendency to bring absolute norms down from their abstract heights and to relativize them appropriately, in order to bring them to the reality of concrete life, is thus well within its rights and should not be confused with shallow relativism, which simply trivializes the ethical demand. It puts itself in the wrong, however, when it surrounds its relativizing

[6] *Catholic moral casuistry* tackles this question in earnest. Pius XII addresses it in detail in his Allocution of 29 October 1951 ("Moral Questions Affecting Married Life"). He asserts in principle that the theory of weighing goods does not apply to a choice between the life of the mother and the life of the child. Nevertheless, the example that follows this assertion shows that in the most extreme case, the (voluntary) sacrifice of the mother for the sake of the life of the child claims the highest ethical status. "Address to the Italian Catholic Union of Midwives," 29 October 1951: *Acta Apostolicae Sedis* 43 (1951), 835-59.

[7] "If, for example, the saving of the life of the future mother, independently of her pregnant condition, should urgently require a surgical act or other therapeutic treatment which would have as an accessory consequence, in no way desired or intended, but inevitable, the death of the fetus, such an act could no longer be called a direct attempt on an innocent life. Under these conditions the operation can be lawful" (*Ibid.*, 855). See also Bernhard Häring, *The Law of Christ*, Vol. III, trans. Edwin G. Kaiser, Westminster, Maryland: Newman Press, 1966, pp. 211-12.

dismantling of the highest moral norms or principles in ever more differentiated determinations, oriented towards every conceivable individual case for its part with the aura of the absolutely valid and thus wishes to standardize the entire domain of human existence legally and morally, as happened, for example, in the pharisaical casuistry of early Judaism. In that case it inevitably becomes an "ethical orthodoxy" that is just as bad as dogmatic orthodoxy,[8] because it must shackle in chains the genuinely ethical, which always has to do with decision that is free, although tied to responsibility.

2.2.4 *Situation Ethics*

One contribution of casuistic ethics is to have demonstrated in its own way that from norms alone, abstracted from real conditions of existence and established absolutely, de facto no normative rules for action-decisions in the context of real life are yet derived. For that reason, it seeks to apply norms to the conceivably possible individual cases of life, in order to state more precisely the sense in which and the degree to which they could acquire normative validity. However, the "*casus*" of casuistic ethics turn out unambiguously to be, though not without empirical background, constructs, and thus artificialities, which still stand far away from the genuinely situation-embedded, at which, according to their intention, they aim. How a person in an actual, concrete, existentially experienced situation should act or decide cannot be constructed or programmed at the outset following the casuistic way.

In contrast to casuistic ethics, *situation ethics* is concerned with real, natural situations, and thus with something that does not let itself be foreseen, at least not in all of its possibilities. Consequently, situation ethicists as a rule understand the "situation" in an existential sense. Accordingly, it is the person in the *existing situation* who first experiences the situation in its entire reality. Correspondingly, it also can never be analyzed independently of that person's own existence and experience. The same situation can, therefore, be experienced entirely differently by different persons. A "situation," therefore, is constituted not only by the ensemble of situated circumstances, but also just as much by the person affected by it and called to action. In other words, *the existing person lives uniquely in the experienced situation*. And

[8] Emil Brunner, *The Divine Imperative*, trans. Olive Wyon, Philadelphia, 1947, p. 92.

because he stands in it uniquely, there also cannot be for him any universally valid and predetermined norms, values, or casuistic guiding principles capable of indicating how he should act in the moment of decision. The normative, understood as the determination of what must be done, only lets itself follow from the situation. More precisely, it only shows in the act of the decision itself. In extremis that leads to a "morality without norms," to a concept of action and decision on the basis of which the person in the demanding situation remains radically left to his own resources, and thus also must answer to himself for what is "now" normative, what *"hic et nunc"* is good and evil. Thus Jean-Paul Sartre for instance, exponent in his existentialist phase of an extreme form of situation ethics, can say that man makes himself; he is not found ready-made; he makes himself (in the situation requiring a decision) by the choice of his morality, and he cannot but choose a morality, such is the pressure of circumstances upon him.[9] And this means that each person in his own existence cannot refer to some professed norms, but must determine the normative himself in the act of decision and in normative solitude. That is only another description of freedom to which, according to Sartre, the human person is condemned.[10] The immediate situation says compellingly that he must act in this freedom. But it never tells him what he must do, only that he must do something. The normative, which arises from the situation, consequently reduces itself to an *empty, silent ought*. The person can decide in his ought one way or another ethically, as long as he accepts responsibility for his actions and never expresses regret. What remains is a heroic ethos of the "ought," which leaves the normative completely open in terms of matter or content.

Because this is the case of the situation ethics approach, it leads in its extreme form, which illuminates only the "that," not the "how," of human responsible decision-making, it leads to pure *decisionism*, which, devoid of predetermined norms, determines the normative on its own authority. But doesn't that mean that consistent situation ethics must lead to a morality of anything whatsoever, which ultimately declares everything permissible as long as the agent resolutely accepts responsibility for his actions?

[9] Jean-Paul Sartre, *Existentialism and Humanism*, trans. Philip Mairet, London, 1948, p. 50.

[10] *Ibid.*, p. 37.

It must, of course, be said that situation ethicists — at least the theologians among them — seldom go this far. As a rule, they recognize, with varying degrees of qualification, something normative that is given to the situation in advance. Even so determined a situation ethicist as Joseph Fletcher cannot avoid explaining: "Situation ethics is willing to make full and respectful use of principles, to be treated as maxims but not as laws or precepts. We might call it 'principled relativism.' To repeat the term used above, principles or maxims or general rules are *illuminators*. But they are not *directors*."[11] In this version of situation ethics, prescriptive norms or moral laws are rejected, but not principles that illuminate the situation and therefore guide one to the correct decision. Were it otherwise, the normative relativism of situation ethics would remain "without an *arch*, an ordering principle" and would be "anarchic," and thus "amoral — rather in the antinomian mode."[12] For that reason, Fletcher emphasizes explicitly in this context that normative relativism must have "its ultimate criterion," and that "true relativity" is possible only "relative *to* something." For Fletcher himself, a Christian situation ethicist, "the ultimate criterion" is "agapeic love."[13] All of this means that with this type of situation ethics there is something normative that precedes every situation-determined decision and illuminates the situation ethically, without the situation being self-illuminated. And this shows once more, from a different perspective, the impossibility of obtaining normative guidelines for ethically responsible behavior from bare being alone, even the being of the situation. What is fundamentally taking place here, therefore, is not the elimination of all predetermined normative entities, but the relativization of the claim to validity of norms that wish to be absolute,[14] with regard to the concrete situation of the agent, without in the process falsifying the relativized itself into a kind of absoluteness. And in this endeavor situation ethics is certainly of relevance, including theological relevance.

[11] Joseph Fletcher, *Situation Ethics: The New Morality*, Philadelphia, 1966, p. 31.
[12] *Ibid.*, pp. 44-45.
[13] *Ibid.*
[14] With Fletcher, however, this relativization goes quite far, so far that he can even set love against the individual commandments in the New Testament, which is certainly contrary to its spirit. See Horst G. Pöhlmann, "Ethik zwischen Tradition und Situation," *Neue Zeitschrift für systematische Theologie und Religionsphilosophie*, 12 (1970), pp. 125-35.

In so far as situation ethics elevates love or some comparable basic attitude qualifying human existence to the level of the ultimate criterion, as it does succinctly with Fletcher, it approaches what is meant by the "ethics of conviction."[15]

2.2.5 *The Ethics of Conviction*

If in norm ethics the good and the right becomes a matter of legal observance of predetermined norms, and in situation ethics a matter of responsible decision in the particular case, in conviction ethics it becomes a question of conviction and, therefore, of the *inner motivation of the agent*. Not merely the action or behavior as such, but the conviction behind it determines whether a person acts rightly or wrongly, morally or immorally. The basis of the normative is thus found here in having the right conviction. The good conviction determines the good person. But what distinguishes a good conviction from a bad one?

If one replies that the goodness or badness of a conviction is determined by specific norms, then conviction ethics becomes a variant of norm ethics. But it can also become a variant of situation ethics, if for instance the good conviction is equated to the courageous determination with which one overcomes a difficult situation. In these variants, conviction ethics shares the specific problems of the aforementioned normative approaches.

There are, of course, other ways of answering the question about the criterion of the goodness of a conviction. One can disregard the normative content or the existential intensity of a conviction and restrict its true nature to its form. In this case, not the content, but the form of the ethical conviction that determines the will is decisive. Thus Kant made duty — *duty as respect, out of conviction, for the moral law*, which manifests itself in the conscience guided by reason — the innermost motive of the ethically good action.[16] Human will acts well in so far as it allows itself to be led by the principle of duty understood in this way, instead of by personal inclination. That only says how the will must be shaped or "formed" in order to be a good will, but not what it should will. The danger of ethical formalism

[15] Thus Fletcher can say explicitly, *inter alia*, that a lie can be made "right" by its "loving purpose" (p. 65).

[16] Kant, Immanuel, *Groundwork for the Metaphysics of Morals*, trans. and ed. Allen W. Wood, Yale University Press, 2002, p. 13f.

arises here, which in its consistency would again be incapable of giving instructions for action that have ethical content and, therefore, can be concretized. The extent to which Kant's approach itself suffers from this deficiency is certainly a matter of dispute.

Of course, ethical conviction can combine itself with particular goals in such a way that pursuing them becomes a matter of conscience. Thus there are conscientious objectors, but also those who perform military service for reasons of conscience; those who support a socialist, planned economy out of conviction, but also those who support a capitalist market economy from conviction. In this case, conviction ethics avoids formalism. The person acting out of his spirit knows what he wills. But doesn't the fact that very different, even self-contradictory objectives can join forces with conviction of disposition or conscience indicate its ultimate vagueness? Can't one do anything whatsoever with reference to conviction, and is everything that is done from conviction or conscience truly good? Are not terrorists of both the right and the left persons motivated by conviction, whose acts cannot be ethically justified simply because they were not performed with a criminal intent, but from "conviction"? The shrewd word of Pascal is apposite here: "We never do evil so fully and cheerfully as when we do it out of conscience."[17] From all of this we can see that also conviction ethics cannot be the last word.[18] To be sure, genuine ethos will always express itself subjectively as moral conviction in its demand of the absolute that strikes the conscience. All conviction ethics is right about this. Yet the normative does not show itself in the conviction itself, but in the call of the absolute, which strikes the conscience that is awake to conviction. If the relationship is reversed and acting from conviction in its subjectivity becomes the basis of the absolute, then it is almost inevitable that conviction ethics too will degenerate into a morality of permissiveness, for which ultimately everything is permitted, as long as it takes place out of conviction.

2.2.6 *The Ethics of Responsibility*

Norm ethics, situation ethics, and conviction ethics all aim at a determination of the ethically normative, without thereby taking into consideration the consequences of a decision or action that is justified in

[17] Pascal, Blaise, *Pensées*, Frg. 895, trans. A. J. Krailsheimer, Harmondsworth, 1966, p. 272.

[18] See the examples that Georg Wünsch offers in *Evangelische Wirtschaftsethik*, Tübingen, 1927, pp. 17-18.

their terms. For the absolute advocate of one of these types of ethics, what can be gathered from the following verse of the poet Theodor Storm holds true:

> One asks, "What will result?"
> The other asks only, "Is it right?"
> And in this way the free
> Distinguishes himself from the slave.[19]

This conception of the ethical, which limits itself to following high precepts, subjective conviction, or one's own courage of decision, and then watching to see what happens, is decisively opposed by the ethics of responsibility. It requires, in the process of finding the normative, also *including the consequences* of an action or decision justified by it and *accepting responsibility* for it. This is of greatest consequence especially for political and economic ethics.

It is no accident that Max Weber, the initiator of the ethics of responsibility,[20] was prodded to develop this concept by dealings with ethics in the domain of politics and economics. Anyone who has to make political and economic decisions that can affect the fate of many people will see himself again and again obligated — if he is not out of his mind — not only to account for the motives of conviction that guide him, but also to assess as best he can the foreseeable consequences of his actions. If his actions lead to terrible political and social consequences, he cannot excuse himself simply by saying that his motives were good. That would amount to pure irresponsibility in the real world of political and social life.

Since the time of Weber, acceptance of responsibility for the foreseeable consequences of one's actions has been called the *ethics of responsibility*. Weber himself describes its antagonistic relation with the ethics of conviction as one of

> two maxims, which are fundamentally different from, and irreconcilably opposed to, each other," without , however, identifying the ethics of convictions with irresponsibility nor the ethics of responsibility with a lack of conviction. But there is "a profound antithesis

[19] Theodor Storm, *Sämtliche Werke*, ed. Friedrich Düsel, Vol. 2, Berlin, no date, p. 814: "Der eine fragt: Was kommt danach? / Der andre fragt nur: Ist es recht? / Und also unterscheidet sich / Der Freie von dem Knecht."

[20] See above all "Politics as a Vocation," trans. E. Matthews, in W. G. Runciman, ed., *Max Weber: Selections in Translation*, Cambridge, 1978, pp. 212-25.

> between actions governed by the ethics of intention, where to put it in religious language 'The Christian acts rightly and leaves the outcome to God', and actions governed by the ethics of responsibility, where one is answerable for the (foreseeable) *consequences* of one's actions.[21]

According to that, responsible assessment of the foreseeable consequences of action must take priority normatively, especially in the area of politics and economics, and indeed with conscious recognition of human imperfection, which conviction-ethicists of all shades so easily ignore,[22] in order then to march if necessary in a sterile long-term protest to the existing world or to turn away from it with resignation.

Unquestionably, especially from the perspective of the Christian business and economic ethicist — as will be seen — the ethics of responsibility must be of great importance.[23] Certainly, it makes it evident that the question of the normative status of an action cannot be considered in isolation from its consequences.[24] It would be wrong, again, to see in it the entirety of ethical obligation. One could not get along with the ethics of responsibility alone. And Weber frankly admits as much: "It is true: politics is made with the head, but certainly not *only* with the head. In that respect those who advocate the ethics of intention are absolutely right. No one can tell anyone else whether they *ought* to act according to the ethics of intention or the ethics of responsibility, or when they should follow the one and when the other."[25] But one must go even further here: The ethics of conviction — the same goes for norm ethics and situation ethics — has its right not only *beside* the ethics of responsibility, but also in the ethics of responsibility itself. Anyone who wishes to assess the consequences of a decision that must be made or an action that must be taken can do so only with awareness of the situation. And anyone

[21] *Ibid.*, pp. 217-18.

[22] *Ibid.*, pp. 218-19.

[23] Christofer Frey writes concisely, "To discuss questions of business and economic ethics from a theological perspective means giving priority to an *ethics of responsibility*" ("Theologische Kriterien für die Gestaltung und Entwicklung der Wirtschaft," in *Zwischen Wachstum und Lebensqualität*, Munich, 1980, p. 125).

[24] With Hans Jonas this aspect is radicalized in such a way that "now and until further notice, responsibility for what has been set afoot and is kept moving by ourselves, takes precedence before everything else" (*The Imperative of Responsibility*, Chicago, 1984, p. 129).

[25] Max Weber, "Politics as a Vocation," pp. 223-24.

who is really prepared to bear responsibility for it in ethical certainty will rely in the process on norms formed from convictions that cannot be derived from the responsible act itself, at least not from it alone. Otherwise, the ethics of responsibility would risk being concerned with only the intended outcome of an action, thus conferring normativeness on achieving the result, or at least promising the result, and declaring everything else, including the choice of the means, to be ethically irrelevant. And that would mean the pragmatic sanctioning of the outcome, which would no longer have anything to do with ethically qualified responsibility.[26]

2.3 Preliminary Summary

The *tour d'horizon* of the bi-dimensionality of ethics, as well as its directions of research and main schools of thought, outlined in the first two chapters led implicitly to the conclusion or, more precisely, to the question that will be of importance for the principal observations that will be made in the second main part of this volume. For that reason, it may be appropriate at this point to summarize them explicitly, albeit briefly.

2.3.1 One of the most difficult problems in all of ethics is *the question of the validity* of unconditional ethical demands in the realm of the conditional — thus the question of the relationship between absolute and relative moral norms. Aren't relative norms ultimately self-contradictory, submissive constructs of a compromise ethic that seeks to avoid the absolute demands of the ethical? The inner problematic, to which the summary excursus into the main schools of thought in normative ethics already points, shows that one can neither rashly answer this question affirmatively with the ethical rigorist nor casually answer it negatively with the ethical relativist. If the question is casually denied, whether in the trivial sense of empiricist ethics or in the non-trivial sense of the situation or responsibility ethicist, that is to say by uncoupling human actions in one way or another from the absolute demand, then the *pragmatic emptying of the ethical* is inevitable. But if the question is rashly

[26] Cf. Trutz Rendtorff, *Ethics*, Vol. I, trans. Keith Crim, Minneapolis, 1986, pp. 112-13.

affirmed, if one permits only the absolute to be valid in our imperfect world and its ever-contradictory situations, one maneuvers into *terrible ethical apories* and destroys or renders impossible relatively humane rules, which, despite being dubious in principle, are still better than none at all. Seen in this way, it is inevitable that one must choose between two kinds of basic norms: those that belong to the dimension of the unconditional and those that belong to the dimension of the conditional.[27]

But distinction need not mean separation. The conditionally valid norms must take into account the concrete situations, the given relations with their legalities, as well as the imperfection of the world, in which it is valid to make decisions and to find one's way. But not in fatalistic resignation that submits to the dictate of the factual, rather in responsible orientation to the demand of the unconditional, which always means moving in the direction of the better and more just. The unconditional, to be sure, never lets itself be shown to its best advantage in its normativeness that stirs the conscience time and again directly and purely, but it has to work indirectly as the inherent power of the absolute ethos, which of course does not prematurely abolish the relative norms in morality, law, social agreement, etc., but still seeks to prevent the person from being absorbed into it, in order to be at peace. If, on the other hand, absolute and relative ethos are played against one another as a false dichotomy, then one simply destroys both of them. The relative ethos degenerates into rigid legal norms, which, by their inflexibility, put life in chains. The absolute ethos ideologically becomes a set of utopian postulates that eventually can only deny what exists and in its actual effect must work nihilistically.

2.3.2 An additional main problem of ethics is the *justifiability of its norms*. Are they justifiable at all in an intersubjective sense, or does decisionism have the last word here? Metaethics, as we

[27] Cf. Otfried Höffe, "Sittliche Grenzen psychologischer Forschung," in Lenelis Kruse and Martin Kumpf, eds., *Psychologische Grundlagenforschung*, Bern, 1981, pp. 251ff. Höffe similarly distances himself from both "rigid rule dogmatism" and ethical "relativism" and distinguishes between "moral principles" of universal validity and "rules of thumb" or "orientation aids" in concrete moral praxis, which are of merely general validity. This kind of orientation aids arises from the "interplay of an empirical element with a normative element, as the mediation of each new set of situation-conditions with the constant moral principle."

have seen, provides no unambiguous answer. It splits into a non-cognitive direction, which denies the possibility of scientific knowledge in the domain of morality, and a cognitive direction, which affirms it.[28]

If a distinction is made between norms in the unconditional, only prescriptive sense and norms in the conditional, also descriptive sense, then the aforementioned question presents itself in two ways. What is the scientifically rational justification of norms of the first and of the second sense? This question can be asked, but can not yet be answered, at this point. Nevertheless, it is already clear that it must be addressed at two different levels.

2.3.3 A third main question concerns the *boundaries of ethics*. The discussion of the fundamental alternatives in normative ethics has shown that none of them is able to claim to be anything like the "last word." But what does that imply? That ethics cannot be the last word at all? Even as determined an ethical thinker as Immanuel Kant was led beyond ethics, when the most important philosophical question for him was not "What can I know?" "What ought I to do?" or "What may I hope?" but "What is man?"[29] In the glance at this question ethics will in the end only be able to bring to light, whenever it begins deeply enough, that no ethos is able to lead man beyond himself, but rather leaves him by himself together with the difficult dilemmata of his existence, and that salvation cannot lie in the mere morality of the ought, either in the character of the absolute or in that of the relative. It is true that human existence is unavoidably demanding, and in that respect, ethical existence, in which the good should happen. But the conduct of the good does not already come from the demand of the obligatory itself, not from the normative that can only demand, but rather from a being that is more than morality, which demands by giving, which even in failure still lifts and gives courage to new beginnings.

As we now address questions of business and economic ethics from a theological perspective, this will have much to do with the boundary of everything ethical.

[28] See pp. 19-20.

[29] Immanuel Kant, *Lectures on Logic*, trans. and ed. J. Michael Young, Cambridge, 1992, p. 538.

3. BASIC ASPECTS AND MAIN FIELDS OF THE ETHICAL

Now that the fundamental questions and main research directions and normative forms of ethics have been summarily examined, it remains to stake out its elementary problem field.

The elementary problem field with which ethics is concerned — and to say it sounds banal at first — coincides with the *reality of the human person in the entire complexity of one's existence.* This complexity can be seen most clearly in its fundamental structure if one reduces it to the primary relationships, i.e. all of relationships in which the human person stands from the beginning of his life and which thus coincide absolutely with the relationship field or problem field of ethics. All of this must now be clarified.

3.1 The Relationship Field of Ethics

The relationship field of ethics is thus, to put it succinctly, the human person. Ethics is always concerned with human beings, more precisely, with the responsibility of human persons to each other, whether one's "own" person or "another" person, as well as to everything that belongs to humanity. Not only the human person belongs to humanity, not just the "I" and the "Thou," but also the world, the world as the quintessence of cosmic nature, in and with which he lives, which he can of course utilize to a certain degree, but upon which he nevertheless remains dependent in an elementary sense. The responsibility area of ethics consequently contains not only what is human in a narrower and common sense of the word, it also extends over and above the anthropological to the *cosmological dimension.*

It can now be said in anticipation that the human person stands in a threefold, objectively given, and therefore indisputable, fundamental relationship. He behaves as "I" to himself, to his "Self." He behaves as "I" to other persons, to his "Thou." And he conducts himself as "I" or "We" to his environment, as to his "It." If these three fundamental relationships are considered one after another in the following, because it cannot be otherwise, that does not at all mean that one has a higher priority than another. They are all equally original and represent functionally an inseparable unity.

3.1.1 *The First Basic Relationship: I-Self (The Individual Aspect)*

The first fundamental relationship in which each person finds himself — not the psychological genesis, but according to the system chosen here — is the relation of the "I" to its "Self." "I" is understood here to mean that which accounts for man in his separateness, and thus the subjectivity that underlies his individuality. The child who begins to say "I" already means himself in his particularity from all others, from the things of his environment and from the narrowest circle of persons with whom he lives as a family member. He is "I" from the moment he experiences himself consciously in his individuality.

In distinction from the "I," it is now necessary to say more about the "Self." To be sure, the "Self" is always also "I," which is, as subject, the basis of all individuality. It is "I" not only in its individuality that has become self-conscious, but also as the quintessence of all the possibilities, most of them unconscious, that slumber within it and still need to be realized. Simply put, the "I" is something given, while the "Self" is something leaping up, still becoming, which can in this respect face the "I" as its target. If the "I" misses its target, if it becomes unrealized rather than realized in its "Self", then it arrives at "self-alienation" and with it — in extremis — at a loss of identity, at a conflicted existence. Only to the degree that "I" stands in agreement with its "Self," thus each corresponding to the other, does man find his identity and consequently his full individuality. That is why human individuality is based upon the I-Self relationship.

3.1.2 *The Second Basic Relationship: I-Thou (The Personal Aspect)*

The human person in his individuality as I-Self stands, in accordance with his being and essence, in a wider fundamental relationship, that of I-Thou (which may be one-one or one-many; note of G. Enderle). There is no humanity in pure particularity, even though the human person is always uniquely and distinctively an individual. He never stands as an individual in and of himself without support. He lives instead by a human opposite number, the Thou.[1] This is not meant merely biologically and socially in the trivial sense that everyone is descended from physical parents whose protection and care they require for their rearing, and that they can survive only in association with others. After all, that is true of non-human life as well. No, the human person is dependent upon other persons in yet another, completely different way, above the biological and the social. Precisely the specifically human characteristics, like upright-walking, open-mindedness, decision-making possibility, reason/language, aptitude for culture, etc.,[2] fall to him, according to recent anthropological research, in Thou-like, communicative interaction with others of his own kind.[3] This fundamental fact was really always somehow well-known to the immediate, scientistically not yet affected feeling, as when it suspected that the human person needs love in order to become "human" and consequently himself. This insight, proposed decisively by Kierkegaard, was profoundly and radically developed at a philosophical level by Ferdinand Ebner,[4] and above all, Martin Buber.[5] They see the human person as an "I," who stands opposite the "Thou," and furthermore becomes at all possible in his selfhood

[1] Edward Schillebeeckx, *Christus und die Christen*, Freiburg im Breisgau, 1977, p. 718, with reference to Emmanuel Levinas, correctly draws attention to the fact that there is "not only the I-Thou relationship. The presences of a *third person*, of a 'he,' is the basis of the origin of *society*, which cannot be traced back to an 'I-Thou' relation and a 'We' relation." Therefore, I speak here of an "I-Thou" and an I/We-It relationship.

[2] Cf. Adolf Portmann, *Biologische Fragmente zu einer Lehre vom Menschen*, Basel, 1944, p. 85.

[3] This has been established convincingly with reference to human phenomena such as crying and laughing, by Helmuth Plessner, *Laughing and Crying*, trans. James Spencer Churchill and Marjorie Grene, Evanston, 1970, p. 21: "To understand laughing and crying as forms of expression means to proceed from man as a whole.... Man is accessible to us as a whole, that is, as our fellow man, and we are accessible to ourselves, in the context of behavior, in commerce with our own kind and with the environment."

[4] See above all Fragments 1-5 of "Das Wort und die geistigen Realitäten," in Ferdinand Ebner, *Schriften*, Vol. I, ed Franz Seyr, Munich, 1963, pp. 84-132.

[5] Martin Buber, *I and Thou*, trans. Ronald Gregor Smith, 2nd. Ed., New York, 1958: "But how lovely and how fitting the sound of the lively and impressive *I* of Socrates! It is the *I* of endless dialogue, and the air of dialogue is wafted around it in all its journeys, before the judges and in the last hour in prison. This *I* lived continually in the relation with man which is bodied forth in dialogue. It never ceased to believe in the reality of men, and went out to meet them. So it took its stand with them in reality,

from the "Thou." Accordingly, there is no "I" without "Thou." "I" and "Thou" fit into a whole, one that does not abolish the individual, but is more than individuality.

This entirety of human existence, which always contains individuality, without being established by it, will conceptually be called personality here. Thus individuality and personality, according to my usage, are not identical. Individuality is the "I" in itself; personality is relative to the "Thou," in either the mode of the singular or that of the plural. These facts now make it possible to see clearly the two fundamental relationships that now stand in view.

The structure of the I-Self relationship is characterized by the *element of wordlessness*. I relate to myself in wordless immediacy. Were I to begin to speak, not merely to myself, but with myself as if my self were another person, a kind of pseudo-Thou, I would have at least a crisis of my identity. The I-Self relationship has this kind of adialogical structure.

The I-Thou relationship, in contrast, has a thoroughly dialogical character. Anyone really wishing to associate with someone else as a human person requires the medium of language, where "language" is not limited semantically to the word alone. Indeed, there can be a mutual relationship between "I" and "Thou" that no longer requires linguistic communication, as in wordless love. But those are rare moments, and would be impossible without prior dialogical communication. So it is still the case that the structure of the I-Thou relationship is characterized by the dialogical element. One person can relate to another in a truly human manner only in dialogical existence. This ethical significance of this truth can hardly be exaggerated.

If the I-Self and I-Thou relationships must be distinguished structurally, this distinction does not mean separation. These two fundamental relationships do not at all walk beside one another, as if the "I" related first of all to itself and then also subsequently or additionally to the "Thou" of its fellow human beings, or vice versa. They are, instead, equally primary and exist within one another. The "Thou" belongs to the "I" just as the "Self" belongs to it. A disturbance of one fundamental relationship inevitably has an effect on the other. Thus the schizophrenic has not only a disturbed relationship with himself, but also a disturbed relationship with other persons — and with reality in general. And it is difficult or impossible

and reality forsakes it no more. Its very loneliness can never be forsakenness, and if the world of man is silent it hears the voice of the daimonion say *Thou*" (p. 66).

in individual cases to determine with which of the two disturbances the illness began. Therefore, anyone concerned about having good relationships with others must try just as hard to have a healthy relationship with himself. And, of course, the reverse is just as true. There is an interdependence of fundamental importance here.

After all of that, it is important to record that the I-Thou relationship, in contrast to the I-Self relationship, has a dialogical structure, and that human personality is rooted in this structure. Thus, I am never a person in this sense only for myself, but always in a relationship, where I find myself an I-Self to the Thou of the other person and accept him as a Thou, and where the other person is a Thou to myself and accepts me as an I-Self. From that it becomes understandable why personality is not the same thing as individualism. Individualism means the individualization of the "I" into the isolated Thou-less individual, who considers himself to be everything, thereby necessarily excluding the personhood of the human being. In other words, individualism fails to recognize the communal character of all personal existence and leads ultimately into the impasse of I-solitary isolation, which leaves the human person in emptiness. It is desperately necessary to emphasize this today, when so much emphasis is placed on individual self-realization.

Personality, as it is understood here, means not only the *opposite of individualism*, but also the *opposite of collectivism*. Someone who fails to appreciate the communal character of human personal existence also misjudges the personal character of all true communal life. Collectivism means the collectivization of the "I/We" into an anonymous mass, which in its hopeless monotony produces no less loneliness[6] than the isolated, self-absorbed individual. Human loneliness, to which emancipated individualism and socialized collectivism, despite their supposed contradiction, both lead, may also explain why either one can be transformed so easily into the other.[7] To the isolated individual, collectivity looks like the saving isle; but then when mass-loneliness is experienced, one seeks salvation in individualistic self-realization, which usually leads to disappointment and

[6] See David Riesman, *The Lonely Crowd*, New Haven, 1950, which is as important today as ever.

[7] Nikolai Berdiajev, in his pioneering work *Von der Bestimmung des Menschen*, Bern, 1935, already saw the closeness of individualism and collectivism and their distance from the personal understanding of the human person.

another cycle of the vicious circle. An *anthropology* that understands the relationality of the fundamental relationships of I-Self and I-Thou must defend itself resolutely against both individualism and collectivism, as two elementary transgressions of human existence. That this truth has important implications for the foundation of economic ethics is again obvious.

3.1.3 *The Third Basic Relationship: I/We-It (The Ecological Aspect)*

A third basic relationship of human existence remains to be considered. The human person is not only an "I" related to his own Self and to the Thou of his fellow human beings; he is also always related to the natural environment that surrounds him, and indeed is from birth or, strictly speaking, even before birth. If the "Self" is the individual inner world and the "Thou" is the dialogical environment of the human person, that which is called "It" here is the ecological outer world, the physical life-basis of his existence. In so far as man, like all organisms, has his vital basis in the ecological total household of nature, the "I/We-It relationship" could be understood as the most elementary of all the relationships in which we stand. The structure of this basic relationship is characterized by two elements, which should be examined at least fleetingly.

The first element is that of *absolute dependency*. Like all living beings — again, a banal observation — the human person is situated in a relationship of elemental dependency upon his natural environment. He lives from the oxygen of the atmosphere that has accumulated around our planet in millions of years, from the stocks of energy that we receive from the sun and the earth, from the natural resources that lie in the ground, and from the foodstuffs that we produce through or with the help of nature, etc. He can use this fundamental basis of existence in totally different ways — simplistically or ingeniously, wastefully or frugally — but he will never be able to detach himself from it. While his imaginative spirit always seeks to expand the boundaries that restrict him, the human person remains bound in the ecological basic data, which should already have made him aware long ago that his opportunities are finite, not infinite.

The fundamental relationship of man to his natural environment is characterized by a second element, which appears to contradict the first one. Not only is man ecologically dependent upon the world in which he lives, he also can *rise above* it by, as "I/We," making the natural world an "It," an object, which he can alter according to his will, his wishes and interests, and thus can remold almost as he pleases. This process of controlling nature or the world began at the time our earliest ancestors, sometime in the *Mesolithic period*, made the transition from the appropriating to the producing lifestyle, from being gatherers, hunters, and nomadic herdsmen to being settled farmers. It initiated real human cultural development.

The original meaning of the word "culture"[8] is farming, care of fields, and thus agriculture. With the emergence of agriculture, man really began to "cultivate" the natural world, and consequently to use it actively and to alter it rationally to his own ends. One of agriculture's legitimate children is modern technology, which, in the course of a long history with various intermediate stages, has climbed only in the most recent period to a breathtaking, but also menacing level. Nearly all areas of our lives, from the raw-materials economy to human medicine, are greatly altered today by technology. Not only the face of the earth, but also conventional living conditions, have been changed in such a way that this is appropriately labeled with the succinct term "revolution." Even limitations to which man previously was absolutely subject as supposed natural necessities could, at least in the so-called "developed" nations, be largely reduced by technology: limitation by hunger, by material want, by infectious diseases, by geographical distances, by information crises, to name only a few. Relative to earlier times, contemporary man has really become more powerful in his natural environment, much more powerful. Despite his unbridled will to emancipation, however, he has not escaped his dependency on it. And the more violently he behaves in it with his technical power, the more recklessly he depletes its energy sources, weakens its natural-resource reserves, pollutes its air and water, decimates its forests, and devastates its grasslands with his expressways and concrete constructions, in short, the more he permits his cultural capability, which could be something large and beautiful, to deteriorate into barbarism, the more ominously this dependency becomes apparent. It is indeed no longer dependency on the original world, but on the world that

[8] The term "culture" (derived from the Latin "*colere*" = to cultivate, plant, look after) was adopted at the end of the seventeenth century and, indeed from the beginning, in the twofold sense of agricultural cultivation and the spiritual care of language, the sciences, the arts, in short the spiritual culture. Cf. Friedrich Kluge, *Etymologisches Wörterbuch der deutschen Sprache*, 18th Ed., Berlin, 1960, p. 411.

he has altered and denatured, and that consequently reacts to him. But it is dependency nonetheless, and indeed, at this point in time, a dependency to whose deadly consequences man has contributed.[9]

These indisputable facts, in the small hints with which they have been outlined here, already make it obvious what explanation the structure of the I/We-It relationship must have. It is, to use a current term, of a *dialectical kind,* with "dialectical" understood here in the sense of the *reciprocal overlapping of subject and object*. The "I/We" as subject can in fact make the "It"-world its object and in this respect gain power over it. But the "It"-world as the ecological basis, which underlies human physical existence and in this respect is and remains precisely its "subject" in the original meaning of the word,[10] keeps the "I/We" in a state of dependency. There is a kind of reciprocity with this dependency, as is also encountered, of course only distantly comparably, with the relationship of the "I" to the "Thou." There is also reciprocity in this relationship. While the reciprocity of "I" and "Thou" has a dialogical-personal structure, however, that of "I/We" and "I" has a non-personal, adialogical, simply dialectic structure. In so far as the I/We relationship is adialogical — we do not speak with nature, but at most, in a metaphorical sense, to nature — it is like that of I-Self. But, again, there is a fundamental difference here. The human person in his historicity as cultural human being does not have a direct relationship with his environmental nature. That is still true of the animal living in the wild as a part of nature identical with itself, and it may also have been true of pre-cultural "natural human being," as long as he did not begin to experience and understand the world as an "It." But whenever the world is experienced as an "It" and, consequently, as an object malleable by humans, to be altered and also already altered, the relationship to it is no longer direct, but rather is an indirect, culturally indirect, and in this respect also

[9] Cf. Hans and Thea Schulze, *Zwischen Technik und Gott*, Stuttgart, 1982, p. 13: "The human person as creator of this second genesis [the universal mechanization of life, A. R.] is at the same time powerful and dependent. That is the moral of the story. He creates something new, on which he is dependent, however, by which he can be exploited, and which even threatens him with annihilation."

[10] The original meaning of "subject, " derived from the Latin "*subiectum*," is that which underlies (everything). Descartes was the first to make the "I" the starting point of his philosophizing and in that respect made it what underlies everything. Modern subjectivism begins with him. Before Descartes, "subject" was not associated only with the "I."

institutionalized relationship. For "culture," in both the original and the developed sense of the word, is a human institution.

Now that the relationship-field of ethics has been staked out in outline, a new question arises, that of the basic relationships of persons in their institutional mediation.

3.2 The Basic Relationships in their Institutional Mediation

Before this additional question can be addressed, we must precisely fix the use of the terms "institution" and "institutional." The term "*institution*" will be used here in a very wide sense, to include all institutions, establishments, and settings that are based on human organization.

There are institutions that do not stem from the human person, but are indispensably given to him. Such institutions come to light, for instance, in the bi-sexuality of the human species or in the need for association in hereditary society, as well as in general social union, which led Aristotle to call man a "political animal" (*zōon politikon*).[11] One could reasonably call them institutions of nature or creation.

That applies *by no means*, however, to the concrete, historical forms of these institutions. They are not imperatively, and thus immutably predetermined, but instead yield the most diverse, even conflicting structures. As far as the social or governmental forms are concerned, they range from strictly autocratic to anarchic. The same can be said of marriage and the family. In addition to the monogamous order, there are polygamous marriages. Families may be matriarchal, patriarchal, or partnerships. Even the traditional division of roles between the sexes can hardly refer to gender-specific and thus inevitable foundations. It is certain only that the biological, maternal role can be assumed only by the woman and the corresponding paternal role only by the man. Everything else, however, is up for grabs. In view of these and similar forms, to speak of natural forms of order would be erroneous and would lead into hopeless contradiction. It is instead a matter of historically developed structures, in whose formation man was and is actively involved. In other words, it is ultimately a matter of organizations into which man is for the most part already born as an historical individual and which in this respect are also

[11] Aristotle, *Politics*, I, 2, 1253a, trans. Carnes Lord, Chicago, 1984, p. 37.

given to him, but not in a natural-immutable sense, only in an historical-alterable sense. The term "institution" will hereafter encompass all of these ordering organizations that man has the power to reshape.

I thus understand institutions to be organizations that are historical-human, and therefore alterable in structure, even if they may also be based on natural orders and thus conform to natural laws with an unalterable character. As such they belong to the domain of the *cultural*, not just the *natural*. They are, consequently, settings that are achieved only with the participation of the human person. Such settings also have their inner conformity to natural laws or their driving tendencies — one may think of the "compulsions" that originate in technology, the economy, the state, etc. Concerning this Marx speaks of "the fixation ... of what we ourselves produce into a material power above us."[12] Although the institutional is and remains a creation of man, it reacts upon him, and indeed in the totality of his fundamental relationships.[13] Since the human person cannot live otherwise than culturally in the world, which always includes the institutionalizing forms of his living conditions,[14] he never acts only directly to himself, to the Thou of his fellow human beings, and to the It of the environment, but always also indirectly through the institutions that are of his own creation. And from that it follows that the basic human relationships also may never be viewed merely in themselves, as they appear immediately, that, in order to avoid romantic illusions, they must be considered in the realism of their institutional mediation. That leads to additional steps.

3.2.1 *The Institutionalizing Effect in the I/We-It Relationship*

It should be sufficiently clear, given the dialectical character of the I/We-It relationship, that for a long time we have no longer been dealing with the "natural" world, but with an environment that we

[12] Marx and Engels, "The German Ideology," in *Collected Works,* Vol. V, New York, 1976, p. 47.

[13] Edward Schillebeeckx, *Christus und die Christen*, Freiburg, 1977, p. 719.

[14] It is assumed here that there cannot be a society that is unstructured, and thus without institutions, a thesis that was vehemently disputed, not for the first time, during the student revolts of 1968, but has been in neo-anarchist circles since then. See, for example, Franco Basaglia, ed., *Die negierte Institution oder die Gemeinschaft der Ausgeschlossenen*, Frankfurt am Main, 1971.

ourselves have altered and will continue to alter even more. The entire process of this alteration will be understood here as "*culture*" or "*culturizing*," where culturizing can assume a structure that amounts to pure environmental destruction, and thus to "unculture." From the very start, culturizing the natural environment has a twofold relationship, caring for and using, and this is, again, connected to the dialectic of the I/We-It relationship. If a piece of land is to be useful in the long run, it must be cared for in a manner corresponding to its nature. And if it is cared for in a manner corresponding to its nature, there can be no maximization of utility, because that would require going beyond its natural limits. At the same time, it would be a mistake to maximize care of the land at the expense of its usefulness, because that would lead to a minimization of our basis of living. Either extreme would be an offense against the dialectic of the I/We-It relationship, and thus a betrayal of the cultural commission of man in his world.

The betrayal of this cultural commission has already become — to our undoing — a harsh reality. A focus on utility has overridden the obligation of care, leading to unrestrained exploitation of the sources of energy and raw materials, our forests and fields and, last but not least, our co-creating life through the modern economy. And this is true regardless of whether the exploitation organizes itself politically as "capitalistic" or "socialistic." In both forms the economy was and is oriented structurally towards such an extent of quantitative growth that becomes an unbearable burden for the environment. Therefore, it makes little sense in the present context to ask what this fatal development is really based on, whether it is based on the ever-rising, material level of demand of the individual person, group, or nation, or upon the growing, sales-seeking, productive power of the modern economy, which created the material covetousness in the first place. All that is of importance here is the fact that the economy has in the meantime become a powerful, not to say all-powerful, institution, which works over us by the momentum of its typical structure like an "objective power" and involves us as its accomplices — whether as employers or employees, producers or consumers — in its effects that destroy the environment, even if the individual does not at all intend this destruction subjectively and even opposes it passionately. Thus we ourselves can treat nature with extreme care, seek to minimize harmful emissions from our own households, plant and maintain our gardens according to biological principles, and abstain from environmental pollution conscientiously in the open air, but collectively, as members of a highly industrialized society, participate in massive environmental destruction. Whether the I/W-It relationship has a disastrous effect on our environment depends not only on our individual attitude towards it, but even more on the structure of the institutionalized activities of our society, in which we are entangled and from which no one, not even the "dropout," can simply walk away. The institutionalizing effect in the I/We-It relationship certainly becomes comprehensible here.

3.2.2 *The Institutionalizing Effect in the I-Thou Relationship*

The case of the I-Thou relationship is similar to that of the I/We-It relationship. Indeed, it may appear at first glance that this relationship, because of its dialogical-personal basic structure, would have a dissimilarly greater immediacy than the I/We-It relationship, which from the start is culturally mediated and thus dialectically structured. In a certain respect, that is correct.

There is a wide range of relationships among persons, which unambiguously carry the *sign of the immediate*. Some examples are the relationships of like-mindedness, friendship, and love. Such relationships, if they are of a genuine nature, materialize completely spontaneously and can also exist without any external statute. Thus one perceives, for instance, agreement of convictions with others and joins together without coercion. Or one experiences friendly feelings for certain people and is fond of them in full freedom. And someone is seized by a deep, erotic affection and remains faithful to the beloved, again not from any external necessity, but because this belongs to the dialogical nature of love itself. All of this takes place immediately and does not require any external, i.e. statutory or institutional, mediation.

Not all human relationship, however, can have this character of immediacy of persons. They can only in so far as they operate within the private sphere of love, friendship, conviction, and neighbors, as well as close cooperation with those nearby, etc. To the degree, however, that they, despite their intimate character, are dragged into the medium of social powers, interests, class differences, etc. — and in reality they always are — they are subject to legal or quasi-legal regulations, even if they are, as with family, marriage, and "free" relationships, rooted primarily in the domain of the immediate. Therefore, in considering human social existence, whether of individuals or of groups, one must distinguish between relationships that have an essentially *person-immediate character* and those that are *institutionally* mediated in a specific sense.

While this distinction is extremely important for ethical reflection, it should not result in a false dichotomy. It is not at all the case that person-immediate and institutionally-mediated relationships must or could stand opposed to one another as alternatives, and it certainly is not true that either kind of relationship as such should be identified with the ethically good and the other with the ethically bad. The anti-institutionalist sentiment of neo-anarchism, with its "death to the institutions," which strongly moves the younger generation of today, misses the target of reality. In his social existence, the human person needs institutions just as much as the soul needs the body for its existence. There is no either-or here, only both-and. In other words, our social life in its reality takes place both in person-immediate and in institutionally mediated existence-relationships. This can be clarified by considering the situation in an industrial enterprise.[15] The industrial firm is, roughly speaking, organized cooperation in the production of specific goods by persons with different educations and different positions. There is a wide range of personal — or in the language of industrial sociology, informal — contacts within it. Workers spontaneously form groups of comrades. Perhaps some of them belong to the same clubs as some of their superiors, forming additional relationships of an immediate nature. If the firm is small, its owner knows his employees personally, at least to a significant degree. This can lead again to a widening of the spectrum of immediate contacts, this time to the top. But even in a work organization of this kind, in which the conditions necessary for the cultivation of personal relationships among co-workers of the same and different positions is optimal, it would never be only person-immediately. In the end every firm is and remains an institution with a statute that formally regulates the horizontal and vertical relationships among all participants in the production process and that remains in force no matter whether someone likes it personally. Furthermore, the firm for its part also stands in a network of interwoven institutions. As an economic enterprise, it must obey the governmental law of corporations, and in general the legal regulations

[15] Cf. Arthur Rich, *Christliche Existenz in der industriellen Welt*, 2nd Ed., Zürich, 1964, pp. 62ff.

relevant to it. The workers are employed according to labor contracts that have a public-legal character. That includes industrial agreements with labor unions, etc. And, finally, the firm operates under the conditions of the existing economic order, which in Western, industrialized societies is based on the institution of the market, as well as that of private ownership of the means of production.

The structures of all these institutions have an effect on the I-Thou relationship within the firm and influence its quality to a high degree. Thus, for instance, the relationship between workers and their supervisors is determined not only by the way the immediate personal relationship plays itself out between them, but often even more by the structure of the leadership style or the way decisions are made in the workplace. The case is similar with the market mechanism, which no business enterprise can ignore. During an economic downturn, a manager may find it necessary to dismiss people with whom he has a thoroughly human, person-immediate relationships. The heart may spontaneously say no, but the structural market situation compels a contrary decision. It reaches a point of conflict between personal inclination and structural necessity. In such a conflict, it can be seen drastically how greatly person-immediate and institutionally-mediated relationships are interwoven with one another in social reality and to what a high degree personal social existence and collaboration also can be and is determined by the structure of the social institutions within which the cooperation is to take place. The institutionalizing effect in its often extremely bitter reality, therefore, cannot be overlooked in the I-Thou relationship.

3.2.3 *The Institutionalizing Effect in the I-Self Relationship*

The title of this section may seem irritating. If there is anything that cannot be institutionalized, it is the I-Self relationship, the individual inner life.

There is a possible objection here, whose relative legitimacy cannot be denied. My relationship to myself exists in an immediacy that requires absolutely no mediation, unless this relationship turns out to be disturbed in such a way that psychotherapeutic help from outside is absolutely necessary. But even such mediation would still be of a non-institutional kind, because of its character, since as medical aid, if it is to succeed, it must be based upon personal confidence between the one who helps and the one who is helped.

This notwithstanding, the world of the institutional is also entitled to influence on the interiority of the I-Self relationship. For the I, which relates to itself, always stands at the same time in the I-Thou and I/We-It relationships. And the way these relationships are formed in the social reality of the structure of the institutions in which we live and work together also has repercussions on the "I" in its immediate relationship to the "Self," if only because the basic relationships of our existence form an inseparable unity.[16]

This connection appears most immediately in the relationship of the person to the institution of social labor. To the degree that social labor provides space for independent decisions, spontaneous opportunities for co-creation, and thus individual responsibility, the human person is also able to experience himself in it as a "Self," and thus as individuality. And to the degree that it is lacking, because the structure of production condemns the worker to operations that he programs and, consequently, must perform mechanically, he will have to exist, not as an individual "Self," but simply as a mechanized "It." Marx and Engels stated in 1848 in an accusatory spirit:

> Owing to the extensive use of machinery and to division of labour, the work of the proletarians has lost all individual character, and, consequently, all charm for the workman. He becomes an appendage of the machine, and it is only the most simple, most monotonous, and most easily acquired knack, that is required of him.[17]

Even if this judgment remains problematic in its generalization, it is more than merely an ideological assertion. It reflects a serious factor in the process of the advancing rationalization of socially organized work, which is characterized by an even higher degree of reality today than 150 years ago, and which has been substantiated by the most recent industrial-scientific research in countless variations as the self-alienation of the human person in work.[18] In any case, there are facts of great ethical consequence here,[19] which also come to light

[16] *Ibid.*, pp. 79ff.

[17] Marx and Engels, "Manifesto of the Communist Party," in *Collected Works*, Vol. VI, New York, 1976, pp. 490-91.

[18] Cf. Arthur Rich and Eberhard Ulich, ed., *Arbeit und Humanität*, Königstein, 1978, especially the chapters by Charles Lattmann, pp. 33-46; Hansjürgen Daheim, pp. 65-80; Friedrich Fürstenberg, pp. 81-92; and Eberhard Ulich, pp. 185-93. (The latter also lists the most important literature on this theme.)

[19] Cf. Charles Lattmann, *Die verhaltenswissenschaftlichen Grundlagen der Führung des Mitarbeiters*, Bern, 1982, pp. 517ff.

with other institutionalizing effects, especially those of the code of industrial relations.[20] This can be brought up in more detail, however, only in later contexts.

3.3 The Main Aspects of Ethical Responsibility and their Integration in Social Ethics

The discussion thus far in this chapter has led to the following conclusions: There are three basic relationships in human existence: the I-Self, the I-Thou, and the I/We-It relationships. Each of these basic relationships is found in both an immediate and an institutionally mediated form, where the institutional mediation can never be ignored, because the human person as a natural creature and as a person and an individual is and always remains a social being. These three basic relationships in their immediate and mediated forms mark the main aspects of ethical responsibility in the concrete existence of the human person.

The three basic relationships, understood in their immediateness, also let three fundamental aspects of responsibility become apparent: the responsibility that the human person has immediately for his "Self," for his "Thou," and for his "It," i.e. for the natural environment, which he must cultivate. From that follows the distinction between individual-ethical, personal-ethical, and environmental-ethical responsibility, which should be observed during the rest of the argument. Consequently, I will write in the following of individual, personal, and environmental ethics — though not in the usual terms.

These three basic aspects, with the differentiation assigned to them within the complete discipline of ethics, however, do not yet contain the entirety of human ethical responsibility. The human person is responsible not only for his behavior towards himself, for his personal interaction with those around him, and for the use or misuse of the environmental goods necessary for existence, in so far as all of this concerns him directly; he is also responsible, in so far as he is indirectly affected in all of that by the structures of the social institutions within which his life concretely takes place. And that means that if we have a tendency to be pushed or compelled in the immediacy of our existence towards behavior that conflicts with our own

[20] See Arthur Rich, *Mitbestimmung in der Industrie*, Zürich, 1973, pp. 18ff.

awareness of individual, personal, or environmental responsibility, but which we are unable to avoid, because it is socially-structurally conditioned, then we cannot simply talk our way out of it by saying that it has to do with a "*force majeure*" that transcends the realm of human responsibility. To be sure, it has to do here indeed with a "superior power," with "objective forces" or conditions that exert pressure on us; but it is about objective forces or circumstances that are caused through human machinations and for which, consequently, human persons must accept responsibility. One would do well in this context to consider the following words of Karl Marx: "If man draws all his knowledge, sensation, etc., from the world of the senses and the experience gained in it, then what has to be done is to arrange the empirical world in such a way that man experiences and becomes accustomed to what is truly human in it ... If man is shaped by environment, his environment must be made human."[21] Even if one rejects the historical-materialistic philosophy that stands behind these words as a system and thinks much more modestly than Marx does about the possible ways of altering social circumstances in a genuinely human sense, there still remains much truth in these words. They make it clear that the human person himself is responsible for the institutional ordering of his society and, therefore, must also accept responsibility collectively for its structural consequences on individual, personal, and environmental behavior. This responsibility, which is concerned about social structures and their consequences for the qualitative formation of the basic human relationships, constitutes the specifics of what is called here "social ethics." *Human responsibility is integrated into a whole only in social ethics understood in this sense.*

After these words of anticipation, it now remains to explain individual, personal, and environmental ethics, as well as their integration in social ethics, more precisely.

3.3.1 *Individual Ethics*

As has already been indicated, the individual-ethical aspect of responsibility is concerned with responsible interaction of the "I" with its "Self," as this takes place directly. I must be concerned not

[21] Marx and Engels, "The Holy Family," in *Collected Works*, Vol. IV, New York, 1975, pp. 130-31.

only for others, but also for myself. For the "Self" can become a victim of inconsiderate I-assertion just as easily as can the "Thou" or "Ye." This is inevitably the case when the maximization of I-desires becomes one's purpose in life. Thus many persons, in the choice of a career or the acceptance of work, allow themselves to be guided by whether the expected payment is capable of satisfying their I-prestige, without considering the underlying needs of the self that always seek more in work than merely money, namely satisfaction and a sense of fulfillment. The consequence is that with all of the I-successes, such as career, material prosperity, even achievement of power, the self comes away empty handed and falls into inner desolation. This bitter experience contains the deeper reason many people, mostly young people, turn away from the cult of "having" today[22] and ask for more "being" or, as the slogan goes, "self-realization." A meaningful and necessary individual-ethical reaction appears in this. The "Self" revolts against being dominated and pushed to the wall by the "I." In other words, the inward person with his particular values rebels against the I-obsessed, avaricious success-nature.

The context that can only be intimated here makes it understandable what responsible interaction of the "I" to its "Self" wishes to say. It wants to say that the "I" does not live from merely possessing, but must commit itself to an existence in which the person can himself exist as a person, and thus does not have to achieve his individual importance from something associated with prestige, such as career, prosperity, power, etc. If the "I" that forgets its being runs over its "Self" by leaving being to the mercy of the will to have, then it degenerates without fail into egoism. Egoism is not only I-assertion directed against one's neighbor; it is also I-assertion that fails itself, i.e. that sacrifices true life to external success. This also makes it clear that true self-realization cannot join forces with I-assertion, but must instead oppose it.[23] But like the wolf in sheep's clothing, sheer egoism, concerned only about

[22] See especially Erich Fromm, *To Have Or To Be?* New York, 1976, pp. 154-67.

[23] Cf. Helmut Barz, *Stichwort: Selbstverwirklichung*, Stuttgart, 1981. With reference to C. G. Jung's theory of individuation, he understands self-realization in contrast to egocentrism: "Self-realization is the opposite of egocentrism, because it seeks to move the ego out of the center. But when the I is relieved of its central position, then not only the nearness to the self, but also the relationship to the Thou of the other person increases" (p. 83).

achieving its own aspirations, often walks around in the shimmering garment of self-realization. One should not allow oneself to be deceived here.

Being obligated to take care of one's "Self," consequently, has nothing to do with a moral justification of egoism, even in its most sublime forms. For all of this can never mean isolation from the "Thou." Quite on the contrary, proper care for the "Self" always includes care for the "Thou," and vice versa. It has already been pointed out explicitly that the "Thou" belongs to the "I" that wishes not to fail itself, just as indispensably as does the "Self."[24] And for that reason one will understand how to treat the "Thou" responsibly only when that also happens with the "Self." This is expressed succinctly in the biblical command "Love your neighbor as yourself."[25] With that the personal-ethical horizon also appears.

3.3.2 *Personal Ethics*

While individual ethics is about the direct responsibility of the "I" for its "Self," personal ethics is about the concern of the "I" for its "Thou," that is, the obligation to interpersonal humanity.

The concept of *interpersonal humanity* should not be understood here in too narrow a sense. It goes beyond direct service of man to man, in the sense of Christian charity for instance. Kant's categorical imperative, "Act so that you use humanity, as much in your own person as in the person of every other, always at the same time as end and never merely as means,"[26] comes closest to it, at least in a formal respect. To honor and to respect the other as a person like oneself means the practice of dialogical existence as the basis of all personality.[27] In this kind of ethical praxis I can always meet the other only as "Thou," as a thou, to whom I understand myself to be directly addressed and demanded. And in this kind of ethical praxis I will be intent first and foremost on accepting him as "Thou," as my personal opposite number, whom I may never use as a mere means to the pursuit of my own ends. If that happens, if

[24] Cf. p. 38-39.
[25] Leviticus 19,18; Mark 12,31; and parallels.
[26] Immanuel Kant, *Groundwork for the Metaphysics of Morals*, ed. and trans. Allen W. Wood, New Haven, 2002, pp. 46-7.
[27] Cf. p. 41.

the other person is regarded only as a means serving to attain my self-chosen and self-legislated ends more easily, then he is inevitably robbed of his personhood and is degraded to the level of an "It," a thing, which can only have the value of a thing. In this case, it remains ultimately inevitable that dialogical existence will be converted into monological existence, since the "I" in monocratic corruption silences the "Thou" and desires to dominate it like a dead thing. But this leads to the destruction of the basis of all personal existence.

Monocratic existence is the irreconcilable opposite of interpersonal humanity. It proves to be the other form of I-assertion, directed against the "Thou" rather than against the "Self." It is encountered concretely in various forms, for example, degradation of one's sexual partner to a mere object of lust, as well as the abuse of political or economic power, leading to personal oppression and exploitation of subordinates. Other examples, however, are the countless small and petty attempts in everyday life to force the other person down, even in the pursuit of his necessary, basic interests, in order to maximize one's own space for life, development, and freedom. Responsible interaction with the "Thou" can only mean here that we must be on our guard against our I-assertions and must respect the rights of those with whom we live no less than our own, whether this means one's own wife, husband, children, or one's neighbors, colleagues, subordinates, and superiors in the business firm, etc. And that simply means "dialogue." Only to the degree that we mutually reconcile our claims and demands with one another and respect them in common, do we practice interpersonal humanity, does the other person cease being merely a means in the calculation of our ends, and can common life really become personal. That is why all humanity stands or falls with dialogical, in strict contrast to monocratic, existence.

Dialogical existence, understood as responsible interaction of the "I" with the "Thou," however, does not stand in contradiction only to egoistic I-assertion, but equally as well to altruistic I-sacrifice. The one just as much as the other means the denial of human personality. In other words, the altruist behaves no less monologically than does the egoist. With him also everything rotates around one pole, around the falsely understood "Thou," to which like an idol the "I" is sacrificed and which is consequently negated and thus becomes an unperson. From that it follows that altruism is easily joined by a secret feeling of superiority and, in its supposed opposition to egoism, behaves in a morally "oppressive and exacting"[28] manner, as if it were the epitome of the ethical. Anyone who has understood the dialogical character of interpersonal humanity, and thus the complex aspect of personal-ethical responsibility that includes the "I" and the "Thou," will no longer allow himself to be dazzled by altruistic presumption.

3.3.3 *Environmental Ethics*

Just as I am responsible for immediate interaction with myself and immediate interaction with the persons with whom I directly live, I am also responsible for immediate interaction with the natural environment as the elementary basis of existence of all creation. That is ethics' third basic aspect of responsibility.

This third aspect of responsibility is distinguished from the other two in that the responsibility does not refer to something human, but rather to something non-human, not to the "Self" or "Thou", but to an "It." Therefore, it is also more difficult to explain than the individual-ethical or the personal-ethical aspect of responsibility. We understand ourselves, as a rule, to be responsible for things in so far as they belong to ourselves or to a "third person," but not for things that do not formally belong to anyone, such as water, air, flowers in the open country, etc., and therefore are not immediately related to human persons. That is undoubtedly related to the fact that monocratic I-assertion meets no resistance with objects. They can, therefore, become pure power objects more easily than can the "Self" or even the "Thou." For rule of men over men will always meet with opposition sooner or later and thus reveal the fact that it is ethically problematic. The situation is different with rule over things, so long as they are not or are not claimed to be the property of others, whether individually or collectively. For things cannot protest; they are a mute world.

That is also true of the "It" of the natural environment within which we live. Although it is the elementary basis of existence of all life, it has fallen prey to an enormous process of seizure by humans, with the objective of minimizing their natural dependency. The more this happens, however, the more it becomes clear that we are sawing off the branch on which we are sitting. In spite of all our efforts to

[28] Dietrich Bonhoeffer, *Letters and Papers from Prison*, 3rd Ed., New York, 1971, p. 287.

emancipate ourselves through science and technology, we still remain dependent upon the natural environment. It is so to speak our *partner*, not a personal partner, of course, but indeed an ecological partner. Seeking to run over it in monocratic I- or We-assertion amounts to irresponsibility, which must lead to total catastrophe, threatening both nature and human beings.[29]

Environmental-ethical responsibility begins with the insight that we must relate to the environment as if it were a partner, and that means here in a manner that is ecologically-just. Each individual person must become aware that he may not deal with nature, its powers, its treasures, and its life goods exploitatively, but instead must treat them like a partner, considerately and carefully. At this point I can only emphasize this principle as the quintessence of environmental ethics, without going into details. That will be done later.

The awareness of responsibility in interacting with the natural environment belongs to the *cultural commission* of man and must, as has already been indicated, be undertaken by each and every person immediately, in so far as he directly uses nature, whether as a farmer, as a gardener, as a house occupant, as an automobile driver, as a hiker, etc. It is ethically relevant to the highest degree whether this use happens with consideration of nature or devastates nature. The *indirect use* of nature, first of all the use of natural spaces and resources by the modern, socially organized economy, is incomparably more crucial. If each individual took seriously the ecological responsibility arising from his direct use of nature, but we collectively were to regard this responsibility for indirect use — whether over economic or over political institutions — as something imaginary, because it does not make demands on us directly, this would be like "strain at a gnat and swallowing a camel," avoiding small devastations painstakingly, but tolerating large ones fatalistically.[30] That would mean, in other words, that one would understand oneself to be responsible only in the area of direct relationships, but not in that of indirect relationships, which actually determine the quality of our existence and, therefore, are of crucial importance. And that would

[29] It is truly troubling that only the alarming reports of the Club of Rome (Donella H. Meadows, *et al.*, *The Limits to Growth*, New York, 1972; Mihailo Mesarovic and Eduard Pestel, *Mankind at the Turning Point*, New York, 1974) led to a publicly perceptible process of rethinking. Cf. Erich Fromm, *To Have Or To Be?* p. 8-9.

[30] Cf. the important remarks of Hans Jonas, *The Imperative of Responsibility*, Chicago, 1984, pp. 136-40 ("The Future of Mankind and the Future of Nature").

amount to self-castration of the ethical. Thus the environmental-ethical problematic of today makes it clear, as through a magnifying glass, *that the ethics of the immediate must integrate itself into the ethics of the mediate,* if ethical responsibility is to be perceived in its entirety, and thus radically.

3.3.4 *Social Ethics*

In contrast to individual, personal, and environmental ethics, as has already been suggested in anticipation, social ethics is concerned specifically with the aspect of responsibility that arises from the fact that the basic relationships in which every human person immediately stands are always also mediated by the structure of the social institutions within which they concretely develop.[31] Therefore, since social ethics is concerned with responsibility for the how of the structural ordering of the institutions of our social lives, which influence the ethical quality of the I-Self, the I-Thou, and the I/We-It relationships, it is the *ethics of the mediate,* or *social-structural ethics.*

It would be erroneous, however, to push this distinction to the point of separation and place social ethics beside or even against individual, personal, and environmental ethics. It is all of this, of course, but in the mediate sense that it reflects the responsibility for the "Self," for the "Thou" of one's neighbors, and for the "It" of the environment in the total context of the social ordering structures that represent the indispensable context of human existence. This can be clarified most easily in relation to personal ethics.

Personal ethics, in the sense presupposed here, is concerned specifically with responsibility for the relationship to persons with whom one is immediately concerned. Thus, for example, the managers in a firm are immediately responsible for good human relationships with their subordinates. Someone who behaves autocratically and treats his subordinates as mere recipients of orders will inevitably fail. It is also possible, however, for a manager to take great pains to form personal-dialogical relationships with his workers, but to make little

[31] Cf. Wolfgang Huber, "Freiheit und Institution," *Evangelische Theologie,* 40 (1980), p. 308: "Institutions must serve the indispensability of human persons and protect them; they should leave open a space that people can shape by virtue of their freedom; they should promote common human action."

progress, because the corporate structures are authoritarian and notoriously thwart his good will. There exists a relation of interdependence between the personal and the institutional.[32] The one can either hinder or promote the other in regard to facilitating or organizing good, ethically responsible, inter-personal relationships — in this case among workers at different levels within a corporation. If the corporate structures are authoritarian, socially disturbing relationships will be predominate and a manager's good will to create a humane, i.e. personally-dialogical, corporate climate will also accomplish little. If the situation is reversed, then the favorable structural relations will place these personal-ethical efforts on a realistic basis and promote them. On the other hand, even very developed, humane corporate structures can be largely condemned to ineffectiveness, if the people who are to implement them fail in terms of personal ethics, while in turn their suitability increases to the point of the humanization of corporate relationships if those involved prove their worth in this respect.[33] Consequently, social ethics can do justice to the entire extent of its responsibility only to the degree that it knows how to take in the personal-ethical concern.[34]

What is true of personal ethics is, of course, also true of individual and environmental ethics. It must also be taken in by social ethics. Social ethics asks in a universal sense about *the structural order of institutionally mediated existence*, which is able to promote, rather than hindering, the responsible life of individuals, groups, societies, etc. in all orders of human existence. And in this respect it also aims directly at facilitating individual, personal, and environmental ethical, responsible behavior in the sphere of institutionally mediated relationships. Thus, for example, someone affected by self-alienation in work can only cope with his fate in terms of individual ethics and once again

[32] Cf. Gerhard Weisser, *Beiträge zur Gesellschaftspolitik*, ed. Siegfried Katterle, Wolfgang Mudra, and Lothar F. Neumann, Göttingen, 1978, p. 663.

[33] Cf. Rolf-Peter Callies, "Dialogisches Recht," *Evangelische Theologie* 25 (1965), p. 311: "A person *is* only in an institution; he or she is only in the law, just as, in reverse, the law is only in personal action. An institution is a *dialogical* law."

[34] On the other hand, personalism, if it begins with sufficient anthropological depth, must take in the social-structural dimension. That is decidedly the case with the socialist personalists Nikolai Berdiajev (1874-1948) and Emmanuel Mounier (1905-1950). On the German side, something similar can be said of Dietrich von Oppen's and Stephan H. Pfürtner's personalism. Cf. Wolfgang Huber, "Sozialethik als Verantwortungsethik," in Alberto Bondolfi, Werner Heierle, and Dietmar Mieth, eds., *Ethos des Alltags*, Zürich, 1983, pp. 55-76.

experience work as something that has to do with his "Self" when structures of production are developed through which work can be humanized. And, similarly, it will only really make sense to call upon the individual to shape his direct relationship with nature in terms of environmental ethics when that goes hand-in-hand with a structural reorganization of technology and the economy that meets the demands of environmental consideration. In this comprehensive perspective, social ethics as structural ethics means the integration of all the main aspects of ethical responsibility.[35] Thus, it can be said with Heinz-Dietrich Wendland that "*all* ethics is finally and ultimately 'social' ethics."[36]

3.4 Business and Economic Ethics as a Special Case of Social Ethics

Business and economic ethics is not concerned with a separate aspect of responsibility of its own. It turns out to be merely *one component of social ethics*, albeit — in terms of its importance and complexity — probably *the most important and also the most difficult*. As analogous components, marriage ethics, family ethics, and political ethics can be cited. Ecological problems, on the other hand, are too interwoven with business and economic ethics and political ethics, to some degree also with family ethics (family planning, population growth), to be singled out as a special component of social ethics.

Business and economic ethics is thus nothing other than the application of social-ethical questions, perspectives, and principles to fundamental problems of business and economics. This brings with it the fact that working it out concretely must go ahead of grounding and developing the social-ethical approach, as it is advocated here and should be applied. At the same time, the concept of the responsibility assigned to it must be substantiated in terms of its content, which could be mentioned only more formally thus far, just as earlier the closely related normative foundation of social ethics was substantiated. That leads to a series of foundational reflections and excursuses, which will be taken up in the second part of this volume.

[35] Cf. Hans and Thea Schulze, *Zwischen Technik und Gott*, Stuttgart, 1982, p. 11, where the necessity of an integrative social ethic is similarly pointed out.

[36] Heinz-Dietrich Wendland, *Einführung in die Sozialethik*, 2nd Ed., Berlin, 1971, p. 7.

II. FOUNDATIONAL CONSIDERATIONS

4. SOCIAL ETHICS IN THE CONTEXT OF THE SOCIAL SCIENCES

4.1 The Relationship to the Social Sciences

The very concept of social ethics, as it has been developed in the preceding chapter and is understood to include business and economic ethics, manifests a close relationship to the social sciences. *Social ethics,* to emphasize the point once again, *is the theory and practice of the responsible existence of human persons in relation to their fellow human beings and to the environment, in so far as this relation does not have a direct character, but is instead mediated by social institutions.* Its specific, basic question is: How should the social institutions that mediate social coexistence be structured, so that in all of the basic relationships of human existence the manner of the mediation does not hinder, but rather promotes, human and environmental justice?[1] Since the nature of this basic question entails that it can be properly asked only in the context of social reality, social ethics is naturally dependent on the findings and insights of the theoretical and empirical social sciences that have this sphere of reality as their object of study. It thus turns out to be a discipline related to, and consequently also conscious of, empirical research.

Establishing that social ethics stands in a necessary relationship to the empirical social sciences says nothing about the nature of this relationship. Therefore, some clarification and precision is necessary. The special nature of the relationship — to anticipate the crucial point — is related to knowledge of the subject, or discipline-related. Social ethics can responsibly explain how fundamental

[1] To the best of my knowledge, the social-ethical question is first encountered in precisely this form with the American theologian Reinhold Niebuhr. See, for example, *Young Reinhold Niebuhr: His Early Writings, 1911-1931,* ed. William G. Chrystal, St. Louis, 1977, p. 172. See especially *Moral Man and Immoral Society,* New York, 1932. See also John Philip Wogaman, "Towards a Method for Dealing with Economic Problems as Ethical Problems," *Concilium,* 140 (1980), p. 80: "Economic structures can either aid or hinder a genuine sense of fellow humanity within the human community."

institutions or rules, or rather rule-functions, of social reality should be structured, only when it is supported by the required expertise (both theoretical and practical). Without sufficient expertise, social ethics has no legitimacy to speak about it. It then becomes, at most, a supplier of utopian blueprints for society, that may well inspire imagination, arouse emotion, and raise a critical consciousness of social reality as it is. Although that is certainly more than nothing, it is less than a constructive and practicable contribution to the development of realistic, humanly just institutions and rules. If social ethics sees its specific task in that — and, according to my conception of it, it does — then it must always relate to knowledge of the subject and, therefore, in the concise sense of the word, be "objective." It can do this, however, only in dialogue with the empirical, practical social sciences. And this is exactly what is meant by social-scientifically informed.

To make the point in a different way, social-ethical statements about what should be done in social reality are concerned with the conditions of "social-scientific correctness" in general and, in the context of business and economic ethics, with the conditions of "economic correctness" in particular. Social ethics will be able to accept responsibility for its judgment- and decision-maxims[2] in the social context in which it stands only in so far as it meets the standards of the social sciences. It is not sufficient here merely to have good intentions; expertise must be involved if anything substantial, enduring, and attainable is to be achieved. Of what use are, for example, the most ideal plans for new regulations about corporate governance and industrial relations, if they prove to be illusionary in terms of the discipline of economics? Are they anything other than a kind of mirage that feigns what is unreal and can never become real? But if this is the case, if social ethics must orient itself to the social sciences, does it not run the risk of submitting to a foreign principle, and thereby simply ceasing to be ethics?

It must be said in reply that in reaching its judgment- and decision-maxims, social ethics must always meet the standards of the social sciences, *but that the social sciences can never provide its guiding principle.* If social ethics were to seek normative guidance from the social sciences, it would have to submit to a foreign principle and give itself up for lost. In that case, the question of human justice

[2] On maxims for judgment and decision, see 8.1-8.5.

would be lost in questions of the social sciences. But social ethics, as understood here, stands or falls with exactly this question. It must ask persistently and relentlessly, with full expertise, about human justice in the realm of the socially-scientifically correct, and thus not only, for instance, whether one structured social concept or another is functional and efficient, but first and foremost, whether its realization would augment or diminish human well-being.[3] In short, its specific function is *to tie social-scientific correctness to human justice*, where that is understood to mean human justice in its full sense, which can never disregard environmental justice. Further clarification of this thesis is now required.

Since the time of Max Weber there has been a prevailing tendency in the social sciences to divorce social scientific-correctness from human justice, in order to make it (as much as possible) "value-free." That is, I believe, correct up to a point; a scientifically-objective basis of ethical values is impossible, unless one broadens the concept of scientific rationality in such a way that it could also include intuitionism. (This view is also supported by the findings of contemporary metaethics.[4]) Thus, if the postulate of the value-neutrality of the social sciences is understood to mean that the grounding of ethical values cannot be a matter of rigorous science, and that, consequently, it is necessary to distinguish between the scientific and the evaluative in the social sciences, which is Weber's basic concern here, I agree. From that, however, it does not follow that ethics is simply irrelevant to the rational sciences, including economics: "To be sure, it is impossible to prove the rightness of any ethical principle, or even to argue in its favor in just the manner in which we argue in favor of a scientific statement. Ethics is not a science. But although there is no 'rational scientific basis' of ethics, there is an ethical basis of science, and of rationalism."[5] Or, to put it differently, no matter how hard they strive methodologically to operate from the principle of value-neutrality, the social sciences can never determine what is social-scientifically

[3] Cf. Gibson Winter, *Elements for a Social Ethic: Scientific and Ethical Perspectives on Social Process*, New York, 1966, p. 262. According to Winter "social science is a theory of the conditioned character of practice" and "social ethics is evaluative interpretation of the intentional character of practice."

[4] See 2.1.3.

[5] Karl R. Popper, *The Open Society and Its Enemies*, Vol. II, 5th Ed., Princeton, Princeton University Press, 1966, p. 238.

correct without values — though as a rule these values are not reflected upon, but rather are left in the gray area.[6]

If values are introduced into social-scientific analysis in this manner, under the table, then a fatal falsification of what must be considered "social-scientifically correct" can easily arise under the heading of what is proper, legitimate, and necessary. The following considerations will attempt to elucidate this.

As far as the subject matter of the economy is concerned, in so far as it is taken as a whole, the business corporation's orientation towards profitability is undoubtedly imperative. If a firm wishes to survive, to safeguard the jobs of its employees, to reward its shareholders, to provide any benefit at all to society as a whole, then it must meet its expenses. In other words, it must be profitable. This is true regardless of whether the societal structure is "capitalist," "socialist," or some other alternative.

At the same time, the necessary profitability-orientation of a corporation does not at all mean that this interest in profit-maximization should dominate all other interests. That is imperative only if one thinks, in agreement with the capitalist tradition, purely in terms of an acquisitive economy and makes attainment of maximum profit the ultimate objective of doing business.[7] The principle of profit maximization is thus based on a value judgment and, therefore, cannot be absolutely valid as an economic imperative — though this point is often contended.

Thus, whenever certain economic particulars, such as profit maximization, are claimed to be economically rational under the rubric of economic propriety or economic necessity, social ethics must ask critically what is really imperative economically and what can be attributed to a value system that is concealed, because it has been accepted for so long and identified with economic rationality. Accordingly, the relationship of social ethics to the social sciences is twofold.

[6] Siegfried Katterle makes this point convincingly with the example of welfare economics: *Sozialwissenschaft und Sozialethik*, Göttingen, 1972, pp. 11-46. See also Herbert Giersch, *Allgemeine Wirtschaftspolitik*, Vol. I, Wiesbaden, 1961, pp. 125-26.

[7] See Folkert Wilken, *Das Kapital: Sein Wesen und seine Geschichte und sein Wirken im 20. Jahrhundert*, Schaffhausen, 1976, p. 41: "In the large economy, however, the pursuit of profit, as it has emerged from English economic thought, increases until it becomes the fundamental, primary motive of all economic activity. In it the motive of profit maximization achieves a supra-economic dimention." Peter F. Drucker, to be sure, argues to the contrary: *The Practice of Management*, New York, 1954, p. 35.

In learning from the social sciences, it must impartially sharpen its awareness of that which is genuinely social-scientifically correct. At the same time, it must be careful not to accept uncritically the values that are possibly equated with correctness in the social sciences, but that conflict with the criteria of human justice. Were social ethics not to do so, its self-destruction would be inevitable, because in supposedly taking social-scientific correctness seriously, it would in fact be assimilating values essentially foreign to it. Incidentally, in such an endeavor both to respect fully the principle of social-scientific correctness and to distinguish it from the normative, social ethics aligns itself closely to the *normative social science*[8] of Gerhard Weisser and his methodological distinction between "explicative" and "practically (normative)" statements.

Just as the social ethicist must take seriously, albeit critically, what is accepted as socially-scientifically correct, so the social scientist (as the case of Weisser provides evidence) cannot be excused from ethical questions. As soon as he voices warnings, recommendations, or judicious criticism — and he cannot in fact avoid doing so — he already faces the normative problem and, therefore, the ethical question.[9] Thus, his retreat from active participation in the process of values-education in society would be fatal. Moreover, he would run the real risk, from which recourse to "value-free science" could not protect him, of accepting indiscriminately, not to say dogmatically, the value-orientation that is brought subliminally into play in the economy and is disguised as social-scientific correctness.[10] Seen from that perspective, social ethics has the function of warning, and in this sense is of lasting relevance to social science, which is indelibly related to the ethical question, just as, on the other hand, social ethics, through its necessary relationship to social reality, finds itself permanently dependent on social science.

[8] On (Gerhard Weissers') normative social science, see 4.3.4.

[9] Friedrich A. Lutz, in his subtle investigation *Politische Überzeugungen und nationalökonomische Theorie*, Tübingen, 1971, p. 11, also reaches the conclusion: "One will not be able to dismiss completely such influences (scil. "political convictions"), certainly not in the normative branch of science, where at least the goal that one sets will always be influenced by general-political ideas. That will not do any harm, assuming that one is aware of it and openly acknowledges it."

[10] Cf. Bruno Fritsch, "Private und volkswirtschaftliche Kosten," in Erwin von Beckerath and Herbert Giersch, eds., *Probleme der normativen Ökonomik und der wirtschaftspolitischen Beratung*, Berlin, 1963, p. 235.

4.2 Economic Rationality and Human Justice

The relationship between social ethics and social science has implicitly raised the question of the relation of social-scientific correctness and human justice in the economy. This relation must now be addressed explicitly.

The concept of the scientifically correct is primarily joined in ordinary usage with that of the *objective*. Thus, whatever is considered objective is scientifically correct. In this sense, for example, a bridge is constructed with scientific-correctness in so far as its method of construction complies with the objective laws of statics. Such scientific correctness in itself has nothing to do with ethics or ethical evaluations. The categories of "correct" and "incorrect," not those of "good" and "evil," are appropriate here. It is good, however, for a bridge to be constructed "correctly," and thus scientifically correctly, so those using it are not in danger of having it suddenly collapse. If the scientifically correct is in this sense ethically indifferent, it nevertheless belongs to ethical responsibility to subject itself to the scientifically correct, because scientifically incorrect conduct — in this example, conduct that disregards the laws of nature — would be directed ultimately against human persons, and consequently, against human justice. Thus one can say here that the genuinely scientifically correct, though its character is in principle non-ethical, can also correspond to what ethics requires as humanly just. Does that also hold of the scientifically correct in the economy?

This most difficult question leads to a prior question. Are there laws of economics with the same or comparable objectivity as that which characterizes natural laws?[11] It appears that there are indeed such laws, though not on a large scale: "Limits to all human activities are drawn by external nature. There is no question that economic life in its productivity strongly depends upon these external conditions (location, boundaries, landscape, climate, soil conditions, what grows on the land or what is in it), upon these genuine natural laws.

[11] Modern physics has, of course, called into question the objectivity of natural laws in the sense of their absolute universal validity and interprets them statistically, not deterministically. This, however, has no practical significance for events in the macro-cosmos (as distinguished from those in the micro- and possibly the mega-cosmos).

One must sometimes even speak of real iron laws."[12] Thus one must speak of a natural, and consequently a "natural-lawful" dependence of the economy in this specific sense.

These conformities to natural laws that simply indicate the ecological dependence and objective boundaries of all economic activities, however, are to be contrasted with the regularities or economic necessities encountered in the economic organism itself. The economy, as we have already seen,[13] is not ruled by an iron law of nature, but rather is an historical, cultural product. In other words, it is a structure of institutions created by humans, which, however, often enough behaves like an objective force, controlling its creators in such a way that the economic subjects see themselves as under the control of supposedly objective constraints that may limit their scope of action quite narrowly. The "objectivity" of such constraints, however, is of a kind different in principle from the objectivity of natural laws. It does not come into being independently of man, but rather as a consequence of human decisions. This objectivity, therefore, is historical and ultimately man must accept responsibility for it.[14] In short, man himself both determines this objectivity and subordinates himself to it.

The trend towards rationality in economic life undoubtedly belongs to this objectivity,[15] because it is ingrained in the rational nature of man himself. Always and everywhere man has attempted, albeit with varying degrees of success, to shape his economic activity rationally, that is, to achieve an optimally high benefit by means of factor investment (human labor, raw materials, means of operation, entrepreneurial capabilities) that is as thrifty as possible, and thus to increase the efficiency of the economy. This need not in itself have anything at all to do with the pure pursuit of profit. Even if the purpose of the economy is understood, not in terms of acquisition,

12 Friedrich Karrenberg, "Das Problem der 'Eigengesetzlichkeit'," in Karrenberg, *Gestalt und Kritik des Westens*, Stuttgart, 1959, p. 120. See also Martin Honecker, "Das Problem der Eigengesetzlichkeit," *Zeitschrift für Theologie und Kirche*, 73 (1976), pp. 92-130.

13 p. 46-47.

14 Friedrich Karrenberg, "Das Problem der 'Eigengesetzlichkeit'," pp. 120-26, introduces with good reasons the term "historical laws," in the sense of law-governed regularities of historical, economic, and legal life, in order to clarify this question.

15 On the controversial concept of economic rationality and the necessity of critically restricting it by including normative aspects of human justice, see Helmut Kaiser, "Normative Erweiterung ökonomischer Rationalität," *Zeitschrift für Theologie und Kirche*, 28 (1984), pp. 285-320.

but in terms of meeting the vital human needs of all and improving the quality of life, as is true especially of the Christian understanding, the rational necessity of efficiency, together with the accompanying momentum, remains. An inefficient or unprofitable economy will be useless in meeting the necessities of life.

A major impetus for the pursuit of rational efficiency is competition. When economic actors stand in a relationship of competition with one another, it becomes inevitably clear from the income statement who is and who is not managing efficiently. That is acknowledged almost everywhere today, so that even for non-doctrinaire supporters of a "socialist" satisfaction-of-needs economy, the economic problematic tends to concentrate on finding forms that constructively combine the principle of market-economic competition to the idea of collective planning.

With the concept of planning, a third economic necessity is addressed. It must have a forward-looking perspective: "By its very nature, all economic activity is forward-looking, calculated, goal-directed, and therefore planned activity. The element of planning is already inseparably tied to the concept of economic activity."[16] Consequently, classifying the possible economic systems as "planned" and "unplanned" proves to be misleading. The crucial difference does not lie in planning itself: "The distinguishing criterion of economic orders is...not whether an economy is planned or unplanned, but instead who the subjects of the planning and control are."[17] In the free market economy (to the extent that it even exists), the agents of planning and control are individual firms or groups of firms; in the communist state economy, it is the central party-state planning authority. And between these two extremes there are mixed forms of decentralized and centralized, individual and collective, indicative and imperative planning. Planning is necessarily at work everywhere, however, even if we choose to call it something else.

On the basis of this discussion, it can now be said that efficiency, competition, and planning are economic necessities related to the rational structure of man and his economic activities[18] and in this

[16] K. Paul Hensel, "Planwirtschaft," *Handwörterbuch der Sozialwissenschaften*, Vol. VIII, Stuttgart, 1964, p. 325.

[17] *Ibid.*, p. 326.

[18] A contrary opinion is expressed by André Gorz, *Farewell to the Working Class*, trans. Michael Sonenscher, London, 1982, p. 175. This author considers efficiency and competition to be necessary only for the rationality of the economy that is now

respect, despite the constraints that also go out from them, by no means need to contradict human justice. That is not true, however, of every form of rational efficiency, nor of every form of competition or planning in the economy.

In order to understand this clearly, one must remember that human economies can be determined by quite different fundamental interests. Thus the fundamental interest of the economy oriented towards acquisition is profit, in the sense of either individual or collective enrichment. But that does not at all preclude, but instead includes, as a side-effect, an ample satisfaction of socially determined economic needs. In fact, the will to acquire can unleash enormous productive powers, as modern capitalism quite alarmingly proves. If this fundamental interest becomes the prevailing structural principle of the economy, then there will also arise necessities or constraints that are not connected to the rational structure of the economy, but instead to a particular form or ordering of the economy that is shaped by the dominance of the motive to acquire. In this case profit is not primarily a gauge of economic efficiency, but an end in itself that encourages, as experience shows oppressively, senseless growth in production, far exceeding the reasonable satisfaction of needs, and also extremely damaging to the environment. And competition in a market economy is then not only a stimulant and regulator of productive and consumptive economic activities. It degenerates all too easily into an aggressive, unbridled driving out of competition, which does not decide the firm's ability to compete, but instead its economic power position over market share, which in turn encourages the formation of cartels in resistance to it. With all of this a network of constraints is created, which the individual economic agents can scarcely evade without suffering economic loss, if not complete catastrophe. They thus have the appearance of firm economic necessities, which are then suddenly misinterpreted as objective economic laws. For one actually tends summarily to equate what is experienced in economic processes as super-human coercion with economic necessities, even when they are in fact constraints based only on the structure of an economic system or economic policy created by

passing away and has already become outdated by the industrial revolution (automatization), for which reason he argues for a "new economic rationality," which would be appropriate for the age of automation. But does that not throw out the baby with the bathwater? Is automation not closely related to the rational pursuit of efficiency?

particular, for the most part unacknowledged, value judgments, and that could be mitigated, if not abolished, by altering them.[19]

For this reason, one must distinguish between genuine and merely putative economic laws, between conformities to economic law that are grounded in the rationality of economic activities themselves, such as efficiency, competition, planning, and, on the other hand, inevitable consequences that are based on the structure-determining dominance of certain misdirected basic interests, whether they are, for example, the most extreme acquisition principle in the "capitalist" economy or the most extreme party-state power-maximizing principle in the "communist" economy. Rationally grounded conformities to economic law need not contradict the claims of human justice. This differs in the case of inevitable economic consequences following from economic structures in which social-ethically problematic basic concerns or interests objectify themselves, or when they have the appearance of rationality within the given economic order. Thus, in an expanding acquisition-economy, it is "rational" to invest even more following the general trend, in order to take maximal advantage of anticipated opportunities for profit, even if the economy experiences exponential growth as a result, as was decidedly the case in the years 1945-73. Yet this kind of economic growth, with its cult of material values, its consumption of raw materials, goods, and energy, as well as its rapid environmental destruction, stands under an omen that is not humanly just, but rather inhuman. And indeed it is not only inhuman, but also irrational.[20] It is utter nonsense that: "In comparison with what is going on now and what has been going on, progressively, during the last quarter of a century, all the industrial activities of mankind up to, and including, World War II are as nothing. The next four or five years are likely to see more industrial production, taking the world as a whole, than all of mankind accomplished up to 1945."[21] It is obvious to all reasonable persons that it neither should nor can continue like this.

These observations can now be summarized: *That which is not economically rational cannot really be humanly just, and that which conflicts*

[19] See also Friedrich Karrenberg, "Das Problem der 'Eigengesetzlichkeit'," pp. 123-26: "What presents itself as conformity to laws of social, legal, and economic life is frequently nothing other than a sum of habits, rules, and conventions...that are subject to change."

[20] See Hans Christoph Binswanger, Werner Geissberger, and Theo Ginsburg, eds., *Der NAWU-Report*, Frankfurt am Main, 1978, esp. pp. 27-39.

[21] E. F. Schumacher, *Small Is Beautiful*, New York, 1973, p. 18.

with human justice cannot really be economically rational. This is a guiding principle of great relevance to social ethics, and specifically business and economic ethics. Its thrust is directed in two quite different directions.

It is directed against the utopian disregard of the economically correct in economic questions. It is thus unrealistic, as has already been stated, to think that profitability interests are tied only to the capitalist economic order and can be eliminated in a socialist economy. Even Karl Marx, who thought about this matter realistically, asserted with emphasis in his *Critique of the Gotha Program* (which, under the influence of Lassalle, called for unrestricted distribution of the proceeds of labor to workers, and thus for the renunciation of profit in a socialist society) that even in a socialist economy, deductions from the product of labor must be made for the replacement of the means of production consumed, for the expansion of production, and for reserve and insurance funds. Thus, profit must be made. And he added, "These deductions from the 'undiminished proceeds of labour' are an economic necessity and their magnitude is to be determined according to available means and forces, and partly by computation of probabilities, but they are in no way calculable by equity."[22]

This guiding principle is also directed against the elimination of human justice as a social-ethical postulate from the economic sphere, in the name of the frequently invoked "autonomy" of the economy. Taken in the strictest sense of the word, the autonomy of the economy does not exist, as should already be clear. For the economy did not emerge from nature, but rather arises from the activity of human persons. Its "law-governed regularities," if one wishes to use this expression at all, are determined by man's human spirit or pernicious ideology, even if secondarily they face the economic subject as an objective force. In so far as they are rooted in rationality, they are necessary, also carry in their necessity human justice, and prove themselves to be, in their economic necessity, ethically responsible. But in so far as they are based on and related to certain social-political ordering structures that have been prejudiced by extreme value judgments and are thus more or less inevitable, while standing in notorious resistance to human justice, not only must they be called into

[22] Karl Marx, "Critique of the Gotha Program," in *Collected Works*, Vol. XXIV, 1989, p. 84.

question ethically, but their supposed economic correctness must be examined critically. Can an economic order that is functioning well on the whole, seen purely technically, really be economically rational, if for structural reasons it necessarily violates human justice? More concretely, can such an economic order really be economically rational if it produces horrendous social inequality? if it brings about mass unemployment? if in production and consumption it is interested in persons only, or at least predominantly, as workers and consumers, so that the feeling of self-alienation spreads and many of those affected by it seek to escape from it? Must it not in that case, at least in the long run, destroy itself? In this sense human justice and economic rationality are, though they belong to totally different spheres, in the final analysis inseparably related to one another in such a way that everything ethical has a factual component and everything factual has an ethical component.[23] With that the complete complexity of the social-ethical, that is to say the economic-ethical, formulation first comes into view.

4.3 The Problem of the Normative in the Social Sciences

The concept of "scientific correctness" belongs to the vocabulary of the *descriptive-explicative* sphere. Descriptive-explicative expressions state how something is, how it behaves, how it happens or functions. For example, what are the essential law-governed regularities of a competitive economy? What are its specific consequences in the past, present, and probably in the near future? Is a competitive economy still a possibility in a world of increasing concentration of economic power and the accompanying penetration of power in all market relations? And if it is, to what degree and under what structural conditions? Statements answering questions such as these must follow from analysis of the subject matter itself. In so far as they actually correspond to the facts of the matter and do not secretly assume value judgments, they can lay claim to objectivity and can be generalized. The concept of "human justice," in contrast, proves to be a

[23] Cf. John Philip Wogaman, "Towards a Method for Dealing with Economic Problems as Ethical Problems," p. 81: "Christians cannot hope to contribute to the ethical solution of economic problems without acquiring technical competence, any more than economists and policy-makers can expect to accomplish this without giving serious thought to the value considerations which lie beyond economics."

prescriptive-normative category. It states how something should be, behave, happen, or function, and therefore is not only scientifically correct, and thus practical, but can also at the same time, in its systemic structures, meet the demands of human justice.

The concept of human justice has been used thus far only in a formal sense, with its content undetermined. Purely formal norms are, however, empty and thus without determining, let alone obligating, power. The merely formal, social-ethical demand for a humanly just economic order within the framework of imperative economic conditions is something about which everyone can agree, because it remains in the domain of the undetermined. One is likely to become involved in an argument only if material definiteness is brought to the value category of "human justice," thereby making it concrete. Experience shows that liberals, Marxists, Christians, etc. can have quite different conceptions of the fundamental demands of human justice, and that these differences lead in theory and in practice to controversial economic-ethical consequences. What, then, is the possibility of reaching a decision social scientifically concerning the material determination of human justice? Are there objectively justifiable, universally valid norms here? And, if not, what other ways are social-scientifically defensible, without abandoning the claim of the ethical? It is, of course, not possible in the present context to go into all of the various attempts to answer these questions. Only a few approaches will be discussed, selectively and succinctly, in order at least to shed light on the problem situation and, in its contradictions, to show a passable path.

4.3.1 *The Natural Law Approach*

The concept of the "humanly just" is associated somewhat inevitably with that of "*human rights*." One could say, therefore, that the content of human justice is concretely determined by human rights and, indeed, is generally valid to the degree that it is universally recognized. Without question, universality is claimed by the "Universal Declaration of Human Rights,"[24] which was adopted without opposition by the General Assembly of the United Nations on 10 December 1948 (though the East Block Nations, South Africa, and Saudi Arabia abstained). Granted, universality does not mean here universal validity, in the sense of a law binding all member nations. The UN Declaration sees itself as

[24] United Nations, "Universal Declaration of Human Rights," 1948.

> a common standard of achievement for all peoples and all nations, to the end that every individual and every organ of society, keeping this Declaration constantly in mind, shall strive by teaching and education to promote respect for these rights and freedoms and by progressive measures, national and international, to secure their universal and effective recognition and observance, both among the peoples of Member States themselves and among the peoples of territories under their jurisdiction.[25]

The universality and universal validity claimed here, therefore, relate more to the ideal or the idea of human rights than to their individual concretizations themselves. Upon what is the normative substance of the intended idea based?

The idea of universal human rights grew from the soil of Western natural law thought.[26] "*Natural law*" means generally the system of legal norms that are binding for all human beings, everywhere and always, because of their common essential nature and without, or in the event of conflict even against, all positive law, especially national laws and legal decisions. This is, therefore, a matter of norms that must lie in human nature itself. But what does "nature" mean in this context? Depending upon how this question is answered — whether one understands it naturalistically as biological-vital spirit-nature or idealistically as its spirit-nature, directed teleologically at the good and perfect, whether one thinks in Christian terms of the created nature or rationalistically primarily of the rational nature of human persons — totally different natural law approaches ensue. In the modern era, the rationalistic approach has above all developed into an historically effective idea.

Modern, and especially the most recent, declarations of human rights have, therefore, also grown from the soil of rationalistic natural law thought — though its content was enriched by assimilation of Stoic and Christian ideas — which intentionally equates natural law with rational law. In this sense, the Virginia Declaration of Rights of 12 June 1776 declared that "all men are by nature equally free and independent and have certain inherent rights."[27] In a similar manner,

[25] *Ibid.*

[26] On the origin and development of the idea of natural law, which can be comprehended in its complexity and disparateness only with difficulty, see the concise but well-informed orientation of Karl Heinz Ilting, "Naturrecht," *Geschichtliche Grundbegriffe*, ed. Otto Brunner, Werner Conze, and Reinhart Koselleck, Vol. IV, Stuttgart, 1978, pp. 245-313.

[27] "Virginia Declaration of Rights," 12 June 1776.

the French Declaration of the Rights of Man and of the Citizen of 26 August 1789 speaks of "natural," "unalienable," and "sacred" human rights.[28] When "equal and inalienable rights," based on the "recognition of the inherent dignity...of all members of the human family," are invoked in the Preamble to the United Nations' Universal Declaration of Human Rights, it sounds like an echo of these historically significant statements.[29]

These declarations of human rights are written in the grammatical form of the indicative, and, consequently, have the formal appearance of descriptive-explicative, and in this respect universally valid statements: "All men are by nature equally free and independent," "Men are born and remain free and equal in rights." In other words, an "ought" is supposedly inferred from an "is." Human beings should be free, independent, and equal in rights, because they already are, on the basis of their own nature as the true and original norm. But this raises the question: If that really is the case, why is the "ought" not realized? Why are freedom and equality so frequently foreign to actual human existence? Apparently, because human persons in their empirically perceptible and thus objectively describable nature do not correspond to what they "by nature" should be. There exists, therefore, a gap between the historical-social reality of their true nature and the concept of nature in the idea of natural law. To put it differently, *in human persons nature is self-alienated*. And behind that stands, when all is said and done, either the idealistic difference between noumenal and phenomenal nature or, quite simply, the Christian distinction between the original and the fallen creation of God.

This explanation of the natural law is the reason that declarations of human rights based upon it are only apparently descriptive explications of facts that are "natural" and consequently objective, and thus observable and recognizable by everyone. Actually they are normative, *prescriptively practical* requirements. *Human beings should obey the commands of their true or original nature*. In this way, however, the concept "nature" gains a definite ethical qualification. Taken by itself, of course, this concept remains ethically indefinite and thus ambivalent. It can mean both actual, biologically-determined and socially-modified human nature, with its inequalities and the resultant domination of men over men, and postulated ideal nature, on

[28] "Declaration of the Rights of Man and of the Citizen," 26 August 1789.
[29] United Nations, "Universal Declaration of Human Rights," 1948.

the basis of which all men have the same dignity and rights. Thus in the long history of natural law argumentation, not only the principle of the equality of all men, but also the right of the stronger, has been based on natural law. The same is true analogously of both slavery and its abolition, of both private property and common ownership, etc. Whenever declarations of human rights in the sense of ideals of freedom and equality were based on natural law thought, some confessional certainty stood in the background — whether in the form of Christian faith that all human persons are created in the image of God or in the manner of the Enlightenment idea of humanity, where such beliefs live on in a secularized form.[30] The universal recognition of traditional human rights, and human rights developed further in their spirit, as the norm for human justice, therefore, continues to exist only to the extent that the declaration of belief in humanity behind it stands up for itself effectively and gains recognition. Only within this certitude of conviction do human rights find their inner evidence, not already in an objectively describable and verifiable being of human nature. So far as the conception of natural law seeks to provide an objective foundation for human justice, reasonable to every rational or scientifically-thinking person, and not merely to bring to light the fact that positive law, valid in state and society, must always orient itself to a norm of the just that transcends itself, it will hardly be able to withstand critical examination.

4.3.2 *The Approach of Critical Theory*

The concept of natural law is problematic, not only for the reasons summarized above, but also because it is based upon a timeless, ahistorical concept of nature and norms, which can be related only tenuously, if at all, to historical, positive law. Thus, no positive law covers completely what the natural law principles of the freedom and equality of all persons require. Pascal even said, "Nothing will be just if weighed in these scales."[31] Even if this pessimism may be exaggerated, one thing is certain: the strength of the traditional idea of natural law exists in its legal-critical function, not in its function of

[30] Cf. Jan Milič Lochman and Jürgen Moltmann, eds., *Gottes Recht und Menschenrechte*, Neukirchen-Vluyn, 1976.

[31] Pascal, Blaise, *Pensées*, Frg. 294, trans. A. J. Krailsheimer, Harmondsworth, 1966, p. 47.

actually establishing laws. There will always be the critical distinction between claims motivated by natural law, which have little to do with the historical context, and the actual law. And an insecurity of the existing legal order cannot be avoided in this way — one thinks today of the "Green" movement. That is the dilemma! Is it not also possible to follow the opposite path, that is, to find the universal validity intended by natural law, and therefore human justice, not in the stasis of the timelessly-ahistorical, but in the historical-temporal itself? Friedrich Hegel followed this path.

From the Hegelian "philosophy of right," which begins with the rationalistic natural law thought of the Enlightenment, one undoubtedly can gather — to follow Karl Heinz Ilting — that with "this work the idea of historicity again and again gains the upper hand."[32] Thus in 1818 the philosopher could still declare concerning the demarcation of natural law and positive law: "The positive right in its content, though, can be partly irrational and illegal." In the version of 1820 it reads, on the contrary, in the same place: "Right in this positive form acquires a positive element in its *content* ... through the particular national character of a people, its stage of historical development, and the whole complex of relations connected with the necessities of nature." And from this one can see that Hegel replaces the thesis that positive law is irrational and unjust if it opposes natural-law principles with the idea that differences arising between natural law and positive law are to be understood, and thus also to be justified, by the particular historical components. An *historicization* of the natural law takes place, therefore, in such a way that it is understood as an admittedly dialectic, nonlinear, continuing process of development, through which the standard and sense of the historical come to light. In this way, then, the history of the world finally becomes with Hegel "progress in the consciousness of freedom."[33] It is the course of world history, which unfolds the normative orientation as a reason-guided process of liberation in the dialectic oppositions of reality and also makes it the norm of human justice.

Despite reservations, especially concerning Hegel's idealism, critical theory, represented primarily by Max Horkheimer, Theodor W. Adorno,

[32] Karl Heinz Ilting, "Naturrecht," p. 307. The following discussion of the historization of the idea of natural law by Hegel is based on Ilting's work (there also the references of the citations).

[33] Georg W. F. Hegel, *The Philosophy of History*, trans. J. Sibree, New York, 1956, p. 19.

Herbert Marcuse, and Jürgen Habermas, now also stands in the Hegelian tradition — though mediated and accordingly modified in essentials by Karl Marx. Also with it the historical prevails over nature. And also with it the process of the emancipation of humanity is the purposeful sense of history.

In the *Habermasian variant of critical theory,*[34] emancipation, understood as an historical process that drifts towards unconstrained communication in "mankind's evolution towards autonomy and responsibility," becomes the fundamental interest that guides all knowledge.[35] This fundamental interest is like the "transcendental subject" of history. It serves functionally in the place of the proletariat in Marx and already has its basis "in the natural history of the human species."[36] Originally an "instrument of self-preservation," it transcends by far the naked will to survive and "is subject to the criterion of what a society intends for itself as *the good life.*"[37] Consequently, the good life, understood as dialogical life, freed from all constraints and in that respect autonomous, becomes the measure of that to which man must understand himself to be challenged, if the emancipation of the human species is ever to be achieved. And "to this extent," as Habermas explicitly says, "the truth of statements is based on anticipating the realization of the good life."[38] It seems fair to conclude from all of this that the cognitive discovery of truth, including the truth of ethical norms, and the emancipatory realization of the "good life," wherein the driving fundamental interest of history manifests itself, coincide. To the extent that universal history, with its guiding fundamental interest in emancipation, is the history of the entire human race, the normative orientation, which brings itself

[34] The extent to which Jürgen Habermas should be classified among the representatives of critical theory is a subject of debate. Carl-Friedrich Geyer, *Kritische Theorie*, Freiburg im Breisgau, 1982, considers him not to be one in his main ideas, because Habermas "shows only a qualified interest in the central positions of Horkheimer and Adorno" (p. 168). Nevertheless, he deals with him in the concluding section, "Further Development of Critical Theory," and certifies that he, "despite all discontinuity," takes up "central concerns of critical theory" in two areas, "that of a philosophy of history starting from materialist premises and that of the relationship of cognition and interest" (*ibid.*). Precisely these concerns are important.

[35] Jürgen Habermas, *Knowledge and Human Interests*, trans. Jeremy J. Shapiro, Boston, 1971, p. 315.

[36] Habermas, p. 312.

[37] Habermas, p. 313.

[38] Habermas, p. 314.

about in anticipation of the successful life, must also have universal meaning. As is the case with "nature" in natural law theory, human "history" becomes here, in its single-minded process, the ultimate basis of the normative that claims general validity.

But what has been said of the natural law approach is true here as well. From the actual, describable course of history as such, it can no more be gathered that it is, according to its inner logic, "progress in the consciousness of freedom" or, in its fundamental interest, "mankind's evolution toward autonomy and responsibility," than it can be concluded from human nature as such that all men should be "equally free and independent." When history is understood in this way, there is once again a convictional certitude, which does not result from its process itself, standing ultimately behind it. With Hegel, that is revealed immediately by his apocalyptic construction of the history of the world,[39] which would be inconceivable without the adoption of essential elements of Christian eschatology, and which is at play when the philosopher understands world history as the permanent "world's court of judgment,"[40] and indeed not as the "non-rational inevitability of a blind destiny," but rather as "the necessary development, out of the concept of mind's freedom alone, of the moments of reason and so of the self-consciousness and freedom of mind," a development which is "the interpretation and actualization of the universal mind."[41] In critical theory, this connection is found less directly, yet with it also, historical-theological implications are undoubtedly encountered as rationalized basic convictions.[42]

4.3.3 *The Approach of Critical Rationalism*

Both the natural law approach and that of critical theory are based on a concept of rationality that orients itself according to the methodological principle of an absolute foundation, and yet ultimately must refer back to a certitude that is not rationally grounded, but rather (though this is not admitted) has the character of a confession or conviction. In one case, it is the certitude of rights that are irrevocable, inherent in human nature, and timeless. In the other case, it is the

[39] Cf. Karl Löwith, *From Hegel to Nietzsche*, trans. David E. Green, New York, 1964, pp. 31ff.

[40] Hegel, *Hegel's Philosophy of Right,*" §340.

[41] Hegel, *Hegel's Philosophy of Right,*" §342.

[42] Michael Theunissen, *Gesellschaft und Geschichte*, Berlin, 1969.

certitude that emancipation, in the sense of liberation of man from all oppression, corresponds to what the historical process as such intends, and therefore includes the fundamental interest by which all socially-relevant knowledge is supposedly led. Since, in both cases, the norm-containing certainty fuses with rational truth, it presents itself in its normative content in the mode of certain, objective truth that claims universal validity.

Critical rationalism, as it was inaugurated by *Karl R. Popper* and found an influential interpreter and spokesman first and foremost in *Hans Albert*, developed precisely from the critique of this self-confident rationalism, in this respect characterized as classical. It sees itself then as a "revised rationalism" or "criticism" that "begins with the assumption of the in-principle fallibility of human reason, and therefore of human problem-solving behavior in general — regardless of the type of problem to be solved — and rejects as illusory the claim to return to a sure foundation, and therefore replaces the classical principle of the adequate — that is, the absolute and sure — foundation with the principle of critical examination."[43] In other words, with critical rationalism, not the verifiability of a theory or statement, but its falsifiability becomes the scientific criterion of rationality. In short, a theory or proposition can raise a claim to scientific validity only so long as it permits no exceptions to itself. The statement, for example, that all swans are white is untenable if only a single non-white swan is found. There can be, therefore, no absolute validity. Each new scientific discovery will be considered in turn only as material for the ongoing critical process of falsification. Even if a scientist establishes something experimentally a thousand times, it still remains uncertain whether it will be the case the ten-thousandth time. Thus, if he were to put forward more than a hypothesis on the basis of his empirical experience, and instead seek to ground a law inductively, he would only dogmatize the result of his previous experiences. In this sense, permanent critique methodologically replaces the procedure of establishing or justifying.[44]

From this it can now be said that critical rationalism is guided by efforts to exclude every kind of dogmatism from scientific problem-solving behavior. And indeed that is true not only for the field of the

[43] Hans Albert, "Aufklärung und Steuerung," in George Lührs, *et al.*, eds., *Kritischer Rationalismus und Sozialdemokratie*, Berlin, 1975, pp. 108-9.

[44] Cf. Hans Albert, *Treatise on Critical Reason*, Princeton, 1985, pp. 111-12.

physical and social sciences, but also for the problematic of moral- or legal-philosophical norms. Hans Albert states this explicitly: "Our criticism of the classical methodology of sufficient justification may..., in principle, be applied to the problem of the basis of ethics, for it applies to the general structure of foundationalist thinking, regardless of the kind of convictions discussed."[45] It goes without saying that this accuses both the natural-law approach and that of critical theory of dogmatism, for both approaches are based on procedure of establishing and both, consequently, ultimately refer back to conviction-certitudes, which as such are neither verifiable nor falsifiable scientifically, and thus, measured according to critical rationalism's criterion of rationality, are clearly dogmatic in character. But if only what meets this criterion can survive, isn't every ethical concept that somehow refers in the question of the normative to value convictions that are creedal, and thus subjective, absolutely condemned?

Answering this new question is not as easy as it may appear at first glance. In any case, it would be incorrect to think that for Hans Albert subjective "value convictions" are already as such absolutely suspect and, therefore, must simply be ruled out in every attempt to solve a problem, and, consequently, also in the discussion of norms. Such convictions, on the contrary, stand in a necessary relation to objective cognitions: "Particular value convictions always appear in combination with knowledge. They are intimately intermixed, 'bound up with' factual convictions — a situation that everyday thought takes into account with its Platonism of value."[46] That agrees, incidentally, with the correlation of "economic rationality" and "human justice," as it was introduced in Section 4.2. "It is necessary," according to Albert, "to make continual use of both [factual convictions and value convictions] in solving the problems of our existence, to constantly test them and, if need be, to revise them."[47] For "new ideas and experiences can lead us to restructure our cognitive system [and thus our level of knowledge] in some particular manner and in this way also to change our system of values. It is true, as we know, that one cannot without more ado deduce a value judgment from a factual statement; but particular value judgments can certainly turn out to be *incompatible* with particular previously

[45] Hans Albert, *Treatise on Critical Reason*, pp. 92-93.
[46] Albert, pp. 99-100.
[47] Albert, p. 100.

held value convictions *in the light of a revised factual conviction.*"[48] Value convictions, consequently, have a place in critical rationalism. Indeed, this is declared openly — in contrast to natural law theory and critical theory — and, moreover, their status is of a different nature.

Albert's subtly-differentiated arguments have primarily a dual focus: "Thus it is possible to overcome positivist resignation in questions of moral philosophy without lapsing into the existentialist cult of commitment, which replaces rational discussions of such problems with irrational decisions."[49] *Positivist resignation* consists in completely separating value convictions from the realm of the empirical-rational and leaving the field to the irrational, whereby the normative existing in society, if it does not simply succumb to the verdict of pure fiction, is accepted uncritically as an indispensable premise that can be neither defended nor questioned on rational grounds. And *existentialism* makes a virtue of the irrationality of the normative in that it, in a putatively value-free manner, lets the committed decision in the concrete situation coincide with that which should be done. Both lead to dogmatizing in the sense of critical rationalism, to dogmatizing given norms, in one case, and to dogmatizing arbitrary decisions, in the other. And according to Albert, his criticist philosophy is able to go beyond both of them, in that it indeed holds to value convictions, though "not as *dogmas* but as *hypotheses*."[50] That means, as normative content, to which an ethical obligation may well be befitting, but that must remain in principle revisable, and thus open. In this way, this criticist philosophy lays claim to "moral content itself": "Whoever adopts it does not decide for an abstract principle with no existential significance, but for a way of life." And in unconcealed irony Albert adds, "One of the immediate ethical consequences of criticist philosophy is the conclusion that unshakable faith, impervious to rational argument, valued so highly by many religions, is not a virtue, but a vice."[51]

One undoubtedly must grant to critical rationalism that in relentlessly warning us of all dogmatism, it has an important role to play, particularly in ethical discussion. For there is always a great danger

[48] Albert, p. 100.
[49] Albert, p. 101.
[50] Albert, p. 96.
[51] Albert, p. 101.

that ethical argumentation — especially when supported by strong conviction — will proceed dogmatically in concrete factual questions, in that it knows *a priori* what should be regarded as good and just, no matter how complicated and difficult the situation in which decisions must be made. If in such situations one is concerned with finding operational guidelines for judgment and decision, and thus practical instructions for action, which are called "maxims" in our terminology, then one cannot pay too much attention to critical rationalism's critic of dogmatism.[52]

The question remains, however, whether critical rationalism does not run the risk of summarily dismissing as "dogmatic" that in the field of normative discussion which is essentially not dogmatic. First of all, there is the question of the status of the certitude of value judgments. As has already become obvious, Albert does not dispute that there are value convictions, and that they exist legitimately in conjunction with factual cognitions. But they must not claim absolute validity, in order to evade critical examination. That, however, is inevitably the case when normative convictions attach themselves to a certitude that transcends the rational. Behind this, if I am not mistaken, stands a confusion of certitude (*Gewißheit*) and certainty (*Sicherheit*), which may also underlie the passage above about "unshakable faith, impervious to rational argument, valued so highly by many religions."

That is to say, one should avoid simply conflating certitude and dogmatic certainty.[53] The certitude of the faith that, for example, God's word manifests itself definitively in the word testified in the Bible, is by no means identical to the certainty in which, for instance, fundamentalists indiscriminately claim all commands in the Bible to be absolute expressions of God's will.[54] But the certitude of the faith has no doubt that human justice is to be found — please note, to be found — in realistically dealing with the normative potential of the

[52] See 8.2.5 and 8.3.

[53] The distinction between religious certitude and dogmatic certainty stems from Pascal, who knew about the certitudes of the heart (understood as an organ to which God makes himself perceptible), which have their own reasons that are inaccessible to reason (*Pensées*, Frg. 277: "Le cœur a ses raisons, que la raison ne connaît point"). But he never attempted to reinterpret such certitude (*certitude*) as dogmatic certainty (*assurance, fermeté*) in such a way that reason would also have to agree with it, if only reason would use its intellectual ability properly. Pascal explicitly distanced himself from such an interpretation: "Ne cherchons donc point d'assurance et de fermeté. Notre raison est toujours déçue par l'inconstance des apparences." (Frg. 72).

[54] Cf. Gerhard Ebeling, *Critical Rationalism?* Tübingen, 1973, esp. pp. 75ff.

Holy Scriptures, not by reading biblical passages mechanically. In this sense, it places its trust entirely in the truth of God's Word. Yet the criteria of human justice gained in this manner are not dogmas laid down once and for all, about which there can be no change, but rather are guidelines borne by conviction that must prove themselves and thus prove their truth again and again in contact with both the instructions of the Bible and human social reality. To be sure, this assumes that such a by no means uncritical finding of the normative, which seeks to obligate absolutely, not merely hypothetical, must rely on certitudes to which one ultimately can only be either open or closed. Is this not dogmatism? If it were, then critical rationalism would also have to fall under this verdict; for it also rests ultimately on a certainty, on the incidentally quite-paradoxical certainty, that fallible reason, by virtue of the permanent falsification of its cognitions, will not miss the way to truth.[55]

4.3.4 *The Approach of Gerhard Weisser's Normative Social Science*

Normative social science, as it is associated today with the name of Gerhard Weisser, and critical rationalism stand in a relation of both proximity and distance to one another. Symptomatic of this is the fact that Hans Albert was an assistant to Weisser early on, but later clearly distanced himself from Weisser.

The orientation of Weisser's normative social science is decidedly "practical." It seeks to enable the social scientist "to advise and to warn"[56] in the shaping of contemporary social life, as it constantly becomes more complex. Seen from the perspective of practice, social scientists would be less and less able to avoid service of this kind.[57] That would mean, however, that there are also *value judgments* in their discipline.

Weisser understands quite clearly, of course, that with this postulate he will encounter great resistance from his colleagues: "Since

[55] If I am not mistaken, Paul Feyerabend's immanent critique of critical rationalism also points in this direction: "We have to conclude, then, that *even within* science reason cannot and should not be allowed to be comprehensive and that it must often be overruled, or eliminated, in favour of other agencies. There is not a single rule that remains valid under all circumstances and not a single agency to which appeal can always be made" (*Against Method*, 3rd Ed., London, 1993, p. 158).

[56] Gerhard Weisser, *Beiträge zur Gesellschaftspolitik*, ed. Siegfried Katterle, Wolfgang Mudra, and Lothar F. Neumann, Göttingen, 1978, p. 21.

[57] Weisser, pp. 21ff.

Max Weber, the aversion to the value judgment is so strong that it is frequently considered incompatible with a distinguished scholarly attitude for a scientist to strive for anything other than purely explicative research."[58] Value judgments would have nothing to do with being scientific.

Though this opinion is still common, Weisser resolutely opposes it. In addition to explicative social science, which must analyze social or economic events and bring them to theorems that are universally verifiable and thus valid, practical social science should be developed, so that the difficult problem of evaluative advice and decision in the sphere of the social can be addressed in a scientifically defensible manner.[59] It would not be permitted, as happens in reality, that time and again when decisions must be made, *ad hoc* value premises would be brought in or even that practical maxims would be fabricated out of the social sciences by means of mostly unconscious logical deception, and that these premises or maxims would then give the appearance of being purely scientific.

"The following specific tasks may be assigned to the practical social sciences, which are also called normative social sciences:

a) Demonstration of the practical axioms that are needed for social-scientific recommendations, warnings, and the evaluative critique of given situations;
b) Application of basic teachings of the explicative social sciences as theoretical axioms, as well as elementary anthropological statements, analyses of the time period, historical-theoretical theorems, theoretical statements about otherwise empirical rules of social life, especially statements about the limitations of what can be enforced in particular historical situations;
c) Derivation of a general preliminary decision, arising from a) and b), about the historically applicable basic type of the order and in general the shape of social life, which is based on the intended recommendations and warnings;
d) Development of recommendations and warnings of a specialized kind that arise from a)-c) and empirical knowledge of the concerned specialized fields of society and serve particular social sciences, including political science, economics, etc., as their practical axioms."[60]

[58] Weisser, p. 30.
[59] Weisser, p. 16.
[60] Weisser, pp. 16-17.

For the present context, of course, point a) stands in the foreground. How does Weisser proceed methodologically with the demonstration of the practical axioms or norms for social-scientific recommendations and warnings in practice?

First, it must be understood that Weisser, just like the critical rationalists, refuses to surrender to the method of establishing these axioms, which are based on ultimate "fundamental concerns," scientifically, and thus universally. He clarifies this decisively: "In the following, therefore, it is assumed that either the content of these fundamental concerns cannot be established scientifically or that there is no scientific system at our disposal now from which the universal validity of the most important fundamental concerns could emerge convincingly."[61] He also seeks, however, to avoid making himself a "sceptic in questioning the possibility of 'practical' [i.e. normative, A. R.] philosophy." He may be thinking at this point primarily about positivist resignation, but then also about Albert's criticist philosophy. He holds, on the contrary, in connection to the school of the Kantian Friedrich Fries, that there exist axiomatic fundamental concerns that have their place in subjective convinction-experiences containing "direct cognition," and therefore neither can have nor need a foundation. He understands this to correspond absolutely to the current situation in epistemology. Even "from the standpoint of modern logic, for example, from a consistent further development of the Vienna School's position, nothing stands in the way of developing systems of advice whose normative foundations, as here recommended, *consist of confessionally-introduced axioms*."[62] Consequently, Weisser's normative social science is concerned with *systems of propositions that consist of confessionally-introduced, interpreted basic concerns, required theoretical axioms, and conclusions from both groups of axioms*."[63]

The contentious point in Weisser's conception, not astonishingly, is the confessional introduction of fundamental concerns or normative axioms into social science. Hans Albert objected to it and considers these logically-ultimate value premises to be determined dogmatically, because they are taken from critique.[64] There are some

[61] Weisser, p. 29.

[62] Weisser, pp. 29-30.

[63] Weisser, p. 30.

[64] See, for example, Hans Albert, "Normative Social Science and Political Rationality," *Archiv für Rechts- und Sozialphilosophie*, 55 (1969), esp. pp. 568-72.

statements within Weisser's works that actually could give the impression of dogmatism, in that for him confessional certitude and dogmatic certainty occasionally merge. He asserts, for instance:

> If human persons wish to attain certitude, they are not exclusively dependent upon science. The idea that they remain in uncertainty as long as science does not confirm their matters of concern is grotesque, if one thinks about the shortness of the phase of human history in which it can be said that science has had meaning in the life of human persons. Neither was the human race lost in uncertainty without a compass during the previous thousands of centuries nor can new relativizations of the foundations of science threaten us with the loss of all certainty.[65]

It becomes clear, however, on closer examination that Weisser does not intend confessional certitude to mean a claim of certainty removed from all critique. According to him fundamental concerns should certainly be interpreted and clarified, which includes, rather than excludes, dealing with them critically.[66] He even remarks later that "upon reflection, the fundamental concerns themselves and their ranking can be corrected."[67] And he does not claim that his "fundamental concerns," "practical axioms," "value premises," or whatever he chooses to call them, have objective, universal validity, and therefore does not claim that they are "scientific" in the traditional sense of the word.[68] All in all one may be able to say here with Siegfried Katterle: "Weisser's practical social science does indeed go beyond the limits of Popper's philosophy of science; however, it remains within his more general conception of critical rationalism."[69]

An additional question may still be raised at this point. Is Weisser's attempt in the field of ethical norms to get beyond both the dogmatism of the method of establishing and the scepticism of the method of falsifying ultimately nothing other than pure subjectivism, which leaves it up to each individual subject to decide what will be

[65] Weisser, *Beiträge zur Gesellschaftspolitik*, pp. 33-34.

[66] Weisser, p. 24.

[67] Gerhard Weisser, "Die 'praktischen' Aussagen von Politologie und Wirtschaftswissenschaft," in Carl Böhret and Dieter Grosser, eds., *Interdependenzen von Politik und Wirtschaft*, Berlin, 1967, p. 112.

[68] Cf. Gerhard Weisser, "Glaubensgewißheit und heutige Wertens- und Erkennenskritik," in Theodor Strohm, ed., *Christliche Wirtschaftsethik vor neuen Aufgaben*, Zürich, 1980, pp. 120-21.

[69] Siegfried Katterle, *Sozialwissenschaft und Sozialethik*, Göttingen, 1972, pp. 61-62.

normatively valid or invalid? And does this not lead logically to hopeless ethical relativism, according to which all ethical norms must ultimately become equally valid?

To this it must be said that, for Weisser, subjectivity and mere subjectivism cannot be equated: "'Confessional' introduction of the fundamental postulates means only that the scholar introduces the content of certain basic assumptions of his claims, the validity of which he is convinced without scientific basis. Nothing forces him to hold that his postulates are '*therefore*' subjective"[70] and, consequently, to regard them as arbitrary. Convictions have nothing to do with arbitrariness, but rather have to do with inner certitude. "If the scholar, through the confessional introduction of his fundamental concerns, restricts himself to the communication of his convictions, *he nevertheless communicates a conviction*, not possible points of view to be chosen arbitrarily. He has certitude, but only cannot establish compellingly in the manner of science that others should also have this conviction with certitude."[71] That is, of course, quite different from ethical relativism. On the contrary, this means standing up definitely, even confessionally, for the fundamental concerns or value judgments that are perceived to be certain and necessary for a change to the better: "There are...ways other than the scientific way to convince other persons. We mean 'giving testimony' of an inner bond that lets others perceive that they also have this bond."[72] In this way all conviction-certitudes are for Weisser now "person-related." By that he means — in total opposition to subjectivist arbitrariness — "not derived, but rather simply affirmed..., just as the empiricist affirms that what he sees is valid. This is naturally — exactly like the perception of empirical phenomena — person-related."[73] This, then, is the explanation of Weisser's subjectivity: It is directed against the positivists' objectivism, which seeks to separate the validity of perception-cognitions from the perceiving and recognizing subject. That is an unrealistic abstraction, because all perception and recognition, including the empirical, is based on a personal subject. Consequently, the fact that inner experience-certitudes are subjective in this way

[70] Gerhard Weisser, *Beiträge zur Gesellschaftspolitik*, p. 34.

[71] *Ibid.*

[72] *Ibid.*

[73] Gerhard Weisser, Comment in Heiner Flohr and Klaus Lompe, eds., *Wissenschaftler und Politiker — Partner oder Gegner?* Göttingen, 1967, p. 54.

does not count against their validity, even if they are, unlike outer experience-cognitions, inaccessible to an objectified generalization. Weisser's objective is to enable the process of reaching conclusions in the social sciences to benefit from this insight.

Finally, it can still be asked by what right a normative concept that introduces basic value judgments for systems of practical advice "confessionally" is entitled to the attribute "scientific." For Weisser himself, this is ultimately of little relevance: "If someone should place great value on not calling such systems 'scientific' in the strong sense, little would stand in the way of speaking in this manner. What matters is that scholars themselves undertake this task, even if one may call it non-scientific. For only the scientifically-trained researcher is in a position to serve this public interest of the highest significance."[74] "Normative social science," as Weisser understands it, by no means intends to suggest that fundamental norms in the social sphere can be proven to be scientifically objective and therefore universally valid, but rather to suggest that it is possible, in scientific responsibility and honesty, to treat them as conviction-certitudes.

4.3.5 *Conclusions*

The present considerations of the problem of normativeness in the social sciences have taken as their starting point the question whether there are norms of human justice that are objectively establishable and thus universally valid in the scientific sense and, if not, what other paths are passable, as seen from the social-scientific as well as the ethical point-of-view. The conclusions can be summarized as follows:

a) *It is impossible to ground human justice as a materially-definite norm in the sense of scientifically-objective, universally-valid rationality.* Behind attempts of this kind ultimately stand rationalized conviction- or experience-certitudes of a confessional character, as is evident both from the natural-rights approach and that of critical theory.[75] In so far as these certitudes nevertheless claim to be objective principles, verifiable either by human nature or by human history, they are marked with the stigma of dogmatism. Yet even with these certitudes ethical dogmatism cannot persuade, but on the contrary will

[74] Weisser, *Beiträge zur Gesellschaftspolitik*, p. 30.
[75] That is even true of Rawls' theory of justice. See 7.3.3, esp. pp. 210-11.

lead to well-founded scepticism, if it embodies noble and indispensable values in its substance, as with "natural" and "universal" human rights.

b) Such ethical dogmatism is contradicted in principle by *critical rationalism,* immediately from its methodological approach, which replaces the procedure of verification with that of falsification. Accordingly, fundamental ethical value judgments concerning human justice that may not be called into question permanently are also impermissible. Value convictions have their legitimacy, because they are necessary and are always contained in cognitive findings, but only in a hypothetical form. Doesn't this, however, mean an impermissible relativization of ethics? Isn't ethics as a requirement of the absolute excluded from the start, if ethics itself, even in the final decision-premises, comes to stand on a basis that is only hypothetical and, therefore, always questionable? Ethical scepticism, as these questions already show, cannot be the correct response to ethical dogmatism, however little ethical dogmatism is in turn the answer to ethical scepticism.

c) *Gerhard Weisser's normative social science* opens up an escape from the dilemma in the question of norms between a dogmatist procedure and the method of falsification, which "methodically seals the permanence of the critique."[76] The basic concerns, as well as the basic value judgments for a humanly-just social or economic policy associated with them, are introduced there confessionally, and thus with obligation in mind. However, they are not to be understood dogmatically as principles secured once and for all and claiming objective, universal validity, but rather as critically revisable certitudes, capable of self-reflection and in need of interpretation on the basis of relevant traditions and experiences. Although the persuasiveness of such normative certitudes is subjective and not universally valid, they nevertheless aim, for those who have those certitudes, at least possibly, at general evidence and, consequently, at universal obligation. The lack of evidence for their universal validity is not equivalent to evidence of the necessity of this deficit. In short, it is a matter here of certitudes that seek to prove themselves to be certain in their tendency for other persons as well. Nevertheless, that must happen by means of testimony and argument, not dogmatically and authoritatively.

[76] Gerhard Ebeling, *Critical Rationalism?* p. 45.

d) Decision maxims or action orientations for social-political praxis can no more be obtained directly from the normative basic concerns of human justice than normative value convictions can be derived from the basic theories of the explicative social sciences. That is possible only indirectly, by means of *factual communication with the social sciences*. Thus, the interplay between empirical social science and normative ethics is needed here. With Weisser, that is completely clear.[77] In principle, Hans Albert also thinks similarly.[78] Consequently, it is necessary to distinguish between norms of different natures — between those that stand beyond scientific verifiability and assessment in their ethical substance, not simply in their logical form, and those that are to be found only in conjunction with discoveries of the empirical social sciences, which must meet the conditions of operationality and, accordingly, must subject themselves in principle to examination, even to the point of their falsification. Our discussion of the main types of normative ethics has, incidentally, already led to an analogous conclusion (2.3.2), which only confirms from another problem-situation the appropriateness of the distinction made here between norms that are based on an absolute conviction-claim and those that are in principle relative.

It now remains to draw from these conclusions methodological implications for laying the foundation of social, or business and economic ethics.

4.4 Methodological Consequences

Social ethics, as it is understood here, must assert not only personal-ethical responsibility in social existence, but also human justice in the social structures and processes of society. Furthermore, this should take place in a manner that takes social and economic rationality into account, in so far as it proves really to be socially and economically rational, not merely an ideological veiling of interest-bound goal-ideas that mistakenly raise an ethical claim. Social ethics, consequently, cannot be satisfied with developing norms of human justice that exist in principle; it must be able to convert them into a form

[77] See p. 89.
[78] Hans Albert, "Aufklärung und Steuerung," pp. 111-16.

that can take up the requirements of social and economic rationality, and thus that is operational and practicable. That leads, with the help of the preceding considerations, to quite definite methodological guidelines.

a) The starting point of social-ethical judgment- and decision-finding are constitutive criteria that can articulate the fundamental concerns of human justice in a principled and thus obligatory sense. As the preceding considerations have shown, fundamental criteria of this kind arise by way of neither a rational verification procedure nor a rational falsification procedure. They are a matter of personal and meaning-giving experience-certitudes, which lie beyond all scientific assessment and condemnation. Scientific honesty can, therefore, only say here that one should lay one's cards on the table and candidly account for the experience-certitudes that stand behind the fundamental social-ethical criteria to which one is committed.
b) Although the fundamental criteria of human justice rest on experience-certitudes, they may not and cannot take on a dogmatic character. That is true for various reasons:
   First, one has to distinguish between the inner substance of an experience-certitude and its character as expressed in the form of verbalized criteria. One may encounter differences that will require revision of the criteria.
   Further, experience-certitudes never exist in a vacuum, but instead always occur in an historical context and must be interpreted, and therefore understood, in view of it. Changes in the historical context can lead to new interpretations of the substance of the experience-certitudes, and to the development of new criteria.
   Finally, the criteria of human justice should by no means prove to be helpful and valid only inwardly, but also outwardly, in other words, with respect to criteria that stand in other ranges of experience. In contrast, dogmas do not need to prove themselves valid. They are simply decreed. Therefore, if the aforementioned criteria are not to degenerate on the quiet into inflexible dogmas, then one must go to the trouble of that kind of proof, which is possible only on the basis of persuasive argumentation. And that means that not the identification, but the mediation of the basic criteria of human justice must take place unauthoritarianly in the medium of arguing reason.
c) The criteria of human justice, understood not as dogmatically determinable once and for all, but rather as experience-certitudes

that are never completed and are constantly in need of hermeneutical clarification, are the highest principles of social ethics. They must guide the critical question of human justice in the social and economic rationality of social structures and processes, but they are not yet themselves the concrete answer to this question. Guidelines for action that seek to accentuate the humanly just — or, more modestly, the more humanly just — in the midst of the structures and processes of social events cannot simply be deduced from principles, as mathematical theorems can be deduced from axioms. There is no social ethics *"more geometrico demonstrata,"* a project upon which Spinoza (in vain) based his ethics. Such guidelines can be acquired only on the basis of sound analyses of social and economic facts that take up the discoveries of the theoretical and applied social sciences, and indeed, that do so in a manner such that the fundamental criteria are brought into the analyses as guidelines for assessment and decision. In this respect, social ethics is in its methodological approach resolutely aware of and related to empirical discoveries.

d) These guidelines for action, which are called "maxims" here, must be clearly distinguished from "criteria." Criteria must prove themselves to be norms of a purely prescriptive nature. They express in the range of a definite experience-certitude what must in principle be valid ethically. Maxims, on the other hand, constitute norms of a character that is prescriptive and at the same time also explicative. They are prescriptive in so far as they are guided by the criteria. And they are explicative in so far as they orient themselves to social-scientific discoveries in the interest of economic rationality. At the same time, this means that their degree of certainty, even in the best case, can be only relative, because the validity of the maxims is dependent upon discoveries of the social sciences, which must be fundamentally falsifiable.

The clear distinction between the "criteria of human justice" and their practical "maxims," with equally clear demonstration of their necessary connection, is of fundamental significance for the methodology of social and economic ethics.

These methodological guidelines already indicate the wider course of the in principle considerations of the basis of business and economic ethics. Next, it is necessary to account for the experience-certitudes that stand behind the whole.

5. HUMANITY ORIGINATING FROM FAITH, HOPE, AND LOVE

5.1 The Horizon of General Human Experience Rooted in Faith, Hope, and Love

The very words "faith," "hope," and "love" reveal clearly in which experience-certitude the understanding of human justice to be discussed here is rooted. It understands human justice as experienced by the persons who get involved in the comforting and demanding words of the biblical proclamation and gain in it the decisive orientation of their personal and social existence.

Faith, hope, and love are, of course, key words that concern general human experiences, not just specifically Christian experiences. After all, non-Christians also know about faith, hope, and love in their own, indeed elementary, way. When these words are used, non-Christians do not encounter them with a complete lack of understanding, but rather with a certain understanding. If that were not true, the Christian experience-certitude expressed by them could not be communicated. It makes sense, therefore, to begin here with the horizon of general human experience rooted in faith, hope, and love.

Let us begin with the original meaning of the word "faith" [*Glauben*]. It does not at all mean, as contemporary worn-down usage suggests, holding unproven propositions for true or an esoteric, religious knowledge that transcends everything rational. The Gothic "*galaubjan*," from which the New High German "*glauben*" is derived, has instead the basic meaning of friendly trust.[1] Thus the genuine meaning of faith is *an act of trust supported by love*. To love other persons means, therefore, to put one's trust in them.

From that it can also be understood why the word faith expresses something that belongs to the horizon of general human experience.

[1] German Academy of Science, ed., *Deutsches Wörterbuch*, Vol. IV, Sec. I, Part 4, Leipzig, 1949, col. 7820.

Without fundamental trust, life ceases to be human. Even the most ordinary steps, actions, and decisions presuppose trust. Who would even get out of bed in the morning, go to work, prepare for the day's business activities, if he did not have a certain trust in surviving until evening? This is true especially of agreements between individuals, social groups, economic associations, nations, etc. They would all be senseless if one could not have at least a minimal trust in the partner's contractual fidelity. Without "good faith," therefore, even the best laws and the most helpful social structures are robbed of their effectiveness. It can thus be said that a human ordering of life is based upon good faith and where good faith is lacking, there is no humanity in life. That is no mere assertion, with which one could also compare the opposite assertion with good reasons. It is, instead, an experience-certitude of great evidential power.

Faith, understood as trust, is closely related to hope. One could understand hope as a special form of trust, trust in the future. Without trust in the future, there is no hope. Therefore, it is also anchored in the horizon of general human experience. This can be seen in the fact that the person who sees no future for himself experiences his life as a hopeless, absurd, and therefore ruined existence. If human life is to be more than merely a meaningless eking out of a miserable existence, characterized by random events, then it must orient itself towards hope. With Ernst Bloch, in his famous work *The Principle of Hope,*[2] it coincides with humanity in general. Being human means for him having hope, and the human race comes through it to its goal of realizing the great hope as it manifests itself in the fantastic utopia of religious and non-religious visions of the future. The fact of the matter is that without hope, the human powers of constructing and sustaining necessarily break down. What then remains are resignation, despair, and nihilism, in which humanity gives itself up for lost. That is also a compelling certitude, as Albert Camus, for example, was able to point out with special, impressive power.[3]

What then is the case with love? What is experienced in it, beyond faith and hope? *Love is first of all trust and hope in one.* Whenever it is found, trust and hope will always be there as well. A child trusts his

[2] Ernst Bloch, *The Principle of Hope,* trans. Neville Plaice, Stephen Plaice, and Paul Knight, 3 vols., Cambridge, Mass., 1995.

[3] See especially "The Myth of Sisyphus," in *The Myth of Sisyphus and Other Essays,* New York, 1991.

parents and places his hope in them, if it experiences their love. If it does not experience such love, then trust and hope must also disappear for it, and the fundamental state of its life becomes anxiety.

This is related to something further: Trust and hope are present in love, as surely as love can always be exercised and experienced only as something present. Someone who loves and is loved, lives truly in the present; and someone who knows nothing about it runs the risk of fleeing from the present. On the other hand, someone who flees from the present will be incapable of true love. For one who does that lives either in a dreamlike utopia of the past or in an illusionary utopia of the future. And what he is then capable of loving is at most an idealized picture of the human person, not the human person as he presently is, as he genuinely lives in his entire non-ideal reality. This genuine person is instead abandoned, whether in the name of a conservative or a progressive ideal of humanity. Genuine love, however, always has to do with the present, actual person, who is not at all ideal, but rather is often enough repulsive and sometimes even abhorrent. And it is precisely this love that is widely understood as the epitome of humanity. That also belongs to the horizon of general human experience. How different it would otherwise be to explain that one — whatever one may think of the Christian faith — commonly sees as it were in Jesus of Nazareth, who did not push anyone, not even the guilty, away from himself, the human person in whom human justice has found a valid form.

In this way faith, hope, and love can already be experienced in the horizon of general human experience as basic categories of human existence. It is by no means a matter of esoteric words, whose meaning would be intelligible only to the Christian. They instead express something that can be the experience of every human person. Consequently, one can arrive at seeing in faith, hope, and love the indispensable existentials of human existence even outside Christian experience-certitude. There are countless indications of this. It must be all the more shocking for the insightful that our life, especially life that is mediated by social, economic, and political institutions, is not based on that kind of humanity — that, on the contrary, a completely different basic constitution of humankind comes to power here: mutual distrust, resigned acceptance of existing practical constraints, class, racial, national, and ideological hatred, the will to use other persons for one's own advantage or to dominate them, etc. How can humanity originating from faith, hope, and love, in short human justice oriented towards them, exist at all in the real world in which we live? Is this not a pure utopia, therefore doomed from the outset to failure, just as in the end Jesus himself failed? In these realistic questions a universal human experience also comes into play: the experience of the hard fact of the inhuman or, more succinctly, of *evil*. Can we exclude this experience, full of temptations, from social-ethical reflection?

5.2 The Experience of Evil

It has become anachronistic today to talk about the experience of evil, especially of "radical evil."[4] One senses that an unenlightened, obscurantist, unscientific attitude is behind it.[5] After all, science is concerned with empirical, unambiguously ascertainable facts. But is evil such a fact? Is it not merely a prescientific mindset, interpreting misunderstood facts, "so-called evil," as Konrad Lorenz puts it in the title of one of his books? In other words, focusing on the central thesis of this author, are we not ultimately dealing with a fiction, at most a human deficiency, but never an efficiency, with which one would also have to reckon in the sense of an historical constant in the empirical behavioral and social sciences? There are many theories today that *mutatis mutandis* follow this formulation of the question and, in principle, play down evil in human history to the level of a variable that as such did not always exist and by virtue of the evolutionary historical process's own tendencies will someday disappear, or at least can disappear.[6] One assumes that everything is scientifically

[4] Even the quite commendable *Handbuch der christlichen Ethik*, 2 Vols., Freiburg im Breisgau, 1979, omits this theme. It is mentioned, to be sure, in the 3rd (Supplementary) Volume, 1982, under "Guilt and Conversion" (Chap. 2), though only in passing (pp. 146-55).

[5] Goethe already harbored this prejudice, when he raised the censure against Kant that he had "disgracefully slobbered on his philosopher's cloak with the blot of radical evil, so that even Christians would be enticed to kiss its hem" (Letter to Herder, 7 June 1793), *Artemis-Gedenkausgabe*, Vol. 19, Zürich, 1949, p. 213.

[6] Two authors, who may be cited here as typical, have had much to say in the last two decades and, because of the wealth of essential information, are already important even for those who do not share the presuppositions of their worldviews: the behavioral researcher Konrad Lorenz, *On Aggression*, trans. Marjorie Kerr Wilson, New York, 1966, and the cultural critic Arno Plack, *Die Gesellschaft und das Böse: Eine Kritik der herrschenden Moral*, 7th Ed., Munich, 1970. As much as these two works differ from one another in their starting points and methods, they are similar in their basic biological orientations, as well as in their efforts to explain evil scientifically and

understandable, and consequently learnable and also feasible: the good person, the good society, liberation from all constraints, the total pacification of humanity until the realization of universal peace in the world.

to overcome it. (Literal translations of the German titles of these two books would be *So-Called Evil: On the Natural History of Aggression* and *Society and Evil: A Critique of Present Morality*, respectively, D. Lutz.)

For Lorenz, the impulse to aggression is the basic biological condition. But even in its intra-specific form (the impulse to aggression within the same species) this drive is not simply evil, but only "so-called" evil, and as such is even a condition of the good: "Intra-specific aggression can certainly exist without its counterpart, love, but conversely there is no love without aggression" (p. 217). Real evil is the impulse to aggression when it has been deprived of its natural inhibitions and thus has become excessive. The development of modern military technology, with its imbalance between weapons and the natural inhibition of aggression has created a highly critical situation. Nevertheless, this situation is not hopeless: "The natural inclinations of man are not so evil. Man is not so evil from his youth up. He is only not quite good enough for meeting the demands of modern societal life" (based on 7th — 16th German edition, S. 349, trans. G. Enderle). And, on the basis of the contemporary theory of evolution or selection, "it does not require considerable optimism to assume that from us human beings something better and higher may evolve. Far from seeing in man the irrevocable and unsurpassable image of God, I assert — more modestly and, I believe, in greater awe of the Creation and its infinite possibilities — that the long-sought missing link between animals and the really humane being is ourselves!" (p. 229). "Evil" will be overcome in the truly humane person of future evolution.

In contrast to Lorenz, the vital impulses, especially sexuality, are for Plack the basic biological data that determine the character of human existence. For present morality, the vital impulse-nature, to which aggression does not originally belong, is regarded as "supposed evil." In reality, however, it is precisely the good, and its suppression produces "true evil, which threatens our health and all of our lives" and the "chaos of aggression." In this way aggression, as a manifestation of real evil, becomes a variable of the suppression of impulse by morality, and thus disappears with the disappearance of this suppression. The impulse-nature itself, if it is only left free, holds the principle of the good, which takes evil's basis from it. And that gives rise to a completely new ethics, disregarding all values and virtues, which Plack calls "scientific": "Scientific ethics does not propagate any values: it is confident that human nature, if it is only left in peace and is not warped from an early age, develops on its own a form of behavior that best corresponds to both the individual and the community" (p. 345).

In the background of these two "scientific" attempts to cope with evil stands ultimately the confidence, which is not scientifically verifiable, in the wisdom of evolution or in the goodness of original human nature, which is not culturally depraved. In both cases it is a matter of anthropologically optimistic assumptions, which, when examined closely, lead to a concealed value judgment.

On the theological side, Gerhard Ebeling above all has recently criticized this view of evil, which is ultimately optimistic, and also ultimately plays down evil: "Das Problem des Bösen als Prüfstein der Anthropologie," in Ebeling, *Wort und Glaube*, Vol. III, Tübingen, 1975, pp. 205-24.

This optimistic expectation, however, completely contradicts the experiences of the human race thus far. Evil has, until now, in so far as we see its effectiveness in the oppression, exploitation, destruction, etc. of human persons by human persons, held up with eerie constancy. Epochs have come and gone: ancient slave society, medieval feudal society, modern mercantile-absolutist society, and both capitalism and socialism today. But evil has not gone away; it has only changed its form and above all — one could think of the mass destruction in our century through war and civil war — taken on even more colossal dimensions. "Contemporary humanity is subject to an enormous experience of evil," to say it with Gerhard Ebeling.[7] All that remains is the astonishment that, despite this harsh experience, about which everyone can have knowledge, the fundamental character of evil is repeatedly veiled.[8]

The evil of the human person can be identified in a first anticipation: from our fundamental experiences we could know it absolutely and also know how much human justice is essentially the humanity originating from faith, hope, and love, but nevertheless we notoriously deny faith, hope, and love through our actions and base our actual existence on totally different factors: underhanded distrust, fatalistic resignation, inconsiderate self-assertion. It is the contradiction between the essence of humanity and the existence of the human person.[9] *The human person exists in contradiction to himself, both as a person and as a society.*[10]

The primary focus of this last statement is on the simultaneity of person and society. One cannot divorce the person of the human being from his societal context, nor the structure of a society from the persons and groups of persons that constitute it. Let us be reminded here of the analysis of the fundamental human relationship that has

[7] Gerhard Ebeling, "Theologie zwischen reformatorischem Sündenverständnis und heutiger Einstellung zum Bösen," in Ebeling, *Wort und Glaube*, Vol. III, Tübingen, 1975, p. 197.

[8] In the field of psychotherapy Erich Fromm warns against this tendency towards covering up: "Clinical analysis must not be used to obscure the moral problem of evil. Just as there are evil and benign 'sane' men, there are evil madmen and benign madmen. Evilness must be seen for what it is, and moral judgment is not suspended by clinical diagnosis" (*The Anatomy of Human Destructiveness*, New York, 1973, p. 432).

[9] Cf. Erich Fromm, *The Heart of Man*, New York, 1964, p. 148: "Evil is man's loss of himself in the tragic attempt to escape the burden of his humanity."

[10] See the still significant work of Emil Brunner, *Man in Revolt*, trans. Olive Wyon, New York, 1939, which reflects on this problem theologically.

shown the ontological interdependence of the person and the institution, of the personal and the structural, as a social-ethical state of affairs of the highest relevance.[11] This state of affairs includes the fact that the existential alienation of the human person from what is essentially human as the fundamentally evil must meet the human person in the totality of his existence, namely, to repeat it in an abbreviated way, as person *and* society. In short, there exists not only of a personal kind, but also evil of a structural kind.[12] Repeated attempts to reduce it, whether to the personal-human or to the social-structural dimension, lead to a contraction and therefore play down the existence of evil as a reality to be experienced today.

The reduction of evil to the personal-human dimension in the Christian tradition, especially in its pietistic form, has become predominant, even though the New Testament clearly understands the transpersonal character of evil or "sin."[13] According to the purely personalistic view of the matter, the core of evil is found in the "heart," representing the center of the human person. Deliverance from evil means conversion of the heart, inner change. If only persons would become different inwardly, would be converted to faith, to hope, and to love, then their outer existence, their life in and of society and the world, would inevitably also experience a fundamental transformation. Society and the world, consequently, must be healed within persons themselves. That is the credo of this personalism that is encountered one time in Christian, another time also in idealistic, psycho-analytical form, etc.

[11] Cf. Section 3.2.

[12] For a more detailed discussion, see Arthur Rich, "Sachzwänge und strukturell Böses in der Wirtschaft," *Zeitschrift für Evangelische Ethik*, 26 (1982), pp. 62-82.

[13] In the New Testament, especially with Paul, "sin" is often understood as the power of sin. Seen in this way, it almost gains the character of a transpersonal power, even to the point of appearing like an objective power. Thus, he speaks of a reign of sin (Rom. 5,21; 6,12). And indeed its reign is understood in such a way that those ruled by it become veritable slaves of sin. See Ernst Käsemann, *Commentary on Romans*, trans. Geoffrey W. Bromiley, Grand Rapids, 1980, p. 147. Also related to this is the awareness of being subject to the rulers of this age (e.g. I Cor. 2, 6 & 8), who belong to the *"s'chema"* (form) of this world (I Cor. 7,31) and thus dominate the world as well as the human persons in it. Nevertheless, it would be mistaken to understand statements of this kind simply to mean an objective-impersonal power of sin. For Paul, in any case, sin remains the act of the human person, even when this act objectifies itself to become a structurally evil force that gains power over the human person in his historicity. All of this points to a dialectical relationship between personal and structural evil.

There is, of course, truth behind all of this. There really can be no fundamental change of society and the world without change in the persons and groups of persons that belong to them.[14] However, is the outer, structural transformation of society and the world a *mere function* of the internal-personal reality of persons, in such a way that the latter would, so to speak, automatically entail the former? That is out of the question.

Granted, a large and still growing number of citizens, motivated by an inner change of attitude, seek to orient their personal lifestyle deliberately towards the needs of the third world in the attempt thereby to contribute to evening out the discrepancy, which on the whole cries to heaven, between the standard of living of the developing nations and that of the industrialized nations. They thus prefer to buy products from the third world, despite higher prices, and to donate part of their income, even of their savings, to financing sensible development projects. That is without question a highly respectable act of the heart, a visible sign of ethical seriousness. But if one disregards the non-trivial demonstrative meaning of such generous decisions, their influence on the inherited structures of the world economy will not be substantial. It is, however, just these structures that favor the industrialized nations in their economic position and handicap the developing nations.[15] And as far as evil grows from this situation, it is precisely of a structural kind, and thus cannot be dismantled by means of personal charitable assistance, even if performed on a grand scale. A change of these structures themselves is required, which can be accomplished, if at all, only against strong resistance. Anyone who underestimates the aforementioned dimension of evil, therefore, underestimates it in its radicalness and underestimates that we ourselves still participate in it massively when we fight against it in the personal realm in full seriousness, and not without effect.

It is, then, among perhaps the most meaningful achievements of Karl Marx, to have awakened the sense of the reality of structural evil in his time and to have sharpened the eye for it. Indeed, the chief

[14] In this respect I agree with Walter Mostert that "the will to overcome evil as an objective power must concentrate on the sinner" ("Gott und das Böse," *Zeitschrift für Theologie und Kirche*, 77 [1980], p. 468). But "concentrate" should not be understood to mean that the will should focus only on the sinner.

[15] Cf. Hans-Balz Peter, Hans Ruh, and Rudolf Höhn, *Die neue internationale Wirtschaftsordnung*, Bern, 1979, esp. pp. 65ff. and the bibliography, pp. 95-96.

proponents of Marxism rarely uses the term "evil." He was opposed to traditional ethical concepts of that kind. He, nevertheless, completely addresses the subject by calling structural evil the "perverse world" and personal evil the "perverse world conscience": "Man is *the world of man,* the state, society. This state, this society, produce religion, an *inverted world-consciousness,* because they are an *inverted world.*"[16]

Two things stand out in this passage. First, for Marx, there is not only personal or consciousness-related perversity, but also political-social perversity. Second, consciousness-related perversity, which corresponds to personal evil, is merely a product of structural perversity.

The first statement of the passage cited above mentions what we are calling "structural evil." It implies that the fundamental perversity of the world is not to be found ultimately in the subjectivity of human persons, but in the objectivity of the structural constitution of society and nation, which for its part (still according to Marx) depends on the prevailing structure of the economic conditions of production. Accordingly, the individual participants in society — and that obviously includes "capitalists" — are not to be held personally responsible for the evil that results from their activities in society and the nation. Marx writes explicitly: "My standpoint, from which the evolution of the economic formation of society is viewed as a process of natural history, can less than any other make the individual responsible for relations whose creature he socially remains, however much he may subjectively raise himself above them."[17] The human person, therefore, is caught up in objective structural processes, which, according to their nature, can be captured with quasi-natural-scientific precision. If these structural processes have consequences that are harmful to human persons, the existence of the subjects joined together in society, whether "capitalist" or "proletarian," will also be objectively anti-human, even if they endeavor to comply subjectively, i.e. in the personal-ethical sense, with the demands of human justice. Consequently, they are also, seen purely subjectively, not to be held responsible for the objective evil in the world that

[16] Marx, "Contribution to the Critique of Hegel's Philosophy of Law," in *Collected Works,* Vol. III, New York, 1975, p. 175.

[17] Marx, *Capital,* "Preface to the First German Edition," in *Collected Works,* Vol. XXXV, New York, 1996, p. 10.

stems from social structures. And from that it is clear that Marx ultimately denies the personal dimension of the reality of evil and, in complete opposition to the personalistic position, reduces it to structural evil.

There is some truth even in the Marxist view of evil. Since human persons in the totality of their existence can never be detached from institutions and their structural conditions, the evil that they cause must likewise be found in the structural dimension. As has already been said, Marx, in his complete radicalness, recognized that. It is for this reason that he belongs to those who early on came upon the specific sense of the social-ethical question. He himself reduces that to the following impressive common denominator: "If man draws all his knowledge, sensation, etc., from the world of the senses and the experience gained in it, then what has to be done is to arrange the empirical world in such a way that man experiences and becomes accustomed to what is truly human in it ... If man is shaped by environment, his environment must be made human."[18] And from that it follows, again to use Marx's own words, "*the categorical imperative to overthrow all relations* in which man is a debased, enslaved, forsaken, despicable being."[19] Thus, it is not inner transformation of the human person that restores what is essentially humane to effectiveness, but revolt of the outer, socially real conditions of his existence, which Marx calls "materialistic."

In this form, which dissolves the reality of personal evil into a mere function of structural injustice in society, Marx's insight into the reality of structural evil, which contains essential truth, also becomes untruth. *To expect that the structural transformation of social conditions would automatically change the person of the human being in his character is just as untrue as the expectation that the inner transformation of the human person by itself would lead to elimination of the structural injustice in society.* The evidence of this is supplied by historical experience. More than a half-century of "real socialism" in the U.S.S.R. did not make Soviet man "more socialistic," i.e. more concerned about common-economic thought and conduct, in his personal values.[20] There

[18] Marx and Engels, "The Holy Family," in *Collected Works*, Vol. IV, New York, 1975, pp. 130-31.

[19] Marx, "Contribution to the Critique of Hegel's Philosophy of Law," in *Collected Works*, Vol. III, p. 182.

[20] See Michael S. Voslensky, *Nomenklatura*, New York: Doubleday, 1984.

is little essential difference between his elementary values, needs, and desires and those of persons in non-socialistic societies. And that simply means that one can no more do away with personal evil merely by making structural changes in society than one can do away with structural evil merely by making changes in inner outlook. Evil clearly proves to be something so fundamental that it can be covered up in neither of these ways, and precisely when one believes one has it under control, its many-faced nature is encountered once again.[21] This old and yet ever-new experience is taken into account by traditional church teaching that speaks of "original sin" as persisting evil, which nonetheless never frees persons from their responsibility.[22] But if that is the case, if evil turns out to be something persistent, fundamental, and consequently radical, isn't the humanity originating from faith, hope, and love then merely a beautiful dream, which can to be sure edify idealistic minds, but which must in the real world scatter like spray and foam? Or is there nevertheless a radical good that transcends both the horizon of universal human experience of humanity rooted in faith, hope, and love and that of radical evil, which constantly opposes humanity in the person and in the structure of society? That is the new question that now arises.

5.3 The Experience of the Totally Other

This question is not new. It has always been confronted by persons who have wrestled earnestly with the experience of evil. In the inter-

[21] Gerhard Ebeling, *Dogmatik des christlichen Glaubens*, Vol. I, Tübingen, 1979, p. 294, reduces this question to the theologically concise formula: "The evil in evil is sin."

[22] Dorothee Sölle, *Political Theology*, trans. John Shelley, Philadelphia, 1974, p. 88, accurately explains the relationship between personal and structural evil thus: "I have not selected this world for myself, I have been born into it. Every historical understanding of man is constituted by his bondage to the past; there is no zero point at which he could begin, for at every point he is already stamped by and grounded in the world from which he comes. At the same time, however, freedom is presupposed in the concept of original sin, which means that man has the capacity for guilt. I collaborate with what has already been placed at my disposal; there is an 'I' which acts, regardless of whether the action is aggressive or passive.... We must think of compulsion and freedom, 'inheritance' and sin, as standing in a dialectical relation to each other."

est of continuity with the previous argumentation, it might be referred to Karl Marx.

According to Marx, the fundamental evil that impacts on history, similarly to the discussion in the preceding section, lies in the contradiction between nature and reality, essence and existence of the human person, or what is for him synonymous, between "*human interest*" and "*private interest*." Consequently for him "the principle of all morality ... [is that] man's private interest must be made to coincide with the interest of humanity."[23] Marx thus understands "*communism* as the *positive* transcendence of *private property*," within which the principle of all morality is realized as "the true resolution of the strife between existence and essence, between objectification and self-confirmation, between freedom and necessity, between the individual and the species." From this the assurance, which confirms the whole, immediately follows: "Communism is the riddle of history solved, and it knows itself to be this solution."[24]

Just as the conflict between private and general interest, between individual and species, in short between existence and nature, will be sublated in this way in the future society of communism, the human person of the existing, i.e. bourgeois, society in his concrete existence has become entirely alienated from himself, and thus stands in contradiction to his true nature. And indeed this is true of the entirety of this society: "The propertied class and the class of the proletariat present the same human self-estrangement."[25] There is no residue of the good. All are committed to the same state of decay. Wherein, according to Marx, in view of this miserable situation, is the possibility of liberation from ubiquitous alienation as the epitome of evil to be found?

> *Answer*: In the formation of a class ... of civil society which is not a class of civil society, an estate which is the dissolution of all estates, a sphere which has a universal character by its universal suffering and claims no *particular right* because no *particular wrong* but *wrong generally* is perpetrated against it; which can no longer invoke a *historical* title but only the human title ..., a sphere, finally, which cannot emancipate itself without emancipating itself from all other

[23] Marx and Engels, "The Holy Family," in *Collected Works*, Vol. IV, New York, 1975, pp. 130-31.

[24] Marx, *Collected Works*, Vol. III, New York, 1975, pp. 296-97.

[25] Marx and Engels, "The Holy Family," in *Collected Works*, Vol. IV, New York, 1975, p. 36.

> spheres of society and thereby emanicipating all other spheres of society, which, in a word, is the *complete loss* of man and hence can win itself only through the *complete rewinning of man*. This dissolution of society as a particular estate is the *proletariat*. [26]

This amazing quotation lets one thing be seen clearly: For Marx, at least for the young Marx, there is the possibility of liberation from the fundamental evil of society, which is based upon the class-formed conflict between the universal nature and the particular existence of man, between his general and his special interests. This possibility exists, because with capitalistic society something completely other, revolutionarily new, has attained historical effectiveness: the industrial-worker proletariat. In it — which as a class of bourgeois society already decisively transcends this society, and which, suffering injustice as such, can no longer defend any special interests, but rather resorts only to justice as such, and consequently can refer back to the complete recovery of what is human — the essentially humane must therefore uniquely come to existence, and thus the good must occur in the midst of the decayed reality of the present world. What is expressed by this incredible expectation? Historical experience or historical ideology?

It cannot possibly be historical experience. For Marx never experienced the actual proletariat as the completely other, in whom the real human person, who no longer can defend any private special interest, already announced himself. He attributes to it, rather, as has already become obvious, the same self-alienation and in that respect the same depravity as the opposing class. Thus in his letters he not infrequently calls the proletarians of his world of experience "knots" and "bristles." And in his "Communist Manifesto," which he wrote with Engels, he even writes the evil words "lumpen proletariat" to describe the rottenness of the lowest layer of the old society, which was supposed to be more willing to let itself pay for reactionary activities than to serve the proletarian revolution.[27] If Marx can, nonetheless, in his theory of class struggle, elevate the proletariat to a class of a totally-other quality of nature from the bourgeois, he can do so only by virtue of dialectical deviousness. It remains indeed true

[26] Marx, "Contribution to Critique of Hegel's Philosophy of Law," in *Collected Works*, Vol. III, New York, 1975, p. 186.

[27] Marx and Engels, "Manifesto of the Communist Party," in *Collected Works*, Vol. VI, New York, 1976, p. 494.

that the "possessing class" and the "class of the proletariat" exhibit the same human self-alienation:

> But the former class feels at ease and strengthened in this self-estrangement, it recognises estrangement as *its own power* and has in it the *semblance* of a human existence. The latter feels annihilated in estrangement: it sees in it its own powerlessness and the reality of an inhuman existence. It is, to use an expression of Hegel, in its abasement the *indignation* at that abasement, an indignation to which it is necessarily driven by the contradiction between its human *nature* and its condition of life, which is the outright, resolute and comprehensive negation of that nature. [28]

However intellectually stimulating this dialectically-proceeding argumentation may be, it certainly has nothing to do with experience-based proof that the "totally other" has come to historical reality in the contemporary industrial-worker proletariat, that the liberation of man from all evil has begun with the revolution from the ground up against previous society. Provided that Marx himself should have been of a contrary opinion here, which, however, remains unknown,[29] his view of the matter would be based on pure illusion. However that may be, he wishes in any case in his way to bring to evidence that for such a liberation there would be need of an historical event transcending everything previous, separating time into a before and an after, and thus announcing something completely new. In that respect something is expressed which coincides closely with the experience of Christian faith.

Christian faith, understood in its originality, is based on experience, precisely, on faith-experience, not on ideology. That is by no means to claim that there is no ideologized Christianity. This kind of Christianity does exist, foremost in the form of a supernatural world-view and conception of society that wishes to have answers to all riddles of existence that are valid once and for all. It is thus recognizable that

[28] Marx and Engels, "The Holy Family," in *Collected Works*, Vol. IV., New York 1975, p. 36.

[29] André Gorz, *Farewell to the Working Class*, trans. Michael Sonenscher, London, 1982, p. 19: "It is worth noting that this theory [of the proletariat as the realization of a human universal] did not grow out of empirical observation but developed from a critical reflection, carried out in reaction to hegelianism, upon the essence of labour. For the young Marx it was not the existence of a revolutionary proletariat that justified his theory. Instead his theory enabled him to predict the inevitable emergence of the revolutionary proletariat."

it makes claim to absolute truth directly in questions of worldview and social questions. All vigorous ideologies postulate such claims and react allergically to all experience-convictions that critically contradict them. For that reason they are opposed in principle to pluralism and strive, whenever possible, to achieve autocracy. Christianity turns out, consequently, to be an ideology to the extent that it exerts social and world-view pressure in the question of truth, or at least seeks to do so. And it proves itself to be conviction-experience to the extent that it professes its faith self-critically and yet resolutely to its subject matter, without wishing to exert anything like a forced confession. In this sense, Christian faith is not to be understood as a preconceived ideology of religious worldview, but rather as a conviction, behind which real experience stands.

What is the basis of the experience by which what is genuinely Christian lives? At the beginning of the Christian movement stands *Jesus of Nazareth*, unquestionably an historical personality,[30] who has singular significance in the history of religions. In contrast to Buddha and Mohammed, however, he is not actually to be included among the founders of religions. He did not proclaim a new God, but rather the "God of Israel, the Creator and Ruler, Lawgiver and Judge."[31] And he brought no new doctrine, but rather followed the Old Testament prophets, as well as the Mosaic Law, the latter to be sure in an absoluteness and freedom that brought him into the sharpest conflict with the Jewish scribes, the law-ideologues of his day.[32] What was really and radically new with Jesus was that he proclaimed with full power the breaking out of the Kingdom of God, the eschatological revolution originating from God, called the people to change, and joined all of this with his person in such a way that in his speech and conduct God's comforting and demanding call itself attained transparency and the coming became already a present event. "If it is by the finger of God that I cast out the demons, then the Kingdom of God has come to you."[33]

Furthermore, it can be proven historically of the beginnings of Christianity that Jesus found disciples who placed their trust in his

[30] Rudolf Bultmann, *Jesus*, 2nd Ed., Munich, 1965, p. 14: "Doubt concerning whether Jesus actually existed is unfounded and not worth a word of refutation. It is fully clear that he stands as the initiator of the historical movement whose first concrete stage was the oldest Palestinian community."

[31] Hans Conzelmann, *Jesus*, trans. J. Raymond Lord, Philadelphia, 1973, p. 54.

[32] *Ibid.*

[33] Luke 11,20.

message of the coming of God's kingdom and followed him, in short, believed in him. But it is just as certain that these disciples eventually became mad at him, and indeed in the complete sense of the word. For Jesus as an historical personality failed in his project and ended up on a cross, the gallows of Roman antiquity. For the disciples, all of whom were Jews and for whom, therefore, the Torah stood as steadfast divine law, that must have been an unimaginable shock. The Torah says plainly: "Anyone hung on a tree is under God's curse."[34] How then could Jesus, in view of his accursed death, still be the one in whom the Kingdom of God, liberating from of all evil, happened, is happening, and still will happen? Wasn't the verdict of the law unambiguously against him? In the consciousness of the Jewish people, the crucifixion of Jesus could only mean definitively that God Himself, and not just the religious and political opposition of the Crucified One, put his project on trial, on the final trial. Only that explains why the disciples, as the historical failure of Jesus became ever more drastically evident, became completely discouraged, fully abandoned his project, and finally scattered in all directions.[35]

One must look at these historically verifiable facts in their full reality. Only then can one comprehend how completely it goes against all historical reason, and even amounts to a paradox, that the cause of Jesus came to life all the more after its total catastrophe and that the same disciples who just fled out of inscrutable resignation, once again, and indeed absolutely — also again an historical fact — placed their trust in the Crucified One and his cause and went to their deaths for them. How could that be?

There are many attempts to provide a plausible explanation of these paradoxical events, from the crude thesis of the disciples' self-deception to refined psychological interpretations. But none of them has had much staying power. Everything remains ultimately incomprehensible without the experience that the Christians unanimously and categorically testified to have really had, namely, the experience of the resurrection of the Crucified One.[36] "*Resurrection*" is a metaphorical word that tries to express in a symbolic, figurative sense something that fundamentally cannot be expressed. In other

[34] Deuteronomy 21,23.

[35] Mark 14,50.

[36] Regarding this entire complex of questions, the reflections of Hans Küng, *Christ sein*, Munich, 1974, pp. 332-39, are helpful.

words, it seeks not actually to explain what happened on the third day after the crucifixion; it only wishes not to remain silent about what happened. What happened remains inexplicable. That something must have happened, something surprising, incredible, unique, which filled the discouraged and despairing disciples with certainty — Jesus lives — can hardly be questioned. For without that it would remain completely incomprehensible that the project of the Crucified One would go forward, that there is Christianity at all, Christianity as the conviction that God acted precisely in the historically-failed Jesus of Nazareth and that there is consequently a future of God as the coming of His kingdom, which cannot be refuted by any historical failure of man, even if it happens in as absolute and final a form as death. This faith found expression from the very beginning in the simple profession, "The Lord has risen indeed."[37] He lives and what began in him goes further: the coming of the Kingdom of God, redemption from all evil, personal as well as structural, and true humanity originating from faith, hope, and love.

From that, the specifically Christian, the "totally other," proves to be resurrection faith. *Faith as the experience of resurrection is faith originating from resurrection, not simply faith in the resurrection.*[38] The two must be distinguished from one another. Faith in the resurrection can merely mean taking for true a dogmatic proposition. One can also consider the resurrection to be true in the way one considers any miracle to be true. That can found a supranaturalist worldview, according to which the dead can unexpectedly come back to life, but not existential trust in the God of Jesus Christ. Faith originating from resurrection, however, is faith that persons and the world have a future in God's future advent, even if they themselves fail in the reality of personal and structural evil. This faith experiences in the cross and the resurrection certainty that God, as the totally other, transcends all

[37] Luke 24,34.

[38] See Eduard Schweizer, *The Good News according to Mark*, trans. Donald H. Madvig, Richmond, Va., 1970, p. 371: "In the New Testament the fact that the mystery of God's action cannot be seen or described by anyone is always of decisive significance. Neither the miracle of the resurrection nor the incomprehensible discovery of the empty tomb produces faith. Faith is created only when the living One encounters his disciples. Faith in God's miraculous intervention will always be based upon such an encounter. Only those to whom the resurrected One has appeared alive can understand the report of the empty tomb."

human possibilities and makes possible what for human persons is impossible: that life becomes lord over death, light over darkness, being over nothingness, good over evil, in short, that his kingdom comes. It is one with the faith in the living God, in whose life Jesus lives, today as in former times. And so resurrection faith proves to be present reality, which again and again surprisingly comes to effect exactly where it is least expected. As Vladimir Maximov, one of the most significant Russian poets of our day and raised completely in proletarian circumstances, spontaneously answered when asked in an interview how he came to profess Christianity: "My parents were naive atheists of the 1920s, seduced by the political arbitrariness that developed before their eyes and that they felt as freedom. They understandably could awaken no religious feeling in me. But the temptation of arrogance proves to be powerless before the magnitude of the redemption. As the young shoot breaks through the asphalt road, so also the gospel breaks through in persons held down by depressing, time-contingent stratifications. It reached the point of a breakthrough even in me and lit everything that surrounded me with the everlasting light of expectation and hope."[39] That and nothing else is resurrection faith: *the experience of the totally other in the middle of the reality of our world.*

5.4 The Specifically Christian in the Humanity originating from Faith, Hope, and Love

On the basis of the preceding excursus, the specifically Christian of this humanity can now be determined, to the point that it is insolubly related to resurrection faith as the experience of the totally other in human reality, with its personal and structural evil. Humanity originating from faith in the Christian understanding proves accordingly to be humanity *that has its place in resurrection faith.* In that, and only in that, lies its specialness. This specialness must not be played off in theological hubris against the humanity that exists in the horizon of general human experience, as if that were a matter of triviality. Humanity is absolutely not a triviality. For in it lives the fundamental knowledge that without trust in the human world, without hope in the future, and without love that lives from trust and from hope,

[39] *Deutsche Zeitung*, 28 June 1974, p. 22.

life cannot be human. But trust, hope, and love that are rooted only in what is human shatter easily at the experience of evil, or even change into their opposites. And if that happens, it is the end of humanness.

Resurrection faith, in contrast, grows out of a trust based primarily on the faithfulness of God, not only on human faithfulness. The cross and the resurrection substantiate in ultimate radicalness what Joseph experienced in dealing with his unfaithful brothers: "Even though you intended to do harm to me, God intended it for good."[40] On the cross of Jesus, the evil human machinations raged to the bitter end. But the end brought about life, not death. God himself identified with the Crucified One, whose suffering he made his own suffering, and took all horror of evil upon himself in order to unmask it in its complete, demonic power, to weaken it, and to lay bare the way to its coming defeat. And that means that God does not leave human persons, neither the victims of evil nor its originators, to the entanglements of their wicked machinations. He unconditionally holds on to his creation, which threatens itself, in order to make his justice obvious in his absolute faithfulness, which are synonymous terms in biblical language. The faithfulness of God, which becomes known in the cross and resurrection, brings about courage and confidence, where this is grasped in faith, even in a world that experiences daily the effectiveness of personal and structural evil, to preserve trust, to stand by human persons despite everything, and to defend the cause of humanity.

That which holds of trust holds also for hope. Hope, as one of the existentials of humanity, is a most fragile matter, especially in our time, since human persons increasingly despair of their own future. The naive progress-optimism, as a legacy of the Enlightenment, has fled abruptly and has made room for a deep pessimism.[41] Is there any future, any good future at all for human persons? In the atomic age, in view of the growing ideological, economic, and political conflicts, doesn't the total self-destruction of the human race instead loom as an ever more menacing possibility on the horizon of world events? In these harsh questions,

[40] Genesis 50,20.

[41] Cf. Gerhard Huber, "Der Fortschrittsgedanke in Philosophie und Geistesgeschichte," in Maja Svilar, ed., *Was ist Fortschritt?* Bern, 1979, pp. 20ff.

inscrutable scepticism, which plunges contemporary man into despair, speaks out against the modern expectation of progress, which was still dominant until recently. Can anyone still honestly talk about hope at all in this situation?

Christian faith is far removed from rashly and superciliously dismissing the temptation that lies within such scepticism. It certainly has nothing to do with mere historical optimism. For it, the time that follows the present, thus the future, which human persons themselves get under way by their deeds and misdeeds, will never be able to bring the "redemption from all evil," even if one assumes a long process of evolution, shaped by difficult setbacks. The future that grows out of what already exists ("*Futurum*"), which to at least a certain degree stands in the power of human persons, is precisely not the future ("*Zukunft*") in which Christian faith hopes, not at all the future ("*Zukunft*") in the genuine sense of the word.

"Future," understood in the original sense, means, to be precise, "*adventus*,"[42] and thus not what corresponds in contemporary language to the future as "*futurum*."[43] And thus *adventus* or advent means arrival, dawning, coming, or more precisely the coming of the kingdom of He who acted in the Crucified and Resurrected One. Consequently, future as advent does not exist because the time that lies in human hands advances, but because God breaks into this time, comes to the world, in order to prepare the way for the infeasible, totally other. Genuinely Christian hope is, consequently, hope for the future as the coming of God, in which the future as *futurum* of human persons need not aim into emptiness and triviality, even if all historical probability speaks against it. It can in this way withstand the hopelessness of the future as *futurum*, no matter how harshly its terrible temptations assail it, in so far as it, now to speak with Paul, trusts in "that God"..."who gives life to the dead and calls into existence the things that do not exist," and therefore always

[42] Cf. Friedrich Kluge, *Etymologisches Wörterbuch der deutschen Sprache*, 18th Ed., Berlin, 1960, p. 893.

[43] The distinction between "*futurum*" and "*adventus*" in the concept of the future is found for the first time, to the best of my knowledge, in Emil Brunner, *Eternal Hope*, trans. Harold Knight, Philadelphia, 1954. It was then taken up by myself and systematically continued in the paper "Die Bedeutung der Eschatologie für den christlichen Glauben," Zürich, 1954, and also later by Jürgen Moltmann and Karl Rahner.

"hopes against all hope."[44] And only with that does what is specifically Christian in the humanity originating from hope come into view. It reveals itself to be "hoping against all hope," which understands itself called to meet this evil also amidst the hopelessness of personal and structural evil in the world, and undauntedly to stand by human persons and their world, who are both its victims and originators in one.

The humanity originating from faith and hope thus substantiates itself in *the humanity originating from love*. Only in the humanity originating from love does faith become real and what is hoped for become present. That at which God's will aims happens in it, "for God is love."[45] And in it what is coming already comes now into power, and what is human, however it may turn out, becomes anticipated reality. In short, in the words of Paul, it is the "new being," the "being in Christ," the being of the Kingdom of God, whose future began in the Crucified and Resurrected One.

As this new being, the love of the hoping faith, called "*agape*" in the New Testament, reaches to human persons in the totality of their existence. In other words, this means that it cannot be identified with any particular form of human capability to love, neither the passionate feeling of erotic devotion nor the sublime sensibility of friendly affection, nor even the empathizing attitude of compassionate pity, though *agape*-love can shine through and become effective in all of them. To be sure, eros, friendship, and compassionate pity belong to the entirety of human existence, to which the love of faith and hope seeks to reach out. But this love itself does not just spring from a capability of that kind. For with all of those it is a matter of potencies that lie in human persons' own possibilities and that are in this respect at their command. *Agape*-love, however, is not at their command. It is something that befalls, a gift of God, which becomes a driving command for those who believe and hope. Or, to say it with a phrase from the Epistle to the Colossians, it is the "energy of God" (*energeia tou theou*),[46] as such an energy in this world that is not an energy of this world. Therefore, it cannot be identified with any historical power, not even with Christianity and Church. Never is it a political party, certainly not a "Christian" party. But it does take a

[44] Romans 4,17-18.
[45] I John 4,8.
[46] Colossians 2,12.

side, the side of the coming, thus of what is called in biblical language the "Kingdom of God," by placing itself uncompromisingly against the powers of personal and structural evil. More precisely, it takes the part of the victims of this evil, of those who fall among thieves, as the Parable of the Good Samaritan shows without parallel. *Agape*-love is, in this concise sense, a partisan and militant love, which stands up for the right[47] and wishes to have nothing to do with the wretched "burying of the right in the dung pit of grace," to take up a drastic expression of Heinrich Pestalozzi.[48] All in all, it understands itself as a "free, resolute act" and "depends primarily on the love of God, the love of the higher that raises the lower,"[49] and thus helps him gain his rights.

As the presentness of that which is coming, this love, whenever it seizes and moves persons, is now already a foretaste of the future, the complete in the incomplete, the ultimate in the penultimate, and consequently that which remains. "Love never ends," as Paul puts it.[50] In this presentness, it proves itself, in strict opposition to radical evil, to be the radical good or radically humanly just. In *agape*-love, therefore, the humanly just comes to its most radical and thus incomparable form, which cannot be identified with any respectable personal or political energy of past or present history whatsoever, except Jesus Christ. He is the perfect personification of the love, for which Paul in his *agape* hymn[51] finds unparalleled words. And indeed he is that, not as a man in whom what is itself human transcends itself, as unorthodox Marxists such as Milan Machovec or Vitezslàv Gardavsky for instance understand Jesus, but rather as a man in whom God has transcended himself in the movement of the high to the low, of the powerful to the powerless, of the living to the buried, thus in the movement from above to below, which significantly is the movement of *agape*-love. Thus Christian faith certainly experiences God.

[47] I Corinthians 13,6. For Paul, truth and justice correspond to one another; see Romans 2,8.

[48] *Sämtliche Werke*, Vol. XII, Berlin, 1938, p. 56. Paul Tillich, *Gesammelte Werke*, Vol. III, Stuttgart, 1965, p. 34, also fights against an understanding of *agape* that does not contain "justice as an essential element and as resistance against degenerating into sentimentality."

[49] Cf. Gerhard Kittel, *Theologisches Wörterbuch zum Neuen Testament*, Vol. I, Stuttgart, 1933, p. 37.

[50] I Corinthians 13,8.

[51] I Corinthians 13,1-13.

Consequently, it is able to define him in the New Testament, if it dares to define him at all, only as this love,[52] which is resurrected in Jesus Christ in the world and history as a thing that lives, that goes onward, that functions in the reality of the personal, as in that of society, as the basic revolutionary, now with Christianity, now against it, now with the revolutions, now against them, but always with human persons who are crucified and who hunger and thirst after righteousness. In this fundamentally revolutionary matter, the imperative is valid: "Do not be haughty, but associate with the lowly."[53] Because and in so far as such love occurs again and again within the world of personal and structural evil, there is not only the possibility, but also the reality, of the humanity originating from faith, hope, and love, in a word, the good.[54]

5.5 The Specifically Christian and the Generally Human in the Humanity originating from Faith, Hope, and Love

There has already been a warning against seeking, in theological arrogance, to claim the humanity originating from faith, hope, and love as, so to speak, a Christian monopoly. To be sure, for Christians this humanity is based on an experience-conviction that is specific, because it is rooted in resurrection faith. But, in its ethical concretion, it is not tied exclusively to Christianity as a religious confession. In other words, that which is specifically Christian is the experience of faith, hope, and love in its radicalness, namely in its rootedness in the totally other of the Christ-event, which awakens trust where distrustfulness spreads, encourages hope where all indications speak against hope, and frees to love where one can expect no love in return, but rather must reckon with hatred and enmity. In short, it is the experience of humanity beyond the normative as an existence-founding power, a power, by the way, that is effective where it

[52] I John 4,8.

[53] Romans 12,16.

[54] This means that Christian ethics can never be understood in its essence merely as normative ethics of "ought" (*Sollensethik*). It is at the same time ethics of "is" (*Seinsethik*), which motivates to the "ought" and reveals the limits of all pure ethics of "ought." In view of this, Walter Mostert remarks correctly that its crux consists in sending into the fight against evil the person who caused it ("Gott und das Böse," p. 468).

wishes, as the spirit moves where it wills, and therefore that also can be at work where no one knows the things of Christ religiously. The New Testament itself brings this to visualization, quite shockingly, in the parable of the final judgment.[55] Significantly, humanity as God's command and offer, coincides there normatively with what is linked generally with the concept of humanity: feeding the hungry, refreshing the thirsty, giving shelter to strangers, visiting the sick, standing by prisoners. And in this respect, i.e. seen now under the aspect of normative concretization, *there is no specifically Christian humanity, only a human humanity*. The humanity originating from faith, hope, and love also belongs to the horizon of general human experience, as has already come to light in 5.1.

If Christian faith takes this insight seriously, it will not simply reflect on its humanity contained in its experience-certitude — one could also call this "conscience" — without accounting for what is encountered as human in some other way, or still claims to be human, no matter how controversial the form in which it may appear. It must expound the normative content of its humanity, which it is first necessary to determine more closely, not dogmatically-apodictically, but dialogically-argumentatively. This means that the humanity originating from faith, hope, and love, in so far as it is precisely a matter of the normative, must strive to make itself perceptible also to those who have different basic beliefs. The prerequisite for this is a way of argumentation that meets the conditions of rational thinking and judging, and that consequently is available to everyone. What Paul said in a different context is valid here as well: "I would rather speak five words with my mind, in order to instruct others also, than ten thousand words in a tongue."[56] First of all, it is necessary to guard against seeking to contrast love and reason with one another,[57] as if one excluded the other. Rather, just as it should be asserted against a rationalistically-narrowed understanding of reason with philosopher Gerhard Huber that "it could be that the deeper reason lies in love,"[58] so, on the other hand, a religiously-emotionalized and view of love that disparages reason should be countered theologically by saying that, quite possibly, the deeper love is found in reason.

[55] Matthew 25,31-46.

[56] I Corinthians 14,19.

[57] Cf. Martin Honecker, "Liebe und Vernunft," *Zeitschrift für Theologie und Kirche*, 68 (1971), pp. 227-59.

[58] Gerhard Huber, *Gegenwärtigkeit der Philosophie*, Basel, 1975, p. 86.

Before we turn to determining the criteria of the humanity originating from faith, hope, and love in continuation of our principal discussions, it may be advisable also to clarify explicitly the theological approach that is implicitly joined to the understanding of humanity that has been brought to bear here. That will take place now in the form of a critical excursus on the theological positions that have been of importance, both positively and negatively, for the author in the development of his own social-ethical concept. Those who shrink from specifically theological considerations may skip the following chapter.

6. THE THEOLOGICAL APPROACH

6.1 The Eschatological Dimension of the Humanity originating from Faith, Hope, and Love

It can be concluded from Chapter 5 that the normative content of the humanity originating from faith, hope, and love is in fact not foreign to the horizon of general human experience, but also that in its Christian specificity it cannot simply be reduced to humanity, for instance in the sense of humane conduct. This kind of humanity is based on an experience-certitude that transcends everything human, in so far as it lives most authentically from the totally other that God set in motion through the event of the resurrection of the Crucified One and will fulfill in the coming of his kingdom. It stands, to put it succinctly, in the eschatological dimension.

"*Eschatological dimension*" means, in this context, not only that the humanity originating from faith, hope, and love is directed towards the Kingdom of God as its ultimate purpose, but even more, that the "energy of God," which seeks to drive human persons towards this goal, becomes effective in it. With this humanity, understood as the ethical aspect of eschatological salvation in the coming of the Kingdom of God, it is a matter of God's action. But it is a matter of God's action in such a way that the actions of human persons do not thereby become irrelevant, but rather attain all the more relevance. "Work out your own salvation with fear and trembling; for it is God who is at work in you, enabling you both to will and to work for his good pleasure."[1] There is thus no mention of a deterministic, automatic mechanism of salvation that must make human conduct irrelevant and ultimately make everything ethical lose its significance. And certainly no mention of an inevitable "happy ending" to the ups and downs of human history. The eschatological faith of the New Testament would be misunderstood if one were to think of it as mere

[1] Philippians 2,12-13.

religious excess of optimistic expectation for the future, as it is found, for example, in Marxism. Human persons, in their individual and collective history, can fall short of that to which they are called through God's salvation will; but they do not have to do so, because God's intention, established through the events of the cross and the resurrection, is that they not miss it. And if they do not fall short, then the glory is due God alone. Thus the enduring request: "Thy kingdom come."

By virtue of its integration into eschatological expectation, the humanity originating from faith, hope, and love gains its driving certitude — certitude, not certainty — that intercession has meaning and promise for the good and the just, even if the reality of evil in the world makes it appear to be an illusion. If it is removed from this context, it loses its motivating power. It becomes, at best, a structure of norms, based on the body of biblical-ethical traditions, for which many rational reasons may speak, but which can never gain its power of motivation from there. For reasonableness is not a sufficient reason for human action,[2] especially in an increasingly irrational world. Siegfried Katterle appears to leave this matter out of consideration when he advocates — particularly in connection with Albert Schweitzer and in the laudable intention to contribute to a better understanding between social science and Christian social ethics — his strict separation of Christology and eschatology "by having 'recourse to the ethics of the Old Testament prophets' in the teaching of Jesus."[3] How could what is centrally Christian still come to fruition in Christian ethics with an undertaking of this kind? This is a question that cannot be avoided.

It is evident from the preceding discussion that the eschatological dimension of the humanity originating from faith, hope, and love has at its core an *existential character*. It involves a certain manner of human existence, namely existence as responsible life in the comfort and demands of the Kingdom of God,[4] which alone can bring

[2] Cf. Martin Honecker, "Vernunft, Gewissen, Glaube," *Zeitschrift für Theologie und Kirche*, 77 (1980), p. 334.

[3] Siegfried Katterle, *Sozialwissenschaft und Sozialethik*, Göttingen, 1972, pp. 178-79.

[4] While in 3.3 and 3.4 responsibility *for* (for the Self, the Thou, the environment) was articulated, here the specifically theological aspect of responsibility, responsibility *to* (to God and his eschatological will) enters the scene. The theological concept of responsibility always has a double structure, as Wolfgang Huber, *Gegenwärtigkeit der Philosophie*, p. 68, correctly emphasizes. This twofold structure differs from Hans Jonas's understanding of responsibility in *The Imperative of Responsibility*, where only

redemption from all evil. But it does not involve the dogmatic adoption of the obsolete cosmology, that is, the historical theology of the late-Jewish apocalyptic, from which the imaginaries in the eschatological statements of the New Testament originate. Indeed, the ethical dimension includes a cosmic-historical aspect, in the sense that human existence, which real experience already reveals, cannot be removed from its historical world-context, and thus existence- and world-transformation stand dialectically in one another. But still, an essential connection to the cosmic picture of history of the late-Jewish apocalyptic is by no means thereby established, at least not in the preaching of Jesus.[5] Just as the central theological message of biblical creation-faith is comprehensible without the necessity of accepting the mythical cosmogonies that stand conceptually behind the Old Testament creation stories, so eschatologically determined existence can be adopted without biblicist reception of the apocalyptic world of imagination in which the early-Christian eschatology is articulated.[6] Ultimately, biblical creation-faith, like New Testament future-hope, are concerned with the real risk of trusting the message of the Kingdom of God and getting involved in the "living God," who is the beginning and end of all existence.

Christian existence as humanity originating from faith, hope, and love is in this way, seen in its eschatological dimension, responsible

responsibility *for* (human persons and the world in the age of technology) is given a chance.

[5] Werner G. Kümmel, in his careful study of Jesus' eschatological prophecy, even comes to the conclusion that, contrary to the opinion of Albert Schweitzer's school, it stands "completely in opposition to the worldview of apocalypticism" (*Verheißung und Erfüllung*, 2nd Ed., Zürich, 1953, p. 97. See also John Wick Bowman, *The Intention of Jesus*, Philadelphia, 1943). Katterle's thesis, based on the argumentation of "logically consistent eschatology," that with the apocalyptic ideas in the New Testament the "eschatological basic attitude" is also to be abandoned (*Sozialwissenschaft und Sozialethik*, p. 177), is consequently unconvincing. On the controversy that Katterle provoked, see first of all Horst Westmüller, "Wie theologisch darf Sozialethik sein?" *Die Mitarbeit*, 22 (1973), pp. 244-54, and Katterle's rejoinder, "Sozialethik im Dialog mit dem Kritizismus," *Die Mitarbeit*, 23 (1974), pp. 353-58. See also Katterle, "Die Kooperation von Sozialwissenschaft und Sozialethik auf der Grundlage einer kritischen Philosophie," *Zeitschrift für Evangelische Ethik*, 20 (1976), pp. 191-206.

[6] In this respect I cannot share the fear of Katterle, "Die Kooperation von Sozialwissenschaft und Sozialethik auf der Grundlage einer kritischen Philosophie," in Theodor Strohm, ed., *Christliche Wirtschaftsethik vor neuen Aufgaben*, Zürich, 1980, p. 140, that "with the understanding of Christian existence as eschatological, misconceptions" based on the apocalyptic thinking of the New Testament and contradicting "the metaphysical framework of our modern worldview" must have been received.

existence facing the comfort and demands of the coming dominion of God amidst the harsh realities of the existing world, with its political, social, and economic structures. In other words, *it is existence in the penultimate, but in such a way that it lets itself be determined and moved in the penultimate by the call of the ultimate, of the "eschaton."*[7] Not in the sense that it wishes to realize the "Kingdom of God" as a metaphor for God's absolute final-will "in heaven as it is on earth" in the penultimate. That remains God's business and cannot be a social-political postulate of man. If one sees it otherwise, then the message of the Kingdom of God is mixed up with a universal utopia, and in this misshapen form it no longer acts as a mediator between politics and scientific rationality.[8] Therefore, if Christian existence has to guard against pursuing a utopia of the Kingdom of God in its social-political engagement, it must all the more protect itself from immobility in regard to the economic, political, and social structures of our world. For in view of the absolute demand of the message of the Kingdom of God, all of these structures are relative and, consequently, capable of and in need of alteration. Thus they are not to be preserved by adapting oneself to them in a conformist manner. "Do not be conformed to the 's'chemata', to the patterns of this world, but be transformed by the renewing of your minds, so that you may discern what is the will of God, that which is good and acceptable and perfect"[9] is how it reads in the Epistle to the Romans. The terms "good," "acceptable," and "perfect" are to be understood here, in the language of Greek popular philosophy, to mean "obligatory in the widest sense of the word," that is to say, the humanly just, which obligates everyone.[10] The passage cited above thus means that Christian existence in the world of the penultimate or relative, must prove rationally according to its own criteria, which can only be the criteria of humanity originating from faith, hope, and love, what is humanly just *hic et nunc*, and how it can become effective in the world of the penultimate. The relative, the question of human justice,

[7] Similarly, Günter Brakelmann, *Abschied vom Unverbindlichen*, Gütersloh, 1976, p. 19-22.

[8] I agree with Siegfried Katterle, understood in this way, when he speaks of the "utopian concept of the Kingdom of God, which is unusable for science and politics" (*op. cit.*, p. 157).

[9] Romans 12,2-3.

[10] Ernst Käsemann, *Commentary on Romans*, trans. Geoffrey W. Bromiley, Grand Rapids, 1980, p. 301.

consequently, does not become meaningless before the absolute as the demand of divine justice, but, on the contrary, becomes meaningful, even though no human justice can exist before the divine. It is, therefore — completely in agreement with the fundamental ethical question as it was developed in the first chapter[11] — not only a matter of the critique of the relative before the demand of the absolute, but also, directly in responsible interaction with the absolute, a matter of assuring the right of the relative — more precisely, of the humanly just, which in its concretion is never unambiguously and thus absolutely definable in a universally-valid manner — without thereby trivializing or even concealing the difference between it and the absolute. The question of the proper mediation between the relative and the absolute, therefore, becomes a central question of Christian ethics.[12] As an ethically, seriously challenged person in the realm of the relative, one cannot simply bustle around with absolute standards, however little the demand of the absolute notoriously lets itself be ignored there. The one would lead to a *moralistic maximalism*, which would no longer allow room for the merely better, yet really possible, because pure negation would then remain the perfect solution, and would have to end in a social-political nihilism. And the other would result in a *pragmatistic relativism*, which, again as the final consequence, would amount to a mere sanctioning of what already exists. It is important, therefore, agreeing with Martin Honecker, to refrain from trying "to deduce from the Kingdom of God as the fulfillment of hope any concrete standards for the shaping of the world,"[13] just as one should be careful to come to terms with existing reality in its relativity, which is all too often evil, since historically there is no absolute alternative to doing so.

6.2 The Absolute and the Relative in the Problem Field of Theological Ethics

The preceding considerations of the eschatological dimension of the humanity originating from faith, hope, and love have yielded *inter*

[11] See pp. 11-15.

[12] Christoph Blumhardt and his friend Howard Eugster-Züst have already recognized that clearly from their experiences in their social-political praxis. See Louis Specker, ed., *Politik aus der Nachfolge*, introduced by Arthur Rich, Zürich, 1985.

[13] Martin Honecker, *Konzept einer sozialethischen Theorie*, Tübingen, 1971, pp. 84-85.

alia the central meaning of the proper mediation between the eschatologically ultimate and the historically penultimate, the absolute and the relative, for the purpose of founding a theory of Christian social ethics. Its fundamental structure, just as its suitability for the responsible social system, depends decisively upon whether and how this mediation succeeds. That will now be demonstrated by means of a critical analysis of several social-ethical approaches, of which the first four have certainly dominated discussion recently, since 1920, and which in their theological typology *mutatis mutandis* still possess their power of attraction.

6.2.1 *The Transcendental-Eschatological Approach (The Early Karl Barth)*

The transcendental-eschatological approach to social ethics is understood here to mean the framework of the early *"dialectical theology,"* associated primarily with the name of Karl Barth, in so far as the radical theological change provoked by it at the beginning of the 1920s also aims at a new social-ethical concept.

Barth's dialectical theology is defined, at least as far as its social-ethical dimension is concerned, by both continuity and discontinuity with Swiss *religious socialism*, from which it has taken its theological-historical starting point.[14] Swiss religious socialism, arising from the thought and work of Hermann Kutter and Leonhard Ragaz,[15] has shown anew the message of the Kingdom of God as the core of the biblical revelation-testimony. To be sure, the concept of the Kingdom of God already played an essential role in Protestant theology.[16] But that took place in the context of idealist-romantic philosophy, i.e. in the sense of understanding the "Kingdom of God" as the ultimate goal of historical-cultural development and, therefore, as a religious cultural good in secularized form. With Kutter and Ragaz, on the

[14] Cf. Friedrich-Wilhelm Marquardt, *Theologie und Sozialismus*, Munich, 1972, esp. Chaps. II and III; Ulrich Dannemann, "Karl Barth und der religiöse Sozialismus," *Evangelische Theologie*, 37 (1977), pp. 127-48; and Arthur Rich, "Theologisch-sozialethische Einführung," in Christine Ragaz, *et al.*, eds., *Leonhard Ragaz in seinen Briefen*, Vol. II, Zürich, 1982, p. 9-22.

[15] On the theological convergence and divergence of Kutter and Ragaz, see Christine Ragaz, *et al.*, eds., *Leonhard Ragaz in seinen Briefen*, Vol. I, Zürich, 1966 and Vol. II, Zürich, 1982; Max Geiger and Andreas Lindt, eds., *Hermann Kutter in seinen Briefen 1883-1931*, Munich, 1983; and Markus Mattmüller, *Leonhard Ragaz und der Religiöse Sozialismus*, Zürich, 1957, pp. 100-7, 119-20, 135-36, 177-80, 189-90.

[16] Cf. Christian Walther, *Typen des Reich-Gottes-Verständnisses*, Munich, 1961.

other hand, the Kingdom of God was understood eschatologically as the radically-new of God, which breaks in as judgment of the bourgeois cultural world, with its social injustice and imperialistic power politics. In other words, they understand it primarily as a *revolutionary power, which calls the existing state of affairs into question.*

Early on, however, there arose between Kutter and Ragaz elementary differences that would have serious consequences.[17] Kutter, deeply rooted in the intellectual tradition of idealism, especially in Plato, gave a transcendental meaning to the Kingdom of God as the revolutionary power of God, in the sense that it faced the world as the ideas face the phenomenon and eternity faces time. Thus, the absolute of the Kingdom of God could not enter into a genuine relationship with the relative in the real world, with its conflicting forces and powers. To be sure, in his beacon "*Sie müssen*" ("*They Must*"),[18] which created quite a stir at the time and was widely influential, Kutter understood social democracy, which at that time still presented itself in a revolutionary way, as an historical tool in the hand of God that had to carry out his judgment on the Christian, i.e. bourgeois, world. It soon became apparent, however, that the ultimately idealized social democracy of "*Sie müssen*" could not be identified with the Social Democratic Party, as it had begun to play its political role as the workers' party with constantly growing weight around the turn of the century. For that reason, Kutter never had a politically positive relationship with the Social Democratic Party of his time. In fact, a few years after the publication of his inspiring book, he characterized formally joining the Party as an outright betrayal of the Gospel.

With Leonhard Ragaz the situation is different. To be sure, the eschatological "from God" of the Kingdom of God, in critical contrast to its merely cultural-Protestant understanding, also gains constituting significance with Ragaz. He says explicitly that it is "in principle and systematically the right thing."[19] Yet this alignment, oriented towards the absolute, does not have sole or exclusive validity for him. The opposite orientation, the "to God" as a human-historical

[17] Cf. Arnold Pfeiffer, "Kutter und Ragaz," *Neue Zeitschrift für systematische Theologie und Religionsphilosophie*, 21 (1979), pp. 160-76.

[18] Hermann Kutter, *Sie müssen! Ein offenes Wort an die christliche Gesellschaft*, Zürich, 1904.

[19] Christine Ragaz, *et al.*, eds., *Leonhard Ragaz in seinen Briefen*, Vol. I, Zürich, 1966, p. 251.

movement, also receives its due.[20] Thus Ragaz then states in the context of the cited passage: "God must not ultimately become for us a mere abstract entity, a word, a schema, but must come to meet us from living reality, must become apparent to us through it."[21] But he did not at all mean by that, as he would often be misunderstood, that God is to be experienced in the coming of his kingdom directly from the course of actual history, dependent on human beings, or at least co-determined by them, as, for instance, of the worker movement. He expresses himself much more subtly and carefully than Kutter does, in that he precisely does not use the preposition "from," but rather "through." The statement means, therefore, that the coming of the Kingdom of God becomes obvious *through* the living reality of history as it is oriented towards God, in so far as — and this is Ragaz's basic intention — this reality of God, more precisely, of the message of the Bible, is seen and understood. The "from God" and the "to God" act dialectically with respect to one another in this way, which has practical consequences of the greatest significance.

Thanks to this dialectic, distinguished from Kutter's, therefore, Ragaz was also able to achieve a relationship to that which is merely relative in the world of the political and social. He was able to see what is relative, in so far as in democracy, socialism, the worker or peace movement, etc., it aimed at greater justice, as a movement towards God. And so he saw himself able to stand by it, despite the inevitable shortcomings that accompany all historical relativities; more concretely, to become active in the Social Democratic worker movement and even, on the occasion of the general strike in Zürich in 1912, to stand up openly for the rights of the striking workers, though not without certain reservations. Not the least because of this incident, events led to the sensational break with Hermann Kutter.

In a letter of biting severity,[22] Kutter harshly accused Ragaz of severely damaging the common cause, because his comments during this strike gave the impression that such occasional crises had something to do with the coming of the Kingdom of God, in a word, with the absolute. Indeed, there exists a connection between this coming and the great march of the proletariat through history, but both are

[20] *Ibid.*
[21] *Ibid.*, p. 252.
[22] *Ibid.*, pp. 308-9.

to be distinguished unambiguously from social and political events of the day, such as strikes. The Kingdom of God in its revolutionary manifestations stands far above those events in their temporal-momentary limitedness as random, isolated, and apparently trivial events. Therefore, its "religious, integral, and universal radicalism…is not to be related to any political radicalism," as happens with Ragaz. But that means, in others words, that Kutter's Kingdom of God radicalism stands beyond earthly ordinariness in its historical relativities, and thus is fundamentally unconcerned with concretely perceived responsibility for social and political-economic decisions.

It is advisable to go somewhat further afield here, because this prehistory is helpful in understanding better the transcendental-eschatological approach in social-ethical theory of the early dialectical theology. The young Barth, as has already been noted, coming from religious socialism, essentially continued to pursue Kutter's line, though, of course, in an entirely original way. With him, Kutter's "from God" comes dominantly into the foreground, while Ragaz's "to God" as the religious, social and political activity of human beings, does not simply disappear, but is left theologically in weightlessness. That can already be seen in "The Christian in Society," a paper that Barth presented at a religious-social conference in Tambach (Thuringia) in 1919.[23] Right at the beginning he declares clearly: "Our concern is *God*, the movement originating in *God*, the motion which *he* lends us — and it is not religion."[24] And, indeed, that is meant in the sense of a radical critique of everything earthly, including for Barth religion especially, not just capitalism, socialism, politics in general, etc.:

> Will the creation of this new life, in which God makes us believe, consist in the last end simply in the annulment [sublation, D. Lutz] of the creaturehood in which, in contrast to the life of God, we live our life on earth? Fundamentally, this is exactly what we mean. "We wait for the redemption of our body" (Romans 8,23). And however remote the annulment [sublation, D. Lutz] may be, it yet influences our life on earth in every part, and the light which rises in our soul with our growing perception of God will less and less allow us at any point to come to an agreement with the ultimately mortal character of our existence here. [25]

[23] Karl Barth, "The Christian's Place in Society," in Karl Barth, *The Word of God and the Word of Man*, trans. by Douglas Horton, London, 1935, pp. 257-327.
[24] *Ibid.*, p. 285.
[25] *Ibid.*, p. 288-289.

The absolute "from God" means, therefore, the "sublation" of the creaturely and with it everything that refers to "our entire earthly life." The domain of the creaturely-earthly, to which human existence belongs and in which it is concretely lived, can then be seen only under the aspect of making vain and therefore becoming vain: "God judges the world by setting over against it his own righteousness ... The *negation* which issues from God, and means God, is positive, and all positives [in original text: all *positions*; trans. G. Enderle] which are not built upon God are negative."[26] That includes all human attempts to cope in life itself, the socialistic just as much as the bourgeois, the religious just as the secular. This means explicitly, in the Second Edition of Barth's *Epistle to the Romans*, which is quite similar in theological substance to the Tambach paper: "There is, no doubt, a great and universal 'building' at which we all in our various ways labour in fear and trembling; but it is a work in which the will of God at no single point touches or overlaps with the will of man."[27] Between the will of God and that of human persons, at whatever the latter may aim, there is here only the relation of non-correspondence, in short, of absolute difference.

It stands to reason that on this basis, if there is still to be any talk of ethics at all, ethics can continue to exist only as the critique of ethics:

> When [a Church which has set its hope upon God only] embarks upon moral exhortation, its exhortation can be naught else but a criticism of all human behaviour, a criticism which moves through every one of the 360 degrees of the circle of our ambiguous life. This means that very great reserve is necessary when judgements concerning human capacity of will and action, whether they be positive or negative, have to be made — not for fear lest the criticism should be too sweeping, but lest it should not be sweeping enough.[28]

In this way the early Barth proclaims the absolute "from God" as *radical, eschatological judgment over this world*. It is encountered, similarly to the case of Kutter, in the mode of the transcendental, which cannot

[26] *Ibid.*, p. 294.
[27] Karl Barth, *The Epistle to the Romans*, trans. Edwyn C. Hoskyns, London, 1933, p. 432.
[28] *Ibid.*, p. 428.

really go into society and the state, neither preserving nor transforming, neither legitimizing that which exists nor revolutionizing it, and which instead has only to maintain critical distance from all social and political powers, the legitimate as well as the revolutionary:

> Occupying some position, positive or negative, on the plane of the existing order, we are bound to have to pay for the fact that all are relative. We attack or defend, we build or tear down, fight or are at peace, affirm or deny; but sooner or later we are compelled to halt before a last threatening danger and a last heavy punishment — the danger that, after all, we are men, and the punishment for being so. God does not yield before our encroachments — and when do we not encroach upon His rights? The encroachments of revolution He meets with the *sword* of government; the encroachments of government with the *sword* of revolution.[29]

Consequently, not only reactionary adherence to that which exists is judged, the same is no less true of its revolutionary removal:

> The revolutionary Titan is far more godless, far more dangerous, than his reactionary counterpart — because he is so much nearer to the truth. To us, at least, the reactionary presents little danger; with his Red brother it is far otherwise. With this danger we are vitally concerned. For the honour of God we have to bring the revolutionary within the orbit of sacrifice; and his sacrifice is a sacrifice of quite peculiar dignity![30]

The previous citation, which at first glance could come from the mouth of a conservative theologian, gently intimates that the early Barth, despite his basic tendency towards ethical clear-felling, nevertheless also occasionally sees himself obligated to distinguish among trees in the dreary world of the relative and, therefore, not to lump everything together, but instead to recognize that there is something like a relative good in the middle of evil. Yes, he can even say of persons who have become conscious of the full incommensurability of their actions with the will of God:

> And yet, in spite of what he sees, he is possessed of sufficient patience and sagacity and humour — it is his critical sense that permits, and indeed demands, this 'interim'! — to recognize that these

[29] *Ibid.*, p. 490.
[30] *Ibid.*, p. 478.

> relative possibilities are, in the midst of their evil, good, and to accept them as shadows preserving the lineaments of that which is contrasted with them. Therefore he takes them seriously; he examines them and participates in them. As routine exercises and representations, they must not be neglected. And so, the existing order is the *minister of God* — and revolution is also the minister of God to those who are not disturbed and punished, but, encouraged by what has been said, imagine that they are in the right — in the sense that, when the negative character of all concrete things has been perceived, then it is that they begin to shine with the positive power of what is not concrete; they begin to shine with the power of God. Calm reflection has thus been substituted for the convulsions of revolution — calm, because final assertions and final complaints have been ruled out, because a prudent reckoning with reality has outrun the insolence of warfare between good and evil, and because an honest humanitarianism and a clear knowledge of the world recognize that the strange chess-board upon which men dare to experiment with men and against them in State and Church and in Society cannot be the scene of the conflict between the Kingdom of God and Anti-Christ. A political career, for example, becomes possible only when it is seen to be essentially a game; that is to say, when we are unable to speak of absolute political right, when the note of 'absoluteness' has vanished from both thesis and antithesis, and when room has perhaps been made for that relative moderateness or for that relative radicalism in which human possibilities have been renounced.[31]

Thus there is also for the Barth of the Epistle to the Romans *sub specie aeternitatis* a quiet question, which appraises critically and reckons with reality, concerning the "just" and the "unjust," a genuine "humaneness and worldliness," which, because it is conscious of the relativity of all its actions, does not bring any absolute tones into its social and political thoughts and actions. In a word, he can also affirm the right of the relative. But the pathos of his theological message is not based upon that. It is actually only conceded secondarily, "interimly," and thus also kept in a peculiarly, almost ironically-playful suspense, which has already revealed that the crucial concepts here, such as reality, justice, and injustice, are put in quotation marks and consequently are again called into question. All of this, therefore, is not really of any effect. Transcendental eschatologism,

[31] *Ibid.*, pp. 488-89.

for which events in the contemporary world are ultimately inconsequential, remains dominant. What does or does not happen among human beings here below is not so important. The one thing that does matter is the "from God," the sublation of the world in the world. And thus Barth's Tambach paper, which rang in dialectical theology, also leads to the question that simultaneously is supposed to be an answer and yet is not one: "What can the Christian do in society other than attentively follow *God's* acts?"[32]

It can be said in summary that the transcendental-eschatological approach, as it is encountered, prepared by Hermann Kutter, in the early Barth in a way not merely theological-historically effective, is structurally defined by the qualitative difference between eternity and time, the absolute and the relative, divine history and human history, and indeed the temporal, relative, human-race historical — despite some dampening stop signs — in a way ultimately falls into triviality. It is here basically only to gain an absolute-critical relationship with the existing world with its processes and institutions. One may not in the process conceal the fact that this position of absolute critique of the relative from the absolute, of the penultimate from the ultimate, is entitled not only polemically to great power, but also theologically to a deep right. It is, reduced to a short formula, knowledge of why human justice can never be divine justice, why even in the best case, to speak now with Zwingli, it will be a "*presten*," thus a fragile, frail thing. From this insight Barth knew in the early 1920s — and the religious socialism of that time, not to mention the cultural-Protestant forerunners and latecomers, had not recognized it — to recite insistently that not only capitalism, militarism, liberalism, and bourgeois culture were in a sorry state, but that socialism, pacifism, democracy and proletarian lifestyle are also to be supplied "from God" with a large question mark. But the danger, the uncanny danger, associated with this kind of absolutely correct critique is that, in the domain of the relative, and thus in the social and political decisions of time, all possible options may be assessed as ultimately of equal validity, and one then can thereby easily be trapped into choosing the worse ones.[33] To dispute that this has actually occurred under the influence of dialectical theology would

[32] Karl Barth, "Der Christ in der Gesellschaft," p. 37.

[33] Similarly Ulrich Dannemann, "Karl Barth und der religiöse Sozialismus," pp. 136-37 and *Theologie und Politik im Denken Karl Barths*, Munich, 1977, p. 118.

be difficult. Barth himself had to acknowledge it occasionally, and indeed with inward rage.[34] Behind it was hidden the factual impossibility of gaining from the absolute a social-ethically constructive relationship to the relative,[35] as is, incidentally, found in Herbert Marcuse, whose critical approach, although essentially Marxist, betrays a structural relationship to the transcendental eschatology of the early Barth.[36] Indeed, this relationship is not only perverted, in that one takes the relative too seriously and, for instance, brings the bourgeois or even a socialist ordering of society into a direct relationship with the will of God. That is also true if one trivializes all socially and politically profound distinctions in the realm of the relative and no longer seriously knows how to distinguish, for example, between using force to promote the rule of law and using it to promote the rule of power, because both are judged according to the absolute, for instance, by the commandment of love, which is essentially incompatible with the use of force for any purpose. And when that occurs, social critique of the existing order is still possible in principle in the best case, but there can be no operational social ethic, according to which it is a matter of obligation concerning justice and injustice in the domain of the penultimate and, therefore, relative. From that it is clear why the early-Barthian approach could not lead to any real social ethic, and why Barth himself, as he had to understand anew under the bitter experiences of National Socialism the decisive meaning of the rule of law for the political and social life of human persons, saw the necessity of proceeding in an entirely different theological way.

6.2.2 *The Creation-Theological Approach (Emil Brunner)*

The creation- or order-theological approach in social ethics is associated first of all with the names of Friedrich Brunstäd, Paul Althaus, Werner Elert, Walter Künneth, and Emil Brunner — the

[34] See, for example, Karl Barth, *Gesamtausgabe*, V: *Briefe*, Vol. II, Zürich, 1974, p. 334.

[35] Cf. Knud Eiler Løgstrup, "Ist die ethische Forderung durch ihre Radikalität destruktiv?" *Zeitschrift für Theologie und Kirche*, 52 (1955), pp. 104-23, who intensively discussed this question in debate with Kierkegaard, with the help of the opposite person of "love of neighbor" and "natural love", of course, with a personal-ethical orientation.

[36] Cf. Hans Heinz Holz, "Der Irrtum der 'Großen Weigerung'," *Blätter für deutsche und internationale Politik*, XIII (1968), pp. 49-50.

latter the only non-Lutheran in this theological quintet. There are three reasons for presenting the structure and problematic nature of this conception by focusing on Brunner. First, the background to creation theology, which the preceding passage has summarized, is most concrete with him. Second, he may be the most sophisticated of the order-theologians of the inter-war period. And third, his chief ethical work, *The Divine Imperative*,[37] which will be examined, belongs to the international standard literature of theological social ethics.

Brunner, who, like Barth, started out from religious socialism — he was Ragaz's student and Kutter's curate — recognized early and clearly the weaknesses of the transcendental-eschatological approach. Foremost among these is that its merely negative mediation between the absolute of the Kingdom of God and the relative of the existing world makes it impossible for there to be any genuine social ethics. There is little room to recognize Barth's passing thesis of the interim that permits the possibility of recognizing the relatively good within the evil of real relationships. That is why Brunner takes up this point, in order to establish social ethics on the basis of dialectical theology, which he supports, but greatly modifies. For him "all genuine Protestant ethics is 'interim ethics.'"[38] And it cannot possibly be otherwise; for in the Kingdom of God there will be no ethics.

The term "interim ethics," derived from the vocabulary of "consistent eschatology," which takes Albert Schweitzer as its starting point, gains a completely unique character and a distinctive theological status with Emil Brunner. It is ethics between creation and redemption, between the original condition and the end times. In short, it is the ethics of reconciliation, where reconciliation is understood as "the centre of history," as the time between creation and redemption.[39]

The confrontation of creation and redemption in their mediation through the reconciliation that happens in Jesus Christ corresponds to a twofold command: "the Command of the Creator and Redeemer."[40] As the Creator, God is the beginning and basis, the

[37] Emil Brunner, *The Divine Imperative*, trans. Olive Wyon, New York, 1937; Philadelphia, 1947.

[38] *Ibid.*, p. 123.

[39] *Ibid.*

[40] *Ibid.*, p. 122-23.

where-from; as the Redeemer, he is the end and the goal, the where-to of all being. The will of God that approaches us from the past differs from the will of God that calls to us from the future goal; yet they do not differ essentially. For the Creator has no other work than the Redeemer. Nevertheless, "The will of God is indeed only one, but we can only understand it in this twofold character."[41]

To the duality of the will of God something further is added: the duality of "command" and "law." For Brunner, "command" is not identical to the law. "What the Bible calls 'the Commandments' do not primarily constitute *the* Command, although, certainly, the 'Commandments' do help us to hear the Command. For us the Commandments are primarily the *Law*, and they only become the Divine Command through faith."[42] Thus, the "commandments" are perceived only within faith as the command which in essence means love, outside faith on the contrary only as law, only as the justice accessible to humans.

"The *Law*, the laws of the Bible and of 'conscience' can," therefore, according to Brunner, "be perceived by everyone; the Divine *Command*, however, can only be perceived by those to whom God Himself speaks His Word, in faith."[43] The law is consequently the command removed from the grace of God, in this respect a pure norm, that is also outside faith and therefore generally recognizable. Thus, "man of himself knows God's Law, it is true, but not His Command, and because he does not know the Law as His Command, he does not rightly know the meaning of the Law, which is love,"[44] the love that is not only a mere norm, but at the same time always also a newly-made gift of God.

It follows from the preceding that the command of the Creator and Redeemer is not only universally recognizable in the mode of the law as demanding norm, it also demands universal recognition. That becomes concretely tangible in God's *orders of creation*. With that the central concept of Brunner's social ethics comes into view. What is to be understood by "order of creation"?

In order to answer this question satisfactorily, we must first take a detour. In its essence, Brunner's ethics is conceived personalistically,

[41] *Ibid.*, p. 122.
[42] *Ibid.*, p. 112.
[43] *Ibid.*, p. 111.
[44] *Ibid.*, p. 115.

with that concept understood in the sense of *Ferdinand Ebner* and *Martin Buber*, for whose understanding of the person the I-Thou relation is essential and in it the responsibility of the I towards the Thou. Therefore, it is true that "the 'I' comes from the 'Thou.'"[45] The power, however, which alone can make the "I" responsible to the "Thou" is, according to Brunner, God. "Our responsibility can only be based on the Divine claim." — "Only as we respond to this claim upon us do we fulfill the purpose for which we have been created."[46]

Human existence in its reality thus means responsible existence facing the claim of the command of God as Creator and Redeemer. It is existence in the relation of Thou and I, of the Thou of God and the Thou of other human persons. In this context, Brunner significantly cites the fine words of Pestalozzi, according to which "God is our nearest relation," in order to add immediately, "But the fact that God is thus related to us means that this intimate relation can only become concrete and real in a relationship with the human 'Thou.'"[47]

In this way human creation reveals itself ontologically as responsible existence, as existence in relationship. The meaning of this relational existence for Brunner is love. "Every human relationship which does not express love is abnormal."[48] That love is the original sense of the intended relation and, therefore, "the whole meaning of our life, and is also its foundation" is, however, recognizable only in Christian faith. "Here the Creator reveals Himself as the One" — and now follows one of the most important passages for understanding Brunner's social ethical approach —

> who has created us *in* love, *by* love, *for* love. He *reveals* to us our true nature, and He *gives* it back to us. In Him it becomes clear to us that our 'natural' life" [despite the Fall] has not ceased to be a human existence, an existence-in-responsibility, one that responds to a summons; it is obvious, however, that we do not make this response positively, but negatively; we do not respond by accepting our responsibilities, by manifesting love; no, our response takes the form of irresponsibility and lovelessness: we still live as human beings, it is true, but we are misshapen human beings. Thus even our 'natural sinful existence, is a kind of *co*-existence, but it is *co*-existence in the negative sense; it means separation from our fellows, and, indeed,

[45] *Ibid.*, p. 295.
[46] *Ibid.*
[47] *Ibid.*, p. 296.
[48] *Ibid.*

> hostility towards them. It is not an unrelated existence, but it is an existence which 'contracts out,' that is, it is an existence which withdraws itself both from God and Man. This explains how it is that in this false definition of co-Existence both the 'I' and the 'Thou' receive a false distorted meaning, but that at the same time the 'I' and the 'Thou' do not sever their relation with one another. The distorted meaning shows itself in this: that henceforth 'self-existence' or 'selfhood' stands in a permanent relation of opposition to co-existence, to the community, that the false 'self-existence' and the false 'co-existence' are in perpetual conflict with each other. On this basis a right definition and realization of the relation between the individual and the community — which could indeed only be an adjustment — is impossible.[49]

The concluding sentence of this passage reveals the unique basic theme of Brunner's social ethics: the individual and the community.

Human existence in its own essence is indeed personal existence, love as concretized responsibility towards and for the Thou. The Thou, however, "does not confront us merely as an individual but as a member and supporter of definite communal 'orders.'"[50] If, however, in the state of sin which makes up the empirical being of man, the original with-existence perverts itself in a contra-existence and now stands "in a permanent relation of opposition to the community," how is social life in the real world at all still possible?

The answer can be inferred from what has already been explained. If recognition of and obedience to the command, and thus the love and community grounded in it, become impossible in unbelief, that is not true of recognition and enforcement of the law. In other words, there is not only the community commanded by the Creator and Redeemer in His command, but also communal orders established, and therefore prescribed, by the law that is recognizable outside the faith. Brunner calls these communal orders, understood in their narrower sense, "*orders of creation.*" By this he means "those existing facts of human corporate life which lie at the root of all historical life as unalterable presuppositions, which, although their historical forms may vary, are unalterable in their fundamental structure, and, at the same time, relate and unite men to one another in a definite way."[51] This has a great deal to do with the "creational inequality," as it comes

[49] *Ibid.*, pp. 296-97.
[50] *Ibid.*, p. 210.
[51] *Ibid.*

to expression, for example, in the gender difference between man and woman and "which renders one dependent upon another, and thus bases life upon 'exchange,' 'co-operation,' and — this alone is decisive — upon community, in the sense of the necessity of being together, or of dependence upon one another."[52]

The orders of creation become concrete in what Brunner calls the "natural communities," which he introduces in Chapter 30 of *The Divine Imperative*. They originate according to their fundamental nature without reference to the Fall. Included with them is, first of all, since it is foundational for all other societies, the community of marriage and family. Then there are the community based on the drive towards nourishment and acquisition, the national and legal community of larger associations, and finally — strangely enough — also the church (though only in so far as it takes on the character of a visible corporation).[53] The state thereby takes a conspicuously intermediate position. To the extent that it behaves as a national and legal community and encompasses the other orders, it is one of the natural communities. To the extent, however, that it has the character of an order of law and power — and it always does — it makes sense only "owing to the fact of sin." For only sin makes "legal coercion" necessary, and with it the order of the state and the law. To the extent that the state serves its elementary functions according to preservation of the natural communities under the conditions of the fallen world, it "points to the same thing as the natural orders."[54]

In their essence the orders of creation are thus in creation itself, and not based upon sin. That holds true, though, only of their prehistorical structure, not of their historical manifestations. These are corrupted through the fact of sin, as we "only know the Divine Creation as it has been marred by sin, and the created human being as a sinner."[55] But it is in light of this very fact that the orders of creation gain their true significance. We know them — the state included — despite their obvious deficiencies, "as means by which the divine wisdom *compels* men to live in community — men, that is, who through their sin have become separated from one another, and in their inmost will have lost the sense of corporate life; this means that

[52] *Ibid.*, p. 212.
[53] *Ibid.*, pp. 331-33.
[54] *Ibid.*, p. 213.
[55] *Ibid.*, p. 210.

human life, which is only possible as a life in community, is continually being made possible once more."[56] Nevertheless, for Brunner, they should not be understood as anything like a perfect world. Because they are *de facto* corrupted by sin, they too are in need of redemption. Also, the command of the Redeemer is, therefore, valid for them. And in that way man stands in his concrete existence in "the interim" between fallen creation and the coming redemption, between law and command, between justice and love, between the orders of creation of the corrupted world and the orders of redemption of the Kingdom of God. As interim ethics, Brunner's social ethics must consistently take into account the already-mentioned duality. It determines conclusively its basic structure.

In the proposition placed at the beginning of the important chapter on "The Natural Orders and the Kingdom of God," Brunner epitomizes this dialectical basic structure to the succinct formula: "As Creator, God requires us to recognize and adjust ourselves to the orders He has created, as our first duty; as Redeemer, as our second duty, He bids us ignore the existing orders, and inaugurate a new line of action in view of the coming Kingdom of God."[57] Both are thus demanded in view of the orders of creation that become tangible in social institutions from marriage and family to the concrete state: acceptance and rejection, conservative and revolutionary basic attitude. Precisely this thesis, full of tension, now reveals Brunner's convergence towards and divergence from the early-Barthian approach in social ethics. The convergence consists in the dialectic between what is factual from human society and what should be and will be from God. The divergence consists in the difference in weight of the two poles of this dialectic.

With Barth the eschatologically determined critique of the existing, or even only striven for, institutional order of society stands unambiguously in the foreground. If one has once affirmed and taken seriously "the great disruption" from God, upon which this critique is based, one may finally secondarily also adapt oneself to this order and thereby ask what can relatively best be made of it. The emphasis here is clearly on the revolutionary, admittedly the transcendental-eschatological revolutionary, who knows very well to launch an attack on both the contemporary-historical "revolutionary" and the contemporary-historical "reactionary." With

[56] *Ibid.*
[57] *Ibid.*, p. 208.

Brunner, in contrast, this is reversed. With him the insertion in the social institutions, whose basic structure, though corrupted by sin, is still always characterized by the orders of creation, stands in front. Someone who recognizes them in their communal demands as absolute divine law can then, likewise secondarily, also expose them to critique through the command of the Redeemer, which is to be understood eschatologically, in order to proclaim that the justice of the order, which should allocate within the current social institutions with their inherent laws "to each its own," is still far from love that seeks not its own. Therefore, what with the early Barth has only regulative meaning, becomes with Brunner constitutive. That gives his social ethics a noticeably *conservative* trait, which later apparently grows even stronger with him.[58] Indeed, the theologian from Zürich can say explicitly, "God's Command requires from us always — but in a very different way — both adaptation and protest, acceptance of the existing order and resistance to it, because our service of our neighbour requires it."[59] Yes, clearly following Zwingli and comparing the existing orders to vessels, he can even declare emphatically: "There are vessels which are contrary to this content of love, and it is quite possible that such vessels ought to be smashed. Where the existing order is no longer useful but harmful, it is ripe for destruction."[60] But, the other immediately precedes it: "The existing orders, behind which stands the Divine order, constitute the framework within which our service of our neighbour is to be performed; they form the vessel which we are to fill with the content of love. We have just said that the first thing necessary is not to alter this vessel but to fill it with the new content."[61] And that rather contains an overtone of Luther. With Brunner, this tone is primary and thus dominant. In other words, the static, the preserving, and the existing remain dominantly in the domain of social ethics as interim order ethics. The existing social structures are, since they are in their basic constitution stamped by the orders of creation, ultimately nevertheless evil-checking, not evil-causing structures. That there is also structurally qualified evil

[58] That indicates similarity between *The Divine Imperative* and Brunner's *Justice and the Social Order*, trans. Mary Hottinger, New York, 1945.

[59] *The Divine Imperative*, p. 218.

[60] *Ibid.*

[61] *Ibid.*

is for Brunner indeed not simply concealed, but strongly pushed into the background. According to the personalistic basis of his social-ethical approach, social evil is nonetheless found ultimately only in persons, which is why as a matter of priority one has to start with their conduct. In a world, however, which directly reveals structural evil of that kind penetratingly, as the modern economic world does, the solution of the primary ordering in the existing must become problematic.

Despite this critical reservation, it is nevertheless to be said that the creation-theological approach of Emil Brunner means a great gain relative to the transcendental-eschatological approach of the early Barth. Brunner overcame Barth's basically only negative relation to the existing and, therefore, on the basis of the new theology co-initiated by him, made possible a theory of social ethics going beyond mere social critique, without thereby removing the social-critical element.[62] Closely related to that, by the way, is his pronounced sense of the social realities, especially the economic realities, which in him — in contrast to Ragaz and Barth — awakened the consciousness that also in a theory Christian social or economic ethics, which in the final analysis wishes to be led by God's command, the element of the economically-correct must play a decisive role. Does Brunner's approach not thereby show all in all a successful mediation between the ultimate and the penultimate, between the absolute and the relative?

At first glance, one would like to answer this question affirmatively. But upon closer examination, certain reservations present themselves.

The mediation between the relative of the historically-concrete orders and that which God ultimately wills ensues with Brunner on the basis of the divine command in the *mode of the Creator's will, not that of the Redeemer's will*. Indeed, according to this intention, the will of the Creator and the will of the Redeemer are identical. But he expresses himself, as has become clear, in a completely different way, which leads to a variation on the two-kingdom theory in his approach. There are basically two absolutes, the absolute of redemption-justice and the absolute of creation-justice. In the ultimate of the Kingdom of God, only redemption-justice is valid. In the penultimate, however, the will of God as creation-justice is constitutive,

[62] What succinct contours Brunner's social critique could assume is showed by, for instance, the critique of capitalism in Chap. 35 of *The Divine Imperative*.

which, though corrupted, becomes tangible in the fundamental structures of existing social institutions. These are, even in their historicity and thus dubiousness, not merely made by humans, but rather are established by divine will. In their relativity, one consequently meets the absolute, to which one owes obedience absolutely. And in this respect the absolute and the relative are mediated with one another here. But, as has already been mentioned, this kind of mediation proves to be problematic.

First of all, it remains restricted to the absolute, which appears in the orders of creation. The absolute demand, which goes out from the redemption orders of the Kingdom of God, stands in opposition, not unlike with the early Barth, beyond the relative, and thus beyond the concrete society in its social, economic and political constitution. It calls for rejection, not acceptance, of life in the social structures, as that applies to the call, which rings out from the orders of creation. And precisely for this reason, according to Brunner, "we have as much right to say that the Christian Ethos is *revolutionary* as to say that it is conservative."[63] The intended mediation between the absolute and the relative is consequently splintered.

In addition, one can hardly overlook the fact that the unsplit mediation takes place merely on the level of creation-justice, at the cost of the actual relativity of the concrete social orders. To these orders, as historical, if also determined by the Fall, objectivation of the creation order of God, a theological dignity is due, which cannot easily be reconciled to seriously understood relativity. That means practically, however, that the basic social order, in which what it constitutes is genuinely sacrosanct, and thus the relative and in this respect mutable only touches the surface. In other words, the relative threatens to disappear behind the absolute.

6.2.3 *The Christological Approach (The Late Karl Barth)*

One could interpret Emil Brunner's creation-theological approach, and order theology as a whole, as an attempt to grant the existing basic orders of society — since its structure, in so far as it perseveres historically, is rooted in the creation-will of God — social-ethically a right of their own, and thus to allow them normative obligation, and

[63] *Ibid.*, p. 127.

in doing so to tone down, both in principle and in practice, the eschatological "from God" in its social-critical relevance. In any event, that is how Barth saw it. He himself wishes to hold on absolutely and undividedly to the eschatological "from God," as it has become apparent historically in the Christ events. Therein, incidentally, lies the fundamental continuity between the early and the late Barth.

On the other hand, Barth also had to recognize that one cannot simply remain standing with the mere opposition of God and man, of Kingdom of God and earthly regime according to the qualitative difference between eternity and time; the decay of human and earthly "*coram deo*" into meaninglessness should be prevented. But how is the relevance of the human and earthly to be established, without abandoning the "*Soli deo gloria*" in its Christologically determined radicalness? This question led Barth to a new *theory of analogy*, which decidedly shaped his later theology, as it is found foremost in his monumental *Church Dogmatics*.[64] What does "analogy" mean in the sense in which one finds it in this work?

To put it succinctly: "In distinction to both likeness and unlikeness 'analogy' means similarity, i.e. a partial correspondence and agreement (and, therefore, one which limits both parity and disparity between two or more different entities)."[65] From that it is evident that, for Barth, "analogy" is to be understood in a relational sense. It means a correspondence, which can be reduced neither to the common denominator of identity, nor to that of non-identity, and in which instead identity limits non-identity and *vice versa*, each thus referring to the other.

This relational concept of analogy becomes decisive for the foundation of Barth's dogmatics, as well as his ethics. In accordance with the fundamental perspective, according to which everything is to be heard, seen, and understood from the God revealed in Jesus Christ, ethics belongs to the teachings of God, according to Barth. It is thus not autonomous, but rather is to be understood *in the framework of the dogmatic*. An additional reason for the subordination of ethics to dogmatics is that the God who claims human persons for himself makes

[64] Karl Barth, *Church Dogmatics*, 4 vols., Edinburgh, T. & T. Clark, 1956-75.

[65] Barth, *Church Dogmatics*, II, 1, p. 224. On Barth's doctrine of analogy, see the impressive and comprehensive study: Horst Georg Pöhlmann, *Analogia entis oder Analogia fidei?* Göttingen, 1965.

himself responsible for them. The ethical behavior of human persons must also, according to Barth, be derived from God's responsibility and, indeed, according to the principle of analogy that has just been formulated. Human existence-relationships correspond in their being and obligation to the divine relation, where that means here primarily the inner-Trinitarian divine relation. That means, first of all, that the Barthian concept of analogy, as its formal basic structure already suggests, is to be understood in the sense of an "*analogia relationis,*" not in that of the "*analogia entis.*" "*Analogia entis*" means that one can infer the nature of God from the nature of man, and thus can establish a natural theology. "*Analogia relationis*" means, on the contrary, that *correspondence exists only between divine and human relationships,* in other words, that, despite the absolute ontological difference between man and God, there are nevertheless relationships in the divine and human realm that can be compared. In doing so, one must start from above, which means at the inner-Trinitarian divine relationship, which one could call "monopluralism" (Horst Georg Pöhlmann) in love.

In so far as Barth's theory of analogy is developed "from God," and that concretely means here "in faith," his "*analogia relationis*" is at the same time an "*analogia fidei.*" That means that analogies of this kind are accessible only to faith, not to reason. Indeed, they are effective in the reality of human relationships, as certainly as God is real. And, therefore, the reality of human relationships in view of the being of God as the basis of all reality is not only capable of corresponding, but also in need of corresponding. But in order for that which they are against the actual appearance in reality to become conceivable, they require illumination in faith and through faith. Only in faith, more precisely, faith in Christ, do these analogies become evident, does humanity prove itself to be similar in its relation to the being of God. Barth's theory of analogy then can also only unfold on the basis of Christology:

> This correspondence and similarity consists in the fact that the man Jesus in His being for man repeats and reflects the inner being or essence of God and this confirms His being for God. We obviously have to do here with the final and decisive basis indicated when we spoke of the ontological character, the reality and the radical nature of the being of Jesus for His fellow-men. It is from this context that these derive their truth and power. The humanity of Jesus is not merely the repetition and reflection of His divinity, or of God's

> controlling will; it is the repetition and reflection of God Himself, no more and no less. It is the image of God, the *imago Dei*.[66]

In this way the interpersonal humanity of Jesus, in which humanity first appears in its complete truth, is an analogy, a replica, a repetition of the divinity of God. Such humanity, such fellow-humanness, as the man Jesus personified it, is man according to his true nature and, therefore, is also what he should be. As surely as it is based on God, ethics, as the quintessence of what the human person is called to be — and for Barth that is fellow-human love — is also based on this same foundation:

> Love is a free action: the self-giving of one to another without interest, intention or goal; the spontaneous self-giving of the one to the other just because the other is there and confronts him. It is not an action which has no ground or basis. The man engaged in it, the Christian, exists as and because God is his basis, and has disclosed Himself to him, and is known by him, as such. He loves on this basis in God, as one who is called and impelled by God to do so by the fact that He has disclosed Himself and is known as the One who first loves, and first loves *him*, in the glory and majesty of His divine essence. It is for this reason, in response to the Word in which God loves him and tells him that He loves him, in correspondence to it, that the Christian may and must and will also love.[67]

In so far as God's action precedes human action in this way, the ethical action of human persons is fundamentally "a posteriori analogue,"[68] ethics thus conceivable only as the ethics of justification.

In the present context, of course, it is not a matter of unfolding Barth's ethical approach *in extenso*. His analogy-conclusion procedure can be of interest here only in so far as it becomes relevant to specifically social-ethical problems and reveals its manner of mediation between the absolute and the relative. Unfortunately, Barth — and it is certainly no accident — only very rarely said anything about specifically social-ethical problems. The most important exception is the problem of the *state*. It is, therefore, advisable to begin immediately at this point.

Barth's doctrine of the state, seen in its historical context, proves to be *conscious opposition* to the form of the state found in order theology. If order theology brings the reality of the state theologically into

[66] Barth, *Church Dogmatics*, III, 2, p. 219.
[67] Barth, *Church Dogmatics*, IV, 2, p. 752.
[68] Pöhlmann, *Analogia entis oder Analogia fidei?* p. 94.

the context of creation and sin, Barth brings it into that of redemption and grace. Like all reality, the reality of the state is also in its originality based on the reign of Christ, by virtue of whom redemption and grace, in a word, justification, takes place. There also exists an analogical relationship between it and the reign of Christ, even when the state itself fails, when it misses its own purpose, namely the safeguarding of the law, which has its basis — again according to Barth — not in the "well full of holes" of the natural law, but rather in justification, thus in the event of grace. That goes so far that even Pilate, as a representative of the repressive Roman state power and Jesus' judge, becomes comparable to the reign of Christ:

> The same pilate, constrained to become the instrument of the death of Jesus, ordained by God for the justification of sinful man — this same Pilate is also forced to confirm the presupposition of this event: to affirm expressly and openly the innocence of Christ, and — of course — it is in this very fact that he is fulfilling his specific function. "Pilate sought to release Him" (John 19,12). For it is in this sentence of acquittal (which he did *not* pronounce), that his duty lies. If he had done so the State would have shown its *true* face. Had it really done so, then acquittal would have had to follow, ... The fact that this did not actually happen is clearly regarded by the Evangelists as a *deviation* from the line of duty on the part of Pilate, as a *failure* on the part of the State. Pilate "delivered" Jesus to crucifixion, because he wished to satisfy the people (Mk 15,15). The political charge against Jesus was for Pilate clearly groundless, but he "gave sentence that it should be as they required" (Luke 23, 24). "Take him *yourselves* and crucify him!" (John 19,6). This decision has nothing to do with the law of the State nor with the administration of justice. The Jews themselves confirmed this: "*We* have a law and by *our* law he ought to die" (John 19,7). It was not in accordance with the law of the State, but *in spite* of this law, and in accordance with a totally *different* law, and in flagrant defiance of justice that Jesus had to die.[69]

From that it is clear that for Barth the state is performing its function when it exercises justice, when it grants legal protection to threatened persons, in short, when it stands up for human persons with its power humanely. However, that proves also to be, as it now understands itself, not a universally-accessible conclusion, achieved on the basis of political experience or by means of consideration of the

[69] Karl Barth, *Church and State*, London, 1939, pp. 19-20.

natural law, but rather a conclusion that can be drawn only if one sees the state in its originality *per analogiam fidei* in correspondence to the reign of Christ, that is to say, the law implemented by him in correspondence to God's justifying love.

The Christological foundation of the state outlined above should not be understood, as it might appear at first glance, as a justification of political power as such. On the contrary, Barth above all strives persistently and uncompromisingly to draw attention to the fact that the state that denies human persons their rights — not only, but nevertheless primarily, in view of Hitler's power-state — is not performing its own function and, therefore, is a failure and resembles Pilate. And in the event that the state does not exercise justice in relationally understood analogy to the justice of God, then it must simply — at whatever the cost — be checked by Christians and held to the preservation of its basic function. Only to the extent that it performs this basic function can the state really be compared to the reign of Christ. And in this respect the Christological basis of the state possesses for Karl Barth an eminently state-critical element, as was hardly possible in Emil Brunner's order-theological approach. According to Brunner: "The essence of the state is not justice but power. Even the unjust state is still a state, but the impotent state ceases to be a state."[70] This difference in the assessment of the fundamental nature of the state is, of course, theologically grounded. According to Brunner, the state must be seen from the perspective of the created order of God, which is corrupted by sin. Its decisive function consists in compelling, under the conditions of sin in the social existence of human persons, a sufficient mass of political order, for which power receives constitutive significance. Barth, on the other hand, sees the state from the perspective of redemption, from the reign of Christ, from grace, which has become and is becoming effective. Therein, not as power-organization against evil, it has its elementary function. As a law-state, which it should be, it is a parabolic correspondence to the justification that takes place in Christ, which is valid, not only for the sinful person in his personal existence but also far beyond for the sinful world in the entirety of its economic, social, and political institutions, as a power already effective now, which opens freer and more human possibilities for the ordering of society.

It goes without saying that with his idea of analogy, otherwise than with his early, transcendental-eschatological approach, Karl Barth

[70] Emil Brunner, *Justice and the Social Order*, p. 196.

understands how to build a bridge from the will of God to the will of man, from the ultimate to the penultimate, from the absolute to the relative. The relation of total non-correspondence no longer prevails here, but instead a relation of correspondence, whereby "correspondence," to emphasize the point once more, does not mean similarity, but also does not mean dissimilarity. To put it differently, Christian ethics is not a mere "critique of all ethos" here, but "the epitome of that to which the human person is called *in actu*," namely, to practice fellow-human love and therein to exercise justice to human persons amidst the relativities of our world.

It is to be said additionally that with Barth, in contrast to Brunner, who mediates the relative basically only with the absolute of the orders of creation, a mediation of the absolute of the redeemed world with the relative of the human world takes place. And that happens, again, not in the merely negative sense that the ultimate stands critically facing the penultimate as its pure sublation, but in such a way that it becomes present in the penultimate, in the case of the actual state, reveals its fundamental justice-function, strives to preserve it, and thus in analogy to the reign of Christ, already anticipates the absolute in the relative. The relative, the existing world in its concrete institutional order, is in this way no longer condemned to triviality before the claim of the absolute, as in the transcendental-eschatological approach, but rather — similarly to the case of Ragaz — the place where God's eschatological redeeming will seeks to happen and does happen. In this way, space is created for social-ethical action that understands its responsibility originating from the demand of the ultimate, for a responsible formation of social relations in the penultimate.

Nevertheless, here too, one cannot avoid critical questions. Is the relative really taken seriously in its relativity in the Christological approach of the late Barth, or only to the extent that it already anticipates the absolute analogically? In other words, isn't the relative here like the state in its basic function bound in a dimension that the relative already transcends and that gives it more solemnity than it is entitled to? It can be said pointedly that, just as with Brunner the absolute of the Kingdom of God is transposed down on the level of the orders of creation, in order to be able to mediate it with the relative, with Barth the relative is lifted up to the level of what is comparable to the absolute of the lordship of Christ, in order to make the mediation possible. The price of this is a somehow transfigured interpretation of reality in its contemporary possibilities. Indeed Christian existence in present-day reality is also for Barth still existence in the "*simul iustus et peccator*," as Luther formulated it, in the simultaneity of being justified and of sin. But with him the "simultaneity" receives an interpretation going far beyond Luther: "The two things which are 'at the same time' are our past and our future. Our sin has been, and our righteousness comes."[71] In so far as one wishes to testify by it that "our" justice, made effectual by God, wishes to and should determine Christian existence as a new life-power, this statement undoubtedly aims at the center of the Christian faith. But in so far as it suggests that this evil actually is in the past, that it has already played itself out, although the world does not yet know it, and that therefore social-ethical thought and action concerning the future possibilities no longer need to take evil seriously, it is otherwise, and the social-political reality, if not the present, so nevertheless that which is expected and sought, is idealistically transfigured. One actually can then easily see the reality of evil only in what is disappearing in the past, for example in the "bourgeois-capitalist" world, ultimately also the "proletarian-communist" world, but not also in the future-oriented, more or less revolutionary alternative concepts or visions of our time. And that would have to lead in the direction of an historical theology that sets the dynamic-progressive in history as an at least higher quality of the relative, compared to the static-conservative, in direct relationship with the eschatological will of God. That is not at all to maintain that Barth's Christological approach is inevitably joined in direct relationship with that kind of tendency, but it is observed that the historical-theological designs of recent times, from Richard Shaull to Jürgen Moltmann, proceed in their own ways from him.

6.2.4 *The Historical-Theological Approach (Theology of Revolution or Liberation)*

The historical-theological approach, as it experienced a powerful renaissance primarily in the 1960s, can best be understood as an opposition to order theology. If order theology is joined with the understanding of human history as a process of degeneration from the original creation-will of God, which must be halted by respecting the

[71] Barth, *Church Dogmatics*, II/1, p. 627.

claims that still proceed from the orders of creation, the historical-theological conceptions, on the other hand, understand history as a process that runs towards the Kingdom of God as the new creation and aims at the redemption or, as one is more likely to say today, liberation or emancipation of the human person. That also explains why the former conception shows, to a more or less articulated degree, an inclination to culturally pessimistic moods, while the latter encourages culturally-optimistic tendencies, provided at least that the cultural development is guided by the emancipating basic interest of liberation. Despite this fundamental contradiction, the two have one thing in common: in both of them God's will becomes tangible in the historical, in the former God's will of creation or preservation and in the latter God's will of redemption or liberation. Hence, strictly speaking, order theology argues in an historical-theological manner. The actual difference does not lie in the evaluation of history as a source of revelation itself, but in the completely different identification of historical forces, wherein God's will expresses itself in its social-ethically constituted demand. With the order theologians — referring back to Emil Brunner — he reveals his identity in that which perseveres in history, even if corrupted by sin, thus in the static and stable, in what does not change at all or changes only insignificantly, and consequently in what establishes solid order. The historical-theological approach, on the contrary, perceives what God basically wants in the opposite way, in the historically dynamic, in what liberates from the present, presses forward, and anticipates the future. In the extreme, the latter leads to a *theology of revolution*, which found a continuation and further-development in the theology of liberation.

It goes without saying that the historical-theological approach can start from Karl Barth, in so far as it decidedly rejects the creation- or order-theological conception, with its conservative basic tendency. There are, however, also positive points of contact. Above all, the crucial point for Barth is not the "has been," the sin related to the fallen nature of human persons, but rather the "should be," the justice of God that has happened and happens in Jesus Christ and effectuates the Kingdom of Christ, and indeed not only dogmatically, but also ethically. Something new began in Christ. Therefore, Christians should stand by it and should also vote for it demonstratively, i.e. symbolically, in social-political events. A revolutionary component is thus inherent in Barth's Christological approach, as the advocates of a historical-theological approach very well recognized.

The revolutionary that Barth means, however, is God himself, his justice, in relation to which the human will to justice can certainly be understood in the political, social, and economic as an analogue, but with which God can never coincide. Where God is, where his justice is brought to reality in the world, that which exists is certainly called into question, new things pave the way, the coming itself already occurs analogically in the now. Yet that is far from meaning that wherever society is revolutionized and attempts are made to anticipate the utopian, God makes himself known in his eschatological will. For Barth's Christologically-conceived doctrine of analogy, there is no manifest revelation of God in world history, in its dynamic tendencies no more than in the static tendencies, even if his sympathies very much went to the forces that seek to change the world in the direction of a human and reasonable socialism. Barth always maintained that God's revelation exists only in the Christ event testified to by Holy Scripture and that, therefore, all dogmatics and ethics also have to establish themselves Christologically. And indeed, he did this in such an anti-modern sense and so provocatively that it became an offense precisely for those whose last word is the enlightenment and total emancipation of the human person. According to all this, the historical-theological approach in social ethics both can and cannot refer to Karl Barth. That will now be shown concisely by means of a significant essay by the American theologian *Richard Shaull*, who may count as one of the most prominent advocates of the historical-theological conception.[72]

Shaull, who worked for a considerable time in the milieu of the South American liberation movement, refers first of all in this essay to what one can call the revolutionary component in Barth's theology:

> When society is at peace with itself and the church at ease in Zion, Christian faith often reveals an unusual capacity for disruption, as it challenges the accepted presuppositions of a culture and violates the norms of thought and action until then taken for granted. The outstanding example of this in our century is provided by Karl Barth, who negated what appeared to be the inevitable thrust of modernity and challenged its then uncontested assumptions in the name of Revelation, communicated through that "strange new world" of the Bible.[73]

[72] Richard Shaull, "Christian Faith as Scandal in a Technocratic World," in Marty and Peerman, eds., *New Theology No. 6*, London, 1969, pp. 123-34.

[73] *Ibid.*, pp. 123-24.

The component that Shaull correctly identifies in Barth, which provocatively calls into question the world up to now, precisely also the modern world in its technocratic orientation and in that respect is revolutionarily effective, is the revolutionary "from God," namely the "strange new world" communicated by the biblical message. On the one hand, Shaull takes this up; on the other hand, he turns it around 180 degrees. For he can suddenly say:

> As we participate in this world, our thought, illumined by the Christian symbols, may lead us to a further conclusion: today we are being pushed to the threshold of a new order; and we have arrived at a moment in which the nature of the struggle for liberation, as well as instruments for its attainment, should be defined in a new way. If there is any truth in this reading of our western history, it will be only in and through this struggle that contemporary man can move to a fuller and richer life.[74]

What Barth calls "revelation" is diluted by Shaull to "Christian symbols," which enable the thought engaged in the struggle for liberation to understand even more clearly, which it could gather anyway from Western history, namely, that the struggle for the liberation of the oppressed today drives the human race towards that "new order" to which the biblical symbol "Kingdom of God" points. And this means that the revolution of humankind must ultimately coincide with the "from God." The "futurist" future, which human persons make, and the "adventic" future, which the faithful expect from God, become identical. What still distinguishes Christian faith-hope from the secular expectation of revolution is ultimately only that it sees in the revolutionary processes of the historical present more than merely secular events, namely, events behind which God stands as the absolute. And so Shaull also writes:

> What this means, I believe, is that Christian faith can provide resources for being authentically revolutionary. It can produce the type of person whose own inward experience of death and resurrection equips him to let the old die when its time has come, and frees him to give form to the new possibilities open before him. This is what we most desperately need today: men liberated for creativity, participating in a community in which they are forced to die daily in order to create new ideas, new perspectives, new

[74] *Ibid.*, pp. 128-129.

> institutions, new political possibilities. In other words, our western world needs cadres of men and women who are as seriously concerned as the Marxists in China or earlier in Eastern Europe, to bury the dead, violate the old and create the new. When such a moment arrives, the distinctiveness of the Christian witness does not lie in its emphasis upon the values to be preserved from the past, but rather in the freedom it offers to bury the dead without remorse, to create the new in response to the future rather than in reaction against the past ...." [75]

The latter citation makes it completely clear that with Shaull the Christian testimony has at least the tendency to coincide with the revolutionary will in contemporary events. It can be recognized in its originality only as the vague invitation to see the "new," which breaks out in these events, less as a "reaction" to the past, and thus to what exists, which should be buried, and more as a response to the call of the "future," and thus what is coming, which represents the absolute final-will of God. That means that the revolutionary new in history, understood as an answer to the future that surges forward, which has with Shaull both a futurist-chronological and adventist-eschatological character, tends to correspond to the claim of the ultimate, which the redeeming-will of God desires. And that is no longer Barth, neither the early nor the late Barth. For the early Barth all time, the preterit-present as well as the future, is incommensurable with the ultimate. And for the late Barth and his way of seeing genuine humanity, which breaks up everything previous, in the sense of the *analogia fidei*, understood as correspondence to the humanity of Christ, that does not mean identity. The critical distance to the fellow-human breaking-up in time, let alone to what revolutionary liberation movements want in their ambivalent multifariousness, is also preserved, at least theologically-fundamentally, by the relationality of his concept of analogy, which always includes the element of inequality. With Shaull, on the other hand, the revolutionary is surrounded by the aura of the absolute, although even revolutions can produce only something relative, sometimes something relatively better, often however something relatively even worse.

The primary problem with this approach is that it brings the relative, in this case the relative of the revolutionary-progressives of our day, very close to the absolute, and in this respect brings today's

[75] *Ibid.*, p. 131.

unconditional obligations closer to the eschatological will of God, if it does not actually equate them. That, however, does not mean mediation of the absolute with the relative, but sublation of the relative by the absolute. Fundamentally, one actually wishes to opt for an absolute alternative to that which now exists, which lies beyond human possibilities and thus disqualifies humanly possible, only relative alterations to the good as mere cosmetic improvements of the old, which can have no future. All historical-theological approaches betray a tendency in this direction. This kind of tone can already be heard occasionally with Leonhard Ragaz,[76] although for the most part he understood the law of the relative. And also Jürgen Moltmann, of whom the same is true, can say: "If there were no hope in the coming of God itself, everything else would be only renovation of the prison, not an actual breakout from the prison into the land of freedom."[77] Even though such remarks are theologically legitimate, in so far as they seek to mark the critical distance of the Christian faith to everything relative, they are nevertheless fatal in terms of social ethics, since they could suggest that the persistent but unspectacular endeavors towards serious, relative changes in the existing economic, social, and political orders are actually in vain. Therefore, a possible mediation between the absolute and the relative that can serve as the basis for concrete social ethics can hardly, if at all, be carried out with this approach, at least with Shaull's version of it.

6.2.5 *The Existential-Eschatological Approach (The New Way)*

The existential-eschatological approach, as it will be expounded in this theological process of laying a foundation for business and economic ethics, has developed in continual examination of the approaches that have been critically presented above. It was and is concerned with finding true mediation, making concrete social ethics possible, between the absolute and the relative, between the ultimate and the penultimate, between the demand in the comfort of the Kingdom of God and the reality of our world, which is still stirred up by

[76] Thus, Ragaz says: "The Kingdom of God should get involved in politics, not in order to become politics... but to sublate politics" (*Die Botschaft vom Reiche Gottes*, Bern, 1942, p. 73). See also Arthur Rich in *Leonhard Ragaz in seinen Briefen*, Vol. II, pp. 52-53.

[77] Jürgen Moltmann, "Existenzgeschichte und Weltgeschichte," in Moltmann, *Perspektiven der Theologie*, Munich, 1968, p. 145.

structural and personal evil, but is nevertheless also already standing in the force field of that which is coming. The difficulty of this kind of mediation is found in the fact that there exists a relationship of difference as well as correspondence between the relative determined in this way and the absolute, and that the mediation, therefore, must fail in its complexity if one factor is diminished or completely disregarded in its weight relative to the other.

The transcendental-eschatological approach of the early Barth emphasized the difference between the relative and the absolute, between time and eternity, between man and God, but in an exclusiveness that actually lets the factor of correspondence become meaningless. On this basis, the critical distance of the Christian faith to the social and political structure of the existing world, and incidentally, also to its revolutions, can be made evident, but not the possibility, let alone the necessity, of its relative acceptance.

The creation- or order-theological approach, in contrast, attempts to explain the factor of correspondence between the absolute of the creating and preserving will of God and the relativity of the orders in the existing world. According to it, this will is still tangible in the traditional fundamental orders of existence, even though they are corrupted by sin. In their binding demands on the human person, they thus correspond to the absoluteness of the creation laws. That essentially establishes a conservatism of orders, which allows the difference and thus the critical distance to the traditional, if it is even discerned at all — which is the case with Emil Brunner — to be articulated only in a moderated manner.

In the historical-theological approach, on the contrary, the critical distance to the relative orders of the existing world is taken seriously and is increased, in the extreme, to the point of their complete rejection. Therefore, only the relation of difference exists between them and what God eschatologically wills in his originality. The existing orders are already doomed to destruction, and not merely eschatologically. On the other hand, there exists a massive correspondence of the final-will of God to the revolutionary powers in the contemporary world, as far as they seek an alternative order. And that is the case in a way that conceals their relativity and in which they approach so close to the absolute that the factor of difference must fade and the critical distance to the revolutionary, if it is still spoken of at all, is minimized. In this way there exists here the tendency to a conformism regarding the order-altering powers in the world, just as in the creation-theological approach there is a tendency towards the order-preserving powers in the world.

The problem of mediation between the absolute and the relative presents itself differently once again in the Christological approach of the late Barth. In contrast to the transcendental-eschatological conception, with its abrupt separation between the human and the divine, the temporal and the eternal, the correspondence relation between the absolute of the reign of Christ and the relative of the state legal system comes to fruition here *per analogiam fidei,* as the doctrine of the state, for example, demonstrates. there exists a relationship of correspondence between the two, whereby, according to Barth's concept of analogy, the factors of similarity and dissimilarity, thus correspondence and difference, set limits on each side. Much more than the other attempts, therefore, this approach allows the decisive acceptance of the relatively just, e.g., expressed concretely, of the state founded on the rule of law, without thereby having to minimize its remaining distance to the absolute of God's justice.

It should be noted, however, that with the late Barth there is a tendency to bring the state in its fundamental existence in line with the reign of Christ in such a way that the factor of critical distance can become indistinct. The fundamental nature of the state is based, according to his view of the matter, on the preservation of the law, which in its originality is to be derived from the justification that take place in Christ.[78] The activity of the state thus resembles, for the most part, the reign of Christ, as it attends to its own affairs, i.e. exercises justice. And it becomes unlike the reign of Christ to the extent that it abandons this project and becomes a power state. The fundamental function of the state, arising from its true nature, namely the exercise of law, consists accordingly in bringing Christocracy to validity in the historical world. But would the state not thereby be expected to leave its relativity behind and become something that it cannot be?

At this point one meets an aporia that is inevitable when one attempts to establish orders that are relative, because they are historical, directly from the absolute, and immediately to obtain from that standards for the shaping of the world, whether the absolute means "orders of creation," "reign of Christ," Kingdom of God," or something else. In such a case, one either will not arrive at genuine acceptance of the relative, because it can never exist in the face of

[78] Barth, *Church and State,* London, 1939.

the demand of the absolute — and the whole thing ends in social-political indifference, if not in something even worse — or one will arrive at acceptance of the relative, because one projects the absolute into social-political processes (the creation-will of God into the basic orders of society, his liberating power into the movements of social and political awakening of the time, and Christocracy into social institutions analogous to those of the state) — and the consequence will be raising, with suspicion of ideology, those kind of forces, with the actual inevitable tendency, whether it be to a conservative or a revolutionary conformism. Both are, however, extremely alarming in terms of social ethics, because both alternatives arrive at a false attitude towards the relative.

From that perspective, it now becomes understandable why even close friends of Barth could not simply remain standing by him. Thus Ernst Wolf[79] has once again accentuated the Christological relation of the political and determined it in such a way that "the weakening of the (daemonic) powers, achieved by Christ, liberates us to 'accepting' the state in its 'worldliness' as a task of *human* action in obedience to God's commands."[80] The state is thus taken completely seriously here in its secularity, and thus relativity. What is true of the state, of course, applies also to other political-social structures. They are all, therefore, to be seen and accepted in their historical relativity and secularity, and thus require neither a theological pro- nor anti-establishment. However, they should also never be received uncritically, with conformism, in their existing structures. On the contrary, it should always be asked how they should and can be structurally ordered, so that they promote the realization of personal and social common life and cooperation, oriented towards the highest possible degree of social justice. That is, thinking in the direction of Ernst Wolf, the specifically social-ethical task of the human person. It includes a consciousness of responsibility that must perceive Christian existence in accordance with the theological-anthropological premises developed here in the horizon of the humanity originating from faith, hope, and love. From that it follows that the social-political setting of goals in the concrete shaping of society and the world must not be primarily established by the comfort and demand of the

[79] On the following, see Martin Bock, *"Politia Christi"*, Hannover, 1983, pp. 186ff.

[80] Werner Schmauch and Ernst Wolf, *Königsherrschaft Christi*, Munich, 1958, pp. 23-24.

ultimate, which has become transparent in the eschatological event, Jesus of Nazareth. That, however, is the case for *Christian existence in the specificity of its social-ethical responsibility*, and thus in relation to the social institutions and their structurally determined repercussions. That leads to a new approach, which, in establishing and concretizing social- and economic-ethical responsibility, starts out from Christian existence in the believing experience of its eschatologically-determined context of existentce and in this respect can be characterized as *existential-eschatological*.

The existential-eschatological approach is about a determination of existence that is concerned with social-ethical responsibility for a humanly just ordering of society, which always remains in the domain of the relative, to make true that the demand of the absolute that God wishes in the coming of his kingdom always remains present as social-critical potential. Christian existence is incompatible with social conformism. The critical distance to everything relative remains, because it can never exist before the demand of the absolute, which still remains true even for the relatively best. But Christian existence also cannot speak out in favor of a notorious position of refusal, just because each society is and remains imperfect. Nothing like perfection is a possible social-political goal. When anything like that is sought, for instance, under the rubric of an order liberated from every constraint and all power, and one thus embraces a social-political messianism or maximalism, the final result can only be a negativism opposed to all social-institutional reality.[81] And that is not a possibility for Christian existence. It must, on the contrary, bear social existence in its imperfection, but in such a way that it thereby insist on a structural order of things, which, despite the remaining difference, can also make the correspondence between the relative and the absolute credible and can combat evil's permanent threat to society.

So, to clarify the preceding, the hoping love of faith, the epitome of that from which and upon which Christian existence lives in its responsibility, must stand up passionately for humanly just law in every social existence-relationship.[82] Every human law is relative. It remains subject to constant change and requires, if it is to be effective, the enforcing power of the state. For that reason, it is also never

[81] See Leszek Kolakowski, *Der revolutionäre Geist*, Stuttgart, 1977, esp. pp. 17ff.
[82] See pp. 119-21.

essentially love, for love does not get along with power. Provided that the law sets boundaries to human arbitrariness, protects the weak from the grasp of the strong, and creates the preconditions of humane communal life among human persons in the penultimate, however, it also seeks what love seeks, it gains the functionality of love, and it thus corresponds to the absolute. In this way, the humanly just law, not the law as a means of mere legalistic self-assertion, but the law as a means to a more fellow-human life, is an adequate mediation between the absolute and the relative, and functions under the demand of the absolute of love, without overplaying its enduring difference of essence to it. Christian existence must ask in its social-ethical responsibility about this more humanly just law, about social-ethically optimal possibilities of order in the concrete existence conditions of society, and seek answers that are also guided by the obligation to economic rationality and, consequently, can be put into practice in the world of the relative.

The hoping love of faith will thus have to fulfill its social-ethical responsibility in this way. It will do so as precisely this love and, therefore, under the demand of the absolute. In other words, in doing so it may not be led by any foreign norms, but instead must receive the fundamental criteria from faith, hope, and love as the existentials of their own humanity, which it experiences by means of example, in a way that provides norms, in the humanity of the man Jesus of Nazareth. We meet here Walter Kreck, who, starting out from Barth, asserts similarly that "the Christian community for its part also must take up the concept of humanity and use social-ethical guideposts," but in such a way that it "seeks to obtain the criteria for genuine humanity in the human person Jesus Christ."[83] Therein also exists agreement that the demand of the absolute cannot be put into effect directly in social orders, the domain of the relative, but that it must become effective there as a power to make relative changes:

> The Christian community cannot be indifferent to how the orders of marriage, of economic relations, and of the state take place, whether space is made here in which human living together is promoted or hindered. It cannot, if it believes in the present reconciliation and the coming redemption, see such orders as static quantities, which are given fatalistically, but must instead ask how its humanity-serving

[83] Walter Kreck, *Grundfragen christlicher Ethik*, Munich, 1975, pp. 211-12.

function can be fulfilled under the particular historical conditions in the relatively best manner. [84]

Because the hoping love of faith must in this way mediate the demand that starts out from the absolute with the relative in concrete social conditions, thus in the state, society, and economy, it must *rely on the use of reason appropriate to it*. There has already been a warning, at the conclusion of 5.5.5,[85] against attempting to place love and reason in a relationship of mutual exclusiveness. Whenever love wishes to reach concrete judgments or decisions in the domain of social relations or processes, it requires the critical capacity of reason. Consequently, it always includes reason. Thus Paul requests for the Christians in Philippi — incidentally, in a context that testifies concisely to the eschatological dimension of Christian existence — that their *agape*-love may always continue to increase in "*epignosis*" and "*aisthesis*,"[86] where the former term can be interpreted more in the sense of theoretical knowledge and the latter more in the sense of practical judgment.[87] And indeed he makes this request so that the Philippians may become capable of examining what "*ta diapheronta*" is, i.e., what essentially matters in concrete existence and the decisions demanded of it,[88] or, as the *Zürcher Bibel* succinctly translates it, "what is right and what is wrong". Thus Paul understands love in its rationality as the capacity to judge critically, which must examine in specific situations what does and what does not correspond to the humanly just, what should be accepted from the ultimate as appropriate in the penultimate and from what it is proper to distance oneself.[89] The criterion here, according to which the humanly just is evaluated in concrete situations, is not *agape*-love itself (which should be

[84] *Ibid.*, p. 212

[85] p. 122.

[86] Philippians 1,9.

[87] Rudolf Bultmann writes concerning *(epi)gnosis* in the sense of Pauline, early-Christian language: "One can always translate *knowledge*. The theoretical element determines the concept, but the practical consequences are always included" (*Theologisches Wörterbuch zum Neuen Testament*, Vol. I, Stuttgart, 1933, p. 707). According to Gerhard Delling, "*aesthesis*" originally meant "sensory perception" (*Theologisches Wörterbuch zum Neuen Testament*, Vol. I, pp. 186ff.). In Phil. 1,9, then, the term means "the ability to make moral decisions, the capacity of ethical judgment" (p. 180), and thus comes close to what Kant understood by "practical reason."

[88] Cf. Konrad Weiß, *Theologisches Wörterbuch zum Neuen Testament*, Vol. IX, Stuttgart, 1973, p. 65.

[89] Cf. Ernst Käsemann, *Commentary on Romans*, p. 301.

heeded precisely, because otherwise the danger of a social-ethical utopia would be evoked).[90] It is, rather, the critical authority, which, according to its own criteria of course, must examine critically what in given situations, conditions, and processes best understands how to satisfy the demand of the humanly just and what for that reason matters in the formation of ethical judgment and decision. Seen under this aspect, love is, to speak with Paul Tillich, "both absolute and relative."[91] It is absolute, because it is oriented in its criteria towards the humanity originating from faith, hope, and love; it is relative, in so far as it, directly for the sake of the well-being of the human person, does not judge abstractly, but instead always takes into account the concrete conditions of existence with their special characteristics.[92]

[90] The understanding of "*agapē*" as "*kritēs*" (examining authority), and thus not as a criterion of human justice, appears for the first time in my essay "Die institutionelle Ordnung der Gesellschaft als sozialethisches Problem" (1960), now in *Glaube in politischer Entscheidung*, Zürich, 1962, p. 124. This distinction, which I consider important, is assumed in my later publications, something that has not always be discerned, as for instance Christofer Frey fails to perceive it in his important study "Theologische Kriterien für die Gestaltung und Entwicklung der Wirtschaft," in *Zwischen Wachstum und Lebensqualität*, Munich, 1980, p. 130.

[91] Paul Tillich, *Gesammelte Werke*, Vol. III, Stuttgart, 1965, p. 37: "For love is, by its very nature, both absolute and relative. It is an immutable principle, and yet it adapts to every concrete situation."

[92] The existential-eschatological approach is similar in its basic structure to the universal-eschatological conception of Heinz-Dietrich Wendland, in so far as with Wendland Christian humanity also lives from the already happening and still to happen eschatological event in Jesus Christ, and in this respect, since it is oriented towards divine justice, it has a revolutionary component, but at the same time distances itself decidedly from the utopia of an absolute revolution or a perfect society, because the Kingdom of God, understood religiously or secularly, can never be a social-political project, and in such a distorted form will wreck havoc. Furthermore, for Wendland, in the time of the penultimate, there are only relatively better possibilities of shaping the state, economy, and society, which, however, must be taken up resolutely by Christian humanity, if they are helpful in achieving a "humanization of the worldly orders," and thus "point to the future." And, finally, for him, finding what is relatively better is also a matter of reason guided by the basic concerns of Christian humanity (cf., above all, *Die Kirche in der revolutionären Gesellschaft*, Gütersloh, 1967, esp. pp. 77-98 and (in concentrated form) *Einführung in die Sozialethik*, 2nd Ed., Berlin, 1971, pp. 17-50). But, while with Wendland the accent is more on working out a socially relevant theology of hope, with my approach, as the following discussion will show, the establishment of social-ethically responsible competence of judgment stands in the foreground.

6.3 The Three Levels of Social-Ethical Argumentation

The existential-eschatological approach, with its unique mediation of the absolute and the relative, agrees with the results and methodological conclusions that the reflections on the problem of the normative in the social sciences have yielded (4.3 and 4.4). According to them, social-ethical argumentation must take place at three levels:

> *first*, at the level of the fundamental experience-certitude of the humane, which with Weisser has a confessional character;
> *second*, at the level of in principle criteria, which, although they are oriented towards the absolute of experience-certitude, should articulate the humanly just in such a way that it can be understood, discussed, and applied even without the fundamental premises;[93] and
> *third*, at the level of feasible, critically-examinable norms, responsible for mediating the absolute and the relative, the prescriptive and the explicative, the normative, humanly just and the situational, economically correct, in such a way that they are able to provide practical guidelines for action, which are both ethically and technically responsible.

The first level is, in this approach, the *hoping love* of faith, with the humanity that belongs to it specifically. This humanity lies beyond rational substantiation and is a matter of personal experience-certitude in the event of the Christian faith, as has been explained in 5.1-5.

The second level constitutes the criteria of *the humanity originating from faith, hope, and love*. Because they are oriented towards the absolute of the faith conviction, they also cannot be established rationally, even though a certain degree of convincingness is appropriate to them, which can and should become rationally effective in social-ethical argumentation.[94]

[93] Cf. Hans Schulze, "Theologische Sätze über soziale Sachverhalte," *Zeitschrift für Evangelische Ethik*, 18 (1974), p. 199.

[94] Honecker, in "Vernunft, Gewissen, Glaube," thinks he is able to say that faith "does not bring any increase in ethical knowledge to a theory of theological ethics" (p. 339). It brings about only "*motivation* to use reason and to carry out the affirmation of the call of conscience" (p. 341). It is necessary to assert in opposition to this that the love of faith has criteria for the humanity corresponding to it and that, consequently, one can very well speak at this level of an increase in ethical knowledge. Honecker himself moderates the strength of his thesis when he writes more precisely somewhat later: "Motivation certainly does not mean any changeable impulse of conscience whatsoever, but a... particular basic attitude towards complete life-reality"

Finally, the third level is that of *practical maxims* that should make ethical judgments possible in concrete situations. They are by no means deducible from the in principle kind of criteria, but are only to be arrived at in such a way that it is asked by means of all reason under what ethical and technical conditions an optimum of human justice can be achieved in the actual circumstances of social life according to these criteria. Their validity will, therefore, despite the orientation towards the absolute, always be only conditional and relative, on the one hand, because they are always related to particular situations, and on the other hand, because questions about the concrete optimization of human justice can be rationally answered differently in good faith in the same situation, under the same conditions, and by application of the same criteria.

If social-ethical argumentation, according to this approach, has a specifically theological relevance at the first level and, to a somewhat lesser degree, also at the second level, it must rely indispensably on reason at the third level. Martin Honecker's thesis that "reason is indispensable as a principle of argumentation for ethics"[95] and "faith brings no increase in ethical understanding for a theological ethic"[96] receives decisive weight here. He writes correctly: "In order to arrive at ethical judgments in concrete situations, appeal to personal certitude is by no means sufficient. Such an appeal is irrational, if it is unable to name the good reasons for an ethical judgment."[97]

The first level of our social-ethical approach has been explained in detail in Chapter 5. The other two levels will now become the central theme.

(p. 341). The humanity originating from faith, hope, and love and the criteria belonging to it are about such a basic attitude.

[95] *Ibid.*, p. 334.

[96] *Ibid.*, p. 339.

[97] *Ibid.*, p. 337.

7. CRITERIA OF THE HUMANLY JUST AND THEIR ORIENTATION TOWARDS SOCIAL JUSTICE

7.1 The Basis of the Humanly Just

According to the theological approach that will be considered here, the foundation of human justice is understood as the humanity originating from faith, hope, and love, which has achieved its fully valid form and has come to historical effectiveness in the event of Jesus Christ. Its primary source of knowledge is, then, the experience of human existence, as it is authentically reflected in the Christ-testimony of the New Testament. Faith, hope, and love are the fundamental existentials of this existence. They have certain criteria, which in their interplay yield normative grounds for the concretization of human justice in social justice. In so far as these criteria prove to be principles of Christian existence, a specifically Christian character naturally befits them. But in so far as Christian existence seeks to be nothing other than genuinely human existence, they must legitimate themselves simply as human criteria, as criteria for true humanity in general. In other words, they do not simply decree dogmatically — to reemphasize what has already been said — they can only be referred to in such a way that they can at the same time in their inner faith-evidence also attain relevance for the horizon of general human experience.

If there is discussion subsequently of seven criteria of human justice, that does not mean that the number is determined forever. On the contrary, this number remains open. Humanity understood as the hoping love of faith is always humanity in the historical world. It must prove itself, therefore, as the epitome of *both* Christian *and* human existence in the historical world and, therefore, must bring its criteria of human justice to effect in the dynamic of the world. To be sure, it is by no means the historical situation, but love in its hoping faith alone, that produces these criteria. But they never show themselves beyond the historical situation. And with an alteration of the historical situation, even more criteria can become apparent to this love at any time. In this indirect and thus secondary sense, then, the historicity of Christian existence is to be relied upon as a further basis of knowledge of human justice.

7.2 Explication of the Criteria of Human Justice[1]

7.2.1 *The Criterion of Creatureliness*

The criterion of creatureliness, as a basic criterion of what is human, arises directly from the self-understanding of Christian, biblical faith. Seen in terms of the history of religion, the word "faith" is first met in Isaiah 7,9.[2] It is characteristic of the biblical understanding of faith that "faith" has nothing to do with holding religious dogmas as true or pious traditions, nor with acts of mere conjecture, but rather with existence-establishing trust in the reality of divine fidelity.[3] At a time of extreme political difficulty, according to the cited passage, the prophet Isaiah went to the despondent king of the small state of Judah in order to tell him: *"If you do not stand firm in faith, you shall not stand at all."* And that means that Israel's existence is based not on

[1] I first wrote about "criteria," as distinguished from maxims, in my own social-ethical work in "Die institutionelle Ordnung der Gesellschaft als sozialethisches Problem," *Zeitschrift für Evangelische Ethik*, 4 (1960), pp. 233-44 and *Glaube in politischer Entscheidung*, Zürich, 1962, pp. 113-31. As a basic social ethical criterion, "*agape*" is found there simply as "fellow- humanness." A process of reflection subsequently took place on a constant theological foundation and in historical or contemporary interaction with concrete social-ethical and business-and-economic-ethical questions, which arrived at a preliminary conclusion in my book *Mitbestimmung in der Industrie*, Zürich, 1973, pp. 49-61. Seven criteria were named there: critical distance, relativity, relationality, radicality, fellow-humanness, participation, and economic correctness. Since then, continuing reflection on these matters has led to a number of modifications (including the criterion of economic correctness in the process of forming humanly-just maxims; including radicality in the criterion of relationality) and also to additional criteria (creatureliness, fellow-creatureliness). From that it can already be seen that the criteria of the humanity originating from faith, hope, and love, although it is concerned with experience-certitudes rooted in Christian faith, should by no means be understood as hardened, non-modifiable dogmas, inaccessible to all critical examination (see pp. 94ff.).

[2] Hans Wildberger writes in a recent and authoritative commentary that this passage is "the birth hour of the biblical idea of faith" (*Jesaja*, Vol. I, Neukirchen-Vluyn, 1972, p. 299).

[3] Hans Wildberger, *ibid.*, "'Faith' is the attitude of calm trust, which counts on the reality of divine fidelity, on the truth of the promise given in the choosing-pledge to the faithful in harsh hours of destiny in the present."

particular historical possibilities of existence, but rather on trust in God alone.

Faith in the biblical-Christian sense means, therefore, "the establishment of existence outside itself."[4] The truth that human existence does not have its basis in itself finds its succinct expression in creation faith. Creation faith proclaims in its central core that human persons do not owe their existence to themselves, that they are creatures and not Creator, in short, that there exists a fundamental ontological difference between them as creatures and God as the Creator.

Old Testament creation faith, with its ontological difference between Creator and creature, also determines the character of the self-understanding of human persons in the Christian faith-tradition, and indeed from the very beginning. When Jesus calls God "Father," the essential substance of creation faith is contained in his doing so. The metaphor "Father" — one could instead say "Mother" — means that our life does not arise from ourselves, that it is produced and, consequently, that human existence, like all other existence, is created existence. This faith must not, of course, be objectified into a worldview doctrine of the origin of humankind, the species as a whole, in competition with the natural-scientific theory of evolution. That would not be consistent with its true intent. It intends, instead, to testify that the world, life, and human beings, however they may have originated, do not exist in and of themselves, as God exists in and of Himself, but rather have a *self-transcending basis*. And that means that this is a matter of ontological difference: human persons are human beings; they are not God. Consequently, humanity measured by such faith can exist, only if one always keeps the awareness of this difference in mind in an existential sense.

The criterion of creatureliness, as a fundamental criterion of humanness, however, is not simply to be equated with the aforementioned ontological difference. The metaphor "Father," as symbol of the Creator, contains yet another aspect, which appears to be opposed to this difference, namely, that of personal correspondence.

The aspect of ontological difference marks the essential equality of human beings with all other created being. "All flesh [i.e. the entire creation, including human beings] is grass and all its splendor like

[4] The formulation is derived from Gerhard Ebeling, *Was heißt Glauben?* Tübingen, 1958, p. 15. Dietrich Bonhoeffer writes similarly in *Ethics*, trans. Neville Horton Smith, New York, 1955, p. 122.

the flower of the field."[5] According to that, no nature is befitting to human beings other than that which animals also possess.[6] But what is different, fundamentally different, is the relationship of God as the Creator to the human creation. The human person is, seen from the perspective of biblical anthropology, the only being among everything created to whom God reveals himself, to whom he speaks with fatherly love, that he thus takes in his comfort and demand and in all of that calls to answer, more precisely, to responsibility as epitome of the image of God.[7] And the concept of personal correspondence means precisely the calling of human persons to responsibility and thus to maturity in their created existence. In other words, in the human person the creature is responsible to God for the created world, without ceasing to be a creature. Responsibility, determined in this manner, in which the human person answers that demand as an active, co-creative agent of the Creator, created in the image of God, is an additional fundamental characteristic of humanity in the sense of biblical creation faith.

Two constituents of humanity thus come into view: *ontological difference* and *personal correspondence*. The two belong to a whole, which must not be split up. If ontological difference is emphasized without the element of personal correspondence, one robs human persons of their essence as personal subjects and reduces them to mere marionette-like objects of the Creator. And if one wishes to accept only their subjective being, without simultaneously taking seriously the ontological difference between them and God the Father, who first establishes their personal subjectivity, they become simply subjects and creators answerable ultimately to no one other than themselves. Both alternatives mean the dehumanization of the human person and his world.

It is not necessary to explain in greater detail that the reduction of human persons to mere objects of the Creator must lead to their total dehumanization. That is obvious. For it is tantamount to condemning them to a thoroughly determined existence, lacking in freedom and consequently incapable of responsibility, which simply contains with itself the negation of the fundamental nature of all humanity.

[5] Isaiah 40,6.

[6] Ecclesiastes 3,19.

[7] That emerges from the context of Genesis 1,27. Cf. Friedrich Horst, "Der Mensch als Ebenbild Gottes," in Horst, *Gottes Recht*, Munich, 1961, pp. 230-31.

It also means, however, the negation of the Creator as the Father himself. For to the metaphor "Father" corresponds the picture of free sons and daughters, provided with mature responsibility, not that of pre-programmed robots that lack free will. It is profoundly meaningful that in both the Old and New Testaments the divine relationship is articulated with the idea of covenant. "The God of Abraham, Isaac, and Jacob, the God of Jesus Christ," to take up Pascal's well-known formulation, is in its fundamental nature a covenantal-dialogical God, *deus amans et loquens*, who lives and speaks, who seeks cooperation with human persons answerable to his demands, thus not the puppets of an absolute being, who, unmoved by himself, moves everything and rules the universe monocratically in such a way that there can be no freedom in the creation. From that it is also clear why Christianity, quite early in its efforts to speak correctly about God, did not profess abstract monotheism, but instead developed the Doctrine of the Trinity. Through the symbols of Father, Son, and Holy Spirit, God should already be testified as a convenantal-covenantal God in His innermost being, and not first in his loving care for human persons.[8] It is all the more unfortunate that Christian creation faith is always bound to the abstract conception of God as absolute power and in that respect with antihumanism that becomes effective therein.[9]

Against this perverted creation faith, which one-sidely stresses the ontological difference between Creator and creation, and darkens, if it does not completely deny, the existence of the human person as an active, and thus free and responsible subject, Karl Marx justifiably protested on the basis of an argument that is humanist in itself. For him "the question about an *alien* being, about a being above nature and man" is "a question" which *eo ipso* "implies the admission of the unreality of nature and of man."[10] From this citation it is undoubtedly evident that Marx can have known creation faith only in the

[8] Nikolai Berdiajev writes similarly: "Christianity is not a monotheistic religion, like Islam; it is a Trinitarian religion. The Trinitarian conception of God overcomes... the enslavement of the human person and establishes his freedom and dignity" (*Von der Bestimmung des Menschen*, Bern, 1935, p. 45).

[9] A similar view is already found within Johann Georg Hamann (1730-88) in §8 of his "*Brocken*" or "Fragments." See also the illuminating essay of Oswald Bayer, "Schöpfung als 'Rede an die Kreatur durch die Kreatur'," *Evangelische Theologie*, 40 (1980), esp. pp. 320ff.

[10] Karl Marx, *Collected Works*, Vol. III, New York, 1975, pp. 305-6.

form that makes God the "*potestas absoluta*," thus the total pantocrator, and reduces the human person to triviality. Understood in this way, humanity and creation faith are certainly incompatible with one another. About that one can undoubtedly agree with Marx.

Marx's argumentation, however, does not stop with the critique of perverted creation faith. He goes on to oppose the absoluteness of the Creator, which negates the human person, with the absoluteness of the human person, which negates the Creator:

> A *being* only considers himself independent when he stands on his own feet; and he only stands on his own feet when he owes his *existence* to himself. A man who lives by the grace of another regards himself as a dependent being. But I live completely by the grace of another if I owe him not only the maintenance of my life, but if he has, moreover, *created* my *life* — if he is the *source* of my life. When it is not of my own creation, my life has necessarily a source of this kind outside of it."[11]

That means that the human person, according to his human constitution, is his own creator; he has his basis of existence in himself.

One could call Marx's position in his critique of creation faith that of an *absolute humanism*, since he makes of the human subject an absolute being, caused by nothing other than himself. That means a basis of existence directly opposed to faith, namely the establishment of existence within itself. This means ultimately that the human person is his own creator.

With his absolute humanist position, Marx stands in the shadow of *Fichte*, who already made the free self-setting of the "I" the basis of his philosophizing.[12] Marx distinguishes himself from Fichte, of course, in that it is the empirical human being in his historical process, determined by the development of human work, not the transcendental "I" of the idealist philosopher, limiting its own absolute freedom, that sets itself: "But since for the socialist man the *entire so-called history of the world* is nothing but the creation of man through human labour, nothing but the emergence of nature for man, so he has the visible, irrefutable proof of his *birth* through himself, of his *genesis*."[13] All in all that means nothing other than the Promethean

[11] *Ibid.*, p. 304.

[12] Johann Gottlieb Fichte, *Grundlage der gesamten Wissenschaftslehre*, Hamburg, 1961, p. 16.

[13] *Collected Works*, Vol. III, pp. 305.

self-elevation of human existence, the negation of the ontological difference between Creator and creation, in short, the enthronement of the absolute human person.

This absolute or Promethean humanism has proved more and more to be a source of totalitarian antihumanism, even of the nihilism of our time.[14] *Friedrich Nietzsche*, though himself a prophet of Promethean humanism, already foresaw prophetically the connection prevailing in it in his oppressive aphorism "The Madman."[15] And *Leszek Kolakowski*, a perceptive interpreter of our epoch, calls Marx's and Nietzsche's conceptions of self-creation, which are of course extremely different in their philosophical foundations, two great ideas of the nineteenth century, which however "served ideological veiling, the justification of the two most disastrous tyrannies that our century has experienced"[16] (meaning, of course, National Socialism and Stalinism). And humanity, in fact, is no less threatened by the ideology of "*homo absolutus*" than by that of "*deus absolutus*."[17] The human person who understands himself as absolute, as lord and creator of himself, and who himself determines in monocratic autonomy, whether individual or collective, what is good and evil, right and wrong, human and inhuman, necessarily becomes the greatest danger to human persons and to humanity.[18]

In that way, the criterion of creatureliness, with its constituents of ontological difference and personal correspondence, proves humanity to be humanity originating from faith. Humanity becomes reality here, where the human person understands his existence to be founded not in himself, but in his Creator, and where he does not experience the Creator as the "*deus absolutus*," before whose omnipotence only human impotence is valid, but rather as the Father-God become transparent in Jesus Christ, who calls us in the personality of dialogical existence with him to covenantal partnership and thus to a life in the freedom of active, creative, and critical responsibility.

[14] That is not at all to say that the Promethean element in Marxist humanism does not also possess a *relative* kernel of truth. See Jan Milič Lochman, *Christus oder Prometheus?* Hamburg, 1972, esp. pp. 65ff.

[15] Friedrich Nietzsche, *The Gay Science*, 125, New York, 1974, p. 181.

[16] Leszek Kolakowski, "Die sogenannte Krise des Christentums," in *Leben trotz Geschichte*, Munich, 1977, p. 182.

[17] On the internal contradiction in absolute humanism, which is not only found with Marx, but is the temptation of human persons, especially the Western persons, as a whole, see Heinrich Weinstock, *Die Tragödie des Humanism*, Heidelberg, 1954.

[18] Albert Camus expresses this fact both originally and surprisingly in his important work *L'homme révolté*, Paris, 1951, esp. pp. 84-105 ("*L'affirmation absolue*").

So the human person is not — as the Promethean misjudgment of his creatureliness seeks to make credible — the lord of creation, but is nevertheless an agent of the Creator, with the mission of bringing his saving will to effectiveness in the world.

7.2.2 *The Criterion of Critical Distance*

The humanity originating from faith not only knows about the created dimension of true humanity, it also knows that the historical human person has fallen from this humanity and attempts repeatedly to establish his personal and social existence by his own power, whether in terms of a religious or a non-religious ideology, of reason, science, or technological-civilizational progress, etc. In the biblical story of the fall, this is expressed in mythical language. What the seductive serpent suggests to the first human persons is nothing other than taking the risk of the existence of the unbeliever, wherein the Bible sees the genuine basis of sin.[19] If you disregard God's command, thereby relying on your own resources, and thus covering up the ontological difference from the Creator and the personal correspondence with him, "your eyes will be opened, and you will be like God, knowing good and evil."[20] If one wishes to grasp this statement in all of its implications, then it must be observed that "knowledge" always also has the sense of "capability" for the ancient world and, furthermore, that the formula "good and evil" in Hebrew can take on the meaning of "everything," in the sense of being able to do anything.[21] From that it follows that it had in mind the existence of total power, emancipated from faith, according to which the human person in the final analysis permits himself to do anything and everything he can, hindered neither by the demands of the Divine nor by those of a human "Thou." What all of this means is an existence in which the human person finally has to reckon only with himself, grants his own needs, wishes, hopes and ambitions highest priority and, therefore, perverts the tendency towards dialogical existence into monological-monocratic existence. This evil, which according to the biblical view of the matter is fundamental, which repeats itself over and over again, and which in Christian dogmatics has taken on

[19] Cf. Romans 14,23.
[20] Genesis 3,5.
[21] Cf. Gerhard von Rad, *Das erste Buch Mose*, Vol. I, Göttingen, 1956, pp. 71-72.

the extremely-misunderstood name of "original sin," is the basis of personal and structural evil in its disastrous dialectic.[22]

Christianly-defined humanity, therefore, does not at all delude itself about the reality of the historical world. It knows that personal and structural evil is at work in it down to its very foundation. The historical world and the created world are not at all the same, not even in their fundamental structures, as order theology or its idealistic analogue believe. A return to the old traditions and their values, and a "return to nature" — however relatively meaningful they may be in a time of loss of world and destruction of nature — do not at all mean a process of finding one's way back to the salvation of God's original world. On the contrary, "the present form of the world," the world in which its historically characteristic form of appearance or structure,[23] "is passing away."[24]

Because this is the case, for Christian faith salvation is a matter of hope alone, hope in the future, succinctly, "adventic" hope in the advent of God in His kingdom, not in the "futuristic future"[25] of the human person in his sometimes progressive, sometimes conservative utopias. Neither backward nor forward illusions, therefore, can be his project. All of this means critical distance from the world, both in its past and its present, or yet emerging structural forms.

Specified on the economic-ethical basic problematic, therefore, critical distance means, in order at least to offer an example, that no economic system of order, whatever its basic structure, can claim to be ultimately valid, even if this is cautiously related merely to the fundamental direction and not to the concrete, historical form of the economic concept of order. It is, consequently, not acceptable to understand on the basis of this criterion, for example, the political-economic basic intention of liberalism — the same holds for that of socialism — as an ordering principle, which, ideal-typically, holds ultimate meaning, because it would coincide with human nature or the emancipating future of the historical process. Whenever anything like that is asserted and practiced, the creaturely is placed absolutely

[22] See p. 108f.

[23] Cf. Johannes Schneider, *Theologisches Wörterbuch zum Neuen Testament*, Vol. VII, Stuttgart, 1964, pp. 956-57.

[24] I Corinthians 7,31.

[25] On the distinction between "adventist" future and "futurist" future, see Arthur Rich, "Die Bedeutung der Eschatologie für den christlichen Glauben," *Aufrisse*, Zürich, 1970, pp. 127-56.

in its historicity, the "system" sets itself above the person, and human justice must be measured according to preconceived ordering structures, rather than the ordering structures being evaluated according to human justice. And it is inevitable that humanity will disintegrate there. Large-scale disintegration of humanity appears, then, both in actually-practiced capitalism, which absolutizes the private economic dynamic, as well as in the actually-existing, governmentally-centrally-planned economy of idealizing socialism. All of these contexts make it evident that the criterion of critical distance expresses an indispensable basic condition for the enabling of true humanity.

7.2.3 *The Criterion of Relative Reception*

The humanity originating from faith, hope, and love maintains critical distance from the existing world and the characteristic structures of its nations, societies, economies, etc. "Do not be conformed to the patterns of this world," writes Paul.[26] This is a matter of an indispensable dimension of everything human. If it fails in that, then tiresome conformism will prevail. In other words, one betrays the coming in the present and abandons the fundamentally revolutionary hope against all hope as the originating-basis of all humanity, which never can come to terms with the world as it is. As long as radical social critics, such as Herbert Marcuse, have that in mind, they are completely in the right. But, the relationship to the world, if it is to remain human, cannot be defined according to the criterion of critical distance alone.

If, in fact, the criterion of critical distance becomes decisive in the world-relationship alone, then this must ultimately lead to mere negativism, which, as with Ernst Bloch, sees evil in that which exists. That already happened with the early Christian enthusiasts, who in their eschatological exuberance saw the present world as already sublated by the future world. The same is true of the "drop-outs" of later times, up to the present day. Their exodus is either only an apparent one — a romantic flight into the residues of a society, far from civilization — or an extremist negation of the existing world as a supposedly radical alternative to it. One seeks to stay out of structural evil by the mere rejection of the existing world under the seductive spell of a total utopia. Such maximalism, however, is also again

[26] Romans 12,2.

a betrayal of what is human,[27] this time a betrayal of the present in a utopian future, of the imperfect in imaginary perfection, of the relative in a pseudo-absolute. It proves to be incapable of actually changing the existing world, in the interest of bringing about more humanity and social justice at the present time, because it can only negate what exists fundamentally, in the unfounded expectation that the positive will arise on its own from the negative, like Phoenix from its ashes. What remains in the end is permanent protest, which suspects the merely relatively-better of sheer system-preservation and which is unfruitful for designing a more concretely humane world.

That means, positively, the relative reception of the relative, the imperfect, the penultimate, rather than its simple rejection. Simple rejection, which means here absolute critique, is, of course, appropriate whenever the relative sets itself up as the absolute and precipitates totalitarian behavior. Thus early Christian faith opposed the Emperor Nero's presumptuous exercise of political power during his later years with extreme radicalness, speaking in encoded language of an animal from the abyss that would absorb human persons totally and whose temptations and compulsions it would be necessary to resist absolutely.[28] But this negation may by no means be generalized and interpreted as justifying *religious anarchism*. In addition to critical distance from the state, which goes in the extreme as far as rejecting it completely, there is also relative reception of the state. The same Paul, in the same epistle in which he calls the Roman Christians to non-conformity with the structures of this world, also admonishes them to submit to the powers that exercise political power in the state.[29] He evidently does that in opposition to those Christian enthusiasts who believed that as citizens of the coming Kingdom of God, they no longer had any genuine obligations to society and the state, and thus were not obligated to pay taxes and tolls. The emphasis of the statement in the cited passage, of course, is on this concrete exhortation and not on the preceding, theological, foundational propositions, which one can interpret metaphysically in the sense of an authoritarian theory of the state[30] and which have also

[27] Fyodor Dostoevsky illuminates this with great inner compelling nature in his fictional character Shigalyov, *The Possessed*, Chap. 7.2.

[28] Revelation 13,11-18.

[29] Romans 13,1-7.

[30] Cf. Ernst Käsemann in his important study "Römer 13,1-7 in unserer Generation," *Zeitschrift für Theologie und Kirche*, 56 (1959), p. 325.

played a disastrous role in the history of Christian interpretation. What Paul ultimately goes about is the relative reception of the Roman governing authorities, because and in so far as he could experience and also had experienced them as "God's servants," that is to say, as "avengers to bring punishment upon those who do evil." He had in mind, therefore, the state as an institution that combats evil, and thus helps those who suffer injustice to achieve justice, and consequently does something, about which the hoping love of faith can only be pleased. But he says nothing about the state having an ultimate claim on persons. He remains in the sphere of the relative. Therefore, according to Romans 13,1ff., no "obedience" to the state is required in the way that the human person owes obedience to God, but rather only a *loyal subordination*, which does not necessarily contradict the criterion of critical distance.[31]

What has been said here by way of example about the state holds true of the historical world and its present structures as a whole. They are not to be rejected, because they, like all existing things, are imperfect and, therefore, cannot meet the demand of the absolute and, consequently, ultimately fall into doubt. Thus, for example, no property right, whether based upon the principle of personal ownership or upon that of the common ownership, can exist before the demand of love. For love does not at all seek to take possession. If, however, a right of ownership has the function of distributing possessions in such a way that no one remains impoverished, thus seeking to hinder the monocratic concentration of property in the hands of private or collective owners and to protect justly acquired property from the expropriating grasp of either individual persons or collective powers, then it can be adopted as a relatively humanly just order from the humanity that is guided by faith, hope, and love, with all of the ambiguities that are still attached to it. For with that kind of right of ownership, property stands ultimately in the service of persons, not persons in the service of property.

In this way, the criterion of relativity teaches us to compare the relative to the relative, as for example a right of ownership, that is, whether and to what degree it is suitable to promote an order of property that is as just as possible, satisfying all members of society.

[31] For more detail, see Arthur Rich, "Die Verantwortung des Christen für Staat und Politik," in *Glaube in politischer Entscheidung*, Zürich, 1962, pp. 133-56, esp. pp. 144-49.

Its reception of the existing or emerging right is thus always relative, in the sense that it never declares the adopted right to be sacrosanct, but rather constantly keeps it critically moving towards a better justice that corresponds more closely to the criteria of human justice. Existence from faith, hope, and love, therefore, has in this criterion's seriousness a twofold battle to fight: the battle against the totalitarian self-elevation of the relative or the existing — whether, again for example, setting either private or collective property as absolute — and the battle against its nihilistic denial, which lives from the utopian principle of a nebulous "propertylessness." And precisely in that its fundamental significance for a humane ordering of society proves itself once again. For without the transformation of the relativity, understood in this way, into politically practicable maxims, society and the world become depraved in the sterile conflict between the immobilism that merely preserves the existing order and the revolutionism that only rejects it, thus between two alternatives that are not alternatives.

7.2.4 *The Criterion of Relationality*

If the criterion of creatureliness is concerned with the illumination of the humanly just self-understanding of the human person in general, and if the criteria of critical distance and relative reception are concerned with the determination of the humanly just conditions of the historical world and its social structures, the criterion of relationality is concerned with humanly just dealings with ethical values or virtues, as they are encountered in the horizon of general human experience.

One of the greatest misunderstandings is that Jesus brought a new morality, in the sense of a new order of values, into the world. He no more brought a new order of values than he brought a new religion. On the contrary, he is the crisis of all morality. Paul puts this into the succinct words: "*Christ is the end of the law.*"[32] For, ultimately, humanity based upon Jesus Christ knows only one imperative, that of love. This imperative, however, cannot be imposed forcefully like a moral law. For it is a matter here of the love of faith, which, like faith itself, has its basis in the free, loving care of God for the human person, and

[32] Romans 10,4.

thus is essentially a gift. "*We love, because he first loved us.*"[33] A moral order of values will come no closer to this command than a society, even at its highest imaginable level, will come close to the Kingdom of God. Therefore, the humanity originating from faith, hope, and love also can never be joined to a particular order of values. It is in that respect ultimately free. But the traditional moral and value ideas that are to be found in a culture should no more be rejected than the social structures of our world should simply be dismissed as relative because of this humanity's interest in the ultimate. In the time of the penultimate, all of this remains indispensable and, therefore, of great significance. Thus Paul exhorted the Philippians to reflect upon "whatever is true, whatever is honorable, whatever is just, whatever is pure, whatever is lovely, whatever is of good repute, anything that is excellent and praiseworthy."[34] All of these are concepts that can be found "in Hellenistic catalogues of the virtues, as well as in Jewish literature," and thus in the existing cultural world.[35] From that it is evident that the humanity to which Paul understands himself to be obligated in faith, hope, and love does not set any specific values, but rather takes them over from his living circumstances. This, however, is not in conformist, but *in critical reception,* which on the one hand relativizes these values and on the other hand grounds them specifically, i.e. relationally. This will be shown more closely with the values "freedom" and "servitude."

The ethical values of freedom and servitude are familiar to the horizon of general human experience. Whenever human persons live together, the question of how this common existence should or should not be structured inevitably poses itself: in freedom or in servitude, in autonomy or in heteronomy? That means that these two values, as they have been circumscribed in the sense of generally customary understanding, have opposite meanings. For autonomy contradicts heteronomy and heteronomy contradicts autonomy.

The antagonism of freedom (*eleutheria*) and servitude (*douleia*) is also a fundamental fact for the Hellenistic world, the cultural milieu of the New Testament.[36] Freedom is opposed to servitude, which is

[33] I John 4,19.
[34] Philippians 4,8.
[35] Gerhard Friedrich, *Der Brief an die Philipper*, Göttingen, 1981, p. 172.
[36] For a detailed discussion, see Alexander Rüstow, *Ortsbestimmung der Gegenwart*, Vol. II, Erlenbach-Zürich, 1952, pp. 11-165.

the epitome of unfreedom. To be sure, the Greeks' view of freedom is always constrained by the political order of their city-state. This order can be liberal (i.e. democratic) or illiberal: "'Life as one wishes'...is called again and again and with complete agreement the genuine palladium of democracy; not merely its ideal, but its true essence. The opposite is true only of Sparta, where 'no one was free to live as he wished'."[37]

Thus "freedom" is understood by the Greeks as "life as one wishes." — "Freedom is...independently being at one's own disposal."[38] Servitude accordingly means "a service that is not up to the person serving, but must be done by him, whether he wishes it or not."[39] It denotes specifically the social status of the slave. Slaves, in contrast to free citizens, have no right of self-disposal or self-determination within the political order. Legally, they are exclusively heteronomous and, therefore, unfree.

This in principle antagonistic understanding of the values freedom and servitude, according to which the latter was naturally an "un-value" in the eyes of the free — and also of the slaves — is the one Paul had to deal with in his cultural world of experience. What, then, is their status in the humanity originating from faith, hope, and love?

We must assume that *for Paul freedom belongs to the quintessence of being human,* which corresponds to the Christ event: "For freedom Christ has set us free."[40] — "You were called to freedom, brothers."[41] The striking formulation *"for freedom set free," "called to freedom,"* expresses the fact that this freedom cannot be about the human person being in control, emancipating control, of himself, but rather about freedom as a gift, which is given to the human person in faith, hope, and love.[42] In other words, it is a matter of freedom in which the human person "understands his life to be based on trust in God,"

[37] *Ibid.*, p. 39.

[38] Heinrich Schlier, *Theologisches Wörterbuch zum Neuen Testament*, Vol. II, Stuttgart, 1935, p. 489.

[39] Karl Heinrich Rengstorf, *Theologisches Wörterbuch zum Neuen Testament*, Vol. II, Stuttgart, 1935, p. 264.

[40] Galatians 5,1.

[41] Galatians 5,13.

[42] On the Christian understanding of freedom, see Trutz Rendtorff, "Die christliche Freiheit als Orientierungsbegriff der gegenwärtigen christlichen Ethik," *Handbuch der christlichen Ethik*, Vol. I, 1979, pp. 378-88 and Wolfgang Huber, "Freiheit und Institution," *Evangelische Theologie*, 40 (1980), esp. pp. 306-8.

and experiences himself "in his creatureliness," and thus "in the limits of his finiteness and his own human ability,"[43] and not as absolutely autonomous existence. In other words, it is personal freedom in dialogical existence with God and leads into dialogical, community-creating freedom with other persons.[44] As such it is "communicative" freedom in the love that, on its own initiative and thus autonomously, allows itself to be determined by what serves the fellow human being in the interpersonal community. Therefore, Paul not only says, "You were called to freedom, brothers," but goes on to add the exhortation: "Only do not use your freedom as an opportunity for the flesh [i.e. self-assertion], but instead serve one another in love."[45] Thus autonomy and servitude are "in love" no longer antagonistic to one another. Or, in the words of Martin Luther: "A Christian man is a perfectly free lord of all, subject to none. A Christian man is a perfectly dutiful servant of all, subject to all".[46] And that also gives the values of freedom and servitude a new status in their socially-relevant context.

For the modern tradition of the concept of freedom, just as for the Hellenistic world, it is typical that freedom is understood primarily as independence and emancipating self-realization, extending to the point of self-assertion. In this view of things, the human right to freedom, which incidently Marx (despite the incompatibility with his absolute humanism) occasionally recognized, "is based not on the association of man with man, but on the separation of man from man." In other words, "it makes every man see in other men not the *realisation* of his own freedom, but the *barrier* to it." [47] But if the other person is only the limit of my freedom, then it is in principle separated, and thus set free from him. In short, it becomes absolutely (for "*absolutus*" means "set free") based on itself.

Christian freedom, understood as freedom in the humanity originating from faith, hope, and love can, in contrast, never understand itself as absolute, but always in relation to its complement of servitude. It is self-determined freedom in loving servitude and loving servitude

[43] Trutz Rendtorff, "Die christliche Freiheit als Orientierungsbegriff der gegenwärtigen christlichen Ethik," p. 384.

[44] Wolfgang Huber, "Freiheit und Institution," p. 307.

[45] Galatians 5,13.

[46] Martin Luther, "A Treatise on Christian Liberty," in Vergilius Ferm, ed., *Classics of Protestantism*, New York, 1959, p. 41.

[47] Marx, "On the Jewish Question," in *Collected Works*, Vol. III, New York, p. 162-63.

in self-determined freedom: "Christian freedom is precisely the given duplication of the existence of Jesus, who as Lord is a slave and as a slave is Lord."[48] And that provides a completely new perspective.

What is new is that in this perspective freedom and servitude become relational values. For both are always present in love. In it freedom and servitude find themselves belonging to a whole. Conversely, in the antagonistic breakup of freedom and servitude in social reality, it turns out that our world conflicts with the demand of love, that it is not as God wills it, that it is, on the contrary, dominated by personal and structural evil as the adversary of fellow-humanness. Set free from servitude, freedom degenerates into libertarian license and produces despotism. And liberated from freedom, servitude is perverted into slavish submission, in which all community spirit necessarily suffocates.

The humanity originating from faith, hope, and love cannot cover up the reality of personal and structural evil in our world, as it appears in the perversion of freedom and of servitude through the tendency towards making them absolutes. There exists no exodus into a perfect world. But it can and should deal with values anew, as it persistently expresses its relational character and resists with decisiveness everything in social reality that seeks to maximize freedom at the cost of solidarist subservience or solidarist subservience at the cost of freedom. Freedom and servitude thus retain their fundamental ethical significance for the person and for society, but do so as relational, and in that respect always also relative, not absolute values. And this means that, despite the factual tension that will always remain between them, they are at the same time to be held firmly, so that the humanity that they contain does not degenerate.

What has just been demonstrated about the value-polarity of freedom and servitude can also be said analogously of other value-polarities. Every instance of the *absolutization* of such a value, as it expresses itself in the value's extremization, which excludes the polar-opposite value, will bring inhumane consequences in its wake. Thus, individual responsibility becomes autistic utility-maximization, and the principle of solidarity becomes comfortable laziness; from frugality comes miserliness, and from generosity extravagance; diligence becomes hectic workaholism, and leisure becomes notorious idleness, etc. Thus value-polarity does not promote the golden mean

[48] Wolfgang Huber, "Freiheit und Institution," p. 308.

as the quintessence of the petty bourgeoisie. There can and should be no more mediation between such extremisms and their open or latent inhumaneness as between despotism and subservience. On the contrary, a clear, decisive "no" is imperative here, and in such a way that through it the deeper sense of the relationality of the unfalsified ethical values is recognizable.

The deeper sense of the relationality of the fundamental ethical values, as they behave in our world of experience, can be seen in the fact that true and real humanity can be reduced to none of them, not even if one places such values next to each other additively, as in the motto of the French Revolution: "Liberty, Equality, Fraternity." In their isolation they are aspects of humanity, and nothing more than that. That is true of the basic liberal value "freedom" as well as of the basic socialist value "solidarity." The whole in which they find their unity is the humanity originating from faith, hope, and love. They themselves can never be this whole. They can, however, refer to it, but only if they understand themselves relationally, and thus do not attempt to become themselves the whole, and therefore that which cures and saves.

Understood as the specific way in which the humanity originating from faith, hope, and love associates with the fundamental ethical values, relationality orients itself in this way towards the whole of humanity and refuses to surrender to simplifying solutions, as they are found in the form of the spectacular extremization of such basic values, as well as in the form of the politics of the mere *just milieu*. Wherever there is an alert, realistic sense of the complexity of the question of a more humane shaping of the conditions in our ever more dubious world, there also exists in some way a view of things closely related to the principle of relationality. Thus the French political scientist Alfred Grosser writes:

> We should know where the renunciation of simple solutions can lead: We will establish that the proclaimed values are by no means always compatible with one another, that the attempt to realize one of them can often bring us into conflict with the demands of the other. From that we will not conclude, however, that there is a golden middle way to walk along. We will instead sharpen our sense for the tensions between opposing imperatives. For the tensions that exist when one feels oneself pulled back and forth between two poles, both of which are rooted in accepted, even revered, moral principles. To approach one of the two poles is to relinquish the principle on which the other is based. To endure such

> tensions, to live with them, does not mean flight into a *juste milieu*, but concrete exercise of freedom, in order to find for oneself the narrow ridge on which one can remain only by permanent effort of will.[49]

Observing the relationality of values is actually like a delicate balancing act. Three things are imperative on this risky way.

It is imperative, first of all — to emphasize the point once again — to renounce all efforts to maximize values that are indispensable in themselves, but whose maximization would in fact lead to their absolutization. Thus the basic value *equality* is indispensable to the determination of human justice. Nevertheless, it would be wrong to think that the more equality there is among human persons, the more justice there is. That is the way extremist thinking argues. It turns the partial truth contained in the principle of equality into the whole truth. Through it, justice and equality become one. In other words, equality is stretched all the way to egalitarianism. Egalitarian leveling, however, never corresponds to human justice, but instead proves itself again and again to be a source of injustices. For human persons are essentially not only equal, but also unequal, in gender, talents, inclinations, health, capabilities, etc. Smoothing over inequalities of this kind in an egalitarian manner inevitably leads to hopeless oppression of human reality.

Relational thinking's interest in the whole of the created reality of the human person does not receive the value of equality without that of inequality, and does not receive inequality without equality. Just as the principle of equality without its complement of inequality leads to an extremist bringing into line of everything human and, therefore, to its fatal desolation, so inequality without equality leads to the ideology of the inferiority of certain human groups relative to others, for example of women to men, blacks to whites, the intelligent to the less intelligent, etc. And that always leads to structures of domination that discriminate to a greater or lesser degree against the disadvantaged groups. The criterion of relationality stands in clear contradiction to every ideology of disadvantage and, therefore, proves to be a basic condition for concretely taking hold of human justice.

It is necessary to clarify further that relationality must not be confused with *balance*. There are situations in which relationality must mean precisely *one-sided partisanship* for particular basic values that

[49] Alfred Grosser, *Der schmale Grat der Freiheit*, Munich, 1981, pp. 27-28.

are neglected or completely ignored. If, for example, foreign workers, who have performed socially important work that serves the general public in good times, are discriminated against as persons with fewer rights than citizens, or are completely expelled in times of economic recession,[50] radical protest must be made and decisive emphasis must be placed on the equality of all, even if one knows that this cannot simply be the last word.

This kind of radicalness — and this is the third point to be made here — differs from extremism in that it aims even with one-sided partisanship at the whole of humanity originating from faith, hope, and love, and does not make partial truths into a pseudo-whole. When it must take one side in a particular situation, it will not simply be an interested party, but instead will agree with Pascal, who pleaded that with every truth, one should imagine the opposite truth.[51] This is with the insight that human truths, to which the common moral values belong, are not identical to the entirety of divine truth, and thus must stand by their relativity. Therefore, this kind of radicalness also cannot be associated with fanaticism, which is the hallmark of extremism in all of its forms. It will instead seek dialogue with the opposing position, even if the tensions are great and a responsible mediation of the opposing views appears to be impossible.[52]

The humanity originating from faith, hope, and love, in the sense just explained, does not create new values, but instead deals with previously found values in a new way, in a way that may be characterized here as "radical," in distinction from "extremist." *Radical ethos* is relational ethos, in a way such that it searches, above value conflicts, against divisions, for the whole of humanity, as it has become

[50] One need only think about the foreign-worker policy of Switzerland that was practiced under great public pressure during the recession of the 1970s. See Marianne Ebel and Pierre Fiala, *Sous le consensus, la xénophobie*, Lausanne, 1983.

[51] Pascal, Blaise, *Pensées*, Frg. 567, trans. A. J. Krailsheimer, Harmondsworth, 1966, p. 224.

[52] That sheds light on the nearness of the criterion of relationality to the integrative category of reconciliation. See Christian Walther, "Die Kategorie der Versöhnung," *Handbuch der christlichen Ethik*, Vol. I, 1979, pp. 459-73. Reconciliation, which ultimately means "cancellation of enmity," is a prerequisite of genuine communication, understood as "clarification of opposing viewpoints" (pp. 472-73). The principle of relationality is linked to this kind of communication, which lives from the process of reconciliation and simultaneously distances itself from the superficially reconciliatory nature of "harmonization," which trivializes the opposites and even seeks to mediate between that which cannot be reconciled.

transparent in Jesus Christ. What contradicts this humanity cannot be understood relationally. Thus neither hatred nor submissive appeasement can be understood relationally. In the humanity originating from faith, hope, and love, one can neither hate notoriously nor be notoriously submissive, as in it one can be free and of service at the same time. One can certainly be angry in this humanity, as Jesus, full of anger, drove the sellers and moneychangers from the forecourt of the temple. To be sure, angry love will always know that gentleness is also imperative, just as gentleness from love does not exclude anger, when it is shamefully misused. The criterion of relationality would be completely misunderstood in its essence if one were to transform it into a dubious means of reconciling the irreconcilable or even the blurring of the boundaries between justice and injustice, truth and lie, good and evil. It has nothing to do with an ethic of ambiguity and even less to do with a half-hearted one. When anger is called for, as for instance with discrimination against other races, foreign workers, the socially weaker in general, then precisely anger, not gentleness, is called for. However, anger will be something else if it, despite the harshness of the immediate confrontation, has gentleness as its indispensable complement, and thus is not dictated by pure hatred that seeks the destruction of the opponent, rather than his turning back. Seen from the perspective of relationality, anger and hatred are ethically totally different patterns of behavior.

7.2.5 *The Criterion of Fellow-Humanness*

To the criterion of relationality corresponds, as may be seen without difficulty, an understanding of humanity that can be reduced neither exclusively to the principles of autonomy, emancipation, self-realization, nor exclusively to those of obedience, servitude, self-moderation, etc. Relationally determined humanity is, in contrast, always fellow-humanness, i.e. being human specifically with others and for others. Only in so far as these and similar values, such as equality and inequality, self-responsibility and solidarity, self-development and self-renunciation, etc., serve the increase of fellow-human life, are they genuinely human. The *criterion of fellow-humanness* stands, therefore, in the closest relationship to the *criterion of relationality*.

As a criterion of the humanity originating from faith, hope, and love, however, fellow-humanness is also anchored in the criterion of creatureliness. Being created in the image of God is in its basic nature dialogical fellow-human existence. The human person is "not created solitarily, but rather is called to the thou of the opposite gender," as Gerhard von Rad says in interpreting Genesis 1,27.[53] True humanness and fellow-humanness are in this perspective identical. So then Jesus, the embodiment of true humanity, is witnessed by the Synoptic Gospels as he who was and is the absolute fellow-human of all, and who himself, in scandalous contradiction to the pious persons of his day, ate and drank with "tax collectors and sinners."[54] All of this can be summarized with the words of Karl Barth: "It is not as he is for himself but with others, not in loneliness but in fellowship, that he is genuinely human, that he achieves true humanity, that he corresponds to his determination to be God's covenant-partner, that he is the being for which the man Jesus is, and therefore real man."[55]

Fellow-humanness in the context of this kind of humanity has an essentially *dialogical* character, since it is always only possible in the correlation of Thou and I. If this correlation is broken, if the Thou is dominated by the I-interest or the I by the Thou-interest in the sense of a principle of existence, then the humanity turns into either exclusive self-love, egoism, or exclusive love of others, altruism. Both however — not just egoism! — are fundamental transgressions of what is genuinely human, either sacrifice of the Thou or self-abandonment of the I. The humanity originating from faith, hope, and love will have to resist both. It is essential to "love your neighbor as yourself." And that includes a life of fellow-human association with both the Thou and the I, in short, a dialogical-communitarian life, in contrast to the extremisms of pure self-realization ideology and self-sacrifice ideology.

There is also a high degree of inner evidence for the criterion of fellow-humanness as a fundamental distinguishing feature of true humanity for the horizon of universal human experience. Somehow everyone knows that humanity in our society stands or falls with the realization of an optimum of fellow-humanness. Without it, the human person is robbed of his personal I-oriented as well as his communitarian Thou-oriented existence. He becomes a slave, sometimes to the individualism that fails to recognize the fellow-human, communitarian character of the person and sometimes to the collectivism

[53] Gerhard von Rad, *Das erste Buch Mose*, Vol. I, p. 47.

[54] Mark 2,16 and parallels.

[55] Karl Barth, *Church Dogmatics*, Vol. III, Part 2, ed. G. W. Bromiley and T. F. Torrance, Edinburgh, T. & T. Clark, 1960, p. 243.

that denies the personal dimension of the fellow-human community. Both, however, individualism that forgets community, as well as collectivism that is hostile to persons, are gravediggers of genuine humanity, as the social reality of today demonstrates globally.

7.2.6 *The Criterion of Fellow-Creatureliness*

The human person in his creatureliness is not only a fellow human, but also a fellow creature. As a fellow creature he stands in a *community of destiny with the rest of creation*.

The community of destiny of the human person with the rest of creation can be expressed quite shockingly in the horizon of biblical creation-faith: "I said in my heart with regard to human beings that God is testing them to show that they are but animals. For the fate of humans and the fate of animals is the same; as one dies, so dies the other. They all have the same breath."[56]

Behind that stands the idea, which is typical in the Old Testament and continues to be effective in the New Testament, of the creation as an order of existence in which "there is no special position marked out for man over against other living things. There is only the confrontation between Yahweh (who transcends the world and brings life and wherewithal into being) and his nonliving and living creations, which he has formed for the benefit of all life."[57] Or, reduced to a common denominator, the human person shares his absolute dependency on Yahweh as the Creator with all other creatures. He proves to be a fellow-creature in the sense that he also is and remains embedded in the whole of the creation-event.

Nevertheless, biblical creation-faith assigns the human person a special place within creation. In the oldest, most-Yahwist creation account, it is already written, "The Lord God took the man and put him in the garden of Eden to till it and keep it."[58] Therefore, the human person is destined for an active role in regard to the creation, that is in the double-function of the active shaper and the guarding protector, as "*homo faber*" and "*homo conservator*."

In the more recent or priestly creation account, this special position of the human person is expressed with even greater intensity.

[56] Ecclesiastes 3,18-19.
[57] Odil Hannes Steck, *World and Environment*, Nashville, 1980, p. 191.
[58] Genesis 2,15.

As created in the image of God, he must, according to this account, subdue the earth and rule the world of animals.[59] When the impact of this passage on the interpretation history is considered, much disaster has come from it. For it was understood primarily as an excuse for the exploitation of nature for the sake of increasing the material welfare and power of the human person, which, seen in the long run, has without question been partly to blame for the present ecological crisis. Such an interpretation is, however, exegetically untenable. The priestly writing means a dominion of the human person under the lordship of God, not autonomous sovereign rule: "He is in fact the agent of God, called to preserve and to enforce God's claim to power on earth."[60] God's dominion will is, however, never dominion against, but always dominion for the creation. Odil Hannes Steck, therefore, is correct in saying: "Just as man himself belongs to the natural world of creation, in that he lives and carries on his life in the world, so his divine stewardship expresses itself precisely in the fact that he has to preserve the right to live and the contribution to life of the natural world and environment as a whole. That is to say, he has to preserve the right to life of living things apart from himself as well." The steady perspective that is peculiar to the creation account of "P" makes it clear that "man and nature have a common history and a common future, and that man's special position does not mean autocratic confrontation, but the active responsibility as God's representative for the natural created world."[61] Only in so far as human persons play the dominion role intended for them by Genesis 1,28 co-creationally for the well-being of creation, can they as a result of this be agents and thus the image of God in the created world.

The meaning of co-creatureliness as a criterion of humanness is, consequently, twofold: the inclusion of the human person in the whole of creation, and his mission in responsibility to God to utilize the creation in a manner that promotes life and to safeguard it reverently. If that is not recognized in its complexity, then, as we see and experience today, the survival of the created nature that still remains and the quality of life that is bound to it is profoundly endangered. The emancipation of nature, as it has been pursued first of all by the unrestrained, progressing technologizing of the economy and has led

[59] Genesis 1,28.
[60] Gerhard von Rad, *Das erste Buch Mose*, Vol. I, p. 46.
[61] Odil Hannes Steck, *World and Environment*, Nashville, 1980, p. 106.

to the displacement of *homo conservator* by *homo faber*, has proved to be a mistake that must not be perpetuated. But the urgently imperative turnabout also cannot take place in the opposite extreme of a displacement of *homo faber* by *homo conservator* that romanticizes nature.[62]

It is necessary, on the one hand, to understand in complete seriousness that we are constrained, for better or for worse, in the pregiven creation-nature and cannot escape from this dependency by a technocratic feat of strength. On the other hand, it remains true that the human person must occupy himself in the creation innovatively and do business in it in such a way that he can exist from and with nature humanly-justly and nature can exist through and with him ecologically-correctly. Promoting an ecological maximalism that blocks the way to a high-performance economy that serves the human person makes no more sense than sacrificing the natural environment to the maximization of economic performance. Co-creatureliness must be understood in this complex sense, if it wishes to be and to remain a criterion of humanity.

7.2.7 *The Criterion of Participation*

Fellow-humanness and co-creation, as criteria of humanity, concern the personal conduct of either the single individual or the single group in dealing with fellow human persons and fellow creatures. Humanity, in so far as it is understood in a radical sense, i.e. considered on the whole, however, must prove itself not only in unmediated personal relationships. It is no less, but even more essential for the institutionally-mediated field of relationships in which our existence as citizens, producers and consumers, pensioners, etc. for the most part takes place. If this social sphere of reality is not structured fellow-humanly, unmediated personal relationships will also suffer severely. This has already been discussed in sufficient detail in 3.2.2. It is, quite simply, a matter of taking seriously the specifically social-ethical dimension of our responsibility.

[62] Otfried Höffe, "Natur als Orientierungspunkt der Ethik," in *Liberal: Beiträge zur Entwicklung einer freiheitlichen Ordnung*, 25 (1983), pp. 326, rightly says: "Therefore nature is, in contrast to a romantic flight from culture, always also an object of being employed to service; it is not only virgin nature, but also cultivated nature; the natural environment of the human person is divided in two: it is, on one hand, natural living space, but on the other hand, living space shaped by human persons."

Fellow-humanness, understood in its unmediated-personal relationship, means nothing other than letting others share in what one is, has, or does. John the Baptist expresses it in the succinct demand, "The man who has two tunics should share with him who has none, and the one who has food should do likewise."[63] Transferred from the unmediated-personal level to the mediated-institutional level, this means that the social structures of power, law, administration, regulations, and property can exist in the face of the demand of human justice only to the degree that they are oriented towards the ability of all involved or affected parties to share in the powers, laws, authorities, and goods founded by these structures and, therefore, already structurally oppose the formation of unilateral privileges. That founds a new criterion of human justice: *participation*.

If the criteria explicated thus far have a clear basis in the New Testament, the Magna Charta of the humanity originating from faith, hope, and love, this cannot be said in the same way of the criterion of participation. This is related to the fact that it has the social-structural components of human justice decidedly in mind. This aspect, however, appears in the early-Christian period only at the very margin. That early period of Christian history was dominated by the expectation of eschatological proximity, the consciousness that the "things" of this world are in the process of passing away, and that the coming of the Kingdom of God is imminent. That made the question of structural changes in society, in so far as it could be raised at all then, appear from the outset to be obsolete. The social-structural element of ethics is thus superimposed in the New Testament almost entirely by the inter-personal element. Therefore, "questions such as those of the assessment of property, wealth, and poverty rarely appear except in the context of the exhortation," i.e., in the form of concrete instructions directed immediately to the persons mentioned in the situations currently determining them.[64]

It is all the more remarkable that the social-structural component of human justice does not simply disappear from the horizon of the New Testament writings. The fact that brotherly love as the specific Christian form of fellow-humanness must also have a social-structural dimension can be expressed surprisingly. Thus Paul indeed

[63] Luke 3,11.

[64] See Heinz-Dietrich Wendland, *Ethik des Neuen Testamentes*, Göttingen, 1970, p. 40.

returned the runaway slave Onesimus to his Christian master Philemon, because, according to the law in effect, Philemon had a claim to Onesimus, but not without vigorously telling him that Onesimus in the reality of Christian existence was now more than a slave, namely "a beloved brother," and indeed "both in the flesh and in the Lord."[65] The term "flesh" (*sarx*) denotes here the earthly sphere, more precisely, the social relationships within it.[66] This striking expression thus means that the brotherliness of the slave Onesimus should be valid not only in the spiritual community with Christ, but also in the social relations of societal life, which Christian existence as human existence can never ignore. If even Paul himself drew no social-structural conclusions from this, and thus did not yet call into question the social institution of slavery, those conclusions are still at least within the bounds of possibility, if one extrapolates historically the lines that announce themselves here.

It is, therefore, not surprising that Luke goes a step further in the Acts of the Apostles and portrays the communal life of the early-Christian parish in Jerusalem in a way that goes beyond the religious dimension and leads into the social: "And the congregation of those who believed were of one heart and soul; and not one of them claimed that anything belonging to him was his own; but all things were common property to them."[67] The degree to which this is an ideal picture or historical reality is, of course, a matter of dispute among researchers. Without doubt Luke idealized. Nevertheless, "that does not necessarily mean that this picture has no basis in historical reality."[68]

Whatever it may be, ideal picture, historical fact, or a mixture of the two, one thing cannot be denied, namely, that the Lucan account seeks to emphasize something important. Wolfgang Schrage expresses it thus: "*The unity of the church cannot be established solely on the spiritual and religious plane.*"[69] Commonly sharing in salvation in Jesus Christ must also lead to common structures that make possible the participation of all in the material goods of the believers, so that

[65] Philemon 16.

[66] Eduard Schweizer, *Theologisches Wörterbuch zum Neuen Testament*, Vol. VII, p. 127.

[67] Acts 4,32.

[68] Heinz-Dietrich Wendland, *Ethik des Neuen Testamentes*, p. 38. See also Jürgen Roloff, *Die Apostelgeschichte*, Göttingen, 1981, pp. 89-90.

[69] Wolfgang Schrage, *The Ethics of the New Testament*, trans. David E. Green, Philadelphia, 1988, p. 161.

no member of the congregation is needy.[70] The humanity originating from faith, hope, and love will never be able to come to terms with conditions in which one has too little and another has to much. It must strive, according to Luke, for its ultimate reason, "the testimony of the resurrection of the Lord Jesus,"[71] with great power for structuring the communal life in a way that can ensure the participation of the poor in the possessions of the wealthy. Yet, it is not decisive in which form the principle of participation is structurally concretized. Luke never elevates the community of property to the level of an absolute law. It is one possible way to realize participation in the area of material goods, but it is not identical to it. Only the principle of participation as such can oblige, because without participative structures in institutionally-mediated communal life — in this case, that of the Christian congregation — there exists no humanity that can be adapted by the humanity originating from faith, hope, and love. And in this respect participation belongs to its fundamental criteria, even though it comes to light in the New Testament, at least in the sense defined above, only in traces.

One of the great fundamental experiences of our time is, in turn, that the social-structurally conditioned diminution of real opportunities for participation in the real life-world of very many contemporary persons means the disintegration of humanity. The more bureaucracy, technocracy, expertocracy, etc. get out of hand in society, the state, and the economy, and the more, as an undeniable consequence thereof, power of disposal and decision is monopolized in the hands of a few people and then entails monocratic structures, the more impotent ordinary citizens find themselves, despite the formally intact political democracy, and the stronger is the protest against a more and more bureaucratized world, about whose macabre possibilities *George Orwell* already warned urgently four decades ago in his visionary novel *1984*. The ever louder call for co-determination and self-administration in the core areas of our society, the countless citizens' initiatives with their often bizarre grassroots democratic ideas, etc. signal in their own way that social structures opposing the spirit of participation are experienced as inhumane and, therefore, intolerable. The humanity originating from faith, hope, and love must take that very seriously according to its own guiding criteria.

70 Acts 4,34.
71 Acts 4,33.

If applying the criterion of participation to the social-structural human sphere presents no special difficulties logically, that is not at all true of their application to the planetary-ecological world that involves the entire created world. Participation, in the sense intended here, assumes the existence of partners who not only mutually rely on one another, but who are also in a position to structure this reciprocal dependency, which is always in need of institutional ordering, in a practicable way that is able to resist its perversion into unilateral dependency and, consequently, can be justified ethically. Human beings, as individual persons and as associated groups, can be such partners immediately. That is not true, however, of animals and plants, let alone of inanimate nature. How, then, can the criterion of participation still be applied at all sensibly in the area of the ecological problematic?

That undoubtedly can take place only in an indirect sense, in which the co-creature is passive. What we must do is also really to begin to take seriously the fact of the mutual dependency of human persons and nature, and to give what we owe to those partners who are unable to claim anything, because they cannot speak. The main trend of historical development thus far has been in exactly the opposite direction. The human person, seen globally, has unilaterally considered nature or his co-creature to be his debtor, from which one may demand whatever one wishes and which can be exploited by any means whatsoever. A radical change of direction is imperative if the criterion of participation is really to be followed in our overall ecological and social behavior. A change of direction, in the sense that we decisively turn away from exploitative access to creation, and that consequently *homo conservator* puts the one-sided, anthropocentrically-oriented dominance of *homo faber* in its place and becomes the advocate of mute nature, which is dominated and maltreated by human persons. To put it succinctly, it is about the assertion of the criterion of participation in the question of how to order the environment, to conceive of structures that further a situation in which not only nature, with all that belongs to it, is there for human persons, but also human persons are there for nature in a spirit of partnership.[72] Incidentally, the degree to which a participative, fundamental orientation of that kind can be found in the extended

[72] Otfried Höffe, "Natur als Orientierungspunkt der Ethik," p. 331, speaks in a similar context of a new "dimension of responsibility for and preservation of the environment," which breaks up the orientation towards "anthropocentrism": "The human

perspective of the biblical ethos with its own humanity[73] appears in the fourth commandment of the Decalogue, according to which not only all human persons, including "the alien resident in your towns," but also "all of your livestock" should participate in the blessing that became the ritual institution of rest from labor on the Sabbath.[74]

7.3 Human Justice Originating from Faith, Hope, and Love and Social Justice

Social ethics is by definition social-structural ethics.[75] Although it integrates within itself individual and personal ethics, as well as environmental ethics, it is concerned specifically with the question of the just structure and function of social institutions. Consequently, it is related primarily to social justice. How, then, is the human justice of the hoping love of faith related to social justice?

7.3.1 *The Criteria of Human Justice as Conditions of Social Justice*

Neither individually nor as a whole do the seven criteria of human justice, as they have been explicated in the preceding section, already yield an practicable concept of social justice. They do outline the criterial conditions that must be met in order for human existence in social life, at least for the hoping love of faith, to be regarded as truly human and thus humanly just. There is thus no humanly just existence if, for example, someone in common work has only labor duties, but no effective civil rights, for instance, in the form of co-determination, or if he lives in depressed material conditions, because for economic-structural reasons, through no fault of his own, he is obviously disadvantaged in the distribution of the commonly-achieved income. Unquestionably, in the former case the criterion of relationality and in the latter case that of participation is not given due attention. In that way it becomes, of course, clear that without the observance of these criteria, social

person feels himself to be a member of the biosphere and seeks a relationship of '*partnership*' to nature."

[73] See Johannes Hempel, *Das Ethos des Alten Testamentes*, 2nd Ed., Berlin, 1964, p. 199.

[74] Exodus 20,10.

[75] See 3.3.4.

justice cannot survive. But it is by no means thereby already determined what a just relationship of rights and duties or just participation in the national income and national wealth means. This concrete decision matters directly, however, if the criteria of human justice are to receive social relevance, and thus are to become suitable for conceiving a practically applicable idea of social justice. It is, therefore, not enough simply to assert criteria of human justice as fundamental humane conditions for the facilitation of social justice. It is also necessary to ask — on the basis of its main idea itself, of course — what can be accepted responsibly as just and proper in view of existing conditions.[76] And that — to emphasize the point once again — is in essence a matter of rational deliberation.

7.3.2 *Social Justice as a Permanent Duty of the Hoping Love of Faith*

The simple fact that the hoping love of faith and social justice are never identical is assumed. "Love seeks not its own."[77] Social justice, on the contrary, seeks to allot to each person precisely that which belongs to him or her, that to which each person has a claim. Love, therefore, can never take the place of this justice, and justice can never replace love. Between the two there exists an essential difference, indeed an essential opposition, which rules out any attempt to equate them. There is, nevertheless, a connection between love and justice. Each is oriented in its own way towards equality.

That the hoping love of faith is oriented in its understanding of humanity towards equality already proves itself from the basic criterion of creatureliness. It accentuates the same ontological difference between all creation and its creator, as well as, above all, the same personal correspondence between each human creature and that which calls him or her into existence. All human beings, without exception, are created in the image of God and, consequently, have this equal status. According to the humanity originating from faith,

[76] Edward Schillebeeckx, *Christus und die Christen*, Freiburg im Breisgau, 1977, pp. 714-15, instead of the concept of "criteria," speaks of "anthropological constants," which point "quite universally to *constant* human impulses and orientations," but "do not *directly* provide us with concrete norms or ethical imperatives, according to which humane and livable humanity must be called into life here and now."

[77] I Corinthians 13,5.

hope, and love, therefore, each person is also to be respected, accepted, and indeed approved as one in God's image, even those who contravene their claim and do evil. Thus Jesus, the prototype of humanity in the image of God, impresses upon his followers: "You have heard that it was said: 'Love your neighbor and hate your enemy.' But I say to you: Love your enemies and pray for those who persecute you, so that you may be sons of your Father in heaven. For he causes his sun to rise on the evil and the good, and sends rain on the righteous and the unrighteous."[78] A more radical formulation of the equality of all who have human faces than this command of love for each and every one does not exist. And from that it is obvious that in the faith-followers of Christ, all inequality-barriers that divide persons from one another and thus violate the criterion of fellow-humanness must ultimately fall. For here is unambiguously in force: "There is neither Jew nor Greek, neither slave nor free man, neither male nor female; for you are all one in Christ Jesus."[79] That expresses the insoluble connection between faith and equality. Emil Brunner may well be right in his thesis that this is "the tenet of faith which underlies the European conception of the same original right of all human beings."[80]

What is true of love is true even more of justice. However one may define "justice" — it is, to be sure, a "variable term"[81] — one thing remains certain: it possesses an indispensable affinity to the idea of equality: "We can imagine no definition, no theory of justice, without including the close relationship of justice and equality."[82] Thus Aristotle, with whom the variability of the concept of justice led to the momentous distinction between "distributive" and "commutative" justice,[83] connects both conceptions of justice to the principle of equality. "Commutative" justice gives each person the same, according to the model of arithmetic proportion (for instance, equal payment for equal work). "Distributive" justice, in contrast, gives to each

[78] Matthew 5,43-45.

[79] Galatians 3,28.

[80] Emil Brunner, *Justice and the Social Order*, p. 34.

[81] Christofer Frey, "Gerechtigkeit," in *Evangelisches Soziallexikon*, 7th Ed., Stuttgart, 1980, col. 490.

[82] Hans Ruh, "Gerechtigkeitstheorien," in Armin Wildermuth and Alfred Jäger, eds., *Gerechtigkeit*, Tübingen, 1981, p. 58-59.

[83] Aristotle, *Nicomachean Ethics*, V, 2,1130b-1131a, trans. W. D. Ross, in Richard McKeon, ed., *The Basic Works of Aristotle*, New York, 1941, pp. 1005-6.

his or her own, whereby equality orients itself according to the scheme of geometric proportion (for example, he who performs better receives correspondingly more pay), and thus takes existing inequalities into account. From that time forward, especially during the European Enlightenment, the idea of equality has determined the theory of justice. The struggle for greater justice was identical to the optimization of the principle of equality in society. That holds true, on the whole, up to the present day.

The *affinity to the equality* of all human persons is, consequently, what connects love and justice to one another. Love, in the form of the humanity that corresponds to it, however, is familiar with not only the right of equality, with its search for social justice, but also the right of inequality. For love, equality and inequality are relational values. The inequality among human persons corresponds to their equality as persons created in God's image: "So God created humankind in his image, in the image of God he created them; male and female he created them."[84] That means that human persons are not in their equality indistinguishable individuals, so many social atoms, but rather distinctive individualities, who are called, precisely in their diversity, to the same personal community in the I-Thou / We relationship and the society that includes them, with its institutions. Moreover, there can be personal humanness only where there is room to move for one's own development and, therefore, also for unequal development; in short, where social freedom exists. Personal rights to freedom in society with their tendency towards inequality are, therefore, just as much a basic concern of the humanity originating from faith, hope, and love as is the principle of social equality. It must, therefore, always keep both in mind in its interest in social justice: "For the secret of the Christian conception of justice is not equality but the blend of equality and inequality."[85] Seen in this way, the fight for social justice cannot simply be about leveling in an egalitarian manner all inequalities among human persons — whether of individuals, groups, classes, complete nations, etc. It is, instead, about treating the created or freedom-associated inequalities in such a way that they can no longer be opportunities for the notorious social disadvantage of those affected by them. The fact that, for example, a woman is a

[84] Gen. 1,27.

[85] Emil Brunner, *Justice and the Social Order*, p. 39.

woman and not a man is not a reason to discriminate against her social-legally or in economic life. And the fact that workers have no means of production property at their disposal, similarly, must not be the basis of the exclusive right of owners to make decisions in the process of production. None of that has anything to do with mechanical leveling down, but rather with *justice,* which strives to create respect for the *right of everyone to be a person* within the conditions of existing inequalities, and indeed extending all the way into the actual core areas of society.

In this way, Christian love sees itself in a position of opposition to both the *elitist* and the *egalitarian* conceptions of society. By "elitist" we mean a view of society from which social inequalities are constitutive and which derives from that the right of the supremacy of an elite, however it may be constituted. "Egalitarian," on the other hand, means a conception of society in which all members, despite their differences, have in principle the same status and, consequently, should be brought into line. The modern idea of justice has for historical reasons — it originated in necessary opposition to the elitist conception of society of the *"ancien regime"* — oriented itself primarily towards the principle of equality. And indeed that happened in essence with reference to the stoic ideal of equality, which the Enlightenment received, along with Christian impulses, to a great degree and which sees equality based on an impersonal spirit-principle, namely universal, uniform reason. Thus the essential conflict with the other great principle of the Enlightenment, individual freedom, was inevitable. For just as individual freedom shows a tendency towards social inequality, generalized equality shows a tendency towards social unfreedom.

This apparently tragic state of affairs had an effect foremost in the area of the economy. The free market not only produced an enormous rise of per capita income in the industrialized nations, but also brought about simultaneously provocative economic inequality, both within the industrialized states and most of all in their relations to the peoples of the third world. It cannot be said at all that the free market economy in its current constitution has solved the problem of distribution in an acceptable manner. That is certainly true for those who measure things according to an idea of justice that neither excludes the principle of equality nor considers it to be only secondary. And one may not seek consolation for this dismal situation in the fact that there are still many, often even massive and moreover growing, economic inequalities in the nations of actually existing socialism.

The centrally-planned economies, on the other hand, in following their ideal of abstract equality of distribution, have practically had to eliminate not only market freedom, but also social freedom overall, which likewise is not made more acceptable by the fact that civil rights are often trampled upon in market societies. The Christian will to justice can come to terms with neither a concept of equality that leads in its consequences to a denial of rights to freedom nor an idea of freedom that perpetuates, or even increases, existing inequalities. It must instead stand up for an idea of freedom that unambiguously stresses the right of every person to participate in the national income and national wealth, which evens out the provoking inequalities and thereby affirms the fundamental value of solidarity, understood in a relational sense. And it must opt for a social solidarity that does not strain the principle of equality in such a way that must kill the right to freedom, including the right to freedom of businesspersons. One may object that this would be like attempting to square the circle. This double postulate does indeed amount to squaring the circle, if one takes it to mean a perfect synthesis. There certainly will not be a perfect synthesis of freedom and solidarity in the time of the penultimate, which happens to be our time. Nevertheless, there exists the possibility of a mutual and effective bringing together of the two fundamental values that humanizes the intended relationships. To meet this challenge is precisely the permanent task of the hoping love of faith in its striving towards social justice. In doing so, it will never be able to reach its conclusion, since ideal solutions are impossible, so long as we must reckon with the ever-changing reality of personal and structural evil — and in the time of the penultimate we will always have to do that. Therefore, when there exists in a society more of a deficit of rights to freedom, and consequently also of development opportunities for businesspersons, it will accordingly have to stand up for more freedom. And when in a society there is more of a lack of the participation of all in the social goods, it will be its duty to stand up for more equality of participation. The Christian will to justice, therefore, must always keep in mind that participative distribution is never about economic goods alone. As Gerhard Weisser repeatedly and correctly emphasized, it is fundamentally *"life situations"* that are distributed.[86] An unemployed person, for example, may be able through insurance benefits to participate to a sufficient degree in the national product of the economy. In the long run, however, he will be disadvantaged in his life situation, and indeed severely. For as long as he cannot participate in socially-productive work, he will have to experience himself, even with sizable economic safeguards, as reduced to the status of "surplus population." And that is one of the worst things that can happen to a person in his society.

If one accounts to himself for all of this, then it will also be understandable that the concept of social justice cannot be reduced to a fixed and handy common denominator. It remains a "variable" term. Depending upon the situation, the accent must sometimes be placed at one location, sometimes at another. It is sometimes equality and sometimes freedom that must be emphasized most. Determining concretely in social and economic relationships how to place the emphasis on the interest of the disadvantaged, who long for more justice, can never be merely a matter of emotional social engagement, but must instead be a matter of critically evaluating reason. For by no means is everything that wanders around under the emotionally-loaded heading of "social justice" really humanly just, that is, suitable to better the life situations of those who actually do not have enough. What is needed here is that *love* which always becomes richer in all reason in order to examine what is just and unjust in a concrete situation that provokes decisions about social justice.[87] The hoping love of faith will, therefore, never ignore what reason has to say regarding what is just in society. It must, on the contrary, consider reason's insights seriously. In this context, for several reasons, the theory of justice of the American philosopher John Rawls[88] deserves special consideration.

7.3.3 *John Rawls' Theory of Justice from the Perspective of the Criterial Requirements of Human Justice from Faith, Hope, and Love*

It is obviously not possible here to undertake a comprehensive, critical examination of John Rawls' fascinating theory of justice.[89] We must be satisfied with examining whether and, if so, in what

[86] Gerhard Weisser, *Beiträge zur Gesellschaftspolitik*, Göttingen, 1978, p. 360.

[87] P. 165-66.

[88] John Rawls, *A Theory of Justice*, Cambridge, Mass., 1971.

[89] Regarding critical evaluation of Rawls' theory of justice, which provoked intensive discussion, especially in the English-speaking world, extending beyond the

sense it could have significance for the humanity originating from faith, hope, and love, with its concern for the concretization of social justice.

In the first place, it should be emphasized that Rawls' theory of justice is tailor-made for the specific question of social-ethics. That already makes it clear that it is relevant to our own project. "For us the primary subject of justice is the basic structure of society, or more exactly, the way in which the major social institutions distribute fundamental rights and duties and determine the division of advantages from social cooperation."[90] In defining the subject of his theory in this way, Rawls is not concerned with a merely formal determination, but with a materially analyzable determination of social justice in the form of basic "principles that free and rational persons concerned to further their own interests would accept in an initial position of equality as defining the fundamental terms of their association."[91] Rawls explicitly calls this way of understanding the basic principles of justice — to come straight to the point — a theory of *"justice as fairness."*[92]

From that one can already see that Rawls develops his theory within the social contract tradition, which is indebted to the idea of natural law and primarily follows Rousseau and Kant: "In justice as fairness the original position of equality corresponds to the state of nature in the traditional theory of the social contract."[93] Therefore, "the original position of equality" means neither an early historical stage nor a primitive step in the development of the human race, but rather a "theoretical situation" that marks the logical conditions under which a rational and fair determination of justice is possible while each person has in mind his own enlightened self-interest.

narrower sphere of ethics and political philosophy to jurisprudence, economics, and the social sciences, only the following titles, besides those cited in the text, are offered here: Otfried Höffe, ed., *Theorie-Diskussion über John Rawls' Theorie der Gerechtigkeit*, Frankfurt am Main, 1977; Otfried Höffe, "A Theory of Justice," *Philosophische Rundschau*, 21 (1974), pp. 187-208; Christian Watrin, "Eine liberale Interpretation der Idee der sozialen Gerechtigkeit," *Hamburger Jahrbuch für Wirtschafts- und Gesellschaftspolitik*, 21, Tübingen, 1976, pp. 45-61; Guido Küng, "Les fondements méthodologiques de la théorie de la justice de John Rawls," *Revue de théologie et de philosophie*, 111 (1979), pp. 279-89; Ernst Tugendhat, "Comments on some Methodological Aspects of Rawls' 'Theory of Justice'," *Analyse und Kritik*, 1 (1979), pp. 77-89.

90 Rawls, *A Theory of Justice*, p. 7.

91 *Ibid.*, p. 11.

92 *Ibid.*, p. 11, passim.

93 *Ibid.*, p. 12.

In contrast to classical contract theory, not only persons who are originally equal, and thus sovereign, and in their sovereignty rational, belong to these logical conditions. Rawls introduces here a modification that is as original as it is significant. The persons decide for the principles of justice that will govern their social relationships in a situation in which all of them are affected by the same *information deficit*:

> Among the essential features of this situation is that no one knows his place in society, his class position or social status, nor does any one know his fortune in the distribution of natural assets and abilities, his intelligence, strength, and the like. I shall even assume that the parties do not know their conceptions of the good or their special psychological propensities. The principles of justice are chosen behind a veil of ignorance. This ensures that no one is advantaged or disadvantaged in the choice of principles by the outcome of natural chance or the contingency of social circumstances. Since all are similarly situated and no one is able to design principles to favor his particular condition, the principles of justice are the result of a fair agreement or bargain.[94]

Under these conditions of original equality, the persons must, according to the Rawlsian argument, choose two fundamental principles of justice. In their final formulation they read:

> *First Principle*
> Each person is to have an equal right to the most extensive total system of equal basic liberties compatible with a similar system of liberty for all.
>
> *Second Principle*
> Social and economic inequalities are to be arranged so that they are both:
> (a) to the greatest benefit of the least advantaged, consistent with the just savings principle, and
> (b) attached to offices and positions open to all under conditions of fair equality of opportunity.[95]

The two principles of justice are supplemented by two priority rules. The first priority rule (the priority of liberty) prescribes that "liberty can be restricted only for the sake of liberty."[96] The second priority

[94] *Ibid.*
[95] *Ibid.*, p. 302.
[96] *Ibid.*

rule (the priority of justice) requires that (a) "an inequality of opportunity must enhance the opportunities of those with the lesser opportunity" and (b) "an excessive rate of saving must on balance mitigate the burden of those bearing this hardship."[97]

The first principle of justice, to which, according to Rawls, all rational decision-makers in the theoretical original position would agree, thus postulates that each should have the same greatest-possible basic liberties. This means, naturally, the classical liberal civil rights, which are inalienable and the same for everyone. Thus each person would, in order now only to offer this example, choose freedom of religion, conscience, and thought, because in the original position one's own fundamental religious or philosophical attitudes remain hidden behind the veil of ignorance and, therefore, no one would risk being discriminated against by the religious or philosophical orientation predominating at the time in a society. It goes without saying that this contains an option for the liberal state, founded upon the rule of law.

The first principle of justice relates primarily to political relationships, the second to social and economic relationships. In this sphere, but only in it, inequalities, even if they arise from differences in natural and social starting conditions, are, contrary to egalitarianism, not simply to be ruled out. But they are also not automatically justified, as the advocates of elitist theories would have it. They are, on the contrary, acceptable, only if they serve — as the first, provisional formulation of the second principle of justice reads — "to everyone's advantage," and furthermore, if the positions and offices attached to them are "open to all."[98] Thus, inequalities in the economic-social sphere, if they cannot simply be eliminated, must promote greater equality. And that does not mean merely in such a way that all the less advantaged can participate in the advantages of the advantaged. Rawls refines and modifies the first formulation of his second principle of justice in accordance with what he calls the difference principle. According to that — and this is precisely the meaning of the final formulation of the second basic principle — economic-social

[97] *Ibid.*, pp. 302-3.

[98] *Ibid.*, p. 60. The provisional formulation of the second principle of justice reads: "Social and economic inequalities are to be arranged so that they are both (a) reasonably expected to be to everyone's advantage, and (b) attached to positions and offices open to all."

inequalities are justified when and only when the "greatest possible advantage to the least advantaged" is attained through them. It goes without saying that for Rawls, in view of the radical note that the difference principle brings into his second principle of justice, it cannot be a matter of justifying the liberal state, governed by the rule of law, and the market ordering of the economy that belongs to it as they actually exist. His theory of justice contains rather, in view of actual relationships in liberal, market-economic societies, an eminently social-critical potential. What it aspires to is a liberal order, based on the market economy[99] (in principle, of course), which, however, must even out as much as possible existing inequalities in the distribution of both material goods and social positions.

Seen from this specific viewpoint, it might appear that Rawls' theory of justice simply coincides in its political-economic thrust with the basic tendency of welfare economics. This appearance, however, is deceptive.

"The purpose of welfare economics is to demonstrate the conditions under which the greatest possible economic prosperity can be realized for the macroeconomy as a whole."[100] From that much alone it is already obvious that it stands in the ethical tradition of *utilitarianism*. According to utilitarian theory, then, social institutions correspond structurally to the principle of justice when they are able to maximize total utility. This conception is encountered in two essentially different variants. According to one variant, that of Jeremy Bentham, it is a matter of realizing "the greatest possible happiness for the greatest possible number of people," which is equivalent to realizing the highest possible total utility. For the other variant, that of John Stuart Mill, in contrast, the goal to be strived for is not the maximization of the sum of utility as such, but rather the maximization of the average utility per capita of the population. Consequently, neither reading of the utilitarian theory excludes mistreating at least a small minority in the interest of economic utility maximization — whether of the greatest possible sum or of the highest possible

[99] *Ibid.*, pp. 274ff.

[100] *Dr. Gablers Wirtschaftslexikon*, ed. R. and H. Sellien, 6th Ed., Vol. VI, Wiesbaden, 1976, col. 2345.

[101] On the Pareto Principle (or criterion), see Helmut Hesse, "Ökonomische Kriterien zur Beurteilung konkurrierender Lösungsmodelle," *Handbuch der christlichen Ethik*, Vol. III, 1982, pp. 340-41.

average prosperity — and in addition possibly even having to accept a severe restriction of personal civil rights. The *Pareto Principle*,[101] which is exercised with special preference as a supposedly purely rational, and thus generally recognized, value judgment of welfare economics,[102] also follows the utilitarian line of thought. According to it, the welfare of a community increases if the quantity of utility of all members except one remains constant and that member experiences an improvement. An economic change of existing conditions is thus justified, according to this principle, "if by it at least one individual can feel better and no other is disadvantaged,"[103] where it remains unimportant whether the favored individual belongs to a privileged or non-privileged class.

The incompatibility of utility-maximization thought, to which welfare economics pays tribute, and Rawls' theory of justice is obvious. Apart from his difference principle, which seeks to provide in the distribution question the greatest advantage directly to the least advantaged, and consequently runs directly counter to the Pareto principle, no free and rational decision-making person in the original position, as Rawls assumes, would ever agree to a principle that ultimately contains within itself the risk that, along with an overall raised standard of living, he would have to belong to the underprivileged minority, or even spend his life in slave-like conditions. The desired distance from the utilitarian position, and therefore also from welfare economics, is unmistakable. The question remains, however, whether Rawls is not still led by a sublime utilitarianism, since an option for justice in his sense ultimately would also lead only to a prudent utility selection, led by enlightened self-interest. That question will now be addressed.

In order to clarify this new question, we will first consider Rawls' starting point, because it presents the greatest difficulties, at least *prima facie*, for the social-ethical approach pursued here. He begins, as will be recalled, with the "principles that free and rational persons concerned to further their own interests would accept in an initial position of equality as defining the fundamental terms of their association." But does Rawls not appear, in the words of Otfried Höffe,

[102] Cf. Egon Sohmen, "Grundlagen, Grenzen und Entwicklungsmöglichkeiten der Welfare Economics," in Erwin von Beckerath and Herbert Giersch, eds., *Probleme der normativen Ökonomik und der wirtschaftspolitischen Beratung*, Berlin, 1963, pp. 69ff.

[103] *Ibid.*, p. 71.

to miss the mark of justice right from the outset? "Is justice really a derivative of self-interest, or does it not instead mean the negation of self-interest and the recognition of a, however more precisely defined, general interest?"[104] Although such questions are inevitable, they result, as Höffe himself demonstrates, from a misunderstanding of Rawls' basic intention.[105]

It should be observed here that Rawls assumes for the selection of the principles of justice a position of original justice that, even though hidden, is already ethically qualified. To be sure, the decision-makers in this position decide in "their own interests." But self-interest here can have only a formal meaning. For the choosers ignore their materially determined interests, since according to the Rawlsian original-position scenario the status that they will assume in the actual society remains completely unknown to them. "They are conceived as not taking an interest in one another's interests."[106] Thus materially determined interestedness does not at all come into play in the choice of the principles of justice. The information deficit leads, therefore, to the point that the persons in their original choice position, unaware of their strong or weak position in the actual society, recognize themselves as mutually free and equal persons. And that means that the justice decisions that they make in their own interest are at the same time in the general interest of all, so that general validity must attach to the subjective decision of the individuals. Therefore, with Rawls, a morally-oriented rational choice is hidden behind the prudential decision, which is guided by self-interest and is apparently utilitarian,[107] especially since pre-rational assumptions of a moral kind, which codetermine the rational decisions for the justice that pushes towards concretization are contained in his rationally-structured theory of justice.

It might be justified, therefore, to understand Rawls to mean that his choice of the principles of justice has to do not only with reason that prudently considers self-interest, but also with morally-determined convictions of justice that stand in validity from the start with the choice of the principles of justice in the original position and

[104] Otfried Höffe, "Rawls' Theorie der politisch-sozialen Gerechtigkeit," in Otfried Höffe, ed., *John Rawls*, Freiburg im Breisgau, 1977, p. 26.

[105] *Ibid.*, pp. 26-27.

[106] Rawls, *A Theory of Justice*, p. 13.

[107] Otfried Höffe agrees, "Rawls' Theorie der politisch-sozialen Gerechtigkeit," p. 28.

amalgamate themselves with choosing reason. That is stated explicitly in his theory of justice:

> There is, however, another side to justifying a particular description of the original position. This is to see if the principles which would be chosen match our considered convictions of justice or extend them in an acceptable way. We can note whether applying these principles would lead us to make the same judgments about the basic structure of society which we now make intuitively and in which we have the greatest confidence; or whether, in cases where our present judgments are in doubt and given with hesitation, these principles offer a resolution which we can affirm on reflection. There are questions which we feel sure must be answered in a certain way. For example, we are confident that religious intolerance and racial discrimination are unjust.... These convictions are provisional fixed points which we presume any conception of justice must fit. But we have much less assurance as to what is the correct distribution of wealth and authority. Here we may be looking for a way to remove our doubts. We can check an interpretation of the initial situation, then, by the capacity of its principles to accommodate our firmest convictions and to provide guidance where guidance is needed.[108]

Consequently, in his search for an ethically-justifying concretization of the initial situation into real society, Rawls is concerned with argumentation "that both expresses reasonable conditions and yields principles which match our considered judgments duly pruned and adjusted,"[109] where these verdicts are supported by convictions. He himself speaks in this context about a "reflective equilibrium."[110] Rational and pre-rational elements are mutually in play here in a way that clarifies the conviction elements of the argument, but are not given up. This is not simply a circular argument, as is often claimed, but rather a dialectical process.[111] It is ultimately not far from what is also found in the style of argumentation of Gerhard Weisser's normative social science,[112] which has been co-opted in the methodological foundation-laying of the social ethical approach presented here.

[108] Rawls, *A Theory of Justice*, pp. 19-20.
[109] *Ibid.*, p. 20.
[110] *Ibid.*
[111] See Walter Ott, "Grundzüge der Gerechtigkeitstheorie von John Rawls," in Ulrich Häfelin, *et al.*, eds., *Festschrift zum 70. Geburtstag von Hans Nef*, Zürich, 1981, p. 261.
[112] See 4.3.4, especially p. 90-93.

Rawls' approach appears to be compatible with our own, not only methodologically, but also in the respect of what he calls convictions of justice or the "*sense of justice.*" One part of this sense of justice is the fact that persons in the theoretical initial situation recognize one another as free and equal persons and, therefore, are already obligated to "justice as fairness." That indicates a pre-understanding of humanity that is along the lines of the criterion of fellow-humanness, with its dialogical essential-understanding of the humane. At any rate, it can be received without difficulty by the hoping love of faith. The same is true of Rawls' second principle of justice. It corresponds in the highest degree to the fundamental social-ethical concern expressed in the criteria of relationality and participation. Rawls avoids permitting the contrary value positions that express themselves in the principles of equality and inequality to play out against one another in the sense of mutually exclusive alternatives that thus make themselves absolute. He holds to neither an elitist nor an egalitarian ideology. For him, equality and inequality are instead related to one another in an actual society, but again, not merely in the way of a harmonistic reconciliation of the two conflicting values. Just as, in accordance with the standard of the correctly understood criterion of relationality, in a society where the economic inequality of its members prevails, the emphasis should be placed on the element of equality, that happens with Rawls. According to his difference principle, an inequality of that kind is justified only if it provides the greatest possible advantage to the least advantaged, and thus accomplishes an equality that benefits above all those who are the poorest economically and are in the worst position. And that is precisely what the hoping love of faith seeks to accentuate with the criterion of participation. For this love, inequalities are compatible with human justice only when they make possible for the members of the underclass a better situation in life than could be brought about by a socially uniform and mechanical leveling down. Conversely, it must refuse to surrender itself to any in principle striving for equality in society, if the prospect of participation of the disadvantaged thereby decreases, in short, if their situation in life would become even worse. Equality cannot have the sense of becoming equally poor, equally miserable, or equally disadvantaged: "It tends toward improvement of the disadvantaged, toward adequate participation."[113]

[113] Hans Ruh, "Gerechtigkeitstheorien," p. 67.

If the sense of justice and the second principle of justice are to unite in this way with the criteria of the hoping love of faith — and that is obvious for the sense of justice — this raises *reservations about the first priority rule*. According to it, basic liberties may be restricted only for the sake of liberty itself. Liberty appears, consequently, to be an absolute value, which, contrary to the principle of relationality, does not permit itself to be limited by any other value. It is, consequently, entitled to an *absolute priority* in relation to solidarity as a social obligation of the economically stronger for the benefit of the economically weaker. One must indeed agree with Rawls that basic liberties should not be restricted for the sake of higher economic welfare. The human person does not live by bread alone. But neither does he live by liberty alone. Bread and liberty belong together. It is a matter of working for "bread," understood as a symbol for the necessities of life, in liberty and, indeed, in a just social context that permits each person to participate sufficiently in it. There may, however, be circumstances — one thinks first of all about the developing nations — that make it necessary to give priority to "bread" and to restrict certain rights to liberty temporarily for the sake of the extremely disadvantaged. "Rawls may have been at least partially aware of this difficulty, since he himself in some comments restricts the priority of liberty in such conditions that — as in the developed, industrialized societies — guarantee a sufficient supply of the goods important for life."[114] But such restrictions, as they occasionally occur with him, are not sufficient to influence the formulation of the principles of justice or their priority rules.

An additional critical point, which is, of course, closely related to the absolute priority of liberty, is the problem of *liberty and power*. Spaces of liberty are potential spaces of power, provided that they permit human persons to actualize the possibilities within them, which in reality are never distributed equally, according to their own desires and, if need be, to gain significant, even distinct, advantages relative to others. Socially relevant inequalities established in this way cannot be avoided in a free society. But such inequalities are justified, according to the Rawlsian difference principle, only if they are "to the greatest benefit of the least advantaged." Economic power, for example, accordingly, should be used in such a way that it becomes effective in the sense of social equalizing. Experience shows,

[114] Peter Koller, "Rawls' Theorie der Gerechtigkeit und ihre Kritik," *Kriminalsoziologische Bibliographie*, 5 (1978), p. 43.

however, that they do not do that when freely abandoned to themselves, but instead frequently demonstrate the diametrically opposed tendency and, indeed, in both "capitalist" and "socialist" societies. That does not yet need to be a full confirmation of the thesis of Jacob Burckhardt "that power in itself is evil no matter who exercises it."[115] But it does make evident that the exercise of power in society can and often does misuse power. Do Rawls' principles of justice sufficiently take this fact into account? Or do they not need expansion or amendment? Harri Wettstein has looked into this question in a thorough study.[116] In it he reaches the conclusion that they are in need of amendment, and places the *"responsibility principle"* beside them: "Act within your scope of freedom in such a way that no one is thereby harmed."[117] Wettstein understands this to mean that each person makes himself punishable for the socially harmful consequences of the risk associated with his sphere of power and for which he must assume responsibility.[118] The suitability of this expansion for Rawls' theory of justice cannot and will not be discussed here. However one may judge it, Wettstein at least draws attention to the problem that Rawls has left open. Economic liberty is not automatically justified by the principle of liberty as such; it requires the institutionalizable acceptance of responsibility for the social consequences that arise from the use of power that the sphere of liberty makes possible. At least the understanding of liberty that corresponds to Christianly-determined humanity requires that.

7.3.4 *Guidelines for Social Justice*

As a result of our explication of the criteria of human justice in the sense of the humanity originating from faith, hope, and love, of the considerations of the nature of its relationship to social justice, and of the assessment of Rawls' theory of justice from the point of view of this humanity, certain guidelines emerge, which have significance for the concretization of what is called justice in the context of the economy. They will be outlined briefly at this point.

[115] Jacob Burckhardt, *Weltgeschichtliche Betrachtungen*, Stuttgart, 1963, pp. 36, 97.

[116] Harri Wettstein, *Über die Ausbaufähigkeit von Rawls' Theorie der Gerechtigkeit*, Basel, 1979.

[117] *Ibid.*, p. 55.

[118] *Ibid.*

a) The *hoping love of faith* exceeds in its ethos every kind of *social justice*. It is justice that is also valid in the ultimate, in the Kingdom of God. Social justice, on the contrary, can only have validity in the penultimate, only in historically-existing circumstances. The love of faith must, therefore, always observe critical distance from social or human justice. The former can grant the latter no claim whatsoever to absolute validity, even when justice attains its best possible form, as it may appear visionarily in utopian designs.
b) Nevertheless, the hoping love of faith can never approve of the *merely anarchistic negation* of institutionalized social justice, simply because of its imperfection. In the time of the penultimate, there is nothing other than this. If it were to fade away, we would remain completely without tangible justice. In so far as anarchism has in mind the difference between the absolute promotion of justice and all established legal systems, it is in the right. But if it is to have any sense of reality, it must not avoid establishing social order and, therefore, socially determined law,[119] which ultimately no more exists before the claim of absolute justice than that which it calls into question. Because this is true, because we happen to be unable to dispense with social or human justice, the hoping love of faith receives this law realistically, despite its obvious relativity. But it does this in a way that always keeps social justice in its actual legal form critically in motion towards the humanity originating from faith, hope, and love.
c) This means practically that love in its hoping interest in the Kingdom of God must always simultaneously have in mind the *optimization of social justice* on the basis of its own fundamental criteria, and indeed in a way that does not cover up the practical in a utopian manner, but rather takes it into account soberly. And that is essentially a matter of rational reflection. Thus Christian ethics must attempt to persuade on the basis of reason, which under realistic circumstances can and should mean a practicable optimization of social justice. The humanity originating from faith, hope, and love is, therefore, directly and seriously interested in rational theories of justice, such as that of John Rawls, because and provided that they are useful for the intended finding of consensus.

[119] Thus Anselme Bellegarrigue asserts quite provocatively in his anarchistic "Manifesto": "Anarchy is order."

d) Rawls' second principle of justice provides, as has hopefully become clear, a *rational means, which can be adopted by the humanity originating from faith, hope, and love,* of bring the criterion of participation in its essential concerns closer to the concrete world, so far as this concerns the problem of distribution, without limiting its claim to universal validity. According to it, inequalities in the distribution of the national product, life situations, and social opportunities in general meet the requirements of human justice only in so far as the situation of the least advantaged above all is improved by them. The basic tendency of participative humanity can hardly be described more adequately than this. It is, incidentally, also significant in this context that the normative-social-scientist Gerhard Weisser, who, in contrast to Rawls, advocates political-economically a socialist, non-liberal position, arrives at a surprisingly similar principle of justice. Weisser writes in his study of the "principles of distributive politics," which appeared long before Rawls' main work: "The fundamentally equal dignity of human persons requires that advantages of distribution existing in the market economy be not larger than is necessary to attain the culturally determined optimum in national product. The principle of equal opportunity is thus to be corrected in the following way: *Differences in the life situations of the producers (both independent and dependent) should exist to the extent necessary and sufficient within present social circumstances to induce the producers to the desirable benefits.* Those members of society who are not admitted to such distributive advantages can also consent to such a regulation,"[120] provided that these advantages indirectly benefit the disadvantaged. That agrees in reality with the intention of Rawls' second principle of justice, and underlines his theory's great ability to attain consensus.

e) The situation is similar with Rawls' first *principle of justice,* despite the reservations that are to be expressed concerning the priority of basic human liberties, which are conceived absolutely in the sense of the first priority rule, not relationally. Indeed, both the principle and the priority rule deliberately stand within the worldview of the liberal tradition and contain what may be called an *a priori option* for the order-political system of the market economy. Yet it

[120] Gerhard Weisser, "Grundsätze der Verteilungspolitik" (1954), in *Beiträge zur Gesellschaftspolitik,* Göttingen, 1978, pp. 378-79.

remains without doubt that Rawls does not simply adopt the market-economic system in its for the most part existing constitution and certainly does not do so uncritically. First of all, the market-economic order, with its basis on the economic self-interest of economic subjects, is "not indeed an ideal arrangement" for him and, therefore, requires certain "background institutions" in order to remove "the worst aspects of so-called wage slavery."[121] Among these background institutions is "a democratic regime in which land and capital are widely though not presumably equally held." Furthermore, "society is not so divided that one fairly small sector controls the preponderance of productive resources." Moreover, according to Rawls:

> a liberal socialist regime can also answer to the two principles of justice. We have only to suppose that the means of production are publicly owned and that firms are managed by workers' councils say, or by agents appointed by them. Collective decisions made democratically under the constitution determine the general features of the economy, such as the rate of saving and the proportion of society's production devoted to essential public goods. Given the resulting economic environment, firms regulated by market forces conduct themselves much as before. Although the background institutions will take a different form, especially in the case of the distribution branch, there is no reason in principle why just distributive shares cannot be achieved. The theory of justice does not by itself favor either form of regime.[122]

An institutional ordering of the market economy that places more emphasis on the element of solidarity in the liberty-solidarity relationship — for instance, under well-aimed promotion of free-social-economy forms of the firm (for which, by the way, Gerhard Weisser argued[123]) — is thus not ruled out by Rawls. By no means does he tie the principle of the market economy to specific capitalist forms of property ownership. His principles of social justice require, of course, that the optimization of participation takes place by means of fair distribution of the opportunities for life and existence in an order-political setting that can simultaneously bring about an optimum of self-sufficiency and self-responsibility, in short, of liberty, for all who participate in economic events. This,

[121] Rawls, *A Theory of Justice*, p. 281.
[122] *Ibid.*, p. 280.
[123] Gerhard Weisser, "Grundsätze der Verteilungspolitik," esp. pp. 654-72.

however, permits order-politically different, even socialist structure-possibilities of a market-economic constitution. A liberal socialist could, therefore, also agree with this. Thus it is here, again, a matter of a guideline of high capability for consensus. Furthermore, it permits the practicability of the criterion of relationality for order-political yes-no questions to be recognized.

f) Social justice stands not only in the fellow-human dimension, but also in the *fellow-creature dimension*. In other words, this means not only that it is necessary to combat the exploitation of human persons by other human persons by means of a notoriously unequal distribution of liberty and participation rights in the social economy, but also that social justice includes protecting the natural environment from its destructive exploitation by taking the criterion of fellow-creatureliness seriously. Such exploitation is inevitable if a society organizes its economy according to economistic principles, as is also the case with welfare economics. "Economism" is a way of looking at things that assesses all manifestations of social life exclusively from the standpoint of economic rationality and material productivity and, consequently, eliminates the prescriptive-ethical viewpoint from the start as economically non-rational. "The most disturbing form of a refined economism today appears as the thesis that the purpose of the national economy is to *maximize the national product*."[124] This can be advocated in the interest of either capitalist profit-maximization or non-capitalistic welfare-maximization. In either case, one must declare one's belief in a politics of accelerated economic growth. "Continuous economic growth, however, provokes increasing exploitation of the natural environment."[125] A clear rejection of economism also belongs as an indispensable guideline to social justice, as it must be understood in our context of reflection. The economy must observe in its own development-dynamic not only the limits that are set for it by human justice, but also those set for it by ecological justice, because what is not ecologically just cannot truly be humanly just. In short, the challenge is to find the path from an economy of ever-more to an "economy of enough."[126]

124 *Ibid.*, p. 576.

125 Otfried Höffe, "Natur als Orientierungspunkt der Ethik," in *Liberal: Beiträge zur Entwicklung einer freiheitlichen Ordnung*, 25 (1983), p. 328.

126 The expression is found in Harry M. de Lange, "Die Kirchen und die Einheit Europa," *Zeitschrift für Evangelische Ethik*, 27 (1983), p. 47.

With Rawls, in whose theory of justice the ecological viewpoint does not yet appear, the rejection of economism is encountered only *indirectly* in the form of the critique of utilitarian welfare economics. With Weisser, in contrast, it becomes directly tangible.[127] But with him the inclusion of the ecological problematic is missing, because, as a theme of normative social science, it is of a most recent date. Yet it could be introduced to his basic concept without difficulty.

These guidelines of social justice point out only the perspective in which the basic criteria of human justice from faith, hope, and love are to be concretized with regard to social reality, more precisely, the reality of the economy. The actual concretization of practical maxims must take place on a new level, the third and final one.

[127] Gerhard Weisser, "Die Überwindung des Ökonomismus in der Wirtschaftswissenschaft," in *Beiträge zur Gesellschaftspolitik*, pp. 573-601.

8. SOCIAL-ETHICAL MAXIMS

8.1 The Formal Aspect of Maxims

Working out the content of social-ethical, or economic-ethical, maxims in detail cannot be accomplished in this chapter. That will be the concern of Volume II, which will address the problem of structuring the economy. This chapter is concerned with preliminary questions about the *formal aspect* of the maxims, the principal steps leading to their conception, and their claim to validity.

There has already been some anticipatory discussion of the formal aspect of the maxims, as distinguished from the formal aspect of the criteria, in 4.4 and 6.3. Criteria were described there as norms of a purely prescriptive kind. They express, in the horizon of a definite experience-certitude, what must in principle be valid ethically. They can be compared formally with "basic matters of concern" or "fundamental value judgments", as they are encountered in Gerhard Weisser's normative social science. As criteria of the humanity originating from faith, hope, and love, they are also introduced "confessionally," similarly to Weisser's, even though strong rational grounds can be given for them. In their completeness, they mark the absolute orientation point of all social-ethical judgment-formation and decision-making.

The social-ethical process of forming judgments and making decisions has to do not only with the ideal world of principles, but also just as much with the real world of facts, in our case with the economic cosmos, as it actually behaves. Therefore, this process must take place with knowledge about the facts, including the concrete situation, with which one is concerned. In other words, social-ethical judgment-formation and decision-making cannot take place without employing the criteria as their absolute orientation point; but neither can they simply argue deductively, by drawing conclusions directly from the criteria. They require for their reality-aware execution, to repeat, well-founded insight into the actual subject matter about which value judgments are to be made. "These judgments are thus *integrated cognitive and voluntary acts"* — voluntary, because they are oriented towards confessional and thus faith-related or volitional criteria, and cognitive, because they are based upon empirical, specialized knowledge.[1] In our terminology, they are called "maxims."[2] They, too, have a normative character. But their normativeness is of a kind fundamentally different from that of the criteria.

The reason for this difference is that the maxims, in contrast to the criteria, are not only voluntary, prescriptive "ought" propositions, but at the same time also cognitive "is" propositions. They can, to be sure, only be achieved in such a way that it is asked on the basis of the criteria according to which basic rules society, the state, and the economy should be ordered structurally in their central institutions, and fundamental rights and duties should be distributed, so that this is able, on the one hand, to correspond to the conditions of economic correctness and, on the other hand, to let itself meet the demands of human justice. Maxims must, consequently, not only stand up to the supra-rational demand of human justice, they must also prove themselves before the rational demand of economic correctness. Only to the degree that the integration of both elements is achieved are they suitable for practice as social-ethical rules for evaluation and decision. But since an integration of that kind is possible only approximately, the normativeness of the maxims can be no more than relative.[3] This raises the question of which process of reasoning will lead to maxims of this kind.

[1] Heinz Eduard Tödt, "Zweiter Versuch zu einer ethischer Theorie der sittlichen Urteilsfindung," presented at the 1979 Annual Conference of the Societas Ethica in Liebfrauenberg bei Straßburg, *Protokoll der Jahrestagung*, 1979, p. 4. See also "Versuch zu einer Theorie ethischer Urteilsfindung," *Zeitschrift für Evangelische Ethik*, 21 (1977), p. 87.

[2] In Kant's moral philosophy, the term "maxim" denotes the subjective principle of an action, which can be considered moral in the sense of the categorical imperative only if it agrees with the moral law as the objective and absolute principle of all rational beings. The concept of maxim used here differs from the Kantian understanding. It means norms for decision and action that are indeed oriented towards the absolute of the humanity originating from faith, hope, and love, but that in their historicity and relatedness to particular situations can in principle claim only relative ethical validity. It also does not coincide with Walter Schulz's "ethical maxims of the present" (*Philosophie in der veränderten Welt*, Pfullingen, 1972, pp. 378ff.), which have a very universalizing and thus abstract character.

[3] Joseph H. Oldham's "middle axioms" comes closest to what I mean by "maxims": "The middle axioms first give Christian ethics a clear connection. They are an attempt to determine the direction in which Christian faith must work itself out in a

8.2 The Principal Steps in the Formation of Maxims [4]

With a social-ethically conceived economic ethic, as can be recalled, we are primarily concerned with the question of the humanly-justly and economically-correctly structured ordering of the economic, or socially-determined life conditions of the human person, through which the responsible fulfillment of the fundamental existence rights and duties of individuals, groups, entire societies, etc. can be promoted, rather than being hindered or completely nullified. The process of finding the evaluation and decision norms considered here, in order to make them concrete, has already been determined implicitly by the considerations of the preceding chapters. All that remains is to explain the main steps of this process explicitly and systematically. Five of these steps must be fundamentally distinguished.

8.2.1 *Demonstration of the Problem*

The concretization of the absolute demand that is communicated normatively by the criteria of the humanity originating from faith, hope, and love, and thus its operationalization in the form of practicable

particular overall situation. They are not binding for all time, but they are instead interim descriptions of the kind of lifestyle that Christians should live in a particular time and under particular circumstances" (Willem A. Visser't Hooft and Joseph H. Oldham, *Die Kirche und ihr Dienst an der Welt*, Berlin, 1937, p. 200). Oldham's "middle axioms" (development, participation, solidarity, etc.), however, are less concrete than my maxims, as they will be formally determined in the following. In their verbalization, they are closer to my criteria. Moreover, they are conceived in a more personalist context.

[4] The following sketch of the main steps in the development of maxims stands — as far as its procedural structure is concerned — in moral proximity to Heinz Eduard Tödt's theory of moral decision-making (see note 1). His first attempt in 1977 (see note 1) distinguishes six elements: 1. Definition of the problem, 2. Analysis of the situation, 3. Determination of alternative actions, 4. Examination of norms, 5. Decision, 6. Retrospective control. With Tödt's second attempt in 1979 Examination of the communicative binding nature is in fifth position, followed by Decision as the sixth element. In my approach, which was developed independently of Tödt's and whose beginnings go back to the essay "Die institutionelle Ordnung der Gesellschaft als theologisches Problem," *Zeitschrift für Evangelische Ethik*, 4 (1960), pp. 233-44, Tödt's first two steps merge into one. My other steps are comparable to his. On the compatibility of the two approaches, see Christofer Frey, "Theologische Kriterien für die Gestaltung und Entwicklung der Wirtschaft," in *Zwischen Wachstum und Lebensqualität*, Munich, 1980, p. 130-36; and on the critical assessment of Tödt's project, see the essays of Otfried Höffe, Christian Link, and Christofer Frey in *Zeitschrift für Evangelische Ethik*, 22 (1978), pp. 181-213.

norms or rules, which are here called maxims, is the main task of realistic social and economic ethics. Since, if they are to be anything more than idealistic postulation, the maxims must be related to reality, even a theologically-conceived economic ethic must, in its process of finding them, take existing facts as its starting point. It must, therefore, begin with an analysis of the actual political, economic, and social situation, with the aim of clarifying the crucial problems with which it is concerned. The demonstration of the problem and the analysis of the situation or subject matter stand, consequently, insolubly in one another and, therefore, should be brought together in this approach in a single act, which goes ahead of all other steps.

8.2.2 *Examining Existing or Postulated Concepts of Analysis*

The demonstration of problems calls for overcoming them; for problems pose questions, and questions call for answers. Thus, for example, the often horrendously unequal distribution of income and property, seen both domestically and most of all globally, is a fundamental problem that inevitably gives rise to eminently critical questions that can no longer be smoothed over, but instead provoke a substantial and operational answer. Upon what are such inequalities based? Are they, seen from the viewpoint of economic correctness, really inevitable, or can they be, in agreement with the criterial justice guidelines developed above, if not simply overcome, at least effectively mitigated? Which alternative systems of distribution and ownership exist at all, and which are in addition conceivable or desirable in the interests of a just order of distribution and property? Concepts of analysis and formation that actually exist, or are desired and possible, must be examined objectively for the time being in their specific structures and probable effects. This is all the more true, analogously, of order-political systems and conceptions of new models in the economy and the problems they pose, which will be addressed in the second volume. Only if that kind of stock-taking analysis is taken into account are the informational prerequisites for reality-related judgment-decisions in the set of questions under investigation established.

8.2.3 *Norm-Critical Clarifications*

Economic *judgment-decisions*, however they may be made and turn out, are ultimately ethical acts. That is true even of what are alleged to be purely pragmatic choices. One can, for example, opt for the market economy for reasons of economic efficiency, and thus supposedly be motivated in only a technical, pragmatic sense. Such a decision would, nonetheless, never be value neutral ethically. Efficiency is in itself an abstract matter, empty of content. It receives concrete meaningfulness only through the context in which it exists. Does it exist exclusively in the service of profit, or does it include the conscious safeguarding of social interests? Depending upon the answer, the aforementioned decision means not just a choice of the market economy as such, but a choice of one of its possible forms, i.e. the specifically capitalist market economy or a socially-orientated market economy. That is, however, of ethical relevance. Therefore, behind the order-political structures of the economy and the choices for or against them, stand mostly concealed value preferences. These preferences must be revealed and critically clarified in their ethical legitimacy. Norm-critical clarification must, consequently, take place in two ways. First, to remain with the particular problem now under discussion — the ethical implications of each order-political option must be revealed. Second, it is necessary to determine the normative guidelines according to which the decision is to be carried through if it is responsibly to meet the demand of the humanity originating from faith, hope, and love.

8.2.4 *Determination of the Guidelines*

The three steps in the formation of maxims outlined above lead logically to the determination of norm-critically clarified guidelines for making fundamental social or economic-ethical decisions that are intent on concretion. The determination of these guidelines is — to stress the point once again — a volitional act, in so far as they orient themselves normatively towards the criteria of what is human, which is rooted in the experience-certitude of Christian faith. It is simultaneously of a cognitive kind, however, since the guidelines must also exist before the demand of economic correctness in the conditions of the existing situation and, consequently, must rely on empirical, specialized knowledge.

Only if the volitional and cognitive acts go together, can judgments be formed that have the character of maxims and, therefore, can be valid as normative principles in concrete decision-questions. If either of the two elements is neglected, one deteriorates into either an unrealistic ethics of principles or principle-free pragmatism. Neither alternative is acceptable in terms of social ethics.

8.2.5 *Critical Examination*

Because the conception of the maxims as normative guidelines or guiding rules for practical decisions involves both a volitional and a cognitive act, they are determined in a *circular* manner. The ethical substance of a maxim must also be able to prove itself in principle before the demand of economic correctness, just as that which is promoted as economically correct must also be able to prove itself before normative demands based upon the criteria of human justice. Maxims, therefore, always require critical examination and, indeed, in precisely this reciprocal sense, oriented towards both ethical imperatives and technical requirements. If this circular process of examination does not accomplish sufficient agreement between the two elements, then the maxims must remain undetermined.

These facts contain something additional: In the process of forming maxims, motives from an ethics of conviction and an ethics of responsibility must go hand-in-hand. It is not sufficient that a maxim stems from an honorable intention that is guided by the criteria of human justice and is social-politically engaged. It is always necessary to ask in addition about its practicability and — to the extent possible — its foreseeable or already-existing consequences in social reality. If it proves not to be practicable, because it contradicts basic economic data, or if it shows that its actual consequences in a given situation and in view of the desired objectives are humanly, socially, or ecologically counter-productive, then it should be given up as economically-incorrect and ethically indefensible or, when appropriate, should be modified. Conversely, however, neither the economic practicability of a maxim nor its merely social and eco-political efficiency is an adequate basis for its ethical justification. For that it is necessary that it be, in all probability, capable of promoting a style of humanity that can be united with the humanity-convictions originating from faith, hope, and love. In this way (i.e. in the reciprocity of conviction- and responsibility-ethical argumentation) the maxims must be critically flexible in the direction of their always-reexamining optimization, where it must be accepted that unambiguous decisions are oftentimes impossible. So, incidentally, precisely in the process of forming maxims, an opposition of the ethics of conviction and the ethics of responsibility as doctrinaire alternatives proves to be inconsistent, as was already recognizable in earlier discussions of this complex of problems.[5]

8.3 The Maxims' Claim to Validity

This relative character of the maxims inevitably poses the question of their validity or obligatory nature. Can the relative make any claim whatsoever to being obligatory? Doesn't the relativity of the maxims mean *eo ipso* ethical relativism at the practical level, precisely where concrete decisions are to be made and, therefore, where it is most serious? Only someone who confuses relativity with relativism can reach this conclusion. For relativism, *everything* is relative and, therefore, ultimately *everything* is equally valid or, if one prefers, equally invalid. But is the relativistic position really tenable? "A certain type of superior person is fond of asserting that 'everything is relative.' This is, of course, nonsense, because, if *everything* were relative, there would be nothing for it to be relative to."[6] What Bertrand Russell says here about scientific relativism with respect to Albert Einstein's theory of relativity is equally true of ethical, practical relativism. Its basic assertion of the relativity of everything ethically normative is simply impossible, a contradiction in itself, because it is the absolutization of the relative. If, therefore, there was talk of the relativity of maxims in the preceding context, it is always only in the relation to an absolute, namely, the absolute of the humanity originating from faith, hope, and love. The maxims are relative to this absolute. And, as the fundamental theological determination of the conditions of the absolute and the relative has already demonstrated,[7] that means something twofold:

It means, first of all, the absolute difference between the maxims and the humanity originating from faith, hope, and love, in so far as they might pretend to be what is ultimately valid, redeeming, and intended by God. At the level of maxims, there is no perfection, no ethic of the Kingdom of God, the Sermon on the Mount, and suchlike. If one were to aspire to and assert something in this way, only

[5] See 2.2.5 and 2.2.6.

[6] Bertrand Russell, *The ABC of Relativity*, 4th Ed., ed. Felix Pirani, New York, 1985, p. 20.

[7] See 6.2.5.

the collapse of each theory of social or economic ethics that grasps for the concrete would become obvious. The maxims contain nothing heavenly. They are norms of fully earthy smell.

The relativity of the maxims, however, means more than that. It also means the relative correspondence to the humanity that desires faith, hope, and love. In so far as they offer an opportunity for a creation- and humanly-just existence in the world of the penultimate, with its personal and structural evil, as a first glimpse of the coming Kingdom of God, they are directly helpful in their relativity, helping to improve life norms at which Christian humanity also intentionally aims. Furthermore, the more the maxims stand under the impulse of this desire and the more they are interested in greater humanity in the actual core areas of society, the more tangible will be the relation of correspondence to the criteria of humanity and the more universal will be their claim to validity. Consequently, the relativity of the maxims does not exclude, but rather includes their obligatoriness in the time of the penultimate. Although they must rule out all dogmatic fixation, owing to their relativity, and — in the sense of critical rationalism — must leave open the possibility of their falsification, they do not at all establish an ethics of arbitrariness.

This understanding of the relativity of the maxims is based theologically and historically upon the political ethics of Huldrych Zwingli.[8] With the Swiss reformer, one finds the relation of the absolute and the relative in the dialectic of "divine and human justice."[9] Divine justice is absolute; human justice is relative. For Zwingli, divine justice coincides with love. It is unrealizable and unenforceable in the absoluteness of its requirements, whereas human justice, objectified to begin with in positive law, must be realizable and enforceable. Only divine justice, therefore, can be regarded as true justice. Human justice, in contrast, even in its best legal and behavioral norms, is inadequate, "not worthy of being called

[8] The presentation of Huldrych Zwingli's political ethics has, unfortunately, not yet appeared. Some works preliminary to it are available: Ernst Ramp, *Das Zinsproblem*, Zürich, 1949, pp. 59-81; Erik Wolf, "Die Sozialtheologie Zwinglis," *Festschrift Guido Kisch*, Stuttgart, 1955, pp. 167-188; Siegfried Rother, *Die religiösen und geistigen Grundlagen der Politik Zwinglis*, Erlangen, 1956; Arthur Rich, "Zwingli als sozialpolitischer Denker," *Zwingliana*, 13 (1969), pp. 67-89.

[9] See Heinrich Schmid, *Zwinglis Lehre von der göttlichen und menschlichen Gerechtigkeit*, Zürich, 1959.

justice."[10] Nevertheless, God also commanded it as an obligatory guiding rule in a world that does not follow the guiding principle of love, but is instead — in our terminology — still characterized by personal and structural evil. For without this miserable human justice, we would have not justice at all and society would degenerate into the rule of force.[11] It is, therefore, in its relativity a kind of *ersatz function* for the absent divine justice, in so far as it at least knows how to protect the human person in his social existence from arbitrary encroachments, machinations of the powerful, and exploitative practices of the rich. In this way, human justice stands as an opportunity for the humanization of social conditions of existence in agreement with what divine justices also seeks, although it can never attain its height. Consequently, the absolute difference remains.

That said, however, Zwingli by no means wishes to bestow anything like a sacrosanct nimbus to existing legal conditions. Precisely because all merely human justice is only relative, it must remain critically in motion, i.e. must tend towards a form that as much as possible is "similar to" the command of divine justice.[12] In other words, valid orderings that in their effects infringe upon human justice oriented towards the absolute requirement of love should be altered in a way such that they conform as much as possible to the demand of divine justice in existing circumstances. And that releases a potential for social reformation that necessarily has concrete consequences. Thus Zwingli applied maxims in Zürich that aimed at the elimination of the peasants' economic dependency upon the lords of the manor. The heredity interest payment, which brought about the perpetual dependence of the mortgage-debtors on the money-lenders, was made revocable and the interest rate was limited to 5% for the period of transition, i.e. until the conclusion of the process of getting peasants out of debt.[13] That was merely human justice, but better human justice than the *status quo ante*. Incidentally, it led to a fundamental reduction of the tensions caused by peasant disturbances during the Reformation period in the region of Zürich.

The maxims of social-ethical judgment-forming and decision-making receive normativeness in the sense of the human justice of the Swiss reformer. In other words, it is of a fundamentally relative kind,

[10] Huldrych Zwingli, *Sämtliche Werke*, Vol. II, 1908, p. 486.
[11] *Ibid.*, p. 488.
[12] *Ibid.*, p. 343, passim.
[13] Cf. Ernst Ramp, *Das Zinsproblem*, pp. 69ff.

but nevertheless obligatory. Within this fundamentally relative normativeness, it is necessary to distinguish between maxims that lie closer to the criteria of humanity, and thus with what is true in principle, and those that are expressly turned towards the concrete. The maxim that the exercise of power for political, economic, or other purposes, for example, can be justified before the demand of human justice only if it, first, serves common life in society, secondly, takes place with efficient limitation by an order of law that protects basic human rights, and, third, gives a share of it to those affected by it, is of a fundamental nature. The same is true of the maxim that unlimited, and therefore monocratic and absolute power cannot conform to the requirements of human justice. The implementation of the criteria of humanity, especially those of fellow-humanness, relationality, and participation, at the level of maxims takes place here on the whole in the neighborhood of principles. Therefore, maxims of that kind also aim at a more general claim to validity. Maxims, however, that concern the concrete "how" of the distribution of power and its legally-restricted and, participatively-structured administration in the political or the economic sphere — to remain with the set of problems now under consideration — cannot claim such general validity. For they must prove themselves to be, with regard to existing situations, not only practicable and efficient, but also efficient in practical results for the construction of a humanly just society. And that cannot be decided from the outset. Such maxims should, therefore, always be reevaluated and, consequently, operate in the area of the tentative-pragmatic, as far as their suitability is concerned. Their claim to validity is explicitly tied to situations that can change quickly.

With that comes something additional. In the tentative-pragmatic step of forming maxims, various guidelines or rules are conceivable, which possibly are equally valuable. How, for instance, should the humanly just distribution and administration of power in a large business firm be determined? Through economic co-determination rights on the part of the employees, through capital-sharing by the employees, whether in the form of individual or collective participation? Or through combinations of such possibilities, etc.? Answering such questions is by no means easy and definitely cannot be accomplished merely by following principles.

In this sense, as far as their claim to validity is concerned, more principled maxims are to be distinguished from more tentative-pragmatic maxims. When evaluated according to the humanity originating from faith, hope, and love, even maxims that stand in the vicinity of the principled have merely relative validity. Nevertheless, their demand is aimed at universal obligation. The same cannot be said of the tentative-pragmatic maxims. Only to the degree that they are really able to prove their probable suitability for bringing about structures in the realm of the state, society, and economy that promote both economic rationality and human and environmental justice, are they capable of being generalized. At the level of maxims, therefore, the social ethicist must be on guard against any tendency towards dogmatism and must refrain decisively from seeking simply to turn maxims, whose tentative-pragmatic character is unmistakable, into something in-principle or even to make them into something like matters of faith, according to which it would be decided whether one should obey God in questions of economics and politics.

Summa summarum the fact should be stressed that maxims for social-ethical judgment and decision have a relative, though not a relativistic, character. They in no way suggest a decisionistic arbitrariness, for which everything is permissible as long as it stems from subjectively respectable beliefs or comes from a conviction that is resolute to anything whatsoever.[14] They teach, instead, rationally considered conduct, which in its orientation is related to the criteria of humanity originating from faith, hope, and love. But obligation can no more mean legalism than relativity can mean relativism. Maxims are not stark laws, but guidelines for the sphere of the concrete, and must always leave room for free play. Thus they are not committed to any particular economic order. But they offer standards for assessing which existing possibilities of order, or which new ones coming into play, to exclude and which are acceptable. And if it comes to a specific choice among the acceptable possibilities, it does so in only a relative sense.[15] If it were otherwise, a fall into legal-social moralism

[14] Günter Brakelmann also shows convincingly how little that understanding of the relative as an order-political decision in the time of the penultimate has to do with ethical permissiveness, *Abschied vom Unverbindlichen*, Gütersloh, 1976, pp. 19-22.

[15] Hartmut Weber (*Theologie, Gesellschaft, Wirtschaft*, Göttingen, 1970), who undertook a critical examination of my theory of criteria and maxims in one of its early stages, as it is found in my book *Christliche Existenz in der industriellen Welt*, 2nd Ed., Zürich, 1964, pp. 171-86, summarizes his reservations thus: "If one were instead to understand the 'maxims of social decision' as situation-criteria...a category of criteria would be introduced that would also enable us to express our opinions on current situations. It would still have to be clarified, though, how they are related to the 'maxims of love' [which must, of course, mean *criteria* of love, A. R.]. Therefore, the

would be inevitable and in the place of a responsible social-ethical process of assessment and decision-making there would enter a social prophecy or social utopia acting compellingly in the domain of the relative with absolute theses.[16] This, however, would in its consequences be nothing less than disastrous as a relativistic pragmatism that denounces all concern for principles in social ethics as "ideological" and thus degrades the question of truth to the level of anything goes.

8.4 On Dealing with Biblical Maxims

The preceding reflections in this chapter hold true also of ethical maxims in the Bible. There are countless normative requirements in the Bible that operate at the level of what we are calling maxims here. They are recognizable in that they, although fundamentally of a relative character, nevertheless make a concrete, and for the most part — indeed not always — situational claim to validity and, depending on whether the in-principle or the situational prevails, have a more general or a more pragmatic meaning. The *relationship of tension* between their fundamental relativity and their claim to validity, whether in the sense of the distant general situation or the nearby pragmatic situation, poses the question of how to deal with them correctly.

Maxims with a *general*, not situational, claim to validity are, first of all, the *commandments of the Decalogue*, which concern the regulation of fundamental interpersonal-social relationships. Classifying them

maxims cannot be derived compellingly from the criteria" (p. 414). It is obvious that these maxims, especially since they are of the tentative, pragmatic kind, are situation-related. One could call them situation-bound norms. Precisely for this reason, however, they cannot be derived compellingly from the criteria. Compelling derivation is deduction. The maxims exclude *ex definitione* a deductive derivation from the criteria, because they are related not only to the relevant academic disciplines but also to particular situations and, therefore, must remain critically open. It is conceded that this contains an element of indefiniteness, but the reason for that lies in the subject matter itself.

[16] I agree with the warning of Helmut Thielicke, *Einführung in die christliche Ethik*, Munich, 1963, p. 134: "Theological ethics has the task of showing 'what it is all about,' what it is ultimately all about. Consequently, it does not itself make any decisions and does not take them away from the person who listens to the author of a particular ethical theory." Maxims of social-ethical judgment-formation and decision-making cannot take the decision away from anyone; they are to be understood as orientation aids for a responsible decision.

among the maxims and, therefore, within the sphere of the relative, may be disturbing at first glance. To be sure, the Decalogue understands itself as the expression of the will of God, revealed to Moses at Sinai and thus intended as absolute.[17] There can, however, be no doubt that it stands, at least as far as literary specification is concerned, in a concrete traditional history. How far it goes back to the time of Moses in its basic substance is still a question of controversy in the academic literature, even though it appears certain today "that the Decalogue, together with other documents of the apodictic law, had a central position in the life of the Israelites early on."[18] However that may be, one thing is obvious: The Ten Commandments were handed down from the Old Testament in two versions, where Exodus 20,1-17 represents the older and Deuteronomy 5,1-18(21) the newer. Between the two renditions of the Decalogue, "there are more than twenty points of difference,"[19] two of which have ethical significance. In the older tradition the Sabbath command is grounded cultishly; in the more recent one it is grounded socially, or more precisely, fellow-humanly-and-fellow-creaturely. And whereas in Exodus 20,17 ("You shall not covet" etc.) the neighbor's wife is listed after the word "house," in Deuteronomy 5,21 the order is reversed. Since the word in question means the "complete concept of 'property,'" in Hebrew,[20] according to the older version of the Decalogue the wife is included in the husband's possessions, but the newer version excludes the wife and gives her her own right of personality. The preceding points to a critical flexibility of these commandments. In their normative verbalization they are not themselves an absolute demand, but rather the relative, and hence variable, expression of an absolute. The absolute to which they refer can be regarded, one could say, as a humanity-demand that includes the covenant-relationship that Yahweh entered into with Israel. This covenant-faith and the covenant-humanity tied to it are already expressed in the religious-ethical quintessential expressions of the Old Testament Torah as love of God and neighbor.[21] Ultimately, it is the absolute demand of the love that also guides and moves the humanity-commandments of the

[17] Exodus 20,1-2; Deuteronomy 5,6.

[18] Johann Jakob Stamm, *Der Dekalog im Lichte der neueren Forschung*, 2nd Ed., Bern, 1962, p. 31.

[19] *Ibid.*, p. 7.

[20] Martin Noth, *Das zweite Buch Mose*, Göttingen, 1959, p. 134.

[21] Deuteronomy 6,5 and Leviticus 19,18.

Decalogue. Precisely because of that, they are not self-contained, but are in motion towards a better humanity, as comparison of the form of the fourth and tenth commandments in the earlier and later traditions proves.

If the relativity of the Decalogue and, consequently, the fact that it has the character of maxims becomes clear in this way, it does so even more, in radical intensification, with *Jesus* as the epitome of humanity originating from faith, hope and love: "You have heard that it was said to the ancients, 'You shall not kill'; and 'whoever kills will be liable to the court.' But I tell you that whoever is angry with his brother will be liable to the court; and whoever says to his brother, 'You, good for nothing!' will be liable to the council; and whoever says, 'You fool!' will be liable to the hell of fire."[22] And: "You have heard that it was said 'You shall not commit adultery.' But I tell you that whoever looks at a woman lustfully has already committed adultery with her in his heart."[23] The sixth and seventh commandments are thus intensified relative to the traditional demand in such a way that its merely relative meaning, assessed according to what God intends in the ultimate and real, becomes apparent.

Social-ethically relevant maxims of a specifically situational and thus casuistic or tentative-pragmatic kind are found in the Old Testament in great numbers.[24] The New Testament is also not without them.[25] For purposes of clarification, only two of them will be selected.

1. According to Exodus 22,25, the normal taking of interest in the commercial dealings of the ancient Orient was prohibited in dealings with the poor, where that most probably means here "*to extort*."[26] The fact that the maxim in question is situation-bound is unmistakable. It is undoubtedly about consumer loans or, more

[22] Matthew 5,21-22.

[23] Matthew 5,27-28.

[24] First of all, there are the legal statutes of the Book of the Covenant (Exodus 20,22-23,33), then Leviticus 19,9-18, the social regulations of Leviticus 25 (sabbatical year and year of jubilee), as well as the various social instructions of Deuteronomy, especially in Chapters 15-25, etc.

[25] Regulations such as Luke 3,10-14, II Thessalonians 3,10, and II Timothy 2,6 have the character of maxims.

[26] Martin Noth, *Das zweite Buch Mose*, p. 151. — The opposition to interest and extortion in the Old Testament may also be based on the fact that interest was demanded in the Middle East at that time at a rate of 20-25% (Hendrik van Oyen, *Ethik des Alten Testaments*, Gütersloh, 1967, p. 129).

precisely, subsistence loans to ensure the very survival of the borrower. To demand interest from him in his distress would mean exploiting his plight commercially, which would in fact be usury, and would necessarily have disastrous consequences for the disadvantaged. Machinations of this kind undoubtedly conflict with the humanity that understands itself to be obligated ultimately to love and that wishes with determination that each human person, without exception, can participate in the consumer goods that are indispensable for his life. They can, therefore, never be ethically justified. In so far as the Old Testament prohibition of interest refers to consumer loans that a needy person in his predicament must take up like, as it were, a nutrition loan, the maxim in question retains its general validity. But only to that extent. And from that its fundamental relativity becomes apparent.

2. In II Thessalonians 3,10, Paul impresses upon the Christian community the maxim: *"If someone does not want to work, he also will not eat."* This apodictically formulated norm is also not without its completely definite, historically situated background. Paul almost certainly has in mind "eschatological enthusiasts," who have given up working in expectation of the imminent *parusia* of Christ and now live from the charity of the Christian community.[27] They pretend already to be able to emancipate themselves from the conditions of the penultimate, but at the same time take advantage of institutions, such as organized generosity inspired by love, which seek to relieve the worst material poverty in the still-existing world. And that amounts to the abuse of love, to life at the cost of those who recognize their fellow-human responsibility in the time of the penultimate, to which the obligation to work belongs, rather than opting out of it in enthusiastic blindness. In so far as this maxim encounters an analogous situation, it can also claim universal validity, which, however, only proves again its in principle relativity. Dealing with biblical maxims correctly stands or falls with correct mediation between the absolute and the relative, between divine and human justice, between love and law.[28]

[27] Gerhard Friedrich, *Die Briefe an die Galater, Epheser, Philipper, Kolosser, Thessalonicher und Philemon*, 2nd Ed., 1981, p. 274.

[28] Cf. Gottfried W. Locher, "Der Geltungsgrund der Zehn Gebote," in *Zeitschrift für Evangelische Ethik*, 13 (1969), pp. 129-45 and H.-G. Fritzsche, "Die Anfänge christlicher Ethik im Dekalog," *Theologische Literaturzeitung*, 98 (1973), cols. 162-70.

Even biblical maxims are maxims of human justice. Thus Luther himself could speak even of the Decalogue as of *"the Jews' Saxon mirror."*[29] Therefore, these maxims may never be raised to the level of the absolute, may never be equated with divine justice. Divine justice cannot be attained by means of such lofty ethical ambition and effort; it can only attain reality in such a way that God grants it in free grace to the human person and claims him for it. That is not to say that it is already up to the human person to arrive in the perfection of the absolute; but it does mean that he is nonetheless already demanded by the absolute to practice, to practice with social-ethical effectiveness, the humanity originating from faith, hope, and love in the relative of the present world. And that can happen only at the level of maxims. Thus Jesus — it is similar with Paul — by no means abolished the Decalogue through the command of love; he instead adapted it in its relativity as the expression of God's will for the time of the penultimate, though he certainly adapted it with intensity. This, of course, not as a legal path to salvation, as Judaism understood it, but nevertheless as a good path to a more humane life. A path is a good path only if it leads further, and thus does not end in a cul-de-sac. Therefore, the Decalogue should be adapted in view of new life-situations and life-insights in a flexible sense implying something more than itself.[30] Deuteronomy, as has become evident, in its adaptation of the Decalogue already went beyond its earlier version in Exodus. And similarly the Epistle to the Ephesians adopted the fifth commandment, according to which children should honor their parents, with the meaningful addition: "And, fathers, do not provoke your children to anger,"[31] etc. The parent-child relationship is undoubtedly elevated there to a higher fellow-human level through the reciprocal understanding of the fourth demand of the Decalogue. The ethical maxims of the Ten Commandments are to be taken seriously in this critical-flexible, and thus living sense, as Luther also most likely believed when he boldly dared to say that Christians would be authorized

[29] Martin Luther, "Wider die himmlischen Propheten, von den Bildern und Sakrament," 1525, in *Werke*, Vol. 18, Weimar, 1908, pp. 81, 14ff.

[30] Hans and Thea Schulze (*Zwischen Technik und Gott*, Stuttgart, 1982, pp. 81-210) show what that can mean in the contemporary social situation.

[31] Ephesians 6,4.

in faith to draw up new Decalogues, which would be better than those of Moses.[32]

What is true of the ethical commandments of the Decalogue, which are independent of particular situations and thus point toward the in principle, is even truer of the biblical maxims whose situational and thus tentative-pragmatic character is unmistakable. They are statutes of a decisively relative kind, and it would be disastrous to attempt to elevate them to the level of general or even absolutely valid commandments, simply because they are in the Bible. The history of the *canonical prohibition of interest*[33] in the Middle Ages shows where that can and must lead.

The canonical prohibition of interest is theologically based primarily on the maxim of Exodus 22,25, as well as its variant in Deuteronomy 23,19-20, together with the natural law argument, going back to Aristotle, that money cannot produce more money. In so far as it is about interest on consumer loans that are necessary for the survival of the needy, it is and was salutary to a high degree.[34] Loans of that kind have a vital, not an economic, potency. They serve the fundamental cost of living, not economic acquisition with its, albeit risky, opportunities for profit. To weight them down with interest would lead to an even greater burdening of those who are already poor. And that is intolerable for a theory of social ethics oriented towards the humanity originating from faith, hope, and love. In this specific respect, the maxim of Exodus 22,25 contains social-ethical relevance that must have massive implications today, especially for the loan policies of the industrialized nations towards the poorest developing nations.

The situation is otherwise with loans that serve acquisitive motives, and are just as typical as they are indispensable for the developed capital economy — which includes all economies, including socialist

[32] Martin Luther, "Thesen de fide," 1535, in *Werke*, Vol. 39/I, Weimar, 1926, pp. 47, 27ff.

[33] On the canonical prohibition of interest and its consequences in the Middle Ages, see Henri Pirenne, *Economic and Social History of Medieval Europe*, New York, 1956, esp. pp. 13-14 and pp. 116-39; Ernst Ramp, *op. cit.*, pp. 7-21.

[34] Henri Pirenne, *Economic and Social History of Medieval Europe*, New York, 1956, p. 120: "When it prohibited usury for religious reasones, the Church therefore rendered a signal service to the agrarian society of the early Middle Ages. It saved it from the affliction of consumption debts, from which the ancient world suffered so severely."

economies. These loans are about lending as providing economic power (according to Oswald von Nell-Breuning). Interest on such profit-bringing, gainful-employment-serving loans, in whatever form they are found, does not in itself mean the exploitative burdening of the poor. It is, rather, understood as the lender's participation in obtaining corporate profit by careful management, with the help of the loan. Certainly interest on loaned capital can lead indirectly to inhumane exploitation of workers, if the capital-compensations are unusually high and thus work to the disadvantage of the producers or the salary and wage recipients, or also the consumers. That, however, is not really a problem of interest, but one of distribution and redistribution. If one wishes to follow here the basic social intention of the Old Testament regulations prohibiting interest, then distribution or redistribution maxims that prevent the accumulation of wealth by virtue of income without work at the cost of the workers must be developed with the help of guidelines for justice led by the criteria of humanity, and enforced. The generalizing inclusion of productive and commercial loans in the Old Testament prohibition of interest would be, on the contrary, an unsuitable means for this purpose, because it would bring the complex economy of today to a standstill.

Already in the Late Middle Ages, one could recognize the counterproductive effects of the general prohibition of interest. To the degree that the economy developed and the need for loans grew, practices to circumvent it got started, and indeed inevitably, which ultimately the Church itself legalized — often reluctantly enough — through the development of a sublime casuistry.[35] Nevertheless, the

[35] Lending at interest was discouraged throughout the entire medieval period, which is already shown by the fact that the technical expression for it is "*usura*" ("usury"). But with the renaissance of distant trade in the High Middle Ages and the economic transformations connected to it, which made the initiation of trade loans, and later also production loans, indispensable, it became necessary to look at interest in a new light. Consequently, beginning in the thirteenth century, Church teachers searched for ways and means to moderate the absolute ban of interest. "It was discovered that in any advance of money involving either an eventual loss (*damnum emergens*), or a cessation of gain (*lucrum cessans*), or a risk of the capital (*periculum sortis*), an indemnity, or in other words, interest (*interesse*), was justifiable. Thus interest was simply legitimate usury, and it is easy to understand how delicate was the distinction between this tolerated usury and the prohibited usury, and what scope it left for interpretation by the judges. In commerce the 'letting out' of money was authorized by current practice. It was the rule at the fairs of Champagne and in general in the operations of commercial societies. In the fourteenth century the theologian,

interest-businesses, because they had traditionally been discriminated against religiously, remained forced away into an ominous, wild-growth gray zone. And precisely this contributed to medieval interest rates often reaching exorbitant heights of 50% or more.[36]

The case of absolutizing, or at least generalizing, the Pauline maxim that those who do not wish to work should not eat is similar. It has its relative correctness in relation to the enthusiastic wanderers who, like those on whom Paul set his sights in the Second Epistle to the Thessalonians, simply rejected the obligation to work as outdated and abandoned themselves to a parasitic existence. Yet, if understood absolutely, it would have to lead, according to logical consistency, to a legal duty of everyone to work, implemented without discrimination.[37] And that would have, in today's conditions, unacceptable consequences. Thus, for example, an unemployed person, who thoroughly wished to work and seriously strived to find a job that would conform to his level of education, his ability to serve, and his social level, would simply be compelled to accept any work whatsoever, even if it stood in no relationship whatsoever to his previous work and would require altering his personal and familial situation in life in an unreasonable way. The refusal to undertake that kind of a compulsion to work must not be equated with a simple refusal to work. The claim to validity of the maxim, "Those who do not wish to work shall also not eat," must find its limits in such cases. Nevertheless, it still has guiding significance precisely in its relativity. It requires modification only in the sense that working must be more rewarding than not working. Those who refuse to accept a particular kind of work, because they rightly feel that it is unreasonable, should expect a noticeable reduction of income. That leads to the new maxim that income from work is unambiguously to be preferred to income from not working. And, indeed, that must be true not only for income from unemployment, but also for income from capital ownership and pension entitlements. Moreover, the maxim that every person able to work is obligated to work must be amended by the additional maxim

Alvarus Palagius, states that the prohibition of usury is not applicable to the latter." (Pirenne, *Economic and Social History of Medieval Europe*, New York, 1956, p. 138).

[36] *Ibid.*, pp. 128 and 131.

[37] This conclusion was drawn in the 1918 Constitution of the Russian Socialist Federative Soviet Republic: "In order to exterminate all parasitic strata of society and to organize the economic life of the country, general compulsory labor is introduced" ("Constitution of the RSFSR," 10 July 1918, Chap. 2, Art. 3.f).

that each person willing to work has a right to work. It is no accident, but lies rather in the logical consistency of the matter, that the *Didache*, the oldest Christian instructions for the community, originating between 80 and 120 A.D., adapted the Pauline maxim of the obligation of everyone to work with the astonishing and historically-effective, explosive addition that precautions must be taken in the community "according to your understanding" that "no man shall live among you in idleness because he is a Christian."[38]

Therefore, it is necessary to understand and take seriously the social-ethically relevant biblical maxims in this way, not as absolute commandments of God, but rather in their relativity as the path to a better humanity. And, furthermore, it is necessary to examine them to see what they have to say today in their normative requirements, in order to modify them wherever necessary or to arrive at new maxims under this impulse, which is the impulse of the humanity originating from faith, hope, and love. All of that is ethics in the relative space of humanity, on the level of merely human law. But this law has, if it remains critically in motion towards a better humanity, an obligatory nature in its relativity, and indeed precisely from the absolute demand of love. For love does not set itself enthusiastically in the place of law, does not desire in reality-forgetting spontaneity to do without its institutionalization, as if the orderly assistance in the fight against personal and structural evil in society were eschatologically overtaken and therefore already obsolete. Or, in the words of Rudolf Hofmann: "There is no such thing as a path of love distinct from the path of law; there is only a path of love on the basis of and above and beyond the law."[39] Seen from this point of view, finding maxims for a responsible form of existence in the state, society, and economy becomes the most important task of a theory of Christian social ethics.

8.5 The Distinctive Characteristic of Christian Social Ethics

The fundamental considerations of 4.1-8.4 lead to the concretization of the theory of social ethics that will be attempted in the second,

[38] *Didache*, XII, 4; trans. Kirsopp Lake, in *The Apostolic Fathers*, Vol. I, Cambridge, Mass., 1912, p. 329.

[39] Rudolf Hofmann, "Die Bedeutung des Dekalogs, theologisch und geschichtlich, in der Sicht der katholischen Moraltheologie," *Zeitschrift für Evangelische Ethik*, 13 (1969), p. 244.

specifically economic-ethical volume, focusing on the order-political problem of the economy, and that must be treated at the level of maxims. This alone already means, as may have already become obvious, that our goal cannot be to chase after the utopian ideal of a perfect economy, freed from all personal and structural evil. The task that presents itself is far more modest. It can consist only in — and this certainly is already enough —preparing the way, with responsible safeguarding of the demands of human justice and economic correctness, for order-political maxims in the economy that intend a society of the relative good and just, and must in themselves create realistic space for a better humanity, including the economic fundamentals.

One should not, however, misunderstand this fundamental limitation of objectives. It is not at all about coming to terms in resignation with the imperfections in our society, let alone personal and structural evil, as it turns up again and again in economic conditions. If one were to be satisfied in this false sense, the relative would again be turned into the absolute, in that it would under the table become something unalterable and thus ultimate. For the eschatologically oriented humanity originating from faith, hope, and love, however, relative, imperfect, and thus merely human justice is never the ultimate; only the Kingdom of God is. Therefore, it cannot be otherwise than oriented in the relative towards divine justice. And in this orientation, which must manifest itself in critical distance from everything existing, it will develop a hopeful-powerful potential, which urgently strives for greater human justice over and above the status quo, of course always also keeping in mind that the possibly better human justice can never meet the absolute standard of divine justice. But this humanity will not misuse this eschatological reservation to disqualify what is better politically, just because it is not also perfect. It will, quite on the contrary, evaluate it politically, by means of the criterion of relative reception, as the relative compared to the relative, and accept it if it is able relatively to attain progress in the direction of more humanity in society. That is how Zwingli saw it in his day, and in that respect he is still exemplary today.

Finally, all of this means that the humanity originating from faith, hope, and love does not seek to make perfect justice, the Kingdom of God as that which is unenforceable, politically enforceable, but instead awaits it eschatologically as the new creation from God. And therein precisely exists the *specific characteristic* of the social ethics based upon it. This specific characteristic is not found in the maxims that non-Christians can also have as *ius humanum*. It is not found most truly even in the criteria that guide the humanity based on the Christian faith as its characteristic basic ethical principles. Ultimately, it lies in the fact that the humanity of faith with its ethics is never merely ethics,[40] never merely a reflected "ought" that calls for commitment here and now, *but is instead a given "is" that stems from what is coming*. In short, it is never merely an imperative that demands, but rather an indicative that gives and already now moves in the future (*Zu-Kunft*) of the Kingdom of God, which first comes. In other words, it is a gift that, even against all future hope, encourages in the coming hope and authorizes the task of searching for maxims of a better humanity and helping them achieve their breakthrough. Without this other dimension, Christian ethics ceases to be Christian; just as it would no longer be ethical if it attempted to eliminate the dimension of the "ought," in which the criteria and maxims exist, or indeed to rob them of their full seriousness. Only the dialectic of "is" and "ought," of grace and works constitutes the specific characteristic of Christian ethics. It is in that respect always and essentially a commandment, a call to action of the just in the world. But it is a commandment in the horizon of the Good News, from which everything lives.

[40] Gerhard Ebeling, "Luthers Kampf gegen die Moralisierung des Christlichen," *Reformatio*, 32 (1983), pp. 447-56, concludes rightly: "The ethical always runs into problems that are not concerns of ethics, because they cannot be dealt with ethically. The theological...in relation with the moral, is the human life-form, which excels and overflows in all directions" (p. 456).

BIBLIOGRAPHY

Albert, Hans, "Aufklärung und Steuerung: Gesellschaft, Wissenschaft und Politik in der Perspektive des kritischen Rationalismus," in Georg Lührs, *et al.*, eds., *Kritischer Rationalismus und Sozialdemokratie*, 2nd Ed., Berlin and Bonn-Bad Godesberg: Verlag J. H. W. Dietz, 1975, pp. 103-25.

—, "Ethik und Meta-Ethik: Das Dilemma der analytischen Moralphilosophie," in Hans Albert and Ernst Topitsch, eds., *Werturteilsstreit*, Darmstadt: Wissenschaftliche Buchgesellschaft, 1971, pp. 472-517.

—, "Normative Sozialwissenschaft und politische Rationalität: Zur Kontroverse über den Weisserschen Ansatz," *Archiv für Rechts- und Sozialphilosophie*, 55 (1969), pp. 567-82.

—, *Treatise on Critical Reason*, Princeton: Princeton University Press, 1985.

Albertz, Rainer, "Der Mensch als Hüter seiner Welt: Verfügungsrecht und Verantwortungspflicht als Elemente des Schöpfungsauftrages," *Die Mitarbeit*, 25 (1976), pp. 306-21.

Aristotle, *Nicomachean Ethics*, trans. W. D. Ross, in *The Basic Works of Aristotle*, ed. Richard McKeon, New York: Random House, 1941, pp. 927-1112.

—, *Politics*, trans. Carnes Lord, Chicago: University of Chicago Press, 1984.

Barth, Karl, *The Epistle to the Romans*, London: Oxford University Press, 1933.

—, "The Christian's Place in Society," in Karl Barth, *The Word of God and the Word of Man*, trans. D. Horton, London: Hodder and Stoughton, 1935, pp. 272-327.

—, *Church and State*, trans. G. R. Howe, London: Student Christian Movement Press, 1939.

—, *Church Dogmatics*, 4 vols., ed. G. W. Bromiley and T. F. Torrance, trans. G. W. Bromiley, *et al.*, Edinburgh: T. & T. Clark, 1955-77.

—, *Gesamtausgabe*, V: *Briefe: Karl Barth — Eduard Thurneysen Briefwechsel*, Vol. II: 1921-1930, ed. Eduard Thurneysen, Zürich: Theologischer Verlag, 1974.

Barz, Helmut, *Stichwort: Selbstverwirklichung: Ehrenrettung eines Modewortes*, Stuttgart and Berlin: Kreuz Verlag, 1981.

Basaglia, Franco, ed., *Die negierte Institution oder die Gemeinschaft der Ausgeschlossenen: ein Experiment der Psychiatrischen Klinik in Görz*, Frankfurt am Main: Suhrkamp Verlag, 1971.

Bayer, Oswald, "Schöpfung als 'Rede an die Kreatur durch die Kreatur': Die Frage nach dem Schlüssel zum Buch der Natur und Geschichte," *Evangelische Theologie*, 40 (1980), pp. 316-33.

Beck, Ulrich, *Objektivität und Normativität: Die Theorie-Praxis-Debatte in der modernen deutschen und amerikanischen Soziologie*, Reinbek bei Hamburg: Rowohlt Taschenbuch Verlag, 1974.

Berdiajev, Nikolai, *Von der Bestimmung des Menschen: Versuch einer paradoxalen Ethik*, Bern and Leipzig: Gotthelf Verlag, 1935.

Binswanger, Hans Christoph, Werner Geissberger, and Theo Ginsburg, eds., *Der NAWU-Report: Wege aus der Wohlstandsfalle: Strategien gegen Arbeitslosigkeit und Umweltkrise*, Frankfurt am Main: S. Fischer Verlag, 1978.

Birnbacher, Dieter and Norbert Hoerster, eds., *Texte zur Ethik*, Munich: Deutscher Taschenbuch Verlag, 1976.

Bloch, Ernst, *The Principle of Hope*, trans. Neville Plaice, Stephen Plaice, and Paul Knight, 3 vols., Cambridge, Mass.: MIT Press, 1995.

Bock, Martin, *"Politia Christi": Ethik des Politischen bei Ernst Wolf zwischen Zwei-Reiche-Dualismus und Christokratie*, Hannover: Copy Team, 1983.

Bondolfi, Alberto, *Teoria critica ed etica cristiana*, Bologna: Edizioni Dehoniane, 1979.

Bonhoeffer, Dietrich, *Ethics*, trans. Neville Horton Smith, New York: Macmillan, 1955.

—, *Letters and Papers from Prison*, 3rd Ed., New York: Macmillan, 1971.

Boulding, Kenneth E., "Ökonomie als eine Moralwissenschaft," in Winfried Vogt, ed., *Seminar: Politische Ökonomie: Zur Kritik der herrschenden Nationalökonomie*, Frankfurt am Main: Suhrkamp Verlag, 1973, pp. 103-25.

Bowman, John Wick, *The Intention of Jesus*, Philadelphia: Westminster Press, 1943.

Brakelmann, Günter, *Abschied vom Unverbindlichen: Gedanken eines Christen zum Demokratischen Sozialismus*, Gütersloh: Gütersloher Verlagshaus Gerd Mohn, 1976.

Brunner, Emil, *Christianity and Civilisation*, New York: C. Scribner's Sons, 1948-49; New York: AMS Press, 1981.

—, *Eternal Hope*, trans. Harold Knight, Philadelphia: Westminster Press, 1954; Westport, Conn.: Greenwood Press, 1972.

—, *The Divine Imperative: A Study in Christian Ethics*, trans. Olive Wyon, New York: Macmillan, 1937; Philadelphia: Westminster Press, 1947.

—, *Justice and the Social Order*, trans. Mary Hottinger, New York: Harper & Brothers, 1945.

—, *Man in Revolt: A Christian Anthropology*, trans. Olive Wyon, New York: C. Scribner's Sons, 1939; Philadelphia: Westminster Press, 1947.

Buber, Martin, *I and Thou*, trans. Ronald Gregor Smith, 2nd. Ed., New York: Charles Scribner's Sons, 1958.

—, *Zwei Glaubensweisen*, Zürich: Manesse Verlag, 1950.
Bubner, Rüdiger, "Was ist kritische Theorie?" *Philosophische Rundschau*, 16 (1969), pp. 213-49.
Bultmann, Rudolf, *Jesus*, 2nd Ed., Munich and Hamburg: Siebenstern Taschenbuch Verlag, 1965.
Burckhardt, Jacob, *Weltgeschichtliche Betrachtungen*, Stuttgart: Alfred Kröner Verlag, 1963.
Callies, Rolf-Peter, "Dialogisches Recht," *Evangelische Theologie* 25 (1965), pp. 297-323.
Camus, Albert, *L'homme révolté*, Paris: Gallimard, 1951.
—, *Le Mythe de Sisyphe: Essai sur l'absurde*, Paris: Gallimard, 1942.
"Constitution of the Russian Socialist Federated Soviet Republic," 10 July 1918.
Conzelmann, Hans, *Jesus: The Classic Article from RGG Expanded and Updated*, trans. J. Raymond Lord, ed. John Reumann, Philadelphia: Fortress Press, 1973.
Cox, Harvey, ed., *The Situation Ethics Debate*, Philadelphia: Westminster Press, 1968.
Dannemann, Ulrich, "Karl Barth und der religiöse Sozialismus," *Evangelische Theologie*, 37 (1977), pp. 127-48.
—, *Theologie und Politik im Denken Karl Barths*, Munich: C. Kaiser Verlag and Mainz: Matthias-Grünewald-Verlag, 1977.
"Declaration of the Rights of Man and of the Citizen," 26 August 1789.
"Didache," trans. Kirsopp Lake, in *The Apostolic Fathers*, Vol. I, ed. G. P. Goold, Cambridge, Mass.: Harvard University Press, 1912, pp. 303-33.
Drucker, Peter F., *The Practice of Management*, New York: Harper & Row, 1954.
Ebel, Marianne and Pierre Fiala, *Sous le consensus, la xénophobie: Paroles, arguments, contexts "1961-1981"*, Lausanne: Institut de science politique, 1983.
Ebeling, Gerhard, *Dogmatik des christlichen Glaubens*, 3 vols., Tübingen: J. C. B. Mohr (Paul Siebeck), 1979.
—, *Kritischer Rationalismus? Zu Hans Alberts "Traktat über kritische Vernunft,"* Tübingen: J. C. B. Mohr (Paul Siebeck), 1973.
—, "Luthers Kampf gegen die Moralisierung des Christlichen," *Reformatio*, 32 (1983), pp. 447-56.
—, "Das Problem des Bösen als Prüfstein der Anthropologie," in Ebeling, *Wort und Glaube*, Vol. III, Tübingen: J. C. B. Mohr (Paul Siebeck), 1975, pp. 205-24.
—, "Theologie zwischen reformatorischem Sündenverständnis und heutiger Einstellung zum Bösen," in Ebeling *Wort und Glaube*, Vol. III, Tübingen: J. C. B. Mohr (Paul Siebeck), 1975, pp. 173-204.
—, *Was heißt Glauben?* Tübingen: J. C. B. Mohr (Paul Siebeck), 1958.

Ebner, Ferdinand, *Schriften*, Vol. I: *Fragmente, Aufsätze, Aphorismen: Zu einer Pneumatologie des Wortes*, ed Franz Seyr, Munich: Kösel-Verlag, 1963.

Feil, Ernst and Rudolf Weth, eds., *Diskussion zur "Theologie der Revolution"*, Munich: C. Kaiser Verlag and Mainz: Matthias-Grünewald-Verlag, 1969.

Feyerabend, Paul K., *Against Method: Outline of an Anarchistic Theory of Knowledge*, London: New Left Books, 1975; London: Verso Books, 1988.

Fichte, Johann Gottlieb, *Grundlage der gesamten Wissenschaftslehre* (1794), Hamburg: Verlag von Felix Meiner, 1961.

Fletcher, Joseph, *Moral Responsibility: Situation Ethics at Work*, Philadelphia: Westminster Press, 1967.

—, *Situation Ethics: The New Morality*, Philadelphia: Westminster Press, 1966.

Flohr, Heiner and Klaus Lompe, eds., *Wissenschaftler und Politiker — Partner oder Gegner? Gespräch und Dokumentation*, Göttingen: Verlag Otto Schwartz, 1967.

Foot, Philippa, ed., *Theories of Ethics*, Oxford: Oxford University Press, 1967.

Frankena, William K., *Ethics*, 2nd Ed., Englewood Cliffs, N. J., Prentice-Hall, 1973.

Frey, Christofer, "Gerechtigkeit," in Theodor Schober, Martin Honecker, and Horst Dahlhaus, eds., *Evangelisches Soziallexikon*, 7th Ed., Stuttgart and Berlin: Kreuz Verlag, 1980, Cols. 490-94.

—, "Humane Erfahrung und selbstkritische Vernunft: Marginalien zum 'Versuch zu einer Theorie ethischer Urteilsbildung'," *Zeitschrift für Evangelische Ethik*, 22 (1978), pp. 200-13.

—, "Theologische Kriterien für die Gestaltung und Entwicklung der Wirtschaft, in Institute of Social Sciences of the Protestant Church in Germany, ed., *Zwischen Wachstum und Lebensqualität: Wirtschaftsethische Fragen angesichts der Krisen wirtschaftlichen Wachstums*, Munich: C. Kaiser Verlag, 1980, pp. 116-55.

Friedrich, Gerhard, *Die Briefe an die Galater, Epheser, Philipper, Kolosser, Thessalonicher und Philemon*, 2nd Ed., trans. Jürgen Becker, Hans Conzelmann, and Gerhard Friedrich, Göttingen: Vandenhoeck & Ruprecht, 1981.

Fritsch, Bruno, "Private und volkswirtschaftliche Kosten," in Erwin von Beckerath and Herbert Giersch, eds., *Probleme der normativen Ökonomik und der wirtschaftspolitischen Beratung*, Berlin: Duncker & Humblot, 1963, pp. 211-44.

Fritzsche, H.-G., "Die Anfänge christlicher Ethik im Dekalog," *Theologische Literaturzeitung*, 98 (1973), pp. 162-70.

Fromm, Erich, *The Anatomy of Human Destructiveness*, New York: Holt, Rinehart & Winston, 1973.

—, *To Have Or To Be?* New York: Harper and Row, 1976.
—, *The Heart of Man: Its Genius for Good and Evil*, New York: Harper & Row, 1964.
—, *The Revolution of Hope: Toward a Humanized Technology*, New York: Harper & Row, 1968.
Funke, Gerhard, "Ethos: Gewohnheit, Sitte, Sittlichkeit," *Archiv für Rechts- und Sozialphilosophie*, 47 (1961), pp. 1-80.
Furger, Franz, *Begründung des Sittlichen: Ethische Strömungen der Gegenwart*, Fribourg: Imba Verlag, 1975.
—, "Zur Begründung eines christlichen Ethos: Forschungstendenzen in der katholischen Moraltheologie," in Furger, ed., *Theologische Berichte*, IV, Zürich, Einsiedeln, Cologne: Benziger Verlag, 1974, pp. 11-87.
German Academy of Science, ed., *Deutsches Wörterbuch von Jacob Grimm und Wilhelm Grimm*, Vol. IV, Sec. I, Part 4, Leipzig: Verlag von S. Hirzel, 1949.
Geuss, Raymond, *Die Idee einer kritischen Theorie*, Meisenheim: Verlag Anton Hain, 1983.
Geyer, Carl-Friedrich, *Kritische Theorie: Max Horkheimer und Theodor W. Adorno*, Freiburg im Breisgau and Munich: Verlag Karl Alber, 1982.
Giersch, Herbert, *Allgemeine Wirtschaftspolitik*, Vol. I: *Grundlagen*, Wiesbaden: Betriebswirtschaftlicher Verlag Dr. T. Gabler, 1961.
Goethe, Johann Wolfgang, *Gedenkausgabe der Werke, Briefe und Gespräche*, Vol. 19: *Briefe der Jahre 1786-1814*, Zürich: Artemis-Verlag, 1949.
Gollwitzer, Helmut, *Forderungen der Freiheit: Aufsätze und Reden zur politischen Ethik*, Munich: C. Kaiser Verlag, 1962.
Goodpaster, Kenneth E. and John B. Matthews, Jr., "Can a Corporation Have a Conscience?" *Harvard Business Review*, 60, Jan-Feb 1982, pp. 132-34.
Goppelt, Leonhard, "Prinzipien neutestamentlicher und systematischer Sozialethik heute," in Jörg Baur, Leonhard Goppelt, and Georg Kretschmar, eds., *Die Verantwortung der Kirche in der Gesellschaft: Eine Studienarbeit des Ökumenischen Ausschusses der Vereinigten Evangelisch-Lutherischen Kirche Deutschlands*, Stuttgart: Calwer Verlag, 1973, pp. 7-30.
Gorz, André, *Farewell to the Working Class: An Essay on Post-Industrial Socialism*, trans. Michael Sonenscher, London: Pluto Press, 1982.
Grosser, Alfred, *Der schmale Grat der Freiheit: Eine neue Ethik für eine neue Zeit?* Munich and Vienna: Carl Hanser Verlag, 1981.
Guardini, Romano, *Welt und Person: Versuch zur christlichen Lehre vom Menschen*, 2nd Ed., Würzburg: Werkbund-Verlag, 1940.
Habermas, Jürgen, *Knowledge and Human Interests*, trans. Jeremy J. Shapiro, Boston: Beacon Press, 1971.
Häring, Bernhard, *The Law of Christ*, Vol. III, trans. Edwin G. Kaiser, Westminster, Maryland: Newman Press, 1966.

Das Gesetz Christi: Moraltheologie, dargestellt für Priester und Laien, Vol. III, 7th Ed., Freiburg im Breisgau: Erich Wewel Verlag, 1963.

Hegel, Georg Wilhelm Friedrich, *The Philosophy of History*, trans. J. Sibree, New York: Dover Publications, 1956.

—, *Hegel's Philosophy of Right*, trans. T. M. Knox, Oxford: Clarendon Press, 1942.

Hempel, Johannes, *Das Ethos des Alten Testaments*, 2nd Ed., Berlin: Verlag Alfred Töpelmann, 1964.

Hensel, K. Paul, "Planwirtschaft," in Erwin von Beckerath, *et al.*, eds., *Handwörterbuch der Sozialwissenschaften*, Vol. VIII, Stuttgart: Gustav Fischer, Tübingen: J. C. B. Mohr (Paul Siebeck), and Göttingen: Vandenhoeck & Ruprecht, 1964, pp. 325-38.

Hertz, Anselm, *et al.*, eds. *Handbuch der christlichen Ethik*, 3. Vols., Freiburg im Breisgau, Basel, Vienna: Herder Verlag and Gütersloh: Gütersloher Verlagshaus Gerd Mohn, 1979-1982.

Hesse, Helmut, "Ökonomische Kriterien zur Beurteilung konkurrierender Lösungsmodelle," *Handbuch der christlichen Ethik*, Vol. III, 1982, pp. 337-49.

Hoerster, Norbert, Foreword to William K. Frankena, *Analytische Ethik: Eine Einführung*, Munich, 1972; German translation of *Ethics*, Englewood Cliffs: Prentice-Hall, 1963.

Höffe, Otfried, "Bemerkungen zu einer Theorie sittlicher Urteilsfindung (H. E. Tödt)," *Zeitschrift für Evangelische Ethik*, 22 (1978), pp. 181-87.

—, "Natur als Orientierungspunkt der Ethik," in *Liberal: Beiträge zur Entwicklung einer freiheitlichen Ordnung*, 25 (1983), pp. 324-335.

—, "Rawls' Theorie der politisch-sozialen Gerechtigkeit," *John Rawls: Gerechtigkeit als Fairneß*, ed. Otfried Höffe, Freiburg im Breisgau and Munich: Karl Alber, 1977, pp. 16-33.

—, "Sittliche Grenzen psychologischer Forschung: Zur Perspektive philosophischer Ethik," in Lenelis Kruse and Martin Kumpf, eds., *Psychologische Grundlagenforschung: Ethik und Recht*, Bern, Stuttgart, Vienna: Verlag Hans Huber, 1981, pp. 237-61.

—, ed., *Theorie-Diskussion über John Rawls' Theorie der Gerechtigkeit*, Frankfurt am Main: Suhrkamp Verlag, 1977.

—, "A Theory of Justice," *Philosophische Rundschau*, 21 (1974), pp. 187-208.

Hofmann, Rudolf, "Die Bedeutung des Dekalogs, theologisch und geschichtlich, in der Sicht der katholischen Moraltheologie," *Zeitschrift für Evangelische Ethik*, 13 (1969), pp. 230-45.

Hohlfeld, Winfried, *Umweltkrise: Herausforderung der Kirche*, Stuttgart: Quell Verlag, 1974.

Holz, Hans Heinz, "Der Irrtum der 'Großen Weigerung': Zu Herbert Marcuses kritischer Theorie der Industriegesellschaft," *Blätter für deutsche und internationale Politik*, 13 (1968), pp. 46-61.

Honecker, Martin, *Konzept einer sozialethischen Theorie: Grundfragen evangelischer Sozialethik*, Tübingen: J. C. B. Mohr (Paul Siebeck), 1971.

—, "Liebe und Vernunft," *Zeitschrift für Theologie und Kirche*, 68 (1971), pp. 227-59.

—, "Das Problem der Eigengesetzlichkeit," *Zeitschrift für Theologie und Kirche*, 73 (1976), pp. 92-130.

—, "Sozialethik," in Hermann Kunst, Roman Herzog, and Wilhelm Schneemelcher, eds., *Evangelisches Staatslexikon*, 2nd Ed., Stuttgart and Berlin: Kreuz-Verlag, 1975, cols. 2350-62.

—, *Sozialethik zwischen Tradition und Vernunft*, Tübingen: J. C. B. Mohr (Paul Siebeck), 1977.

—, "Vernunft, Gewissen, Glaube: Das spezifisch Christliche im Horizont der Ethik," *Zeitschrift für Theologie und Kirche*, 77 (1980), pp. 325-44.

Horst, Friedrich, "Der Mensch als Ebenbild Gottes," in Horst, *Gottes Recht: Gesammelte Studien zum Recht im Alten Testament*, ed. Hans Walter Wolff, Munich: C. Kaiser Verlag, 1961, pp. 222-34.

Huber, Gerhard, "Der Fortschrittsgedanke in Philosophie und Geistesgeschichte," in Maja Svilar, ed., *Was ist Fortschritt? Kulturhistorische Vorlesungen an der Universität Bern 1978/79*, Bern, Frankfurt am Main, Las Vegas: Verlag Peter Lang, 1979, pp. 9-25.

—, *Gegenwärtigkeit der Philosophie: Vorträge und Aufsätze*, Basel and Stuttgart: Birkhäuser Verlag, 1975.

Huber, Wolfgang, "Freiheit und Institution: Überlegungen zu einem Grundproblem der Sozialethik," *Evangelische Theologie*, 40 (1980), pp. 302-15.

—, "Sozialethik als Verantwortungsethik," in Alberto Bondolfi, Werner Heierle, and Dietmar Mieth, eds., *Ethos des Alltags* (Festschrift for Stephan H. Pfürtner), Zürich, Einsiedeln, Cologne: Benziger Verlag, 1983, pp. 55-76.

Hygen, Johan B., "Das Böse," in Gerhard Krause und Gerhard Müller, eds., *Theologische Realenzyklopädie*, Vol. VII, Berlin and New York: Walter de Gruyter, 1981, pp. 8-17.

Ilting, Karl-Heinz, "Naturrecht," in Otto Brunner, Werner Conze, and Reinhart Koselleck, eds., *Geschichtliche Grundbegriffe: Historisches Lexikon zur politisch-sozialen Sprache in Deutschland*, Vol. IV, Stuttgart: Klett-Cotta, 1978, pp. 245-313.

Jöhr, Walter Adolf, *Gespräche über Wissenschaftstheorie*, Tübingen: J. C. B. Mohr (Paul Siebeck), 1973.

Jonas, Hans, *The Imperative of Responsibility: In Search of an Ethics for the Technological Age*, trans. Hans Jonas with the collaboration of David Herr, Chicago: University of Chicago Press, 1984.

Kaiser, Helmut, "Normative Erweiterung ökonomischer Rationalität," *Zeitschrift für Theologie und Kirche*, 28 (1984), pp. 285-320.

Kant, Immanuel, *Groundwork for the Metaphysics of Morals*, ed. and trans. Allen W. Wood, New Haven: Yale University Press, 2002.

—, *Lectures on Logic*, trans. and ed. J. Michael Young, Cambridge: Cambridge University Press, 1992.

—, *The Metaphysical Elements of Justice: Part I of The Metaphysics of Morals*, trans. John Ladd, New York: Macmillan, 1985.

Karg, Siegfried, "Arthur Richs Sozialethik im Spiegel seiner Publikationen," in Theodor Strohm, ed., *Christliche Wirtschaftsethik vor neuen Aufgaben* (Festschrift for Arthur Rich), Zürich: Theologischer Verlag, 1980, pp. 471-507.

Karrenberg, Friedrich, "Gesellschaftspolitische Probleme bei Karl Barth," in *Antwort* (Festschrift for Karl Barth), Zollikon-Zürich: Evangelischer Verlag, 1956, pp. 357-68.

—, "Das Problem der 'Eigengesetzlichkeit'," in Karrenberg, *Gestalt und Kritik des Westens: Beiträge zur christlichen Sozialethik heute*, Stuttgart: Kreuz-Verlag, 1959, p. 102-33.

Käsemann, Ernst, *Commentary on Romans*, trans. Geoffrey W. Bromiley, Grand Rapids, Eerdmans, 1980.

—, "Römer 13,1-7 in unserer Generation," *Zeitschrift für Theologie und Kirche*, 56 (1959), p. 316-76.

Katterle, Siegfried, "Die Kooperation von Sozialwissenschaft und Sozialethik auf der Grundlage einer kritischen Philosophie," *Zeitschrift für Evangelische Ethik*, 20 (1976), pp. 191-206; and in Theodor Strohm, ed., *Christliche Wirtschaftsethik vor neuen Aufgaben* (Festschrift for Arthur Rich), Zürich: Theologischer Verlag, 1980, pp. 125-43.

—, "Sozialethik im Dialog mit dem Kritizismus," *Die Mitarbeit*, 23 (1974), pp. 353-58.

—, *Sozialwissenschaft und Sozialethik: Logische und theoretische Probleme praktischer Sozialwissenschaften, besonders christlicher Soziallehren*, Göttingen: Verlag Otto Schwartz, 1972.

Kerber, Walter, "Positives Recht versus Naturrecht?" in *Handbuch der christlichen Ethik*, Vol. II, 1979, pp. 300-12.

—, ed., *Sittliche Normen: Zum Problem ihrer allgemeinen und unwandelbaren Geltung*, Düsseldorf: Patmos Verlag, 1982.

Kinsey, Alfred C., *et al.*, *Sexual Behavior in the Human Male*, Philadelphia: W. B. Saunders, 1948.

—, *Sexual Behavior in the Human Female*, Philadelphia: W. B. Saunders, 1953.

Klein, Josef, "Kasuistik, IV: Grundsätzlich," in *Die Religion in Geschichte und Gegenwart*, Vol. III, 3rd Ed., cols. 1169-1171.

Kleinewefers, Henner, "Rationalität und ökonomisches Normalverhalten," Pub. No. 7 of the Institute of Economics and Social Sciences of the University of Fribourg, 1981.

Kluge, Friedrich, *Etymologisches Wörterbuch der deutschen Sprache*, 18th Ed., Berlin: Walter de Gruyter, 1960.

Kluxen, Wolfgang, "Moralische Aspekte der Energie- und Umweltfrage," in *Handbuch der christlichen Ethik*, Vol. III, 1982, pp. 379-424.

Koch, Traugott, "Das Böse als theologisches Problem," *Kerygma und Dogma*, 24 (1978), pp. 285-320.

Kohnstamm, Max, "Person und Struktur am Beispiel internationaler Beziehungen," *Zeitschrift für Evangelische Ethik*, 14 (1970), pp. 193-203.

Kolakowski, Leszek, *Leben trotz Geschichte*, Munich and Zürich: R. Piper Verlag, 1977.

—, *Der revolutionäre Geist*, 2nd Ed., Stuttgart, Berlin, Cologne, Mainz: Verlag W. Kohlhammer, 1977.

Koller, Peter, "Rawls' Theorie der Gerechtigkeit und ihre Kritik," *Kriminalsoziologische Bibliographie*, 5 (1978), pp. 31-43.

Korff, Wilhelm, "Institutionstheorie: Die sittlichen Struktur gesellschaftlicher Lebensformen," *Handbuch der christlichen Ethik*, Vol. I, 1979, pp. 168-76.

Kramer, Rolf, *Die christliche Verantwortung in der sozialen Marktwirtschaft*, Stuttgart: J. F. Steinkopf Verlag, 1973.

Kreck, Walter, "Analogia fidei oder analogia entis?" in *Antwort* (Festschrift for Karl Barth), Zollikon-Zürich: Evangelischer Verlag, 1956, pp. 272-86.

—, *Grundfragen christlicher Ethik*, Munich: C. Kaiser Verlag, 1975.

Kümmel, Werner Georg, *Verheißung und Erfüllung: Untersuchungen zur eschatologischen Verkündigung Jesu*, 3rd Ed., Zürich: Zwingli-Verlag, 1956.

Küng, Emil, *Wirtschaft und Gerechtigkeit: Sozialethische Probleme im Lichte der Volkswirtschaftslehre*, Tübingen: J. C. B. Mohr (Paul Siebeck), 1967.

Küng, Guido, "Les fondements méthodologiques de la théorie de la justice de John Rawls," *Revue de théologie et de philosophie*, 111 (1979), pp. 279-89.

Küng, Hans, *Christ sein*, Munich: R. Piper Verlag, 1974.

Kutter, Hermann, *Hermann Kutter in seinen Briefen 1883-1931*, ed. Max Geiger and Andreas Lindt, Munich: C. Kaiser Verlag, 1983.

—, *Sie müssen! Ein offenes Wort an die christliche Gesellschaft*, Zürich: Verlag Müller, 1904.

de Lange, Harry M., "Die Kirchen und die Einheit Europa," *Zeitschrift für Evangelische Ethik* 27 (1983), pp. 41-49.

Lattmann, Charles, *Die verhaltenswissenschaftlichen Grundlagen der Führung des Mitarbeiters*, Bern and Stuttgart: Verlag Paul Haupt, 1982.

Lefringhausen, Klaus, "Wirtschaftsethik heute," *Theologische Rundschau*, 35 (1970), pp. 164-78.

Liedke, Gerhard, *Im Bauch des Fisches: Ökologische Theologie,* Stuttgart and Berlin: Kreuz Verlag, 1979.

Link, Christian, "Überlegungen zum Problem der Norm in der theologischen Ethik," *Zeitschrift für Evangelische Ethik,* 22 (1978), pp. 188-99.

Locher, Gottfried W., "Der Geltungsgrund der Zehn Gebote," *Zeitschrift für Evangelische Ethik,* 13 (1969), pp. 129-45.

Lochman, Jan Milič and Jürgen Moltmann, eds., *Gottes Recht und Menschenrechte: Studien und Empfehlungen des Reformierten Weltbundes,* Neukirchen-Vluyn: Neukirchener Verlag, 1976.

Lochman, Jan Milič, *Christus oder Prometheus? Die Kernfrage des christlich-marxistischen Dialogs und die Christologie,* Hamburg: Furche-Verlag, 1972.

—, "Das sogenannte Böse: Zur Aktualität des biblischen Sündenbegriffs," *Reformatio,* 32 (1983), pp. 456-61.

Løgstrup, Knud Eiler, "Betrachtungen über die englische Moralphilosophie des 20. Jahrhunderts," *Theologische Rundschau,* 39 (1975), pp. 139-55.

—, *The Ethical Demand,* trans. Theodor I. Jensen, Philadelphia: Fortress Press, 1971.

—, "Ist die ethische Forderung durch ihre Radikalität destruktiv?" *Zeitschrift für Theologie und Kirche,* 52 (1955), pp. 104-23.

Lorenz, Konrad, *On Aggression,* trans. Marjorie Kerr Wilson, New York: Hartcourt, Brace & World, 1966.

Löwith, Karl, *From Hegel to Nietzsche: The Revolution in Nineteenth Century Thought,* trans. David E. Green, New York: Holt, Rinehart, Winston, 1964.

Luther, Martin, "A Treatise on Christian Liberty," in Vergilius Ferm, ed., *Classics of Protestantism,* New York: Philosophical Library, 1959, pp. 39-66.

—, *D. Martin Luthers Werke: Kritische Gesamtausgabe,* 120 vols., Weimar: Verlag Hermann Böhlaus Nachfolger, 1883 ff.

Lutz, Friedrich A., *Politische Überzeugungen und nationalökonomische Theorie: Züricher Vorträge,* Tübingen: J. C. B. Mohr (Paul Siebeck), 1971.

Marquardt, Friedrich-Wilhelm, *Theologie und Sozialismus: Das Beispiel Karl Barths,* Munich: C. Kaiser Verlag and Mainz: Matthias-Grünewald-Verlag, 1972.

Marsch, Wolf-Dieter, "Christologische Begründung des Rechts? K. Barths Theologie des Rechts und die Theorie der Institutionen," *Evangelische Theologie,* 17 (1957), pp. 145-70 & 193-218.

—, "Glauben und Handeln in der 'technisch-organisatorischen Daseinsverfassung'," *Monatsschrift für Pastoraltheologie,* 52 (1963), pp. 269-85.

—, "Institution," in *Die Religion in Geschichte und Gegenwart,* Vol. III, 3rd Ed., cols. 783-85.

Marx, Karl and Friedrich Engels, *The Collected Works of Karl Marx and Frederick Engels,* 50 Vols., New York: International Publishers; London: Lawrence & Wishart; Moscow: Progress Publishers, 1975-.

Mattmüller, Markus, *Leonhard Ragaz und der Religiöse Sozialismus: Eine Biographie,* Vol I: *Die Entwicklung der Persönlichkeit und des Werkes bis ins Jahr* 1913, Zollikon-Zürich: Evangelischer Verlag, 1957.

Meadows, Donella H., *et al., The Limits to Growth: A Report for the Club of Rome's Project on the Predicament of Mankind,* New York: Universe Books, 1972.

van Melsen, Andreas G. M., *Physical Science and Ethics: A Reflection on the Relationship between Nature and Morality,* Pittsburgh: Duquesne University Press, 1967.

Mesarovic, Mihailo and Eduard Pestel, *Mankind at the Turning Point,* New York: E. P. Dutton, 1974.

Moltmann, Jürgen, *Perspektiven der Theologie: Gesammelte Aufsätze,* Munich: C. Kaiser Verlag and Mainz: Matthias-Grünewald-Verlag, 1968.

Moore, George Edward, *Principia Ethica,* Cambridge: Cambridge University Press, 1903.

—, *Some Main Problems of Philosophy,* London: George Allen and Unwin, 1953.

Mostert, Walter, "Gott und das Böse: Bemerkungen zu einer vielschichtigen Frage," *Zeitschrift für Theologie und Kirche,* 77 (1980), pp. 453-78.

Muelder, Walter George, *Religion and Economic Responsibility,* New York: Charles Scribner's Sons, 1953.

Müller, Eberhard, *Bekehrung der Strukturen: Konflikte und ihre Bewältigung in den Bereichen der Gesellschaft,* Zürich: Theologischer Verlag and Hamburg: Furche-Verlag, 1973.

Müller-Armack, Alfred, *Religion und Wirtschaft: Geistesgeschichtliche Hintergründe unserer europäischen Lebensform,* Stuttgart: W. Kohlhammer Verlag, 1959.

Munby, Denis Lawrence, *Christ und Wirtschaft,* Gütersloh: Gütersloher Verlagshaus Gerd Mohn, 1962.

Niebuhr, Reinhold, *Christian Realism and Political Problems,* New York: Charles Scribner's Sons, 1953.

—, *Faith and History: A Comparison of Christian and Modern Views of History,* New York: Charles Scribner's Sons, 1949.

—, "Freiheit und Gleichheit," in Heinz-Dietrich Wendland and Theodor Strohm, eds., *Politik und Ethik,* Darmstadt: Wissenschaftliche Buchgesellschaft, 1969, pp. 257-72.

—, *Moral Man and Immoral Society: A Study in Ethics and Politics,* New York: Charles Scribner's Sons, 1932.

—, *Pious and Secular America,* New York: Charles Scribner's Sons, 1958.

—, *Young Reinhold Niebuhr: His Early Writings, 1911-1931,* ed. William G. Chrystal, St. Louis: Eden Publishing House, 1977.

Nietzsche, Friedrich, *The Gay Science*, trans., with commentary, by W. Kaufmann, New York: Vintage Books, 1974.

Noth, Martin, *Das zweite Buch Mose: Exodus*, Göttingen: Vandenhoeck & Ruprecht, 1959.

Olimart, Karl Edgar, *Der Begriff der Schöpfungsordnung in der evangelischen Theologie der Gegenwart*, Essen: Druck Heinrich Geck, 1933.

von Oppen, Dietrich, *Das personal Zeitalter: Formen und Grundlagen gesellschaftlichen Lebens im 20. Jahrhundert*, Stuttgart: Kreuz-Verlag, 1964.

Ott, Walter, "Grundzüge der Gerechtigkeitstheorie von John Rawls," in Ulrich Häfelin, *et al.*, eds., *Festschrift zum 70. Geburtstag von Hans Nef*, Zürich: Schulthess Polygraphischer Verlag, 1981, pp. 249-62.

van Oyen, Hendrik, *Ethik des Alten Testaments*, Gütersloh: Gütersloher Verlagshaus Gerd Mohn, 1967.

—, "Gesinnungsethik," in *Die Religion in Geschichte und Gegenwart*, Vol. II, 3rd Ed., cols. 1537-38.

Pascal, Blaise, *Pensées*, trans. A. J. Krailsheimer, Harmondsworth: Penguin Books, 1966.

Pestalozzi, Heinrich, *Sämtliche Werke*, Vol. XII, Berlin: Walter de Gruyter, 1938.

Peter, Hans-Balz, Hans Ruh, and Rudolf Höhn, *Die neue internationale Wirtschaftsordnung: Test für die Schweiz*, Bern and Lausanne: Institut für Sozialethik des Schweizerischen Evangelischen Kirchenbundes, 1979.

Pfeiffer, Arnold, "Kutter und Ragaz: Variationen des religiösen Sozialismus," *Neue Zeitschrift für systematische Theologie und Religionsphilosophie*, 21 (1979), pp. 160-76.

Pieper, Annemarie, "Analytische Ethik: Ein Überblick über die seit 1900 in England und Amerika erschienene Ethikliteratur," *Philosophisches Jahrbuch*, 78 (1971), pp. 144-76.

Pirenne, Henri, *Economic and Social History of Medieval Europe*, trans. I. E. Clegg New York: Harcourt, Brace & World, 1956.

Plack, Anro, *Die Gesellschaft und das Böse: Eine Kritik der herrschenden Moral*, 7th Ed., Munich: Paul List Verlag, 1970.

Plato, *The Collected Dialogues*, ed. Edith Hamilton and Huntington Cairns, New York: Pantheon Books, 1961.

Pius XII, "Address to the Italian Catholic Union of Midwives," 29 October 1951: *Acta Apostolicae Sedis* 43 (1951), 835-59.

Plessner, Helmuth, *Laughing and Crying: A Study of the Limits of Human Behavior*, trans. James Spencer Churchill and Marjorie Grene, Evanston: Northwestern University Press, 1970.

Pöhlmann, Horst Georg, *Analogia entis oder Analogia fidei? Die Frage der Analogie bei Karl Barth*, Göttingen: Vandenhoeck & Ruprecht, 1965.

—, "Ethik zwischen Tradition und Situation: Zum Problem der Situationsethik, unter besonderer Berücksichtigung der Situationsethik von J. Fletcher," *Neue Zeitschrift für systematische Theologie und Religionsphilosophie*, 12 (1970), pp. 125-35.

Popper, Karl R., *Logik der Forschung*, 6th Ed., Tübingen: J. C. B. Mohr (Paul Siebeck), 1976.

—, *The Open Society and Its Enemies*, 2 Vols., 5th Ed., Princeton: Princeton University Press, 1966.

Portmann, Adolf, *Biologische Fragmente zu einer Lehre vom Menschen*, 3rd. Ed., Basel and Stuttgart: Schwabe Verlag, 1969.

—, "Von der Idee des Humanen in der gegenwärtigen Biologie," in Portmann, *Biologie und Geist*, Frankfurt am Main: Suhrkamp Verlag, 1968, pp. 342-60.

von Rad, Gerhard, *Das erste Buch Mose: Genesis Kapitel 1-12,9*, Vol. I, Göttingen: Vandenhoeck & Ruprecht, 1956.

Ragaz, Leonhard, *Die Botschaft vom Reiche Gottes: Ein Katechismus für Erwachsene*, Bern: Verlag Herbert Lang, 1942.

—, *Leonhard Ragaz in seinen Briefen*, Vol. I: 1887-1914, ed. Christine Ragaz, Markus Mattmüller, and Arthur Rich, Zürich: EVZ-Verlag, 1966.

—, *Leonhard Ragaz in seinen Briefen*, Vol. II: 1914-1932, ed. Christine Ragaz, Markus Mattmüller, and Arthur Rich, Zürich: Theologischer Verlag, 1982.

Ramp, Ernst, *Das Zinsproblem: Eine historische Untersuchung*, Zürich: Zwingli-Verlag, 1949.

Rawls, John, *A Theory of Justice*, Cambridge, Mass.: Harvard University Press, 1971.

Reiner, Hans, "Gesinnungsethik und Erfolgsethik," *Archiv für Rechts- und Sozialphilosophie*, 40 (1952/53), pp. 520-33.

—, *Pflicht und Neigung: Die Grundlagen der Sittlichkeit erörtert und neu bestimmt mit besonderem Bezug auf Kant und Schiller*, Meisenheim and Glan: Westkulturverlag Anton Hain, 1951.

—, *Die philosophische Ethik: Ihre Fragen und Lehren in Geschichte und Gegenwart*, Heidelberg: Quelle & Meyer, 1964.

Rendtorff, Trutz, "Die christliche Freiheit als Orientierungsbegriff der gegenwärtigen christlichen Ethik," *Handbuch der christlichen Ethik*, Vol. I, 1979, pp. 378-88.

—, *Ethics*, Vol. I: *Basic Elements and Methodology in an Ethical Theology*, trans. Keith Crim, Minneapolis: Fortress Press, 1986.

—, *Ethics*, Vol. II: *Applications of an Ethical Theology*, trans. Keith Crim, Minneapolis: Fortress Press, 1986.

— and Arthur Rich, eds., *Humane Gesellschaft: Beiträge zu ihrer sozialen Gestaltung* (Festschrift for Heinz-Dietrich Wendland), Zürich: Furche-Verlag/Zwingli Verlag, 1970.

— and Heinz Eduard Tödt, *Theologie der Revolution: Analysen und Materialien*, Frankfurt am Main: Suhrkamp Verlag, 1968.

Rich, Arthur, "Die Bedeutung der Eschatologie für den christlichen Glauben," Zürich: Zwingli Verlag, 1954; and in Rich, *Aufrisse: Vorarbeiten zum sozialethischen Denken*, Zürich: Zwingli Verlag, 1970, pp. 127-56.

—, *Christliche Existenz in der industriellen Welt: Eine Einführung in die sozialethischen Grundfragen der industriellen Arbeitswelt*, 2nd Ed., Zürich and Stuttgart: Zwingli Verlag, 1964.

—, *Glaube in politischer Entscheidung: Beiträge zur Ethik des Politischen*, Zürich and Stuttgart: Zwingli Verlag, 1962.

—, "Die institutionelle Ordnung der Gesellschaft als theologisches Problem," *Zeitschrift für Evangelische Ethik*, 4 (1960), pp. 233-44.

—, "Marxistische und christliche Zukunftshoffnung," in Rich, *Aufrisse: Vorarbeiten zum sozialethischen Denken*, Zürich: Zwingli Verlag, 1970, pp. 157-72.

—, *Mitbestimmung in der Industrie: Probleme — Modelle — Kritische Beurteilung: Eine sozialethische Orientierung*, Zürich: Flamberg Verlag, 1973.

—, "Revolution als theologisches Problem," in Ernst Feil and Rudolf Weth, eds., *Diskussion zur "Theologie der Revolution"*, Munich: C. Kaiser Verlag and Mainz: Matthias-Grünewald-Verlag, 1969, pp. 133-58.

—, "Sachzwänge und strukturell Böses in der Wirtschaft: Analysen und Konsequenzen aus der Sicht der christlichen Sozialethik," *Zeitschrift für Evangelische Ethik*, 26 (1982), pp. 62-82.

—, "Die theologische Sozialethik vor dem Umweltproblem," *Reformatio*, 23 (1974), pp. 551-64.

—, "Zwingli als sozialpolitischer Denker," *Zwingliana: Beiträge zur Geschichte Zwinglis, der Reformation und des Protestantismus in der Schweiz*, Vol. XIII (1969), pp. 67-89; and *Zeitschrift für Evangelische Ethik*, 13 (1969), pp. 257-73.

— and Eberhard Ulich, eds., *Arbeit und Humanität*, Königstein: Athenäum Verlag, 1978.

Riesman, David, with Reuel Denney and Nathan Glazer, *The Lonely Crowd: A Study of the Changing American Character*, New Haven: Yale University Press, 1950.

Ringeling, Hermann, "Christliche Ethik im Dialog mit der Anthropologie: Das Problem der Identität," in *Handbuch der christlichen Ethik*, Vol. I, 1979, pp. 474-518.

Ritter, Joachim, R. Romberg, and Annemarie Pieper, "Ethik," in Ritter, ed., *Historisches Wörterbuch der Philosophie*, Vol. II, Basel: Schwabe Verlag, 1972, cols. 759-808.

Roessler, Roman, *Person und Glaube: Der Personalismus der Gottesbeziehung bei Emil Brunner*, Munich: C. Kaiser Verlag, 1965.

Roloff, Jürgen, *Die Apostelgeschichte,* Göttingen: Vandenhoeck & Ruprecht, 1981.

Rother, Siegfried, *Die religiösen und geistigen Grundlagen der Politik Huldrych Zwinglis: Ein Beitrag zum Problem des christlichen Staates,* Erlangen: Palm & Enke, 1956.

Ruh, Hans, "Gerechtigkeitstheorien," in Armin Wildermuth and Alfred Jäger, eds., *Gerechtigkeit: Themen der Sozialethik,* Tübingen: J. C. B. Mohr (Paul Siebeck), 1981, pp. 55-69.

Russell, Bertrand, *The ABC of Relativity,* 4th Rev. Ed., ed. Felix Pirani, New York: New American Library, 1985.

Rüstow, Alexander, *Ortsbestimmung der Gegenwart: Eine universalgeschichtliche Kulturkritik,* Vol. II: *Weg der Freiheit,* Erlenbach-Zürich: Eugen Rentsch Verlag, 1952.

Sartre, Jean-Paul, *Existentialism and Humanism,* trans. Philip Mairet, London: Eyre Methuen, 1948.

Sauter, Gerhard, "Was heißt 'christologische Begründung' christlichen Handelns heute?" *Evangelische Theologie,* 35 (1975), pp. 407-21.

Scheler, Max, *Formalism in Ethics and Non-Formal Ethics of Values: A New Attempt toward the Foundation of an Ethical Personalism,* trans. Manfred S. Frings and Roger L. Funk, Evanston: Northwestern University Press, 1973.

Schelsky, Helmut, ed., *Zur Theorie der Institution,* 2nd Ed., Düsseldorf: Bertelsmann Universitätsverlag, 1973.

Schillebeeckx, Edward, *Christus und die Christen: Die Geschichte einer neuen Lebenspraxis,* Freiburg im Breisgau, Basel, Vienna: Herder, 1977.

Schmauch, Werner and Ernst Wolf, *Königsherrschaft Christi: Der Christ im Staat,* Munich: C. Kaiser Verlag, 1958.

Schmid, Heinrich, *Zwinglis Lehre von der göttlichen und menschlichen Gerechtigkeit,* Zürich: Zwingli Verlag, 1959.

Schrage, Wolfgang, *The Ethics of the New Testament,* trans. David E. Green, Philadelphia: Fortress Press, 1988.

—, *Die konkreten Einzelgebote in der paulinischen Paränese: Ein Beitrag zur neutestamentlichen Ethik,* Gütersloh: Gütersloher Verlagshaus Gerd Mohn, 1961.

Schrey, Heinz-Horst, *Einführung in die Ethik,* Darmstadt: Wissenschaftliche Buchgesellschaft, 1972.

—, *Einführung in die Evangelische Soziallehre,* Darmstadt: Wissenschaftliche Buchgesellschaft, 1973.

Schulz, Walter, *Philosophie in der veränderten Welt,* Pfullingen: Verlag Günther Neske, 1972.

Schulze, Hans, "Begriff und Kriterien einer theologischen Handlungslehre — im Gegenüber zu paränetischer und ordnungstheologischer Ethik," *Evangelische Theologie,* 29 (1969), pp. 183-202.

—, "Theologische Sätze über soziale Sachverhalte," *Zeitschrift für Evangelische Ethik*, 18 (1974), pp. 193-212.

—, *Theologische Sozialethik: Grundlegung, Methodik, Programmatik*, Gütersloh: Gütersloher Verlagshaus Gerd Mohn, 1979.

— and Thea Schulze, *Zwischen Technik und Gott: Lebensführung in den Krisen der Gegenwart*, Stuttgart: Calwer Verlag, 1982.

Schumacher, E. F., *Small is Beautiful: Economics as if People Mattered*, New York: Harper & Row, 1973.

Schweizer, Eduard, *The Good News according to Mark*, trans. Donald H. Madvig, Richmond, Va.: John Knox Press, 1970.

—, "Die Leiblichkeit des Menschen: Leben — Tod — Auferstehung," in Schweizer, *Beiträge zur Theologie des Neuen Testaments: Neutestamentliche Aufsätze (1955-70)*, Zürich: Zwingli Verlag, 1970, pp. 165-82.

Sellien, R. and H. eds., *Dr. Gablers Wirtschaftslexikon*, Vol. 6, 9th Ed., Wiesbaden: Betriebswirtschaftlicher Verlag Dr. T. Gabler, 1976.

Shaull, Richard, "Christian Faith as Scandal in a Technocratic World," in Martin E. Marty and Dean G. Peerman, eds., *New Theology No. 6*, London: Macmillan, 1969, pp. 123-134.

Sohmen, Egon, "Grundlagen, Grenzen und Entwicklungsmöglichkeiten der Welfare Economics," in Erwin von Beckerath and Herbert Giersch, eds., *Probleme der normativen Ökonomik und der wirtschaftspolitischen Beratung*, Berlin: Duncker & Humblot, 1963, pp. 69-98.

Sölle, Dorothee, *Political Theology*, trans. John Shelley, Philadelphia: Fortress Press, 1974.

Specker, Louis, ed., *Politik aus der Nachfolge: Der Briefwechsel zwischen Howard Eugster-Züst und Christoph Blumhardt (1886-1919)*, intro. Arthur Rich, Zürich: Gotthelf Verlag, 1985.

Spencer, Herbert, *The Principles of Ethics*, Part 1: *The Data of Ethics*, 2nd Ed., London and Edinburgh: Williams and Norgate, 1879.

Spiegel, Yorick, *Hinwegzunehmen die Last der Beladenen: Einführung in die Sozialethik*, 1, Munich: C. Kaiser Verlag, 1979.

Stackhouse, Max L., "Gesellschaftstheorie und Sozialethik," *Zeitschrift für Evangelische Ethik*, 22 (1978), pp. 275-94.

Stamm, Johann Jakob, *Der Dekalog im Lichte der neueren Forschung*, 2nd Ed., Bern and Stuttgart: Verlag Paul Haupt, 1962.

Steck, Odil Hannes, *World and Environment*, Nashville: Abingdon, 1980.

Stelzig, Thorhild, "Gerhard Weissers Konzept einer normativen Sozialwissenschaft," *Kölner Zeitschrift für Soziologie und Sozialpsychologie*, Special Issue 19 (1977), pp. 260-89.

Storm, Theodor, *Sämtliche Werke*, ed. Friedrich Düsel, Vol. 2, Berlin: T. Knaur, no date.

Strohm, Theodor, ed., *Christliche Wirtschaftsethik vor neuen Aufgaben* (Festschrift for Arthur Rich), Zürich: Theologischer Verlag, 1980.

Stückelberger, Christoph, *Aufbruch zu einem menschengerechten Wachstum: Sozialethische Ansätze zu einem neuen Lebensstil*, 2nd Ed., Zürich: Theologischer Verlag, 1980.
Stuhlmacher, Peter, "Christliche Verantwortung bei Paulus und seinen Schülern," *Evangelische Theologie*, 28 (1968), pp. 165-86.
Styczén, Tadeusz, "Metaethik: Ein neues Ding oder ein neues Wort?" *Internationale Dialog Zeitschrift*, 2 (1969), pp. 61-67.
Surányi-Unger, Theo, "Wirtschaftsethik," in Erwin von Beckerath, *et al.*, eds., *Handwörterbuch der Sozialwissenschaften*, Vol. XII, Stuttgart: Gustav Fischer, Tübingen: J. C. B. Mohr (Paul Siebeck), and Göttingen: Vandenhoeck & Ruprecht, 1965, pp. 83-103.
Theologisches Wörterbuch zum Neuen Testament, Vols. I-IV, ed. Gerhard Kittel; Vols. V-X, ed. Gerhard Friedrich; Stuttgart, Berlin, Cologne, Mainz: Verlag W. Kohlhammer, 1933-79.
Theunissen, Michael, *Gesellschaft und Geschichte: Zur Kritik der Kritischen Theorie*, Berlin: Walter de Gruyter, 1969.
Thielicke, Helmut, *Einführung in die christliche Ethik*, Munich: R. Piper Verlag, 1963.
—, *Theologische Ethik*, Vol. II, Part 1: *Mensch und Welt*, 2nd Ed., Tübingen: J. C. B. Mohr (Paul Siebeck), 1959.
Tillich, Paul, *Die neue Wirklichkeit*, Munich: Deutscher Taschenbuch Verlag, 1962.
—, "Das religiöser Fundament des moralischen Handelns: Schriften zur Ethik und zum Menschenbild," *Gesammelte Werke*, Vol. III, Stuttgart: Evangelisches Verlagswerk, 1965.
—, "Sein und Sinn: Zwei Schriften zur Ontologie," *Gesammelte Werke*, Vol. XI, Stuttgart: Evangelisches Verlagswerk, 1969.
Tödt, Heinz Eduard, "Versuch zu einer Theorie ethischer Urteilsfindung," *Zeitschrift für Evangelische Ethik*, 21 (1977), pp. 81-93.
—, "Zweiter Versuch zu einer ethischen Theorie der sittlicher Urteilsfindung," presented at the 1979 Annual Conference of the Societas Ethica in Liebfrauenberg bei Straßburg, *Protokoll der Jahrestagung*, 1979, pp. 1-30.
Tonks, Harold, *Faith, Hope and Decision-Making: The Kingdom of God and Social Policy-Making: The Work of Arthur Rich of Zürich*, Frankfurt am Main: Verlag Peter Lang, 1984.
Trillhaas, Wolfgang, *Ethik*, 3rd Ed., Berlin: Walter de Gruyter, 1970.
Troeltsch, Ernst, "Grundprobleme der Ethik" (1902), *Gesammelte Schriften*, Vol. II: *Zur religiösen Lage, Religionsphilosopie und Ethik*, 2nd Ed., Tübingen: J. C. B. Mohr (Paul Siebeck), 1922, pp. 552-672.
Tugendhat, Ernst, "Comments on Some Methodological Aspects of Rawls' 'Theory of Justice'," *Analyse und Kritik*, 1 (1979), pp. 77-89.
Ulrich, Hans G., "Grundlinien ethischer Diskussion: Ein Literaturbericht," *Verkündigung und Forschung*, 20 (1975), pp. 53-99.

"Universal Declaration of Human Rights," 1948.

"Virginia Declaration of Rights," 12 June 1776.

Visser't Hooft, Willem A. and Joseph H. Oldham, *Die Kirche und ihr Dienst an der Welt: Eine ökumenische Kirchenkunde der Gegenwart*, Berlin: Furche-Verlag, 1937.

Voslensky, Michael S., *Nomenklatura: The Soviet Ruling Class*, New York: Doubleday, 1984.

Walther, Christian, "Die Kategorie der Versöhnung," *Handbuch der christlichen Ethik*, Vol. I, 1979, pp. 459-73.

—, *Theologie und Gesellschaft: Ortsbestimmung der evangelischen Sozialethik*, Zürich and Stuttgart: Zwingli Verlag, 1967.

—, *Typen des Reich-Gottes-Verständnisses: Studien zur Eschatologie und Ethik im 19. Jahrhundert*, Munich: C. Kaiser Verlag, 1961.

Watrin, Christian, "Eine liberale Interpretation der Idee der sozialen Gerechtigkeit," in Heinz-Dietrich Ortlieb, Bruno Molitor, and Werner Krone, eds., *Hamburger Jahrbuch für Wirtschafts- und Gesellschaftspolitik*, Vol. 21, Tübingen: J. C. B. Mohr (Paul Siebeck), 1976.

Weber, Hartmut, *Theologie — Gesellschaft — Wirtschaft: Die Sozial- und Wirtschaftsethik in der evangelischen Theologie der Gegenwart*, Göttingen: Vandenhoeck & Ruprecht, 1970.

Weber, Max, "Politics as a Vocation," trans. E. Matthews, in *Max Weber: Selections in Translation*, ed. W. G. Runciman, Cambridge: Cambridge University Press, 1978, pp. 212-25.

Weddigen, Walter, *Wirtschaftsethik: System humanitärer Wirtschaftsmoral*, Berlin: Duncker & Humblot, 1951.

Weinstock, Heinrich, *Die Tragödie des Humanism: Wahrheit und Trug im abendländischen Menschenbild*, 2nd Ed., Heidelberg: Quelle & Meyer, 1954.

Weisser, Gerhard, *Beiträge zur Gesellschaftspolitik*, ed. Siegfried Katterle, Wolfgang Mudra, and Lothar F. Neumann, Göttingen: Verlag Otto Schwartz, 1978.

—, "Glaubensgewißheit und heutige Wertens- und Erkennenskritik," in Theodor Strohm, ed., *Christliche Wirtschaftsethik vor neuen Aufgaben* (Festschrift for Arthur Rich), Zürich: Theologischer Verlag, 1980, pp. 111-24.

—, *Politik als System aus normativen Urteilen*, Göttingen: Verlag Otto Schwartz, 1951.

—, "Die 'praktischen' Aussagen von Politologie und Wirtschaftswissenschaft," in Carl Böhret and Dieter Grosser, eds., *Interdependenzen von Politik und Wirtschaft: Beiträge zur Politischen Wirtschaftslehre* (Festschrift for Gert von Eynern), Berlin: Duncker & Humblot, 1967, pp. 99-127.

von Weizsäcker, Carl Christian, "Die Welt aus der Sicht des Ökonomen," in Heiko Körner, *et al.*, eds., *Wirtschaftspolitik: Wissenschaft und politische Aufgabe* (Festschrift for Karl Schiller), Bern and Stuttgart: Verlag Paul Haupt, 1976, pp. 67-83.

Wendland, Heinz-Dietrich, *Einführung in die Sozialethik*, 2nd Ed., Berlin and New York: Walter de Gruyter, 1971.

—, *Ethik des Neuen Testaments: Eine Einführung*, Göttingen: Vandenhoeck & Ruprecht, 1970.

—, *Die Kirche in der revolutionären Gesellschaft: Sozialethische Aufsätze und Reden*, Gütersloh, Gütersloher Verlagshaus Gerd Mohn, 1967.

—, "Über den gegenwärtigen Stand der Sozialethik," in Wendland, ed., *Sozialethik im Umbruch der Gesellschaft*, Göttingen: Vandenhoeck & Ruprecht, 1969, pp. 15-28.

Westmüller, Horst, "Wie theologisch darf Sozialethik sein? Notwendigkeit und Schwierigkeit des Dialogs zwischen theoretischer Sozialwissenschaft und theologischer Sozialethik" *Die Mitarbeit*, 22 (1973), pp. 244-54.

Wettstein, Harri, *Über die Ausbaufähigkeit von Rawls' Theorie der Gerechtigkeit*, Vol. 13 of *Social Strategies: Monographien zur Soziologie und Gesellschaftspolitik*, Basel: Social Strategies Publishers Co-operative Society, 1979.

Wiebering, Joachim, *Handeln aus Glauben: Grundriß der theologischen Ethik*, Berlin: Evangelische Verlagsanstalt, 1981.

Wildberger, Hans, *Jesaja*, Vol. I, Neukirchen-Vluyn: Neukirchener Verlag, 1972.

Wilken, Folkert, *Das Kapital: Sein Wesen und seine Geschichte und sein Wirken im 20. Jahrhundert*, Schaffhausen: Novalis Verlag, 1976.

Winter, Gibson, *Elements for a Social Ethic: Scientific and Ethical Perspectives on Social Process*, New York: Macmillan, 1966.

Wogaman, John Philip, *The Great Economic Debate: An Ethical Analysis*, Philadelphia: Westminster Press, 1977.

—, "Towards a Method for Dealing with Economic Problems as Ethical Problems," *Concilium*, 140 (1980), pp. 76-83.

Wolf, Erik, "Die Sozialtheologie Zwinglis," *Festschrift Guido Kisch: Rechtshistorische Forschungen*, Stuttgart: W. Kohlhammer, 1955, pp. 167-88.

Wolf, Ernst, *Sozialethik: Theologische Grundfragen*, ed. Theodor Strohm, Göttingen: Vandenhoeck & Ruprecht, 1975.

Wünsch, Georg, *Evangelische Wirtschaftsethik*, Tübingen: J. C. B. Mohr (Paul Siebeck), 1927.

Zwingli, Huldrych, *Sämtliche Werke*, Vol. II, Leipzig: Verlag von M. Heinsius Nachfolger, 1908.

ARTHUR RICH,
BUSINESS AND ECONOMIC ETHICS

VOLUME II:
MARKET ECONOMY, PLANNED ECONOMY, AND GLOBAL ECONOMY FROM THE PESPECTIVE OF SOCIAL ETHICS

Translated by David W. Lutz (chapter 1 to 5)
and Albert Wimmer (chapter 6 to 7)
in Collaboration with Georges Enderle

To the University of St. Gallen,
Patroness of business and economic
ethics within the discipline of economics,
in gratitude for conferring the title of
Honorary Doctorate of Economics

FOREWORD

A good five years have passed since the publication of Volume I of this book, a span of time for which it is difficult to accept responsibility. Besides handicaps of health, the main reason for the regrettable delay is that dealing with the complex, extremely demanding theme presented more difficulties than originally anticipated. Moreover, passages already written were overtaken time and time again by the rapid economic developments and dramatic events in the East. Also, the present version no longer takes into account the most recent, seemingly revolutionary, radical changes in the German Democratic Republic, Czechoslovakia, and Romania. These developments do not, however, restrict the thesis, fundamental in these contexts, that the communist, centrally planned system is irreformable and that every actual reform that goes to the root of the problem leads inevitably to a break from that system. On the contrary, what has already played itself out in Hungary and Poland and then transferred with unexpected suddenness to the other three countries of the East Block only confirm this thesis. The author is thankful that he was, nevertheless, able to bring his project to a conclusion in defiance of all of these handicaps.

This second volume sets its own objective: putting to the test, by focusing on the problem of structuring the contemporary industrial economy, the suitability of the theologically-conceived foundation developed in the first volume for achieving concrete judgment- and decision-maxims, and thus maxims that can accept responsibility before both the demand of human justice rooted in the humanity originating from faith, hope, and love and the demand of technical, economic rationality. The extent to which this testing and, consequently, the comprehensible mediation of the two heterogeneous demands, is successful or unsuccessful will have to be decided by the critique of experts and scholars.

Although the two volumes branch out widely and constitute together a single body, they remain an uncompleted work. The specific questions of business management, which are of direct relevance primarily to the practitioner and are, naturally, difficult to address without preceding clarification of the problem of the economic order, are discussed at best marginally in these two volumes. Doing adequate justice to them may require an additional volume. But, for reasons of health, the author is hardly still in a position to accomplish that. It would be good if a competent scholar were to turn up and jump into the breach.

The author received assistance in writing and editing the text from a variety of experts. He cannot possibly thank all of them by name at this point. Exceptions are, however, noted.

Professor Dr. Hans Christoph Binswanger of the University of St. Gallen and Director Hans-Erich Roth, President of the Board of Directors of Mühlebach AG, Switzerland, examined the entire text continually and carefully, and influenced its final form by their critical comments. Electrical engineer Eduard Murbach checked the correctness of Section 2.3 from a technological point of view. In addition, German-language scholar Dr. Jörg Kielholz subjected the text to examination. All of these persons are sincerely thanked. The author also owes very special thanks to his part-time assistant, pastor BD/ThM Siegfried Karg, in Adliswil. It was his responsibility above all to process the electronic text, to obtain the bibliographic references, to proofread the citations, and to compile the name and subject indices, laborious and time-consuming work, which he performed with exemplary conscientiousness.

Last but not least, the Swiss National Science Foundation also supported the work of Volume II with a substantial two-year subsidy. Similarly, the Association of Higher Education in the Canton of Zürich contributed again with a large contribution for the printing costs. Gratitude is expressed to both of these organizations for their active assistance.

Zürich, New Year 1990 *Arthur Rich*

1. THE QUESTION OF MEANING IN THE ECONOMY

1.1 The Ethical Dimension of the Question of Meaning in the Economy

To seek the meaning of something is to discover its sense and purpose. Something is meaningful, then, when it serves its end or fulfills its purpose. That is also true, of course, of the economy. The question of the meaning of the economy is the same as the questions of its purpose or end. What is the aim of the economy? In what does the end appropriate to its nature consist?

This purely formal determination of the question of meaning in the economy may hardly give cause for controversy. That is not the case, however, the moment one asks to which area of competence its answer belongs: that of economics or that of ethics?

Already prepared by the "classics" of political economy from Adam Smith to David Ricardo, one way of looking at things, usually called "economism,"[1] has established itself in the discipline of economics. It typically evaluates all manifestations of social life exclusively, or at least primarily, from the viewpoint of economic rationality and material productivity. Seen in this way, the economy appears as a *sui generis* order, existing in itself and following its own "natural" laws, as the Physiocrats of the Enlightenment period already asserted in their own way, and as has been reasserted on a natural-scientific foundation in contemporary evolutionary ecology and socio-biology.[2] If one adopts the economistic way of viewing the world, of course, the question of meaning in the economy, if it is even still asked, is to be answered by economics as a positive science,

[1] On "economism" and its conquest in economics see Gerhard Weisser, *Beiträge zur Gesellschaftspolitik*, ed. Siegfried Katterle, Wolfgang Mudra, and Lothar F. Neumann, Göttingen, 1978, pp. 573-601. — Jürgen Mittelstraß, "Wirtschaftsethik als wissenschaftliche Disziplin?" in *Ethik und Wirtschaftswissenschaft*, ed. Georges Enderle, Berlin, 1985, pp. 17-31.

[2] For a concise critique, see Peter Koslowski, *Evolution und Gesellschaft*, Tübingen, 1984.

concerned with the causalities of economic processes and behavior. And it also goes without saying that ethics can then have only marginal significance, if any at all. Thus even Lujo Brentano, who ultimately belonged to the social-reforming powers of his time and did not become involved in the economistic concept without reservations, could conclude his presidential address of 23 November 1901 on "Ethics and Political Economy" with an appeal to the students:

> From that it is evident that all influences on social life can be fruitful and just only to the extent that they do not oppose the nature of things, of which natural development is a part. Therefore, although you must maintain your ideals, do not forget that your first task as academics is to study, without presuppositions, that which exists, with all its causes, and to learn the functions of the individual existing institutions. You will then be able to distinguish that which is necessary from shortcomings that accompany it accidentally. Then, in order to fight the shortcomings, pursue your ultimate ideals within the boundaries determined by necessity.[3]

This view of things is undoubtedly correct in recognizing that every effort to have an ethical influence on the structure of the economy and the behavior of the persons active within it must take economic research into account. Whatever simply contradicts economic scholarship can never be ethically defensible in economic events. That does not at all mean, however, that what should be done in the economy, which articulates itself in its purpose or meaning, can be derived from the empirically tangible, speaking metaphorically, from its "nature." That would amount to a naturalistic fallacy, which is logically absurd.[4] Whenever this is attempted, it is by no means thought "without presuppositions." Evaluative and, therefore, normative premises are instead introduced under the table and naturally receive thereby the appearance of economic rationality, so that they are equated with the rational-natural as the universally valid and necessary. That can also be seen with Brentano. Thus, in the cited presidential address, he simply confronts the Church Fathers' concept of property with that of the Stoics, who taught "the rational, natural life" and approved "striving after riches as wise," from the insight that "wealth is to be preferred to poverty." His sympathy is

[3] Lujo Brentano, *Ethik und Volkswirtschaft in der Geschichte*, Munich, 1902, p. 38.

[4] See Arthur Rich, *Business and Economic Ethics*, Vol. I: *Foundations from a Theological Perspective*, p. 23. Cited hereafter as *BEE*, Vol I.

with it and the underlying view "that if each person preserved his own interest as much as possible, the general interest would be best promoted."[5]

This fundamental thesis, rooted in the Stoic tradition, which, as is well known, Adam Smith adopted,[6] and which then deeply influenced classical economics, is for Brentano on the whole natural and in this respect is to be attributed to that which is necessary in the economy. From that it goes without saying that, since wealth is naturally to be preferred to poverty, the purpose of the economy is "the increase and distribution of earthly goods," and the task of investigating its fundamental conditions falls to the discipline of economics.[7] That, of course, has in itself nothing to do — at least apparently — with ethics. It would merely be a matter of researching the fundamental determinants and mechanisms of increasing and distributing wealth. Certainly, it is necessary to take into account "shortcomings" that "accidentally accompany" economic events, and thus are not determined and, consequently, can also be remedied. Ethical ideals would have their purpose and meaning precisely there as marginal "proof-readers." But only there, not with the fundamental questions whose purpose and meaning the economy must address. But this is incorrect, as has already been made clear.

However the purpose of the economy may be determined, one can never accomplish it without taking the human person into account. There is an economy, because there are human persons. It cannot exist without them, in the way that nature, as the epitome of cosmic reality, could and did exist without us for billions of years. It, together with the law-governed regularities that it possesses, is a historical, cultural product, not an inevitable product of nature. For that reason, also, no economy can ignore the reality of human persons in their needs, desires, hopes, etc. as the indispensable prerequisite of everything economic. The economistic way of looking at things is not excepted from that. It, too, must take the human person into account. Its analysis is based on the model of the "*homo oeconomicus*,"[8] who acts rationally in his economic behavior, in the sense that he lets himself be led by his self-interest, which optimally

[5] Brentano, *Ethik und Volkswirtschaft in der Geschichte*, p. 7.

[6] Adam Smith, *The Wealth of Nations*, Oxford, 1976, IV.ii.9, p. 456.

[7] Brentano, *Ethik und Volkswirtschaft in der Geschichte*, p. 4.

[8] See Hartmut Kliemt, "Der Homo Oeconomicus zwischen Ethik und Biologie," in *Homo Oeconomicus* I, ed., Manfred J. Holler, Munich, 1983, pp. 9-20. See also *BEE*, Vol. II, p. 428.

promotes the general interest, according to the theory. However, this understanding of the human person supposedly agrees with empirical, rational human nature as such and, therefore, is supposed to do without the assumption of pre-scientific value judgments. Yet, the delusion lies precisely in this assertion.

Thomas Hobbes already made the observation that rational-logical thought yields significant, generally accepted results in the field of mathematics, only because in mathematics truth and self-interest do not encroach upon one another's territory.[9] But in the area of anthropology, sociology, economics, etc., no truth is uninterested in this sense. Whenever discussion is of the "true" understanding of actual human persons in their concrete social and economic relationships, interests are always also at play and what presents itself as objective rationality is never absolute, never detached from the interested, subjectively-committed value judgments of persons, groups, classes, etc. I can, thus, regard it as economically rational and, consequently, in accordance with human nature for each person to seek to safeguard his or her own self-interest in economic behavior — as, in fact, most people do. I must only make it completely clear that in doing so I have at the same time made a value judgment, elevating self-interest above the general interest, perhaps with the expectation, arising from a liberal conviction, that it is best for everyone if each individual seeks his or her own advantage. And, in the interest of fairness, I must then also acknowledge that the opposite choice, preference of the general interest before self-interest, perhaps arising from a socialist conviction that preference of the general interest in the economy best secures the interest of each individual, cannot be dismissed as contradicting the principle of rationality, just because it obviously involves a value judgment. Finally, in both cases, it is a matter of evaluations, and thus of fundamental decisions that are primarily ethical, but also secondarily rational and, therefore, also more or less rationally defensible.

[9] Thomas Hobbes, *The Elements of Law, Natural and Politic*, London, 1889, Epistle Dedicatory: "From the two principal parts of our nature, Reason and Passion, have proceeded two kinds of learning, mathematical and dogmatical. The former is free from controversies and dispute, because it consisteth in comparing *figures* and *motion* only; in which things truth and the interest of men, oppose not each other. But in the later there is nothing not disputable, because it compareth *men*, and meddleth with their right and profit; *in which as oft as reason is against a man, so oft will a man be against reason*."

The question of which of these two fundamental decisions has the greater claim to being ethical is not yet under discussion. That is, incidentally — and contrary to a superficial, socially dressed-up view of humanity that rashly votes for the general interest — by no means easy to determine, but requires careful deliberation. In the present context, it is merely a matter of demonstrating that the question of the purpose of the economy cannot be decided in a manner that is "value-free," in the sense of economism, and that it instead lies, and indeed irrefutably, within the sphere of the ethical. Thus one can see, as political economists tend to assume, the primary purpose of the economy entirely as sufficiently meeting human requirements for goods and services, thus in "reducing the scarcity of goods."[10] If this definition of meaning appears at first glance to be value-neutral, it is by no means value-free. It is, on the contrary, guided by the conviction that material scarcity is an evil that must be remedied and that, consequently, maximizing the national product is meaningful. The economist Emil Küng correctly observes "that in the process a *value premise* is established or accepted that is not at all obligatory for everyone," and that it can be justified only "as a *working hypothesis* in reference to the fact that most people in the Western world have held this opinion up to now."[11] One could hardly describe the situation under consideration more accurately. And that means that the question of the meaning of the economy cannot be separated from ethics. Therefore, economic ethics, as understood here, contains the decided rejection of economism in economics.

1.2 The Question of Meaning in the Economy as the Question of Human Justice in the Economy

It turns out that the question of the meaning of the economy exists undeniably in the dimension of the ethical. This is the case, because the economy is not an independent order, as the natural world is, but rather is an institution created by and for human persons. Its purpose, consequently, cannot be determined economistically from its own existence. It can be determined only with regard to human persons and their existential basic needs. The economy has meaning for

[10] Hans-Rudolf Peters, "Ordnungstheoretische Ansätze zur Typisierung unvollkommener Wirtschaftsordnungen," *Hamburger Jahrbuch für Wirtschafts- und Gesellschaftspolitik*, Vol. 18, Tübingen, 1973, p. 49.

[11] Emil Küng, *Wirtschaft und Gerechtigkeit*, Tübingen, 1967, p. 16.

human persons to the degree that it meets these basic needs and, consequently, proves to be humanly just. And to the degree that it fails to meet them, and thus fails to fulfill its purpose, it becomes meaningless and deteriorates into absurdity, even if it attains in the process a high degree of efficiency and appears to be characterized by an optimum of rationality.

If we speak here of human justice that must meet basic human needs, this is not to be understood in an anthropocentrically-restricted sense. The human person is not his own cosmos. He is, as Karl Marx puts it, "no abstract being encamped outside the world. Man is *the world of man*." [12] One can no more separate him from his natural environment than from his social environment. He remains tied to it, for better or for worse. If it is ruined, he is ruined. And if its ecological quality improves, so does the quality of human life. Therefore, anyone who ignores environmental justice while defining human justice inevitably misses the mark; a truth so simple that one hesitates to express it at all. Nevertheless, it is notoriously defied, because in this question one traditionally sticks to a shortsighted anthropocentrism that favors short-term, individual or social interests. Human justice, as we understand it, thus necessarily includes environmental justice.[13] It is fundamentally about *one* thing here, not two different things. In other words, the right of human persons correlates with the right of the environment, of nature, as "the form of life preserved by God for the fallen world."[14] That must be asserted emphatically.

The concept of human justice, however, even in this indispensable expansion, proves to be unsuitable as an ethical reference point for the illumination of the question of meaning in the economy, as long as it remains formally undefined and, consequently, amounts to an empty formula that can mean everything and nothing. It requires a formulation that aims into the subject matter, and thus is more precise. Such a more precise formulation has been accomplished in the first volume of this work, which develops the foundation of business

[12] Karl Marx, "Contribution to the Critique of Hegel's Philosophy of Law," in *Collected Works*, Vol. III, New York, 1975, p. 175.

[13] *BEE*, Vol. I, p. 65 and p. 67. For a fuller picture, see sections 3.1.3, as well as 3.3.3 and 7.2.6. See also the important study of Martin Honecker, "Verantwortung für die Umwelt als Auftrag des Menschen," in *Vorsorge für die Umwelt*, ed. G. Hosemann and E. Finckh, Erlangen, 1984, pp. 9-22.

[14] Dietrich Bonhoeffer, *Ethics*, trans. Neville Horton Smith, New York, 1955, p. 145.

and economic ethics from a theological perspective.[15] The following discussions are based on the criteria of human justice that are developed there and obviously must be assumed here.

1.3 The Criteria of the Humanity Originating from Faith, Hope, and Love as Guidelines for Clarifying the Question of Meaning in the Economy

1.3.1 *The Fundamental Purpose of the Economy*

The most fundamental basic need of human persons is without question the need to live, to grow, to develop themselves, basically synonymous concepts, as surely as life always means growth and development and their termination means death, which is the conclusion of life. We share this basic need with all creatures, plants as well as animals. It quite simply proves our creatureliness as the will to live in the sphere of finiteness.

Creatureliness, as a fundamental criterion of the humanity originating from faith, hope, and love,[16] means that human persons do not have themselves to thank for their existence, that they, like all creation, have been made by the Creator, and that in this created nature, which establishes the finiteness of their natural lives, exists the inextinguishable ontological difference between creation and the uncreated, infinite, eternal God. The criterion of creatureliness, however, means not only this ontological difference, but also at the same time, in biblical dialectic, their personal correspondence to the Creator, namely their status as having been created in the image of God, which is based upon the fact that they are the only creatures called by God's word, and thus have been held responsible. Thus, not merely creaturely life and, therefore, the fundamental basic need to live is ascribed to human persons, as it is to other creatures; they are also called by God to fulfill this basic need consciously, according to their destination, i.e., in a way that brings the will of God to bear in an ethical way. In other words, they occupy a singular place in creation, the place of agents responsible to the Creator and, therefore, the place of personal subjects who should use and rule over the

[15] *BEE*, Vol. I, Chapters 5 (Humanity Originating from Faith, Hope, and Love) and 7 (The Criteria of Human Justice and their Orientation toward Social Justice).
[16] *BEE*, Vol. I, pp. 173-76.

earth, with its treasures and everything that lives on it, in short, who should make it the object of their creating, life-serving activity, which is in that respect analogous to God's creation.[17] That belongs essentially to humanity as the specific dimension of its creatureliness, distinguishing itself from other creatures.

Human persons, consequently, share with all other creatures the basic need to live, to grow, and to develop themselves. But they share this need with other creatures in such a way that they are at the same time elevated above the others. In all of that, they are not simply biologically conditioned, as are other creatures. They have, though not absolute, nevertheless, relative liberty to regulate the fulfillment of this basic need themselves, even to alter its content. The necessities of life of contemporary human persons are fundamentally different from those of our Stone Age ancestors, and so are the methods of meeting them. What the Stone Age has in common with modernity, however, is that human persons already refused at that time to be satisfied with what existed and took it upon themselves to surpass it. Instead of merely appropriating, as hunters or gatherers, the goods necessary for their existence from what they found in their natural world, as had happened over immeasurable periods of time, they began relatively recently to plant, to cultivate the soil, to domesticate animals, to make tools, to invent and develop utensils, and thus to produce what did not already exist. With this productive, culture-founding activity began what we call "the economy," the specific way in which human persons meet their fundamental basic needs, namely, to live, to live with more material security, to multiply, and to develop, both as individuals and as societies. Only human persons engage in this economic activity. They alone are able to produce, beyond natural means of production, such as soil, plants, animals, etc., artificial means of production, which increase their productive power and enable them to produce goods beyond their own needs and to exchange the surplus products for others that they are not able to produce themselves. That generally raises the level of their opportunities in life and awakens new needs that for their part stimulate economic activity, always differentiate it more, but also complicate it, because of the increasing complexity. What meanwhile survives up to our day, since the economy in its world-wide interdependencies has grown up to a tangle of activities, relationships, and networks that

[17] Genesis 1,26 ff.

can hardly be fully perceived and understood, is the fact that, viewed from the perspective of its fundamental purpose, it must stand in the service of satisfying basic human-cultural needs. In the words of economist Walter Adolf Jöhr, "although it appears to constitute a thoroughly self-sufficient area of life, it is entitled to no independent aims, since its mission is one of pure service."[18] This fundamental definition of the meaning of the economy stands in agreement with the humanity criterion of creatureliness. Only an economy that sees its truest purpose as service to life can conform to it. And from that it follows, with compelling logic, that the economy must be oriented primarily towards the needs of human persons, not human persons towards the needs of the economy. In other words, the economy can be only a means, not an end.[19] If that is reversed, if it makes of itself its own purpose, then a fundamental crisis of meaning in the economy is inevitable.

1.3.2 *The Humane Purpose of the Economy*

The fundamental purpose of the economy turns out to be, as has become apparent, service to life. In order to be able to serve life, it unquestionably must see itself as able to meet the elementary necessities of the lives of human persons, which never remain constant, but instead grow with their cultural, collaborative, historical development. That compels the efficiency of human economic activity, which means in principle the production-increasing rationalization and organization of human work as the economy's fundamental factor of production.

Distinct traces of that kind of rationalization and organization of work can be detected as far back as the early Neolithic period, especially in the "flood economy" of the ancient Egyptians.[20] Thus the wooden pickax, later the prototype of the plow, and also the precursor of the rapidly rotating potter's wheel, etc. already appear as instruments to increase productivity. Contemporaneously, the first

[18] Walter Adolf Jöhr, "Wirtschaft und Politik," in *Handwörterbuch der Wirtschaftswissenschaften*, Vol. 9, p. 28.

[19] Similarly, Emil Brunner, *The Divine Imperative*, trans. Olive Wyon, Philadelphia, 1947, p. 402: "The primary purpose of economics willed by God is to minister to human needs, service to life. This implies that the economic order is a means and not an end."

[20] Arne Eggebrecht, *et al.*, *Geschichte der Arbeit*, Zürich, 1982, pp. 32-33.

beginnings of a structuring of primitive economic activities in the direction of a division of labor and the formation of a class-society are encountered. Insofar as all of this promotes the efficiency of human economic activity and in this respect its service to life, it is in accord with the fundamental purpose of the economy and, therefore, also with the demand of human justice. Yet precisely this relative agreement can become the occasion of fatal confusion.

This confusion is based on the fact that the conclusion could be drawn economistically from the mentioned agreement that the fundamental purpose of the economy, its service to life, coincides with the increase of overall efficiency, and thus could ultimately be synonymous with the maximization of the national product. Thus, what should be the means becomes the end under the table, and the end, namely human persons in their fundamental necessities of life, runs the risk of becoming the means.

It goes without saying that if work is the fundamental factor of production in the economy, then the increase of productivity[21] can only take place through its more efficient formation and organization. Productive work is, however, inseparably linked to human persons. Only human persons can produce, create value, and increase value, whether directly by means of their own personal activity or indirectly through the means of production produced by them, from the simplest tools to the highly developed microprocessor-controlled CNC machines of today, which, apart from programming, hardly require human operators. The formation and organization of work, both of which can be summarized under the concept of rationalization, thus means the formation and organization of persons by persons in the service of the increase of productivity and the national product. But do not — and this is precisely the question — the formed and organized human persons inevitably become thereby a kind of means of production, the mere workforce, whose human existence in the work is endangered, and that all the more so, since specialization can also lead to an emptying of the work-task?

This reservation has nothing to do with anti-economic ideologies. Adam Smith already became conscious of the dilemma expressed by our question. Thus, in his well-known pin example, he praises extreme specialization as an excellent means of improving the productive powers of work.[22] He hopes from the division of labor, which

[21] Productivity = gross national product per hour of work.
[22] Smith, *The Wealth of Nations*, I.i.3, pp. 14-15.

analyzes human activity, at least that of manual workers, into ever more specialized and simplified functions, not only a "great multiplication of the productions of all the different arts," but also "in a well-governed society," a "universal opulence which extends itself to the lowest ranks of the people."[23] Therefore, he argues for an economization of work,[24] that is, for its technical formation and social organization in the sense that the viewpoint of the increase of productivity is thereby given the first priority. In another context in comparison, namely, that of public expenditures, he addresses the negative consequences of this kind of division of labor, and indeed in words that could in their substance remind one of Karl Marx and Friedrich Engels:[25]

> In the progress of the division of labour, the employment of the far greater part of those who live by labour, that is, of the great body of the people, comes to be confined to a few very simple operations; frequently to one or two. But the understandings of the greater part of men are necessarily formed by their ordinary employments. The man whose whole life is spent in performing a few simple operations, of which the effects too are, perhaps, always the same, or very nearly the same, has no occasion to exert his understanding.... He naturally loses, therefore, the habit of such exertion, and generally becomes as stupid and ignorant as it is possible for a human creature to become.[26]

Smith thus understands the already much-discussed connection between work and personality[27] and, therefore, the fact that the structures of work are of great importance for the spiritual formation of human persons, that a crisis of meaning of human existence overall is inevitably brought about by the economistic emptying of the

[23] *Ibid.*, I.i.10, p. 22.

[24] See Werner Conze, "Arbeit," in *Geschichtliche Grundbegriffe*, ed. Otto Brunner, Werner Conze, and Reinhart Koselleck, Vol. 1, Stuttgart, 1974, pp. 174-81.

[25] Marx and Engels, "Manifesto of the Communist Party," in *Collected Works*, Vol. VI, New York, 1976, pp. 490-91.

[26] Smith, *The Wealth of Nations*, V.i.f.50, pp. 781-82.

[27] See Arthur Rich, *Christliche Existenz in der industriellen Welt*, 2nd Ed., Zürich, 1964, pp. 59-104; Charles Lattmann, "Arbeit als Selbstentfaltung des Menschen," in *Arbeit und Humanität*, ed. Rich and Eberhard Ulich, Königstein, 1978, pp. 33-46; Lattmann, *Die verhaltenswissenschaftlichen Grundlagen der Führung des Mitarbeiters*, Bern, 1982, pp. 517-19; Peter Groskurth, ed., *Arbeit und Persönlichkeit*, Reinbek bei Hamburg, 1979; Melvin Lester Kohn, *Persönlichkeit, Beruf und soziale Schichtung*, ed. Kurt Lüscher, Stuttgart, 1981; Ueli Kraft, Kurt Häfeli, and Urs Schallberger, "...*natürlich hat mich meine Lehre verändert": Ein Bericht über Zusammenhänge zwischen Berufsausbildung und Persönlichkeitsentwicklung*, Zürich, 1985.

meaning of work. But he does not draw a serious conclusion from that. For him, the principle of economic efficiency in the formation and organization of work as the deciding factor of production in the economy remains predominant.

Seen from the viewpoint of creatureliness, as one of the basic criteria of the humanity originating from faith, hope, and love, the economistic perspective proves to be untenable. Human persons, as beings created for personal responsibility in their entire existence by the Creator, of course, need an efficient economy that is able to secure their material basis of life. Otherwise, the economy would not be of service to life and would fail to attain its fundamental purpose. Yet, beyond that, they are also entitled to a form of economic work that contains a humane structure, in the sense that it gives them room for the development of their determination to be persons in the image of God, not humanly stunted robots. In other words, work never understands itself as only a necessary and, thus, often enough laborious means of earning a living; it understands itself no less as a medium of an activity that confirms the humanness of human persons. Therefore, in its biblical understanding it carries a double face. On the one hand, it is a severe, oppressive command: "By the sweat of your brow you shall eat your bread."[28] On the other hand, it is an uplifting mission that honors human persons more than animals and goes far beyond merely obtaining the necessities of life. The psalmist says it with the following words:

> The young lions roar after their prey,
> and seek their food from God.
> When the sun rises, they withdraw,
> and lie down in their dens.
> Then man goes forth to his work,
> and to his labor until evening.[29]

Both oppressive necessity and uplifting work appropriate for human persons belong to the essence of work[30] from the beginning of its cultural development. As man began to fashion tools, and by doing so to found a productive economy, he unquestionably did so out of

[28] Genesis 3,19.

[29] Psalm 104,21-23.

[30] On the entire complex of the problematic of work, see Dietmar Mieth, *Arbeit und Menschenwürde*, Freiburg, 1985. The author makes a "fundamental phenomenological distinction" between "labor" (*Arbeit*) and "work" (*Werk*) (pp. 11 ff.) and opposes the "spiritual identification of labor and work," as it is found in the encyclical *Laborem*

absolute necessity, in order to alter threats to his existence. However, "He did that not only out of necessity, but also derived pleasure from it. He therefore simultaneously gave into an inclination towards embellishment, through which his labor remained joined to an element of play — which is to be found in all art."[31] If this dimension is excluded from economically organized labor, if it is experienced simply as a harsh necessity that ultimately also justifies the reduction of the human person to a mere means in the process of production, then it stands in contradiction to the humanity originating from faith, hope, and love, to humanity as God wills it, and then even it will inevitably be robbed of its humane meaning.

According to the preceding reflections, it is not sufficient to orient the ordering of the economy according to its fundamental purpose alone. Human persons should not merely live by means of the economy, they should also be able to live humanly within it, i.e., so that they can in the process of laboring and earning a living attain the status of co-designing, co-determining, and in that respect also co-responsible persons, instead of being only workers, hired, used, and correspondingly paid according to the requirements of economic efficiency. That obviously does not mean that, going to the opposite extreme, the humane purpose is to be claimed as the dominating

exercens (1981), "as a theological misunderstanding" (pp. 27 ff.). Labor as human activity meets the necessity for human persons to obtain the economic means to satisfy their basic needs (p. 30). It neither deserves theological dignity nor constitutes the dignity of human persons. This is due only to human activity as work, which has a character like God's work: "The human activity in which the transformation of the cosmos is collaborated" — thus, what is understood here as responsible, productive activity — "does not appear under the rubric of labor, but rather under the rubric of work" (p. 18).

Insofar as Mieth opposes the ideologization of social and economic work, as if the humanness of human persons consisted in it, he is, in my opinion, right. To that extent, the distinction between labor and work is also justified. But that distinction must not become a separation. Separating them from one another would be just as fatal a mistake as identifying them with one another. Indeed labor (I follow here Günter Brakelmann, "Arbeit," in *Christlicher Glaube in moderner Gesellschaft*, ed. Franz Böckle, *et al.*, Vol. 8, Freiburg, 1980, p. 106) does not constitute the humanness of human persons, but it is and remains a fundamental form of expression of human persons. Human labor, therefore, should never have to be experienced merely as severe necessity, but always as also containing the element of work, just as, vice versa, the element of arduous labor is anything but foreign to human work (as is expressed by the Swiss-dialect-German word "*wärche*" or "working hard").

[31] Frans van der Ven, *Sozialgeschichte der Arbeit*, Vol. I: *Antike and Frühmittelalter*, Munich, 1972, pp. 12-13.

objective, if not sole objective in the question of ordering the economy. An economy that is oriented according to humane principles, but is inefficient, missing its mark of elementary service to life, will lead to a crisis of meaning no less than one that demonstrates a high degree of productivity, but whose human structural conditions are nevertheless in a sorry state. One must beware of false alternatives in this direction, just as much as in the other direction.

1.3.3 *The Social Purpose of the Economy*

The preceding considerations have attempted to make it clear that an economy can have meaning only if it is able to do justice to both its fundamental and its humane purposes. It should not only produce the goods and services necessary for humane existence in sufficient quantity and satisfactory quality, it should also do that in such a way that, instead of reifying some of those who work to mere means of production, it enables each willing person to receive in the world of work the status of a co-participative, co-determining, and in that respect co-responsible person. But that is not enough. It is possible for an economy to meet these conditions, but nevertheless to create social inequality of such a kind that there exists, on the one hand, an unnecessary surplus and, on the other hand, a shortage of the most necessary goods, whether within a particular group of persons or the entire human race. Such an economy will be experienced as absurd, and not only by those who are disadvantaged. Consequently, the question of the meaning of the economy also concerns distributive justice.

If distributive justice is mentioned here, it should not be understood in a sense that is too narrow, as if it is only concerned with the distribution of the national product in the form of income and wealth. What are fundamentally to be distributed are "life situations."[32] The life situations of human persons — considered independently of the perspective of their spiritual-psychological resources, which surpass everything economic — do not depend only on income and wealth. Even more is of consequence: that they have education suited to their abilities and corresponding employment opportunities and, beyond activities to earn a living, that they know how to make something substantial out of their lives. If the mere just

[32] Gerhard Weisser, *Beiträge zur Gesellschaftspolitik*, p. 360.

distribution of economic goods and services in the narrower sense of the word is an extremely difficult challenge, that is true even more of the broader understanding of the concept. In any case, one cannot get by with a dogmatic ideology of equality.

In the tradition that sympathizes with economistic thought, there was always the temptation simply to tone down pragmatically the question of distributive justice, which was already restricted to the purely economic, if not to gloss over it completely. That can be recognized as early as Adam Smith. Contrary to the dominant opinion of his time, he found it shameful that the mass of the people of a country should live in poor conditions, and declared explicitly: "It is but equity, besides, that they who feed, cloath and lodge the whole body of the people, should have such a share of the produce of their own labour as to be themselves tolerably well fed, cloathed and lodged."[33] Yet he did not really see in that a social problem, but rather an economic one: "The liberal reward of labour" is for him, as it were, the automatic "effect of increasing wealth."[34] Thus, for him, everything depends on increasing wealth, on the growth of the economy, or the national product. Thus, he continues:

> It deserves to be remarked… that it is in the progressive state, while the society is advancing to the further acquisition, rather than when it has acquired its full complement of riches, that the condition of the labouring poor, of the great body of the people, seems to be the happiest and the most comfortable. It is hard in the stationary, and miserable in the declining state. The progressive state is in reality the cheerful and the hearty state to all the different orders of the society. The stationary is dull; the declining, melancholy.[35]

Karl Marx also still thought along these lines, despite his opposition to Adam Smith at other points. Thus, in the *Manifesto of the Communist Party*, he praises the "modern bourgeois society" of his day "that has conjured up such gigantic means of production and of exchange,"[36] and sees in it the economic prerequisite of the full satisfaction of everyone's needs. Only the conditions of production, i.e. the totality of the order-conditions under which bourgeois society performed economic activities, no longer corresponded to the pro-

[33] Smith, *The Wealth of Nations*, I.viii.36, p. 96.
[34] *Ibid.*, I.viii.42, p. 99.
[35] *Ibid.*, I.viii.43, p. 99.
[36] Marx and Engels, "Manifesto of the Communist Party," in *Collected Works*, Vol. VI, New York, 1976, p. 489.

ductive forces created by it.[37] If these order-conditions were revolutionized in such a way that the means of production passed over from private into social hands and the economic processes were linked extensively and according to planning, then a state of abundance would necessarily be achieved, which would bring to reality the early socialist maxim "from each according to his abilities, to each according to his needs."[38] This also means that with the maximization of national product the problem of distributive justice will solve itself. For it is obvious that if each person can meet his or her economic needs as he or she wishes, because an abundance exists, then the question whether one receives more than the other no longer arises.

That is certainly correct, insofar as the problem of distribution loses its social explosiveness in a growth economy with high production of goods. When much is produced, a high level of employment is present, and profits and wages increase, there is more for all to distribute, which promotes social contentment. From that it can be understood only all to well how the growth of national product has progressed to a kind of economic dogma, and indeed in the Eastern as well as in the Western social orders. Nevertheless, the distribution question does not go out of existence in this way, and certainly not from itself. Even in Western, affluent societies there is still, and recently again, often alarming poverty[39] that cannot be attributed to the fault of the poor themselves — though there certainly is also some that can be attributed to them. Above all, the increasing hunger

[37] *Ibid.*, p. 490.

[38] Marx, "Critique of the Gotha Programme," in *Collected Works*, Vol. XXIV, 1989, p. 87. In Saint-Amand Bazard, *Doctrine de Saint-Simon: Exposition* (1829), ed. C. Bouglé and Elie Halévy, Paris, 1924, p. 94, the dictum is encountered in the version: "*...à chacun suivant sa capacité, à chaque capacité suivant ses œuvres.*" Marx, following Louis Blanc, modified it in the cited variation. On the origin of this saying, see Hermann Pechan, *Louis Blanc als Wegbereiter des modernen Sozialismus*, Jena, 1929, p. 76: "If the followers of Saint-Simon reduced the principle of the future society to the formula: '*à chacun selon sa capacité, à chaque capacité selon ses œuvres*', and if the followers of Fourier expressed their societal ideal with the other rule of distribution, '*à chacun selon sa capital, selon son travail, selon son talent*', Blanc, in connection to Morelly, summarized the picture of the future society in the words: '*De chacun selon sa faculté, à chacun selon ses besoins*'." It can be added that consumer goods are already distributed according to the needs of consumers in Thomas More, *Utopia*, II, 9.

[39] Cf. Enderle, *Sicherung des Existenzminimums im nationalen und internationalen Kontext*, Bern, 1987, esp. pp. 48-59. See also Ulf Claußen, ed., *Die im Dunkeln sieht man nicht*, Bochum, 1985; Hélène Beyeler-von Burg, *Schweizer ohne Namen*, Pierrelaye, 1985;

in the poorest nations of the Third World is shocking, despite enormously increasing production of food in the industrialized nations, that leads more and more to shameful surpluses there. Precisely when one does not ideologically see in all of that a mere monstrous product of "capitalism" and "economic imperialism," but also knows about the economic sins of the impoverished, will one have to experience these facts as a challenge that demands even more justice in the question of distribution, and not simply more economic growth.

It is a matter here of a challenge that imposes itself all the more imperiously today, as may become clear to each insightful person, that economic growth, at least that which is understood quantitatively, pushes against its ecological limits. That must lead to a reorientation of the still-dominant definition of the purpose of the economy. We must ask seriously with Emil Küng: "Is the maximization of national product still appropriate today? Can an economic policy that makes effectiveness relative to this goal its highest priority still always be supported?"[40] If that is doubted (and can one do otherwise than doubt it today?), if therefore the manner and magnitude of economic growth must respect the limits set by ecological conditions, then, since it cannot increase without limit, the quantity of economic goods (to which the number of jobs belongs) must also be distributed as humanly justly as possible, so that the economically weaker are not required to bear the primary burden of a reorientation of that kind, which would be no less meaningless than unjust. That agrees completely with the basic criteria of fellow-humanness and participation as fundamental principles of the humanity originating from faith, hope, and love.[41] To be motivated by its demand means taking on the problem of distribution consciously as an ethical challenge and, indeed, in the sense that it, rather than being merely a matter of personal generosity and helpfulness, leads to the obligatory question of how the society is to be arranged in its economic and legal structures, so that the highest possible degree of participation in the production and the outcome of the national product and in individually suitable educational opportunities can result from it for everyone, especially

National Conference of Catholic Bishops, *Economic Justice for All*, Washington, 1986, pp. 83-105.

[40] Küng, *Wirtschaft und Gerechtigkeit*, p. 16.

[41] *BEE*, Vol. I, Sections 7.2.5 and 7.2.7.

for the disadvantaged. Only in this way can one address distributive justice and the social meaning and purpose of the economy.

1.3.4 *The Ecological Purpose of the Economy*

It belongs to the nature of human persons as creatures that they are a part of the creation, embedded in the ecological cycle of nature, in which everything is related to and dependent upon everything else. And it also belongs to their nature to have a special place within creation that enables them to intervene in the natural world in order to mold it into their world, into the historical-cultural life-world. This duality has already been mentioned.

The economy, as a specifically human phenomenon, is crucially concerned with this duality. Through it human persons intervene actively in that which is given naturally; they become producers of new things, of goods that never before existed. In that way they are able to rise above the natural world, to take possession of it, yes even to set themselves up as lords over it. Nevertheless, they can never escape from the ecological cycle of nature. They remain inescapably embedded in it and the abuse of this order leads to the destruction of the basis of their own lives.

Insofar as the economy means using what exists naturally, such as air, water, plants, animals, natural resources, sources of energy, etc., and through them increasing life opportunities — not only those of humans — without thereby endangering or even destroying nature as the universal basis of life, one can speak of an ecological purpose of the economy. It is, succinctly, to be seen in not only using natural goods in the service of life, but also preserving them, looking after them, and taking care of them. Human persons, however, have long ago abandoned this bivalence in the ecological purpose of the economy and have, for the most part, permitted *homo faber* to triumph over *homo conservator*.

This is not the place to depict this occurrence, which is in its inner chain of events both tragic and culpable, together with the unfortunate historical consequences that have resulted from it. It is appropriate here simply to remark that, in contrast to the humane and social purposes of the economy, the perversion of the ecological purpose, except in the most recent time, has hardly been contradicted. The early socialists already protested vehemently against the economic "exploitation of man by man" and the degradation of the worker to a mere means of production. Yet, as for the exploitation of the natural world by human persons, who had already entered the stage of the lack of restraint in those days, they, too, have found it in order, and almost celebrated it as revolutionary progress: "Man no longer exploits man; but he associated with other men, exploits the world handed over to his power."[42] Socialists of Saint-Simon's school and other early socialists were not the only ones who thought in this way:

> This opposition — exploitation of nature by humans instead of exploitation of humans by humans — was based on the idea, already liberal or generally "enlightened," of the epochal change of work. If previous history was characterized by states of domination and war that were hostile to work, their abolition meant the liberation of human work for progress in a state of peace that was supposed to allow their energies to be used exclusively to conquer nature.[43]

The war of human persons against nature, instead of the war of humans against humans, or, in other words, the inconsiderate basic attitude in the interest of thoughtless maximization of economic growth, intent no longer on the preservation, but only on the exploitation of nature, thus determined both the socialist and the liberal traditions. In their historical consequences, then, "the different social systems in the East and the West are equally involved in the exploitation of nature."[44] This is one of the dominant features of our time and is tantamount to losing the sense of the ecological purpose of the economy.

This loss marks one of the essential aspects of the crisis of meaning in the contemporary economy. Meaningful, long-term, economic activity is impossible if its ecological purpose is continually disregarded by notoriously aggressive treatment of existing nature. The public should have realized that this cannot continue, at least since the publication in 1972 of the Club of Rome's so-called "Meadows Report" on the limits to growth. Although one may argue in detail about the meaningfulness of the statistical data on which it is based, one thing is certain: the twentieth century, especially in the period after the Second World War, has squandered more of the irreplaceable resources of the earth than all earlier periods combined.[45] To that

[42] Bazard, *Doctrine de Saint-Simon*, p. 94. See also Thilo Ramm, ed., *Der Frühsozialismus*, Stuttgart, 1956, p. 75.

[43] Werner Conze, "Arbeit," p. 197.

[44] Oskar Lafontaine, *Der andere Fortschritt*, Hamburg, 1985, p. 15.

[45] Michael Landmann, "Ökologische und anthropologische Verantwortung," in *Gerechtigkeit*, ed. Armin Wildermuth and Alfred Jäger, Tübingen, 1981, p. 164.

is added the extreme overuse of our earth by artificial fertilizer, fatal air and water pollution, the killing of forests, etc., all of which will have catastrophic consequences if they are not stopped. With this kind of economic expansion, which threatens our natural basis of life, we are about to jeopardize, to jeopardize radically, the very fulfillment of the fundamental purpose of the economy, namely its service to life. And that is an unparalleled absurdity that can be countered only by a decisive reversal of direction.

This reversal of direction, however, does not consist in simply denying the modern economy and its highly developed technology, and nostalgically advocating a "post-industrial" age that supposedly would enable the world to return to its natural state. That would lead to refusing the cultural determination of human persons. Human persons are instructed to use nature, with everything that it provides, to make it into their life world, to develop themselves in it, and to make necessary goods available, in short, to achieve that which promotes the fundamental purpose of the economy. Without them, the demand for vital goods and services could not be met and the economic basis for the promotion of welfare, particularly in the destitute regions of our world, would simply fade away. Moreover, the financial means to meaningful conservation of the environment would be lacking. One must soberly take that into account. Therefore, the alternative cannot be zero or negative economic growth,[46] but rather the kind of growth that no longer burdens the environment and instead eases the burden as much as possible.

What is certainly necessary is a conscious rejection of the previous power-arrogance of modern man towards his environment, an aberration that has, not least of all, encouraged the traditionally false understanding of Genesis 1:28. Contrary to the common conception, human persons are by no means entitled to the rank of lord in creation. They are fellow-creatures, of course fellow-creatures who as

[46] Cf. Peter Stolz, "Arbeit, Umwelt, qualitatives Wachstum," *Zeitschrift für Evangelische Ethik*, 30 (1986), p. 196: "In this [ecological] context, zero growth is not the answer. Should we turn back the wheel of economic history and possibly reduce the production of goods? An oppressive scenario could then begin to emerge. Different components of the quality of life could deteriorate; unemployment, and perhaps also criminality, could increase in the face of visibly unmet demands; in the face of growing existential problems, high environmental quality would fatally be declared a luxury; one could or would no longer provide development aid." See also 2.7.3 in this volume.

agents of God must stand up for all of nature as the form of life which God preserved to the fallen world, and thus they must not speak out against it. That arises compellingly from the criterion of fellow-creatureliness as one of the basic determinants of the humanity originating from faith, hope, and love.[47] Fellow-creatureliness, therefore, has a two-fold meaning: the permanent embeddedness of human persons in creation as a whole, and their mission to use existing nature, in responsibility to God, in a manner that promotes life, and to preserve it reverently. Therefore, it is profoundly significant that the Latin verb "*colere*" means both "to cultivate a field" and "to honor God." Economic intervention in the natural world should not take place imperiously, but rather with reverence for God's will and His creation. In addition, the means of production that human persons make and use should consequently be means of service, not means of domination. They must serve human persons and, indeed, in such a manner that the natural world is not shamelessly plundered, maltreated, reduced by them to the status of a slave of an economic world that sees its purpose essentially in itself and, therefore, always risks the danger of throwing money around recklessly and pointlessly. That has definite consequences for the imperative dealing with technology as the most potent instrument of the contemporary economy. It has become a means of domination *par excellence*, through which human persons have gained previously unknown power over both other persons and their entire world of existence, extending all the way to the macabre possibility of their extermination. And precisely that must be changed, if there is to be a genuine reversal of direction, a brighter prospect for the future. Technology must become, to the extent that it has not already done so, an instrument of service to both the natural environment and other persons,[48] first of all, by taking on a form that protects nature. As such an instrument of service, it can and will have positive effects. In technology, and therefore indirectly in the contemporary economy supported by it, there exists not only the potential to destroy the environment, but also, when it is implemented responsibly, the potential

[47] *BEE*, Vol. I, 7.2.6.

[48] The humanity criterion of fellow-creatureliness corresponds to the understanding of nature as the world of other persons. See Pius Hafner, *et al.*, who correctly emphasize the aspect of "nature as the world of other persons" (*Mensch sein im Ganzen der Schöpfung*, Zürich, 1985, pp. 8-9).

to protect the environment.[49] Actualizing this potential, developing it, and using it to protect the naturally given environment all belong to the ecological purpose of the economy. This purpose must not be sacrificed to the other purposes of the economy. In other words, the social welfare of human persons remains an economic goal. But it is to be pursued in such a way that the welfare of the non-human world, on which we are just as dependent as it is on us, remains as unendangered as possible. Ethically, that means abandoning an anthropocentrically-narrowed understanding of the human sphere of responsibility and adopting an integrated perspective that includes the ecological dimension of reality.[50] Only in such a comprehensive horizon can the question of meaning in the economy be raised, without cutting it short.

1.3.5 *The Relationality of the Purposes*

In the preceding sections of this chapter, four purposes of the economy, each contributing to the determination of its meaning, were discussed: the fundamental, the humane, the social, and the ecological purpose. That led to the necessity of a perspective in which the different purposes are combined to form a whole. But is that within the realm of the possible? Is there indeed convergence between these purposes, by means of which an integrated point of view can be justified? When considered realistically, is this not, on the contrary, a case of divergence, if not complete antagonism? What is in fact the truth here? The preceding observations have made it apparent that one can speak of both the convergence and the divergence of these purposes. Thus, the fundamental purpose of the economy, which is aimed, in the interest of amply satisfying needs, at an increase in efficiency and economic growth, converges with the social purpose, because distribution problems can be simplified and more jobs can be created through it. Both of these purposes or goals, however, come easily into conflict in their convergence with the humane and ecological concerns in the economy. An increase in the economic efficiency of firms, which generally means progress in the rationalization

[49] See the reflections of Heinz Eduard Tödt, "Die Ambivalenz des technischen Fortschritts als Thema christlicher Ethik," *Zeitschrift für Evangelische Ethik*, 25 (1981), pp. 18-29.

[50] Cf. Landmann, "Ökologische und anthropologische Verantwortung," pp. 157-78, where he follows a similar path and makes the same point impressively.

or even tighter organization of work, apart from the elimination of jobs and, therefore, of increased unemployment, can lose its human content and thus produce inhumane consequences. And economic growth, at least insofar as it is merely quantitative, leads as a rule to an even stronger burdening of the environment, which is already excessively stressed as it is. These are dilemmata that are only all too well known, and that make our time harsher. Which background realities are behind them?

Behind the four main purposes of the economy that have been discussed here are certain values, each of which must be taken seriously in its own way. For the fundamental purpose of the economy, the value of prosperity is constitutive as the epitome of the life-serving satisfaction of material basic needs; for the humane purpose it is humanity in the concrete work situations; for the social purpose it is balance in the distribution of life situations; and for the ecological purpose it is reverence for nature in the use of its goods. Disregarding one of these values — this has already been made clear — has disastrous consequences and calls into question the meaningfulness of the economy as a whole.

But not only disregarding one of these values, also absolutizing or extremizing one of them, leads to contradictions that lead to absurdity, since this is possible only at the cost of other values. If the economy orients itself one-sidedly towards the value of prosperity, which is honorable in itself, and accordingly towards the maximization of national product, then one takes into account, in case this promotes the realization of the desired goal, that the human quality of jobs deteriorates or the burden on the endangered environment increases even further. If, however, one is intent only on the humanization of jobs, balance in the distribution of life situations is stressed to the point of mechanical leveling down; or if protection of the environment receives absolute priority and values that in themselves command full respect are in turn extremized, then the weakening of meaning for the profitability of the economy will hardly fail to materialize, which likewise must result in severe social disadvantages that only burden others. Taking these values to the extreme is what leads to the dilemmata identified above. Each value that is taken to an extreme or even made absolute, however legitimate and necessary it may be, brings about disaster and contradicts human justice, which in an integrated point of view is never removed from environmental concerns. Only by respecting the opposing values can a value be human. Thus the value of equality, which negates all inequality, deteriorates into a uniformity that oppresses life, discriminates against the extraordinary, and suppresses creative initiatives. On the other hand, if the value of diversity excludes any reconciliation among the various social situations of the people, it degenerates into an elitism that simply sanctions the division of society into the privileged and underprivileged and reduces the disadvantaged to a type of person with fewer rights.

It may be advisable at this point to pose briefly an apparently remote question, which is, however, of fateful significance for the economy and is at least indirectly related to the problem of values, as it has been brought into view here, namely, the question of money.[51]

Money-wealth is also related to values, and indeed to values whose nature is not merely economic. Insofar as money-wealth is a product of diligence, thriftiness, and an innovative entrepreneurial spirit, ethical values stand behind it. In his fundamental, though not uncontroversial work, *The Protestant Ethic and the Spirit of Capitalism*, Max Weber has shown how precisely upholding values of that kind has contributed to economically-relevant capital formation and, consequently, to the development of the modern economy.[52] Capital formation, as such, without which the economy in the contemporary sense — including the socialist economy — would be inconceivable, is thus by no means without an ethically legitimate basis.

It is, however, a different question whether capital formation or the profit motive stands in service to the determination of the purpose of the economy, as it was outlined above, or whether it has been removed from that, has become absolute, and has made itself into a self-purpose. In that case, profit maximization of capital becomes the primary purpose of the economy overall. Even if this may increase economic efficiency, understood purely quantitatively, and in that respect be beneficial for the development of the material standard of living of the society as a whole as an indispensable purpose of the economy, it gets specifically capitalist mechanisms into gear with accumulation drives that run counter to the humane purpose, as well

[51] On the question of money and its consequences for the economy, see the provocative book of Hans Christoph Binswanger, *Money and Magic*, trans. J. E. Harrison, Chicago, 1994.

[52] Max Weber, *The Protestant Ethic and the Spirit of Capitalism*, trans. Talcott Parsons, London, 1930.

as the social and ecological purposes of the economy.[53] Aristotle already understood that "all who engage in business increase their money without limit."[54] Under contemporary conditions, that leads to a boundless expansion of the economy that receives an irrational character, that becomes meaningless, and cannot be united with the demands of human justice.

Absolutized financial capital, with its structural tendency to take the profit motive to an extreme, consequently stands in irrepealable opposition to humanity originating in faith, hope, and love. It is to be subsumed under what is called "mammon" in the New Testament. Mammon, or mammonism, is not simply synonymous with money or the money economy, as naive anti-capitalism believes. Money, as a means of exchange and a potential means of production, remains indispensable for every economy that has outgrown the natural phase. Yet money capital must remain a means, a means in the service of an economy that stands in agreement with the purposes that humanity originating in faith, hope, and love yields. In view of that, Jesus' words, "You cannot serve both God and mammon,"[55] are of fundamental significance to economic ethics. One cannot absolutize the capital interest, released from its humane, social, and ecological obligatoriness, and simultaneously take seriously the humanity to which God calls and obligates human persons. There is only an either-or here. Even when the pursuit of the capital-forming interest serves the efficiency of the economy and, moreover, is joined to high ethical values, such as diligence, thriftiness, individual responsibility, entrepreneurial courage, etc., with the absolutizing of the mentioned interests, these values become absolutes as well. And making any one of these purposes or values an absolute, no matter how high the moral ranking in the consciousness of the society may be, means the annihilation of the human factor and, consequently, disaster.

[53] See 2.7.2-3.

[54] Aristotle, *Politics*, I, 9, 1257b, trans. Carnes Lord, Chicago, 1984, p. 48. Aristotle distinguishes two kinds of acquisitive expertise (*ktetike*) here. One is part of the art of business management (*oikonomike*) and serves obtaining all of the goods useful and necessary for the community in the household and the city-state. The other disengages itself from this purpose and is directed towards the pure acquisition of money or wealth (I, 8-9, 1256b). Aristotle says of this kind of acquisitive expertise that it is not necessary and leads to boundless accumulation of money, while the other, which in accordance with its purpose holds accumulation within limits, is for him economically imperative (I, 9, 1256b).

[55] Matthew 6,24.

The inner basis of explanation of these ethically important facts can be seen in the fact that the relationality of the values is and remains an indispensable criterion for human justice. In any event, that arises from the understanding of the humanity originating from faith, hope, and love.[56]

According to this understanding of humanity, what is humane cannot be reduced to a single basic value. This has already been made clear concerning the values of equality and diversity. Neither the high, liberal basic values of freedom and individual responsibility nor the equally high socialist basic values of solidarity and social duty, taken alone, constitute in themselves the whole of what is humane. According to the concept of humanity that is fundamental here, the whole of what is humane proves to be love rooted in believing hope in the coming of the Kingdom of God. In it, freedom and individual responsibility, as well as solidarity and social duty, are an indivisible whole, and thus a unity.[57] In other words, it is their comprehensive synthesis and, consequently, radical humanity. But such humanity cannot be made, cannot be compelled, because love cannot be compelled by force. One can only orient oneself towards that which is expected and longed for in faith, hope, and love. And one is truly oriented towards it when one deals relationally with such basic values as freedom and individual responsibility, solidarity and social duty, in the fullness of their tension. For, when understood relationally, they refer to love as the epitome of radical humanity. If their relationality is disregarded, however, if one of these pairs of values is made an absolute in such a way that the other pair must back away, then the orientation towards humanity ceases, and the human factor borrowed from them falls apart. That is the meaning of relationality, understood as a basic criterion of the humanity originating from faith, hope, and love. What meaning does this have for the purpose of the economy, which is being considered here, and the values standing behind it?

First of all, the criterion of relationality, as a basic criterion of human justice, illuminates the fact that the mentioned purposes need not stand among themselves in antagonistic opposition and, consequently,

[56] This is discussed in detail in *BEE*, Vol. I, 7.2.4 and 7.3.2.

[57] Galatians 5,13: "For you were called to freedom, brothers; only do not use your freedom as an opportunity for self-assertion (*sarx*), but instead serve one another in love."

must not enter into meaning-annihilating contradiction to what is human, which each of them, in its own way, seeks to achieve. They must do this only insofar as they establish themselves absolutely, degenerate into extremist positions, and thereby pursue a sort of imperialism of a single purpose. As long as the view of the whole is not lost and the purposes, together with the values and interests oriented towards them, are seen in their relations and in that respect also relatively, their compatibility can be asserted pragmatically.

On the other hand, the criterion of relationality makes it equally evident that a perfect harmonization of the various economic purposes, and thus a completely reconciliatory synthesis of the opposites, does not lie within the reach of what human persons can "do." This synthesis belongs to the *eschaton,* the ultimate, the rule of God as the kingdom of love that unites everyone and everything. As long as we exist in the time of the penultimate, and that is our historical period, there will be tensions, serious tensions, between these purposes, which, however, must lead to antagonistic opposites that deny and, therefore, destroy the meaning of humanity, only if their relationality is not recognized and is disregarded. Hence, in the penultimate, no ideal, tensionless economic and social order, liberated from all conflicts of interest, is attainable, as, for instance, the communist utopia of the early Marx dreamed.[58] What will be possible in the best case — and it is necessary to strive towards it with all power — is the pragmatic optimization of the mutual relationship of the economic purposes now under consideration, with the aim of minimizing the opposing tensions. With that, however, one moves into the domain of the relative, which in this context also means that the question of meaning in the economy can never find more than a relative solution.

1.3.6 *The Question of Meaning in the Economy within the Area of Tension between the Relative and the Absolute*

It has already been established in the first section of this chapter, and substantiated by the discussions following it, that the question of meaning in the economy cannot be answered economistically from the actual existence of the economy itself, because it goes far beyond the economic and refers to the ethical dimension. By its very nature,

[58] Marx and Engels, *Collected Works,* Vol. III, New York, 1975, pp. 296-97.

it can be undertaken only in the horizon of the ethical. For this theologically-based theory of business and economic ethics, this simply means, to make the point once again, that when it comes to resolving the question of the meaning of the economy, or the normative question, the criteria of human justice, as understood in relation to the humanity originating from faith, hope, and love, are to be claimed as guidelines.

But the hoping love of faith marks an absolute claim. Let all that you do be done "*en agape*," in love, is how Paul formulates it.[59] There exists no higher demand than that of unconditional love. It is the fulfillment and, consequently, the meaning of the law, and thus of God's will for human persons.[60] If, however, "all" must be done in love, including the existence and activity of human persons in the economy, and if, consequently, its highest meaning should likewise be love as the most radical form of service to life, is not everything economic then condemned by God from the start? No actually existing economic order can claim that it is inspired by the imperative of love in its specific structural principles and their effects. With liberal models of the economy, the principles of freedom, individual responsibility, and self-interest, viewed ideally, stand in the background as determining value factors. With socialist orders, again considered ideally, the same is true of solidarity, social duty, and collective interest. Although the ethical content of both of these sets of values is of high quality, neither comes close to meeting the demand made by love in its radicalness, that is, in its completeness. They are, at best, nothing more than partial truths, aspects of the whole. To the extent that a form of order of the economy claims to have exclusive and absolute validity, with reference to such a set of values, it ultimately usurps what only the order of love can be. And then it certainly enters into radical opposition to it and to the humanity belonging to it as the epitome of human justice.

Towards such a concept of the economy, which toys with the nimbus of the absolute, there is, for the humanity originating from faith, hope, and love, really only the attitude of critical distance, which crystallizes into an unequivocal "no." Critical distance is also a basic criterion of this humanity.[61] It makes it conclusively evident that no

59 I Corinthians 16,14.

60 Romans 13,10.

61 See *BEE*, Vol. I, 7.2.2.

economic system, whether liberal, socialist, or of any other kind, can claim anything like an ultimate character, in the sense of the Kingdom of God. On the contrary, each existing order, again in the words of Paul, belongs to the form of this world, which is passing away.[62] But that must never be confused with simply negating every economy that is structured in one way or another as purely meaningless, just because all of them are relative and, therefore, imperfect and transitory. In the time of the penultimate, which is our historical period, there neither is nor will be perfection. But the imperfect, relative, mutable, and consequently transitory can and will have meaning, when it is in its relative nature directed towards the absolute, when it does not smugly come to terms with existing structures and conditions, but instead keeps them critically in motion towards more justice, in the sense of the humanity originating from faith, hope, and love. Such a critically flexible, and thus open order of the economy can also be respected and adopted from the point of view of the absolute demand of love, because it is just and meaningful to stand up for relatively better justice in the world of imperfections, for the sake of the belittled, the disadvantaged, and the oppressed. For love desires that all who labor and are heavy laden be helped concretely, that they neither be put off until a perfectionist utopia nor be sacrificed to a fate that supposedly cannot be changed.

In addition to the criterion of critical distance, therefore, the criterion of relative reception is to be observed as a constitutive feature of human justice.[63] Without it, pure negativism towards everything imperfect and, consequently, the nihilistic assertion of its total meaninglessness would be the answer to everything. The more an order attempts, certainly often in questionable ways, to reduce existing injustice and to create more space for humanly just exchange structures of society, of which the economy is certainly among the most important, the more meaningful is its reception, because the more humanly necessary. Yet, here also, it will have to be a matter of critical reception, conscious of its relativity, because even the better and more just remains in the sphere of the temporary, and thus may never claim the status of an order to be affirmed absolutely. When the latter takes place, however, when an historical order, invoking theocratic, natural law or historical-speculative ambitions, exempts

[62] I Corinthians 7,31.

[63] See *BEE*, Vol. I, 7.2.3.

itself from fundamental critique and elevates itself to the level of the ultimate, then, with internal inevitability, a totalitarian regime is produced, human persons are sacrificed to the system, and the society is sentenced to meaninglessness. In this way, the criteria of critical distance and relative reception are conditions of each other in order to preserve what is human, and in this way, under the demand of the absolute requirement of the humanity originating from faith, hope, and love, the realization of relative meaning in the economy is possible, as the struggle for structures of order that are based on the relationality of values and that give an increase in opportunities to social participation, to person-affirming fellow-humanness, and to fellow-creatureliness, which turns ecological embeddedness into a partnership. The goal of this theory of economic ethics is the transformation, postulated in all of these opportunities, of the absolute demand manifested in the criteria of the humanity originating from faith, hope, and love into relative maxims that can endure in a world of the imperfect, are practicable, and thus can actually promote human justice in the economy. The fact that these maxims must satisfy not only the demand of human justice, but also that of economic rationality, has been discussed in detail in the first volume, which is devoted to establishing the theory's foundation.[64] The discussions in the following chapters must take that into account as much as possible. A prerequisite for this is a factual grasp of the essential aspects and perspectives of the modern industrial economy.

[64] See above all *BEE*, Vol. I, pp. 94-95, 6.3, and 8.1-5.

2. ASPECTS AND PERSPECTIVES OF THE MODERN INDUSTRIAL ECONOMY

2.1 What is the Economy?

The undertaking of comprehending the nature and reality of the modern industrial economy in its basic structure and primary features requires at least a brief description of the economy in general.

The preceding discussion of the question of meaning in the economy has already stated that the fundamental purpose of the economy is service to life in the historical context of the cultural development of the human race. By analogy, the economy can be understood, quite generally, to be the aggregate of the policies and institutions within the culture as a whole that serve the material preservation, security, and promotion of human life. This means that the economy is concerned with meeting the demand for so-called "scarce goods." A distinction is made in economics between "free" and "scarce" goods. "Free goods," such as air to breathe (though how much longer?) or dead trees lying in forests, are found in nature in supplies that are, for practical purposes, unlimited. Using them has no cost, since for them, "even with a price of zero, the supply exceeds the demand."[1] "Scarce goods" are those for which the demand always exceeds the supply, and which, consequently, must be obtained by careful management and have their price.[2] The main task of the economy is to meet the demand for scarce goods inexpensively with available, though always scarce means of production, and thus to attain the greatest possible supply for everyone.[3]

[1] Helmut Schneider, "Preise," in *Handwörterbuch der Wirtschaftswissenschaften*, Vol. 6, p. 181.

[2] Thus, the economic concept of "scarcity" never relates "to an absolute state, but always to a relation between a limited available quantity and unlimited needs." In other words, the scarcity of a good depends upon the demand for it (Silvio Borner, *Einführung in die Volkswirtschaftslehre*, Diessenhofen, 1980, p. 15).

[3] Macroeconomics consequently operates according to the following definition, which is accepted by economists on the whole: "Economics is the study of how men

Meeting the demand for goods that are scarce and, therefore, not freely available, yet which are necessary for existence, expand opportunities in life, and therefore should be produced, constitutes the basic nature of the economy. If the meeting of demand is restricted to the family (understood to mean the extended family), then one speaks of "household management," a term that expresses the original meaning of "economy."[4] If it relates to the needs of an entire nation or, beyond that, the entire world, then we speak of "political economy" or "global economy." In all of these cases, the concern is with the production and distribution of goods that are otherwise not available, and are also necessary for the elevation of human persons from the level of natural existence to that of cultural existence. All in all, this agrees with the assertion in 1.3.1-4 that the economy, by its very nature, is intended for human persons as service to the life of human persons, by which they can turn the naturally-given into the cultural and can increase and further develop the life opportunities of their own race, despite the continuing dependency upon the overall ecological context.

Simply meeting the demand for scarce goods as such is, consequently, not all that belongs to the fundamental nature of the economy. Accomplishing this efficiently, thereby achieving the greatest possible benefit at the least possible cost, belongs no less to its basic nature. In other words, the economy must function economically. That is, of course, a pure tautology. Yet it illuminates precisely the fact that the rational element of economic efficiency belongs indispensably to the concept of the economy.[5] An uneconomical economy is a contradiction, which, wherever it shows itself, necessarily leads in the long term to situations that are economically intolerable.

Because this is true, there exists in the economy, as its history reveals compellingly, a constant trend operating towards increasing efficiency. Its degree of effectiveness should be measured not only in

and society *choose*, with or without the use of money, to employ *scarce* productive resources, which could have alternative uses, to produce various commodities over time and distribute them for consumption, now and in the future, among various people and groups in society" (Paul A. Samuelson, *Macroeconomics*, Vol. I, 7th Ed., New York, 1967, p. 5).

4 "Economy" and "economics" are derived from the Greek *oikos* = house, and mean primarily housekeeping or management of the household.

5 It is already clear from the explanations in 1.3.2 that, according to this approach to business and economic ethics, the rational element of economic efficiency cannot simply be equated with the principle of profit-maximization.

terms of higher profits, but just as much, if not even more so, in terms of higher salaries and wages, greater social benefits and public expenditures, and less damage to the environment. This trend can be seen in the process of economic rationalization, to begin with, in the form of the industrial division of labor, a process one should qualify in its reality, though not without hesitation, as "progressive," since it can be and often is tied, on the contrary, to consequences that are humanly difficult to bear. It certainly has had epochal effects, and has produced one fundamentally different structural form of economy after another. Thus we speak, to mention only the most fundamental turning points, of the pre-industrial, the industrial, and recently — with those who think alternatively — the post-industrial economy.[6] However one assesses the latter vision, we are still concerned today with the economy that has been shaped by the process of industrialization. It will, therefore, be taken as the theme of the following deliberations, at least in their main aspects.

2.2 Industry and Industrialization

The complex of terms, "industry," "industrialism," "industrialization,"[7] has taken on such a diversity of meanings in the course of history that it can no longer be reduced to a simple common denominator. The Latin word *industria,* upon which it is based, means simply "assiduous activity," "sedulousness," "bustle," "brisk, persistent diligence," etc. It thus means intensively pursued work and, therefore, a quality bordering on the ethical: "Until the threshold of the industrial revolution, '*industria*' still meant the 'virtue of diligence'."[8] This qualitative meaning began to fade quite early, however, in the fourteenth century, and the term "industry" began to take on the meaning of mere commercial occupation or activity.[9] With Leibniz, who

[6] For example, Otto Ullrich, *Weltniveau*, Berlin, 1979, who, however, understands the "post-industrial society" as merely "a reversal of over-industrialization, a relative reversal of industrial structures, tied to a new, qualitative conception of our production methods and way of life" (p. 113).

[7] See Dietrich Hilger and Lucian Hölscher, "Industrie, Gewerbe," in *Geschichtliche Grundbegriffe*, ed. Otto Brunner, Werner Conze, and Reinhart Koselleck, Vol. 3, Stuttgart, 1982, pp. 237-304.

[8] *Ibid.*, p. 249.

[9] *Ibid.*, p. 250.

introduced it into the vocabulary of the German language, its traditional meaning of "diligence" was completely turned in the direction of the expression "ability as a manual worker" and the use of the word "industry" was already restricted to a completely specific form of economic activity, namely commercial production.[10] The term thus gained a classificatory function, instead of a qualitative one and, consequently, could take its place beside "agriculture" and "trade."

With the use of "industry" as a classificatory term in the narrower sense, related only to the increasingly present commercial entity, especially to the form of production of small factories, the path to a further change of meaning was prepared. In the age of mercantilism, the term came to mean the aggregate of the taxable economic activities in a state, and thus a kind of "national industry."[11] Thus, the idea of the economically powerful and extensive is connected with "industry." In this way, the concept came to denote primarily large commercial enterprises and their specific way of producing goods, designed to increase efficiency. This was the point in time when "industry" mutated into what moderns understood and still understand by it, namely large-scale, capital-intensive production.

What qualifies the large mercantilist enterprises as "industry before industry"[12] is a way of production still essentially free of machines, relying only on small factories, on manual work. Through the rapid development of machine technology that went out from England in the eighteenth and nineteenth centuries, it experienced a revolution that was just as radical as it was consequential. Its characteristic feature proved to be the rapid inclusion of machines in the economic production process, together with the increasing competition of mechanical work with manual work, which inevitably accompanied it. In France one spoke for the first time concerning this epochal event of "*révolution industrielle*," a succinct expression, which was then adopted by Friedrich Engels in 1845[13] and has been in general use since Arnold Toynbee's "Lectures on the Industrial Revolution" of 1884. The means-of-production machine as such is not exactly what is decidedly new here. Contrary to popular belief,

[10] *Ibid.*, p. 251.

[11] *Ibid.*, p. 256.

[12] This formulation originated with the historian Jean-François Bergier, *Die Wirtschaftsgeschichte der Schweiz*, Zürich, 1983, p. 147.

[13] Engels, "The Condition of the Working-Class in England," in *Collected Works*, Vol. IV, New York, 1975, p. 307.

machine technology existed, and indeed at a surprisingly high level, in the High Middle Ages, which is why Jean Gimpel can speak, admittedly exaggeratedly, of an industrial revolution of the Middle Ages.[14] What was new was that the technologizing of the process of work became dominant and universal in the modern era. It replaced the era of manual labor and led up to the period of machines and appliances, by which, for the first time, the work process could be "performed almost automatically and, regarding the relationships among sub-processes, continually,"[15] which was supposed to bring about an even greater increase in the productivity of work. In this context, therefore, "industrialization" is synonymous with the "machinization" or mechanization of economic production in the interest of increased efficiency, as a result of which mass production, and therefore the origin of large industrial firms, is inevitably promoted. Because this took place initially in the second main sector of the economy,[16] it happened to be identified with industry and manufacturing firms in general. The process of industrialization did not at all remain restricted to this sector, however, but instead also spread to the other sectors of the economy, first of all to agriculture, which experienced large-scale mechanization in a relatively short period of time and in recent decades even developed the beginnings of the automation of its production.[17]

Since manual labor generally plays a secondary role in the third main sector of the economy, it was less amenable than the other two sectors to mechanization and the form of rationalization determined by it. The traditional method of work was able, therefore, to survive longer in it.

After the invention of the transistor in 1948 and the "semiconductor technology" that resulted from it, by means of which it became possible to produce complex integrated chips in the smallest places, a new stage of rationalization was set in motion, which has already been given the current label "second" or "third" industrial

[14] Jean Gimpel, *La révolution industrielle du Moyen Age*, Paris, 1975.

[15] Walther Hoffmann, *Stadien und Typen der Industrialisierung*, Jena, 1931, p. 1.

[16] In distinction from the primary main sector of the economy (farming and mining) and the tertiary sector (services, including trade, banking, and insurance), the secondary sector encompasses trades, crafts, and industry.

[17] See, for instance, W. Batel and H. Hesse, "Möglichkeiten der Automation bei der landwirtschaftlichen Produktion," *VDI-Zeitschrift, Fortschritt Berichte*, Ser. 14, No. 2, Düsseldorf, 1966.

revolution.[18] In contrast to that of the first industrial revolution, which has recently been mentioned, the newest stage of rationalization is not based on mechanics, but rather on electronics, more precisely microelectronics,[19] which now goes beyond manual labor and also makes, as it were, intellectual labor substitutable. This has led and still leads to a revolution of the entire information and communication sector, which is the basis of the service sector.[20] Thus, not only do large areas of services become extremely rationalizable, but the previous automation in the second economic sector experiences a still higher perfection, *in extremis* to production sites virtually devoid if people, as exists, for example, in Europe with FIAT in Termoli. In view of the universalizing possibilities of microelectronics, which first raised information technology to a qualitatively higher level, the expression "information society," instead of "industrial society," has already been introduced. One must, however, be aware that the process of industrialization, if one understands it in its historically based sense as a method of rationalization directed towards increasing the efficiency of providing economic production and services, is not at all replaced by computer science, but is, on the contrary, magnified. For, according to it, the method of industrial rationalization in the direction of automation can not only be applied even more efficiently in all sectors of the economy, especially the third and second sectors, but it can also be applied, in contrast to the preceding mechanical stages, to production in small lots, even to the manufacture of a single product. Consequently, small and medium firms again receive increased opportunities. Thus, one will also be able and will have to speak of "industrial economy" and "industrial society" in the future, even if large-scale industry is forced back, in favor of medium- and small-scale industry.

[18] If someone speaks of a "third" industrial revolution, that should be understood as equivalent to what I mean by the "second," namely the stage of rationalization introduced by electronics, as distinguished from automation on a mechanical basis. On the "second" or "third" industrial revolution, see Dieter Balkhausen, *Die dritte industrielle Revolution*, Düsseldorf, 1978.

[19] See *BEE*, Vol. II, 2.3.3.2.

[20] Wilhelm Steinmüller reduces this revolution to the succinct formula: "The new technology brings about an 'industrialization of brainwork and communication'" ("Die zweite Phase der Industrialisierung," *Neue Zürcher Zeitung*, 29 April 1987, p. 69).

It is apparent from the above remarks that industrialization is a specific form of rationalization and runs parallel with its development. Since our analyses and perspectives of the industrial economy are guided by ethical interests, it will be advisable to enter more closely the typology of this occurrence in its dominant phases, in order to comprehend the process of industrialization, primarily in its social, human effects.

2.3 The Process of Industrial Rationalization

2.3.1 *Rationalization as a Basic Phenomenon of the Economy*

The extremely close relationship, approaching identity, between the principle of efficiency and the principle of rationalization, has already been referred to in Section 1.3.2, which discussed the humane purpose of the economy. Everything economic possesses a trend towards increased efficiency. But to manage efficiently means nothing other than to do so with foresight, deliberation, and orderliness, in other words, to manage rationally. Rationalization is, therefore, a basic datum of the economy. Its beginnings go back to in the earliest stage of economic development, when human needs began to be differentiated and the demand for scarce goods became both more diverse and more demanding, so that individuals were no longer capable of creating what they needed, but instead found themselves more and more dependent upon the skills of others. From, at the latest, this point in time, which coincides with the origin of trade by barter, it was inevitable that people would begin to ask themselves: Who makes what best? How does one make it most expediently? And where does one make it most advantageously? Questions like these lead inevitably to division of labor as the basic form of economic rationalization. It became tangible very early, more precisely, in the Neolithic period, which has led cultural historians to speak of a Neolithic revolution.

In the above questions, three basic forms of division of labor are already identified. The first question — "Who makes what best?" — refers to product-oriented division of labor; the second question — "How does one make it most expediently?" — to production-oriented division of labor; and the third — "Where does one make it most advantageously?" — to location-oriented division labor. These three basic kinds of division of labor are not really mutually exclusive. Nevertheless, each of them is of a specific, unique kind, which justifies looking at them separately and analyzing each one in its specificity.

In the present context, the first two kinds of division of labor are of importance. Addressing the third must be reserved for a later section.[21]

2.3.2 *Product-Oriented Division of Labor*

Product-oriented division of labor is division of labor with reference to both the product manufactured and the materials used. In the transition from Ice Age hunting to New Stone Age farming, labor, regardless of its gender-specific differentiation, was still undivided. Each person made everything from primitive hand-axes, cutting tools, arrowheads, and earthen vessels to the stone axe, the first farm tools, and fabrics.[22] To the degree that these various forms of manual labor developed into true arts or techniques (originally synonymous terms), however, they gradually became to the same degree the affairs of individual experts or groups of experts. Pottery, weaving, the making of utensils emerged; with the construction of better dwellings, so did carpentry, etc. The bronze founder arrived on the scene as the leading craftsman in the Bronze Age, as did the ironsmith in the Iron Age. All in all there arose during these periods a wide range of primary occupations (the word "occupation" or "vocation" [*Beruf*] understood here in the contemporary sense[23] as the name of a professionally-conducted means of earning a living), each of which was restricted to the production of a specific product. This was a development that characterized the first phase of product-oriented division of labor.

If the formation of primary occupations outlined here marked the first phase of product-oriented division of labor, the second phase may be called specifically the phase of occupational splitting. Occupational splitting means, succinctly, the differentiation of primary occupations into specialized occupations, either according to the kind of material worked with or the kind of product manufactured. Even before the Iron Age there were blacksmiths distinguished from one

[21] See 2.6.2.

[22] See Alex R. Furger and Fanny Hartmann, *Vor 5000 Jahren... So lebten unsere Vorfahren in der Jungsteinzeit*, Bern, 1983.

[23] On the history of the meaning of the word "*Beruf*" see Werner Conze, "Beruf," *Geschichtliche Grundbegriffe*, Vol. 1, pp. 490-507.

another by working with copper, bronze, silver, or gold. With the discovery of iron as the metal of the future, there developed the craft of the ironsmith, which soon subdivided into an ever-greater number of specialized occupations, devoted to making weapons, plows, chains, horseshoes, nails, knives, dividers, etc. In the Late Middle Ages, the classical period of occupational splitting as a form of the rationalization of work, one could eventually count as many as sixty different species of smiths.[24] This kind of division of labor permitted the development of high mastership in a narrow specialty, which contributed to the quality level of the goods produced. The disadvantage lay in the trend towards over-specialization into an ever-narrower group of products, a situation that diminished the mobility of craftsmen and contributed considerably to making the economic structure become rigid, dampening innovations, and impeding structural adjustments as needs changed, as was typical of the guild system, the social objectification of this kind of economic division of labor.

With regard to the particular typology of product-oriented division of labor, the following characteristics should be emphasized:

1. Product-oriented division of labor is extremely labor-intensive. Value is created (ignoring material costs) almost exclusively by the factor of labor. The more simple and meager the tools — and in the classical age of manual labor, they were simple and relatively meager — the smaller the demand for investment, or capital. Furthermore, since the smallest, or at least the small firm corresponds with product-oriented, highly-specialized division of labor, it was possible for many craftsmen to finance their own workplaces. Consequently, the number of actually or potentially self-sufficient workers was large.
2. This first characteristic is accompanied by a second. The master craftsman was proprietor of his workplace, both entrepreneur and worker. The occupational-splitting species of division of labor did not at all lead inevitably to a splitting of the factors of production, labor, capital, and managerial performance into social subjects distinguishable from one another, let alone separate from one another. Therefore, despite the social contradictions between master and journeyman, which of course also existed, skilled craftsmanship formed in its classical phase a relatively homogenous class for a long time.

[24] See Max Rumpf, *Deutsches Handwerkerleben und der Aufstieg der Stadt*, Stuttgart, 1955, esp. pp. 72-74.

3. An additional feature of this kind of division of labor is the integration of the most diverse functions in the work process. It did not lead to a dissection of the work process in its functional components. The worker instead finished a specific product from A to Z. He thus saw something complete being created by his hands, sometimes even a small work of art, which satisfies to a high degree the urge to create and the need for quality, two primeval motives of human work. Labor thus already received, by virtue of the content of its task, a significance that is related to the person of the producer and, consequently, can be experienced directly. That enables the worker to identify with his work to some degree and, therefore, serves as a basis for intrinsic motivation, which is difficult to find today apart from the product-oriented species of division of labor.
4. As the final characteristic feature, it is noted that product-oriented division of labor proves to be division of labor between human persons. Its principle of rationalization creates progressively new, differentiated species of craftsmanship, which however always must be carried on by human persons. In other words, it does not replace human labor with non-human labor. That became possible on a large scale only with the inclusion of machines in the productive work process, as is typical of the industrial age. Through it, a completely new kind of division of labor occurred, the production-oriented division of labor, adapted to machines' way of functioning, which coincided with the industrial rationalization process so much that it is often equated today with rationalization in general. Although the rationalization of economic activities did not begin with industrialization, it nevertheless gains a specific structure with industrialization. That must be examined more closely.

2.3.3 *Production-Oriented Division of Labor*

2.3.3.1 Production-Oriented Division of Labor under the Conditions of Mechanically-Aided Rationalization

If product-oriented division of labor is its division according to occupations that are defined by what they produce and contain in the production process many work activities, and thus display a comprehensive character, production-oriented division of labor dissects the production functions into every more elementary component functions, which, insofar as the component functions are separated and allocated to individual persons or groups of persons, leads to the fragmentation of the work activities. As the former kind of division of labor is typical of the classical-craftsmanship epoch, which survives today only rudimentarily, the latter is typical of recent times.

The age of machines has produced, roughly speaking, two main species of machines, which were fundamental for at least the first phase of the industrial revolution: engines and production machines. The former — such as the steam engine, the generator, the motor, and the nuclear reactor — serve the production or transmission of power; the latter serve the more rational organization of the production process. Only the second type of machine is of importance in the present context. With it human persons share in the industrial rationalization concept in labor, which is characterized by the production-oriented division of labor.

Georges Friedmann distinguishes three developmental steps within the process of industrial rationalization: the step to "dependent" machines, the step to "semi-independent" machines, and the step to "fully-independent" machines.[25] The first step or first level is determined by the inclusion of dependent machines — such as the lathe, the plane, the grinder, etc. — in the work process. They are called dependent, because they still require the constant influence of the human hand. They are, therefore, operated by humans, just as earlier craftsmen handled their non-mechanical tools. They are basically highly developed, expensive tools, specialized to perform a specific basic function, of course, each according to its degree of perfection, and are called machine tools. Therefore, those who work with them, though they no longer produce finished products, but instead perform special operations in cooperation with the machine, such as turning, planing, grinding, etc., still always feel that they are professional craftsmen. And they do so all the more when they require a longer period of apprenticeship or training in order to perform their extremely demanding production functions. The intrinsic work motivation through the task-orientation itself can, therefore, be for workers at such machine tools appropriately high and easily comparable with those of the craftsmen of the old school.

The situation is otherwise with the second step of rationalization, which is characterized by the introduction of semi-independent

[25] Georges Friedmann, *Der Mensch in der mechanisierten Produktion*, Cologne, 1952, pp. 183 ff.

machines or mechanical production equipment. These stand between typical machine tools and automatic production machines, which is why they are sometimes also called semi-automatic. One example is the so-called "revolving lathe."[26] The ideal model of this step of rationalization is the assembly line, as developed by Taylorism, which has become dominant for the traditional conception of industrial rationalization, at least in the area of large-scale industry. Accordingly, the attempt is made "in the sense of the Taylor principle to bring about the separation of thought and action, of brainwork and handwork, to break up complete activities, and to eliminate thought processes systematically from the work activities."[27] That yields a segmentation of work activities according to the following schema:[28]

Table 1: Segmentation of Work Activities

Brainwork	*Handwork*	*Brainwork*
Planning and Preparation	Execution	Maintenance and Control

At this level of rationalization, the division of labor between humans and machines proceeds in such a way that brainwork remains allocated to humans and handwork is reduced to each repetitive residual function that the machine is unable or not yet able to perform. Handwork is thus emptied from the tasks and the craftsman becomes, so to speak, an accessory of the machine. On the other hand, brainwork experiences a division into the highly demanding activities of planning and labor preparation and the far less demanding functions of maintaining the machines and controlling the products produced by them. An intrinsic work motivation at the level of mere execution no longer exists, and at the level of maintenance and control only to a very limited degree. It can be supported only extrinsically, primarily by financial incentive systems, external working conditions, and "human relations." As experience shows, however, and as we know since the research of Frederick Herzberg,[29] those are insufficient motivations, so that the willingness to work and the will

[26] A lathe with a so-called revolving head, *i.e.*, a spin device for fast, primarily automatic changing of tools.

[27] Eberhard Ulich, "Arbeitspsychologische Konzepte und neue Technologien," in *Personalwirtschaftliche Aspekte neuer Technologien*, ed. Klaus J. Zink, Berlin, 1985, p. 138.

[28] *Ibid.*

to perform necessarily suffer in the long term. With that, the limits of this concept of rationalization, which follows the Taylor principle, become visible.[30] It is not only inhumane, because it reduces human persons to non-essential functions in the labor and presses them so far below their level;[31] it can also reduce the efficiency of the work, which should be promoted by the process of rationalization. One is justified, therefore, in speaking here of a "rationalization impasse."

This impasse was pointed out quite early, primarily by work psychologists and work scientists.[32] The traditional, fragmenting rationalization strategy was called into question, because it both squandered human abilities and wasted macroeconomic resources. The goal was and is a new conception of industrial rationalization, which has as its guidelines "overcoming the (Taylorist) fragmentation" of work "in favor of independent activities in the sense of the — at least partial — recovery of the unity of planning, execution, and control."[33] This should proceed in a way that does not abolish the dissection of work into various production functions as such, but instead abolishes its fragmenting separation and concentration on individual persons. And that means that several, as many as possible, work activities are to be integrated in the person of the worker, in order to prevent him or her from being reduced to a mere residual function, depressing the level of personality.

A first step in this direction of "work humanization"[34] is so-called "work expansion,"[35] in the form of either "job enlargement" or "job

[29] See Frederick Herzberg, Bernard Mausner, and Barbara Bloch Snyderman, *The Motivation to Work*, 2nd Ed., New York, 1967.

[30] See Georges Friedmann, *Grenzen der Arbeitsteilung*, Frankfurt, 1959.

[31] That obviously holds true only for the normal case. For persons who are less gifted or mentally handicapped, repetitive work that they are still able to perform can lead directly to an increase of their self-esteem, as well as their personality level.

[32] Besides Friedmann and Herzberg, who have already been mentioned, there is Peter F. Drucker, *The New Society*, New York, 1950. More recently, there is Thomas J. Peters and Robert H. Waterman, Jr., *In Search of Excellence*, New York, 1982.

[33] Ulich, "Arbeitspsychologische Konzepte und neue Technologien," p. 139.

[34] From the perspective of industrial psychology, a work activity is considered humane if it "does not damage the psychosomatic health of the worker, does not diminish his psychosocial well-being (or does so only for a short time), corresponds to his needs and qualifications, facilitates individual and/or collective exertion of influence on work conditions and systems, and is able to contribute to the development of his personality, in the sense of the promotion of his ability to act" (Ulich, "Industrieroboter," in *Technologie und Kultur*, Reinbek bei Hamburg, 1983, p. 112).

[35] Charles Lattmann, *Die verhaltenswissenschaftlichen Grundlagen der Führung des Mitarbeiters*, Bern, 1982, pp. 276-85.

enrichment." These two terms, which have long since become common in the literature, are not sharply distinguished from one another in practice. But "job enlargement" means more of a quantitative expansion of the area of responsibility, and "job enrichment" more of a qualitative expansion. In other words, in one case, the number of activities that the worker has to perform at the level of executing handwork is increased; in the other case, participation occurs beyond this level, in the functions of maintenance and control, or even planning and preparation, in other words, brainwork. That happens, for example, when the worker himself, instead of his supervisor, can set up his semi-dependent or fully-dependent machine and when it is also his responsibility to check the quality of the finished project, which otherwise would be the concern of the controller. In this way, it comes to reunifications of work that are, of course, still quite modest, but that can at least reduce the fragmentation of the production process by industrial rationalization.

A significantly longer and more promising step on the way to the humanization of work is the semi-autonomous work group, as it first came into existence in Scandinavia: "It involves an expansion of space for collective action, within which a work group can be entrusted with distinguishably diverse and extensive tasks, to be completed under its own responsibility."[36] On this basis, Volvo built a completely new kind of automobile factory in the 1970s, with the goal of "organizing production in such a way that the employees can find meaning and satisfaction in their work." In the words of the directive to the project group responsible for planning the project in detail, a factory was to be built that "without any reduction in efficiency or financial consequences, enables the employees to work in groups, to communicate freely with one another, to change their work-tasks, to vary the work speed, to identify with the product, to accept responsibility for quality, and to influence their working conditions."[37] That means consciously and deliberately turning away from the extremely piecework process, in the sense of the Taylorist assembly line method. With Volvo it was motivated — as incidentally also with Saab, which almost at the same time, likewise on the basis of group work structure, built an automobile body factory in Trollhättan[38] — by negative experiences with the

[36] Ulich, "Alternative Arbeitsstrukturen," in *Psychologie und Praxis*, 27 (1983), p. 70.
[37] Cited by Ulich, *Ibid.*, p. 72.

assembly-line system. It became increasingly difficult to find employees who wanted to work on the assembly line, with its inhumane effects. With that came extraordinarily high rates of turnover and absenteeism, all factors that strongly depress the efficiency of production. This is, incidentally, another argument for our *fundamental thesis that whatever contradicts human justice also cannot be economically rational.*

The system of the partially autonomous work group, which opens up more self-accountability, opportunities for interaction, and diversity of responsibilities[39] in production, certainly points in the direction of a more humanly just work structure. According to the above thesis, it should also be economically rational. That actually appears to be the case: "Many examples indicate that this kind of alternative work structure can also make sense economically."[40] They have been accepted more and more, especially in the area of assembly. In addition to Volvo and Saab, Ulich cites Volkswagen and also refers to Japan, where independently conceived, similar work structures are found in many firms.[41]

The most recent stage of rationalization, precipitated by the rapid development of microelectronics, which made previously unattainable perfection in the automation of mechanical work possible, has already been mentioned briefly in section 2.2. Here again, this is about a process revolutionizing the world of work and the economy, which is far from concluded, but instead is actually still beginning. That leads to new questions, about its specific type, about the presumed social effects, and about the opportunities for the more humane work structures just now brought into view under the conditions of the most recent opportunities for industrial rationalization.

[38] For details, see *Ibid.*, pp. 73 ff.

[39] According to Ulich, the scope of responsibility of one work group in the Saab automobile body factory in Trollhättan includes: direct manufacturing, setting up, inspecting, maintenance, administration, training new workers, cleaning, and transport (*Ibid.*, p. 74).

[40] *Ibid.*, pp. 70-71.

[41] *Ibid.*, pp. 76 ff. See also Curt Berg and Barbo Mazurczak, "Autonome Arbeitsgruppen als neue Form der Arbeitsorganisation," *Wirtschaftswissenschaftliches Studium*, 4 (1975), p. 190; and Lothar Seiwert, "Moderne Formen der Arbeitsorganisation (II): Autonome Arbeitsgruppen und Beurteilung der Verfahren," *Wirtschaftswissenschaftliches Studium*, 8 (1979), p. 187.

2.3.3.2 Production-Oriented Division of Labor under the Conditions of Electronically-Aided Rationalization

Every automatic system is essentially about a procedure for processing and use of information.[42] The technical or mechanical use of information, which makes possible the automation of work processes, is nothing new in itself. It may only refer to the electromagnetic relay, a control element that plays a leading role as an information-using component in conventional, mechanical automation. The new factor that electronics brought are circuits of a highly complex kind, which were inconceivable on an electro-mechanical basis. After the invention of the transistor,[43] the electronic equivalent of the electromagnetic relay, semiconductor technology, which is closely related to this achievement, made possible the integration of several transistors on a single silicon chip of a few square millimeters in 1960. That led to the term "integrated circuit," as the microelectronic component of computer technology. As a consequence, an incredible, exponentially progressing process of compression and increasing complexity was brought about by miniaturization. In 1970 there were already a thousand transistors per integrated circuit, in 1980 a million,[44] and in 1990 it probably will be possible to have a billion. It can be said by way of summary: "Modern microelectronics and its applications provide methods with which very large quantities of the simplest information-using elements can be realized with high operational security in the smallest space and at the lowest cost."[45]

From this it can be gathered that the decisive significance of microelectronic technology consists in its "suitability for high complexity." It offers far more than earlier processes in the technical use of information, and not only quantitatively, but also qualitatively. For highly complex pieces of equipment for the use of information become suitable as means to the solution of highly complex problems, and thus, to a certain extent, also to the adoption of "thought functions," which

[42] The following observations are based on the outline of computer scientist Hansjürg Mey, *Mikroelektronik: Möglichkeiten, Gefahren und Grenzen*, Zürich, 1982; and *Mikroelektronik: Grundlagen der Informatik im betrieblichen Einsatz*, Bern, 1985.

[43] A "transistor" (from "transfer resistor") is, strictly speaking, a small electronic component or semiconductor element used as an amplifier, rectifier, or switch. Because there are dozens of such components in portable radios, they are simply (and technically incorrectly) called "transistors."

[44] Mey, *Mikroelektronik: Möglichkeiten, Gefahren und Grenzen*, p. 10.

[45] *Ibid.*, p. 5.

contains a qualitative dimension. Computer scientist Hansjürg Mey, who expresses himself extremely cautiously and circumspectly in this respect, makes the point as follows: "With all reservations about the use of the term 'thought' in technical contexts, it nevertheless cannot be denied that the automatic use of information is beginning to take on, with growing complexity, 'thought-like' characteristics."[46] In other words, devices based upon microelectronics are tools that can replace not only handwork, but also "brainwork." And in this respect they can be called a kind of "thought tool."[47] That is undoubtedly a striking element of the characterization of the specific kind of electronically-aided automation.

But the new industrial revolution that microelectronics has introduced is not based solely on the creation of highly complex integrated circuits, with their new, automated possibilities for using information and control. Their general dissemination required an additional large step, which was taken in 1971 with the introduction of the microprocessor.[48]

Highly complex integrated circuits have one unfortunate disadvantage. They can be sold at low, affordable prices only in large quantities. But, since high complexity is always tied to high specialization and, therefore, great restriction of the area of application, it contradicts the economic principle of producing as much as possible, in order to reduce the unit cost of production. Mey speaks in this context of a "dilemma of microelectronics."[49] This dilemma between the

[46] *Ibid.*, pp. 5-6.

[47] This, of course, does not mean that tools, such as a computer-controlled machine tool regulated numerically by microprocessors, for instance, can acquire the ability to think on their own. They can, however, perform production operations for which a conventional machine would require a thinking human worker. But they can do so only to the extent that they have been programmed by thinking human persons. One could say that they have secondary, but not primary (*i.e.*, self-sufficient) "thinking ability." (See also 2.3.3.3, note 64.)

[48] The microprocessor, to be technically correct, is only a microelectronic component with the function of a computer processing unit. A computer, therefore, consists of more than a processing unit. Other components belong to it, such as memory, input and output components, etc. If one includes all of these components in a single microelectronic circuit, then one has a microcomputer, by which the microprocessor becomes programmable. It is acceptable, though not in accordance with strict terminology, to use the terms microprocessor and microcomputer interchangeable. But their established application to a personal computer, which contains many other things in addition to one or more microcomputers, is technically incorrect.

[49] Mey, *Mikroelektronik: Möglichkeiten, Gefahren und Grenzen*, p. 15.

self-contradictory demand for specialization and mass-production has now been removed to a large extent by the microprocessor or microcomputer. This is, in principle, "a highly complex integrated circuit, with preferences specific to this technology, that is however *universally usable,*" and "by means of programming," by which it "can be applied to the currently specific purpose."[50] Because microprocessors can be programmed in many different ways, they are not only universally usable, they also permit the enormous potential of the computer for using information and solving problems to be continually specified and decentralized.[51] Thus, the computerization of industry has seized as an opportunity for the most recent phase of rationalization not only the area of administration (electronic data processing and word processing), but also those of engineering (computer-aided drawing and construction) and of actual production (computer-aided production) in growing size. With the high capability for simultaneous universalization and decentralization, which even makes it possible today to move jobs from the office into one's home by means of the personal computer, a second basic feature of the electronic type of rationalization is identified.

An additional basic feature has already been indirectly intimated in the preceding discussion. Automation is also advancing on the path of its electronic development and refinement in the area of thought, and therefore of brainwork. Activities of a complexity that previously could be dealt with only with the help of the intellect are now carried out by appropriately programmed computers. This is also nothing new in itself. Mechanized calculating machines, for example, have been in existence for a long time. The first one was constructed by Pascal in 1642. What is new is the magnitude of the mechanization of thought-like functions. It extends as far as the sphere of elementary production. If human persons, generally speaking, shared handwork with machines during the pre-electronic stage of rationalization, today they must also share brainwork with them more and more. The classical kind of segmentation of work activities into handwork and brainwork, as is still typical of the conventional (i.e. Taylorist) form of industrial rationalization, therefore appears to be obsolete. In the future, there

[50] *Ibid.*, p. 18.

[51] "Because it is small, inexpensive, and reliable, the microprocessor or microcomputer has opened the way into a *completely new area of use,* the decentralized control of equipment of almost every size" (*ibid.*).

will be less and less handwork requiring brainwork in the area of industrial production, which already results in the trend of "employees increasingly moving from the factory into the office."[52] On the other hand, in the technical and business offices, as well as in those of administration or services, including research sites and universities, former brainwork will likewise be taken over by computer-aided equipment. Since these for their part must be provided with programs, then must be programmed for their special application, and finally must be operated expertly, new brainwork arises in place of the old. All in all, this brings about an increasing shift of emphasis from handwork to brainwork, and thus is oriented towards activities that are increasingly intellectual and in that respect, as a rule, more demanding, even with many workers in executive positions.[53] It also leads, however, to a labor-dividing segmentation of this brainwork into quite different levels of qualification. The creation of programs (software)[54] through translation of the problem into processes appropriate for computers (analysts) is one, the specification of the program for specific purposes (programmers) is another, and the practical servicing of the programmed computers on the level of use (operators) is yet another. A third basic feature of the microelectronic type of rationalization shows itself in this double-effect of the shift of emphasis from handwork to brainwork and the simultaneous segmentation of brainwork into many different levels of qualification. What are its specific effects on the process of industrial production and its work structure?

[52] *Ibid.*, p. 51.

[53] Cf. Norbert Koubek, "Neue Entwicklungen in der Unternehmens- und Konzernorganisation," *Die Mitbestimmung*, 32 (1986), p. 8: "At first, automation and increased production flexibility lead to a rejection of the stark Taylorist division of labor. First, many jobs are eliminated. Second, for the remaining employees, the control, adjustment, and maintenance of the machines require extensive technical knowledge. Consequently, in many cases *new and increased demands* are associated with the new technologies."

[54] In computer science, one speaks of "software" and "hardware." "Software" means the entirety of the programs fed into a computer by the user, and thus, metaphorically speaking, its "brain." "Hardware," on the other hand, is the entirety of the technical equipment of a computer, as it were, its "skeleton." The French, who in contrast to German-speakers defend themselves from the proliferation of Americanisms, speak instead of "*le logiciel*" and "*le matériel.*" It is, however, not as easy as it may seem to keep these definitions separated from one another in practice. There can be gray areas between them, for example, when a single computer program is built into a machine and, so to speak, belongs to its material existence. For that, the term "firmware" has recently become established.

2.3.3.3 Specific Effects and Possibilities in the Field of Production

With this new set of questions, of course, it is not possible to go into great detail. We must be satisfied with considering only the main aspects, and with doing so summarily.

First of all, computer-aided production will not completely replace conventional production, at least not for some time, and certainly not all at once: "If one compares the opportunities for using microelectronics in the year 2000 and equates this degree of use with 100%, only 15% of these opportunities are being used today."[55] The new wave of technological change may attain its full strength in only thirty to fifty years.[56] But it cannot be doubted that in industrial production, as well as in administrative offices, the future will be determined by microelectronics. In which direction is the trend headed?

This trend can already be foreseen clearly.[57] The new wave of rationalization is based upon the technology of computerized numerical control (CNC). CNC machines are machines whose movements in dealing with products are no longer controlled by hand, by means of levers and cranks, etc., but instead are controlled automatically by programs stored in the computer. Their use is in the process of constant and rapid growth, so that it is already difficult to estimate their numbers. But their flexibility and, therefore, their opportunities for use remain limited.

Industrial robots are more flexible than CNC machines — where the distinction between the two highly developed apparatuses is blurred. Industrial robots are automatic operation systems that can be programmed freely in several axes of movement, are equipped with tools, such as buckets, etc., and can reach every point within their range of production. These properties enable them to carry out a multitude of tasks. In addition, when equipped with an integrated sensor, they are able not only to perform work, but also to check

[55] K. Friebe, "Mikroelektronik — Perspektiven der industriellen Revolution," in *Mikroelektronik — Chancen und Probleme*, Berlin, 1983, p. 10.

[56] See Wassily Leontief, "Den technologischen Schock dämpfen," Interview in *IAO-Nachrichten*, Vol. 19, No. 4, 1983.

[57] The following observations are supported by Walter Bodmer, ed., *Automatisierung in der Industrie*, Zürich, 1984, a publication of the Society for the Development of the Swiss Economy, which compiles information from competent experts concerning the application of microelectronics in industry.

themselves for quality and accuracy. The robotization of industrial production is likewise advancing rapidly.[58]

The next level above CNC machines and industrial robots, and thus above computer-aided manufacturing (CAM), is distributed numerical control (DNC). This is a smaller or larger hierarchically structured computer system, in which a particular subsystem is controlled by a higher system. The connection is accomplished by means of a central processor, which, as the top of the network, already has links, above CAM, to the systems of computer aided design (CAD) and computer aided planning (CAP), and therefore to engineering and management. Such complex systems are advantageous for two reasons. First, an enormous number of control commands — possibly thousands — are necessary even for simple processes. Second, a graduated structure of superordinate and subordinate control units ensures a much greater opportunity for modification of the control of the specific production requirements. Basically, tested human principles of organization are simply transferred to a hierarchy of computers that must simulate human activities. Furthermore, it makes possible flexible manufacturing systems (FMS) that link entire groups of numerically controlled machines and industrial robots and coordinate their activities in an automated production unity.

The extension of the technology of the numerical control of CNC machines to the computer hierarchy of the DNC and the conjoined realization of flexible manufacturing systems does not at all mean the end point of contemporary possibilities for the automation and rationalization of industry. Development, instead, continues. The automatic processing of products can, on the one hand, be preceded by its automatic design by CAD and, on the other hand, be followed by the automatic assembly in a flexible assembling system (FAS). Moreover, flexible manufacturing and assembly systems can be linked by an automatic transport system to an automatic raw materials stock, an automatic finished product stock, and an automatic dispatch stock. To the extent that this is accomplished, there appears the factory completely automated on the basis of computer integrated

[58] In 1985 approximately 100,000 industrial robots (with at least three axes of movement) were in use worldwide, the greatest number in Japan. We can expect a doubling of this number every two years. Japan also has the greatest density of robots. There are 5.0 industrial robots for every 10,000 persons in Japan, 3.6 in Sweden, 1.4 in West Germany, and 0.5 in Switzerland (Society for the Development of the Swiss Economy, ed., *Notizen zur Wirtschaft*, No. 4, Zürich, 1986, pp. 2-3).

manufacturing (CIM). That is, of course, for the most part still a thing of the future. According to Prof. E. Matthias of the Swiss Federal Institute of Technology Zürich, there are in the entire world only partial solutions here, and it would be extraordinarily difficult, indeed impossible, to determine the point in time at which the CIM system will be fully realized.[59] Nevertheless, partial solutions exist. And there can be no question that the trend is in this direction.[60]

In view of the perspective that is only intimated here and that is in certain respects, at least to some extent, open to objection, two questions are posed. First, what role will human work still have to play in the industry of the approaching electronic age, with its long-term trend in the direction of universal automation? And second, can the way of rationalization determining it, insofar as it permits human work to exist at all, be united with humane work structures?

It is certain that the growing use of microelectronics in the workplace and the office will eliminate traditional jobs in ever-greater numbers.[61] On the other hand, it will also create new jobs. Therefore, while the slogan "chips are job killers" contains some truth, it is only one side of the coin. If in actual production the number of products per worker increases enormously, that does not necessarily mean a reduction of the cost per function. This instead shifts, to stress the point once again, from the workplace to the office, from handwork to brainwork.[62]

[59] Bodmer, ed., *Automatisierung in der Industrie*, p. 12. On the present state of CIM technology see Volker Heiner, "Nur keine Insellösungen... Computer-Integrated-Manufacturing (CIM) als Chance und Herausforderung," *Schweizerische Handelszeitung*, 10 November 1988, pp. 85-86.

[60] That is just as true of the "Eastern" as of the "Western" industrial world. At the end of 1985 the Comecon nations signed an agreement with the goal of accelerating technological development in their societies. According to it, the first priority is the development of highly modern computers, and the second priority is the extensive, (*i.e.*, robotized) automation of production processes (Andreas Oplatka, "Der Comecon im Banne des Jahres 2000," *Neue Zürcher Zeitung*, No. 295, 19 December 1985, pp. 15-16).

[61] Ulich offers as a spectacular example the Murata factory in Inuyama, Japan, where "an increase in productivity of four to five hundred percent, with a reduction of the workforce by two thirds," was achieved with the help of flexible production systems ("Arbeitspsychologische Konzepte und neue Technologien," in *Personalwirtschaftliche Aspekte neuer Technologien*, ed. Klaus J. Zink, Berlin, 1985, p. 144).

[62] As early as 1980, only 58% of workers in the primary and secondary sectors (agriculture and industry) in West Germany performed manual production tasks. According to the most recent prognoses, in the year 2000 in the entire economy about 17.7 million workers will perform infrastructure and service tasks, while the number of those who still exercise real production activities will be reduced to 6.6 million

It belongs to the specific peculiarity of computerized machines, industrial robots, and production systems, however, that they are also able to replace human brainwork. That costs jobs no less in offices, of both the technical and the business-administrative sectors, and will cost increasingly more. Even the creation of software may be affected by it, as soon as "intelligent" computers are developed even further. But to believe that machines could simply replace humans, even if only within the area of technical intelligence, would be utopian. No matter how astonishing their "cognitive" abilities may be, as with the latest generation of robots,[63] machines are programmed thinking-things, and nothing more than that. They will never become independent thinking subjects that can think what has never previously been thought, will never be able to learn beyond what is known in creative acts of discovery.[64] Edward A. Feigenbaum, professor at Stanford University, founder of knowledge engineering theory, and pioneer in the area of artificial intelligence, puts it thus: "*Humans are*

(Walther Müller-Jentsch, "Industrielle Beziehungen im Umbruch," *Die Mitbestimmung*, 32 [1986], p. 442).

63 The following standards have been established for the new generation of robots:

- Robots must identify objects and determine their position and orientation. They should also be able to do this when parts of these objects are hidden by other objects. They must recognize configurations of objects, even scenes.
- Robots should be able to understand natural language, so that instructing and controlling them can take place simply and without special knowledge.
- Given certain objectives, intelligent robots should be able to formulate partial objectives and analyze a task to the point of forming a plan of action. In the process, they must make complex decisions, deduce new knowledge from existing knowledge, and even generalize existing knowledge, in the sense of analogous techniques.
- Plans are to be carried out with sensor-controlled adaptation to new or changing conditions (H. Sydow and K.-P. Timpe, cited by Ulich, "Industrieroboter," 1983, p. 114).

64 Quite recently, of course, a new branch of computer science has developed, "knowledge engineering," already called the "transition to the second age of computers." In addition to the Japanese project of the "fifth-generation computer" (see note 63), so-called "expert systems," above all, are characteristic of it. The former project has as its objective, as has already been mentioned, the development of robots that are able, going beyond the mere function of calculating, to draw a kind of logical conclusion. "Expert systems" are systems that can draw formal-logical conclusions on the basis of stored and processed expert knowledge, which enables them to play the role of, as it were, qualified experts within their area of application. In view of this, the term "artificial intelligence" (AI) has been coined. Its usual German translation, "*Künstliche Intelligenz*" (KI), has been the cause of misunderstandings, because the English word "intelligence" does not correspond precisely to the German artificial word "*Intelligenz*." In addition to the uniquely human capacities of knowing,

very good at learning. So, let us build a *human-machine partnership*, in which the machines take over the rapid reasoning and the humans take over the learning."[65] In other words, creative reasoning belongs to humans, but machines do the reasoning incomparably faster. Both together constitute an ideal partnership. This picture of the "human-machine partnership" is, of course, much too high. Ultimately, there can be partnership deserving of the name only between persons or groups of persons of equal value. Therefore, the term is, strictly speaking, not applicable to the work-relationship between human and machine. The machine is not a person and, therefore, can never attain the value of the human person. Either persons remain personal subjects in their work, in which case they cannot be mechanical, or they become mechanical in their work — as the Taylorist rationalization strategy requires — in which case they cease to exist as human persons; they become alienated from themselves as attachments to the machine. It would be more correct to speak of cooperation in the division of labor, according to which humans understand themselves to be dependent in the work process upon the thinking machine as an efficient tool,[66] but nevertheless to remain the

understanding, and evaluating, it also means simply the "collection, communication, and analysis of information" (as in "intelligence service"). Thus AI and KI are concerned essentially with the use, capable of drawing conclusions, of information on the basis of programs created by human intelligence. If one speaks in this context of "intelligence," it must be made clear that this is an intelligence dependent upon humans. Particularly in the construction of an expert system, the specialized knowledge of human experts is required. Such systems, therefore, are not really "intelligent"; they only act as if they were intelligent. One should, therefore, guard against exaggeration concerning its possibilities. See primarily Hubert L. Dreyfus and Stuart E. Dreyfus, *Mind over Machine*, New York, 1986. See also Hans-Jürgen Appelrath and Jirí Kriz, "Wissensbasierte Expertensysteme," No. 251, *Neue Zürcher Zeitung*, 29 October 1986, pp. 91-92, and Ulrich Klotz, "'Künstliche Intelligenz' und Expertensysteme," *Die Mitbestimmung*, 32 (1986), pp. 562-67. A more optimistic outlook is expressed by Bernd Radig, computer scientist at the Technical University of Munich. According to him, expert systems bring about "a creative solution to problems, of which human persons previously were not aware" ("SHZ-Interview," *Schweizerische Handelszeitung*, 16 April 1987, p. 61).

[65] "SHZ-Interview," *Schweizerische Handelszeitung*, 5 December 1985, p. 53.

[66] Dreyfus and Dreyfus, whose basic thesis is that "computers as reasoning machines cannot match human intuition and expertise" (*Mind over Machine*, p. xi), also emphasize their instrumental importance: "It seems obvious to us that there are tasks for which computers are appropriate and even indispensable. Computers are more deliberate, more precise, and less prone to exhaustion and error than the most caring and conscientious human being. Examples of computers as useful tools are numerous and easy to come by" (*ibid.*, p. xii).

determining subjects, since they operate the machines, and since they must remain the determining subjects, if this cooperation is to avoid deteriorating into a meaningless end-in-itself event, à la Tinguely.[67] Human persons, seen in this way, will also remain qualitatively irreplaceable in the economic world characterized by microelectronics, and indeed at all of its levels of activity. The question is, though, to what quantitative degree that will be the case. It should not be casually denied that in this particular respect there exist grounds for great fear concerning the long term.

The second question raised above still remains, namely the question about the prospects for humane work structures under the conditions of electronically-aided rationalization, both in the area of manufacturing and in the office. The answer depends, first of all, on whether this type of rationalization will continue to push the Taylorist fragmentation of work forward — today the fragmentation of brainwork also — or can drive it backwards.

Labor scientist Eberhard Ulich, on the basis of precise knowledge of the situation, is of the opinion that both possibilities are real and, therefore, that "microelectronic technology can be used both to support the fragmenting rationalization strategy and to promote the integrated strategy, according to which the computer has the function of a tool."[68] If that is correct, this technology possesses a potential for humanization, which can be used, but which can also be squandered.[69] It is used, if the new possibilities for rationalization are not dealt with in an isolated way, i.e., only from the viewpoint of technical feasibility and economic profitability, but instead are realized relationally, as the basic conditions of a humanly just work structure.[70] This would have to mean that already in the phase of the conception of work systems, plans would include objective space for freedom of action, permitting workers to assert and to develop their personalities

[67] "Society must clearly distinguish 'know how' and 'know what'.... To confuse the common sense, wisdom, and mature judgment of the expert with today's artificial intelligence, or to value them less highly, would be genuine stupidity" (*ibid.*, p. 201).

[68] Ulich, "Arbeitspsychologische Konzepte und neue Technologien," p. 142.

[69] Norbert Troy shows impressively the extent to which the latter is the case with the traditional use of computers in contemporary office automation: "Computergerechte oder menschengerechte Lösungen," in *Technologie und Kultur*, Reinbek bei Hamburg, 1983, pp. 55-62.

[70] See 2.3.3.1, fn. 34.

in work activities. Ulich speaks concerning it of a "prospective work arrangement" or of "preventive intervention in work," both of which mean structuring work in computerized industry with an orientation towards autonomy.[71]

Approaches to a reorientation of this kind, which simultaneously reduce the Taylorist dissection of work and reunite various activity functions, are already in existence, though it must be said that they are still quite modest. Essentially, this is equally about the attempt to humanize work with mechanically-aided rationalization, about "job enlargement," "job enrichment," "job rotation," and "semi-autonomous work groups," and about the combination of all of these possibilities.

The way in which job enlargement and job enrichment can be implemented in computerized manufacturing technology is illustrated by the following example of the structuring of work concerning the CNC machine, which was introduced in Japan and has now gained entry in Europe and, to a lesser degree, in America:

> The Japanese machine-operator performs *diverse activities* beyond his narrowly defined main task, such as servicing the machine, performing minor repairs, and writing and optimizing NC programs. He also participates in the *organizational* process, by thinking and acting with others in preceding and following production stages.[72]

A work arrangement of this kind, which reunites fragmented functional parts and, therefore, is oriented towards unity, and which enables workers to operate machines as tools and thereby to experience themselves as subjects competent to act, is, of course, based upon some assumptions. First, this assumes a flexible system of work that gives workers room for their own action, allows them to participate in the work of programming, and includes them in the organization of the production process in such a way that they can at least understand its general structure and their function in it. And it is obviously necessary to have well-trained workers, who show a readiness to understand complex systems and are always willing to learn something new.[73] It is

[71] Ulich, "Präventive Intervention im Betrieb," in *Präventive Intervention im Betrieb*, Reinbek bei Hamburg, 1983, pp. 48-70.

[72] Hans Jürgen Ulrich, "Automation ist nicht alles," *Schweizerische Handelszeitung*, No. 36, 5 September 1985, p. 69.

[73] Troy shows that something similar is true of office workers, "Computergerechte oder menschengerechte Lösungen," pp. 62-68.

worth noting in this context that "more than 90% of the Japanese attend a senior high school."[74]

The concept of semi-autonomous work groups as a means to the humanization of work can apparently also be tied to modern production technology. Following a report of E. Gauderon (1984), Ulich refers to an apparently carefully controlled attempt in a factory of the German firm Sulzer-Weise, in Bruchsal, in which so-called "production islands" have been successfully implemented:

> Each production island consists of an NC lathe, an NC drilling and milling machine, a universal lathe, as well as... a work place "for planning and controlling the activities in the production island, with a link to the central micro-processor and connected high-speed printer."[75]

Work in the production island is performed in shifts, with two workers per shift. They perform all tasks independently, from the preparation of materials to the delivery of the completed product. "Work for which no machine or equipment is available in this production island is subcontracted by the workers to other production units. Responsibility for scheduling, however, remains with the group, as does quality control."[76] It is obvious that with a work structure of this kind, the demand on the workers is relatively high and, furthermore, ensures their position as subjects in the production process.

These two real-world examples[77] show that it is possible, even under the conditions of microelectronically conceived rationalization, to realize efficient work structures that counteract the Taylorist strategy of the fragmentation of work, are oriented towards the integrity of the activities, and create room for workers to act responsibly, without requiring the withering away of their personal subjectivity. And this is no less true for office workers than for those engaged in industrial manufacturing.[78] But this does not at all mean that actual development also goes in this direction. It is merely a possibility, not necessarily the reality. The reality often looks quite different. Norbert Troy even finds it necessary to say, "Some developments in the area of office work" suggest "that a form of division of labor dating from

[74] Ulrich, *ibid.*
[75] Ulich, "Arbeitspsychologische Konzepte und neue Technologien," pp. 143-44.
[76] *Ibid.*, p. 144.
[77] Cf. *ibid.*, pp. 144-45. See also Ulich, "Industrieroboter," pp. 113-19.
[78] Ulich, "Arbeitspsychologische Konzepte und neue Technologien," pp. 146-51.

the beginning of this century, Taylorism, has just been brought into action."[79] The same author maintains, "With microelectronics there now exists *the* opportunity to halt the increase of the division of labor, by means of the appropriate introduction of new methods of work, and to begin reducing it,"[80] in order to prepare the way to a more humanly just structure of work. But if the opportunity is missed, if the process of rationalization continues generally down the traditional path of Taylorism, if possible even more strongly, then it will be inevitable that a large number of workers will be completely mechanized and reduced to the status of mere instruments of production, and Walter Volpert's pessimistic description of them, "computer-programming humans,"[81] will be accurate. Technological "progress," if one even decides to continue using this problematic term, does not lead to human justice simply on its own, but only when it gives in to humanly just objectives.

2.3.4 *Socially and Economically Relevant Consequences of the Process of Industrial Rationalization for Human Persons*

The fact that the process of industrial rationalization had to entail far-reaching consequences for society and the economy goes without saying. They have already been mentioned to some extent in the preceding discussion. It will, nevertheless, still be helpful to cite them explicitly, to the degree that doing so will be beneficial for the continuation of our deliberations.[82]

1. First, in contrast to product-oriented division of labor, which survives residually today, primarily in small-scale manual-labor and in arts and crafts, production-oriented division of labor has on the whole an extremely capital-intensive character. The machine system — power-generating, manufacturing, traction,

[79] *Ibid.*, p. 64.

[80] *Ibid.*

[81] Walter Volpert, "Denkmaschinen und Maschinendenken," in *Technologie und Kultur*, Reinbek bei Hamburg, 1983, pp. 10-29. Various other authors are similarly critical: Peter Brödner, Detlef Krüger, and Bernd Senf, *Der programmierte Kopf*, Berlin, 1981; Jürgen Friedrich, Friedrich Wicke, and Walter Wicke, *Computereinsatz*, Reinbek bei Hamburg, 1982; H. Kubicek, "Glasfasernetze als Autobahnen zum elektronischen Büro und zum elektronischen Heim," in DGB Landesbezirk Rheinland-Pfalz, ed., *Medientag 1982*, Mainz, 1983, pp. 15-30.

[82] Cf. Günter Friedrichs and Adam Schaff, eds., *Auf Gedeih und Verderb*, Vienna, 1982.

and information-processing machines — belongs indispensably to this type of division of labor. Machines are, however, incomparably more expensive means of production than the simple tools of earlier craftsmen. Purchasing them, at least in large numbers, is possible today only for a few well-funded persons, groups of persons, societies, etc. This amounts to a significant shift of emphasis from the factor of labor to that of capital. Anyone wishing to produce something in the industrial age must have capital, in order to finance the relatively high investments that production equipment requires. From that, a second point follows.

2. If it was typical of the age of craftsmen that a large number of the producers worked with means of production that they themselves owned, this has become increasingly atypical in the course of modern industrialization. From its very beginning, a strongly declining number of owner-entrepreneurs faced a rapidly growing number of wage-laborers, with the result that the basic economic interests of the two groups were at opposite poles and the formation of economic classes was provoked. The allocation of work between humans and machines, between *wage*-labor and production-*capital*, led to divisions in society along class lines. It simultaneously promoted the tendency towards mass production and thus to the formation of large firms. The larger the firms, however, the larger, more confusing, and less predictable the markets with which they had to relate. And, as the technology on which the labor-divided production was based became more sophisticated, the demands on the manager became greater, because they were more complex. Entrepreneurial capability began to depend upon specialized "know how," just as much as, if not even more than upon sufficient capital. And the two could be possessed by two different people. The management and ownership of firms began to diverge, especially in the stock corporation, which became typical of the industrial age. The corporate manager, who had the corporate capital at his disposal, but did not possess all of it and did not need to own more than a symbolic amount of it, began to dominate, while the owner-entrepreneur, apart from small and, at the most, medium-sized firms, became the exception. In other words, "managerial performance" and "capital," as two of the factors of production, became more or less independent of one another. And in that way production-oriented division of labor (as distinguished from product-oriented division

of labor) is accompanied by a separation of the factors of labor, capital, and managerial performance or, more precisely, a separation of their possession.

3. Furthermore, it is obvious that production-oriented division of labor generally leads to a displacement of human labor by mechanical labor and, therefore, to a separation of production and employment in the industrial sector. This is especially true of the electronic age. To be sure, electronically-aided rationalization, as has already been noted, does not just eliminate old jobs; it also creates new employment opportunities. The increase in productivity appears on the whole, however, to be of a kind such that the gap between the jobs lost and those newly gained will continue to widen. Japan, with its relatively low unemployment rate (which, admittedly, would also be approximately 6% if calculated by European methods), provides no evidence to the contrary. That nation, which leads the rest of the world in rationalization technology, profits from the fact that its market share in the production primarily of hardware,[83] and consequently of CNC machines, industrial robots, consumer electronics, etc., is extremely large today, as a result of which there exists an increase in jobs that cannot simply be generalized and can hardly be sustained for the long term. The more mechanical labor is substituted for human labor, the rarer jobs become in the areas where this takes place. A tendency towards long-term unemployment, caused partially by technology, is looming on the horizon. If the distribution of work to as many people as possible is not achieved, this tendency will inevitably lead to a splitting of society, a splitting into those who are employed and those who are not,[84] into rationalization winners and rationalization losers.
4. Finally, the character of work will also change for many people, insofar as that has not already happened. Work with and on

[83] "It is a fact that Japan's contribution to the world-wide software market is modest and does not compare with its successes in the hardware market" (Mey, "Auch Japaner kochen nur mit Wasser," *Schweizerische Handelszeitung*, No. 22, 29 May 1987, p. 80).

[84] According to one of the results of an ongoing research project, "Manto," at the Swiss Federal Institute of Technology in Zürich and Lausanne, which is investigating the effects of telecommunication, if working hours remain unchanged, 83,000-255,000 fewer workers will be needed in Swiss offices in the year 2025 than are needed today (*Tages-Anzeiger*, No. 82, 10 April 1986, p. 43).

"thinking machines" points to a trend into anonymity and abstractness.

To speak of anonymity is to say that the human partner disappears in the work. Automated production sites are sparsely populated. With electronic communication and the electronic processing of bank transactions, etc., contact with people is minimized. If people work at home by means of the personal computer, they may begin to feel isolated or lonely in their work. Moreover, as the sensory connection to the events and products of work fades, work becomes abstract. Operators who program their CNC machines do not need to "handle" either the tools or the products. With electronic communication, a message does not need to be brought "tangibly" to paper. Even when it places considerable demands on the worker, many people have difficulty experiencing such work even as work, at least as work capable of satisfying them directly, i.e. intrinsically, with its sensory-discernable content. That is not to say, of course, that this will always be the case. Even work whose traditional character has altered can be associated with a new, subjectively experienced sense of work. The extent to which this will happen, the degree to which it will be accepted, not merely as lucrative, but also as humanly fulfilling work, remains to be seen. A similar situation exists with new kinds of stress that are partially already known and partially still anticipated.[85] There are problems here that we certainly have not already overcome and that, therefore, only make our efforts to humanize work in the shadows of contemporary rationalization methods all the more urgent.

2.4 The Factors of Production

2.4.1 *On the Taxonomy of Terminology*

The preceding analysis of the process of industrial rationalization has concluded, among other things, that production-oriented division of labor is related to a separation of the various factors of production or, more precisely, of the possession of those factors. But what are factors of production?

[85] Concerning the field of technical construction, see Manfred Burr, "Computer Aided Design (CAD)," *Die Mitbestimmung*, 30 (1984), pp. 91-96.

Speaking quite generally, the term serves as a label for the material and immaterial inputs necessary for the production of economic goods and services (output). The way in which the various factors of production are systematically classified in economics depends upon the viewpoint from which they are examined.

In economics, the classification of the factors of production as labor, land, and capital has been established since the time of the classical political economists. This taxonomy of factors serves principally to explain the distribution of income. The kind of income corresponding to the factor of labor is wages; to the factor of land, rent; and to capital, interest or profit. A different taxonomy, originating from Erich Gutenberg, has gained acceptance in business management theory. With it the factors of production are seen from the perspective of production performance. Gutenberg[86] accordingly makes a distinction between elementary and dispositive factors. The elementary factors are working capital (production equipment together with the production site), material, and (object-related) work performance. The dispositive factors are management, planning, and organization, with the goal of using the elementary factors in an economically efficient manner. Recently, technical progress and its innovative power have been mentioned as another factor of production.[87] Labor and capital (invested in the working capital and material) are thus considered to be elementary factors according to this taxonomy, in contrast to the dispositive factors, which are related specifically to managerial activity.

Managerial performance or dispositive labor can, of course, also be encountered as a factor of production in macroeconomically-oriented taxonomies. Jean-Baptiste Say (1767-1832) already identified it as a specific factor and placed it beside land, labor, and capital. It can, of course, be objected that managerial activity is a specific labor function in the macroeconomic perspective, which should in principle be classified as belonging to the factor of labor. That is correct in principle. But differentiating between implementing and dispositive activities within the factor of labor may be advisable, because the two

[86] Erich Gutenberg, *Grundlagen der Betriebswirtschaftslehre*, Vol. I: *Die Production*, 12th Ed., Berlin, 1966, pp. 3 ff.

[87] See Helmut Walter, "Technischer Fortschritt in der Volkswirtschaft," in *Handwörterbuch der Wirtschaftswissenschaften*, Vol. 7, pp. 569-83; The Federal Minister for Research and Technology, ed., *Technischer Fortschritt*, Düsseldorf, 1981.

ways of functioning are quite different and cannot simply be attributed to one another.

2.4.2 *An Overview of the Factors of Production*

The "factors of production" are thus understood to mean the entirety of the material and non-material resources necessary for the production of goods and services. Their employment takes place as a process of factor-combination, from which the product emerges, ready for consumption.[88] Although the factors of production are related and cannot always be clearly distinguished from one another, it is expedient to consider each of them separately.

2.4.2.1 The Factor of Land, or Nature

"Land" has traditionally been considered the original factor of production, because it is found in nature and, therefore, is not produced and cannot be derived from anything else. For the Physiocrats,[89] history's first organized school of political economy, the soil had a dominant position in the process of production. They did not claim, however, as is often asserted, that it was the only factor of production. It is true, of course, that according to the teaching of their master, François Quesnay (1694-1774), this natural good was considered to be the primary source of wealth, and agriculture was regarded as the only way to increase it. Behind this, incidentally, is a theory of production rooted in the scholastic tradition of the Middle Ages, according to which production is understood as an increase of matter, which can be achieved only by agriculture, together with the delivery of raw materials.

Land, as a factor of production, is defined today in a much wider sense. It means not only areas of land useful for agricultural or mining, but also everything provided by land above and beyond that: forests, bodies of water, mineral resources of every kind, recreation areas, land for building, advantages of location, etc., in a word, nature. Consequently, this factor is no longer a homogenous good. But what characterizes all categories of this good is the fact that land,

[88] Artur Woll, *Allgemeine Volkswirtschaftslehre*, 7th Ed., Munich, 1981, p. 54.

[89] Fritz Karl Mann, "Physiokratie," in *Handwörterbuch der Sozialwissenschaften*, Vol. 8, pp. 296-302.

as the epitome of the "natural resources," is "fundamentally unincreasable" and, therefore, its degree of scarcity increases, despite the constant amount of existing land, "when the endowment of work in the economy increases."[90]

In opposition to this, to be sure, some authors assert that land is increasable, since nowhere near all of the land in the world, including the raw material reserves within it, is now being used. The theory of the increasability of this good, however, is not valid for land as a whole, but only for individual categories of its use, and then only relatively. Thus, land that is unsuitable or not very suitable for agriculture can be developed to provide more land for industrial or residential purposes. But that does not change the in-principle and relatively always-growing scarcity of land in the contemporary economic scenario.

Another question is whether, as the American political economist Henry Charles Carey (1793-1879) held, land is not just as much a produced factor of production as machinery, and should be classified as belonging to the factor of capital.[91] Ultimately, even for agricultural use, it must at first be cultivated at some expense and be prepared in some other way. For specific categories of land, such as well-located industrial zones, which require high investment for their preparation, this is unquestionably correct. What is considered primarily here is not simply land, but capital invested in it for production. Thus, the ownership of land appears in balance sheets under the rubric "capital assets." But, again, that does not change the fact that land as such pre-exists and, therefore, is not produced. Erich Carell is thus correct: "The fact that human beings have worked the earth for centuries does not turn it into a human creation."[92] And for this reason it nevertheless remains advisable, even in the conditions of the contemporary industrial economy, to consider land, or nature, to be a separate factor of production, even though it is often no longer possible to distinguish it clearly from capital.[93]

[90] Erich Carell, "Boden," in *Handwörterbuch der Sozialwissenschaften*, Vol. 2, p. 318.

[91] This view was later developed by John Bates Clark (1847-1938) into a theory that ultimately reduced all of the production functions to capital and labor, and thus excluded land and its resources as a factor of production.

[92] Carell, "Boden," p. 316.

[93] Therefore, simply subsuming land or nature within the category of humanly-created capital is a serious mistake, because it leads to the misconception that "nature is increasable to the same degree as the other components of capital (machines, buildings, and equipment)," which in turn encourages using this factor in a way that

All in all, it can be said that the factor of land or nature, as the epitome of the natural goods that go into the economic process, cannot simply be absorbed into the factor of capital. Furthermore, it is substitutable only to a limited degree, since substitution goods, such as synthetic materials, which are able to replace natural goods, find themselves dependent for their production upon nature as the contributor of raw materials and energy. It is and remains a scarce good for the long term, even if certain natural goods are still amply available at the moment and are considered to be quasi-free goods, because, with regard to the future, their prices are undervalued.

2.4.2.2 The Factor of Labor

Like "land" as a representative of nature, "labor" is an elementary, and thus non-derivable factor of production.[94] It is goal-directed economic activity that serves to meet human needs. This goal-directedness distinguishes labor (*Arbeit*), as a factor of production, from work (*Arbeit*), as understood in physics (work = force x distance). As it is understood in physics, work is also performed by animals and machines. But labor as productive activity, with the goal of satisfying the need for life-serving goods, remains reserved for humans alone.

The singularity of labor as a factor of production follows directly from that. It is inseparably connected to the human person, a fundamental form of the expression of human nature itself.[95] It is a factor that does not have the function of a mere means, as do land and (real)-capital (which are identified unambiguously as means of production), but instead earns the position of a personal subject. In short, labor, as a factor of production, is always more than a mere means. It is the subject of production and in that respect — "factor" means "producer" — the true "factor" in general. If the factor of labor is reduced in its anthropological-personal dimension and demoted to the rank of a mere means of production, to the "commodity of laborer," that leads inevitably to the dehumanization of

causes inordinate damage to the environment. (See Hans Christoph Binswanger, *et al.*, *Arbeit ohne Umweltzerstörung*, Frankfurt, 1983, p. 25.)

[94] See Carell, "Arbeit," in *Handwörterbuch der Sozialwissenschaften*, Vol. 1, pp. 229-34; Josef Weis, *Wirtschaftsunternehmen und Demokratie*, Cologne, 1970, pp. 20-23; Bernhard Külp, *Grundfragen der Wirtschaft*, Cologne, 1967, pp. 285-86 and 295 ff.

[95] See *BEE*, Vol. II, 1.3.2, esp. note 30.

the human person, as Karl Marx expressed it with the term "human self-alienation."

For the Physiocrats, who from their basic point of view understood the process of production consistently as a natural process, only agriculture, in the sense of the physical cultivation of the land, was productive. Accordingly, only those who participated in cultivating the soil belonged to the productive and thus value-creating class (*classe productive*). Those who were not involved in agriculture, but instead in trade or manufacturing, were regarded as belonging to the unproductive class (*classe stérile*).[96] The classical political economists, Adam Smith first of all, brought a complete reversal. For Smith, "the annual labour of every nation is the fund which originally supplies it with all the necessaries and conveniences of life which it annually consumes, and which consist always, either in the immediate produce of that labour, or in what is purchased with that produce from other nations," as he maintains in the very first sentence of the Introduction to his epochal work, *The Wealth of Nations*.[97] Labor is thus the origin of wealth. Consequently, labor in every form becomes a factor of production and thus the epitome of a creator of wealth. Furthermore, it also becomes a measure of the value or price of goods produced (the labor theory of value), an opinion that was developed further by David Ricardo and also taken up, in its essence, by Karl Marx. Without tacit reception of the anthropological-personal dimension of the factor of labor (a long-term effect of Calvinism?), the classical economists' assessment of it as paramount — though, to be sure, underestimating the productive significance of the factor of land or nature — would hardly be conceivable.

From that it follows that the working person, in collaboration with other working persons, as the cooperating I-Thou, understood precisely in his or her personality,[98] is the basis and purpose of economic production and the economic prosperity made possible by it. Prosperity exists only to the degree that people produce it, and people perform productive work in order to achieve prosperity, as the measure of the sufficient satisfaction of their demand for necessary and desired goods. Through this indispensable anthropological-personal

[96] See Karl Georg Zinn, *Wirtschaftszusammenhänge verständlich lehren*, Munich, 1976, pp. 96 ff.

[97] Adam Smith, *The Wealth of Nations*, Oxford, 1976, Introduction, p. 10.

[98] On the concept of the personal that stands behind this, see *BEE*, Vol. I, 3.1.2.

relationship, the factor of labor proves to be a good distinguishable from all other economic goods. But may one understand human labor as an economic "good"? Is its humane dimension really perceived at all in this way? Does this not mean from the outset that human work is made into an economic entity, a commodity and, therefore, that it is dehumanized?

Treating labor as an economic good, as is customary in the academic discipline of economics, actually contains a self-contradiction, which must be endured. Economic goods have the character of things. But human work, in its humane dimension, cannot be reduced to the status of a thing. Nevertheless, it is also in its reality a thing or means, more precisely, a means of production.

Labor is a means of production, because human persons produce, must produce, *by means of* their work technology, which entails — as the process of the division of labor clearly shows — that they continually attempt to increase the productivity of this means. To the extent that this is accomplished, their economic value increases and is also better rewarded, as an economic good in great demand. Incidentally, this contains the deeper reason human persons cannot become completely absorbed in their productive work without abandoning themselves, even though it belongs to their specific human nature. Insofar as it is merely a material means, work technology, which working persons make use of and which can, like every other good, be marketed commercially, cannot be the goal of their lives, because if it were, the end would become the means and the means the end, which is to say that the person would be reified.

To the degree that it is a means, labor stands in competition with other economic goods, first of all, the good of leisure time. To work more means giving up the benefit of more leisure time, just as to wish to have more leisure time means giving up the benefit of more work. The one good thus limits the other. In this way labor becomes a good among other goods, precisely, a scarce good, which has its price. For scarce goods are those that are not available without limit. And the factor of labor is neither unlimited nor available without cost, not even in times of extreme underemployment.

Labor is understood in economics as a scarce good in precisely this economic sense. And, as may already be clear, that is completely legitimate. It is only necessary to be on guard against converting its economic aspect into an absolute. If one fails in that, if one sees labor only from the perspective of a scarce good, then its humane dimension disappears and so does its special status as a factor of production, which consists precisely in its being more than a mere economically-calculable means of production. In other words, in dealing with this factor only as a scarce good, the question of human justice will be missing, just as, on the other hand, if one decides to let only the humane aspect be valid here, economic rationality can no longer have any bearing and the door is opened to utopian reveries. This will have to be addressed in more detail in subsequent contexts.

The factor of labor, understood as a means of production, is also not a homogenous good. Production-oriented division of labor already led in its mechanical phase to a splitting of productive activity into "handwork" and "brainwork." The more manual work was mechanized, and thus was brought closer to work as understood in physics, the more easily it could be taken over by machines. The electronic phase of the rationalization of work produced, and is still producing, an incomparably increased substitution of human labor by the use of real capital, while brainwork, at least the less demanding varieties, is also now affected by it to an increasing degree. To the extent that the factor of labor concerns areas of activity that have been exposed to the substitution of labor, a reduction of its degree of scarcity and, consequently, also of its economic significance takes place. At the same time, the demand for performing and disposing work, requiring special technical knowledge conforming to the present state of technology, is growing. In view of that, "know how" is also spoken of today as a specific factor of production, whose degree of scarcity is on the increase, because its significance is constantly increasing in the modern industrial system.[99] The same is true, if not to an even greater extent, of specifically managerial activity, in whose domain the genuine planning, leading, and decision tasks fall. But it is becoming increasingly difficult to distinguish this lower-level managerial ability from the "know how" of the middle and higher cadre, because the former is increasingly dependent on specialized commercial, technical, and organizational knowledge. In this sense, which can only be intimated here, the factor of labor also builds, under the conditions of contemporary production performance, an

[99] According to John Kenneth Galbraith, "trained and educated manpower" is now "the decisive factor of production" (*The New Industrial State*, 2nd Ed., Boston, 1971, p. 394).

integrated whole that is no longer homogenous, but is nevertheless coherent.

2.4.2.3 The Factor of Capital

In contrast to land and labor, capital is an increasable good, and is not tied to persons. How has this concept developed and what does it mean, especially when understood as a means or factor of production?

The term itself is derived from the Latin word *capitale*,[100] which meant in the late Latin period a stock of animals, which were measured in terms of the number of heads (*capita*). According to the extent and duration of barter relationships, the primary object of exchange, the "commodity by which all other commodities were appraised,"[101] was livestock. In short, "livestock assumed the function of money and served as money already at this stage."[102] In this way, the word *capitale* gained a monetary meaning as early as the period of the barter economy, and increasingly took on the meaning of "money" as a means of exchange.

Equating "capital" and "money" is typical of the era of the Western money economy, as it already began to develop in the Middle Ages. The concept thus loses its "concrete reference to that which is counted by the head," and comes to mean, in contrast to interest, the primary or original good.[103] In other words, it is an interest-bearing and, therefore, profit-bringing investment. Such investments in the service of mercantile enterprises, which promise profit on the basis of the "*industria*," diligence, and enthusiasm of the merchant, were already distinguished by scholastic moral theologians (*e.g.*, Bernard of Siena and Antoninus of Florence) from money lent to the needy, on which the prohibition of interest and usury was based.[104]

[100] On the historical development of the concept of capital, see Marie-Elisabeth Hilger, "Kapital, Kapitalist, Kapitalismus," in *Geschichtliche Grundbegriffe*, Vol. 3, pp. 402-3. See also Leonhard Männer, "Kapital," I: "Theorie, volkswirtschaftliche," *Handwörterbuch der Wirtschaftswissenschaften*, Vol. 4, pp. 346-59; Otto Weinberger, "Kapital," I: "Geschichte der Kapitaltheorie," in *Handwörterbuch der Sozialwissenschaften*, Vol. 5, pp. 480-88.

[101] Engels, "Origin of the Family, Private Property and State," in *Collected Works*, Vol. XXVI, New York, 1990, p. 260.

[102] *Ibid.*

[103] Hilger, "Kapital, Kapitalist, Kapitalismus," p. 403.

[104] *Ibid.*, p. 404.

Out of the money-economy grew the commercial society, in which individuals could meet only a fraction of their needs with the products of their own labor, and depended largely upon goods made by others, which they purchased with the money they received in exchange for the surplus products of their own work.[105] "The practice of equating capital and money is widely preserved."[106] Two main kinds of capital are distinguished: that which is invested in business for profit, and that which is lent at interest.[107] To have capital at one's disposal, then, means simply to own money of one or the other of these kinds, in addition to cash, bills of exchange, etc.[108] This is an understanding of the term "capital" that has roughly survived — and not just in everyday language — up to the present day.

The industrial society brought about a significant change in the understanding of the concept of capital: "As early as the eighteenth century, the common, frequently-repeated distinction between capital lent and capital invested in business was broadened by taking into account the investment opportunities in *manufacturing*, in a *factory, or in another type of trade*."[109] With this there begins to develop a turning away from the purely monetary concept and a turning towards the commodity conception of capital. It becomes concrete with those economists, beginning with François Quesnay, who discovered the connections of economic life and attempted to understand them as a process of circulation. According to that, the economy is understood as a complicated, labor-dividing process of the circulation of goods and money, with many intermediate stopping places. Generally speaking, goods flow from producers to consumers and money from consumers to producers. Seen in this way, capital is like blood, which circulates in the body and maintains its life. It turns out to be money that is converted into commodities and serves production. Its products, consumer and capital goods, are converted back into money when they are sold, whereupon the cycle begins anew. Adam Smith, in contact with the Physiocrats and the first to reflect scientifically upon these economic connections, speaks of "circulating capital," in contrast to stationary, i.e., "fixed capital," which

105 Cf. Smith, *The Wealth of Nations*, I.iii.1 ff., p. 31 ff.
106 Hilger, "Kapital, Kapitalist, Kapitalismus," p. 409.
107 *Ibid.*, p. 410.
108 *Ibid.*, pp. 412-13.
109 *Ibid.*, p. 415.

can be used productively without having to change owners,[110] as is the case with the circulation of commodity-money-commodity, etc. In both cases — and this is important — the concept of capital gains the meaning of real capital, as a means of production, and thus a factor of production.

Seen in this way, capital converted into tools, machines, equipment, etc., proves to be tied to real assets and is in a position to produce future goods for the market, which will serve purposes of investment and consumption. It is distinguished from "money capital," and thus from cash, savings books, securities, etc., in short, from the total savings of a nation's economy. Although money capital does not constitute a factor of production in the genuine sense of the word, it is nevertheless often subsumed under them, because it actually or potentially establishes power of disposal over real capital.[111] In this respect, the concept of capital in contemporary economic theory is heterogeneous, not to mention controversial. Sometimes it denotes a produced factor of production and sometimes simply money. Yet the difference may not be as great as appears at first glance: "The first group looks at capital from the side of its use, the second from the side of its origin."[112] If that is correct, the difference between real capital and money capital has less to do with differences in the thing itself than with looking at it from different points of view.

However that may be, with the real-assets-like conception of capital, its merely monetary understanding, as it arose in the commercial society, is surpassed. On the whole, it defines the concept of capital of the industrial society, regardless of whether it is oriented along bourgeois or socialist lines. Even Karl Marx's thought was essentially based upon it. But for him, oddly enough, the means of production are capital only when they are found in the private property of the industrialist class; as social property in the hands of workers, they are not capital.[113] Furthermore, he no longer understands "capital" merely as a means or factor of production, as it denoted the bourgeois era: "However, capital is not a thing, but rather a definite social production relation, belonging to a definite historical formation of

[110] Smith, *The Wealth of Nations*, II.ii.5-6, pp. 286-87.
[111] Artur Woll, *Allgemeine Volkswirtschaftslehre*, p. 54.
[112] Külp, *Grundfragen der Wirtschaft*, p. 298.
[113] Joseph A. Schumpeter, *Capitalism, Socialism and Democracy*, 3rd Ed., New York, 1950, p. 45; Hilger, "Kapital, Kapitalist, Kapitalismus," p. 420.

society, which is manifested in a thing and lends this thing a specific social character."[114] This production relationship is, according to Marx, by virtue of the private ownership of the means of production, inevitably characterized by the subsumption of labor under capital. This is, by the way, the quintessence of his critique of capitalism. That raises the question of the determination of the relationship between the factors of "capital" and "labor" in general.

2.4.3 *The Question of Determining the Relationship between "Capital" and "Labor"*

Our analysis has concluded that the factor of labor should be looked at from a dual aspect: the anthropological-personal aspect and the general-economic aspect. From the latter aspect, which ignores as much as possible concrete human persons with their needs — spiritual as well as material — interests, longings for power, etc., and seeks to make economic processes rationally penetrable with the help of abstract conceptual models, labor appears to be a means of production among other means of production and, consequently, a scarce good. Within labor, a distinction is usually made between produced and non-produced means of production. In contrast to land and labor, capital is a produced means of production, because it does not preexist, but is instead created by human labor, with the help of natural resources. One might call it incarnated labor. David Ricardo, following Adam Smith, succinctly called capital "accumulated labour."[115] And when Karl Marx calls it "past, materialised, and dead labour,"[116] he merely follows the classical liberals. As stored-up, reified labor, capital becomes itself a factor of production. Thus Marx, adapting a line from Goethe's *Faust*, can sarcastically interpret it as "a live monster that is fruitful and multiplies."[117] But that is obviously to think primarily of the mechanical equipment plus accessories, which performs quasi-labor *with* human persons and even, in the case of perfect automation, *in their place*, and thus produces by creating value. In this way, capital can be substituted for human labor secondarily, as the process of the rationalization of work

[114] Marx, *Capital*, in *Collected Works*, Vol. 37, New York, 1998, p. 801.
[115] Hilger, "Kapital, Kapitalist, Kapitalismus," p. 426.
[116] Marx, *Capital*, in *Collected Works*, Vol. 35, New York, 1996, p. 205.
[117] *Ibid.*

shows. But that is not all. Capital can also serve to make human labor resources able to perform better, by providing the means to optimal training of qualified technical workers at all levels of production and service, which in our time of highly-developed technology is already of crucial significance. One speaks in this context, and not without justification, of "human capital." This expression could suggest the conclusion that the contemporary kind of production performance is essentially a function of capital, and consequently that capital is actually the basis of productive labor, not vice versa. This, however, would be a fallacy. All that can be concluded is that capital and labor, as means of production, are inseparably connected to one another. In other words, in the modern industrial society, labor without capital can be no more productive than capital without labor. At the level of scarce goods, the two factors have the same rank and, consequently, should not be played off against one another.

This empirically substantiated truth, however, does not change the fact that the factor of labor, seen from the anthropological-personal perspective, takes precedence over the factor of capital. It cannot be denied, even if one wishes to permit only the economic aspect to be valid, that labor goes ahead of capital. Capital is primarily a produced means of production, achieved by human persons, even if a productive power befits it secondarily. In that respect, however, it turns out that, in the words of Erich Preiser, "there is only one subject in the economy and — seen economically — only the human person works, not the ox that pulls the plow and not the machine, though, to be sure, it performs work in the technical sense."[118] If "work" is understood in the technical sense of the word, as it is used in physics, it is possible, of course, to substitute machines (much more than animals) and thus real capital, for human workers. But this is possible only because the capital has been created previously by humans. Labor, therefore, as personal-social performance, is and remains the original factor of production in the economy. Any supremacy of capital over labor lacks justification and stands in contradiction to both human justice and economic rationality: to human justice, because the priority of capital would mean the subsumption of labor under a thing and thus the sacrifice of the human person as a subject, as the basis and purpose of the economy; and to economic rationality, because

[118] Erich Preiser, *Nationalökonomie heute*, 4th Ed., Munich, 1963, p. 34.

giving capital a higher rank than labor, as a means of production and a scarce good, cannot be justified economically.

2.5 Economic Subjects

According to the preceding discussion, the entire economy proves to be an organization of the human person for the human person. The human person is its subject, who *underlies* it, to use the original meaning of the word "*subiectum*."

Although the certainty of this statement is unquestionable, it is nevertheless an abstraction. In reality, *the* human person does not exist. There are, instead, human persons, persons in the diversity of their gender, skin color, gifts and talents, positions in society, statuses in the economy, spiritual, social, and material interests, etc. Consequently, the human person must be understood as the subject of the economy in this diversity.

If one starts out from the circulation of goods and money as the fundamental process of the economy, then human persons, seen formally, appear as economic subjects in three forms: as producers, as consumers, and as the state. As producers, they create goods and services and offer them to the market. As consumers, they purchase these products and compensate the producers for their work. And as citizens — again, considered formally — they prescribe the elementary conditions under which economic processes are to proceed in their own nations. Although every worker is both a producer and a consumer, and every producer and consumer, with the exception of foreigners, is also a citizen, it is nevertheless advisable to speak here of separate economic subjects, since their particular positions and interests are quite diverse and, consquently, can and do come into conflict with one another.

2.5.1 *Producers*

The term "producer" is understood here to include everyone involved in the production of goods and services, which is to say summarily, those who possess the factors of land, capital, and labor. Those who possess these factors of production are always human persons,[119] either individual persons or groups of persons of some

[119] That is, of course, true of land, the quintessential natural resource, only insofar as someone appropriates this good. The original owner is nature. From that it follows

size, up to and including the state. But, there are various classes of producers, which are in constant motion and have their basis in the changing nature of the interplay of the various factors of production and the particular persons or groups of persons who possess them.

Someone who owns land or capital can work productively with these means of production, and thus can produce goods or services. Those who can claim only the capacity to work as their own, who have neither land nor capital at their disposal, are not able to produce goods or services. Labor becomes productive only in combination with the other means of production. One should not offer as a counterexample the creative powers of poets, artists, and scientists, whose "productivity" is tied to neither land nor capital, but depends instead upon their creative ability. They, too, do not exist in an economic vacuum. The performance of creative work indispensably requires the means of subsistence as its material basis, and they result from land and capital. This has nothing to do with economic materialism. The material basis is not what creative work produces, but the two nevertheless cannot be separated from one another.

In this universal sense, the subject of the factor of production labor is bound up with the means of production land and capital. That is not true of those who possess these other means of production, at least not in the same way. To be sure, natural and capital goods are productive only when someone works with them. Without human production, no value can be created. The owners of land and capital, however, do not have to perform the work themselves. They can transfer it, either partially or totally, to others by means of compensation in the form of wages. In this sense, they have a high degree of independence. If they are still productively active themselves, they constitute within the category of producers the class of independent producers, as distinguished from that of dependent producers, who have only their own labor at their disposal and, therefore, must do whatever the owners of the other means of production, or their agents, decide by virtue of their status.

A fundamental distinction, not to mention conflict, in terms of status consequently exists between those who work independently and those who work dependently in the process of production, and also

that human persons must use this factor in an ecologically proper manner, and thus must adjust their consumption of it to its limited availability, not to unlimited human production and consumption needs.

in the process of distribution. Those who work dependently have a status dependent upon their wages. One could, of course, also speak of the labor-dependency of the owners of the means of production and distribution, since land and capital are no more productive without labor than labor without land and capital. But this does not mean that there exists a state of symmetric, mutual interdependency. Those who decide what others must do stand in the stronger position. In the event of a reduction in the supply of workers, those who work independently can work to offset the deficit by means of investments in rationalization or, ultimately, they can also reduce production and trade. Those with no capital at their disposal, however, are normally (leaving aside the social security system for the time being) absolutely dependent for the means of their subsistence upon offering their potential labor to those who demand the factor of labor. In such a situation, they have no other alternative. And precisely in that consists their dependent status. It goes without saying that a reduction of their actual subject-position in the work world is connected with it.

If wage earners, who are dependent in the processes of production and distribution, make up a relatively homogenous group, insofar as they perform activities of execution as blue- and white-collar employees, that is not at all true of the other class, which stands facing them in status. Differentiations are, therefore, indispensable here.

Under the conditions of the pre-industrial division of labor, to call to memory what has already been mentioned,[120] the master craftsman was, as an independent producer, both the entrepreneurial owner of the means of production and, whether with or without journeymen, the executer of work in one person. This integrated type of producer has become, through the specifically industrial division of labor, with its growing capital-intensity, more and more of a peripheral figure and is still present only in the small-firm and agricultural spheres. In the course of the emergence of large-scale firms, which produce on the basis of social cooperation, the separation of the functions of leading and executing in the production process has become generally established. Both functions are as such indispensable, regardless of the principle according to which a national economy is organized. In other words, the industrial production-organization, whatever the social ordering structure within which it functions,

[120] *BEE*, Vol. II, 2.3.2 (characteristics 1. and 2.).

requires *eo ipso* management that plans, leads, and makes the fundamental decisions. Even Marx says as much:

> All combined labour on a large scale requires, more or less, a directing authority, in order to secure the harmonious working of the individual activities, and to perform the general functions that have their origin in the action of the combined organism, as distinguished from the action of its separate organs. A single violin player is his own conductor; an orchestra requires a separate one.[121]

The industrial age led up to the specific type of manager who, as the owner of the means of production, released from executing activities, concentrates on performing the managerial functions of leading and decision-making in the productive organization.

The entrepreneurial owner is the classical figure of the emerging industrial society. In it the factor of labor, more precisely, of executing labor, separates itself from managerial performance, which is, of course, also a form of labor: dispositive-autonomous labor, not heteronomous labor. He is, therefore, in virtue of his function (still considering small-scale-firm relationships), an economic subject to an incomparably greater degree than is the dependent subject, who produces within a wage-relationship.

Since, with the entrepreneurial owner, managerial status is directly related to the ownership of the means of production, it may appear that he is nothing more than a function of capital. Thus Marx also said: "It is not because he is a leader of industry that a man is a capitalist; on the contrary, he is a leader of industry because he is a capitalist."[122] But this assertion does not stand up to reality. The entrepreneurial function proves instead to be detachable from the ownership of capital. Even though the entrepreneurial owner was typical of the nineteenth-century industrial economy, he is not typical today, at least not in large industry, with its stock corporations. The dominant figure there is the professional manager, who performs his managerial function, not by virtue of ownership of capital — of which he often has only a marginal share, if any at all — but rather owing to his existing or expected strength of knowledge, imagination, and leadership, and thus on the basis of specifically managerial power. In his person, managerial performance, as a specific factor of

121 Marx, *Capital*, in *Collected Works*, Vol. 35, New York, 1996, pp. 335-36.
122 *Ibid.*, p. 337.

production, separates itself from the factor of capital. The manager is no longer the owner of capital and the stockholder is no longer the manager, but instead merely a capital provider who shares in profit and loss, which is to say, a "capitalist" in the genuine sense of the word. One of the weaknesses of Marxist theory is that it was, from the start, not in a position "to distinguish the entrepreneur from the capitalist."[123]

Professional managers thus enter contemporary industrial society and take their place, as economic subjects, beside the true capitalists. They are not specifically subjects of the factor of capital, but instead of the factor of managerial performance. On the one hand, they perform their salaried function on behalf of shareholders, to whom they must account for their actions. In this respect, they are also, in terms of labor law, in a relationship of employment and, if one wishes, dependency. On the other hand, they have managerial power of disposal over the means of production, including the factor of labor, because they are responsible for using them productively. Consequently, their status in the economic process is extremely powerful, and they often have far more opportunities for decision-making in the firm than do the shareholders. Therefore, one could hardly go wrong by seeing modern management as the dominant subject of production and service firms in our economy.

It would again amount to an over-simplification, however, if one were simply to see in management, as the head of the firm, the subject upon which it depends absolutely in production and the marketing of production. More and more, with the growing complexity of production and economic relationships, economic, technical, and scientific "know how," upon which managers must rely in coping with their managerial tasks, plays a central, if not the leading role.

[123] Schumpeter, *Capitalism, Socialism and Democracy*, p. 32. Marx had indeed already seen that with the development of industrial cooperation a "special kind of wage labourer" developed, whom he could call "officers (managers), and sergeants (foremen, overlookers)" (*Capital*, in *Collected Works*, Vol. 35, p. 337). Managers, even at the highest level, however, are entitled to no special status. They are only enforcers of the will of "capital, just as in feudal times the functions of general and judge were attributes of landed property" (*Ibid.*, pp. 337-38). Later (in the posthumously published third volume of *Capital*), however, Marx goes beyond that and speaks of the "manager, administrator of other people's capital" as the "actually functioning capitalist," as distinguished from the mere "money capitalist," who is only an "owner" (*Capital*, in *Collected Works*, Vol. 37, p. 434). Managers are here, however, also capitalists, the genuine capitalists, who represent only capitalist interests.

Decisions, and often more than merely decisions, are prepared, as a rule, at low levels in the firm. Therefore, it is not easy to say precisely what "management" means today. A prominent Swiss executive, who has received an excellent business education, offers the following: "If someone were to ask me whom I consider to count as a manager, I would answer: top-level executives, but also the 'network' of lines of communication to the many participants in decision-making processes, which sees the entire firm through."[124] John Kenneth Galbraith intends something similar when he speaks of a rapidly developing "Technostructure" in large corporations, an extensive leading group that guides the entire organization and is described as its "brain."[125] In reference to this, the pejoratively colored term "technocrats" has become accepted. However one understands it, it brings to mind that the actual decision-making power in the firm no longer rests with top management alone, but instead passes down to those who possess scientific, economic, technical, and otherwise professionally-qualified "know how." They, first of all, embody the innovative potential of a firm, which is, again, an increasingly important factor of production. The path of today leads to genuine "knowledge based industries" (Peter F. Drucker).

In light of the above, it becomes clear that producers, as subjects of the factors of capital and labor, represent a heterogeneous and tension-filled network: entrepreneurial owners who also perform some executing work; entrepreneurial owners in exclusively leadership positions; professional managers without effective participation in capital; "capitalists" who, as co-owners of the firm's original stock or merely as holders of participation certificates, have at their disposal only the capital resources for production and marketing; and workers, at the dispositive and carrying-out levels, who contribute according to their functionally and qualitatively diverse work tasks. What they all have in common is that they are subjects in the process of production or distribution, yet subjects in completely different positions and of totally different degrees of importance, which can be seen in the inequality of opportunities for self-development in work processes, as well as in the security of the jobs themselves, and above

[124] Christian Gasser, "Das Mitbestimmungspostulat aus der Sicht der Unternehmung," in *Mitbestimmung in der Unternehmung*, ed. Charles Lattmann and Vera Ganz-Keppeler, Bern, 1972, p. 113.

[125] Galbraith, *The New Industrial State*, p. 71.

all in the financial compensation for the factor contributions. This conflict-laden diversity of positions and interests cannot — as always happens in dogmatic Marxism — simply be traced back to the antagonistic opposition of two classes, the exploiting owners of the means of production (capitalists) and those who have been robbed of their ownership of the means of production and, therefore, are exploited (proletarians). Regardless of the fact that it is difficult, at least in welfare states, to identify the concept of exploitation so concretely, the two-class schema, which was created in the previous century, has become much too crude to capture contemporary reality. There are also conflicts of interest between managers and shareholders (for example, in deciding whether to use distributable corporate profits for investment, dividends, or building reserves), between workers in management or leadership positions and those in only executing positions, etc. Moreover, totally new classes are developing today within the world of work, primarily as a consequence of electronically aided rationalization. Highly qualified workers, especially those who are knowledgeable about information processing, profit from their relative scarcity in terms of status and compensation and, consequently, are privileged. Less qualified and completely unqualified workers are superfluous, and thus are unemployed or, at best, are forced into unattractive, stultifying, and poorly paid activities. But this means nothing other than the establishment of an employee middle class and an employee lower class. Basic interests diverge widely there, too. If the new middle class has a relatively high situation in life, which is tied to prosperity and which they certainly would like to maintain, the lower class finds itself in a "new poverty" and, once more, in marginalization, which is simply unacceptable for them. A festering social sore is opened up here and will create increasing challenges for the industrial society in the electronic age.

2.5.2 *Consumers*

The goal of all production is consumption. Producers wish not only to make products, but also to sell them. Production for its own sake would make no sense. Its end and purpose consists in consumption, as Adam Smith emphasized.[126] And it goes without saying that the subjects of consumption are consumers.

[126] Smith, *The Wealth of Nations*, IV.viii.49, p. 660.

The goods produced by an economy are, in the most elementary listing, capital goods, consumer goods, and services. Strictly speaking, buyers of capital goods are also consumers. Customarily, however, only the users of consumer goods and services are called "consumers," and then only insofar as private, not public, use is involved. The term will be understood here in this narrower sense.

Because production and consumption comprise a complete cycle, which is fuelled by the entirety of economic forces, it can be said that producers and consumers ultimately coincide. Producers are really also consumers, and consumers, if they are already or still working, are also producers.[127] Consumers can consume only what they have previously co-produced, and producers cannot produce unless at least their essential consumer needs have been met. Since, however, in the modern industrial society, with its universal, highly-differentiated division of labor, human persons, considered concretely and thus individually, do not directly produce what they themselves consume, nor consume what they themselves produce, producers and consumers in fact diverge as different subjects with different interests, at least in a society where exchanges between those who supply and those who buy take place under market conditions.

In the market, more precisely, in the consumer goods market, producers and consumers encounter one another as subjects who are both different from and opposed to one another. Consumers would like to buy necessary goods of high quality at the lowest possible prices. Producers are intent on making their products at minimal cost and selling them for as much profit as possible.

According to the classical liberal view, which dealt with simple and transparent market relationships that were still oriented towards the pre-industrial economy and approached perfect competition,[128] the conflict of interests between producers and buyers balances out. The contrary demands mutually limit themselves by means of the laws of the market, so that neither side can seriously disturb the

[127] "Each of us is both a consumer and a producer of factor outputs. We are consumers when we purchase commodities or make use of services. As producers, we offer various products, consisting of work performance, capital use, land use, or managerial function" (Borner, *Einführung in die Volkswirtschaftslehre*, p. 29).

[128] "Perfect competition" is an ideal type of market in which entrance is free, very many buyers and sellers enter, goods are homogenous or uniform, and no price-fixing agreements between the market participants are made.

balance in the long run. If prices are set too high, consumers will exercise restraint in buying and producers will have unsold products. If, on the other hand, prices are set too low, if producers cannot cover their costs, they must cease, or at least reduce production and consumers will no longer be able to meet their needs for those goods. Furthermore, it is assumed that the consumer is the king of the market. Consumers are ultimately free in their buying decisions and, consequently, producers must be guided by them, especially since the goal of production is consumption, not vice versa.

With the progressive industrialization of the economy, however, market relationships have become incomparably more complex, more complicated, less transparent, and — most significantly as far as the power play is concerned — more unbalanced, so that the classical liberal view is now correct only to an extremely limited degree. For many goods, especially those of high quality, the path from production to sale is long, costly, and full of uncertainties. It is often uncertain whether the demand for a particular good, once it finally appears on the market, will correspond to the original sales prognoses. Furthermore, competing products may have come into play in the meantime, severely frustrating the producer's calculations. In addition, the structure of consumers' needs is dynamic. Their desires are diverse, only roughly outlined, and constantly changing, which makes it much more difficult to plan production and creates a situation loaded with risks. Development has thus taken a turn leading to increasing influence by firms on market events, as they promote the profit interest. Some examples are price-fixing agreements among producers, the formation of cartels to reduce competition, monopolistic mergers to gain greater market power, as well as indirect manipulations of consumers' desires by means of refined advertising and sales methods. But this means that the situation of the consumer in the market becomes precarious. The much-invoked sovereignty of consumers, which is supposed to enable them to choose independently the goods that are least expensive and best for themselves, is called into question: "He must be afraid that instead of buying the goods that are best in terms of usefulness, quality, and price, he will buy those that maximize the seller's profit, at the cost of usefulness and quality."[129] In reaction to the tendencies on the part of sellers

[129] Erich Egner, "Konsumentenschutz," in *Handwörterbuch der Sozialwissenschaften*, Vol. 6, p. 151. The German Federal Cartel Office makes this point even more strongly:

towards influencing, or even controlling markets, steps have been taken to protect consumers. Nothing makes the existing conflict of interests between consumers and producers more obvious than this state of affairs. To be sure, one cannot speak of an absolute antagonism between these two economic subjects. As employees in the manufacturing and marketing of products, the consumers are, nevertheless, also fundamentally interested in good compensation for their work, which is for its part dependent upon the firms' opportunities for making a profit. Nevertheless, it remains undisputed that there exists here a situation of divergence, which leads again and again to conflicts of interest.

2.5.3 *The State*

The activity of the state plays an increasingly important role in the modern industrial society. As early as the age of mercantilism,[130] whose close coincided with the beginnings of the process of industrialization, the influence of the state over the economy was great. But it was based primarily on the setting of political-national, not economic-social goals. The leitmotiv of mercantilism as the economic system of the absolutist nation-state of the seventeenth and eighteenth centuries was defined "by efforts to gain political and military power by developing the economic power of one's own nation at the cost of economic growth in all other nations."[131] In the course of the development of industrialization, which tended towards an open exchange of goods and which weakened national borders, because it was globally orientated, mercantilism was put on the defensive — in England first of all. The Physiocrats and, somewhat later, Adam Smith provided theoretical-economic support to this process.

The era of liberal economic policy began with the Physiocrats. They rejected the activity of the state in the economy and,

"In most consumer good markets of developed national economies, suppliers find themselves in a superior position. They are the active exchange partners; consumers are merely the reactive exchange partners. Instead of consumer-sovereignty, producer sovereignty often rules" (German Federal Cartel Office, *Bericht des Bundeskartellamtes über seine Tätigkeit im Jahre 1972 sowie über die Lage und Entwicklung auf seinem Aufgabenbereich*, Bundestags-Drucksache 7/3574, Bonn, 1972, p. 11).

130 See Fritz Blaich, "Merkantilismus," in *Handwörterbuch der Wirtschaftswissenschaften*, Vol. 5, pp. 240-51.

131 *Ibid.*, p. 240.

consequently, its control of economic subjects as unnatural, and introduced the powerfully-effective maxim: "*Laissez-faire et laissez-passer, le monde va de lui même.*" But there never has been and never could be an economy completely free of the state.

Adam Smith, who by and large accepted the laissez-faire principle, already found himself compelled to allow the state some, though narrowly limited room for action in the economy. In the "system of natural liberty," the sovereign would have to fulfill three duties of great importance:

> First, the duty of protecting the society from violence and invasion of other independent societies; secondly, the duty of protecting, as far as possible, every member of the society from the injustice or oppression of every other member of it, or the duty of establishing an exact administration of justice; and, thirdly, the duty of erecting and maintaining certain publick works and certain publick institutions, which it can never be for the interest of any individual, or small number of individuals, to erect and maintain; because the profit could never repay the expense to any individual or small number of individuals, though it may frequently do much more than repay it to a great society.[132]

It is noteworthy that, according to this passage, the state, as an economic subject, must be active above all in two directions. It must create the legal framework within which the processes of life, and thus also economic processes, take place. And it must itself intervene in the process when the economy does not on its own produce certain goods and services necessary for the nation as a consequence of the free interaction of market forces, because doing so would be unprofitable or insufficiently profitable for the private entrepreneur.

Therefore, the extreme individualist-liberalist position, according to which the state must simply be eliminated as an economic subject, cannot appeal to Adam Smith for support, even though the primary thrust of his economic thesis is unambiguously aimed at mercantilism and, in general, at any attempt to make state activity primary in the economy. It has in its exclusivity an ideological character, just as does the opposed, extreme collectivist-socialist position, which elevates the state to the position of the dominant (not to mention sole)

132 Smith, *The Wealth of Nations*, IV.ix.51, pp. 687-88.

economic subject, since it becomes the central-planning subject, which, with the elimination of market sovereignty, makes the decisions concerning production, and indirectly, consumption as well.[133] Both positions, which, of course, are never encountered in their pure forms in social reality, are unrealistic. The state, as the collective economic subject, can no more replace the individual market subjects, who, considered in abstract differentiation, behave as suppliers and demanders, than the individual subjects, in their conflict-laden market interplay, can make the state, as the collective subject of the economy, superfluous. Therefore, it is necessary to start out from the plurality of the market subjects and their various interests, which differentiate them from one another and thus from the market-economic — yet governmentally relevant — character of the industrial economy. And that all the more so, since the structural elements provided by it are still predominant in the context of our own (i.e., the "Western") world, and since the alternative model for structuring the industrial society that opposes it, namely the strictly state- or centrally-administered economic model, presupposes the market-economic model historically and in principle. For the socialist model is based on the critique, first set in motion by Marx, of the (capitalistic) market economy that chronologically preceded it.

All in all it can be said — and this may at first glance seem paradoxical — that with the progressive development of industrial society, state activity in the economic sphere and, therefore, the significance of the state as an economic subject, has steadily increased, even in the context of ordering conditions that are liberal and thus moderate the state.[134] The growth of governmental expenditures relative to those of national product[135] is sufficient to reveal this. In this century, state expenditures considered generally have grown more

[133] "With central planning, political leadership is necessarily the subject of all formulations of demands and objectives, for which reason one can also speak here of state planning of economic processes" (K. Paul Hensel, "Annäherung der Wirtschaftssysteme?" in Hensel, *Systemvergleich als Aufgabe*, ed. Hannelore Hamel, Stuttgart, 1977, p. 229).

[134] In general, see Paul A. Samuelson, *Macroeconomics*, Vol. I, 7th Ed., New York, 1967 (Chapter 8: "The Economic Role of Government: Expenditure, Regulation, and Finance"), pp. 139-153. On the Swiss situation in particular, see René L. Frey, *Wirtschaft, Staat und Wohlfahrt*, Basel, 1985, pp. 65-81.

[135] "National product" is a measure of the output of a nation's economic activity during a given period of time. It is the value of all goods (commodities and services) produced and placed on the market during the period, less the value of the goods

quickly than gross national product.[136] And, indeed, the government expenditure ratio[137] is highest precisely in highly developed industrial societies.[138] In Switzerland, which can serve as a representative example, between 1960 and 1983, the net government expenditure ratio climbed from 16.9% to 26.8% and the gross government expenditure ratio from 27.4% to 40.2%.[139] These are meaningful facts, which one may welcome or regret, but which in any case emphasize the growing significance of the state in the economies of the industrialized nations.

One might draw the conclusion from the above that an inner inevitability prevails here, directly related to the effects of the process of industrialization in the recent past. The more complex the industrial economy, the more complicated and unclear the market relationships, the more conflicting the interest-politics of individual economic subjects, the stronger the tendencies towards market control, the more unequal the distribution of life situations within a nation's population, the more demanding and expensive the infrastructure of society, the more global the economic exchange relationships, and the more polluted, not to mention more ruinous, the entirety of economic activity for the natural environment — the more wide-ranging the economically relevant activities of the state must become. It manifests itself as the coordinator of contrary objectives and interests, as the guiding authority of economic processes, particularly in finance, monetary, currency, and also subsidy politics, as the opponent of monopolistic market power, as the holder of the social security system or redistribution of income, as the provider of collective goods, such as education systems, medical services, care for the very young and very old, postal service, communication, public transportation, sewage treatment plants, and other environmental protection institutions, which, if left to the market, would be uneconomical or

consumed in production. In contrast to net national product, gross national product includes depreciation (capital consumption allowance).

136 Samuelson, *Macroeconomics*, p. 140.

137 The "government expenditure ratio" is the percentage of the gross national product controlled by the government. The net government expenditure ratio contains only the administrative expenditures of the government, as a percentage of gross national product. The gross government expenditure ratio also includes expenses for governmental institutions and enterprises, as well as social insurance.

138 Samuelson, *Macroeconomics*, p. 141.

139 Swiss Federal Statistical Office, ed., *Öffentliche Finanzen der Schweiz, Dezember 1985, wf-Dokumentation zur Wirtschaftskunde*, Zürich, 1985.

insufficiently economical, or would result in costs beyond the means of most people, etc. All in all it appears that under today's conditions the market economy cannot be left to itself, that it instead requires an economic policy implemented by the state and an ordering framework ensured by it, at least if it is to achieve the purposes, as they have been outlined in 1.3.1 ff. How narrowly or widely the margins should be set, without calling the system of the market economy into question, is, to be sure, hotly debated among its advocates themselves. Supporters of a state-controlled market economy are opposed today by powerful forces, which speak out in favor of decisive "deregulation" of the market. With that the specific order-political problem already comes into view. Dealing with it, as the basic economic-ethical question, will be the main concern of this book.

2.6 Industrial Economy as the Economy of Markets

2.6.1 *The Concept and Morphology of the Market*

The term "market" is derived from the Latin word "*mercatus*," which means trading, buying, and selling. In everyday usage, a market is understood to be an arrangement in which buyers and sellers meet one another at a specific time and place in order to acquire or sell goods. A market, in this ordinary-language sense of the word, is an ancient institution. Markets have existed for as long as human persons have exchanged goods with one another — first without, then with the use of money as a means of exchange.

In economic theory, the ordinary-language concept of the market is greatly modified and becomes highly abstract. In that context, it is a "conceptual synthesis of all demanders and suppliers of a good within a specific economic *period*."[140] When understood in this way, it encompasses all exchange relationships between supplying and demanding economic subjects, "who, with regard to their selling or buying opportunities, stand in such a close relationship of mutual dependence that the price and quantity decisions reached by each economic unit can be explained only within the context of the exchange group."[141] Thus, the market means here an economic

[140] Bernhard Külp, *Grundfragen der Wirtschaft*, p. 72.

[141] Rainer J. Willeke, "Marktformen," in *Handwörterbuch der Sozialwissenschaften*, Vol. 7, p. 136.

exchange system of scarce goods that determines the basic relationships of the economic subjects and their basic decisions as consumers or producers and, therefore, the price level and product quantity of a good. According to the kind of good handled, different markets, such as consumer goods markets and factor markets, can be distinguished.

In addition to the conceptual distinction among markets according to the kind of good handled, differentiation according to market form is encountered in economic theory. The most frequently used criterion of classification is the number and relative size of the sellers and buyers. "Relative size" means "the share of the market's total supply possessed by an individual seller or the share of its total demand possessed by an individual buyer."[142] If one assumes symmetry, according to which the market participants on both the supply side and the demand side of the market either do not differ in size or differ only insignificantly, and if one takes into consideration that either one large actor, a few medium-sized actors, or many small ones can appear on each side of the market, then nine possible market forms result, as the following schema shows:[143]

Table 2: Market Forms

Sellers / *Buyers*	*One Large*	*A Few Large*	*Many Small*
One Large	Bilateral Monopoly	Demand Monopoly and Supply Oligopoly (Limited Monopsony	Demand Monopoly (Monopsony)
A Few Large	Supply Monopoly and Demand Oligopoly (Limited Monopoly)	Bilateral Oligopoly	Demand Oligopoly (Oligopsony)
Many Small	Supply Monopoly (Monopoly)	Supply Oligopoly (Oligopoly)	Perfect Competition (Bilateral Polypoly)

142 Alfred Eugen Ott, "Marktformen," in *Handwörterbuch der Wirtschaftswissenschaften*, Vol. 5, p. 107.

143 This schema results from a combination of the figures in Alfred Eugen Ott (*ibid.*) and Henner Kleinewefers and Regula Pfister, *Die schweizerische Volkswirtschaft*, Frauenfeld, 1977, p. 193.

With this schematic overview, it can already be seen that the different market forms express different power relationships in the market. In the case of perfect competition, where many small sellers face many small buyers, no market participant, whether producer or consumer, can have a powerfully relevant influence on market events. But the situation is otherwise with a supply oligopoly and especially with a monopoly. In that case, buyers find themselves in a weak or completely powerless position. As individual economic subjects, they must accept the oligopolistic or monopolistic market conditions and can only choose between buying and not buying. That does not mean, of course, that there can be market power only on the side of sellers. It can also be found on the demand side, if a buyer possesses a demand monopoly, such as, for instance, the state-owned PTT (post, telegraph, and telephone) company in Switzerland does relative to the producers of telephones.[144]

"The subdivision of market forms according to the number and relative size of sellers and buyers must be supplemented by an examination of the features of the goods handled in the market in question."[145] When that is undertaken, the question whether it is easy or difficult to replace a product offered by one provider with one made by another proves to be decisive.

If the goods that reach the market are homogenous, i.e., uniform, then buyers can be indifferent concerning where they make their purchases. The situation is different, however, when goods are not homogenous. In that case, the buyer will wish to choose selectively. The more heterogeneous the species of a particular product, electric razors for instance, the more difficult their substitution by competitive products and the greater the market power of the producers. Consequently, firms attempt to modify goods that are in fact similar in such a way (often only by face lifting) that they have the appearance of diversity. "Despite these efforts to make the products heterogeneous and thereby to improve their own power position, substitution competition almost always remains. A monopolist who can exploit his market without any kind of substitution competition is,

[144] This monopolistic position of the Swiss PTT company ended legally on 1 January 1988. But only the future will tell the degree to which it actually disappears.

[145] Kleinewefers and Pfister, *Die schweizerische Volkswirtschaft*, p. 194. The following is based on the discussion found there.

therefore, an extremely rare figure,"[146] which of course does not solve the problem of monopoly, but does defuse it (with "monopolistic competition").[147]

2.6.2 *The Multiplicity and Borderless Expansion of Markets*

The word "market" as a general term is also an abstraction. In reality *the* market does not exist; there exists a multiplicity of markets.

As early as the pre-industrial era, in which the production-oriented division of labor specifically developed, there was a plurality of markets. That is not intended to mean the number of local markets, but rather the multiplicity of products provided in them. Larger cities had various marketplaces or market streets for various goods. It thus came about that special markets were created, such as the grain, cattle, horse, vegetable, hay, and fish markets, or that individual handicrafts were consolidated in particular streets: Baker, Butcher, Weaver Street, etc.

In the age of the origin and development of industrialism, with its dominance of the production-oriented division of labor, the process of market differentiation progressed and new dimensions were opened up in an incomparably intensified manner. According to production levels, markets for raw materials and for semi-finished and finished products arose; according to the way the products were used, consumer goods markets and capital goods markets originated. In the wake of the separation of the factors of production typical of the industrial form of the division of labor, these goods markets were joined by separate factor markets: the land, capital, and labor markets. These markets in turn separated into sub-markets (e.g., the labor market into markets for unskilled, skilled, and highly-specialized workers, etc.). The more machines overtook the physical labor of animals and humans and the demand for mechanical production grew in the resulting expanded economy, the more strongly the energy markets (fossil fuels, electricity, atomic energy) continued to develop. Along with these came the financial market, in which a genuine finance industry established itself and continuously grew in size and importance. This merely rough enumeration only points out

[146] *Ibid.*

[147] On monopolistic competition, see *BEE*, Vol. II, p. 445.

how much the fully developed industrial economy developed as a complex network of markets and sub-markets, which, despite their wide variety and dissimilarity, are connected to one another and, consequently, when seen functionally, make up an inseparable, complicated whole that is difficult to understand.

But the modern industrial economy has not only led to a previously unseen multiplicity of interconnected markets; it has also demolished, merely by the tendency to extensiveness typical of it, the local limitations of the markets. That is related, above all, to the location-oriented division of labor, which would always gain importance in the course of the rationalization of economic processes and would be determined by the question of where one could produce most advantageously. Steel, for example, can be produced practically anywhere. Apart from the necessary "know-how," one needs only the essential raw materials, the required energy, the necessary production equipment, and the right workers. If one considers the question of cost, however, it becomes apparent that not all locations are equally economical. There exist comparative advantages and disadvantages, which are crucial. Thus, the emerging German steel industry, still before the turn of the century, concentrated itself in the Ruhr region, because coal, a source of energy, was obtainable there directly, and thus at the lowest price, and, furthermore, iron ore, an essential raw material, could be transported to the steel mills by water, and thus, again, at relatively low cost. With such concentrations of location, the providers of steel and semi-finished steel products and their purchasers are inevitably separated from one another geographically, which obviously had to lead to the expansion of the aforementioned market.

If that kind of location-oriented market expansion first took place within the boundaries of national economies, the national markets soon also proved to be too small for the increased economic power of specific lines of production and trade. The national expansion of markets pushed outward by virtue of their inner dynamic to international expansions and to the development of the macro-economy beyond national borders. Adam Smith was already of the opinion that the wealth of nations was promoted not only by the intranational division of labor, but even more by the international division of labor.[148] It is supposed to lead to the production of each good

[148] Smith, *The Wealth of Nations*, IV.i.31 ff., pp. 446 ff.

at the location where the costs of its production are the lowest. In other words, a nation exports the goods that it can produce at an absolute cost advantage in comparison to another nation, which, again according to Smith, must in the long run be advantageous for everyone. This is, of course, an optimistic expectation, which has been appropriately relativized by hard facts.

The internationalization of the economy through the growing globalization of markets, under the influence of free trade efforts, which are linked to the location-oriented division of labor and which, of course, must fight hard again today against the growing protectionist tendencies of individual nations and their national economies, is the most prominent characteristic of contemporary industrial society, which is growing in global dimensions. The many international economic organizations[149] that have been established since the Second World War bear eloquent witness to this fact. To begin with, there are those of the United Nations, such as the United Nations Conference on Trade and Development (UNCTAD), a special organ of the UN General Assembly founded in 1964, primarily at the request of the developing nations for better representation of their specific interests; the Food and Agriculture Organization (FAO), at work since 1945; the International Monetary Fund (IMF) and the World Bank (IBRD), two complementary financial institutions active since 1947, which exert a strong, although highly controversial influence on international economic relations. The General Agreement on Tariffs and Trade (GATT) — not an organization of the UN, but required to report to it — has been in power since 1948. In contrast to UNCTAD, it orients itself towards the needs of industrialized nations, even though two-thirds of the ninety-two signatories are developing nations. Independent of the UN, but maintaining various relationships with the GATT, IMF, FAO, UNCTAD, etc., the Organization for Economic Cooperation and Development (OECD), a convention in force since 1961, has as its goal the healthy economic growth and employment rate of its member states, as well as non-member nations, while maintaining financial stability. Also international, though not having a global character, are the European Community (EC), including the European Community for Coal and Steel (Montanunion), 1951; the European Atomic Energy Community

[149] Cf. Carlo Schelhammer, *Internationale Wirtschaftsorganisationen*, 2nd Ed., Zürich, 1982.

(Euratom), 1958; and the European Economic Community (EEC), 1958; as well as the Council for Mutual Economic Assistance (COMECON), existing in the East Block states since 1949.

All of these international organizations reflect the epochal process of the internationalization of the economy, directly or indirectly elicited by the expansion of markets from the local to the national and regional (or continental) up to the global sphere, which actually already constitutes the sole market for many capital goods typical of contemporary industrial society, such as, for example, energy generating plants.[150] That is even truer today of financial firms and the service sector, whose globalization (within which the revolution of communication technology effected by electronics plays a crucial role) increasingly converts national markets into subsystems of a global market. In this way, the contemporary industrial economy proves to be both an extremely differentiated network of diverse but interrelated individual markets and a highly complex structure, which includes local, regional, national and international markets and always continues to grow in global dimensions.

2.6.3 *Multinationalization*

Closely related to the borderless expansion of markets on the road to the international division of labor is the formation of corporations or conglomerates, known primarily as "transnational" or "multinational" firms.[151] They characterize to a high degree the picture of the global economy since the Second World War.

Processes of economic internationalization are, of course, phenomena not only of recent times. Long-distance trade already existed in ancient times. Banking companies have also been managed since the Middle Ages at an international level. The East India Company, which already had the features of a transnational corporation, was

[150] Cf. Emil Küng and Erwin Bielinski, in *Die Zukunft der Industrie in Europa, Brennpunkte*, Zürich, 1976, pp. 89-90.

[151] There is no universally recognized definition of the terms "multinational" and "transnational" firm. In the *Handwörterbuch der Wirtschaftswissenschaften*, Vol. 8, p. 85, it is described as follows: A multinational firm is a group of firms, which "(1) are subject to unified control to some extent, (2) are active in geographically different markets that are influenced by different political, legislative, and cultural factors, and (3) stand in a relation of interdependence on one another involving capital sharing." According to current linguistic usage in Western Europe, a multinational is simply a firm with subsidiary corporations in two or more nations.

founded in England during the reign of Queen Elisabeth I. And completely within the nineteenth century, the age of the industrial development of the economy, "companies from Britain, the U.S., and several European countries were conducting huge international trading operations." Additionally, in approximately 1860, "manufacturing companies began to establish production facilities outside their own countries, and by 1914 many of today's giants were already operating in several countries."[152]

The existence of transnational firms in the economy, therefore, is not at all something new. But there are huge differences, which should not be underestimated, between the firms of earlier times and the multinational conglomerates of today.

A first noteworthy difference concerns the kinds of foreign investments. According to Christopher Tugendhat, they had already achieved enormous dimensions before 1914.[153] Thus, at the outbreak of the First World War, the overseas investments of Great Britain amounted to four billion pounds. Those of Germany were 1.2 billion pounds and those of the United States 600 million. International corporations, however, accounted for only an insignificant share of these sums. Furthermore, it was a matter of investments in securities, which included no property rights to the real capital of the firms — except by stoppage of payment. Therefore, the goal of investment was, as a rule, not control, but rather participation in the companies' profits. With the multinational firms of our day, the situation is entirely different. They predominantly conduct direct investments. And this means that they are concerned to establish subsidiary firms and production facilities in foreign countries that belong to them and that they can control. As Tugendhat comments, however, there is "a world of difference" between the purchase of shares of a foreign corporation and the establishment of a subsidiary in a foreign country.

Another characteristic feature of modern multinational firms, as distinguished from earlier international corporations, is the centralized structure of their management:

> However large it may be, and however many subsidiaries it may have scattered across the globe, all its operations are co-ordinated from the centre. Despite frequent assertions to the contrary, the subsidiaries are not run as separate enterprises each of which has to

[152] Christopher Tugendhat, *The Multinationals*, London, 1971, p. 10.
[153] *Ibid.*, pp. 10-11.

> stand on its own feet. They must all work within a framework established by an overall group plan drawn up at headquarters, and their activities are tightly integrated with each other. They are judged not by their individual performance, but by the contribution they make to the group as a whole. Thus a subsidiary which records a loss but whose operations prevent a rival from moving into one of its parent company's more profitable markets may be fulfilling a more valuable task than a subsidiary with a better financial record.[154]

The centralization of management thus means here at the same time directing the economic activities of the firm with direct consequences for market events.

An additional fact, which is typical of the contemporary multinational firm, is related to the development of centralized management structures. A prerequisite of this centralism is the developed industrial economy's achievements of high technology. Without contemporary means of air travel, the extremely accelerated transmission of information, and, above all, electronic data storage and processing, the central leadership of large transnational companies, with their global branching out of individual dependent firms, would be completely unthinkable.[155] That is part of the explanation of the fundamental affinity between the multinationals and high technology. They are its most important carriers. Together with the construction of a powerful, technological, internal structure, they usually maintain large research and development departments, which put them in a position to use the factors of production of scientific-technological progress optimally. That certainly does not mean that they also produce the most and the most important inventions: "This frequently happens in small firms, while the large ones mainly work on improvements of existing technologies and products."[156] Large firms nevertheless remain, because of their international expansion, the most significant translators of technological knowledge, which is also the reason many foreign countries, especially in the Third World, fear technological dependency on a few multinational corporations.[157]

[154] *Ibid.*, p. 11.

[155] Louis Turner, "The Multinational Company," *Journal of Business Policy*, 2 (1971), p. 50. See also Tugendhat, *The Multinationals*, p. 11.

[156] Gerhard Prosi and Jörn Biel, "Unternehmen, multinationale," I: "Volkswirtschaftliche Probleme," in *Handwörterbuch der Wirtschaftswissenschaften*, Vol. 8, p. 89.

[157] *Ibid.*

The most striking difference between the multinationals of today and their predecessors during the period before the Second World War, however, can be seen in the expansion of their economic power. The comparative statistics of the direct investment of American corporations in Europe before and after 1945 may serve as an indicator: "In 1929 their total book value, including ventures of every sort, amounted to only $1,400m.; by 1946 it had fallen to $1,000m. Then came the post-war boom, and by 1969 it had risen to $21,554m, of which manufacturing companies accounted for $12,225m., and oil companies for $4,805m."[158]

The largest multinational firms of our day have taken on dimensions that justify speaking of them as of genuine economic empires,[159] whose annual sales approach or even surpass the gross domestic product (GDP) of smaller European states. The following table[160] makes that clear.

Table 3: Sales of Multinational Firms

GDP — 1986	*$ Billion*	*Sales — 1986*		*$ Billion*
Sweden	220.75	General Motors	USA	102.8
Switzerland	144.98	Exxon	USA	69.9
Greece	130.57	Royal Dutch/Shell	NL/UK	64.8
Denmark	118.38	IBM	USA	51.3
Austria	110.72	Toyota Motor	Japan	31.6
Norway	104.47	Unilever	NL/UK	25.1
Portugal	86.63	Volkswagen	W. Germany	24.3
Ireland	37.84	Nestlé	Swiss	21.2
		Hoechst	W. Germany	17.5

From that it is apparent that a large concentration of economic power takes place in the large multinational firms of today.[161]

[158] Tugendhat, *The Multinationals*, p. 12.

[159] IBM, for example, employs a total of 390,000 persons on five continents. It conducts its business in one hundred currencies and thirty languages. Its gross revenue from other countries increased from $51 million in 1950 to $29.3 billion in 1987. Overseas business accounts for more than half of IBM's total gross revenue ($54.2 billion). Source: IBM, *Annual Report*, 1987.

[160] Source: National Accounts, OECD, Department of Economics and Statistics, Paris, 1988; *Fortune*, Vol. 115, No. 8, April 1987, and *Fortune*, Vol. 116, No. 3, August 1987.

[161] The dominant economic theory pays too little attention to the factor of power. See Volker Bornschier, *Wachstum, Konzentration und Multinationalisierung von Industrieunternehmen*, Frauenfeld, 1976, esp. pp. 32-36. In contrast to neoclassical economic

This state of affairs, of course, should not simply lead to equating multinationalization and the gigantic power concentration of enormous conglomerates. In a world whose economy has grown into global dimensions through the interrelationships of national and international markets, the multinationalization of firms is an objectively-based, quasi-natural process, whose advantages in international economic policy even the industrial states of the COMECON have recently begun to discover.[162] It applies, then, not only to the mammoth conglomerates. Many medium and small, even very small multinationals can hold their ground surprisingly well against the large ones, because they know how to adapt more quickly to changing market conditions, precisely because they are smaller and thus are more flexible and quite often also more innovative.[163] There can hardly be a determinative relationship between the multinationalization process as such and the giant power concentration of the multinational giants. There must also be other factors in play, not the least of which is fascination with the colossal companies.

This interjection is by no means intended to minimize or trivialize the power problem presented by the concentration of large multinational firms. It is merely intended to counter the fallacy that multinationalization and economic power concentration are simply synonymous. The power problem itself remains in existence in its complete complexity. Not even the managers of important multinationals

theory, which he, with Hans Albert, accuses of "ritual power blindness" (p. 32), Bornschier places the aspect of power in the foreground in his analysis of the multinational firm.

[162] See Kurt H. Biedenkopf, "Auf dem Weg zu einer freien Weltwirtschaftsordnung," in *Multinationale im Nord-Süd-Konflikt, Brennpunkte*, Zürich, 1976, p. 21. On the "Advance of the 'Red Multinationals'" (*"Vormarsch der 'roten Multis'"*) see *Schweizerische Handelszeitung*, No. 15, 13 April 1978, p. 45.

[163] Thomas P. Gasser and Jacques A. Rossier, "Multinationale Expansion," *Neue Zürcher Zeitung*, No. 460, 4 October 1973, p. 21. The authors explicitly maintain: "The *controversies* concerning the multinationals are always about only the *large firms*. The many genuinely multinational *small and medium firms*, which have been active with great success, sometimes for decades in many markets, remain unnoticed. Thus, for example, from a Swiss perspective, Mettler, Hero, Charmilles, Juvena, Luwa, Unikeller, Firmenich, Wild, Continentale Linoleum Union, and Griesser.... They compete successfully in international competition, even though their financial means are relatively modest, their staffs of managers are limited, and the research and development potential at their disposal cannot compare with the resources of the large American, German, or even Swiss firms."

can completely avoid it,[164] because every form of accumulation of power has its fatal aspects. Three of these aspects will now be discussed:

1. First of all, there is the possibility of market domination. Multinationals, in the sense of large conglomerates that cross national borders, control a multitude of firms and create entire oligopolies, if not complete (quasi-)monopolies. The markets in which they are active exhibit "an oligopolistic structure for the most part and are characterized by oligopolistic patterns of behavior."[165] As large suppliers facing many demanders, they can have decisive influence on the prices of their goods and services, both at home and abroad. The same is true of the prices of suppliers' goods and services, as well as those of raw materials and factors of production, insofar as they are not fixed by cartels or, as with the labor wage in industrial states, by tariff pay agreements. For in this respect they are large demanders that must often deal with many small suppliers. They are thus able to use the advantages of both the supplier monopoly and the demander monopoly, and thus to achieve a competitive advantage relative to smaller firms, which may not be based on better performance, but instead on market power.[166]

To be sure, it must be granted here that the multinational conglomerates, insofar as they do not hold an actual monopolistic position in some area of business, also stand in a relationship of competition with one another in the markets where they are active, which limits their opportunities for profit and special ambitions. Yet, as Adam Smith already recognized: "To widen the market and to narrow the competition, is always the interest of the dealers."[167] That is also true of the managers of large oligopolies. In order to avoid oligopolistic fights,

[164] Thus, for example, Arthur Fürer, Vice-Chairman of Nestlé's Board of Directors, "Die Multinationalen in einer Welt des Umbruchs," *Neue Zürcher Zeitung*, No. 52, 3/4 March 1979, p. 37. Not without concern does he refer to the enormous concentration of the economy in the United States, where in 1955 the five hundred largest firms already obtained 44.5% of all profit from industry and agriculture and possessed 40% of all assets, while by 1970 the percentages had climbed to 72% and 70% respectively.

[165] Prosi and Biel, "Unternehmen, multinationale," I: "Volkswirtschaftliche Probleme," p. 91.

[166] In this context, the comments of Charles-Albert Michalet deserve attention: "In these unruly times, in which domestic economic activity is atrophying, islands of prosperity still obviously exist, above all multinational corporations" (*Multinationale Unternehmen und die Wirtschaftskrise*, Frankfurt, 1986, p. 10).

[167] Smith, *The Wealth of Nations*, I.xi.p.10, p. 267. One could cite as an impressive example today the cartel agreement among the Swiss banks.

multinational firms attempt to reduce the risk by means of mutual participation and branches in the nations of rivals.[168] This readiness for joint action expresses itself in countless cartel agreements, which tend to limit the spheres of interest against one another and — because they include not only the parent corporation, but also its affiliates — lead to far-reaching reductions of competition in national and international markets.[169] That is, of course, not at all to say that there is no longer any competition at all among the large multinationals. It does exist — one need only think about the large conglomerates in the automobile and aircraft industries — but the tendency is unmistakably to distribute the market shares among themselves on the basis of power positions created in the market: "The 'market,' as an anonymous, public and relatively power-free controlling authority, is thereby eliminated… in ever wider spheres of industry."[170]

2. Another aspect of the economic power of large multinational firms concerns the high degree of freedom in investment policies and in the choice of the locations where their economic activity will take place. Thus L. E. J. Brouwer, as the highest-ranking executive in the Royal Dutch/Shell Group, said frankly in the 1960s, "Internationalism gives us the ability to choose where and when we will invest."[171] There is obviously no absolute freedom here. Even the multinationals are constrained by the governmental economic legislation of both their home countries and the foreign countries in which they do business. As Tugendhat stresses, however: "A government can prevent a new investment in its country, but it cannot force an international company to build or expand. The company, for its part, can select whichever country offers the best industrial, economic, sales, and political prospects for its new plants and facilities."[172]

One could, of course, reply that this fact, which is accompanied by, inter alia, direct effects on the labor market,[173] only reflects the

168 Georg Koopmann, "Warum gibt es multinationale Unternehmen?" in *Multinationale Unternehmen*, ed. Dietrich Kebschull and Otto G. Mayer, Frankfurt, 1974, p. 46.

169 Cf. Prosi and Biel, "Unternehmen, multinationale," I: "Volkswirtschaftliche Probleme," pp. 91-92.

170 Bornschier, *Wachstum, Konzentration und Multinationalisierung von Industrieunternehmen*, p. 188.

171 Cited by Tugendhat, *The Multinationals*, p. 164.

172 *Ibid.*, p. 164. See also Michalet, *Multinationale Unternehmen und die Wirtschaftskrise*, p. 34.

173 See Peter J. Buckley and Patrick F. R. Artisien, *Die Multinationalen Unternehmen und der Arbeitsmarkt*, Frankfurt/New York, 1986.

possibilities that lie in the borderless expansion of the markets to the global economy and the international division of labor connected to it. These opportunities can be used not only by large multinationals, but also by small ones. Therefore, it is merely a question of economic prudence, not one of economic power. But is this simply the case?

Realistically, one will have to answer this question in the negative. Above all, when it is a matter of nations, primarily of the Third World, that are extremely interested in large direct investment by a multinational corporation, because they hope that it will promote their domestic economies (through the creation of new jobs, the transfer of technology, increased educational opportunities for their own young people, etc.), the multinational firm, in its negotiations with the governmental authorities, "can use its extra-territorial nature to great effect."[174] This succeeds all the more, the greater the means, the international room for action, and the range of real alternatives that it has at its disposal. In other words, powerful multinationals have not only the opportunity to select freely the most favorable locations for their investments, but also, if necessary, to change the existing conditions of locations to their favor (by tax reductions, safety precautions for the sales of their own products in the foreign country, concessions concerning the repatriation of profits, etc.). That does not at all mean that there will be only negative consequences for the host county, nor even that some of the consequences will be negative. But it is possible that they will be. For the firms' executives, when making their investment decisions and their business decisions in general that refer to the foreign country's affairs, ultimately have their own interests in mind, at least primarily, not those of the host country. It goes without saying that a virulent potential for conflict is contained therein.

3. At this point a third aspect finally appears, that of the conversion of economic power into political power. In the modern industrial society economics and politics co-exist in an interdependent relationship.[175] On the one hand, the economy is dependent upon politics; on the other hand, politics is dependent upon the economy.

[174] Arnaud de Vogue, President of the French chemical and glass company St. Gobain, as cited by Tugendhat, *The Multinationals*, p. 175.

[175] See Bruno S. Frey, *Theorie demokratischer Wirtschaftspolitik*, Munich, 1981, pp. 2-19.

Dependence of the economy on politics exists through the economic, fiscal, monetary, and environmental policies of the state, which can extend to the allocation, i.e. the distribution and use, of the resources or factors of production at its disposal (especially in the agricultural sector).

For its part, the politics of the state is dependent upon the economic situation, especially on the growth of the national (or domestic) product. Direct and indirect tax revenue, which is the basis of all governmental activity, is determined by its size. Because they decisively influence the course of the economy, the goals, decisions, and tactics of economic power are of the utmost political significance. That is true, of course, not only of large multinational firms, but also of influential economic associations, not the least of which are labor unions.

By virtue of their multinationality, however, international corporations occupy an extraordinary position relative to the state. They are not tied to the framework established by it and the economic policies pursued by it to the degree that nationally-confined firms and commercial associations are: "When companies co-ordinate their activities on an international scale the individual affiliates necessarily become far less responsive both to government policy and to other influences within their own country."[176] Accordingly, production is shifted from one country to another and market share is redistributed among the subsidiary corporations — while there can be, of course, refractory affiliates that thwart the plans of the central corporation. In general, however, it can be said that the multinationals have enormous means of pressure at their disposal, especially relative to weak, unstable countries, of which there are many in the Third World. But even in large, established industrial states, they are able to use the relation of interdependence between the economy and politics to their advantage. John Kenneth Galbraith even maintains, especially in view of circumstances in North America, that large industry, with its transnational corporations, clearly control politics: "Where the industry is powerful, government responds strongly to its needs."[177] Even if this view of things is exaggerated in its sweepingness, the fact nonetheless remains that the multinational conglomerates' economic power has political relevance.

[176] Tugendhat, *The Multinationals*, p. 119.
[177] Galbraith, *Economics and the Public Purpose*, Boston, 1973, p. 283.

These three aspects, which are inseparable from one another, illuminate in general the question of power that arises with the appearance and dissemination of multinational conglomerates. The real problem is not simply that they have power. Power itself is not necessarily reprehensible. It becomes reprehensible, however, because it exceeds the human measure, whenever it expands and takes on centralist-monocratic structures and when those affected by it lose the ability to control or influence it. In this way, perverted power inevitably enables the law of the jungle to gain ground — a process that can also work to the detriment of multinational firms themselves, and against which they seek to protect themselves by forming cartels. At the political-national level, such perversions of power are opposed somewhat by the separation of powers, as a prerequisite of rule-of-law, democratic power control. In the liberal, national economies, the framework established by the state to prevent such perversions, as well as the economic policy pursued by it, have a similar function. International markets, however, are without an analogous apparatus, because there is a lack of international authorities capable of creating it obligatorily and employing it effectively. National economic legislation can jump into the breach only inadequately:

> The essence of the problem lies in the structural inadequacies of national legal orders to comprehend the commercial activities of multinational firms. The aggregate of the components of a firm that conducts international commercial operations appears to be an individual decision-maker, since it follows an integrated strategy. Yet each individual part of the firm comes under a different governmental jurisdiction, which possess neither the practical means nor the legal jurisdiction to cross national boundaries, and therefore can monitor the firms' activities only fragmentarily.[178]

The necessity of efficient integration into a transnational framework and economic policy becomes all the more evident.

The negotiations concerning a code of conduct for multinational firms within the United Nations Commission on Transnational Corporations constitute a first approach to this kind of integration, while,

[178] H. Schwamm, "Verhaltenskodex," *Schweizerische Handelszeitung*, No. 23, 4 June 1981, p. 2. See also Jack N. Behrman, "Können nationale Regierungen die multinationalen Unternehmen unter Kontrolle bringen?" and Gerd Langer, "Können multinationale Unternehmen international kontrolliert werden?" in *Multinationale Unternehmen*, pp. 203-18 and 219-44.

of course, internationally active banks must also be taken into account. They make headway, however, only with difficulty, if at all. To begin with, the ideas of the developing nations and those of the industrialized nations concerning the substantial determination of such a code still diverge widely. Furthermore, the nations of the East Block resist permitting their own transnationally-active state firms to be regarded as multinationals, which is considered unacceptable by the West. But even if the negotiations, despite these and other difficulties, should lead to a workable consensus, one would still have to ask whether a mere code of conduct would be sufficient to deal with the problems presented by multinational firms. These border-crossing corporations are an obvious indication that the economy of the industrial age has become the global economy. And in terms of global economics, if it is not to lead to chaos, in which the weaker economic subjects — one thinks primarily of the developing nations — must from the outset be the ones who suffer, a transnational economic agreement between the multinational corporations and the involved states,[179] guided by a technically and humanly just alignment with the new realities, must be able to defend the exploitation of the weak by the strong.

2.7 Economic Growth

2.7.1 *The Magnitude and Stimuli of Economic Growth*

The most striking aspect of modern industrial society is unquestionably the economic growth tied to it.[180] The age of industrialization led up to a magnitude of economic growth, to which nothing in the past is comparable. Especially in the period after 1950, when the multinational conglomerates began to grow rapidly and the network

[179] Cf. Michalet, *Multinationale Unternehmen und die Wirtschaftskrise*, p. 81-82: "The national control instruments are no longer appropriate, because the nation-state itself has experienced a change of function in the course of multinationalization. But any control exclusively dependent upon the multinational conglomerates, without governmental support, would be too vulnerable and would contain too many uncertainties. This two-fold impasse requires a fundamental solution that cannot be found in a simple juxtaposition of the contemporary protagonists: the state and the multinational conglomerate. The solution will be determined by the dialectical relationship between these two poles. The reality that will come from this interaction will be of an original character."

[180] On the causes of modern economic growth, see also Christoph Stückelberger, *Aufbruch zu einem menschengerechten Wachstum*, Zürich, 1979, pp. 6-25.

of international trade became incomparably more dense, global industrial production increased in such a way that one must really speak of "exponential growth." This development, which by now has become common knowledge, can be seen at a glance with the following graph.

Growth of World Industrial Production[181]

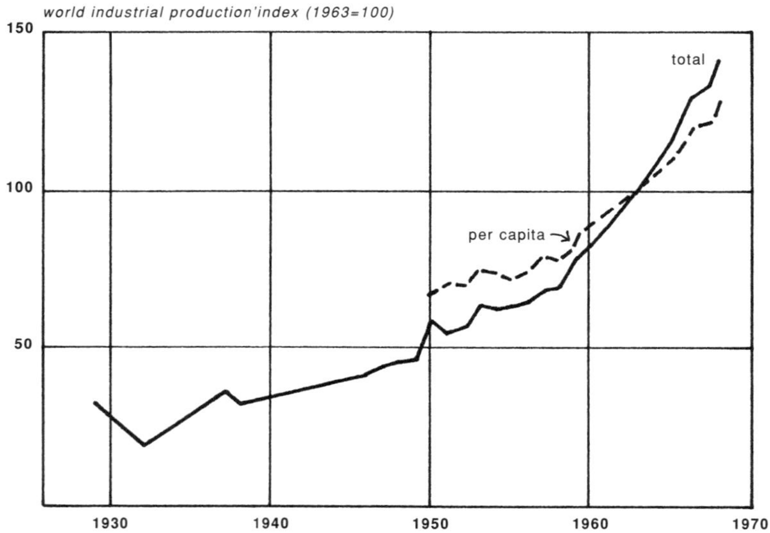

The fact that there is a direct correlation between a nation's degree of industrialization and its rate of economic growth is obvious. The higher the level of industrialization, the higher has also been until now, on the whole, an economy's rate of growth.[182] That, of course, does not yet clarify the specific stimuli that have led to worldwide, though regionally quite different, economic growth.

A primary stimulus of industrial economic growth is found without question in the demographic development of the world population. It proceeds roughly in step with the process of industrialization. As the second graph shows, this growth can be represented until

[181] Donella H. Meadows, *et al.*, *The Limits to Growth*, New York, 2nd Ed., 1974, p. 38.

[182] Ibid., p. 40.

Growth of World Population[183]

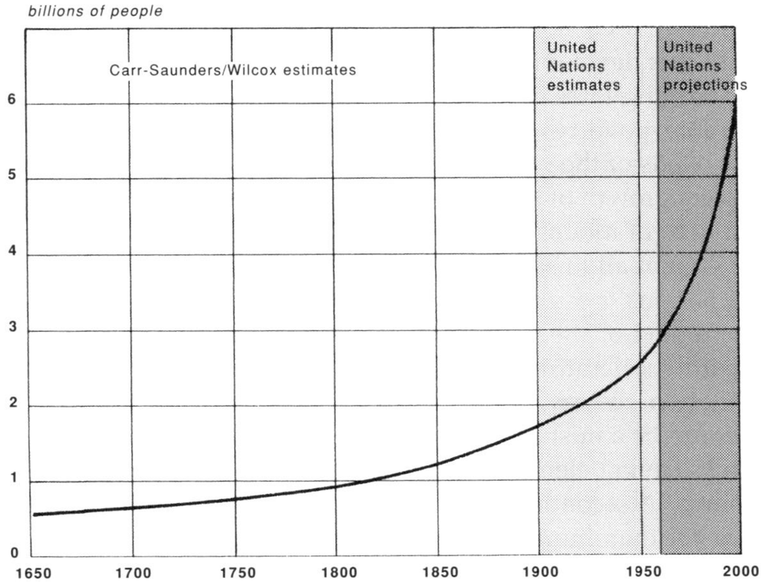

about 1800 by a straight line. After 1800 it becomes more and more a steep curve, and since 1950 an exponential curve, so that one can speak of a genuine population explosion. At this point, of course, the question is raised whether the rapid population growth of the last two centuries advanced the process of industrialization or, conversely, whether industrial culture itself possesses a structurally based growth effect. There is a plausible argument for each of these alternatives. Scientific-technical progress, especially in the fields of medicine, health care, nutritional practices, etc., which cannot be separated from industrial culture understood in the broadest sense, has decisively accelerated the rapid growth of the world population by greatly increasing average life expectancy. And, on the other hand, this growth has made increased production necessary, in order to meet the accompanying increase in basic material needs, just as it also made industrialization possible. There exists an interactive relationship here between two factors. To attempt to play the two elements against one another would be a mistake.

[183] Ibid., p. 33.

However one may evaluate the details of this interactive relationship, a direct correlation between the growth of world population and industrial-economic growth is indisputable. If one also takes into account that developing nations — such as India, for instance — with their alarming rates of population increase, together with the related intolerable poverty of broad population groups, still have many unmet needs of the most elemental kind and, therefore, must rely on per capita growth of their economies, then the demographic stimulus component of modern economic growth imposes itself imperatively. That is not at all to say that the solution to the problem of the developing nations' poverty lies in the industrialization of the economy on the model of the First or Second World. It merely makes it clear that with accelerating population growth, economic growth is also absolutely necessary.

It would be a mistake, however, to see world population growth as the only driving element of the exponential growth of the industrial economy: "A second quantity that has been increasing in the world even faster than human population is industrial output."[184] The first of the graphs above shows the growth of global industrial production relative to the production figures of 1963: "The average growth rate from 1963 to 1968 was 7 percent per year, or 5 percent per year on a per capita basis."[185] Moreover, precisely in the industrialized nations, the average annual population growth rate lies well below that of real GDP.[186] There must, therefore, be factors other than demographically conditioned factors involved in modern economic growth.

One such factor is undoubtedly the greatly increased demands of the populations of industrialized nations with regard to their standard of living. Thus, more than a few young people today wish to live independently of their parents. Individual persons, unmarried couples, and families want to have more spacious and, above all, more comfortable residences. Owning one's own automobile, expensive entertainment equipment, mass tourism, but also a seemingly carefree *dolce far niente*, and many other things are further indices of

[184] Ibid., p. 38.

[185] Ibid., p. 39.

[186] According to Bruno Fritsch, *Wachstumsbegrenzung als Machtinstrument*, Stuttgart, 1974, p. 149, the annual population growth rate in the industrialized nations between 1963 and 1969 was 1.1% and that of real GDP was 3.7% (1960-1970).

the spreading rise in demands. Insofar as they are not artificially provoked, they stem from a life-emptiness that can never be filled by purchased goods and that, precisely for this reason, can provoke endless desires. That is related to industrialization insofar as it has life-desolating consequences for many persons in both their world of work and their world of leisure. It is obvious that such maximization of demands can cause growth impulses in the economy. There are, however, not only subjective but also, even more often, objective reasons for them.

Our preceding analysis of the industrial economy has determined that industrialization and rationalization go hand in hand for the purpose of increasing worker productivity. If, however, worker productivity, understood as output per hour of work, increases, then a barely growing or no longer growing national product leads to a reduction in the number of labor hours necessary to produce it. And the result of that is a tendency towards unemployment.

Unemployment can be mitigated, at least in terms of mathematical calculations, by the distribution of the work hours that are still necessary among more shoulders or heads, in other words, by a reduction in the number of hours worked per person. But to what consequences would this lead?

If a reduction of working hours entailed a corresponding forfeiture of pay, the income of the workers would sink directly and their future retirement pensions would do so indirectly. This consequence is difficult to accept socially, and would lead to labor and distribution conflicts, especially in a society with growing demands for its national product.

If, on the other hand, working hours were reduced with full or nearly full wages, then a huge increase in labor costs would be inevitable and a reduction of profits, which are necessary for the survival of firms, would be possible, or even probable. And the consequences would be either the closing of factories, the reduction of production, or even more substitution of expensive human labor by mechanical labor, in other words, forced rationalization. That, however, would inevitably mean a loss of jobs, which is to say, increased unemployment.

The conflict only intimated here possesses a strong, long-term, structurally situated necessity for constant growth of the economy. If the national product of the economy grows to a sufficient degree, then the loss of jobs resulting from the increased productivity of labor can be balanced by increased production, without a reduction of pay or social services and without putting the economic viability of firms at risk. And that not only justifies the economic stimuli, it also suggests the logical conclusion that socially desired full employment, with a profitable way of managing that ensures the continued existence of firms, and consequently economic and social stability, can be attained only under the conditions of "appropriate" economic growth. Traditional economics, classical, neoclassical, and post-Keynesian, as well as Marxist and neo-Marxist, agrees with this on the whole.[187] The goal of the economy thus becomes indirectly its own growth. But does that not contradict our basic thesis that the economy cannot have an independent goal, determined by itself, because its purpose is one of service, to provide the goods necessary for human existence, and in a way that can be justified humanly, socially, and environmentally?[188] A differentiated answer will be required to deal with this crucial question.

First of all, it should be said that one must guard against the simple alternatives of an economy that meets needs and a growth economy. The magnitude of the need for economic goods is flexible, not fixed. It varies according to the number of those who need the goods and according to the quantity, kind, and quality of their needs. In other words, if the size of the population increases, the economy must also grow correspondingly, both in order to provide for the growing need for goods and in order to account for the growing demand for employment. As long as population increases, which it is still doing today, the economy must likewise grow correspondingly. Furthermore, the needs of human persons change legitimately. Unlike nature, we have, as cultural beings, an elastic structure of needs. With our historical development, new and increased needs arise. All of these factors require economic growth, if the economy is to perform its fundamental task of meeting needs.

Another question, however, is whether the growth of the economy is oriented towards legitimate human needs, or whether it itself conditions the needs. In the former case, the growth of the economy extends to the limits of human needs, including not only the need of goods and services necessary for life, but also the need of human

[187] Binswanger, *et al.*, *Arbeit ohne Umweltzerstörung*, p. 15.
[188] *BEE*, Vol. II, 1.3.1-4.

work conditions, sufficient employment opportunities, and an environment that is as unscathed as possible, in other words, what is meant by "quality of life." In the latter case, growth assumes the character of extreme boundlessness, which evades regulation.

2.7.2 *Industrial Capitalism*

Economic growth, in this dynamic sense, correlates with the dominant position of the factor of capital in the industrial production of goods and services. Land (or nature) and labor are, to be sure, limited as factors of production, because, considered from a long-range perspective, they are not at our disposal without bound. And human workers cannot be used without limit. Artificial materials can be partially substituted for natural raw materials, which of course entails the utilization of available resources, just as human workers can be replaced by machines. Yet both require capital investment. The scarcity of capital, however, has no limits determined by creation or nature, as do the scarcity of the other two factors of production. In other words, monetary or real capital is not pre-existing, but "produced," a means of production created by human persons: "He can also therefore *increase* the money and the money values."[189] And this increase or "value creation becomes all the greater, the more money flows into the economy *and* the more things are transformed into money values."[190] But this means that the greater the investment of capital, the greater the possible creation of value and profit. And the greater the profit, the more there is to be reinvested in the economy. In this way, profit maximization and the maximization of national product go hand in hand as the economic desirables — whether at the cost of the integrity of nature or of humanly just working and social conditions — and thus as untiring engines of modern economic growth. They constitute the essence of what one could call "industrial capitalism," which — it should be emphasized in this context — is not restricted to the West, but exists wherever — as in really existing socialism — the possession and utilization of capital do not rest in private hands, but instead in the hand of the state, or, more precisely, the hands of its planning authorities.

[189] Binswanger, *Money and Magic*, trans. J. E. Harrison, Chicago, 1994, p. 35.
[190] *Ibid.*

It is the economic growth of industrial capitalism, which — in the East as well as the West — stands in contradiction to the fundamental purpose of the economy and has provoked a cultural crisis. Marx understood this contradiction with great vision when he explained, in a passage concerned with the consequences of "large industry": "Capitalist production, therefore, develops technology, and the combining together of various processes into a social whole, only by sapping the original sources of all wealth — the soil and the labourer."[191] By that he meant that industrial capitalism, by making production more dynamic and more rational, which made possible the economic growth of that time — which also astonished him — did violence to the bearers of the factors of production of land and labor. They were taken advantage of and exploited by it in such a way that they stopped playing a part in the long term. If, however, the elemental nature and the creative person no longer play a part in the economy, then social prosperity is struck at its root. One would be ill advised to make light of Marx's critique of industrial capitalism just because it has turned out to be incorrect in some respects.

Thus, the industrial worker, generally speaking, contrary to the prognosis of the Marxist theory of impoverishment, has not become economically poorer, but instead richer, although in the industrialized nations there is still persistent, sometimes even new, poverty, especially in connection to unemployment. But the concept of impoverishment, as Marx understands it, has in addition to its economic dimension, an anthropological dimension, namely the human pauperization that the wage laborer can and often does suffer as "self-alienation," as the reduction or even loss of one's humanity in economic conditions. To the extent that workers, as human factors of production, are reduced to the status of mere material means of production, who are to be used as productively as possible according to the requirements of a profit-maximizing economy, or even be replaced, they will feel reduced in their humanity, whether consciously or unconsciously, and will be vulnerable to an attitude of refusal, sometimes open, sometimes hidden. Industrial capitalism encounters here, despite its merit regarding the economic increase of prosperity, a human veto that is expressed for the most part only in a diffuse malaise, but which should be taken seriously as a social

[191] Karl Marx, *Capital*, in *Collected Works*, New York, 1996, Vol. 35, New York, 1996, pp. 507-8.

warning sign. That is even more true of an ecological veto, that can no longer be ignored today.

The facts that led — and that had to lead — to this veto have become so widely known to the public by now that they hardly need to be referred to in detail.[192] It is sufficient to refer to the overuse and destruction of renewable resources, to the over-exploitation of non-renewable resources, to pollution of air, land, and water by harmful chemicals and waste materials, to the related harm to health and threat to fauna and flora — with the death of forests in the foreground — and, last but not least, to the flood of noise, the ruination of nature, and the decrease of recreation areas. This is about acts of violence, for which nature, both human and non-human, is not a match and which, therefore, must be directed against the cause itself, the limitlessly-expanding economy. For all human economic activity stands or falls with the natural foundation, from which it cannot free itself. But does this mean that the industrial economy, with its growth that undermines the foundation of the natural environment, has reached the end of the road?

This pointed question expresses one of the greatest dilemmas that distress the present age. The industrialization of the economy sprang from a historical necessity, because a growing population with growing needs also requires a growing economy. The industrial economy created growth, but growth of a kind that is now about to undermine its own foundation, human persons and the natural world, and thus the creation, the ecosystem in which everything is interrelated. Does a disastrous fate loom here? Is economic growth itself destructive? The immediate feeling fights against that. Growth is an expression of life. If growth ceases, then life comes to its end. That is also true of the economy. Simply to forbid it to grow would be to sentence it to death. But not all growth promotes life. After all, cancer cells also grow. But with their growth they destroy life, the very life upon which they themselves depend. Therefore, distinctions must be made between different kinds of growth. When seen from that perspective, the distinction that has recently been made between *quantitative* and *qualitative* growth is important and forward looking.[193]

[192] See the well-documented study of Klaus Michael Meyer-Abich, "Die ökologische Grenze des herkömmlichen Wirtschaftswachstums," in *Die Zukunft des Wachstums*, ed. Henrich von Nussbaum, Düsseldorf, 1973, pp. 163-86 (including a list of references).

[193] See Frey, *Wirtschaft, Staat und Wohlfahrt*, pp. 110 ff.

2.7.3 *Quantitative and Qualitative Economic Growth*

Quantitative growth means growth in the magnitude of gross national product as such. If the economy is to grow, in order to be able to fulfill its fundamental, life-serving purpose, but only this kind of growth is available, then everything that increases the national product, the total value of goods and services that are produced within a time period (usually a year) in the formal sector of a national economy and go on the market, is ultimately justified economically.[194] The question whether the increase is based on actual creation of value is of no importance. Someone who "makes" a traffic accident, and thus injuries other persons, "creates" damage to vehicles, receives the services of the police, brings about costs for medical treatment, hospital care, automobile repairs, administrative activities, etc., all of which are provided through the market and, consequently, contribute to increasing the national product, even though no true creation of value, only at best the restoration of value destroyed, takes place.

Quantitative economic growth, therefore, pays no attention to the components of national product. But it also pays little attention to the demands on environmental goods, insofar as they do not enter into the calculation of costs and detract from profit maximization. The term "environmental goods"[195] is understood to include, besides sunlight, air, water, etc., natural or mineral resources in the broadest sense of the word. All of these goods, with the exception of sunlight, are in the long run, though to varying degrees, scarce goods. But only in the long run: "As long as any supply at all of these goods still exists, they appear to the *present-day* owner to be plentiful and, therefore, quasi-free goods. As long as the supply of nature is greater than the *present-day* demand, there is no reason to worry."[196] Thus they are, in view of their future scarcity, undervalued in the present — petroleum is a striking example at the present time (1986) — and can be obtained easily, because their prices are low. Quantitative growth of the economy, which overuses environmental goods, does not receive sufficient braking from the market side. In other words, the environment-harming economic growth of the capital-intensive, industrial

[194] It is not possible here to enter into a fundamental critique of national product. But see Alois Steiger, *Sozialprodukt oder Wohlfahrt?* Diessenhofen, 1979.

[195] Binswanger, "Eine umweltkonforme Wirtschaftsordnung," in *Umweltschutz und Wirtschaftswachstum*, ed. Martin P. von Walterskirchen, Frauenfeld, 1972, p. 129.

[196] *Ibid.*, p. 130.

economy is not held within the ecologically imperative limits on its own by market forces. Thus Binswanger, for instance, can say bluntly: "The more capital-intensive — the more 'capitalistic' — the economy, the greater the burdening of the environment."[197] That is, of course, not to say that the industrially-capitalistically oriented market economy is solely responsible for the environment-damaging, quantitative growth of the economy. Thus Binswanger and co-authors maintain explicitly: "The promoter of quantitative growth today is no longer the market alone, but far more the state, with its various possibilities for influencing the economy, which tends to remove rather than to strengthen the 'self-regulating mechanism' inherent in the market."[198]

Economic-political praxis for the most part, even still today, equates the welfare of the population, the classical economic goal, with the gross national product of every resident, whereby it can cite long-dominant economic theory: "An increased use of the factors of production (labor, capital, nature, technical progress) leads to the increase of real gross national product ('economic growth') and with it the increase of the welfare of the population."[199] Corresponding to the concept of quantitative growth, therefore, there is a quantitative understanding of welfare, since welfare coincides with the increase of goods, the increase in wealth of a national economy. Given this concept, the quality of welfare does not apply, since it is not quantifiable. In view of that, Emil Küng says:

> The prescriptions of economic and social policies, with respect to the quality of life, are extremely meager.... One could call the dominant view: *Wealth as the guarantee of happiness*. The conceptual foundation of most economic activity and political-economic measures can be characterized by prosperity as a synonym for subjective human welfare.[200]

In contrast — and with it a genuine paradigm shift takes place — the concept of qualitative economic growth is tied to an understanding

[197] *Ibid.*, p. 132.
[198] Binswanger, *et al.*, *Arbeit ohne Umweltzerstörung*, pp. 211-12.
[199] *Ibid.*, p. 217.
[200] Emil Küng, "Die Qualität des Lebens als Ziel der Wirtschafts- und Gesellschaftspolitik," *Schweizer Monatshefte*, 54 (1974), pp. 22-23. He has, of course, been decisively contradicted recently by Josua Werner, "Qualitatives Wachstum — was is das?" *Neue Zürcher Zeitung*, No. 13, 17/18 January 1987, pp. 17-18: "Few economists have explained that every form of growth always also leads to the improvement of more fully understood welfare" (p. 17).

of "welfare"[201] that is oriented towards quality of life. That, of course, does not mean that this understanding of welfare is directed in principle against material wealth. Poverty, in the economic-material sense, is certainly not an indicator of quality of life. But qualitatively better life also cannot simply be reduced to mere economic wealth, as a measure of the quantity of goods available. It goes far beyond that and includes, among other things, humanly just working and social conditions and environmentally just conditions of life. This includes, for example — at least according to the criteria of the humanity originating from faith, hope, and love — more humane forms of work or participative corporate structures, as well as living places freed from harmful emissions, restored forests and fields with an animal and human world that can live. None of these are quantitatively measurable goods, but goods without which any economic wealth as the material basis of welfare loses its meaning, and ultimately is foundation as well.

Of course, just as quantitative economic growth, understood as the mere increase of gross national product, does not tend to produce welfare that is humanly and environmentally just, so the mere zeal for more quality of life in the industrial society does not automatically mean qualitative growth in the economy. There is even an emotionalized and ideologically dressed-up ado about quality of life that simply amounts to pure hostility towards the economy. In opposition to that, it must be maintained that qualitative economic growth, if the word is to avoid being reduced to absurdity, must certainly also be growth, economy-affirming growth, but growth of a kind for which the level of gross national product can no longer be the general standard.[202] This includes three things:

[201] A distinction will be made in the following between the terms "wealth" (*Wohlstand*) and "welfare" (*Wohlfahrt*).

In Smith's *Wealth of Nations* the directly measurable and thus quantifiable supply of goods (standard of living) stands in the foreground, in order to characterize the term "wealth." Determining welfare, however, involves not only the quantity of goods available, but also their just distribution and, beyond that, the satisfaction of a quantity of immaterial (i.e. qualitative) needs that is not definitively determined (quality of life).

[202] The report of the expert commission of the Swiss Federal Department of National Economic Affairs, Federal Office for Economic Policy, Study No. 9 (Bern, 1985), p. 15, provides the following definition: "Qualitative growth is any lasting increase in the overall and *per capita* quality of living that is attained with low, or at least non-increasing, use of non-renewable or non-regenerable resources, as well as with a reduction, or at least no increase, in environmental burden."

First, this means that qualitative economic growth must facilitate the economy and, indeed, the efficient economy, which is able to fulfill its fundamental mission of supplying human persons sufficiently with life-serving and life-promoting products, whether goods or services.[203] If it fails to meet this basic condition, it will have no future.

Furthermore, it means that qualitative economic growth, which treats human persons humanely in their working conditions and conserves the environment, may have no negative effects for the rate of employment, but instead must show itself capable of creating sufficient "work without environmental destruction."[204] If the step towards qualitative growth of the economy leaves unemployment, as a worldwide evil, in its present state, or even increases it, then it will certainly fail.

Finally, from all of that it follows that one must avoid a doctrinal opposition of quantitative and qualitative economic growth. Qualitative economic growth cannot mean that there should be no more growth of gross national product, but instead that its components should be changed.[205] As long as the national product is composed of products that avoid notorious damage to human persons and the environment, as well as the over-use of resources, it is welcome to grow.[206] What can no longer be tolerated, though, is growth of the national product for which the qualitative composition has no relevance, and thus is not connected to the limits that arise from the conditions of human and environmental justice and, consequently, can

[203] A detailed establishment of the concept of qualitative economic growth, with concrete recommendations for its realization, is found in Hans Christoph Binswanger, Holger Bonus, and Manfred Timmermann, *Wirtschaft und Umwelt*, Stuttgart, 1981, esp. pp. 80-83. See also Binswanger, *et al.*, *Arbeit ohne Umweltzerstörung*, pp. 209-328.

[204] This is discussed in the NAWU-Report, *Wege aus der Wohlstandsfalle*, ed. Binswanger, Werner Geissberger, and Theo Ginsburg, Frankfurt, 1978, as well as the works cited in the preceding footnote.

[205] Egon Tuchtfeldt, "Wirtschaftspolitik," in *Handwörterbuch der Wirtschaftswissenschaften*, Vol. 9, p. 190.

[206] A singular, and thus non-generalizable example of possibilities for economic growth, without using raw materials and energy in a way that pollutes the environment, is presented by software production, which is gaining ever-greater significance, especially for the tertiary sector: "Software is distinguished from other technical products above all by the *character of the materials* from which it is made and by the possibilities for *costless reproduction*. The material from which software is made is *language*... which is gratis" (Jochen Ludewig, "Software Engineering," *Neue Zürcher Zeitung*, No. 209, 10 September 1986, p. 113). It can also be added that the energy used in the production of software is of a mental kind.

expand without bound. To the extent, however, that quantitative economic growth meets these conditions, it is not opposed to qualitative growth. Therefore, this is by no means a matter of a regressive economy of renunciation, but of the way from an economy of *always more* to one of *enough*."[207]

2.8 The Double Face of the Industrial Economy

If one considers the development of the industrial economy, from its beginnings until the present day, and asks how it should be evaluated from the perspective of human welfare, to which every kind of humanity is committed, one encounters a dilemma. There is no unambiguous answer to this question.

If the idea of human welfare is oriented according to material indicators, the verdict will be positive on the whole. The material standard of living in industrialized nations has, generally speaking, climbed exceptionally, not only in the West, but partially also in the East, though to a much lesser degree. Work itself, for which material wealth is to be thanked, has become incomparably less arduous physically and is shifting — most obviously since the electronic turn — more and more in the direction of activities that use, above all, human intelligence and powers of invention. The enormous increase of labor-productivity through modern methods of rationalization and the growth of the economy coupled to it permitted an improvement of the social security system that widely surpasses everything before, even if one takes into account the considerable differences that exist here between one industrialized nation and another. To be sure, the objection can be raised that, despite all of this, there exist poor classes of the population even in industrialized nations. One can think of the USA, which is highly developed industrially, but in which 15.2% of the population was poor at the end of 1983.[208] But the reason this situation obtains is not found in the lack of value-creating capacity of

[207] See Harry M. de Lange, "Die Kirchen und die Einheit Europas," *Zeitschrift für Evangelische Ethik*, 27 (1983), p. 47.

[208] National Conference of Catholic Bishops, *Economic Justice for All*, Washington, 1986. It is to be noted that in the United States the poverty line for a family of four is $11,600, and thus cannot be compared with poverty in Third World countries. See also *BEE*, Vol. II, pp. 394-95 and pp. 410-13.

the industrial economy itself, but instead, for the most part, in structural defects that hinder just distribution of the national product. The industrial economy, with its multiple technical possibilities, also including soft technologies that conserve the environment but are also efficient, would itself be in a position to create the material goods necessary to meet the needs of everyone humanely. That is also true of the Third World, provided that population growth is held within limits.

Man, however, does not live by bread alone. An understanding of welfare that is measured only according to material indicators falls far short of being able to satisfy human persons in the long run. It leads ultimately into nothingness and, therefore, reduces itself to absurdity. Thus, the growing feeling of unease towards the contemporary industrial economy; thus also the nostalgic dreams of many who sometimes look back at the supposedly good old days, but sometimes also speak progressively of a vision of an alternative post-industrial society. One well knows that the industrial economy has produced much material wealth, but one also begins to realize that it has been purchased at a high price. In short, the industrial economy forcefully presents its other face.

The other face of the industrial economy is associated today by the greater part of the population above all with the ecological crisis that it has brought about. Many also feel, however, increasingly threatened by the change in the quality of work in the course of the process of industrial rationalization. This also shows a double face,[209] and all the more openly as it is supported electronically. On the one hand, it pushes humans even more "into the center of the production process, where robots are programmed, new, innovative programs are invented, and, above all, the management of the entire system also takes place." And, on the other hand, they are pushed "even more to the periphery, where the points of contact between production and social life exist."[210] In other words, this means that some persons are confronted in their work by even higher demands and responsibilities, and thus also that the position of the subject can be raised in it, while others, who are not or are no longer able to meet the new demands are shoved to the margin, that is, are thrown to work that

[209] See Joseph Huber, *Die zwei Gesichter der Arbeit*, Frankfurt, 1984, pp. 13 ff.

[210] Klaus Michael Meyer-Abich and Bertram Schefold, *Wie möchten wir in Zukunft leben*, Munich, 1981, pp. 32-33.

is poor in content, which reduces their personality level, if they are not completely eliminated from the work process entirely. It is already typical of most industrialized nations today, as in the Federal Republic of Germany, that with a pronounced shortage of well-qualified personnel there is also a high ratio of unemployment. The more capital-intensive the production processes, or the more extensive the replacement of the factor of labor by that of capital, the more human persons are pushed out of the sphere of production (goods and services) — whether by reduction of working hours or elimination of positions. If the present trend continues, they will also cease being producers and will be reduced economically to the role of consumer. Even with sufficient provision by purchasing power, which is not only possible, but in fact indispensable in a developed industrial society, this means a severe restriction of the entire situation in life of those affected. Consumption, even when it restricts itself only to material goods, can never compensate for the reduction in status of a person in the working world. Again: Man does not live by bread alone. With that a crucial limit of the industrial economy comes into view. It has brought much to many persons; but it has also taken much from many — or is about to do so.

At this point, the cultural critique of the industrial society begins. The former accuses the latter of a one-sided economistic-materialistic basic orientation, intent only on economic efficiency and the increase of material wealth. It lacks a view of humane, cultural, ecological, and other unquantifiable values. Nothing is easier than supporting this with cogent arguments. Nevertheless, one should avoid concluding fallaciously, as with the cultural-critical syllogism,[211] that if something is missing, then that which does exist is not good. To be sure, much is lacking in modern industrialism. But it has also led economic activity to a level of productivity that makes material welfare possible for everyone, even if far from everyone participates in it. The fact that it is able to do this does not cease to be good just because it exhibits great deficits in other respects. Man, indeed, does not live by bread alone, but he does also live by bread. Thus, the request for daily bread in the "Lord's Prayer." The material component remains a fundamental component of human existence, a fact that must be taken seriously, especially by a theory of business and economic ethics that orients itself towards human justice as a matter

[211] *Ibid.*, p. 13.

of priority: towards human justice as demanded by the humanity originating from faith, hope, and love. For this reason, while maintaining critical distance from the double-faced, and in that respect also dubious, industrial economy, it must refrain from simply passing judgment on it overall. Yet this two-sidedness also confronts business and economic ethics with new, irrefutable questions regarding the meaning and lack of meaning, the rightness and wrongness of the order-political structures of the industrial society of today, in the East and in the West.

These questions finally come to a head in the question of meaning, understood as the question of human justice in the economy overall. This question has been discussed in the first main section. In its horizon, the next step is to go about setting out the critical points on which it decides the extent to which economic orders can or cannot exist in the industrial age before the criteria of human justice, which contains, as the humanity originating from faith, hope, and love, creation justice. In order to be able to undertake this central task in the concreteness necessary, an explicit examination of the economic-ethical main problems is first required, as they are already partially contained by implication in the second main section, with its illumination of essential aspects and perspectives of the industrial economy. The next step is consequently marked out. In the process, certain overlappings are unavoidable.

3. AN ANALYSIS OF THE PRINCIPAL PROBLEMS IN BUSINESS AND ECONOMIC ETHICS

3.1 Fundamental Questions of Economic Order

According to Paul A. Samuelson, any economic society, regardless of its level of development or systemic structure, finds itself facing "three fundamental and interdependent economic problems: 1. WHAT commodities shall be produced and in what quantities?... 2. HOW shall goods be produced?... 3. For WHOM shall goods be produced?"[1]

The first question thus refers to the "What?" and "How much?" of production. What should the economy produce? Consumer goods, investment goods, services, goods for military purposes, etc.? How much of them should it produce? And which goods are to be given priority?

The second question concerns the "How?" of production. How should the economy produce? The primary concern here is with the purpose and manner of using the available resources or factors of production (land, raw materials, energy, labor, capital, entrepreneurial and technological innovative power, etc.), and thus with the so-called problem of allocation.

Finally, the third question has to do with the "For whom?" of production. "That is, who is to enjoy and get the benefit of the goods and services provided?"[2] Investors? Producers? Consumers? And how should the shares of aggregate output be distributed to the various members of society? According to performance? According to need? According to the position of power or powerlessness of the participants in the economic process? Should one accept gross economic inequalities in the distribution of wealth and income, or should the attempt be made to apply the principle of equality as much as possible?

[1] Paul A. Samuelson, *Macroeconomics*, Vol. I, 7th Ed., New York, 1967, pp. 15-16.
[2] *Ibid.*, p. 16.

3.2 Ethical Implications of the Three Fundamental Questions

The three questions cited above are of a specifically economic nature. They indicate explosive ethical implications, however, as is immediately apparent in the case of the third question. Nevertheless, that requires explicit clarification.

3.2.1 *Ethical Implications of the First Fundamental Question (What and how much should be produced?)*

The first of the three fundamental questions appears to be of purely economic relevance. It arises from the fundamental purpose of the economy, the optimal reduction of scarcity restrictions, with the life-serving goal of guaranteeing that the needs of a population are met. If that is correct, then it is also human needs that decide what and in what quantities and according to which priorities goods and services will be produced. The more a good is desired and, consequently, the greater the demand and the degree of scarcity, the higher the priority of production. Therefore, the scarcity rule is decisive, and that has little or nothing to do with ethics.

This opinion would be correct, if human needs were a matter of objective, and thus natural quantities. That, however, is only partially, only slightly true. It is true only to the degree that they are aimed at goods that are simply necessary for life. If they go beyond what is necessary for life — and for the most part they do precisely that in the industrial, affluent society — then they have subjective foundations. This is true not only of individual needs, but also of collective needs, such as needs for schools, hospitals, homes for the elderly, social security systems, public transportation, etc., in short, the need for a well-constructed infrastructure that increases the quality of life. Insofar as these needs are of a subjective kind, the question of their legitimacy, as well as their priority, is also raised. For not all "needs" are needed. In order to offer an extreme example, the need for good housing is not the same as the need for illegal drugs. The former need aims at a better quality of life, the latter leads to the diminution, if not the complete destruction, of the personality and the social relationships of the person who possesses it. Therefore, they are to be assessed completely differently; and to be precise, not only in the sense that they pose the personal question whether one can take responsibility for needs whose satisfaction has disastrous consequences for both one's own existence and social existence. No, they must also be assessed in the way that raises a question relevant to political order: Should the economy really meet all needs, even those that damage individuals, society, or the environment, just because they create demand and thus produce corresponding scarcities, whose remedying promises a profit? However one may answer this question, it cannot be ignored. And, therefore, it is obvious that the first fundamental question of economic order has ethical implications.

The question of "What?" and "How much?" still lets production be tackled from the other side, that is, from the supply side. Should everything that can be produced be supplied? In purely economic terms, the answer is: Yes, if there exists a demand for it.

But it is by no means the case that only demand, more precisely, the need for a good standing behind it, prompts its production; the reverse is also possible. Supply can precede demand and first arouse the desire for it. That is precisely the case in the modern industrial economy, with its enormous ability for innovation. It constantly produces new products that did not previously exist and for which, therefore, no actual demand — at most only a potential demand — could have existed. One need think only of the immeasurable palette of new mass goods that have come into the market with the origin and development of electronics. Transistors, pocket calculators, digital clocks, to name here only these commonplace products, are possessed today by almost every child. And that simply means that, if the charm of novelty entices or if they promise increased utility, supplies can themselves create demand. With that, however, supply is no longer determined by demand. It has, instead, the tendency to expand indefinitely.

This tendency is supported by the theorem formulated by Jean-Baptiste Say (1767-1832)[3] and also accepted to a great extent by contemporary economic theory, though it is not undisputed, according to which any supply of goods leads, through the creation of income or increase in purchasing power brought about by their production, to a corresponding demand. Assuming that this is correct on the whole, it is difficult, again considered in terms of economics, to see why a

[3] See Gerhard Graf, "Beschäftigungstheorie," in *Handwörterbuch der Wirtschaftswissenschaften*, Vol. I, pp. 515 ff. Say's theorem or law, of course, did not remain uncontradicted. In addition to Marx, who rejected it from the start, it was criticized as early as Malthus and, more recently, by Keynes.

selection or restriction of products would be advisable. Nevertheless, it would remain imperative to answer the question whether everything that is technically and economically feasible, is able to provoke a potential need, and probably could also be sold, thanks to the demand effect tied to it, may really be produced. Even goods that pose severe risks for human beings, society, or nature that are difficult to calculate? Moreover, one must ask where the boundaries of at least quantitatively-fashioned economic expansion actually lie, in view of the consumption of scarce, non-regenerable natural resources conditioned by it, together with the burdening of the ecosphere that it implies. In any case, what amount of material prosperity is still compatible with an economy whose most characteristic purpose would still have to consist in service to life, understood universally, to include all of nature. Again, all of this points to enormous ethical implications associated with the first fundamental question.

3.2.2 *Ethical Implications of the Second Fundamental Question (How should goods and services be produced?)*

The second fundamental question of the economy, which is about the "How?" of production, concerns the allocation problem, which has already been mentioned. How should the scarce resources or factors of production — land, labor, and capital — be utilized? Seen from the economic point of view, the answer must be that they are rationally utilized in a way that derives from them the maximum utility for the entire economy with the minimum costs. That means, on the one hand, the thriftiest treatment of the resources and, on the other hand, the greatest possible productive result in terms of quantity and quality, and thus optimal efficiency[4] as the measure of the degree of impact of economic activity. This is true of every economy, regardless of its structure; for no economy can afford to function inefficiently for any length of time. It would not be able to fulfill its most fundamental purpose in society, serving life. And in this respect efficiency,

[4] Efficiency means, on the one hand, *effectiveness* (setting and achieving goals, creating utility, producing results) and, on the other hand, *economizing* (rationally and prudently deciding, working, acting, optimizing the use of means). See Peter Schwarz, *Management in Nonprofit-Organisationen*, Bern, 1986, p. 27. With efficiency in the sense of economizing, a distinction is made between *allocation* efficiency (the best-possible use of the factors of production) and *corporate* efficiency (the lowest-cost manufacture of a particular quantity of goods).

as an economic imperative, is a requirement that is also in accordance with human justice in the broadest sense of the word.

When addressing this subject, however, it is necessary to be on one's guard against a fallacy. To say that an inefficient economy cannot be humanly just does not at all mean that every concern with economic efficiency as such is in line with human justice (where, again, it is to be remembered that our concept of human justice always also includes environmental justice).

That is to say that with the employment of the factors of production in the firm, it is never simply a matter of the mere employment of material goods. Capital, in the form of a produced, easily increasable means of production, is simply a thing. With the factor of land / nature, however, one can no longer simply talk about a thing understood in this way. Natural goods, in contrast to material goods, cannot be increased as much as one wishes. Their availability is absolutely, not merely relatively, limited. The more one employs them for economic purposes, the scarcer they become. If one wishes to talk about them and use them as things, one must do so extremely carefully. Furthermore, nature, as an ecosystem, is vulnerable, and *in extremis* irreversibly so. Therefore, interventions in its activities — and they are inevitable with economic activity — must be taken with caution, so that the threshold of its vulnerability is kept as low as possible.

That is true even more directly of the factor of labor. To employ labor as an economic good in the economic process means to employ human beings, who are destined for personhood[5] and, therefore, if this fact is respected, may never be used merely as means to the fulfillment of economic purposes, but are entitled to be regarded as responsible personal subjects in this process of fulfilling the economy's purpose. Consequently, human persons are vulnerable in a completely different way than nature: not only physically-instrumentally, but also psychologically-personally, to the extent that their personhood is disregarded. Respect for human beings in their personhood is a fundamental ethical postulate, similar to respect for nature and its goods, which are predetermined for human beings, are entrusted to us, and, therefore, may not be treated as manufactured means of production, as capital goods. As much as the efficient allocation of the means of production may appear to be a purely economic affair, it also has definite ethical implications. The way in

[5] On the concept and nature of personality, see *BEE*, Vol. I, 3.1.2 and 3.3.2.

which the command to conduct economic activity in the most efficient way possible is followed, therefore, cannot be a trivial matter. The question is whether it will take place on the basis of narrow rationality, which is only economically calculated, or on the basis of an economic sensibility that understands that the economically rational and the human and environmentally just cannot be short-circuited and separated from one another.

3.2.3 *Ethical Implications of the Third Fundamental Question (For whom should goods and services be produced?)*

The third fundamental question — Who should derive the utility from the goods and services produced, or how much should be paid for the contributions of the bearers of the various factors of production? — gives rise to the problem of distribution. It is most closely connected to the problem of allocation. The way in which the distribution of aggregate output is tackled in terms of political and economic order will have consequences for the allocation of resources. And conversely, the way in which the allocation of resources is conceived in terms of the political and economic order will yield repercussions for the distribution of aggregate output. The present purpose is not to probe these complex relationships, but to point out the ethical implications in play, which means that the discussion will be restricted to a few small, crucial points.

The starting point, again, is the efficiency of economic activity, with the concept now understood not only in its restriction to a single economic actor, but even more in its expansion to the entire economy.[6] The more efficient a national economy, the better the relationship between input and output, the more there is to distribute, and the more effectively its fundamental purpose is fulfilled. Efficiency, to emphasize the point once again, is a presupposition of humanly just economic activity; but it does not by itself solve the problem of distribution.

Even an efficient economy, which produces enough goods and services that everyone can live a life of human dignity, is not free of the problem of distribution. The question of the appropriate distribution of aggregate output to the individual factors of production, or more

[6] See *BEE*, Vol. II, p. 590.

precisely, to those who possess them, remains — with capital and labor standing traditionally in the foreground. Should this distribution be left to the anonymous game of supply and demand in the factor markets, and thus to the rule of scarcity, or should human-social elements be decisive, or at least partially decisive? That is both an economic and an ethical question. Experience shows that a notorious disrespect of the laws of the market necessarily leads to inefficiency of economic activity. But it also shows that "market justice" as such is not automatically brought into agreement with what one commonly understands by justice.[7]

The question of distribution, however, does not refer only to the problem of economically rational and humanly just compensation of the factor outputs; it concerns no less the question of how aggregate output should be divided up among the economically active segment of the population and the segments that are not yet or no longer economically active. An efficient economy, according to its nature, is oriented towards output. But everyone, even those who are not able to ensure their existence by their own effort, are entitled as human persons to having their existence safeguarded.[8] The fact that even in a country as prosperous as Switzerland there are "several hundred thousand persons who for the most part live visibly poor or hidden in poverty"[9] is certainly inconsistent with human justice. Even if this number is excessive, and even if in some cases the poverty is partially the person's own fault, it nevertheless presents a social challenge that reveals once again the ethical dimension of the question of distribution.

[7] See *BEE*, Vol. II, pp. 406 and 458-59.

[8] Georges Enderle, *Ein Leitbild für die Sicherung des Existenzminimums in der Schweiz*, St. Gallen, 1986, pp. 2-5. Enderle even wishes to understand the safeguarding of existence as an "independent, fundamental, social right," which should "be established in the constitution."

[9] *Ibid.*, p. 3. This estimate is based on a definition of the poverty line that is accepted by many social scientists today: 50% of the net available income per consumption unit. In Switzerland this line was 10,150 francs for single persons in 1976 and 15,000 francs in 1984 (*ibid.*, p. 14). Both this kind of estimate and the definition of the poverty level upon which it is based are, however, problematic. They have been criticized by Werner Ulrich, "Zum Stand der schweizerischen Armutsforschung," *Neue Zürcher Zeitung*, No. 168, 22-23 July 1989, p. 21, as well as Robert E. Leu, "Bedürftigkeit und Armut als relative Begriffe," *Neue Zürcher Zeitung*, No. 193, 22 August 1989, p. 33. According to Leu, the establishment of the poverty level is "a *purely political* decision." Depending upon the poverty level used, the percentage of the Swiss population living in poverty fluctuates between 1.6% and 10.3%.

This statement is true even more in view of the scandalous disparity in the distribution of income between industrialized and developing nations, which is still constantly increasing:

> In 1953 the annual per capita income of the developing nations was \$101, compared to \$985 in the industrialized nations. This ratio of approximately 1 to 10 changed in 1972 to 1 to 13 in favor of the industrialized nations. The per capita income of the industrialized nations climbed to \$3,670. Despite the expansion in Latin America and a few other countries, primarily the oil-producing nations, the developing nations achieved only \$280.[10]

The conditions in the poorest regions of the Third World, where sheer hunger prevails, are catastrophic and completely intolerable. According to minimal estimates, the number of those who are starving was already 500 million in 1970.[11] It has increased since then. According to information from the World Bank, a total of about 750 million people (not counting China), 33% of the population of the Third World, lived in absolute poverty in 1980.[12] Even if the misery manifested in these numbers is partially caused by factors for which the developing nations themselves must accept responsibility,[13] the question is nevertheless imperative whether and to what extent the structures of economic-exchange relationships between the industrialized nations and the Third World are primarily to blame for it. It is legitimate to speak of "blame," because economic structures do not grow naturally, but are instead created by human persons — and thus human persons must accept responsibility for them.[14] And, to be precise, not only with regard to their economic efficiency, but also just as much with regard to the way in which resource allocation and the distribution of the global aggregate output between the industrialized

[10] Jürgen Gerhard Todenhöfer, *Wachstum für alle*, Stuttgart, 1976, p. 14. These numerical relationships are, however, to be relativized in the sense that a statistically low per capita income does not necessarily mean mass wretchedness. Similarly, a statistically high per capita income does not necessarily exclude impoverishment of entire segments of the population. As signs of a trend, however, they remain meaningful.

[11] *Ibid.*

[12] World Bank, *World Development Report 1981*, Washington, 1981.

[13] It is important to point out in this context the high annual population growth rates in precisely the developing nations with the lowest incomes, which are even higher than the high Third World average of 2.5%. In the industrialized nations, the corresponding growth rate stands at only 1% (Todenhöfer, *Wachstum für alle*, p. 15).

[14] *BEE*, Vol. I, p. 71.

nations and the developing nations are favored or handicapped by them: whether in a way that makes the rich even richer and the poor even poorer, or in a way that balances out the provocative difference between the two, and thus seeks to attain more distributive justice? That is also among the ethical implications of the third fundamental question.

3.3 Principal Ethical Problems in View of the Question of Ordering the Economy

Now that the ethical implications of the three fundamental questions of economic order have been clarified at certain points and paradigmatically, it is necessary to categorize systematically the principal ethical problems[15] that arise from them in view of the facticity of modern industrial society and from the normative viewpoints of the criteria of the humanity originating from faith, hope, and love. Because this undertaking must relate main sections 1 and 2 to one another, it is impossible to avoid some repetition.

3.3.1 *The Fundamental Problem*

In Section 1.3.1, the fundamental purpose of all economic activity was determined, with the help of the human criterion of creatureliness, to be service to life. Every economy that wishes to avoid failing in its fundamental purpose must serve life, more precisely, human life embedded ecologically in the entire life of nature and, therefore, never to be separated from it. This primarily includes providing to all persons, regardless of their skin color, nationality, social status, etc., the goods and services that are necessary for existence, are desirable, and all in all increase the quality of life. To the extent that the economy fulfills this fundamental purpose, and thus is able to meet the life-serving fundamental needs, it also exists in harmony with itself.

From that it is evident that the economy may not be its own purpose. In other words, it must not serve itself, the development of its own possibilities, but instead must set itself in the service of promoting the welfare of everyone. And that means that the quality of a

[15] See also Peter Stolz, "Arbeit, Umwelt, qualitatives Wachstum," *Zeitschrift für Evangelische Ethik*, 30 (1986), pp. 191-210.

national economy is to be measured neither solely by the degree of effect of its productive and distributive output, nor by the level of the growth rate or the magnitude of its gross national product, but by whether and in which way it is able to increase the quality of life, i.e. is able to produce as a first priority the goods that promote the general welfare, with maximum consideration for natural resources and the environment. All self-purpose thinking in the economy, which is ultimately about its own expansion, ultimately as far as into the immeasurable, regardless of whether its production promotes or hinders welfare, and which, therefore, assesses natural goods, even the human person, as mere means to the achievement of this pseudo purpose, is a fundamental reversal of things and stands in direct contradiction to the principle of service to life. The fundamental problem of business and economic ethics is to combat this real or possible alienation and to promote the genuine purpose of the economy, not only in personal-appellative terms, but also in structural terms of the political and economic.

3.3.2 *The Problem of Efficiency*

Another problem closely linked to the fundamental problem of business and economic ethics outlined in this way is that of efficiency.

If the economy is to be able to do justice to its fundamental purpose of service to life, it must first be effective, i.e. actually be in the position to achieve this purpose. And secondly, it must meet the requirement of economic efficiency, i.e. achieve the greatest possible utility with the least possible expenditure. Effectiveness and rational business management are fundamental determinants of economic efficiency.[16] And in this respect the economy's efficiency and service to life, as has already been emphasized in several passages, are not to be separated from one another. One must be on guard here against false oppositions, as they can be found in critiques of the industrial performance-oriented society that do not hold water, because they are unsophisticated, but nevertheless easily impress people for precisely that reason.

Conversely, it is no less necessary to be careful about — as has already been mentioned — uncritically equating efficiency and service to life with one another. Equating them is problematic to the

[16] See 3.2.2., note 4.

extent that the degree of efficiency of economic activity is measured by the level of the profit ratio that can be achieved by an individual firm. Efficiency, which orients itself only to the manager's cost minimization or profit maximization in the individual business firm and, therefore, ruthlessly rationalizes away jobs, for example, ignores the possibility of more humane forms of work, pushes wages and social benefits downward, seeks to hold the costs for environmental-protection measures as low as possible, etc., will inevitably produce external effects that, instead of having life-serving consequences, have consequences that are hostile or, in the worst case, even devastating to life.[17] If efficiency is to lead to an economy that serves life, then it must be brought into relation with the command of human justice, which includes environmental justice, and thus must open itself to the ethical dimension.[18] That delineates a principal problem in business and economic ethics. How is economic efficiency to be understood and which consequences for structuring the economy are to be drawn from it, so that it is not from the start caught in hopeless opposition to the basic requirement for a life-serving economy, which also means an economy oriented towards the criteria of human justice, not only towards economic rationality?

3.3.3 *The Problem of Human Justice in the Economy*

A concept of efficiency that understands how to assimilate the ethical requirement of human justice is not the only thing that belongs to the economy's service to life. Conversely, human justice is also to be understood in such a way that it takes into account objective necessity in the economy, which is not simply identified with so-called inherent constraints,[19] and to which economic efficiency belongs. In other words, this means that what is concretely commanded by human justice cannot be deduced from abstract principles, forgetting

[17] On the entire problem connected to it, see K. William Kapp, *The Social Costs of Private Enterprise*, Cambridge, Mass., 1950.

[18] Cf. Helmut Kaiser, "Ansatzpunkte für eine normative Erweiterung der ökonomischen Rationalität," *Zeitschrift für Evangelische Ethik*, 28 (1984), pp. 285 ff. This project is discussed comprehensively and from a new perspective by Peter Ulrich, *Transformation der ökonomischen Vernunft*, Bern, 1986. Just as there is no rational business ethics beyond economic rationality, for Ulrich, there is also no "well-understood economic rationality this side of practical (ethical) reason" (p. 344).

[19] See Rich, "Sachzwänge und strukturell Böses in der Wirtschaft," *Zeitschrift für Evangelische Ethik*, 26 (1982), esp. pp. 68-72.

reality, and thus remaining outside economics. It is only to be determined in such a way that its criteria are imparted with the facts, together with their uncertainties, which make up the reality of the contemporary industrial economy. Only with this kind of imparting is it possible to examine more closely the additional principal problems of the economy that follow from the claim of human justice, as it produces the humanity originating from faith, hope, and love with its specific criteria.[20] With that, resulting from the subject matter itself, the criterion of participation must step into the foreground beside those of fellow-humanness, fellow-creatureliness, and relationality. The additional steps are predetermined by it.

3.3.4 *Human Justice from the Perspective of Fellow-Humanness*

Fellow-humanness, understood as a criterion of human justice, turns out to be a personal category. The fellow human person is the person in relationship to you, i.e. in dialogical coexistence with other persons, with the comfort and demands (*Zuspruch und Anspruch*) of the Creator. This establishes, in contrast to individuality, one's personality as the basis and purpose of responsible, mature existence.[21] As such existence in the I-Thou relationship, the human person is always the purpose of the human person. To respect the human being as a person means, therefore, to use Kant's words, to regard the human being "always at the same time as end and never merely as means."[22] When human beings are respected only as means, not as ends, they are robbed of their personality, of their ability to be responsible, and, consequently, of their autonomy. Their existence then ceases to be humanly just. That is true not only of direct personal relationships among human beings, but just as much of institutionally mediated relationships, in this case of relationships within economic structures.

The ways in which work is organized are included within economic structures. Industrially organized work, with the goal of increasing its productivity, is subject to the conditions of highly rationalized division of labor. That presupposes completely different levels of qualification, with corresponding stratification in the allocation

[20] *BEE*, Vol. I, 7.

[21] *BEE*, Vol. I, 3.1.2, 3.3.2 and 7.2.5.

[22] Immanuel Kant, *Groundwork for the Metaphysics of Morals*, ed. and trans. Allen W. Wood, New Haven, 2002, p. 47.

of responsibilities. According to Taylor's principle of the rationalization of labor, with its division of work activities into brainwork and handwork, this tends to lead to a reduction of the handworker to purely order-obeying, alienating, mechanical activities and, therefore, to work that is similar in quality to the ways machines function. Thus, he becomes in his work a machine-serving means of production, instead of also being an end, that is to say, a co-planning, co-deciding, co-responsible person in the production process. To the degree that the aforementioned reduction gains ground, it brings about the depersonalization of the human being in his or her work, which is never consistent with human justice and is expressed strongly in the flight from work into recreational life.[23] Developing and promoting structures of the organization of labor that make it possible for everyone active in production, distribution, and management, and thus also those at the order-obeying level, to attain a status by which they can become or remain co-workers, co-humans, even persons with genuine joint responsibility in the work places, is included in the principal problems of the economy that does not evade the ethical demand of human justice. It has already been shown in earlier contexts that the opportunity for such economically rational humanization of labor also exists under the conditions of mechanical, as well as electronically supported rationalization.[24] That refers, putting it summarily, to the co-determination of workers in their workplaces, in the sense of participation in the dispositive functions that have to do, directly and indirectly, with their work. With that, participation comes into view as an additional basic criterion of human justice.

3.3.5 *Human Justice from the Perspective of Participation*

While fellow-humanness as a criterion of human justice is a primarily personal category, participation is a primarily structural category.

[23] For a detailed discussion, see Rich, *Christliche Existenz in der industriellen Welt*, 2nd Ed., Zürich, 1964, pp. 113-23.

[24] *BEE*, Vol. II, 2.3.3.1 and 2.3.3.3. The humanization of work is assessed sceptically by Manfred J. Holler and Claus J. Tully, *Arbeit und Mensch*, Munich, 1981. According to these authors, the humanization of work stands under the primacy of economic efficiency and, therefore, proves not at all to be universally advantageous for workers.

In other words, it elevates what is meant by "fellow-humanness" from the immediate-personal level to the mediate-institutional level.[25] It means that living and working together in social institutions can meet the demand of human justice only to the degree that their structures are oriented towards the ability to participate of everyone involved in or concerned with the institutionally conditioned forces, rights, goods, and authorities. What principal ethical problems arise from that for the institution of the economy? That will be explained in more detail under three essential headings.

3.3.5.1 Participative Cooperation

The question of the structure of economic cooperation presents a first principal problem here. Every developed economy — again, regardless of how it is organized — is based upon cooperation. The fundamental economic subjects — producers (including distributors), consumers, and the state — cooperate.[26] Within the productive sphere there exists cooperation between, on the one hand, investors and managers and, on the other hand, the specific owners of the factor of labor, who today are multilayered.[27] Cooperation is a basic presupposition of the modern industrial economy, as is explicitly held even by Karl Marx.[28]

Cooperation can take place, however, in completely different structural forms. One possibility is that the multilateral dependence of those cooperating, as it constitutes the basic nature of cooperation, is converted into unilateral dependence, in which one party imposes upon the other the conditions of their collaboration. Another possibility is that those cooperating determine the conditions of their collaboration in common, and thus strive for a consensus. The former case is one of confrontational cooperation, the latter of participative cooperation.

Industrial cooperation becomes confrontational, therefore, if one group — whether producers or consumers, the advocates of the interests of investors and managers or of the interests of workers and society — seeks to impose its will upon the others and to impede, if

[25] *BEE*, Vol. I, 7.2.7, p. 194.
[26] *BEE*, Vol. II, 2.5.
[27] *BEE*, Vol. II, p. 336 and 2.5.1.
[28] Marx, *Capital*, in *Collected Works*, Vol. 35, New York, 1996, Chapter 11.

not to make completely impossible, the legitimate pursuit of contrary interests. The fact that self-interests are pursued at all, instead of being sacrificed altruistically, does not violate human justice. But the interest-monocracy that tends to place one's own demands, aspirations, and goals above everything else and, consequently, to convert them into absolutes, contrary to a humanity that is dialogically and participatively obligated, does violate human justice. Every kind of monocracy, whether it is pursued by one side or the other, violates human justice and, when it becomes embedded in the structure of social relationships, brings about structural evil, inherent constraints that institutionalize injustice.

Cooperation that accepts confrontational structures is, therefore, not only opposed to human justice; it is also contrary to economic rationality, because it contradicts its own nature and thus leads to self-dissolution. In view of the capitalistic structure of industrial cooperation, with its dominance of capital interests relative to worker interests, Marx speaks of "twofoldness."[29] Cooperation then would also have to be twofold, if the situation became one of a monocracy of social and environmental interests, i.e. if all of this were pursued in such a way that the interests of capital formation in the economy, which are required by the economy's very nature, whether in cases of individual firms or of the entire economy, could no longer or only insufficiently be pursued. For the sake of both human beings and economic efficiency, business and economic ethics must clarify this unmistakably and insist on participative forms of industrial cooperation that oppose every kind of interest-monocracy and make it possible for all corporate bodies involved in economic processes to participate in the coordination of interests and, consequently, in the establishment of the conditions of cooperation. A decisive prerequisite for this is the restriction of economic power, with the goal of being able to control and dominate it. Any accumulation of power in the economy that pushes its way towards a monopoly, whether in the hands of private investors or associations of managers and firms such as large multinationals, even in the hands of the state or labor unions, leads to confrontational structures of industrial cooperation and impedes, or even prevents, participative forms of collaboration. This is, again, a principal problem of business and economic ethics: Which available or possible structural orders in the economy are best

[29] Marx, *Capital*, in *Collected Works*, Vol. 35, New York, 1996, p. 337.

able to take into account this demand for participation as a criterion of human justice and, therefore, are to be preferred to others?[30]

3.3.5.2 Participative Distribution

The question of distribution presents additional principal problems in business and economic ethics from the perspective of participation.

1. While the problem of distribution was until recently concerned primarily with the just distribution of the aggregate output resulting from economic cooperation, today, in view of the high rate of unemployment in most industrialized nations,[31] it is increasingly concerned with the question of the just distribution of the available work, so that everyone who is willing and able to work can participate in this cooperation.[32] Someone in the modern industrial economy who has work, generally speaking, already possesses thereby a better situation in life and, consequently, a higher quality of life than someone who wishes to work, but lacks the opportunity. And that is the case not only because the unemployed, despite insurance claims and social welfare benefits, are as a rule much worse off than those who have work. Involuntary long-term unemployment leads with the majority of those affected by it beyond the economically oppressive situation in life to human impoverishment, which contributes to social and personal disintegration, and which cannot be compensated even by larger monetary payments.[33] Thus, what is called "new poverty" today belongs to the same species as long-term unemployment. Therefore, in discussing the distribution problem, it is appropriate to begin at this point.

[30] With regard to the constitutional structures of firms, I have undertaken this in my book *Mitbestimmung in der Industrie*, Zürich, 1973.

[31] In the OECD region alone, more than 30 million persons are unemployed today (1987).

[32] This opinion is also shared even by liberally oriented economists. Thus Josua Werner, "Beziehungen zwischen Beschäftigungspolitik und Arbeitslosigkeit," *Das Wirtschaftsstudium*, No. 5, 1985, p. 258: "The fight against unemployment becomes at the same time the task of giving, under the existing conditions, the total necessary *volume of work* as much as possible to all those who wish to work. In other words, *employment policy* presents itself in a certain respect *as distribution policy*." Likewise, Hans-Jürgen Krupp, "Lohnpolitik und Vermögensbildung," in *Wirtschaftspolitik in den 80er Jahren*, ed. Alex Möller, Bonn, 1984, p. 145.

[33] Oskar Negt says bluntly: "Unemployment is an act of violence, assassination of physical and mental-spiritual integrity, of the intactness of the persons affected by it" (*Lebendige Arbeit, enteignete Zeit*, Frankfurt, 1984, p. 8).

This is, of course, not the place to raise the question of the causes of unemployment. The opinions are, incidentally, highly conflicting. The only thing certain is that it cannot be explained in terms of a single cause.[34] And that is precisely why combating it is so difficult. As much as this is true, it is equally true that one can never resign oneself to the phenomenon of unemployment, if participation is really taken seriously as a criterion of human justice. Everyone who wants to work has a right, according to this criterion, to receive his share of the income-generating work and, of course, also the duty, insofar as his gifts and abilities make it possible, to acquire the qualifications that contemporary industrial society, with its division of labor, requires and that, consequently, are demanded in the labor market.

The greater the number of jobs in existence, the more easily the division of labor takes place. That leads to the demand for full employment, or the highest possible level of employment, which is linked to economic growth. Economic growth, however, even if it is of a more qualitative kind, has its anthropological and ecological limits. Furthermore, a growing economy today does not necessarily lead to a decrease in unemployment.[35] The increase in the productivity of labor through rationalization reduces the number of jobs. In addition, the most recent, electronically supported wave of rationalization, with its shift in emphasis from handwork to brainwork, has profoundly altered the structure of demand in the labor market, and will continue to do so even more. Qualifications that are modified, and sometimes completely new, are now required. Above all, in the coming years, workers, even those identified as the best professionals according to the standards that obtained until now — for example, those in the typographic industry — are becoming superfluous or find it difficult to adjust and keep up, a fate that they experience as the expropriation of acquired abilities, as the destruction of their human capital. Moreover, there are the considerable number of poorly qualified and naturally handicapped persons, who have even

[34] See Walter Adolf Jöhr, *Zur Arbeitslosigkeit der Gegenwart*, Tübingen, 1986, esp. pp. 45-112. The most recent annual conference of the Verein für Socialpolitik in Berlin (Sept. 1987), which was devoted to the theme "employment problems of highly-developed economies," and where the classically inspired "real-wage hypothesis" (unemployment as mainly the consequence of insufficient wage flexibility) was especially under discussion, brought the polycausality of unemployment to light once again (*Neue Zürcher Zeitung*, No. 219, 22 September 1987, p. 39).

[35] Binswanger, *et al.*, *Arbeit ohne Umweltzerstörung*, pp. 139 ff.

more difficulties with the new structure of qualification in the industrial work world. Thus, in addition to new opportunities, there are new risks for workers.[36] One already speaks fatalistically of structural unemployment and means by it the more or less fixed, continued existence of unemployed persons in the formal production and service society, who, because they are no longer needed, have no employment income, only transfer income, which is usually only sufficient for a minimal existence, at their disposal. As a consequence, the class separation of the industrial society between those who possess gainful employment and those who do not is present. And that is confrontational division of labor, not participative division of labor based upon solidarity.

It is not possible to make the division of labor more participative simply by shortening the hours of the existing work, in order to spread it out to more people. If that takes place with no loss of pay, the gain in the productivity of work achieved by rationalization becomes the property of those who possess the gainful employment, in the form of reduced working hours. That can indeed lead to a more balanced distribution of profit between capital and labor, but it favors those who are active in the economic process, and thus those who are already privileged, and does not create new jobs. If, on the other hand, no corresponding increase in productivity precedes the reduction of work, this will simply lead to a rise in the price of the factor of labor. And then it is to be feared either that jobs will migrate to low-wage countries or that additional, work-saving rationalization will cause even more work to be replaced by capital. In that case, unemployment will be increased, not reduced.

In reality, we will only be able to arrive at participative distribution of labor if the increases in productivity made possible by the rationalization of industry are used beforehand to create environment-friendly and labor-intensive goods and services, which have been neglected until now, but are necessary in the interest of the general welfare, and for that reason promise jobs that are long-lasting, but also employment-effective in terms of the demands for qualification of precisely those who are structurally unemployed. This includes,

[36] This has already been pointed out by Alfons Sonderegger, "Die existentiellen Risiken des Arbeitnehmers," in *Christliche Wirtschaftsethik vor neuen Aufgaben*, ed. Theodor Strohm, Zürich, 1980, esp. pp. 341 ff.

above all, collective goods, such as environmental protection and conservation, expanded cleaning and waste disposal services, etc.[37] Favoring them would directly and indirectly contain a high degree of diverse employment opportunities, not the least, for less qualified persons, which is important here. That does not mean, of course, that only or mainly less-qualified personell would be required in the cleaning and waste disposal services, which are still to be created. The future environmental technology will also require many qualified people and, where the danger of wrong decision exists, will have to use systems that can take over the work of unqualified persons. What, then, are the order-political prerequisites that permit the effective realization of these kinds of concepts to be expected with the highest probability? This question is not at all a neutral one for business and economic ethics.[38]

2. The humanly just distribution of aggregate output among those who participate in producing it, as well as the others, who, for whatever reason, have not contributed to it, is the other principal problem in the distribution question. How is it posed from the perspective of the criterion of participation?

For classical macroeconomics, it was important to ask in regard to the distribution problem which share would go to the three factors of production — land, capital, and labor — and thus, on the one hand, to those who employ the land or capital and, on the other hand, to those who have nothing to contribute but their labor.[39] Ricardo believed that he was able to show that the scarcity of land brought about by population growth would make it possible for landowners to appropriate a constantly increasing share of the output of production. But scarcity would also be decisive for its distribution to capital and labor. The scarcer the supply of workers in the market with greater availability of capital, the more expensive the labor and the smaller the return on capital. And conversely, the greater the supply of workers under conditions of scarcity of available capital, the higher the compensation of capital in the form of interest, etc., and

[37] See Binswanger, *et al.*, *Arbeit ohne Umweltzerstörung*, pp. 169 ff.

[38] See Karl Ernst Wenke, ed., *Ökonomie und Ethik*, Frankfurt, 1984.

[39] Cf. Oswald von Nell-Breuning, "Die Arbeitswertlehre in der scholastischen Theologie, in der katholischen Soziallehre und nach Karl Marx," in *Christliche Wirtschaftsethik vor neuen Aufgaben*, pp. 57-74.

the lower the wages. Therefore, it is the relationships of scarcity between capital and labor in the factor markets that decide their price and, consequently, decide what share of the aggregate output they will receive. If these relations are well balanced, then the distribution will be also. Since the market, by virtue of the interplay between supply and demand, i.e. by virtue of its own mechanism, would tend towards evening out the scarcities, including those in the relationship of capital and labor, it would, insofar as it functions in agreement with itself, distribute to everyone what is his by providing each factor the price proper to it. And thus it would bring out, as it were automatically, distributive justice. Does that not converge with the basic request of participative distribution?

It is true that the principle of the market economy as such does not necessarily exclude distributive justice, understood in terms of participation. Oswald von Nell-Breuning says in this context: "As long as there is no reason to view the market as distorted by bad machinations (as misled or violated), one may demand and accept the market price with a clear conscience."[40] But the pure, undistorted market economy, as it is ideally presented in its classical model of harmony, has never existed in reality. In its historical facticity, the participative elements within it have been superimposed by confrontational elements, so that the existing market economy is in fact characterized by the confrontation of capital and labor.

This predominantly confrontational structure is essentially related to the fact that the labor side participates in the productive or interest-generating capital either not at all or only to such a limited degree that it can practically be disregarded. Productive capital is, however, a produced means of production, which has been produced on the basis of industrial cooperation together with the possessors of the factor of labor. But if the co-producers of this capital have no share in the proportion of the output of production that falls to the capital side according to the distribution mechanism of the market economy, then the distribution mechanism has a confrontational structure, because it favors one side and puts the other at a disadvantage. This prejudges nothing about the kind of participation of labor in the productive capital and the profit resulting from it. A variety of alternatives are conceivable. What matters is the practicable dismantling of

[40] *Ibid.*, p. 61.

the confrontational relationship of capital and labor in the question of distribution.[41]

The theory and practice of distribution that refers to the vulgar-Marxist labor theory of value, however, also proves to be confrontational.[42] According to it, only labor creates value, and something is worth as much as labor puts into it. Consequently, the capital employed in production creates no value at all. But if the capital-possessing or capital-risking manager claims the profit that goes above the cost of labor or wages and other essential expenditures, the so-called "value added," whether for himself or for the capital formation necessary for production, that would be exploitation of workers, expropriation of "proletarians" by "capitalists." In contrast to that, it would be imperative — the extreme postulate of socialization of all the means of production excepted — to maximize the wage and social claims, so that the value added that has been created in industrial production goes to those who created it. This fails to recognize that, apart from managerial productivity, real capital (tools, equipment, machines, electronics, etc.) also contributes to the creation of value, that labor can be no more productive without capital than capital without labor, and that, therefore, the wrong in the distribution does not consist in capital receiving a share of the total return of the production, but in the fact that the productive capital is distributed extremely one-sidedly, and thus not in a participative manner.

The criterion of participation is opposed to both of these confrontational structures in distribution. With the former, the rich become even richer. The latter impedes legitimate capital formation, which is indispensable for the survival and development of a humane economy. The participative distribution of productive capital would be capable of fighting against both of them. Furthermore, with additional capital income to the people previously excluded

[41] See Wolfgang Drechsler and Martin Wansleben, *Mitarbeiter-Beteiligung in Unternehmen*, Frankfurt, 1986.

[42] A distinction is made here between the vulgar-Marxist labor theory of value and that of Marx himself. The latter is scarcely comprehensible in its subtlety. It is also not free of contradictions and, therefore, can be interpreted in various ways. It was highly effective in its vulgarized form. See von Nell-Breuning, "Die Arbeitswertlehre in der scholastischen Theologie, in der katholischen Soziallehre und nach Karl Marx," pp. 64-69. A subtly differentiated presentation of the Marxist (labor) theory of value in its dialectic of labor value and use value of products is found with Ota Šik, *Der dritte Weg*, Hamburg, 1972, pp. 129-49.

from it, the shortening of work time would be made easier without reduction, or at least without full reduction, of pay, which would in turn support a participative-solidarist division of labor.

3. The problem of the humanly just distribution of aggregate output is concerned not only with distribution between capital and labor, but also with distribution between the diverse occupational groups that can be subsumed under the economic heading "labor."

As has already become evident from 2.3.4 and 2.4.2.2, the factor of labor in contemporary economic events represents an extremely differentiated and constantly growing diversity of qualifications and performances among people. It extends from top managers to semi-skilled and unskilled workers. The level of compensation of these most diverse levels of activity decides what share of the aggregate output each individual will receive. On the basis of what criterion should it be calculated?

If one assumes only market-economic premises, then one will see performance as the just measure of the wage level, and also refer there to scarcity rules. The scarcer some particular qualification, the more the person possessing it is sought and the higher its price, which is expressed by the level of compensation. But qualification and performance are not the same thing. It can turn out that someone who is most highly qualified in terms of training will perform poorly, or at least worse than expected. In addition to qualification, performance includes commitment, endurance, conscientiousness, loyal conduct in relation to coworkers, etc. All of these are values that cannot be quantified. It matters even more that the production of performance in industrial cooperation happens socially, and thus produces a "social product," which cannot be separated out individually in order to determine its value. Therefore, the reputation of arbitrariness and social injustice is always attached to the performance wage, and indeed all the more as the wage discrepancy between those who possess different qualifications becomes larger. It is certainly not identical with humanly just distribution.

The principle contrary to the performance wage is the need wage: "To each according to his need!" Whatever level of qualification a worker may belong to or whatever his production of performance may be, as a human being he has a right to have his basic natural and cultural needs satisfied in a manner consistent with human dignity. The wage should accomplish no less, but also no more, than this for everyone. This includes the leveling out of wages and is felt by many persons to be quintessentially humanly just, because it would lead to a minimization of differences in income and would promote economic equality for all. The drawback — apart from the impossibility of objectively determining the individual needs of individual wage and salary recipients with respect to their situations in life — is that this severely weakens or even eliminates the incentive to perform well. And experience proves that this has negative consequences for worker productivity, reduces the efficiency of the economy, and diminishes aggregate output.[43] In the long run, this causes the economically weak classes in particular to suffer. The participative and, consequently, humanly just distribution of income from work can, therefore, be reduced neither to the common denominator of the performance wage nor to that of the need wage.[44] In the industrial production and consumption society, which is organized for open cooperation, neither individual performance nor individual needs can be verified objectively. Moreover, these two wage principles (justice of need and of performance), when they are alternatively understood and practiced, have endangering consequences for the welfare of the weaker and weakest social strata. The proper objective is a sharing out of the cooperatively-achieved output of labor in such a way that each worker can live in human dignity by his or her wage and inequalities of income are permitted to the degree that they produce incentives to perform, ensure the efficiency of the economy, and thus form the prerequisite for a better position for precisely the poorest social groups in society. That will be possible only to the degree that the performance and solidarity principles mutually affirm one another. There are and must be inequalities in every performance society, because the individual members' abilities to perform are unequal. It does not contradict participation as a criterion of human justice for the one who produces more to participate in the return of greater production. But participation is contradicted when the more capable person is indifferent to those who are less capable and uninterested in improving their economic positions. Meeting the demand of participation indispensably includes that the stronger are in solidarity with

[43] This fact is receiving increasing attention in the camp of actually existing socialism, including the Chinese reform politicians. See Xue Muqiao, *Sozialismus in China*, Hamburg, 1982, pp. 77-105.

[44] See P. J. Roscam Abbing, *Ethiek van de inkomensverdeling*, Deventer, 1973.

the weaker. Raised from the personal level to the structural level, this means the correlation of a performance-oriented industrial economy and welfare state, which acknowledges the priority of its obligation to the command of solidarity. With that, as far as the question of distribution is concerned, a fourth point comes into view.

4. The welfare state is an indispensable consequence of the industrial age, above all for two reasons.

The first reason can be found in the orientation towards performance, at least in the case of the industrial economy structured as a market economy. Anyone who produces results, of whatever kind, has a claim to income. Anyone who does not forfeits this claim.

There are always some persons, however, who cannot be productive, or at least cannot be fully productive. Apart from the young and the old, there are also those who are unemployed, invalid, sick, mentally or physically handicapped, and finally those who are incapable, including failures. No nation that acknowledges its responsibility for the welfare of all its citizens — and without that, it would lose its humane, legitimating purpose — can disregard these people. It must ensure that they receive an income, unrelated to their personal work performance, with which they receive at least a minimum of social security. That requires creating and financing an appropriate social security system.

The other reason is that the economy's orientation towards performance in the industrial age leads to very different incomes. In view of the complexity of industrial cooperation and the social character of its production of results, which makes it impossible to measure the individual contributions to this production objectively, these differences are controversial, at least with regard to their appropriate magnitude. Moreover, one must take into account the confrontational structure in the distribution of the aggregate output between capital and labor. Both circumstances are causes of social conflicts, which the state must at least seek to defuse, in the interest of internal stability. This can be accomplished by socially oriented fiscal policy. It must distribute the necessary state expenditures — with the financing of the social security system receiving high priority, if the state is really a welfare state — in such a way that the economically strong are heavily burdened and the economically weak are lightly burdened. In reality, this leads to a subsequent redistribution of the aggregate product distributed by the market in favor of the weaker earning classes and that part of the population that has no earned income at all.

The redistributive policy of the welfare state is a prerequisite of participative distribution of the aggregate output that meets the demand of human justice. But not every kind of redistribution satisfies participation as one of the basic criteria of the humanity originating from faith, hope, and love.

Redistribution can be participative in this succinct sense — as has already been stated above — only if it is led by the conscious solidarity of the economically stronger towards the economically weaker and not by opportunistic calculation, which follows the law of least resistance. This means that the first priority is ensuring that the poorest group within the population derives utility from the redistribution.[45] That does not happen automatically. In cases of redistribution, factors of political power are always involved. For example, among the weaker members of the society, those who are organized in labor unions can promote their interests better than those who are not.[46] But those who are really poor are usually not organized; they are also politically and socially weak.[47] Therefore, they require support by the welfare state as a high priority. Only to the extent that the entire situation in life of the poorest citizens is elevated should the other weak people, who are less weak, also receive support. That is solidarity, understood in terms of participation, in view of the question of distribution.

Participative solidarity in the redistribution question of the welfare state means, therefore, that the life situation of the weakest members of the population is raised as a matter of priority. Without doubt, these are the persons who have very little employment income, or none at all, at their disposal. It has already been stated above which social groups are to be counted among them. If they are to achieve a

[45] The fact that poverty is still a problem even in industrial countries is frequently suppressed. If one accepts the 50% threshold as the standard for poverty (3.2.3, note 9), then in 1981 11.4% of the households in the European Community (excluding Greece) were poor. The corresponding figures are 6.6% for West Germany and 8.7% for Switzerland (Enderle, "Sicherung des Existenzminimums für alle Menschen," in Enderle, ed., *Ethik und Wirtschaftswissenschaft*, Berlin, 1985, p. 169). For criticism of this perspective, see BEE, 3.2.3, note 9.

[46] See Heiner Geißler, *Die Neue Soziale Frage*, Freiburg, 1976, p. 15.

[47] According to Michel Mollat's definition, a poor person is someone "who continually or temporarily is found in a situation of weakness, dependence, or humiliation, in a situation of need characterized differently according to the time and form of society, a situation of impotence and social contempt" (*Die Armen im Mittelalter*, Munich, 1984, p. 13).

humanly just situation in life, then their minimal existence must be ensured. In the developed welfare states of the industrialized nations, this happens to a large extent through social insurance for the old, the invalid, and the sick. Life is difficult for those who are unemployed for a long time, especially the young among them, the handicapped, those who lack ability or have failed, not to forget refugees. In order to secure their sheer existence, it is not sufficient to provide them with transfer income. It belongs without doubt to a humanly just life-situation — to which everyone who possesses a human countenance has a claim, according to the humanity originating from faith, hope, and love[48] — to enable the members of these groups, whenever possible, also or again to participate in employment income on the basis of performance. Employment income is to be preferred to transfer income for reasons of self-esteem, whose absence signalizes human impoverishment. With that, the other aspect of participative solidarity already comes into view.

Participative solidarity does not mean a one-way street. It not only gives to those who are weak, but also requires something of them. It requires that they remain aware that social-political solidarity may not be separated from responsibility. If that is lacking in one group or another, then the principle of solidarity is strained and is reduced *ad absurdum* in the long run. One might think of alcohol and nicotine abuse, for instance, and of preventable, health-endangering practices, which lead to social costs in the billions and must be borne for the most part by the general public in solidarity. Anyone who simply has a good time, with confidence that health insurance and social insurance will pay for the health-damaging consequences, does not participate in full solidarity, but instead commits an act of non-solidarity against those who responsibly safeguard their health. Unilateral solidarity, which demands only from those who are stronger, without those who are weaker participating to the degree that they are able in the production of results or reduction of social costs, only contributes to the maximization of governmental expenditures, which must be met by direct and indirect taxes. The ability of productive citizens to bear taxes, however, has limits. When taxes are too high, this has consequences that endanger the welfare state at its foundation. Among them, in addition to other methods of tax evasion, is the

[48] See Enderle, *Ein Leitbild für die Sicherung des Existenzminimums in der Schweiz*, pp. 4 ff.

shadow economy, which can be explained to a great extent as avoidance of the burden of taxes and is spreading in all industrialized nations.[49] From all of that it follows that solidarity understood as a one-way street is solidarity cut in half, and is ultimately directed against itself, because it is self-contradictory. Consequently, there can be participative solidarity only with the inclusion of the responsibility and willingness to perform of those who are its immediate beneficiaries. At this point, it must be asked once again which specific way of ordering the welfare state must be adopted, if it is to stand up to the criterion of participation.

5. Given the preceding four points, it should now be clear how the question of distribution appears in its main aspects from the normative perspective of the criterion of participation. Humanly just distribution of labor and of aggregate output must be directed towards ensuring that everyone is helped to achieve paying work, that everyone who participates in producing it can participate in the productive capital, that, in addition to the market price of individual output, the material, social, and cultural needs of the workers are taken into account in the calculation of income from work as one good produced cooperatively in the industrial economy, and that, all in all, the life situation of those in the worst position is improved as a first priority. Inequalities, which can never be avoided, are, therefore, justified only insofar as they promote this primary goal, which, incidentally, is in agreement with John Rawls' second principle of justice.[50] Which principles of political order in the economy are compatible with the demands of human justice arising from the criterion of participation and which are not? The primary ethical problem can be summarized in this way with reference to the question of distribution.

[49] According to Bruno S. Frey, the shadow economy more than doubled between 1960 and 1978 in Sweden, Belgium, Italy, West Germany, Finland, and Spain; tripled in Denmark; and even quadrupled in Switzerland ("Licht auf die Schattenwirtschaft," in a bulletin edited by the Swiss Credit Institution, 1 February 1987, pp. 6-8). Nevertheless, in absolute terms, the share of the shadow industry relative to the official national product is lowest in Switzerland (1978 = 4.3%) and highest in Sweden (1978 = 13.2%). See also Hannelore Weck-Hannemann, Werner W. Pommerehne, and Frey, *Die heimliche Wirtschaft*, Bern, 1986.

[50] John Rawls, *A Theory of Justice*, Cambridge, Mass., 1971. See also Hans Ruh, "Gerechtigkeitstheorien," in *Gerechtigkeit*, ed. Armin Wildermuth and Alfred Jäger, Tübingen, 1981, pp. 55-69.

3.3.5.3 A Participative Global Economy

As has already been maintained in 3.2.3, the problem of distribution, which is extremely explosive today, depicts the glaring disparity in the distribution of income between the industrial states and the developing nations. The numbers cited there speak for themselves. They contain a worldwide potential for social and political danger, which has a singular character in its explosiveness.

Since the beginnings of the colonial period, the developing nations, the majority of which are former colonial regions, were included in the process of international division of labor and, consequently, in the global economy: "Until the beginning of decolonization, it was a widely-held opinion in the industrialized nations that an optimal international division of labor required the specialization of the developing nations in primary goods,"[51] and thus in providing mainly mineral and agricultural raw materials. Since demand for these goods existed almost entirely in the economies of the industrialized nations, they were in a quasi-monopsonistic position (i.e. a "demand monopoly") in relation to the suppliers of raw materials, which resulted in low prices and a corresponding low standard of living for their citizens. This already established a unilateral and, therefore, confrontational economic dependency of the colonial or developing nations on the developed, industrial economies. One-sided dependency contradicts the human right to participation and builds confrontational structures, which favor the strong and place the weak at a disadvantage. Even after the colonies had become politically independent, the young nations remained trapped economically in the traditional structures — suppliers of cheap raw materials, buyers of expensive industrial products — and thus the new Third World stood and still stands in the shadow of the powerful industrialized nations of the northern hemisphere. Can it come out of this shadow, which means hunger, enormous unemployment, and poverty in many of its nations?

One prerequisite, obviously, is the economic development of the Third World. The contemporary "widely accepted goal of development policy is *to integrate the mass of people into productive employment and to satisfy their basic needs*."[52] That must be accompanied in parallel

[51] Lutz Hoffmann and Hermann Sanders, "Entwicklungspolitik," in *Handwörterbuch der Wirtschaftswissenschaften*, Vol. 2, p. 398.

[52] Georges Enderle and Ambros Lüthi, "Ökonomische Abhängigkeit und Dissoziation," *Concilium*, 16 (1980), p. 704.

by a dismantling of the economic dependency on the First and also Second Worlds, accomplished by an expansion of economic activity. How should one approach these goals?

Two opposing strategies rival one another as the answer to this question: the strategy of expanding exports and the strategy of self-focused development in its different varieties.[53] According to the former strategy, the first priority is to improve the ability of the developing nations to export, in both the agricultural and the manufacturing sectors, in order to remove the profit-minimizing one-sidedness that has existed until now from the exchange of goods with other countries. The second strategy focuses on domestic agriculture. It is essential to be oriented towards the nation's own economy, most of all, to create work and the necessities of life for everyone, even if on a very modest level. Thus, in the former case the relationship to the global economy is associative, in the latter dissociative.

The dissociative or self-focused strategy reacts to the confrontational structure of the global economy. Since the global market is far from a level playing field, the terms of trade have notoriously developed to the disadvantage of the Third World nations.[54] An improvement of these terms can be accomplished only by uncoupling from the global economy.

To date, only China has followed this path with a measure of success. (Because of its enormous integration into the Soviet economy, Cuba will be disregarded here.) Countries such as Tanzania, Sri Lanka, and, to a limited degree, also Burma were able to eliminate neither poverty nor unemployment by their policies of uncoupling from the global economy. In view of the global integration of all economic processes, it is obviously extremely difficult, in fact impossible, for a country to develop itself independently of the global economy. Even China, which comes closest to being in a position to do so, because of its size and giant domestic market, has found itself required for

[53] Hoffmann and Sanders, "Entwicklungspolitik," p. 405.

[54] See Binswanger and Jäger, "Ökonomie und Ökologie," in *Zwischen Wachstum und Lebensqualität*, ed. Sozialwissenschaftlichen Institut der EKD, Munich, 1980. According to these authors, economic expansion since 1950 has been based on "*low prices of raw materials and low energy costs*.... In the last three decades, therefore, the raw-material nations had to hand over more and more of their natural wealth in order to receive the same quantity of industrial goods; the exchange relationships sank to their disadvantage" (p. 83).

years, and indeed at a rapid pace, to find strong connections to the global economy. That goes as far as forming a great number of joint ventures between the socialist state and the "capitalist" world.[55]

On the other hand, the strategy of expanding exports has also encountered severe handicaps under the present conditions of the global economy.[56] To be sure, a few countries, especially South Korea, Taiwan, Malaysia, and Hong Kong, have made good economic progress along this path and have moved up into the ranks of the "newly industrialized countries." Others, however, and indeed precisely the largest among them — one thinks of Brazil, Argentina, and Mexico — have suffered obvious failures, in part because of incorrect economic policies. Modernization of agriculture and industrialization of the branches of industry in the manufacturing sector that are capable of exporting are prerequisites of a policy of expanding exports. Both call for an enormous amount of capital, which must be met in the international financial markets. If interests rates are high and, in addition, access to global markets is difficult,[57] if the interest burden consequently increases, if the level of exports remains below expectations, and if there is a collapse of the prices of the primary goods that are so important for the export of these nations, then high trade deficits, and in their wake horrendous indebtedness, with its difficult social consequences, are inevitable.[58] The following table shows this unmistakably:[59]

This shows that a negative transfer of resources (from the debtors to the creditors) in the amount of $66 billion has taken place since 1984, a completely unbearable situation for the developing nations.

[55] Guo Yiming, President of the China Economic and Trade Consultants Corporation, explained at a conference of the Institute for International Research in Zürich (Dec. 1986), that up to July 1986, 6,814 joint ventures, with a planned capital commitment of $18 billion, had been founded (*Neue Zürcher Zeitung*, No. 286, 9 December 1986, p. 21).

[56] Hoffmann and Sanders, "Entwicklungspolitik," pp. 401 ff.

[57] Thus the agricultural protectionism of most industrialized nations (primarily the European Community, the USA, and also Switzerland) has led to a situation in which the developed countries increase their share in the world market for food considerably to the burden of the developing countries" (*ibid.*, p. 399). The General Agreement on Tariffs and Trade (GATT) is intended to be a counterbalance to protectionist tendencies in the global economy.

[58] As is well known, the total debt of the developing nations surpassed the billion dollar level ($1,035 billion) in 1986. It has continued to increase since then (in 1988 to $1,200 billion).

[59] *Neue Zürcher Zeitung*, No. 48, 27 February 1987, p. 23.

Table 4: Debt Service (in billions of $)

	1982	1983	1984	1985[1]	1986[2]
Heavily Indebted Countries [3]					
Long-Term Indebtedness	276.5	329.2	354.0	367.6	382.0
Gross Inflows	60.1	39.7	32.3	22.4	21.0
Amortization	25.8	19.1	18.4	17.1	16.0
Interest	30.8	29.1	33.3	33,0	31.0
Net Transfers	3.5	−8.5	−19.4	−27.7	−26.0
All Reporting Countries [4]					
Long-Term Indebtedness	551.2	630.2	673.4	730.9	775.0
Gross Inflows	115.8	96.5	88.3	81.7	72.0
Debt Service	97.4	90.8	99.0	108.0	101.0
Net Transfers	18.4	5.7	−10.7	−26.3	−29.0

1 Provisional
2 Estimated
3 Argentina, Bolivia, Brazil, Chile, Colombia, Costa Rica, Côte d'Ivoire, Ecuador, Jamaica, Mexico, Morocco, Nigeria, Peru, Philippines, Uruguay, Venezuela, Yugoslavia (The 15 "Baker Countries" plus Costa Rica and Jamaica).
4 109 World Bank Reporting Countries
Source: World Bank

It is altogether devastating when in countries with pronounced primary production, such as those in the regions south of the Sahara, the modernization of agriculture in the service of agricultural export leads to an extensive or even complete elimination of the subsistence economy.[60] Its price is the total impoverishment of complete strata of society.

All of these are facts that have brought the export strategy in development policy into disrepute and have lead to strong arguments in favor of the strategy of dissociating the developing nations from the industrialized nations. Nevertheless, this strategy has lost more and more ground. It fails to appreciate the interdependence in contemporary, worldwide, interlinked economic events and, therefore, starts out from unrealistic presuppositions. Even an expert as intimately familiar with the existing problems as Andreas Bänziger,

60 Andreas Bänziger, *Die Saat der Dürre*, Bornheim-Merten, 1986, pp. 97 ff.

who regards the market-oriented, let alone the export-expansive conception of development with proper scepticism, distrusts a pure subsistence economy, even for the poorest nations of the African continent. He names the alternative that he recommends "subsistence plus."[61] And that means that there must be, in addition to production for each country's own needs, which receive the highest priority, also production for the market, in order to be able to obtain through careful management the means that are necessary for earning the goods and services that it cannot itself produce. But this includes at least the indirect integration of even the economically weakest developing nations in the global economy.

If the interweaving of the developing nations into the global economy is consequently inevitable, that does not at all mean that the prevailing structures of the contemporary global economy and its present conditions are acceptable. They are determined in their essentials by the industrialized nations, and thus favor their particular interests. And in this respect the interdependencies in the global economy are directed towards power relationships that are laid down unilaterally, and thus towards confrontation. If interdependency as such belongs to the economic rationality of the contemporary economy, then it must, if it is to converge with human justice, be participative in structure, i.e. must be able to dismantle unilateral dependency and balance out the economic power relationships. Business and economic ethics, therefore, requires that the structural conditions of the global economy be participative, allowing for the effective participation of the developing nations, so that they no longer have to fight in the markets with shortened spears. Therefore, an additional fundamental economic problem with regard to the question of ordering the economy is raised: What fundamental conditions must be met in order that global economic cooperation, instead of confrontation, can take on a participative structure?[62]

3.3.6 *Human Justice from the Perspective of Fellow-Creatureliness*

Just as the fundamental purpose of the economy, meeting our material, social, and cultural needs, is derived from the creatureliness of

61 *Ibid.*, pp. 112 ff.
62 This will be discussed in detail in 7.3.

human persons,[63] the criterion of creatureliness determines this basic purpose in the complete context of the entire creation, in which human persons are embedded with all created beings.[64]

Fellow-creatureliness means, first of all, that the human person is a "member of nature,"[65] not lord over it:

> We humans are only apparently the lords of this earth. As with most lords, we are only all too dependent upon there being enough productive slaves to make our lordly status possible. All lords are dependent upon these slaves. For us, they are the innumerable species of plants, animals, and microbes, on whose life activity not only our nourishment and material support is dependent, but also, for example, the maintenance of an atmosphere that is supportive of life.[66]

Human economic activity, of course, also stands in the web of this reciprocity of all creatures.

Fellow-creatureliness, however, does not mean merely this evident fact. As an ethical category, it expresses an "ought." Human persons should respect the will of the Creator and stand by their fellow-creatureliness.[67] This is a basic condition of the humanity originating from faith, hope, and love. It essentially includes human and environmental justice. Anything that is not environmentally just cannot be humanly just in the long run. And environmental justice without concern for human justice becomes illusory. From that a three-fold specific responsibility of the human person as a fellow-creature emerges.

3.3.6.1 Stabilization of Population

The human justice of the economy fundamentally includes the ability to create the material basis of meeting the life needs appropriate to the nature of the human person. If it does not accomplish this, if hunger and misery prevail in large regions of the world, as is the case today, then the organization of the economy as a whole is not

63 *BEE*, Vol. II, 1.3.1.

64 *BEE*, Vol. I, 7.2.6 and Vol. II, 1.3.4.

65 Hubert Markl, *Natur als Kulturaufgabe*, Stuttgart, 1986, p. 195.

66 *Ibid.*, p. 217.

67 Martin Honecker, "Verantwortung für die Umwelt als Auftrag des Menschen," in *Vorsorge für die Umwelt*, ed G. Hosemann and E. Finckh, Erlangen, 1984, pp. 9-22, is theologically significant.

humanly just. The popular answer to this kind of deficiency is more production and, if necessary, a more just distribution of the goods produced.

This answer, as much as it contains an element of truth, can be justified only to the degree that it considers the environmental consequences, more precisely, the limits of the earth's carrying capacity, that arise from it. Looking from the perspective of the productive capacity of the modern industrial economy, the adequate production of the food and consumer goods necessary for an appropriate quality of life is not a problem, at least for the time being. The dilemma exists at the ecological level. Additional production of these goods means increased consumption of raw-material deposits, growing use of sources of energy, which is accompanied by a proportionally climbing production of factors that pollute and even destroy the environment, in other words, an unmeasured consumption of the natural basis for the exclusive and short-term survival aims of the human genus. For centuries, at a constantly increasing pace, humans have thoughtlessly pursued the overexploitation of non-renewable resources and have taken the catastrophic consequences for other persons and the created world into account only casually, often with erroneous appeal to Genesis 1:28. To be sure, according to the first creation account in the Bible, the human person is allotted a privileged position in the created world, but not as an autocratic, sovereign ruler who may do with it whatever he wishes. The human person is, instead, the responsible mandatory of God, who must play a role that serves and maintains the creation.[68] "Be fruitful and multiply," as well as "Subdue the earth," are to be understood only in terms of this mandate, which is tied to responsibility and, therefore, limits power, by no means as a license for unrestricted population growth and economic-technological expansion. In view of the growing scarcity of resources and the increasingly-threatening environmental pollution, fellow-creaturely conduct today means, on the contrary, limiting population growth, which has become excessive and extremely threatening to the natural world and, therefore, to the human race itself. Unless it is stabilized,[69] which especially concerns

[68] *BEE*, Vol. I, p. 192.

[69] The following statistics show how increasingly unstable the world population has become in about the last three hundred years: 10,000 years ago it was 10 million, 5,000 years ago 50 million, 2,000 years ago 250 million, in 1650 500 million, in 1850

the developing nations, the economy cannot fulfill its purpose, at least not in the long run. That would entail the ruinous price of a destruction of nature that would call into question the biological basis of all life. The stabilization of world population growth, which makes a reduction of the birthrate in the interests of other persons and the environment inevitable, is, therefore, a first command of the fellow-creaturely responsibility of the human person.

3.3.6.2 Stabilization of Demands

Fellow-creaturely conduct, however, includes more than responsibility for environmentally just population growth. Even if its stabilization were within reach, that alone would not alter the intolerable fact that the standard of living of large segments of the world population is already intolerably low and, therefore, must urgently be raised in the coming decades, if we are to avoid a social explosion of global proportions. This requires economic development of the suffering regions of the world that is suited and appropriate to their elementary needs, which in any case must entail much greater demand for the natural resources by the nations of the Third World.[70] But it will be possible to cope with that ecologically — seen now from the perspective of the necessary stabilization of population growth — only "if the small segment of the human race that is well-to-luxuriantly provided for will be satisfied with maintaining its present standard of prosperity, rather than — as in the past — increasing it over proportionally."[71] Everything else, to say nothing about the counter-participative distribution of prosperity in the world, violates fellow-creatureliness as a criterion of human justice, including environmental justice. Again, the specifically fellow-creaturely responsibility of the human person includes ensuring that the material level of prosperity — and this is true especially for the industrialized nations — has adjusted itself to the earth's carrying capacity, and not

1 billion, and in 1980 4 billion (Markl, *Natur als Kulturaufgabe*, p. 135). An analogous rate of growth in the near future would open up apocalyptic perspectives.

[70] In 1985 the per capita consumption of petroleum in the developing nations was 0.5 tons. It was 7.6 tons in the USA, about 5 in the USSR, and 3.4 in the other industrialized nations. It is obvious that if the Third World nations are to develop economically, these statistical relationships must be changed significantly in their favor. Sources: for energy consumption: *BP Statistical Review of World Energy*, June 1986, p. 34; for population: *United Nations Monthly Bulletin of Statistics*, January 1987, Table 1.

[71] Markl, *Natur als Kulturaufgabe*, p. 313.

vice versa. At the same time, one must remember that "prosperity" and "welfare" do not mean the same thing,[72] that limiting prosperity in the "affluent society" can lead directly to an increase of welfare and quality of life.

3.3.6.3 Stabilization of the Environment

Restricting demand for prosperity in the regions that already have high levels of prosperity and minimizing the growth rate of the world population are, under the present conditions, prerequisites for an environmentally just economy. But that cannot be the entirety of the responsibility that arises from fellow-creatureliness as a basic criterion of human justice. Such acts of renunciation in themselves lead nowhere, especially when they suggest — and some committed environmental protectionists do suggest — that salvation is to be sought in an economy without growth. An economy without growth, in a world where the greater part of humanity lives in wretched conditions, could never fulfill its fundamental purpose of service to life, even if the global population could be approximately stabilized and the prosperous societies, in consciousness of solidarity, would renounce a continued increase of their prosperity, or even accept its reduction. It must be stressed emphatically, therefore, "that it is not a matter of the question 'Growth or no growth?'..., but of the *characteristics* of this growth,"[73] and thus of its quality. With that, the third and most weighty aspect of fellow-creaturely responsibility comes into view.

Qualitative, in contrast to quantitative, economic growth has already been discussed (2.7.3). With qualitative growth, it is not a matter of indifference how it takes place, if it only increases the gross national product, which, of course — in contrast to a purely ecological type of economy — assumes that the contemporary industrial economy "cannot simply renounce further investment and thus possible increases in return with simultaneous increases in costs, without actually entering into a crisis,"[74] which, however, for all that, aims at a massive reduction of the use of non-renewable resources and the emission of materials that pollute the environment. In short: qualitative growth means continuing the process of investment, but, to be

[72] See *BEE*, Vol. II, pp. 381-83.
[73] Binswanger and Jäger, "Ökonomie und Ökologie," p. 89.
[74] *Ibid.*, p. 90.

sure, with decoupling from the increase of the national product and growth of the use of energy and raw materials. If the economy is actually to be able to fulfill its fundamental purpose, without destroying the ecological basis on which it itself rests, then it must switch over to qualitative growth. Whether and to what degree that is accomplished is one of the biggest fateful questions of our time.

Fellow-creaturely responsibility for the industrial economy, therefore, cannot be restricted to remedying the environmental damage tied to it as much as possible after the fact, while retaining the traditional theory and practice of growth. It must reach much deeper, grasp the evil at the root, and look for "radical" solution in this succinct sense. A prerequisite for a radical solution of this kind is that the vital purpose of the economy is maintained in its entirety,[75] and consequently that the ecological purpose of economic activity (1.3.4) is taken seriously and given effect economically with the emphasis proper to it.

In this context, Hans Christoph Binswanger has offered the suggestion, which is most highly noteworthy in relation to business and economic ethics, to replace the "old" magic triangle of economic policy (balance of payments equilibrium, full employment, price stability) with a "new" magic triangle.[76]

Table 5: The New Magic Triangle

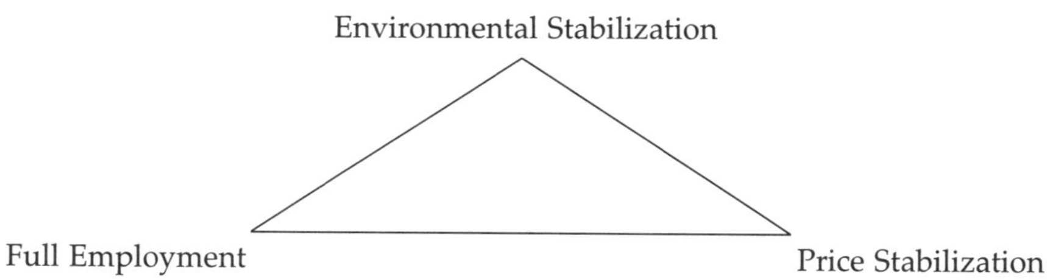

[75] See *BEE*, Vol. II, 1.3.5.

[76] Binswanger and Jäger, "Ökonomie und Ökologie," pp. 78-82. Binswanger's magic triangle replaces the goal of balance of payments equilibrium with environmental stability. According to him, the goal of balance of payments has lost significance since the gold-dollar standard and fixed exchange rates were given up in 1971 and the transition was made to so-called floating exchange rates. The place in the magic triangle that this freed up should be taken over by the stabilization of consumption of the environment as a goal of economic policy (pp. 81-82). See also Hans Christoph Binswanger, Holger Bonus, and Manfred Timmermann, *Wirtschaft und Umwelt*, Stuttgart, 1981, pp. 3-7.

Both the "old" and the "new" triangles of economic policy are called "magic" because the different objectives identified by them partially contradict one another, and the power of a magician, so to speak, is needed to achieve them completely and simultaneously. If, however, the magic triangle, or the objectives established by it, are to be meaningful, then, despite the tension or even conflict that exists between them, it must be possible to bring them into relative harmony. There is good reason to believe that this is possible in the case of Binswanger's triangle, and thus that environmental stabilization based on qualitative economic growth with the goals of full employment and price stabilization, understood as the minimization of unemployment and inflation, can be brought into relative harmony.[77]

The shift in emphasis from quantitative to qualitative economic growth, therefore, demands a profound reorientation of economic policy, with environmental stabilization adopted as one of its principal objectives. With that, however, the highly relevant question of business and economic ethics arises: Under what ordering conditions can such an ecologically aware and thus environmentally just economic policy be implemented most effectively? Do market laws push towards this kind of reorientation in response to price signals? Or is external intervention necessary? Our experience thus far suggests the latter. Thus, today, an environmental good such as clean air has undoubtedly become a scarce good, which, therefore, should have its price. It is considered to be a free good, however, which costs nothing and, consequently, is consumed without restraint. Therefore, even decisive supporters of market-economic environmental policy, such as Professors Robert E. Leu and René L. Frey of the University of Basel, advocate governmental intervention: "Since the market assesses environmental resources in themselves as free of charge, *governmental intervention* is absolutely necessary. Only in this way can it be ensured that the steering signals of the market also express, in addition to economic scarcity, *ecological scarcity*."[78] If, however, the self-regulation of the market is insufficient and, consequently, outside intervention — it does not necessarily have to be initiated by the

[77] *Ibid.*, pp. 82-88. The strategies of an economic policy of qualitative growth are developed comprehensively in Binswanger, *et al.*, *Arbeit ohne Umweltzerstörung*, pp. 209-352.

[78] Robert E. Leu and René L. Frey, "Mehr Umweltschutz mit geringeren Kosten," *Neue Zürcher Zeitung*, No. 230, 4/5 October 1986, p. 17.

government — is necessary, this poses the additional question of what type they should be (internalization of external costs according to the polluter pays principle, emission taxes with the character of control, energy taxes, energy rationing, etc.), and to what extent they need to take place. Is the existing framework of the market economy at all adequate for the required reorientation, or must it be modified drastically, or if necessary, even abandoned? Again, these question identify principal problems of business and economic ethics, which absolutely cannot be avoided today.

3.3.7 *Human Justice from the Perspective of Relationality*

3.3.7.1 Relationality of the Basic Values

The problem of human justice within the technological and economic contexts of the contemporary industrial economy has been reflected upon thus far in sections 3.3.3-3.3.6 from the viewpoints of the criteria fellow-humanness, participation, and fellow-creatureliness, and with the goal of showing the principal problems of business and economic ethics that emerge from it in specific orientation towards the question of order. The question still remains: What significance does relationality have in this context as an additional basic criterion of humanity?

An introduction to the answer, which is referred to here, has already appeared in section 1.3.5. The following discussion starts from those considerations.

In the case of relationality, understood as a fundamental criterion of the humanity originating from faith, hope, and love, we are concerned about dealing with the basic ethical values in a humanly just manner, as they occur in the general-human horizon of experience.[79] Even values of this kind, no matter how high their rank in the particular moral consciousness of a society, can be dealt with in a way that contradicts the command of human justice. That is inevitably the case when contrary values, such as individual liberty and solidarist relationship, for instance, which have particular relevance economically, separate from one another and thus become absolutes, and in such extremity lay claim to being the fulfillment of true humanity.

[79] For the theological foundation, see *BEE*, Vol. I, 7.2.4 (The Criterion of Relationality).

In the biblical horizon of faith and hope, humanity is fulfilled in love. It is the epitome of human justice. This human justice can be reduced neither to the common denominator of liberty alone nor to that of solidarity, neither to emancipation nor to service. For in love all of this remains unseparated; it is always accepted at the same time. You were called to be free, serve one another in love, as Paul put it.[80] Only in such relationality can contrary value attitudes, such as free self-determination and binding service, responsibility for oneself and solidarity, interest in one's own welfare and interest in the welfare of others, be humanly just. If, on the contrary, they are deprived of their relationality, separated from one another, and thus turned into absolutes, then they turn into the opposite of human justice understood in terms of the humanity originating from faith, hope, and love. Free self-determination is converted into emancipating self-assertion, binding service into collectivist bringing into line. Individual responsibility degenerates into autistic rule of interests, and solidarity into comfortable dependence upon social services. In this way, relationality proves to be a fundamental criterion of human justice.

The criterion has crucial significance for business and economic ethics. To be precise, not only for the individual and personal ethical conduct of the persons as economic subjects, but first of all for what concerns the problem of political and economic order. Neither the value-principle of liberty / self-interest nor that of relationship / solidarity can, according to its demand, become the exclusive or even dominant ordering principle of the economy. Both must instead be understood relationally and must mutually relativize one another in this definite way. This has absolutely nothing to do with a mere cult of the middle or even with sheer balancing out. And relationality does not at all mean an opportunistic maneuver between opposing positions, only in order to escape as unscathed as possible. On the contrary, situations can arise where in the interest of the economy's service to life, a temporary overbalance must be given to one value-principle relative to the other. An asymmetry of this kind, situational, not principled, gets along well with relationality as a criterion of human justice, as long as the relatedness of the two value-principles is fundamentally maintained and respected. It is then a matter of a pragmatic asymmetry, which is aware of its one-sidedness and also can be justified only as long as on the whole the quality of life, first

[80] Galatians 5,13.

of all that of the underprivileged, can thereby be improved. This kind of one-sidedness, because it is rooted in the relational, has nothing to do with absolutizing particular values, which are in themselves worthy of respect, but are sometimes carried to an extreme and then threaten humanity from the ground up. It is, instead, rooted in the entirety of human justice and, in this concise sense, is certainly radical humanity.

Because relationality is, in this way, a matter of the entirety of human justice,[81] seen from this perspective, a highly important question for business and economic ethics is posed: What structures of political order in the economy are to be favored, if this criterion, now sharpened to a point by the relationality of liberty and relationship, of self-interest and universal-interest, of individual responsibility and solidarity, despite the contrarieties arising with it, is to be respected?

3.3.7.2 The Relationality of Human Justice and Economic Rationality

For the humanity originating from faith, hope, and love, the criterion of relationality determines not only the relationship with the general-human values, but also the relationship between human justice and economic rationality, between ethical "ought"-statements and economic "is"-statements, between ethics and economics in general.

The fact that the economy, at least as it is understood in economic theory, has something to do with ethics is still anything but self-evident.[82] The neoclassical theory that dominates today understands itself as autonomous (Hans Albert) or as pure economics (Joseph A. Schumpeter), definitions that are bound up with the principle of the

[81] Jäger develops a similar, relationally-determined view of (human) justice in Binswanger and Jäger, "Ökonomie und Ökologie," pp. 107-115.

[82] In the medieval period, economics as a science belonged to moral theology. The fathers of classical-liberal economics, such as Adam Smith and John Stuart Mill, were moral philosophers. The separation of economics and economic ethics arose only with the neoclassical economic theory of the late-nineteenth and twentieth centuries. It has, however, gained broad acceptance. The countercurrents on the side of economics date from the recent past. Thus Gunnar Myrdal and, above all, Gerhard Weisser have taken a stand against economism and denied that there is a "purely economic standpoint." Influenced by Karl-Otto Apel's theory of communicative ethics, Peter Ulrich has recently argued forcefully, in comprehensive philosophical-social-scientific argumentation, for reconnecting economic rationality to (life-)practical reason and, therefore, against the economistic separation of economics and ethics (Ulrich, *Transformation der ökonomischen Vernunft*).

value-freeness of economics. At its center stands the empirical-rational explanation of the processes of the allocation and distribution of scarce goods to satisfy existing needs and of the conditions of stabilizing these needs.[83] Of course, it must at the same time, contrary to the economistic presupposition that social processes are to be reduced to economic processes, also take into account the tiresome fact that it is concrete human persons, not abstract processes, who have needs. In order to be logically coherent, it makes do with the assumption that human needs are themselves given empirically and are, as objective facts, liberated from ethical judgments. And that means: "In the framework of the customary definition of economic rationality, the empirical nature of the human person is seen as essentially 'fixed,' an order of needs is regarded as the natural order."[84] This supposedly empirical nature of the human person and the order of needs established by it corresponds to the construct of "*homo oeconomicus*,"[85] who is considered in the economic process of satisfying material needs to be both a demander and a supplier of scarce goods for the maximization of his own utility, and who in this sense acts rationally or economistically. Thus, we are concerned here with economically determined rationality, whose academic concern is not with what human persons should do *normatively*, but with what they *actually* do. Consequently: "The strict separation of (economic) rationality and normativity belongs to the idea of *homo oeconomicus* under economistic conditions; the former is a matter of science, the latter of ethics (in competition with aesthetics and religion)."[86] In other words, rational economics and ethics, technical correctness and human justice, separate from one another diastatically in this area.

This diastase of economics and ethics, as it is depicted in neoclassical economics, however, stands in contrast to reality. The very fact that the basic economic questions are full of ethical implications points this out.[87] Economic rationality also possesses an ethical dimension, as

[83] See Jürgen Mittelstraß, "Wirtschaftsethik als wissenschaftliche Disziplin?" in *Ethik und Wirtschaftswissenschaft*, ed. Enderle, Berlin, 1985, p. 17.

[84] *Ibid.*, pp. 17-18.

[85] See *BEE*, Vol. II, 1.1. "Homo oeconomicus," as a heuristic, artificial construct, has experienced differentiated further development with the new term "REMM" (resourceful, evaluative, maximizing man), but without breaking free of its economistic narrowness (see Ulrich, *Transformation der ökonomischen Vernunft*, pp. 234-43).

[86] Mittelstraß, "Wirtschaftsethik als wissenschaftliche Disziplin?" p. 19.

[87] *BEE*, Vol. II, 3.2.

classical thinkers from Adam Smith to John Stuart Mill very well understood.[88] This can be concealed, but cannot be eliminated. That will be made clear with an example from welfare economics.

In its basic orientation, which attempts to be value free, welfare economics assumes, completely in the sense of *homo oeconomicus*, that all persons in economic events of exchange by nature wish to maximize their own utility. The pursuit of utility takes place according to the law of decreasing marginal utility, which says that the last unit of a large amount of income creates less utility for the recipient than the last unit of a small amount of income. It is supposed to follow from that, as a rational consequence, that high income should be redistributed to low-income classes, because the common good or sum of all single utilities will be optimized. From the theory of marginal utility, however, assuming that it is correct, it can be concluded rationally only that the redistribution of high income, because of its decreasing marginal utility, does not contradict economic rationality and with increasing prosperity would be easier to carry out, but by no means that it also is actually to be performed. Only those who value the sum of all utilities higher than individual utility will believe that this redistribution should be carried out. And behind that stands — whether it is admitted or not — an ethical value judgment in accordance with the altruistic variant of utilitarianism.

If this is the case, the ethical dimension cannot practically be excluded from the economy.[89] But, if its theory is to maintain value-abstinence, this suggests the escape of limiting the economy to the domain of (allegedly) pure economic rationality and leaving the establishment of extra-economic demands of human justice to business and economic ethics. Accordingly, business and economic ethics would have at best a mere supplementary function in its relation to economics, which would compensate for the latter's normative deficit and be relevant only for the conduct of the economic agent within the economic structures, but not for the shape of these structures. It would not be possible to arrive at a real (i.e. dialogical) link between economics and ethics. The fatal error of this sideline-concept, which has advocates not only among economists, but

[88] See Ulrich, *Transformation der ökonomischen Vernunft*, pp. 187-95. See also *BEE*, Vol. II, 5.2.1.2.

[89] See Helmut Kaiser, "Ansatzpunkte für eine normative Erweiterung der ökonomischen Rationalität," *Zeitschrift für Evangelische Ethik*, 28 (1984), pp. 285 ff.

also among philosophers and theologians, consists in the fact that it separates human justice and economic rationality, the ethical-normative and the economic-rational, from one another. They would belong to separate spheres, which can and does lead, on the one hand, to technocratic views and, on the other hand, to utopian views in economic questions. Peter Ulrich speaks in this context with justification of a "two-world conception," which a "scientific economic ethic" must overcome. His significant book[90] is directed at the methodological reconciliation of economic rationality and ethical reason: "The fundamental theme of economic ethics *as an academic discipline* can be nothing other than economic reason itself: *There is no reasonable economic ethics beyond economic rationality — and no well-understood economic rationality this side of practical (ethical) reason.*"[91] Therefore, economic rationality and reasonable normativity are ultimately identical in economic reason, or that at least appears to be the case.

With regard to this concept of the reconciliation of economic rationality and ethical reason, the humanity originating from faith, hope, and love stands in a relationship of both divergence and convergence.

The divergence arises from the fact that its criteria of human justice,[92] since they are oriented towards the absolute of Christian faith-conviction, are not established by scientific rationality, although they are supported by a degree of evidence, which makes them capable of communication at the level of reason. In this respect, human justice of the faith-humanity contrasts with the world-reality in its rational understanding, including the economy, as the epitome of an absolute requirement. From a theological perspective, this demanding and judging opposition will be abolished, the real-worldly will be humanly just and human justice real-worldly, and ethics and economic rationality will coincide only in the "eschaton," only in the finality of the Kingdom of God. In the penultimate of our historical time, on the other hand, there exists no identity, no harmony, between the two, only tension and conflict. Neither one already preexists in the other.

[90] Ulrich, *Transformation der ökonomischen Vernunft*.

[91] *Ibid.*, p. 344.

[92] For the theoretical foundation, see *BEE*, Vol. I, 7. The criteria are creatureliness, critical distance, relative reception, relationality, fellow-humanness, fellow-creatureliness, and participation.

Christian existence, understood as existence of hope in the coming of the Kingdom of God, however, can never accept this difference, which in biblical language is called "sin," and thus means evil. It is, if it is to avoid failure, directed in the penultimate at the ultimate, and in this orientation towards economically rational orders, which come as close as possible in their rationality to the demands of human justice and aim at human justice, which has to seek to realize itself as economically rationally as possible, because it is within the contexts of social and ecological life, to which the economy fundamentally belongs. Therefore, love, as the quintessence of human justice in the sense of faith-humanity, is not uninterested in reason. It is, on the contrary, intrinsically attached to reason. It should — this is said in reference to Paul[93] — always become richer in all reason, in order to be able to investigate the concrete decisions, which in the domain of the economy always include technical questions, and approve what is excellent, so that they are made justly.[94] Human justice and economic rationality thus stand in an inseparable relation with one another, not in a relation of identity, but in one of relationality. Whenever tensions and conflicts between the ethical assertion of human justice and the rational claim to economic rationality appear, one must be called into question critically by the other, to ask whether it is really humanly just or really economically rational, in order to arrive by such examination at maxims that are capable of standing up sufficiently to the demands of economic rationality and, nevertheless, are capable of existing before the demand of human justice, if not absolutely, at least relatively. It is a matter here of a tension-filled process, which is never concluded and is always intent on better solutions, and which acknowledges its simultaneous obligations to the truth of the normative and the right of the operational in the sense of economic rationality.[95] For the fundamental proposition is valid at the level of maxims: That which is not economically rational cannot really be humanly just; and that which contradicts human justice cannot really be economically rational. And in that exists convergence with Ulrich's basic concept, despite the divergent starting points.

[93] Phil. 1,9 ff.

[94] See *BEE*, Vol. I, pp. 122, 165-66, 203.

[95] Mittelstraß writes similarly: "Normativity...no longer appears to be the backside of (scientific) rationality, but its (normative) foundation" ("Wirtschaftsethik als wissenschaftliche Disziplin?" p. 24).

From all of that it can now be gathered unambiguously that business and economic ethics — as it is designed with criteria in the Christian horizon of the humanity originating from faith, hope, and love — must undoubtedly argue at the level of maxims within, not outside, the economic contexts and their own logic.[96] It is part of the intention of this work to take this into account decisively (with what success, to be sure, must remain an open question). For that reason, the criterial horizon-outline of the whole stands at its beginning under the aspect of the question of economic meaning. For that reason, the analytic sketching of central aspects and perspectives of the modern industrial economy follows immediately. And, for that reason, this is followed by the examination of principal problems in business and economic ethics, of course with the help of the criteria of faith-humanity, but definitely within the emphasized economic contexts, and indeed in such a way that — as may have become apparent — the relationality of economic rationality and human (including environmental) justice has already become the guiding focal point. The critical relationship between the life-serving or life-practical fundamental purpose of the economy and its structures that optimize practicability and efficiency, as this is in accordance with correctly-understood economic rationality, follows from that, to conclude 3.3, as a basic problem of business and economic ethics.

All of this condenses into the crucial question: What consequences does this relationality have in view of the problem of ordering the economy, and which economic-ethical maxims for judgment and decision can be derived from them? As the next step, the fundamental concepts of economic systems will be considered.

[96] If Ulrich, admittedly in slight attenuation, moves my economic-ethical approach to the side of the "two-world conception," then this fact is misjudged ("Die sprachpragmatische Wendung der ökonomischen Rationalitätskonzeption als Grundlegung einer Ethik der Unternehmung," unpublished manuscript, p. 4, n. 5).

4. BASIC ECONOMIC SYSTEMS

4.1 Preliminaries

4.1.1 *Transition*

The modern industrial economy, with its unprecedented division of labor in production and services, with its perfecting of information and communication systems, its growing differentiation and internationalization of the most diverse markets, and with the clashes of economic interests, social conflicts, and ecological threats that have originated and continue to originate from it, has become so complex, interdependent, and unstable that one can ask in all seriousness whether it can still be "ordered." Numerous are the voices that speak of chaotic relationships in contemporary economic events. Of course, no matter how justified such pessimism may be, it does not release us from the question of order. On the contrary, the question is posed with all the more urgency. For the economy can exist only as somehow ordered. The question of which "system" or which "order" of the complexity and interdependence of the contemporary economy, together with the explosive human, social, and ecological problems that it creates, is most probably able to be adequate is a question that no one who wishes to meet the challenges connected to this can avoid.

The present topic is the "system" and "order" of the economy. How should these two concepts be understood?

4.1.2 *"Economic System" and "Economic Order": Demarcation of Terminology*

The terms "economic system" and "economic order" are not used consistently in the economics literature. Some authors use them synonymously; others make a distinction between them. When the terms are distinguished, "order" usually means the ideal ordering principles and "system" usually refers to economic structures that have actually been realized.[1] In contrast, K. Paul Hensel speaks of "basic systems" (*Grundsystemen*) of the economy, which are actualized by a kind of mixing of accidental elements in a multitude of "concrete economic systems."[2]

The following remarks are oriented towards this use of terminology, except that they will use "economic order" instead of "concrete economic system." Therefore, "economic system" will mean the basic system, the foundation of an economic order, and "economic order" will mean the actually or possibly concrete form of a particular economic system.[3]

This raises the question of what constitutes an economic system in its fundamental nature.

4.1.3 *Theories of Economic Systems*

The market economy and the planned economy are usually distinguished from one another as contrary, mutually exclusive, and fundamentally different economic systems.[4] This gives the false impression that there are planned economies and unplanned economies.

If it belongs to the basic nature of every economy to reduce the scarcity of goods of human need in the interest of the "common good," however that may be understood, then it goes without saying that the scarce means that are needed to fulfill this purpose are to be employed in such a way that they produce an optimal result. In other words, the allocation of the means that coincide with the factors of production or resources is to be planned rationally, in accordance with its purpose. Therefore, all economic behavior turns out to be, according to its nature, dispositive behavior, which coordinates the different factors, along with the activities they involve — in short, planned action. Consequently, the element of planning is already

[1] Egon Tuchtfeldt, "Wirtschaftssysteme," in *Handwörterbuch der Wirtschaftswissenschaften*, Vol. 9, p. 329.

[2] K. Paul Hensel, "Annäherung der Wirtschaftssysteme?" in Hensel, *Systemvergleich als Aufgabe*, ed. Hannelore Hamel, Stuttgart, 1977, p. 230.

[3] This is also consistent with Ota Šik, who speaks of "different economic orders within a system (*Wirtschaftssysteme*, Berlin, 1987, p. 52). Admittedly, his terminology is not consistent.

[4] Cf. Volker Nienhaus, *Kontroversen um Markt und Plan*, Darmstadt, 1984, and René L. Frey, *Wirtschaft, Staat und Wohlfahrt*, 4th Ed., Basel, 1985, pp. 162-74.

inseparably tied to the concept of the economy. The decisive point of difference between economic orders, or the feature that constitutes an economic system, therefore, cannot be the "presence or absence of planning in the economy, but instead who does the planning and control (of the economy)."[5] Consequently, the question of who are the actual or possible subjects of economic planning is raised.

The basis of planned economic decisions — there is wide agreement about this in economic theory today — must be the degree of economic scarcity of the individual species of goods. According to Hensel, who takes Walter Eucken as his starting point in his theory of economic order, only two forms of indicating the degree of scarcity have been provided economically thus far:

> The degree of scarcity can be shown in the form of *the prices of goods*, which are formed in markets and which signal, as it were, the respective difference between the quantities of supply and demand, as well as their changes. The total degree of economic scarcity can also be seen in the *account balances of macroeconomic planning*,[6] which are worked out in central planning departments.[7]

In accordance with the two ways of indicating the degree of scarcity, it follows that only two basic economic systems are possible: the system of decentralized, market-oriented planning of economic processes, and the system of centralized planning dictated by the appropriate governmental authorities.[8] In the former case, individual corporate units, guided by the purchasing behavior of consumers, are — ideally — the subjects of economic planning. And in the latter case the subject of economic planning is the state, with its imperative economic plans. Therefore, what fundamentally constitutes an economic system

[5] Hensel, "Planwirtschaft," in *Handwörterbuch der Sozialwissenschaften*, Vol. 8, p. 326.

[6] The account balances of centrally planned economies contain revenue and demand for a particular good or for a category of goods in the planning period. See *BEE*, Vol. II, p. 475-76.

[7] Hensel, "Annäherung der Wirtschaftssysteme?" p. 228. Likewise, Helmut Leipold, *Wirtschafts- und Gesellschaftssystem im Vergleich*, 2nd Ed., Stuttgart, 1980, p. 54. Henner Kleinewefers, "Theorie der Wirtschaftspolitik" VI: "Wirtschaftsordnungstheorie," unpublished lecture notes, 1986, p. 89, asserts to the contrary, in addition to prices and quantities of goods, "additional signs of scarcity (delivery times, waiting lines, storage movements, political protests, etc.)."

[8] Hensel, "Wirtschaftssytseme," in *Systemvergleich als Aufgabe*, ed. Hannelore Hamel, Stuttgart, 1977, p. 243.

is the specific way in which planning takes place within it, whether it is market-economic, decentralized planning or state-economic, centralized planning. In other words, there are two basic economic systems: the market system and the centrally planned system.

This duality of possible basic economic systems, as it was comprehensively established in terms of order theory for the first time by Eucken, and then met with wide approval, is, of course, not undisputed among economists. It is considered by some economists to be too schematic, and consequently too unrealistic.[9] Eucken himself refers to John Maynard Keynes,[10] who, in *The End of Laissez-Faire* (1926), considers yet a third system of coordination to be promising: that of the balancing out of interests between "semi-autonomous corporations," also called the "corporative system." But he passes over it quickly as an alternative that is non-discussible for him. This alternative is treated more positively by Walter Adolf Jöhr, who at least, even if with reservations, includes the "coordination system of corporativism" as a third possibility in his discussion of theories of order.[11] The planning subjects in this basic system are neither individual corporate units or private or public households, as in the market economy, nor collective governmental planning authorities, as in the centrally planned economy, but autonomous groups (e.g. trade associations, labor unions, groups of manufacturers, communes, etc.), which — again ideally — are self-organized and self-lead and strive for a consensus of interests for the benefit of everyone. Apart from the question of the practicability of corporativism, one can ask whether it or similar concepts[12] actually represent a sui generis system of coordination, or whether they ultimately amount to a decentralized system that is planned

[9] Cf. Kleinewefers, "Theorie der Wirtschaftspolitik" VI: "Wirtschaftsordnungstheorie," pp. 71-110, who, from the perspective of the decision-theoretical approach, prepares for a comprehensive critique of Walter Eucken's order theory and, in continuing it, K. Paul Hensel's and Helmut Leipold's. See also Kleinewefers, *Grundzüge einer verallgemeinerten Wirtschaftsordnungstheorie*, Tübingen, 1988, pp. 58-76.

[10] Walter Eucken, *Grundsätze der Wirtschaftspolitik*, ed. Edith Eucken-Erdsiek and K. Paul Hensel, Tübingen, 1960, p. 244.

[11] Walter Adolf Jöhr, "Das Problem der Wirtschaftsordnung," in *Individuum und Gemeinschaft*, St. Gallen, 1949, pp. 257 ff.

[12] "Corporativism," as it is understood here, should not be confused with the "*stato corporativo*" of (Italian) Fascism, where it merely served to veil the totalitarian one-party state. It comes, instead, from the anarcho-syndicalist variant of socialism, which stands in contrast to centralistic Marxism and which, obligated by the

by group agreement rather than by individuals. Finally, group agreements are possible on a poly-centered basis, not on a mono-centered basis. But whatever may be the answers to these questions, openness to this third possibility of economic coordination is advisable.

The next step is to consider more closely the fundamental structures, conditions, and consequences of these alternative economic systems. That is easier with the decentralized market system and the centrally planned economy than with the corporatist system. For the former systems actually exist, even if in quite different concrete forms. That cannot be said of the corporatist concept. It is, at least for the time being, more of an idea still in need of clarification and realized only in beginnings. From that it is clear that the market economy and centrally planned economy must stand in the foreground.

4.2 The Basic System of the Market Economy

4.2.1 *On the Concept of the Market Economy*

All discussion of the market economy is burdened by the attributive range of variation in which this concept is used. It meets with all possible attributes. Thus, people speak of the "free," "liberal," "social," and even "socialist" market economy. Karl Marx labeled it simply with the term "capitalism," which has found common usage among both Marxists and liberals.

Neither linguistic arbitrariness nor pure accident is hiding behind this attributive diversity. There are, on the contrary, reasons for it.[13] The market economy as a basic economic system does not express itself in a single form, but in a plurality of forms, which are also correspondingly differently qualified, a fact that only ideological narrow-mindedness can fail to recognize. Thus Germany's social market economy cannot be simply reduced to the same denominator as

federalist principle, seeks to promote corporate-democratic or soviet structures in society. In practice, it is similar to the concept of the "socially-arranged economy." Cf. Hans G. Schachtschabel, "Die sozialgeordnete Wirtschaft als Grundgestalt der Gegenwart," in *Methoden und Probleme der Wirtschaftspolitik*, ed. Hans Ohm, Berlin, 1964, pp. 65-85. See also 5.2.2.5, n. 80.

[13] Hensel, *Grundformen der Wirtschaftsordnung*, Munich, 1978, p. 27.

the free market economy of the USA, to say nothing of the Manchester capitalism of the nineteenth century, which Marx analyzed and criticized. There exist here, despite the common systematic foundation and although the boundaries in the details are fluid, definite order-political differences, which prevent such a reduction. One must be careful not to identify the market economy with one of its existing or possible forms.

When this is understood, the common practice of equating "capitalism" and "market economy" should also be called into question. There have been and still are capitalist market economies, if the shifting concept of "capitalism" is understood primarily as the dominance of capital interests, together with high accumulation of capital and a corresponding concentration of power in the hands of private entrepreneurs or profit-making corporations.[14] But that is not part of the essential substance of the market economy. On the contrary, capitalism in this sense is capable of becoming highly dangerous to the market economy. It cannot be said that the market economy and private ownership of the means of production are indissolubly bound to one another:[15] "A market economy can exist even without private property. It is possible for it to involve new alliances, which are difficult to imagine today, for instance, with the common ownership of everyone employed by a particular business corporation."[16] Therefore, a distinction will be made here, contrary to common usage, between the market economy and capitalism. Capitalism is one particular form of the market economy, not the market economy as a whole, even though the market economy has developed historically under the sign of capitalism and also in places where it betrays itself with deliberate and intentional socially modified capitalistic characteristics.

When the basic market economic system is discussed in the following, it will be considered for the time being in the sense of its in-principle, ideal, and thus model structure, which indeed is not to

[14] On the understanding of capitalism presupposed here, see *BEE*, Vol. II, 6.2.1.

[15] Tuchtfeldt, "Wirtschaftssysteme," p. 334.

[16] Helge Pross, "Kapitalismus in der demokratischen Gesellschaft," in *Meyers Enzyklopädisches Lexikon*, Vol. 13, Mannheim, 1975, p. 423. See also Kurt W. Rothschild, "Kritik marktwirtschaftlicher Ordnungen als Realtypus," in *Zur Theorie marktwirtschaftlicher Ordnungen*, ed. Erich Streißler and Christian Watrin, Tübingen, 1980, p. 15: "A market economy can be a capitalist market economy or a socialist market economy."

deny it definite content in reality, though this content only comes close to and only fragmentarily reflects market-economic reality.

4.2.2 *The Coordination System of the Market Economy (Order through Competition)*

4.2.2.1 The Basic Principle

The market economy — as has already been shown in 4.1.3 — stands or falls as a decentralized basic system. Decentralized planning presupposes a diversity of responsible economic subjects standing in an economic relationship of exchange with respect to one another, with opportunities for free and effective decision-making in economic activities. Therefore, its basic principle, "the freedom of individual economic subjects to be able to develop themselves in the economic sphere according to their own desires,"[17] is individualistic. This individual freedom of economic actors, which balks at all external binding claims, especially those of the state, is undoubtedly the highest value of a pure or free market economy. It seeks to create for individuals a path to their own economic interests with a minimum of hindrances. In terms of motivation, therefore, the market economy is based on individual interests, not on the general interests of individual economic subjects. More precisely, the "general welfare" becomes a function of the maximization of individual or private interests. This suggests seeing in the value basis summarized by it (whether correctly or incorrectly remains open for the time being) a justification of economic egoism, which has widely discredited the market economy among socially engaged persons.

4.2.2.2 The Economic Subject or Planner

The economic subjects in the decentralized system of the market economy are logically the "individual units of production and consumption, thus especially the business firm and the household."[18] They must work out their own economic plans and make the corresponding decisions. It is up to the firm or supplier to determine what, how, and in what quantity it will produce. And the household must make

[17] Tuchtfeldt, "Wirtschaftssysteme," p. 332.
[18] Kleinewefers, *Reformen für Wirtschaft und Gesellschaft*, Frankfurt, 1985, p. 406.

up its mind about how much of the income at its disposal to spend and how much to save. Therefore, microeconomically-oriented[19] economic planning corresponds to the market-economic individualistic principle. And that is true, not only because individual economic subjects are the planners in the pure market economy, but even more because, according to its fundamental principle, the planning decisions are based on individual-economic interests, not on the interests of the economy as a whole. Coordination of the individual plans is required, however, so that the individual planning decisions mesh with one another, i.e. so that supply and demand attain macroeconomic agreement and a disparity between the two — whether that too much or too little is produced, or too little or too much is purchased — can be avoided. It is constitutive for every form of market economy that the coordination takes place primarily over the market itself by virtue of the mechanisms prevailing in it, with or without a minimum of intervention from outside, either governmental or corporativist. According to what principle does this automatic coordination take place?

4.2.2.3 Market-Economic Coordination

The market economy exists only as a competitive economy. Accordingly, "competition is the guiding principle of the politics of ordering the market."[20] In other words, the coordination is produced by competition.

The (neo)classical economy theory of the model of perfect competition sheds light on the mechanism of this coordination.[21] It serves primarily heuristic objectives. According to this theory, many (small) suppliers stand facing many (small) purchasers, where the goods involved must be homogenous, and thus uniform. Neither suppliers nor purchasers have market power, so that there is no possibility of influencing prices. Moreover, the economic subjects act rationally, in the sense of economic theory, which means

[19] *Microeconomics* is small-scale economics, and is concerned with individual economic actors (firms, factories, households, suppliers, consumers, etc.). *Macroeconomics*, on the other hand, is large-scale economics, and is concerned with the entire economy. It deals with, for example, national product, national income, consumption, exports, imports, money supply, infrastructure, etc. *Mesoeconomics* is intermediate, and is concerned with regional or sectorial level, branches of industry, etc.

[20] Hensel, *Grundformen der Wirtschaftsordnung*, p. 61.

[21] See 2.5.2, fn. 128.

that they are primarily concerned with maximizing their own utility: the suppliers by seeking to attain the highest possible profit and the purchasers by striving to acquire the desired goods as inexpensively as possible. The competitive relationship between the suppliers and purchasers with respect to one another is thus qualified by making gains, and achieving gain is not determined by economic power positions, but by performance factors such as commitment, initiative, market prudence, etc. In addition, it is assumed that money behaves "neutrally"; there is neither inflation nor deflation. How does the coordination process take place with such ideal assumptions?

Analogously to the individualistic basic principle and the accompanying microeconomic planning structure of the market economy, the need of individual persons for scarce goods is assumed as a starting point. How can the degree of scarcity and, therefore, the priority of need of a particular good be measured? The market-economic answer is: by its price. The more a good is demanded and, therefore, the scarcer it is, regardless of whether it is a product or a service, the higher its price in the free market. Market prices are thus clear signals, which show reliably which goods receive priority in the market. And, because high prices promise high profits, the profit-maximizing manager will not fail to produce as a priority precisely the goods for which there is great demand in the market. The allocation of resources takes place, therefore, in accordance with the market or the economy. Overproduction is not to be feared, at least in the long run, because with increasing supply the goods' degree of scarcity is reduced and, consequently, prices decrease and, with the prices, the opportunities to earn a profit decrease, which automatically compels an adjustment of production. On the other hand, when there is underproduction, goods become scarcer, prices climb, and the opportunities for profit increase. This again produces an incentive to produce, which the profit-oriented manager will not pass up. In this way, the flexible market prices establish an automatic equilibrium mechanism, which regulates the relation of supply and demand without compulsion, controls the allocation of resources efficiently, and leads to an optimal provision of goods and services to society. But is this coordination of market-economic competition, since it is based on the principle of profit maximization, not achieved at the cost of a profit economy, which must on the whole one-sidedly benefit entrepreneurs as economic subjects?

According to the model theory of the pure market economy, this question is also to be answered negatively. Under conditions of perfect competition, the entrepreneur must contend with a multitude of competitors in the exploitation of less expensive market opportunities. But the more competitors pounce on the production of a profitable good, the greater its quantity in the market, which infallibly means price pressure. Under such conditions, the profit-oriented entrepreneur must ask himself how much of the good in question he can still produce with the prevailing price and still remain within the profit zone and avoid being eliminated as a competitor. This is decided by the marginal cost. "Marginal cost" is "the increased cost brought about by the increase of the quantity of the product," related to the last unit produced.[22] "As long as the market price is higher than the marginal cost, and thus is higher than the cost caused directly by the last unit produced, production is worthwhile."[23] Once he is in the vicinity of the marginal cost, therefore, the entrepreneur must demand a price higher than the market price for his product, in order to get beyond the indispensable minimal profit. But his competitors oppose this. With perfect competition, therefore, the opportunities for profit move towards the marginal cost. And that means that in the pure market economy the "tendency to eliminate profit" exists.[24] Therefore, limits to producers' and suppliers' striving for profit maximization are established by the market mechanism. They intentionally seek their own utility, and only that. But competition brings it about that in the process they also must produce utility for those who are interested in an optimal provision of goods with the lowest consumer prices. In other words, individual self-interest serves at the same time the collective total interest. This mechanism, which balances out the conflict of interests between the various economic subjects, moved Adam Smith, who was still dealing with market relationships that were actually close to perfect competition, to make the famous statement:

> As every individual, therefore, endeavours as much as he can both to employ his capital in the support of domestic industry, and so to direct that industry that its produce may be of the greatest value;

[22] *Dr. Gablers Wirtschaftslexikon*, ed. R. and H. Sellien, 9th Ed., Vol. 2, Wiesbaden, 1976, col. 1857.
[23] Frey, *Wirtschaft, Staat und Wohlfahrt*, p. 31.
[24] *Ibid.*, p. 33.

> every individual necessarily labours to render the annual revenue of the society as great as he can.... And he is in this, as in many other cases, led by an invisible hand to promote an end which was no part of his intention.[25]

The automatically functioning coordination of individual efforts to pursue utility or interest, or of the correlative plans of the individual economic subjects to achieve a microeconomic interplay that optimizes the efficiency of the allocation of resources, and thus indirectly promotes the prosperity of everyone, as it is encountered for the first time as a theory with Smith, has without doubt much support in reality. And, to be sure, that may be the case all the more as it approaches the ideal of perfect competition. But even under such ideal conditions, the coordination of the market economy, especially the inevitable convergence of individual and common interests, would be only relative. In other words, the market economy, as the basic system of decentralized planning or economic calculation, has its limits. Adam Smith was already aware that the market economy was not able to do justice to the *collective needs of society*.[26] This means, according to his view, apart from the citizens' need for external and internal security, infrastructure in the sense of public institutions, without which a national economy cannot exist. This includes public goods — one of the founders of modern economics himself refers to transportation, culture, and education[27] — which, because they are not very attractive for private-sector profit-seekers, cannot be produced by the market economy, or at least not sufficiently. Therefore, providing them — also agreeing with Smith — can only be the job of the state.

Another limit or "weak point of market coordination is the existence of *externalities*."[28] Externalities are (negative) side effects, such as pollution of the air, water, ground, or forests, which originate from the production of a particular good and damage other goods. Since we are dealing here with public goods, the costs that result from remedying this kind of damage are not borne directly by those who cause it and, therefore, are not automatically included in economic calculations. If one leaves things to themselves and it does not come to direct governmental demands against those who cause such

[25] Adam Smith, *The Wealth of Nations*, Oxford, 1976, IV.ii.9, p 456.
[26] *Ibid.*, IV.ix.51, pp. 687-88.
[27] *Ibid.*, V.i.e.1-V.i.i.6, pp. 731-816.
[28] Tuchtfeldt, "Wirtschaftssysteme," p. 334.

effects, then the costs originating from it must be shouldered by the general public, which not only burdens the governmental budget, but also leads to a distortion of prices and, consequently, to incorrect market signals.

Finally, "a third weakness of the market is its short-term orientation."[29] The theory begins with the assumption that the sum of all individual interests harmonizes with the aggregate interest of society. However, the pursuit of individual interests is oriented towards the present situation of the market. Thus, for example, it can be in the economic interest of an individual to be extravagant for the moment in the use of energy, because its present price is at a relatively low level and it appears for the time being to be a less scarce good. In the long term, however, there is good reason to believe that energy will become a considerably scarce good for ecological reasons. Therefore, it is in the general interest of society, not only that of consideration for the environment, to be extremely sparing in the use of energy today, even if that means for the economy a perceptible increase in present costs. But the market economy cannot achieve such a coordination of individual and common interests on its own, since future scarce prices, because of the short-term orientation, can barely enter into the calculation or planning decisions of individual economic subjects.[30] Ordered interventions from outside are also needed here.[31]

All in all it can be said with Jöhr: "Even if the model of perfect competition could be realized, the state would still have to intervene in order to attain objectives that cannot otherwise be accomplished."[32] This is true even more of the actual market economy, which is far from this ideal.

4.2.2.4 The Actually Existing Market Economy

It can be gathered from the observations above that the market-economic system reckons with economic subjects who, for reasons of "economic rationality," wish to maximize their own utility, but also

[29] *Ibid.*

[30] That is, of course, disputed by many economists. See Helmut Gröner, "Deregulierungsansätze im Energiesektor," *Neue Zürcher Zeitung*, No. 237, 13 October 1987, p. 37.

[31] Cf. *BEE*, Vol. II, pp. 426-27.

[32] Walter Adolf Jöhr, "Das Problem der Wirtschaftsordnung," p. 241.

— because they are held within limits by the mechanisms of competition — contrary to their subjective intentions, must objectively promote the prosperity of everyone. Thus, in his fundamentally egoistic behaviour, the market-economic "homo oeconomicus" proves to be, as it were, an altruist *contre coeur*. But does that not mean that the profit-seeking person, who is thinking only about maximizing his own interests, must experience this as contradictory coercion, which will drive him if possible to reduce, if not to remove, the structural limitations that the mechanism of competition establishes for the profit-seeker? Even Smith saw himself obligated to remark caustically: "People of the same trade seldom meet together..., but the conversation ends in a conspiracy against the public, or in some contrivance to raise prices."[33] That agrees with the statement cited above: "To widen the market and to narrow the competition, is always the interest of the dealers."[34] Obviously, already in Smith's time, perfect competition was not simply the rule, since the formation of price or profit is left to the "invisible hand" of market laws. In the contemporary industrial society it is simply the exception. Actually, there is only imperfect, frequently highly aggressive, but nevertheless restricted competition, since quite visible hands manipulate the market enormously to the advantage of their own utility maximization. How is that to be understood?

According to Paul A. Samuelson, "the economic definition of 'imperfect competitor' is *anyone who buys or sells a good in large enough quantities to be able to affect the price of that good.*"[35] Therefore, imperfect competition is about the formation of market power. The extreme form of market power is the pure monopoly or monopsony.[36] If there is only a single large supplier or a single large purchaser of a particular good in the market, and consequently neither producer competition nor purchaser competition, then direct competition is eliminated and the monopolist or monopsonist can, at least theoretically, determine the price, and thus maximize his own high-handed utility. This state of monopoly or monopsony, devoid of competition, is even more rare than perfect competition. Both cases are extremes, between which actual economic life is played out as "a blend of competitive

[33] Smith, *The Wealth of Nations*, I.x.c.27, p. 145.
[34] *BEE*, Vol. II, 2.6.3, fn. 167.
[35] Paul A. Samuelson, *Macroeconomics*, Vol. I, 7th Ed., New York, 1967, p. 46.
[36] Cf. *BEE*, Vol. II, 2.6.1 (Market Forms).

and monopoly elements."[37] One speaks, therefore, of "monopolistic competition" as the form of competition typical of the actual contemporary market economy. It is a state of more or less conflicting interplay between the economic subjects' market power, whether monopolists or oligopolists, and the laws of the competitive market.

It would amount to an impermissible oversimplification if one wished to connect imperfect, even monopolistic or oligopolistic competition only with the absolutizing of the striving for profit or power of the participants in the economic process, i.e. with subjective reasons. Behind that stand not less important factors of an historical-structural, and thus objective kind.

The ideal coordination system of perfect competition is formed ahistorically, in so far as it ignores the element of time and, consequently, of development. It presupposes stationary conditions, under which the equilibrium between supply and demand arrives immediately and "in which the available resources — labor, land, capital, and above all technological and organizational knowledge — as well as preferences do not change."[38] All of that changed radically with the beginning and progressive development of industrialization, with its continuous mechanization of production. A relatively stationary economy became a decisively dynamic-evolutionary one, which necessarily had profound consequences for the structure of competition in the market economy. In a stationary economy, profits are earned as indicators of the success of the entrepreneur or manager through competitive achievements, which can be immediately imitated by competitors, because they take place in the sphere of the traditional and are generally known. Consequently, their ability to compete remains unrestricted. In a dynamic-evolutionary economy, as it developed in the course of the industrialization process, on the other hand, profits become — and this becomes increasingly true with the passage of time — mainly produced by innovative achievements, which can be imitated, if at all, only difficultly and at least not immediately.[39] That intensifies the competitive pressure and requires less innovative competitors to cut back or to leave the market entirely. The result is an inevitable reduction of the number of competitors, for the most part linked with a concentration of production

[37] Samuelson, *Macroeconomics*, p. 46.
[38] Kleinewefers, *Reformen für Wirtschaft und Gesellschaft*, p. 371.
[39] *Ibid.*, pp. 374-75.

and capital, which makes the formation of oligopolistic and monopolistic market conditions, as today's economy typifies them, more than merely understandable. Therefore, the actual coordination system of the market economy is no more capable of being realized under today's economic-technological development conditions than it is able to satisfy the conditions of perfect competition. That speaks decisively against dogmatizing this ideal model of competition into a normative principle that could or should be universally aspired to in a developed industrial society.[40]

If perfect competition is not in accordance with the actual market economy of the industrial age, which is characterized by a dynamic-evolutionary structure, also for objective reasons, that does not at all mean — as is often asserted, that competition as a principle of economic coordination is in reality completely finished. Monopolies and quasi-monopolies do indeed tend towards the concept of the elimination of competition. Nevertheless, they are not able simply to abolish competition in a decentralized basic system of the economy. Even in the extreme case of absolute monopoly, where there are no direct competitors, it will remain, at least as a restriction through the purchasers' budgets:

> Even if a monopolist has no direct competitor who produces the same product, if he does not have to fear any potential competition through the market entry of new producers, and if there is no substitute for his product, his actions are still restricted by the budgets of his customers. Because of their budget restrictions, he is in indirect competition with every other supplier of his customers, even if their products have nothing to do with his own.[41]

In this respect, each monopolist experiences his or her limitations. Moreover, the absolute monopolist, released from direct competition, as already emphasized above, is extremely rare. That is especially true of micro-monopolies.

A "micro-monopoly" is the exclusive production or sale of individual, heterogeneous goods, which consequently have their specific, distinctive features or preferences and cannot be imitated by any

[40] In contemporary economic theory, perfect competition is finished as a model. Competition is "regarded not as an equilibrium situation, but as a dynamic and evolutionary process" (Ernst Heuß, "Ordoliberalismus," in *Liberalismus im Kreuzfeuer*, ed. Hans G. Nutzinger, Frankfurt, 1986, p. 28.

[41] Kleinewefers, *Reformen für Wirtschaft und Gesellschaft*, p. 366.

other producer over a relatively long period of time, because of patent protection or because production of the good requires special knowledge. As long as the monopolist can maintain his advantage in knowledge or innovation, he is in the position, thanks to this superiority, to maintain the high price of his monopoly product and to receive a monopoly profit, one similar to a pioneer profit. Monopoly profits, however, provoke other producers, as long as the product cannot be simply imitated, to bring a similar product, one capable of substitution, into the market. To the degree that this is achieved, substitution competition begins for the monopolist, which has the effect that, analogously to perfect competition, the opportunities for profit sink, which means that they gravitate to the marginal cost or completely disappear. And in this sense the micro-monopolist must also take direct competition into account, at least in the long run, which presents for him a hindrance in thoughtlessly exploiting his temporary monopoly situation.

The circumstances of macro-monopolies are different. With a macro-monopoly, there is monopolistic production or marketing, not merely of an individual good, but of entire groups of goods, and indeed "in exclusive conditions of production that cannot be achieved by other producers over a relatively long period of time."[42] In contrast to micro-monopolies, with which the singular market advantage is based on the legal protection of a unique product, special knowledge, or distinctive features of the production method that cannot be simply repeated, and thus on exclusivities that can be achieved by small firms, "macro-monopolies stand in a direct relationship to the existence of giant corporations."[43]

Macro-monopolies, consequently, are the things of mammoth corporations. Such firms usually produce a wide range of products, including products that can be easily imitated and, therefore, that do not have a monopolistic character considered in themselves. But they are usually manufactured in such large quantities that the investment for technological, highly developed, rationalized production facilities, which can be built only by industrial giants, pays off. Therefore, the decisive market advantage with a macro-monopoly consists above all in the superiority of the technological production conditions, completely apart from the enormous means that they

[42] Šik, *Der dritte Weg*, Hamburg, 1972, p. 159.
[43] *Ibid.*

have at their disposal for innovative research in the design of production and products. A potential competitor would be able to catch up with this head start, which is provided by the conditions of the mass production, only if he could achieve analogous mass production. But since, with macro-monopolies, the demand for products in its branch of industry is already met to a high degree, this could easily lead to a surplus of supply, and thus to massive price reduction. And these are risks that the market newcomer, because of his weaker starting position in this kind of competitive situation, can hardly undertake. Thus, macro-monopolies make market entry more difficult for potential competitors to a much higher degree than do micro-monopolies.

There is also another way in which macro-monopolies can exploit their market power much more than is possible in the case of micro-monopolies. It is possible that individual products of a macro-monopolistic corporation can be successfully imitated by resourceful producers or that a potent substitution competition for them arises. Under the conditions of perfect competition, if the market price of a product facing this competition fell below marginal cost, the large monopolist would have to reduce, if not complete cease, its manufacture and sale. But since the total profitability of his firm is not dependent upon the manufacture and sale of this one product, he also has the possibility of marketing it for some time at a price below marginal cost, and thus at a loss, in the hope of driving competitors out of the market and maintaining the monopolistic position, together with the resulting monopoly profits, for the long term. In this case, as in the first case cited above, it is the stronger market power, not better performance in production or marketing, that determines the market share and, therefore, the profit. The competition and price mechanisms of the market economy, which reward performance according to their built-in systemic function and at the same time are supposed to set "natural" limits to corporate profit-maximization, are not simply abolished even in this case, but are suppressed as much as possible. And that means that in the actual market economy, the coordination of the different interests of the various economic subjects cannot proceed on its own in the sense of optimizing the "common good." This requires instead the deliberate restraint of the monopolistic elements by the competitive elements. But with that we encounter a fundamental dilemma of market-economic coordination.

4.2.2.5 The Coordination Dilemma

According to its basic principle, the market economy is based, to emphasize the point again, on the decentralized coordination of the individual plans of the different economic subjects active in it by means of competition. The competition, which is motivated by the self-interest of the economic subjects, leads via the price mechanism to an efficient, optimal allocation of the resources or factors of production, which simultaneously, because of the productivity of the economy originating from it, is in the interest of the general welfare of everyone. Consequently, the purer and more undistorted the competition, the more optimal should be its automatic coordination.

It has been seen, however, that even under conditions approximating the ideal model of perfect competition, deficits of coordination will arise in the market economy (see pp. 443-44). This is all the more true of the actual market economy, with its imperfect competition and the related formation of market power in the form of oligopolies and monopolies. They tend to call competition into question as a principle of coordination in general. With that, the coordination dilemma of the market economy is succinctly identified.

In other words, this dilemma is based on the fact that the market economy releases forces that ultimately turn themselves against it. According to the principle of competition, as has already been pointed out, better performance is honored by the market and worse performance is eliminated by it in the long run. In the course of their utility maximization, consumers prefer high-quality, low-priced products. And if they wish to maximize their own utility, producers must provide such products. In this way, the interests of the two different groups of economic subjects are coordinated and resources flow primarily to the site of better performance. At the same time, however, this results in a selection among the producers or among those who trade their products. And this tends to reduce the number of suppliers, insofar as they must depend upon other firms to deliver their products, and also the number of buyers. All in all, this means a tendency towards oligopolistic and, *in extremis,* monopolistic market forms, along with the industrial and capital concentrations inherent to them. Therefore, competition and its sanction mechanisms themselves are not the least of the reasons oligopolies and monopolies originate. Insofar as they are the result of better market performance, which benefits consumers, they have a positive side for society as a whole. On the other hand, they become, because of their size and capital power, economic power factors, which make it more difficult, if not impossible, for new, innovative, and thus potentially dangerous competitors to enter the market. This has already been discussed with regard to macro-monopolies. The oligopolist also pushes towards the market form of the monopoly, either by cartel agreements, partnerships or mergers of industrial giants, or marketing policies. To the degree that monopolistic tendencies progress and market performance is accompanied by market power, the self-interest of the supplier absolutizes itself by the monopolistic profit, and the coupling of self-interest and the general welfare, which distinguishes the principle of competition as Adam Smith understood it, is illusory. In this way, the mechanism of competition contains self-destructive forces, a fact that can hardly be disputed. In any case, "the question whether the competitive system destroys itself cannot be answered with a decisive 'no'."[44] Nevertheless, if one is, like Henner Kleinewefers, of the opinion that even an imperfect competitive system with its tendency to oligopolize or monopolize markets does not have to die out and, despite everything,

> has on balance large advantages and can be replaced by no other method of coordination with even approximately comparable characteristics, the question is still posed with great urgency how one can ensure its survival and, indeed, in such a way that its advantages outweigh the disadvantages as much as possible.[45]

That clearly outlines the basic coordination problem presented by the actual market economy of today. The challenge is to preserve competition that is capable of functioning and that permits profit on the basis of true entrepreneurial and managerial market performance, which is also in the interest of society as a whole, but effectively prevent profit from non-performance, which is based upon market power and seeks to hinder or completely eliminate competition.[46]

[44] Kleinewefers, *Reformen für Wirtschaft und Gesellschaft*, p. 387.

[45] *Ibid.*

[46] On the model of competition capable of functioning, see Wilhelm Henrichsmeyer, Oskar Gans, and Ingo Evers, *Einführung in die Volkswirtschaftslehre*, 7th Ed., Stuttgart, 1986, pp. 243-44: "While the allocation of the factors of production, according to the ideal model of perfect competition, is optimal only in the situation of zero profit, with profits thus being "tolerated" as a temporary phenomenon, in competition capable of functioning, performance-profit takes on the role (among others) of making *technological innovations* and improving the allocation of factors more

The survival of competition that is capable of functioning in this sense is never automatically secured by itself. Competition proves to be an ambivalent process: "It is possible as performance-competition and as non-performance-competition,"[47] as competition that forces the competitor to function efficiently, and thus lets him have a chance, and as competition that drives him out of the market without an opportunity, because the stronger market power decides: "If the socially detrimental effects of non-performance-competition or battles to eliminated competitors are to be hindered, then the competition itself must be ordered; thus not only order by, but also order *of* competition is required."[48]

This "ordering of competition" means that the competition can perform its ordering and coordinating function in the economy only insofar as it itself is ordered in a way that holds the market power of the oligopolies and macro-monopolies within limits, and prevents, or at least strongly hinders, the utility maximization of the different groups of economic subjects (producers, consumers), including those who personally bear the factors of production (workers at all levels of quality, "know how" specialists, managers, investors) from assuming an absolute character. That would mean, consistently with the etymology of "absolute," becoming detached from one another, and thus being counter-solidarist, placing self-interest above everything. The "market mechanisms" that achieve this by bringing about a balancing of interests, according to the ideal model of perfect competition, are not self-compelling natural laws, but instead — as the school of ordo-liberalism already recognized — regulations established and designed by humans. Therefore, they can also be structured and manipulated by humans, and indeed for good and for evil. The market economy requires, therefore, if it is to be capable of functioning in the sense of its own, interest-balancing-out expectations, not only people who are ready to perform, who behave loyally to competitors

strongly than with discrimination against profits. The more capable of performing the competition is, the faster are performance profits reduced. The producer of a new product, such as the electronic pocket calculator, makes a high profit in the initial phase, which is primarily a performance-profit. The pioneer supplier, however, has at best a *chronological monopoly*, since competitors ('imitators') quickly enter the market. The increased supply depresses prices and profits to the normal level; the *pioneer profit or head-start profit* disappears."

[47] Hensel, *Grundformen der Wirtschaftsordnung*, p. 61.

[48] *Ibid.*

and to other economic subjects in general. It requires above all a legal and economic framework that urges, through its structural effects, market participants to pursue their own utility in such a way that they do not seriously harm others, and — what is one of the highest commandments today — do not burden the natural environment, which is already so seriously maltreated. And that is a task of shaping the economic order that can hardly be accomplished without calling in the state and the societal forces that support it. But this means nothing less than modifying the decentralized system of coordination by an all-embracing element. And with that the fundamental limitation of the pure market economy comes into view.

4.2.3 *The Limitations of the Market Economy*

The fundamental limitation of the market economy — as may have become apparent in the preceding discussion — has to do decisively with its specific interest problems. The market economy presents itself, according to its own intention, as the system that is able, thanks to the competitive coordination mechanism, to bring individual economic interests, with an optimum of room for freedom, at least for the managing and consuming economic subjects, into broad agreement with the interest of society as a whole. However, the market-economic interest problem contains, as has already been implicitly indicated, not only a positive aspect, but also a negative one:

> If the realization of individual economic interests is dependent upon achievements that are to be accomplished, then economic behavior is motivated by just these interests and is at the same time urged all the more strongly the more important the interests are to people and the closer the relationship is between performance and success. Seen in this way, the partial interests, having regard to the total interests, can become a highly useful or even indispensable allocative potency. The interests can produce large and creative achievements, and experience teaches that the solution of the allocation problem still depends on whether and in what amount it succeeds in legalizing and activating the interests, and making them useful as a moving and driving force of economic behavior. — Experience also teaches, however, that the negative aspect of this interest problem is that the same interests always tend to realize themselves as much as possible, even if this happens on the basis of inadequate performance and at the cost of the interests of partners, as well as ultimately the common interest. The interests hardly know any limit to their self-realization,

> or at least should not be considered to have such an immanent self-restriction. As useful as the interests can function, they can at any time become the source of asocial distortion and provoke strong contradictions between partial and total interests.[49]

Therefore, the fundamental limitation of the market economy, more precisely, of its system of coordination, becomes apparent in the fact that the reconciliation of the individual interests of the various economic subjects and the aggregate interests of society, which is immanent and, therefore, is supposed to take place automatically according to the model-idea of competition, cannot be relied upon in reality. One speaks in this context of weaknesses, shortages, contradictions, or simply "market failure."

Such market failure has already been discussed under conditions of perfect competition.[50] It is sufficient here to point out briefly once again the weak points mentioned there: insufficient satisfaction of collective needs, the appearance of negative externalities, and the short-term orientation of individual-economic planning decisions, which do react to present scarcities, but not to future scarcities. In the real market economy, with its imperfect competition, therefore, even greater deficits are encountered.[51]

In addition, one must point out that a competitive order and monetary stability are closely related: "Without stability of the value of money, there can be no competition capable of functioning. They depend upon one another."[52] In the real market economy money proves not to be "neutral," but instead to be inflationary or deflationary, which means instabilities of the price level, and thus of the value of money, with all its economic and social consequences. Whether this is to be attributed essentially to market failure or to incorrect monetary policy is disputed in the theory. Keynesianism vs. monetarism. Whatever may be the case there, it shows in any case

49 Hensel, "Das Verhältnis von Allokations- und Wirtschaftssystem," in *Systemvergleich als Aufgabe*, p. 13.

50 *BEE*, Vol. II, pp. 443-44.

51 It is noted that deficits or failures of the market economy are disputed in contemporary economics, inasmuch as a requirement for control of the market-economic system is concluded from them, as is the case here. According to Milton Friedman, there would be a requirement for control only if it could be proved that the interventions actually achieved the desired effect and thus a net utility, which he denies. Cf. Kleinewefers, *Reformen für Wirtschaft und Gesellschaft*, pp. 126-27.

52 Heuß, "Ordoliberalismus," p. 29.

that the market economy is unable to produce on its own an ordering of the money supply that takes economic and social interests into account, but instead that it is dependent upon the coordinating activity of the central bank as the instrument of governmental and, in the indirect sense, centrally controlled monetary policy.[53]

An additional deficit is the cyclical repetition of economic upswings and downswings, which are typical of the market economies of the industrial age, together with related employment problems: "The total economic sequence of events of a market economy left to itself does not automatically regulate itself in a way that avoids significant fluctuations in the degree of occupation of the macroeconomic productive forces and a level of unemployment that appears to be socially intolerable."[54] Apart from the great economic crisis of the 1930s, the massive unemployment rates in most market-economic industrial states of today speak an unusually clear language. Consequently, the stabilization of the complete economy's course of events as a central problem of economic policy is difficult, if not impossible, to achieve without influence from outside, and thus of the state.

The situation is similar with the problems of the environment, which are becoming increasingly urgent today. Even the imperative stabilization or reduction of environmental damage does not arise inevitably — at least not in the medium and short term, as must be the case today — from the incentives of the mechanisms of the market economy. These press primarily towards an efficient, profit-maximizing use of the factor of production land/nature, as well with that of labor and, obviously, of capital, which, according to past experience, makes previously quantitatively organized economic growth dynamic, along with the environmental dangers tied to it.[55] The mechanisms of the market economy could indeed have a decelerating effect, if the use of the mentioned factors also had to be qualified ecologically and socially, and thus according to a kind of economic rationality that includes the ethical and, consequently, if the costs of

[53] On the problematic and praxis of this kind of control, with the example of the Swiss central bank, which orients itself, of course not in a dogmatic way, according to monetary thinking, see Georg Rich, "Ist die schweizerische Geldpolitik wirklich monetaristisch?" in *Geld, Währung, Konjunktur*, ed. Swiss National Bank, Vol. 2, No. 3 (September 1984), pp. 53-60.

[54] Henrichsmeyer, Gans, and Evers, *Einführung in die Volkswirtschaftslehre*, p. 357.

[55] *BEE*, Vol. II, 2.7.2.

externalities, whether of a kind that is environmentally, socially, or in some other way damaging, enter into the individual-economic financial plans. But this, in turn, will never happen on its own. It will happen only if the market economy is ordered and steered from outside in such a way that is able to put the individual interests of economic subjects in relation to the overall interests of society.

Finally, "the distribution of income, as it comes about on the basis of market forces, is not satisfactory."[56] It is still "perceived by an overwhelming segment of the population to be unjust."[57] This is especially true of income in the form of wages.

Wages are the monetary compensation of the bearers of the factor of production labor for the production of their economic output. Considered purely in terms of the market economy, a wage is the price that the manager who seeks workers is prepared to pay in the market, or vice versa, the price that the worker who supplies his labor demands for it. Just as commodities are handled in commodity markets, so workers are handled in the labor market. In both cases, prices are scarcity prices, and thus are subject to the same mechanisms as they are set. In this way, as Karl Marx critically diagnosed, human labor becomes the "commodity of worker." Even if one brackets this dehumanizing effect, which should be taken seriously, problems arise.

Labor markets have not only their anthropological, but also their economic "peculiarities," as K. Paul Hensel emphatically points out.[58] While the supply of goods has a lower limit determined by the cost of their production and, therefore, must adjust to the marginal cost in order to avoid ruinous loss and elimination from the market, there is "no such lower cost limit for the supply of labor, or at best it would consist in the minimum physical existence of workers."[59] To be sure, no one in the market economy is legally compelled to accept work at a wage that he considers too low. Everyone has the freedom to decline it, just as a supplier in a goods market has the freedom to refrain from a sale if the price seems to him to be too low. Nevertheless, there is an important difference here. In the event of an oversupply of labor, the freedom of workers is restricted — always seen

[56] Frey, *Wirtschaft, Staat und Wohlfahrt*, p. 127.
[57] *Ibid.*, p. 143.
[58] Hensel, *Grundformen der Wirtschaftsordnung*, pp. 65-69.
[59] *Ibid.*, p. 66.

under the condition of a pure market economy — either to becoming unemployed and accepting the accompanying human and social loss of status or to accepting the work at a very low wage. Therefore, "the economic right to freedom in labor markets can mean something essentially different from what it means in goods markets."[60] In turn, this identifies a deficit of the market economy, which works itself out *in concreto* for the supplier of labor all the more fatally, the more he faces a situation of oligopolistic or monopolistic demand for labor by corporations. Precisely this situation both gave the social question of the arriving industrial age its specific explosiveness and led to the monopolization of the labor supply through the formation of labor unions as counterweights to the quasi-demand monopolies of large firms in the labor market. Therefore, the automatic mechanism of a labor market left to itself works to the advantage of employers, unless scarce qualifications are supplied or the general demand for workers is too large. Because of the peculiarities of this labor market, the wage-suppressing disparities possible within it do not disappear on their own, or at best disappear only in the long run. In terms of order theory, consequences must be drawn from this. Hensel himself names two of them. First, there must be legal limitation of the supply of labor (e.g. reducing the work week, early retirement), so that the wage cannot sink below a certain level, if necessary, by setting a minimum wage. Second, there must be, on the basis of this kind of regulation of the labor market, collective agreement between the social partners about employment conditions, with legally enforced minimum conditions for concluding individual labor contracts,[61] in which the labor unions must play an important role. There can, of course, be disagreement about the appropriateness and adequacy of these conclusions, but not about the fact that regulative interventions in the labor market are necessary in order to maintain income from labor at a socially tolerable level.

Even if this level is achieved in general, of course, the claim to distributive justice is not yet satisfied. An earlier context (see pp. 408-09) has already shown that, if the problem of distribution is to be tackled in a humanly just manner, both the viewpoint of performance-justice and that of needs-justice must be observed. Disregarding, or even merely neglecting, one of these viewpoints inevitably leads to

[60] *Ibid.*, p. 67.
[61] *Ibid.*, pp. 67-68.

injustices. The market economy, with its primacy of the principle of individual performance, "corresponds at best to performance-justice, but not to needs-justice."[62] This shows again one of its limitations, which, as early as approximately the end of the nineteenth century, called into life opposing forces, which aimed decisively at a secondary redistribution, oriented towards needs-justice and, consequently, favoring the disadvantaged classes of society, and thus at the creation of the welfare state.

The shortcomings of the market economy are obviously not exhausted by these few, rather summarily presented examples. It can be added, above all, that it has a tendency towards the specific capitalistic structure of the market economy,[63] as recent developments in the financial markets especially show. Yet it is sufficient here to point out the paradigmatic concretization of the mentioned limitations in orientation towards the social-ethical deficits that arise from them. The fact that such deficits exist is unquestionable. They are also not at all concealed by resolute advocates of the market economic system. Thus Otto Schlecht, German Federal Minister of Economics, for instance, maintains unmistakably: "Social ethics must still be injected into the pure market economy by a corresponding form of order-framework."[64] This means concretely, according to Schlecht:

1. Governmental regulation of the structure of competition,
2. Amendment by social and labor law protection,
3. Overall control of the entire process, in the interest of stability and employment,
4. Provision of infrastructure: education, transportation network, city planning, etc.,
5. Regulation of what is obligatory and forbidden, and market-economic incentives for protection of the environment.[65]

It is striking that, in addition to order-political provisions in the narrower sense, there are also fiscal measures here. In other words, comprehensive elements of planning and control, in the sense of planning the framework or of (indicative) overall control are taken up,

[62] Frey, *Wirtschaft, Staat und Wohlfahrt*, p. 143.
[63] Cf. *BEE*, Vol. II, 6.2.1.
[64] Otto Schlecht, "Ethische und ökonomischen Ziele im Konflikt," in *BMWI Dokumentation*, ed. Federal Minister of Economics, No. 266, Bonn, 1985, p. 7.
[65] *Ibid.*

and the pure or free market economy is transformed into the controlled market economy. That, to be sure, does not mean, as old-liberal purists fear, abolition of the specifically market economic coordination system.[66] But it does mean relativizing it in consideration of its limitations. What would such relativization look like in principle?

4.2.4 *Relativization of the Market Economy*

The relativization of the market-economic coordination system has its empirical basis in the fact that it can have no continued existence in reality in the sense of its ideal conception, namely as purely decentralized economic planning, determined by the interests of the individual economic subjects. It can actually exist, especially under the conditions of the modern industrial society with its characteristic imperfect competition, only when macroeconomic correctives, based on the opposing principle, even on the central principle of coordination or planning, come into play. The *pure* market economy is, therefore, a utopia, which has never existed in reality. To the degree that — failing to recognize its limitations — it seeks to transform itself absolutely into reality, it will bring disaster, come antagonistically into conflict with human justice, and ultimately be directed against itself. There are, however, not only empirical reasons, but even more in-principle reasons for this.

The fundamental principle of the market economy as a decentralized planning system, according to 4.2.2.1, is based on the individual freedom of individual economic subjects and on the right, by virtue of this freedom, responsibly to pursue properly understood self-interest, whether it is a matter of natural or of legal persons. Therefore, it is based on universal values: on the values of freedom, responsibility, and self-interest. Since the subject of all economic activity is and remains the human person, there is no humanly just economy without the recognition of these values. The ethical right of the market-economic basic principle consists in that.

[66] Cf. Leipold, *Wirtschafts- und Gesellschaftssystem im Vergleich*, pp. 58-59: "The state can restrict itself to establishing a legal framework, but can also move beyond that to the global control of macro-economic quantities. These interventions do not yet necessarily mean a transformation to the centrally-coordinated system. They mean instead indirect regulation or control of decentrally-decided processes in the interest of governmental objectives."

Human values such as freedom, responsibility, and self-interest, however, can be humanly just only if they are realized complementarily to the opposing, also elementary human values of social duty, solidarity, and total or collective interest. That arises, in any case, from relationality as a basic criterion of human justice in the sense of the humanity originating from faith, hope, and love.[67] This was already addressed, apart from 1.3.5, in 3.3.7.1. It is sufficient to repeat here that, from the perspective of relationality, these value complexes, which are contrary in themselves, are hints of the entirety of faith-humanity as the quintessence of human justice, but only in their mutual relationality. If they divorce themselves from their reciprocal relationship, in other words, if they are extremized into absolutes that exclude the opposing human values, then they share the fate of all extremisms, namely becoming the gravediggers of all that is human. Freedom that seeks to free itself from every binding obligation becomes self-assertion at any price, ultimately also at the price of the freedom of others. And that radically destroys the humane sense of freedom as the basis of the market economy. What is true of freedom is true analogously of all human values. In their isolation they are never human justice, but merely aspects of human justice. Therefore, they can also be humanly just only in such relativity, arising from their relationality. That by no means robs a human value of its validity, but does rob it of being ideologized into a totality that is not a totality. In this way, relativity and relationality are indispensable criteria of true human justice. The necessary and actual occurrence of the relativization of the market economy understands itself from that as a concise hint of the reality-content of the criteria of the humanity originating from faith, hope, and love.

In this relative sense, the value-foundation of the market economy and the coordination system based upon it can be received from the criteria of human justice.[68] Such a reception inevitably includes critical distance from the existing market economy, as well as the search for more humanly just possibilities within its order, and indeed in openness to the value-foundation opposed to it. At the same time, this identifies the horizon in which the system of the centrally controlled economy, also again in critical distance, can be objectively challenged.

[67] *BEE*, Vol. I, 7.2.4.

[68] Cf. *BEE*, Vol. II, 1.3.6., where the theological, in-principle establishment of these facts can be found.

4.3 The Basic System of the Centrally Planned Economy

4.3.1 *Terminology*

As already explained in 4.1.3, "centrally planned economy" is understood to be an economic system in which the economic processes are centrally planned and managed by a central authority. Just as the market economy is commonly equated with capitalism, the centrally planned economy is usually identified with socialism. In both cases, there are historical reasons for doing this. When they are considered theoretically, however, identifying the two systems in this way is problematic. A centrally planned economy can exist without a socialist system of ownership, just as a market economy is conceivable without capitalist private ownership of the means of production. Significantly, centrally planned national economic control did not develop "for the first time in a socialist economy, but in the capitalist economy of Germany during the First World War."[69] We should respect this and take it into account terminologically. In contrast to common usage, then, the terminological conflation of the centrally planned or governmentally directed economy and socialism will also be avoided here, just as with the market economy and capitalism, even though actually existing socialism has centrally planning as its foundation and, until recently, considered it to be indispensable.[70] It is possible, of course, that this deviation from common terminology can lead to difficulties of understanding.

4.3.2 *Beginnings and First New Approaches of the Theory of Central Planning in Marxism-Leninism* [71]

Although there is no necessary relationship between socialism, understood as a social order with mainly common, rather than private ownership of the powerful, productive means of capital, and the principle of central planning, its theoretical beginnings go back — of course, developed just as sparsely as vaguely — to genuine Marxism's concept of socialism. They are already laid out in its specific

[69] Šik, *Wirtschaftssysteme*, p. 62.

[70] This dogma has been shaken only recently — first in Yugoslavia, then in Hungary, and finally in the rest of Eastern Europe.

[71] Cf. Šik, *Wirtschaftssysteme*, pp. 60-72.

analysis and critique of the capitalist manner of structuring the market economy, with ideological-utopian and empirical-technical arguments balanced in a rare mixture.

The general horizon of the Marxist-Engelist view of and critique of capitalism proves to contain ideological-utopian impregnation. According to it, there exists an in-principle (i.e. existing *a priori*) relationship between capitalistic private ownership, which as such already exploits those who possess no property, and the industrial division of labor, which ties workers to a particular, narrowly limited activity, as well as the market exchange of commodities, which degrades labor as a factor of production into an exchangeable commodity to be used by capital. So, for Marx: "Division of labour and private property are, after all, identical expressions: in the one the same thing is affirmed with reference to activity as is affirmed in the other with reference to the product of the activity." [72] The division of labor, for its part, induces, according to Engels, the "division into classes"[73] with the antagonistic opposition of capital and labor. And this antagonism ultimately correlates, again according to Marx, with the capitalist market, which is not at all concerned about satisfying human needs, but about the "production of profit" as the "purpose of capital," which must lead, on the one hand, to the progressive exploitation of workers and, on the other hand, to overproduction and, consequently, to chaotic conditions in the economy.[74] All of that creates compulsions, of which the producer, whether an entrepreneur or a worker, is at the mercy of "foreign powers." These powers can be overcome only if capitalist private property and the market production of commodities, in their hopeless connection, are eliminated at the same time and replaced by the socialization of the means of production and the planned organization of the economy. Thus Engels says: "With the seizing of the means of production by society, production of commodities is done away with, and, simultaneously, the mastery of the product over the producer. Anarchy in social production is replaced by systematic, definite organisation."[75] And he emphatically adds to that somewhat later, using a phrase of Marx: "It is the humanity's leap from the kingdom of necessity to the kingdom of freedom."

[72] Marx and Engels, "The German Ideology," in *Collected Works*, Vol. V, New York, 1975, p. 46.

[73] Engels, "Anti-Düring," in *Collected Works*, Vol. XXV, New York, 1987, p. 268.

[74] Marx, *Capital*, in *Collected Works*, Vol. 37, New York, 1998, p. 250.

[75] Engels, "Anti-Düring," in *Collected Works*, Vol. XXV, New York, 1987, p. 270.

If the principle of social economic planning already arises in this way from the ideological general horizon of the Marxist-Engelist critique of capitalism and from the related socialist understanding, it is also decisively supported, with Marx especially, by empirical-analytic arguments. The author of *Das Kapital* displays a sharp, critical eye for the afflictions of the real market economy, as has been mentioned paradigmatically in 4.2.3. This is especially true of the cyclical economic swings that lead in the extreme to serious economic crises and lay bare, beside the aggregate-economic reduction of efficiency, anarchic, self-destroying forces in the market economy. In view of this, Marx performed pioneering work. According to Joseph A. Schumpeter, "practically all the elements that ever entered into any serious analysis of business cycles" are already found in Marx. Schumpeter explicitly calls this "a great achievement."[76] This should be taken into account. Therefore, it would certainly be short sighted and fatal to reject the Marxist critique of capitalism and the market economy simply as ideologically prejudiced. Despite all implications of this kind, it has real, economically based support. To that belongs his deep scepticism about a structuring of the economy, which, with appeal to liberty, provides unrestricted room to the utility-maximization of individual economic subjects and wishes to be subject to the power of market laws as the only regulator, which for Marx means "complete anarchy."[77] This scepticism, however, is of a kind that changes into dogmatism and is able to confront market freedom only with an antithetical alternative: "Freedom in this field can only consist in socialised man, the associated producers, rationally regulating their interchange with Nature [a paraphrase of the basic process of the economy — A. Rich], bringing it under their common control, instead of being ruled by it as by the blind forces of Nature."[78] But this means, in short: a planned economy with dismissal of the market.

Therefore, considered all in all, Marx and Engels call for an economy that is subordinate to social control and is organized in detail according to plan, instead of market-economic self-regulation, which was anarchic in their eyes and, therefore, also inefficient. But they did not concern themselves with the difficult question of the "how" of

[76] Joseph A. Schumpeter, *Capitalism, Socialism and Democracy*, 3rd Ed., New York, 1950, p. 40.

[77] Marx, *Capital*, in *Collected Works*, Vol. 37, p. 867.

[78] Marx, *Capital*, in *Collected Works*, Vol. 37, p. 807. Cf also *Collected Works*, Vol. XXII, p. 335.

such total planning. They appeared to be of the naive opinion — in any event, this is true of Engels — that such a plan could be drawn up easily. Daily experience already shows, and indeed directly, not only via the market, how much social work is required for the production of an individual product, and thus for meeting needs.[79]

The question of the true subject of the planning also remains unclarified. But a tendency towards planned centralism in the transition period between the dictatorship of the proletariat and the dreamed of end state, with its stateless "association, in which the free development of each is the condition for the free development of all,"[80] is unmistakably present with Marx and Engels. The *Manifesto of the Communist Party* of 1848 already demanded from the advanced countries, after the seizure of power by the working class, the "centralisation of credit" and of "the means of communication and transport in the hands of the state," as well as the "extension of factories and instruments of production owned by the State; the bringing into cultivation of waste-lands, and the improvement of the soil generally in accordance with a common plan."[81] With that, for Marx and Engels, the course was set in the question of planning the economy.

As Lenin found himself standing before the huge task of building anew the economy of a socialist society after the 1917 October Revolution, only extremely minimal beginnings of a Marxist theory of planning were available.[82] The only things standing firmly were the unity of socialist property and overall economic planning, as well as the state as the temporary bearer of both. That did not offer a firm foundation for the new beginning for which he was striving. Lenin had to look elsewhere for practicable models. Thereby, the praxis and theory of German wartime economic planning gained decisive importance.[83] The founder of the Soviet Union, in the words of Ota

[79] Engels, "Anti-Düring," in *Collected Works*, Vol. XXV, New York, 1987, 294.

[80] Marx and Engels, "Manifesto of the Communist Party," in *Collected Works*, Vol. VI, New York, 1976, p. 506.

[81] Marx and Engels, "Manifesto of the Communist Party," in *Collected Works*, Vol. VI, New York, 1976, p. 505.

[82] In his review of Marx's *Capital*, Engels candidly admits in an ironic tone that the reader can find no information in this work about "what the communist Millennium would actually be like." "Indeed, he learns here how things should not be." (Engels, [Review of Volume One of *Capital* for the *Düsseldorfer Zeitung*], in *Collected Works*, Vol. XX, New York, 1985, p. 216.)

[83] On planning theory in the wake of the German war economy, see Walther Rathenau, *Die neue Wirtschaft*, Berlin, 1918.

Šik, "owed very strong inspirations" to them.[84] He emphasized them on various occasions as examples for the socialist planned economy.[85] This was followed by the phase of so-called "war communism," which lasted until 1921. It was defined by drawing on a centrally planned natural economy without money and, therefore, also without prices for investment goods, consumer goods, and services. This was in accordance with both the ideas of Marx and Engels — insofar as they did not ultimately aspire to the nationalization of capital, but instead to its abolition altogether[86] — and those of the German planning theorists. Therefore, there was no longer any market in existence, not even in the formal sense. The means of production and consumer goods were rationed according to plan and correspondingly distributed to factories and the population. The experiment ended in total failure, because, especially in agriculture, there were no incentives to production.

The consequence of this catastrophe was a marked reorientation in the question of economic order. Lenin inaugurated the New Economic Policy (NEP). It brought, following Šik once again, the return of the money economy with monetary wages for performance and prices for goods. But that did not mean a turn away from governmental planning policy. On the contrary, in the industrial sphere, in contrast to the agricultural sector,

> an extremely centralized planning organization was constructed, which, with the first plan for the electrification of Russia, already laid foundation stones for the further development of Soviet planning. What was new in this planning was the transition from ideas of natural planning to planning of both production and the distribution of goods with the help of price categories.[87]

[84] Šik, *Wirtschaftssysteme*, p. 64.

[85] "Germany. Here we have 'the last word' in modern large-scale capitalist engineering and planned organization, *subordinated to Junker-bourgeois imperialism*. ... Socialism is inconceivable without large-scale capitalist engineering based on the latest discoveries of modern science. It is inconceivable without planned state organization, which keeps tens of millions of people to the strictest observance of a unified standard in production and distribution. (V. I. Lenin, "'Left-Wing' Childishness and the Petty-Bourgeois Mentality," in *Collected Works*, Vol. XXVII, London/Moscow, 1965, p. 339).

[86] Engels, [Review of Volume One of *Capital* for the *Düsseldorfer Zeitung*], in *Collected Works*, Vol. XX, New York, 1985, p. 216.

[87] Šik, *Wirtschaftssysteme*, p. 65.

Nevertheless, this meant practically the instrumental establishment of a market-economic element in the central planning system, and thus a kind of "plan-market connection." And this fact necessarily gave fresh impetus to a new theoretical development of the question of planning.

It is not possible here to go into this new development of theories in the Soviet Union during the 1920s, which should also be of significance for the contemporary reform efforts in the countries of real socialism. Anyone interested in learning about this quickly may read Šik.[88] It is merely noted here that the problem of the relationship between planning and the market stood at the center of the theoretical discussions. It was asked whether and in what sense plan and market could be linked, even whether in the process the market would be subordinate to the plan or the plan to the market. The explosiveness of such questions is obvious. Both include far-reaching consequences, which are, of course, quite different qualitatively. In the case of the subordination of the market to planning, the market would still have the instrumental role of a corrective to planned production activity, which would mean a drastic modification of the centrally planned economy. In the other case, the market would even become constitutive for the order of the economy, while planning would find itself restricted to a merely regulatory function. And that already would no longer be a planned economy in the centrally planned sense of Marxism-Leninism. It goes without saying that the ideologically-bound forces in the Soviet Union had to pursue this theoretical development with great mistrust and growing disapproval. At the same time, it happened that it strictly opposed the political views and goals of Stalin, who knew how to assert himself fully against his intra-party rivals and to consolidate his power conclusively towards the end of the 1920s: "The advocates of coupling plan and market were quickly labeled as anti-socialists; discussion in this direction was broken off and the theoretical scene was dominated from that point on only by party-conforming apologists of 'socialist conformity to plan'."[89] The centrally conceived plan, which was sanctioned by the party, was regarded from that point in time as infallible and received a

[88] *Ibid.*, pp. 65-70.
[89] *Ibid.*, p. 69.

binding-legal character. In this respect, the era of Stalin went beyond Lenin. To be sure, the monetary economy, as already introduced by the NEP, remained and, accordingly, the prices of commodities were also retained formally. But they became governmentally, administratively fixed quantities and ceased to be the beginning of a market instrument. In short, an almost pure centrally planned economy was created.

If one is interested in shedding light on the coordination system of the centrally planned economy in its elementary, essential features, one can start out from the Soviet economy's model of order.[90]

4.3.3 *The Coordination System of the Centrally Planned Economy (Order through Central Planning)*

4.3.3.1 The Basic Principle

Just like the market economy, the centrally planned economy, as it was realized to a considerable extent in the Soviet Union, is based on a basic principle of social-ethical relevance.[91]

If the basic principle of the market economy is to be characterized individualistically, in the sense that it declares as a fundamental value the right of freedom of individual economic subjects, whether producers or consumers, to pursue their individual utility, the basic principle of the centrally planned economy can be characterized as collective, insofar as not the economic interests of the persons or corporations participating in the economic process, but instead that of society constituted as the state is decisive for it. In other words, in the place of individual economic subjects there is the collective state, more precisely, the classless state of Marxist socialism, which *eo ipso* embodies the universal interest and thus the interest of everyone, because individual special interests have disappeared in it, along with the bourgeois classes. Therefore, the collective pursuit of interest by the communist state economy is also in the interest of

[90] Leipold assumes, but also notes explicitly, in his analysis of the central planning of the German Democratic Republic's system, that it corresponds to "that of other administratively planned socialist countries, especially that of the Soviet Union" (*Wirtschafts- und Gesellschaftssystem im Vergleich*, pp. 193-94). Because of the extensive systemic agreement, no decision between the two models will be made here.

[91] Kurt Dopfer, *Ost-West-Konvergenz*, Zürich, 1970, pp. 180 ff.

each individual. Thus, if in the market economy, as was noted in 4.2.2.1, the general welfare becomes a function of the individual or private maximization of interest, in the centrally planned economy, individual welfare becomes a matter of the governmental-social maximization of the collective interest. This means that the basis of the individual's share of aggregate output should no longer be individual performance, as with the basic principle of the market economy, but instead objective need, which is to be determined and met according to the plan of the collectivity: "The individual must put his self-interest last and hand over his personal performance output to society in its abstract entirety. Then he receives from the collectivity the share that corresponds to his objective need."[92] In short, distribution takes place according to justice of need, not justice of contribution. For many socially engaged persons, this means in terms of social ethics — whether correctly or incorrectly is left open for the time being — an in-principle, of course not always actual, superiority of this collectivist planning system relative to its market-oriented antagonist, which is trapped in individual self-interest.

4.3.3.2 State Collective Property and Central Planning

It has already been mentioned that there is no necessary relationship between the centrally planned economy as such and socialist collective ownership, as its predecessor, the German war economy during the First World War, shows. To be sure, strong reasons of a pragmatic nature speak for a coincidence of this kind. The more the means of production are found in the hands of the state, the greater is its direct commanding and planning power over production. Consequently, a relationship of affinity between central planning and state collective property can be established in actuality.

For its Marxist-Leninist form of realization, which has in the meantime become the historical type of the centrally planned economy in general, however, the relationship between state collective ownership and central planning is not merely of a pragmatic nature, though that, of course, plays an important role. It is, instead, in accordance with an order-specific logic. That already emerges from

[92] *Ibid.*, p. 181.

this system's basic principle. If the collectivity has absolute priority over the individual, and if individual interests must radically give way to the aggregate interest of society, then this also means that individual ownership, at least of the means of production, must be transformed into collective ownership. Especially according to the Marxist conception, economic inequality among the members of society, and with it the possibility of exploitation of one person by another, can be eliminated only in this way. But even more than this social-ethically inspired argument for the necessity of collective ownership in the centrally planned economy, the rational argumentation of the historical development of society in the sense of Marxist theory has weight. According to it, the organization of productive forces gains an increasingly social character in advanced industrial countries, thanks to the technological-functional division of labor. The large corporations, which accordingly must plan far ahead, increasingly become the powerful bearers of the economic production. But this produces a contradiction between the already social ways of production and the conditions of production in the capitalist economy, which are still based on individual ownership of property. That inevitably leads to anarchy and with it, judged by the enormously grown forces of production, to an inefficient economy. This contradiction cannot remain in existence. Its elimination lies in the historical necessity of the dialectically ongoing process of history. The transfer of private into social ownership of the means of production is, seen from this perspective, completely inevitable. To be sure, social property does not necessarily need to mean nationalization. The cooperative form is also possible. But this proves to be less compatible with the system of central planning and, moreover, has a lesser degree of social unity and equality. Only in the form of nationalization does the universal uniformity and equality of collective ownership fully reach its potential and is it totally available for central planning. Therefore, it unambiguously enjoys priority ahead of the cooperative form.

From all of that it emerges that the coincidence of state collective ownership and central planning is much more than a pragmatic matter for the communist central planning system, and also more than the consequence of a postulate of social ethics. It is, because and insofar as the economic theory of history of Marxism-Leninism raises the claim of scientific rigor, a kind of scientific dogma, which obligates the economy ideologically.

4.3.3.3 State Economy and Power Monopoly of the Communist Party

The Marxist-Leninist central planning system presents itself as a total state economy, insofar as the state not only possesses the planning monopoly, but also actually has the entire ownership of the means of production at its disposal. In any event, state ownership, as has already been pointed out, is the favored form of ownership. In relation to it, cooperative ownership, which exists primarily in the agricultural sector, plays a minor role.[93]

Despite the formal position of power, however, the state with its bureaucracy is not the highest decision authority in this system of central planning. The true decision authority rests in the hands of the Communist Party. In comparison to it, the authority of the state has merely instrumental and, consequently, subordinate importance.[94] Although a fair amount of party-bureaucratic pragmatism stands behind that, the reasons for it are, again, ultimately ideological in nature.

As early as Marx and Engels, the communists have special significance. According to the *Manifesto of the Communist Party* they have, as the only working-class party, "no interests separate and apart from those of the proletariat as a whole."[95] In order to appreciate this assertion and its consequences fully, one must understand that in the Marxist view the proletariat is the class of bourgeois society whose legal rights coincide with human rights in general,[96] and thus for whom, to put it differently, self-interest and aggregate-interest are unified. Consequently, the uniqueness of the communists consists in the identity of their interests with the aggregate welfare of society, even of humanity in general. Furthermore, they "have over the great

[93] Šik, *Wirtschaftssysteme*, p. 44. On 1 July 1988, however, the Supreme Soviet passed a law that places private cooperative societies, in which 700,000 persons worked on 1 October 1988 according to official figures, beside the state economy as a sector having equal rights, and thus enhances the status of cooperative ownership. Nevertheless, the state economy with its ownership structure remains the backbone of the Soviet economy.

[94] Šik, *Das kommunistische Machtsystem*, Hamburg, 1976, esp. pp. 145 ff. (The Leading Role of the Party).

[95] Marx and Engels, "Manifesto of the Communist Party," in *Collected Works*, Vol. VI, New York, 1976, p. 497.

[96] Marx, "Contribution to Critique of Hegel's Philosophy of Law," in *Collected Works*, Vol. III, New York, 1975, p. 186.

mass of the proletariat the advantage of clearly understanding the line of march, the conditions, and the ultimate general results of the proletarian movement."[97] All of this means, in plain language, that the Communist Party, thanks to its objective agreement with the aggregate welfare of everyone and its singular theoretical insight into the historical necessity of the revolutionary present and, consequently, as the embodiment of historical reason, must be ascribed a claim to leadership with the seizure of power by the working class and with the realization of socialism as the triumph of the collective interest over the class-bound individual interest. Lenin took over this claim and intensified it. Later, especially under Stalin, the Communist Party became the infallible power that also deserved to rule over the new state that springs from the revolution, because only under the party's leadership could the state coordinate, and thus plan, the economic process of society optimally in the interest of everyone. The structure of power that has originated in this way can be outlined as follows:

> The political power hierarchy consists of the apparatus of the party and of the state. The party takes over the leadership role in the economy and society. The power of the government serves as the main instrument of political leadership. It has the task of translating political and economic directives into concrete programs of action. There is a close union of personnel between the party apparatus and that of the state.[98]

Consequently, it can be said in summary that the monopoly of power in the party and state collective ownership are indispensable attributes of the Marxist-Leninist conception of the centrally planned economy. It is essential to state this fact, because it must be referred to in later discussions.

4.3.3.4 Economic Subject and Planner

It can be gathered from the preceding remarks that in the centrally planned system, as it has developed on the basis of Marxism-Leninism, there can be, strictly speaking, only a single economic subject:

[97] Marx and Engels, "Manifesto of the Communist Party," in *Collected Works*, Vol. VI, New York, 1976, p. 497.

[98] Leipold, *Wirtschafts- und Gesellschaftssystem im Vergleich*, p. 194. Today (1989/90) the power monopoly, though not the party's claim to leadership, has been given up.

the state, or its bureaucracy, which stands with that of the party in a relationship of personal union. There are, to be sure, in addition to the state, producers and consumers. But these groups lack the status of genuine economic subjects. The producing concerns are not business firms that, as in the market economy, have the responsibility of working out their own economic plans. Not only do they find themselves, apart from the unimportant cooperative sector, in the direct ownership of the state, but they are, whether cooperative or state concerns, subordinate to the directives of the planning authorities. And consumers, again excluding the marginal gray area of the black market with its high prices, have no freedom of choice in purchasing; they are instead allocated the consumer goods that the state offers them through its distribution network. Consequently, "The state is the only subject of economic policy and simultaneously the sole economic actor."[99] It controls both production and consumption. The planning of the entire economy lies ultimately as a whole in its hands. To be sure, the planning process takes place not only from the top down, but also from the bottom up. The individual concerns are involved in drawing up the national economic plan of the central government in the sense that they, on the basis of the planning project, work out a draft plan for themselves and must submit it to the top for approval, which, if necessary, also includes changes in the overall plan before its sanctioning by the competent party authorities. But this happens on the basis of centrally determined, though preliminary, data and plan-tasks about the production program and the use of the factors of production of the concern in question, so that the individual planning of the concern is actually prejudiced by the planning guidelines of the highest governmental planning office.[100] The decisive planner is and remains, consequently, the governmental bureaucracy, which is ruled by the party, as the genuine and exclusive economic subject.

4.3.3.5 Problems of Coordinating in the Centrally Planned Economy

In contrast to the system of the market economy, with its plurality of economic subjects and planners, in the centrally planned economy

[99] Walter Heinrich, *Wirtschaftspolitik*, Vol. I, 2nd Ed., Berlin, 1964, p. 113.
[100] Cf. Leipold, *Wirtschafts- und Gesellschaftssystem im Vergleich*, pp. 203-4.

there is only *one* economic subject, the party-controlled government, and only *one* plan, the one worked out by the governmental planning authority. But this monocentric basic system also faces the same fundamental economic questions as the polycentric system: What commodities should be produced and in what quantities? How and for whom should they be produced? These are questions that contain diverse coordination problems and that centrally structured planning must deal with in its own way. It is not possible here to develop their technique and process in detail.[101] That would lead too far and, above all, demand too much of the author. Consequently, restriction to the points that I consider most essential for our particular project is advisable.

1. The question of the what and how much of production concerns the elementary purpose of the economy in general, namely sensibly and sufficiently meeting the need for scarce goods that exists in society. In order to be able to fulfill this basic purpose, first of all, the economic degree of scarcity of the individual kinds of goods and, consequently, the respective magnitude of demand for them must be known. Only then can the problem be addressed, where and how the factors of production are to be employed, so that the greatest possible degree of agreement in the relationship between supply and demand is achievable with the different goods. In the market economy, it is the prices of goods that signal the difference between the demanded and supplied quantities. The higher the price, the scarcer the good. In the centrally planned economy, where the plan replaces the market, this indicator of scarcity is missing. As alternative determinants of scarcity there are, as already mentioned in 4.1.3, only macroeconomic planning balance sheets.[102]

Macroeconomic planning and accounting are, summarily speaking, the methods used in the centrally planned economy to ascertain for all goods, relative to a particular planning period and the respective planning region, the available and required quantities,[103] whereby — an unrealistic assumption — the latter must also be

[101] A detailed presentation of the macroeconomic planning and accounting process can be found in *ibid.*, pp. 199-245. See also Hensel, *Grundformen der Wirtschaftsordnung*, pp. 115-34.

[102] Cf. Šik, *Wirtschaftssysteme*, p. 55.

[103] Hensel, *Grundformen der Wirtschaftsordnung*, p. 121.

objectively determinable. In principle, this is a matter of preparing for each individual kind of good a planning balance sheet of such a kind that the stocks at the beginning of a planning period are recorded on the income side, while the budgeted stocks at the end of the planning period appear on the expenditure side. The difference between the revenue stock and the budgeted stock reports the degree of scarcity of the good in question. Only when the degree of scarcity is definite can the central planner decide what quantity of a good is to be produced in order to meet the need, and how the factors of production are optimally to be allocated, i.e. to be distributed and applied. Helmut Leipold explains impressively with a simple example, which can only be referred to here, how difficult an accounting and planning process of this kind is with a single good.[104] But in order to be able to calculate thoroughly the entire economic process and to construct a total economic plan, which also includes the micro-level, theoretically "just as many such macroeconomic planning balance sheets must be worked out as there are kinds of goods."[105] But that cannot be accomplished in practice, because it would require millions of planning balance sheets. Therefore, only large aggregates, not individual species of goods, are planned. But this means that micro-planning, capable of bringing the concrete relationship of supply and demand into even only approximate equilibrium, is impossible for this system, which the proverbial queues of customers in the Soviet Union drastically confirm. This makes obvious the coordination dilemma of the centrally planned economy, which cannot be remedied even by the best methods of electronic financial accounting, because it is tied to the system. Ota Šik points out the absurdity of this state of affairs concisely: "Working out a plan containing the quantity of every single product, even with the help of the most modern computer systems, would last longer than the time for which the plan is intended."[106] Thus, roughly speaking, the coordination dilemma of the pure market economy is that the merely decentralized-microeconomic planning approach leads to macroeconomic instabilities, and that of the centrally planned economy is that the central, macroeconomic planning system necessarily fails microeconomically.

[104] *Wirtschafts- und Gesellschaftssystem im Vergleich*, pp. 208 ff.
[105] Hensel, *Grundformen der Wirtschaftsordnung*, p. 127.
[106] *Wirtschaftssysteme*, p. 23.

2. For the coordination system of the centrally planned economy, not only the question of how the "what" and "how much" of production can be ascertained and planned in the best way in terms of needs-justice is posed. Just as important is the problem of realizing the plan: How should commodities be produced, so that the plan can be realized as well as possible? Even the best plan, if it is not fully realized, misses the basic goal of all economies: supplying society with scarce, and thus economically limited goods, whether commodities or services, sufficiently in terms of both quantity and quality. The realization of a plan, however, requires economic output. The more output is produced, the more optimal the realization of the plan. In this elementary sense, the centrally planned economy must also be a performance economy.

Output can be produced in one of two ways: efficiently or inefficiently. An economic output is inefficient if the expenditure required by it is larger than its yield, and efficient if the yield exceeds the expenditure. The degree of efficiency of an economic output grows to the degree that the yield exceeds the expenditure. This is measured objectively in terms of profit. Profit can be roughly defined as the difference between the proceeds from the sale of goods produced and the total costs that must be expended for their production and sale. And from that it becomes clear that the centrally planned economy must also pay attention to profit as the measure of the efficient production of output, in the interest of optimal realizing its plans.

In the system of the market economy, the profit interest of producers is simply of fundamental importance. According to its basic principle, corporate and individual profits on the labor side are not only permitted, but also justified, if they are based on genuine market performance and, therefore, benefit producers and consumers, as well as society as a whole. In this sense, they are regarded as motivation-incentives and indicators of efficiency for competitive economic activity and, consequently, as something positive. The centrally planned economy, as it appears here, has, on the contrary, a confused relationship with profit. From its basic principle and the ideological premises according to which the market economy and capitalism form an inseparable unity, the profit interest can be qualified only as a capitalist monster, as inhumane exploitation of labor by capital, in short, as a social sin that must be eliminated by a non-profit-oriented kind of economy. In fact, however, it was impossible for the concerns and their workers to get by, for the cited reasons — and quite early — without veiled appeal to the profit interest based on the performance idea. That includes, besides more political-psychological stimulations such as the Stachanov Principle,[107] wage differentiation, which was originally scorned, but then introduced nevertheless, but above all the bonus system. According to it, concerns are paid considerable bonuses, which flow down to workers of all categories, for realizing their plans, and especially for exceeding them.[108] With this kind of output incentive, which, in contrast to the capitalist species of competition, was dressed up as "socialist competition," but was in fact profit-oriented nonetheless, an attempt was made to increase the economic efficiency of the centrally planned economy. Successes did not fail to appear. But they never achieved the efficiency of production, and did not even come close to the degree of consumption-correct production, of goods as in the market-economic system. Again, this has an explanation that is immanent to the system.

The primary reason is that, according to the centrally planned economic system, increases in income, which are not based upon effectively higher or better outputs, are the order of the day.[109] In the end, it depends only on realizing or, better yet, exceeding the formal plan. And that is also achieved when concerns manipulate the information for the central authority in such a way that plan targets originate from them that can be relatively easily realized or exceeded, and thus indirectly program the bonus profit. Furthermore, the reference numbers in the planning targets can tempt concerns to wangle comfortable bonus allowances and, consequently, profit advantages. If, for example, the gross production of a particular good is expressed for purposes of plan realization in units of weight, then it will be in the self-interest of the concern to produce primarily heavier products: "In a screw factory, whose gross production target was prescribed in tons, the tendency was to manufacture the heaviest screws that it could; if the target was stated in terms of the number of screws, it could be realized most simply with the most and the smallest screws possible."[110] These are meaningful examples, which can be increased

[107] Named after the Soviet mineworker Aleksei G. Stachanov (1906-77), whose legendary productivity was publicized and was celebrated propagandistically as a model performance target (Hero of Labor).

[108] Cf. Hensel, *Grundformen der Wirtschaftsordnung*, p. 138.

[109] *Ibid.*, pp. 138-39. See also Šik, *Wirtschaftssysteme*, p. 33.

[110] Hensel, *Grundformen der Wirtschaftsordnung*, p. 142.

as much as one wishes. They all show that in the centrally planned system, even with the formal observance of plan instructions, the production of goods can easily ignore the real need for them in society and, consequently, the concern's realization of the plan can be combined with inefficient employment of the factors of production. That, of course, is far from an economically and socially acceptable solution to the problem of allocative coordination. Thus, one must say in summary with Ota Šik: "A macroeconomically central planning organ is not in a position to ensure the optimal development of the production of individual goods to satisfy the needs of consumers (individual, concerns, institutions), with the most effective use and qualitative development of the factors of production."[111]

3. Finally, the basic system of the centrally planned economy also has to do with the third basic economic question: Who should derive the utility from the economic activity? In other words, the problem of the distribution of the national product is also posed here.

From the doctrinaire Marxist-Leninist perspective, it can be said, of course, that there can no longer be any problem of distribution resulting from interests in the centrally planned economy according to the socialist pattern. This kind of society produces with socialized means of production for a society without classes, and thus without partial interests, whereby the distribution question, in contrast to the case of the capitalist class economy, is unnecessary from the start. But this claim does not stand up to reality: "The employment of scarce resources is also subject to the competition of partial interests in socialism."[112] Leipold names three different interested parties: "first the *party bureaucracy*, second the economic *bureaucracy*, and third the *consumers*."[113] Each of these "socialist interest groups" attempts to influence the economic-political formulation of goals in such a way that the distribution of resources and goods takes place to its own advantage.

In itself it would be the responsibility of the Communist Party, which represents the common good according to the Marxist-Leninist self-understanding, to coordinate this actually existing competition of interests in a way that serves the aggregate interest of society. But

[111] Šik, *Wirtschaftssysteme*, p. 79.
[112] Leipold, *Wirtschafts- und Gesellschaftssystem im Vergleich*, p. 200.
[113] *Ibid.*

this kind of coordination, which favors none of the different interest groups, is far from the reality. It is no more than a dream.

As Šik is able to say from intimate knowledge of the actual state of affairs, the party leadership is in fact dependent upon the party bureaucracy, because "in the *long term*, the party apparatus has the greater share of the power."[114] Without its support, the party leadership could hardly survive in the long run. Thanks to this interlinking, the interests of the party bureaucracy have the greatest power to assert themselves when it comes to establishing economic goals. Its demands, which are directed "primarily towards the distribution of resources for its own management apparatus, for police and security institutions, and for defense and armament organizations,"[115] which also includes safeguarding the privileges that the members of the party and state bureaucracies enjoy, have decisive priority. All of this is expressed in over-proportional growth of the bureaucratic apparatus and a corresponding increase of the public spending ratio,[116] which is, of course, also a growing tendency in the market economies (see *BEE*, Vol. II, pp. 353-54).

The interest-defined party or state bureaucracy must compete with the economic bureaucracy. The latter aims "at a constant expansion of the accumulation fund," i.e. investments as "the guarantee of being able to realize plans and simultaneously as the prerequisite of high rates of growth in the given sphere of output."[117] These interests also have great importance, since the party and state ultimately live from the output power of the economy. Nevertheless, the conflict of interests remains. The higher the public spending ratio of the national product, the fewer the means for economic investment, especially in the sphere of the production of consumer goods. This opposition of interests, which is also encountered mutatis mutandis in market economies, is thus by no means remedied in the centrally planned economy, but is of a kind that awards the party and state bureaucratic interests a system-specific overemphasis.

The weakest position is occupied by consumers. Their specific interests also depend in the centrally planned economy "on the increase of real income and with it a qualitatively and quantitatively

[114] Šik, *Das kommunistische Machtsystem*, p. 87.
[115] Leipold, *Wirtschafts- und Gesellschaftssystem im Vergleich*, pp. 200-1.
[116] Šik, *Das kommunistische Machtsystem*, p. 237.
[117] Leipold, *Wirtschafts- und Gesellschaftssystem im Vergleich*, p. 201.

good supply of consumer goods."[118] Its ability to assert itself, however, is small.

Decisions about the level of real income rest unilaterally with the party and state bureaucracy, which sovereignly has the socialized ownership of the means of production at its disposal and, therefore, also has the distribution of the total yield of the economy in its hands. Independent labor unions, which at best could gain recognition for the interests of workers by political or economic means of exerting pressure, such as strikes, do not exist.

On the other hand, as far as the supply of consumer goods is concerned, it is established by the compulsory plan. Because market mechanisms are absent, its influence over the purchasing behavior of consumers remains "relatively ineffective."[119] The party and economic bureaucracies also have the say here. One consequence is the traditionally notorious discrimination against the production of consumer goods relative to military and industrial goods.[120]

All in all, the question of distribution also proves to be a sore point in the communist, centrally planned system. It is mitigated by the artificial maintenance of low prices for basic groceries, free education, free medical and other services, etc. Nevertheless, explosive tensions arise from it, which, despite the repressive mechanisms of the party and state, can even lead to open political unrest, as happened in Romania during the difficult supply crisis of late autumn 1987. Although it appears to be stabile internally, the Soviet Union is not excepted from this. There have repeatedly been violent social protest actions there on the part of frustrated workers,[121] which, because they have been concealed, have not become well known in the West. Thus, not only in the real market economy, but also in the real centrally planned economy, there are, in contradiction to communist ideology, fundamental economic conflicts of interest in the question of distribution and, therefore, an additional deficit of coordination.

4. A final point needs to be made in this context. Similarly to the case of industrial capitalism, a compulsion to economic growth also exists

[118] *Ibid.*, p. 202

[119] *Ibid.*

[120] Cf. Michael Kaser, *Wirtschaftspolitik der Sowjetunion*, Munich, 1970, pp. 202 ff.

[121] See Karl Schlögel, *Der renitente Held*, Hamburg, 1984, esp. pp. 47-66 and 91-127. In the meantime (1989) the strike movement in the Soviet Union has taken on proportions that are serious for the regime.

in the communist, centrally planned system. The higher the rate of economic growth, the more easily the aspirations of the different "socialist interest groups" can be taken into account and the more stabile is the system. One prerequisite of economic growth is a certain degree of capital formation, because the investment possibilities of the individual industries depend upon the quantity of capital formation, and the growth potential of the economy as a whole is in turn dependent upon the investment possibilities of the individual industries. An interest in capital formation, therefore, also plays a dominant role here. It is not pursued by private persons, firms, and corporations, but by the state or party bureaucracy, which directs the economy according to its plans. At the same time, however, instead of private profit maximization, the maximization of soviet power, in which, together with the connected material privileges, the ruling class of the nomenklatura participates, is the driving stimulus. It is not without justification that one speaks in this respect about "state capitalism." But capitalism, in whatever form, means the priority of the interests of capital formation ahead of human, social, and ecological interests. Whether this priority stands in the service of private or state utility, the consequences for people, society, and the environment are analogous. Therefore, it cannot be maintained that in the state planned and directed industrial economies of the Soviet type, the economic coordination mechanisms have more humanly and environmentally just consequences than in Western industrial capitalism. Contrary to the ideological view of the situation, the empirical results point in the opposite direction. The real opportunities for participation in the active formation of the economy are minimal for those who are active at the lowest level within this centralized system.[122] The standard of living, flagrantly so in housing, is on the average significantly lower than in the Western industrial nations,[123] in part because of the inherent lower economic efficiency of the economy, in part because of the priority of industrial goods, heavy, and military industries relative to the production of consumer goods, which is explained by the interest in the maximization of power. And since for a long time the communist central control system had to do with an economy that stood in a pronounced, extensive phase, and

[122] Cf. Nutzinger, "Marktliberalismus und Produktionsorganisation," in *Liberalismus im Kreuzfeuer*, p. 123.

[123] See Otto Hörmann, *Von Breschnew zu Gorbatschow*, Graz, 1987, pp. 246-62.

for that reason was oriented as a high priority towards increasing the quantity of particular goods, an extremely quantitatively-oriented concept of growth came into practice, with enormous wear and tear of natural resources,[124] which necessarily led to serious environmental damage.[125] Consequently, the imperative to coordinate the elementary factors of production in this way, and thus to structure them in such a way that the lowest possible burdening of the environment emerges from them, is of no less urgency in the Eastern industrial society — cautiously expressed — than in the Western counterparts.

4.3.4 *The Limits of the Centrally Planned Economy*

Like the market economy, the centrally planned economy is also a reality. Both systems have been realized and, consequently, have also provided proof of their actual ability to function, even if to very different degrees, obviously not in ideal, but in incomplete and, consequently, limited forms of order.

For theoretical reasons, central planning, even in the most favorable, theoretical cases, can never be more than extremely imperfect.

Perfect planning presupposes, first of all, that the economic process in its entirety follows definite, rationally recognizable, and practically applicable laws. Moreover, it would presuppose perfect knowledge, capable not only of recognizing these law-governed regularities infallibly, but also, beyond that, being in a position to record all of the basic economic data that determine the present state of the economy, to foresee the possible interactions of the persons acting in the economic process, and to predict future development exactly. Even if the economic process were in its essence actually of a rational nature, and thus, in principle, also rationally fully ascertainable, the possibilities of knowledge would nevertheless remain limited. For complete knowledge in this sense does not exist. And it is all the less capable of existing, the more complex the economy and, therefore, the interlinking of its process become.

[124] "The Soviet economy is extremely inefficient, because it consumes one and a half times as much energy and material per unit of national product as an industrialized country of the West. At least, Gorbachev declared that during his visit in the port city Murmansk on 1 October 1987" (Adam Zwass, "Gorbatschews Reform im Rahmen des Systems," *Neue Zürcher Zeitung*, No. 20, 26 January 1988, p. 39).

[125] This is impressively documented by Boris Komarov, *Das große Sterben am Baikalsee*, Reinbek bei Hamburg, 1979.

From these facts it follows, on the other hand, that complete knowledge is less essential for the planning of a less complex economy. This was still largely true of the beginnings of the Soviet economy. For a long time, it found itself in a pronounced, extensive phase during which it mostly had to deal with a restricted number of industries and to produce in the highest possible quantities relatively few products, which were easily definable in terms of planning data, such as cement or steel. Under such relatively simple conditions, central planning not only was easier, it even had its merits, because, for example, "politically desired, preferred production development can be obtained more quickly with the help of governmental redistributions, following plans, than in an economy without central planning."[126] The Soviet Union has achieved indisputable economic progress, not only, but primarily, in the construction of heavy industries relevant to armament and with the accomplishment of the space program[127] — of course, at the expense of agriculture, consumer goods industries, and services. To the degree that the economy developed, however, the demands upon it grew, the number of planning data increased astronomically, and the intensive rather than extensive growth factors, especially the new technologies, became ever more important. In short, to the degree that it increased in complexity, its rational knowledge deficit increased and with it the fallibility of the central economic planning. There are, of course, also constantly wrong decisions by individual firms with decentralized planning of the economy, because the knowledge deficit is also in play, somewhat differently, there. But they become noticeable relatively quickly, because of the negative consequences for the market, and require firms to correct their economic plans in the interest of their own survival. "Feedback from unpredicted developments to the plan during its time period" in the central planning system, however, is "practically impossible." Therefore, "centralized decisions are either correct or incorrect and, accordingly, the entire system is then controlled correctly or incorrectly. In view of the previously cited problems, cases of correct control will be rare, and the lacking flexibility hinders timely reactions to mistakes."[128]

[126] Šik, *Wirtschaftssysteme*, p. 78.

[127] Cf. Kaser, *Wirtschaftspolitik der Sowjetunion*, pp. 190-201 (Economic Growth), Šik, *Wirtschaftssysteme*, pp. 77-78.

[128] Kleinewefers, *Reformen für Wirtschaft und Gesellschaft*, pp. 443-44.

The fundamental limits of the centrally planned economy are revealed, therefore, in the impossibility of being able to plan a highly-complex economy all the way down to the subtle sphere of the microeconomy, in the absence of perfect knowledge about "complexly organized phenomena."[129] They are based on the serious "shortages of the Soviet directed planned system,"[130] as they express themselves in the above mentioned coordination deficits and, based on that, in a less efficient use of resources, a pronounced weakness of innovation, and a distribution of the national product between the state and households that discriminates against consumers. Moreover, there are the consequences of the system for persons: the lack of room for free initiative, entrepreneurial action, responsibility, etc., completely apart from the minimization of personal rights to freedom, and related possibilities of political participation in the formation of the state, society, and economy. All of that includes potential and already emerging instabilities, which lay open the limits of the communist central planning system. The necessity of profound reforms is, therefore, increasingly indispensable.

All seriously intended reform efforts of national economies with central planning, as they have gotten going for years, apart from Yugoslavia, in Hungary, China, Poland, and most recently under Gorbachev[131] in the Soviet Union, have one thing in common: they are all directed, even if in different degrees, towards market modification of the planning system. Lenin's "New Economic Policy" was already characterized by it.[132] Since then, the explosive question of the possibility and necessity of connecting plan and market is no longer silenced. The Prague Spring of 1968 stood decisively under its sign. Even though it was silenced by the military intervention of the Soviet Union in Czechoslovakia, it has arisen anew elsewhere. This is an unmistakable indicator that a plan-obsessed centrally planned economy must lead into a dead-end street. This shows that, as the limits and deficits of the market economy led to their relativization by a governmental safeguarding ordering or planning framework, so also that of the centrally planned economy led to its relativization by

[129] On the fundamentals, see Friedrich A. von Hayek, *Die Theorie komplexer Phänomene*, Tübingen, 1972.

[130] Šik, *Wirtschaftssysteme*, pp. 78-84.

[131] Mikhail Gorbachev, *Perestroika*, New York, 1987.

[132] *BEE*, Vol. II, p. 467.

market-economic correctives. But this means, in other words, that the centralized coordination system is just as incapable of being absolutized in the economy as the decentralized system.

4.3.5 *Relativization of the Centrally Planned System*

The ideal, pure centrally planned economy, just like the pure market economy, has never existed. During the period from Stalin to Brezhnev, however, it approached its pure form. But even then it did not go off without concessions in the direction of the market economy. One only needs to think about the formal retention of the prices of commodities, which were introduced by Lenin, or the marginal toleration of the black market.[133] In the meantime, the correction of the central planning system by market-economically inspired reforms in many Eastern national economies has already progressed to a considerable extent. There are not only theoretical and empirical-practical arguments for this, but also principled-ethical reasons. This still requires clarification.

As has become apparent from 4.3.3.1, the basic principle of the communist centrally planned system can be characterized as collective. Not individual self-interest, but collective general interests should be decisive here. In the place of the liberal value-complex of self-interest, responsibility, and liberty, there is the socialist value-structure of collective interest, social duty, and solidarity. It also marks out universal human values, without which there can be no humanly just order of the economy. But, as the absolutization of the liberal value-complex — which was already mentioned in 4.2.4 — leads to the perversion of humanity in the market economy, the absolutization of the socialist value complex does the same to humanity in the system of centrally planned and centrally controlled socialism.

133 As is well known, the kolkhoznik in the Soviet Union, going back to the time of Stalin, may cultivate up to 0.5 hectares as private land. A large share of the resulting production is sold over the not-governmentally-controlled commerce under market conditions. The case is similar with the small, secondary-job cooperatives — constituting a genuine shadow economy — which have had a turnover in recent years of more than 350 million rubles worth of goods and services annually (see also 4.3.3.3, fn. 93). This is according to Vladimir Pankov, Leader of a Section of the Institute for World Economy in Moscow, Interview of the *Tages-Anzeiger* (Zürich), 22 June 1988, p. 2. After its legalization by the new laws (see 5.2.2.4, fn. 54) the value creation of the shadow economy contributes 14 to 16 billion rubles annually (*ibid.*).

The collective interest without self-interest degenerates into minimization of the desire to perform; social duty without liberty leads to the paralysis of the powers of initiative; and solidarity without individual responsibility leads to an anti-communitarian parasitism. All of this offends against a humanly just and economically rational order of the economy and society. It should be noted that the offense does not lie in the cited values themselves. Collective interest, social duty, and solidarity as such are just as essential basic values as the liberal values. The problem is in dealing with them non-relationally. For only in relationality to their opposites values can they safeguard their humanly just substance. And for that reason their absolutization, as if each of them on its own were already the epitome of humaneness, is out of the question.

In other words, all of this means that the basic principle specific to the communist planning system can exist only in relation to the liberal system. And that explains its in-principle relativity. The empirical result is that, speaking succinctly, "planning and market" are not absolutely opposed, but instead are mutually dependent upon one another. It has already been emphasized in other passages that this fact refers to the reality-content of relationality and relativity as basic criteria of the humanity originating from faith, hope, and love.

It can now be said in summary that in this relational and, consequently, also relative sense, the value basis of the communist planning system, like that of the liberal market economy, is acceptable from the demand of human justice, as it is understood here. What is not acceptable, however, is one value basis or the other, if it claims absolute validity for itself. But from that it follows that the humanity originating from faith, hope, and love must keep critical distance from the two contrary basic economic systems to the degree that they extremize their fundamental principles — the principle of economic liberty, on the one hand, and the principle of economic attachment, on the other hand — and thus must understand them alternatively. Or, expressed positively, it must speak out in favor of a coupling of freedom and attachment, of spontaneous market and regulated macro-planning. The question of what this coupling can and should look like is an essentially technical one, whose answer, consequently, is also based on the criteria of economic rationality, not only on those of human justice. This new problem of the ethically and technically responsible relationship between "market and plan," wherein the systematic question of the economy becomes focused, must now be addressed at a level at which the "should be" and the "can be" are reflected and thus make possible normative guidelines that take human justice and economic rationality into account. In our terminology, such guidelines are maxims. The next step, then, is to turn to the establishment of maxims that relate to the systematic question in the economy.

5. EVALUATION AND DECISION MAXIMS FOR THE SYSTEM QUESTION IN THE ECONOMY

5.1 On the Concept of Maxims

As far as their formal, fundamental aspect is concerned, the maxims of social- and economic-ethical decision-making have been discussed in detail in the first volume of this work.[1] Nevertheless, it will be beneficial for understanding the following discussion better to summarize once again the comments made there.

While the criteria of the humanity originating from faith, hope, and love (creatureliness, critical distance, relative reception, relationality, fellow-humanness, fellow-creatureliness, and participation) are norms of a prescriptive kind that express what must take place in the principled-ethical sense and, therefore, absolutely, maxims are concerned with norms of both prescriptive and descriptive content, because they are related to real and, in that respect, empirically-establishable states of affairs. In other words, this means that they cannot be derived deductively from the criteria — which would merely produce nice-sounding empty formulas — but that they are to be found, though under the criteria's normative guidance, by means of perceived states of affairs and in virtue of a rationally provable process of judgment. Therefore, maxims must not only stand up to the super-rational claim of human justice, as the humanity originating from faith, hope, and love produces it; they must also prove themselves in the face of the rational claim of economics. In this respect, they are subject to the principle of falsification and, therefore, are already of only relative validity. Consequently, their obligatory force, in contrast to that of the criteria, is not irrevocable, for which reason they also can by no means be anything like absolute structural principles of a "Christian economic order." They understand themselves, much more modestly, as

[1] *BEE*, Vol. I, 8.1.

normative guidelines, which constantly require critical checking when it comes to answering the question of which order possibilities of the economy can best be answered by Christian humanity in the time of the penultimate.

This double character makes it necessary that in the process of finding the maxims, basic considerations that are twofold, though objectively inseparable from one another, are also to be used: some under the viewpoint of human justice and some under that of economic rationality.

5.2 Basic Considerations for Finding Maxims

5.2.1 *Basic Considerations from the Perspective of Human Justice*

With the basic considerations for finding maxims with respect to the systematic question in the economy, it is at first a matter of the ethical evaluation of the two fundamental order systems, as they have been clarified in the previous section. The contrary basic principles, on which they specifically support themselves, stand at the center. As has already been explained (4.2.2.1), the market system is based on the individualistic principle of the self-interest of the individual economic subjects, the pursuit of which under conditions of competition contains the best guarantee of the increase of general social welfare. In contrast (4.3.3.1), the centrally planned system is based on the collectivist principle of the general social interest, in the belief that its directed planning necessarily also optimizes the welfare of individuals. In the latter case, the values of collective interest, social duty, and solidarity are emphasized, while in the former case, the values of self-interest, economic freedom, and individual responsibility are stressed. In the process, the market economy has the reputation of an in-principle egoistic system, the centrally planned economy on the contrary has that of an in-principle altruistic system. Not only socialist social critique, but to a great extent also Christian social critique, whether conservative or, as with liberation theology, revolutionary in character, consequently, is directed, at least for the most part, against the principle of the market economy. And does that not get to the core of the problem? Is it not humanly just that self-interest, because it is egoistic, must give way to the altruistically-oriented common good?

5.2.1.1 Self-Interest and Common Good

It is already clear from the previous discussions[2] that, when the question under discussion is addressed from the viewpoint of human justice as it satisfies the criteria of the humanity originating from faith, hope, and love, one must be on guard against a rash answer. When self-interest, individual responsibility, and economic freedom are evaluated according to the criterion of relationality — to emphasize this once again — they are not simply to be equated with egoism. These values degenerate into egoism, however, if, denying their relationality, they separate from the opposing values of universal interest, solidarity, and economic relationships, and thus become absolutes. But not only egoism is a transgression of humaneness in the sense of the humanity originating from faith, hope, and love. That is no less true of altruism, which, turning the common good into an absolute, replaces egoistic self-assertion with self-sacrifice. Love as humanity, as God intends it, no more sacrifices the I to the Thou than the Thou to the I. It says: "Love your neighbor as yourself!" This integrative love, in which the antagonism of love of self and love of neighbor is sublated, also surpasses altruism.[3] It is the way of being of perfection, the eschatological ultimate, namely the Kingdom of God and, therefore, is not attainable in the penultimate, in our world of imperfections with its personal and structural evil. When one nevertheless seeks to compel them in moralizing legalism, for instance by violent elimination of self-interest from the real economy, the outcome will not be an increase in humanity, but the opposite. As Pascal perceptively put it, "Man is neither angel nor beast, and it is unfortunately the case that anyone trying to act the angel acts the beast."[4] But what is possible and in all decisiveness imperative is relational dealing with self-interest and with the interests of others, with individual responsibility and solidarity, with economic freedom and economic relationships. And that means critical distance from any attempt to absolutize these values, and thus their limitation by the present and, consequently, their conscious relativization. In this sense, which brings their specific criteria into effect, the humanity

[2] Especially *BEE*, Vol. II, 1.3.5/6, 3.3.7.1, 4.2.4, and 4.3.5.

[3] I Cor. 13,3: "If I give all my possessions to the poor, and if I surrender my body to be burned, but do not have love, I gain nothing."

[4] Blaise Pascal, *Pensées*, Frg. 358, trans. A. J. Krailsheimer, Harmondsworth, 1966, p. 242.

originating from faith, hope, and love quite simply has normative relevance for the ethical decision in the question of ordering the economy at the level of maxims.

It has already been explained in an earlier context that the market economy can be received ethically only with this kind of relativization of its basic principle, and also that it actually can exist only in this way. An extreme deregulation of the market, when individual economic subjects can assert their self-interest without consideration for others, and thus the weaker are abandoned without protection to competition for markets with the stronger, must lead ultimately to the self-destruction of the market economy. It stands — whatever one may say to the contrary — in contradiction to its original self-understanding. This certainly proves itself with Adam Smith's concept of the market economy, with which classical economic theory begins, and which is undoubtedly embedded in an ethical context that limits self-interest.[5]

5.2.1.2 Adam Smith's Concept of the Market Economy

Adam Smith is the author of not only *The Wealth of Nations*, the epochal work of classical market theory, but also *The Theory of Moral Sentiments*, which was the more important work according to his own estimation. If one takes only the former work into account, then it is certainly understandable that Smith holds to the egoistic image of the human person as utility- and profit-maximizing *homo oeconomicus*." He can boldly declare that the person who "intends only his own gain" in commercial transactions is "led by an invisible hand," so that "by pursuing his own interest he frequently promotes that of the society more effectually than when he really intends to promote it."[6] For Smith, self-interest is in fact a fundamental motive for efficient commercial activity and, therefore, for the formation of national prosperity. But he does not mean that in the sense of absolutizing self-interest into egoism.

[5] See especially Horst Claus Recktenwald, Introduction to his German translation of Adam Smith's *The Wealth of Nations* = *Der Wohlstand der Nationen*, Munich, 1974, pp. xv-lxxix; Recktenwald, "Ethik, Selbstinteresse und *bonum commune*," in Georges Enderle, ed., *Ethik und Wirtschaftswissenschaft*, Berlin, 1985, pp. 143-61; Recktenwald, "Ökonomische und christliche Ethik," *Neue Zürcher Zeitung*, No. 48, 27/28 February 1988, p. 95; and Hermann Sautter, "Wie moralisch ist der Markt?" *Evangelische Kommentare*, 16 (1983), pp. 602-5.

[6] Adam Smith, *The Wealth of Nations*, Oxford, 1976, IV.ii.9, p. 456.

As early as the first paragraph of his *Theory of Moral Sentiments*, we read:

> How selfish soever man may be supposed, there are evidently some principles in his nature, which interest him in the fortune of others, and render their happiness necessary to him, though he derives nothing from it except the pleasure of seeing it. Of this kind is pity or compassion, the emotion which we feel for the misery of others, when we either see it, or are made to conceive it in a very lively manner.[7]

By generalizing, Smith also calls this emotion "sympathy."[8] According to him, sympathy is a natural inclination to empathize with other persons, to understand them, and to accept their interests, in short to behave in solidarity.[9] But that means, in other words, that the solidarist interest in the other person is just as much a part of the basic substance of human nature as the self-interest that thinks about one's own welfare. It would hardly be an exaggeration of the outlined situation if one were to conclude from it that self-interest and interest in others are understood relationally here and, therefore, that the self-interest relevant to the market economy, without its relative right to deny altruistically, is coupled to the respect for social duty of the counter-interests, and thus the common good. Horst Claus Reckten-wald, a scholar of Smith, also arrives at a similar conclusion:

> There is no trace of *absolute* freedom in human conduct, of unrestricted egoism, in this sober analysis. On the contrary, a sense of duty even forms a cornerstone of his ethical system. But also from the other extreme, there obviously can be no talk in Smith's model of an exclusive or rapturous altruism or even an abandonment of the personal for the sake of a community.[10]

This is unmistakably about a concept that reckons with people who are certainly not altruists, but also not egoists, and with whom, instead, the interests of others restrict self-interests and self-interests must promote the common good. But that points in the direction of human justice, as it is defined under the criterion of relationality.

[7] Smith, *The Theory of Moral Sentiments*, Oxford, 1976, p. 9.
[8] *Ibid.*, p. 10.
[9] Cf. Franz-Xaver Kaufmann, "Solidarität als Steuerungsform," in *Markt, Staat und Solidarität bei Adam Smith*, ed. Kaufmann and Hans-Günter Krüsselberg, Frankfurt, 1984, pp. 158-84.
[10] Recktenwald, Introduction to Smith, *Der Wohlstand der Nationen*, p. xxxviii.

There is still something additional to be noted. The market, as Smith understands it, is not constrained morally only in the sense that the market subjects, by virtue of the basic sentiment of sympathy, are demanded in terms of personal ethics to pursue the interests of other persons relationally, especially the disadvantaged, together with their self-interest. This demand also has its structural-ethical side. Ultimately, it achieves a harmonization of contrary interests only because a concealed order exists that is able to control the conflicts of self-interest in the competition of the market economy in such a way, i.e. in a morally qualified sense, that this serves the aggregate welfare. Smith, however, never systematically works out what this order is. He merely intimates it in a few passages, most succinctly with the metaphor of the "invisible hand." It is the invisible hand that drives the balancing of interests towards the utility of the whole, even if the individual fails in terms of personal ethics and egoistically has only his own advantage in mind. Neoclassical economic theory simply identifies this puzzling hand with the market laws. But there can be no doubt that Smith himself saw a higher power behind it. Thus, he speaks in *The Theory of Moral Sentiments* of the self-seeking of unfeeling land owners, who are concerned only about "the gratification of their own vain and insatiable desires," but nevertheless must "divide with the poor the produce of all their improvements," because "they are led by an invisible hand to make nearly the same distribution of the necessaries of life, which would have been made, had the earth been divided into equal portions among all its inhabitants."[11] And why is this true? Only because there are market laws that supposedly compel this on their own, if not at every moment, at least in the long run? Smith sees it differently: "When Providence divided the earth among a few lordly masters, it neither forgot nor abandoned those who seemed to have been left out in the partition."[12] Thus, a providential order, a kind of pre-established harmony of interest, is the true reason that, in a world of economic inequalities, the market works to balance them out.

This means that the market as such does not create order oriented towards balancing out, thanks to its own mechanism and, consequently, on its own. On the contrary, it leads to harmonization of contrary interests, because and insofar as it is embedded by providence

[11] Smith, *The Theory of Moral Sentiments*, pp. 184-85.
[12] *Ibid.*, p. 185.

in a moral order. In opposition to neoclassical theory, therefore, the market, according to Smith, as Hermann Sautter correctly emphasizes, "does not make morality unnecessary, but is instead dependent upon it, if it is to perform its 'socially-irenic,' conflict-defusing function and steer the individual-economic endeavors for success towards common goals."[13] And, indeed, this is true, as may already have become clear, both in the personal-ethical and in the structural-ethical sense of the word. In short, Smith opts for the competitive-market economy, because, according to his conviction, it is ordered in such a way that it orients the self-interest of the economic actors towards the increase of the common good and, consequently, supports the humanly just conduct of the individual economic subjects.

Consequently, one will hardly be able to reproach Smith, at least from the point of view of economic ethics as it is understood here, for having failed to recognize the ethical relevance of the market-ethical order problem. He was fully aware of it. But what remains questionable with him is the anchoring of the ethos in nature. The relationality of self-interest and the interests of others or the universal interest is rooted, according to his theory, in the natural constitution of the human person. And the evening out of these contrary interests is based on a natural order. Therefore, market order must not be created, it must only be discovered. This is basically a matter of facts, not tasks. This fatal tracing back of the ethical "ought" to a natural "is" includes the fallacy that the "should be" "is," and thus releases an anthropological and economic optimism that obscures its view of the reality of personal and structural evil in the economy. The problem with his concept of the market consists in that, not in its supposed idolization of economic egoism. It offers handles to an idealization of market reality, even the formation of an ideology that makes the market taboo.[14] The often-heard reproach that he had no sense whatsoever for the disharmonies, conflicts of interest, and contradictions, and thus the limits of the market economy is, of course, exaggerated. He was completely in the open about the fact that all of this exists, and that one cannot simply rely on the "natural" ethos of

[13] Sautter, "Wie moralisch ist der Markt?" p. 604.

[14] Cf. Knud E. Løgstrup, *Norm und Spontaneität*, trans. Rosemarie Løgstrup, Tübingen, 1989, p. 244, who, citing Jørgen Pedersen, notes with justification that nothing could have harmed the liberal system of the market economy more than this, that its pioneers "pronounced it a natural order and that interfering with it was a kind of desecration." [translated by G. Enderle]

economic actors or on the "natural" order of the market. Therefore, he was also open to institutionalized regulations in the economic process. In particular, he granted the state, as has already been mentioned,[15] positive tasks of preserving order, partially to created the framework conditions for competition capable of functioning and partially to meet existing or possible market deficits.

On the whole, it can be said with Recktenwald that Smith's classical market concept is incompatible with extreme answers to the question of economic order, whether they are based on unbridled self-interest, on absolute freedom, or on unrealistic altruism and collective compulsion.[16] In any event, it is far from a kind of competition that follows the law of pure self-assertion in a social-Darwinist manner and balks at both personal-ethical and structural-ethical commitments in the economy. Economic amorality was not the project of the moral philosopher Adam Smith. It had completely different fathers, such as the cynic Bernard de Mandeville, whose notorious *Fable of the Bees* makes vice the origin of the common good.[17] Under such conditions — Manchester liberalism can be offered as an example — though, the market economy stands in strict opposition to the humanity originating from faith, hope, and love.

5.2.1.3 Basic Conditions of the Reception of the System

It is evident from the preceding discussion that the fundamental principle of the market economy, if it is understood in relation to its counter principle and, consequently, as relative, as it is in the case of Adam Smith, can be accepted by human justice in the sense of the humanity originating from faith, hope, and love. The basic condition for its possible reception is thus the acknowledgement of its relativity in openness to the relative truth of the value-meaning opposed to it.

What is true of the fundamental principle of the market economy is no less true of the fundamental principle of the centrally planned economy. It is also to be received under this basic condition. Evaluated at the level of criteria, neither of these two principles is better than the other. One can decide individually for either one of them, as

15 *BEE*, Vol. II, 2.5.3 (p. 352).

16 Recktenwald, "Ethik, Selbstinteresse und *bonum commune*," pp. 153-54.

17 Cf. Alois Riklin, "Mandevilles Bienenfabel," in Riklin, *Verantwortung des Akademikers*, St. Gallen, 1987, pp. 173-89.

long as the reception remains relative and, consequently, is attested that it does not represent an ultimate value, and thus is not to be equated with the humanity of the Kingdom of God, but remains the humanity of the penultimate, with all the imperfections and questions attached to it.

With that, it is stated at the same time that relational dealing with these basic principles never means their reconciliation in a comprehensive synthesis. A synthesis of this kind would be the entirety of humanity, the humanity of the Kingdom of God, the absolute orientation point, towards which all ethical efforts and endeavors in the personal sphere and in the institutional sphere of politics and economics have to be directed. But this humanity is a promise, not a feasible, ethical agenda. What can be "done" ethically is the renunciation of playing the basic principles of the two contrary economic systems against one another ideologically, as if they were absolutes, absolute goodness on the one hand and absolute evil on the other. Dealing with them relationally means the decisive rejection of every attempt to turn them into ideologies, of evaluating them as "*verités opposées*," as Pascal would say, to which one is only able to do justice in such a way that one lives with the paradox of their contradictoriness in the penultimate and respects both of them at the same time. That does not mean a cheap compromise, and even less an illusionist covering up of the explosive conflict of values, as constantly happens in our world, and thus by no means a comfortable balancing out.[18] It means instead that the inevitable conflicts in society are resolved undogmatically. Depending upon the particular situation, one fundamental principle can clearly receive priority over the other in such a way that it is given predominance temporally, not in principle. But it must keep its predominance within limits and be open to necessary corrections from the other side, which in the best case will lead to better opportunities for solutions, but, judged according to the absolute, never to solutions that are simply just, but instead always to solutions that are marked by structural evil and, therefore, cause guilt. The decisive question now is how this ethically-based relativity of the fundamental principles of the two contrary economic systems squares with their reality, in other words, whether these systems can be relativized according to the subject matter in the same way, or whether differences of a fundamental kind exist here. This is

[18] See *BEE*, Vol. I, pp. 187-88.

a question in which the viewpoints of human justice and economic rationality interconnect with one another, but which, for systematic reasons, is to be addressed from the latter perspective.

5.2.2 *Basic Considerations from the Perspective of Economic Rationality*

It has already been explained (4.2.4 and 4.3.5) that neither the decentralized market system nor the central planning system exists in its pure form. Market economies without any comprehensive (i.e. oriented towards the entire economy) planning element no more exist than centrally planned economies without connections to markets. One often speaks, therefore, in view of actual situations, of mixed systems. It is also said that, by virtue of the inner dynamic of the modern process of industrialization in the East and the West, a tendency of convergence exists between the two contrary basic systems, which must lead in the long term to their mutually approaching one another. Is there such a convergence? Can the decentralized market system and the central planning system mix at all with one another? And do "convergence" and "mixing" coincide with what is understood here by the term "relativization"? Or does this mean something fundamentally different? These are the question that must now be addressed.

5.2.2.1 The Question of the Convergence of the Decentralized Market System and the Centralized Planning System

The theory of the convergence of the two basic systems, always rejected by Marxism-Leninism, has found its advocates above all in Jan Tinbergen[19] and John Kenneth Galbraith.[20] It says, to put it succinctly, that as a consequence of parallel technological developments and the general use of analogous planning and coordination techniques, the Western market economy and the Eastern planned economy have a tendency to become a single system.

[19] (1) Jan Tinbergen, "Kommt es zu einer Annäherung zwischen den kommunistischen und den freiheitlichen Wirtschaftsordnungen?" in *Hamburger Jahrbuch für Wirtschafts- und Gesellschaftspolitik*, Vol. 8, Tübingen, 1963, pp. 11-20; (2) Tinbergen, "Die Rolle der Planungstechniken bei einer Annäherung der Strukturen in Ost und West," in *Wirtschaftsplanung im Ostblock*, ed. Erik Boettcher, Stuttgart, 1966, pp. 35-53.

[20] John Kenneth Galbraith, *The New Industrial State*, 2nd Ed., Boston, 1971; and *Economics and the Public Purpose*, Boston, 1973.

For Galbraith, technological development stands in the foreground. It led, in his opinion, in the United States to the separation of macroeconomics into two totally different spheres: the sphere of "around twelve million smaller firms" controlled by individual managers and the sphere of a "handful of giant corporations" led by collective organizations. He calls the former sphere the "market system" and the latter the "planning system."[21]

The "market system," as Galbraith defines it, includes the part of the economy that is characterized by a large number of small or medium-sized firms. In its "admixture of monopoly and competition," it conforms "in broad outline to the neoclassical model" of imperfect competition.[22] In other words, approximately free market conditions are found in it.

In the Western industrial society, the "planning system" stands opposite the "market system" with increasing weight. It embodies, even if not exclusively, at least specifically, the world of the large firms, the giant corporations. The replacement of the "individually guided firm" by the "decision-making group," or, more precisely, the collegial or collective organization, is characteristic of it.[23] The guiding intelligence of such a business firm, "for product planning, to devise price and market strategies, for sales and advertising management, procurement planning, public relations and government relations," is "not an individual but a complex of scientists, engineers and technicians; of sales, advertising and marketing men; of public relations experts, lobbyists, lawyers and men with a specialized knowledge of the Washington bureaucracy and its manipulation; and of coordinators, managers and executives.... This is the technostructure."[24] Thus the "technostructure," which Galbraith also calls "collective intelligence,"[25] makes the managerial decisions. And it does not do this spontaneously, as does the individual manager, but rather deliberately, on the basis of its economic plans. The "planning system," therefore, means the domination of a scientific-technocratic oriented bureaucracy in the leadership of the firm.

Thanks to the superior informative, cognitive, and financial power that is unified in the large concerns, according to Galbraith, the

21 Galbraith, *Economics and the Public Purpose*, p. 43.

22 *Ibid.*, p. 44.

23 *Ibid.*, pp. 79-80.

24 *Ibid.*, pp. 77-78.

25 *Ibid.*, p. 77.

"planning system" now possesses the leadership in the entire economy of Western industrialized society: "The planning system strongly dominates its environment; the market system accommodates itself to forces that it does not control."[26] The market loses its importance as a coordinating factor. Thus, in the "planning system," the conditions of competition are no longer decisive for price formation; they are instead subject to its control.[27] All of this and more leads Galbraith to the thesis that, not only do the firms of the capitalist and the communist world, as bureaucratic oligarchies of their participants, constantly become similar to one another, but also the industrial system of capitalism, since planning takes the place of the free market within it, constantly becomes more like the centralized industrial system of the communist sphere.[28]

If Galbraith starts out in his argument for his convergence thesis from parallel technological-economic developments in Western and Eastern industrial society, Tinbergen begins with the fact that after the Second World War in the West, market economies have taken on a character indicative of master planning or global control, while in the East, under the pressure of reform discussion, a change of direction of imperative detailed planning towards indicative global control is partially taking place.[29] Above all, he discovers in the Soviet system a process of coming together in the techniques of planning and coordination through the acceptance of refined, econometrically-based methods, such as input-output analysis, which was developed in the West by Russian emigrant Wassily Leontief. This process of coming together in planning methods also implies, according to Tinbergen, a similar process in social mechanisms.[30] The question is posed, however, whether the convergence tendencies diagnosed by him — the same is true of Galbraith — are actually substantial or only accidental tendencies.

As far as Galbraith's thesis is concerned, although it says much that is true in the details, its starting point, the dichotomy of "market system" and "planning system" in Western industrial society, is

[26] *Ibid.*, p. 173.

[27] *Ibid.*, p. 106 ff.

[28] Galbraith, *The New Industrial State*, pp. 392 ff.

[29] Cf. Egon Tuchtfeldt, "Wirtschaftssysteme" (IV: "Konvergenz der Wirtschaftssysteme?"), in *Handwörterbuch der Wirtschaftswissenschaften*, Vol. 9, pp. 346-50.

[30] "Die Rolle der Planungstechniken bei einer Annäherung der Strukturen in Ost und West," p. 48.

highly problematic. It is indeed correct that a small number of large corporations stand facing a large number of small or medium firms, and that the former are as a rule able to exercise unequally important market power relative to the latter. Likewise, one can hardly fail to recognize structural similarities in the organization of the large corporations in the West and the giant combines in the East. And, likewise, it cannot be disputed that wide-reaching managerial planning is of decisive importance in the large Western firms. But in view of that, to speak already of a "planning system" that finds itself in principled opposition to the "market system" does not get started. For this suggests, on the one hand, the idea that the market economy as such is a non-planned economy and, on the other hand, the idea that the large corporations were simply removed from the competitive market conditions in their economic decisions. Both are inconsistent with reality.[31]

It has already been explained in 4.1.3 that planning must and does also take place in the market economy, as in every economy. But there, in contrast to the governmentally, centrally planned economy, the subjects of the planning are the individual, private corporate units, which, whether large or small, must create their economic plans, unless they wish to produce out of the blue. Even in Galbraith's planning system, planning is performed by the individual industrial giants, not by central planning authorities. Therefore, the planning structure remains fundamentally decentralized. Consequently, there can be no discussion of a fundamental approach to the centrally planned system of the Soviet economy.

To the other assertion, that large corporations, thanks to their monopolistic position in price formation, are able to withdraw from market forces, the deciding point has likewise already been worked out.[32] Actually Galbraith points there to one of the biggest sore points of the market economy. Monopolies and quasi-monopolies exploit their market force to establish their prices autonomously through elimination of direct competition. But, in the process, they always run into effective market limits. Even if every immediate competitor is eliminated, they are still at least subordinate to restriction by the declining budgets of their actual or potential customers. If the prices

[31] On the entirety of Galbraith's convergence thesis and its critique, see the detailed study of Walter Adolf Jöhr, *Galbraith und die Marktwirtschaft*, Tübingen, 1975.

[32] *BEE*, Vol. II, pp. 450-51.

are set too high, nothing will be purchased, because those who are interested lack the money. Therefore, "Restriction arises, which Galbraith nowhere says, from the fact that a large number of firms compete for the income of the last consumer."[33] And in this respect, his "planning system" remains bound by the decentralized coordination mechanism of the market economy.

Similar comments are to be made concerning Tinbergen's convergence argument. It also starts from unquestionably correct observations. On the one hand, Western market economies have, in order to optimize and to restrain socially their decentrally structured coordination systems, reached for methods of master planning, even overall planning. And, on the other hand, with the mathematically based planning techniques or instruments applied in the West and in the East, "certain tendencies of moving together are perceivable."[34] It must be asked here, however, whether the common application of mathematical coordination techniques should already be regarded as the product of a fundamental transformation of the two basic economic systems. A comprehensive and careful investigation of East-West convergence arrives at an unambiguous "no" to this question:

> It is the respective *scheme of distribution of economic decision authority* that give the mathematical methods in the respective economic systems their *material* content. In the market economy with master planning, economic decision authority is assigned to the individual economic actors and the market mechanism takes over the securing of the consistency of the total execution of economic coordination, as well as the selection function relevant to the optimal allocation of the factors of production.... It is different in a socialist economic system of the centralized type, where decision authority lies largely in the hands of the central authority. The rationality of the total execution of economic coordination is measured there exclusively by the rationality of the predisposed plan norms."[35]

But that means that it does not depend upon the formal kind of planning. It depends upon their material execution, which also determines the social order of the system in question. And the material execution is fundamentally decentralized in one system and fundamentally centralized in the other. At this fundamental point, it does

[33] Jöhr, *Galbraith und die Marktwirtschaft*, p. 36.
[34] Tuchtfeldt, "Wirtschaftssysteme," p. 349.
[35] Kurt Dopfer, *Ost-West-Konvergenz*, Zürich, 1970, p. 457.

not come to a convergence of the opposing systems, despite the similarities of their planning techniques. Therefore, Kurt Dopfer arrives at the unambiguous conclusion: "If the techniques of economic coordination and optimization are merely a formal container, which has no meaning in terms of content, then obviously we cannot from a *common application of such techniques* in the Eastern and Western economic orders reach a conclusion about a *coming together of their 'social mechanisms'*."[36]

Consequently, a material or fundamental convergence of the two basic systems has not taken place and, in principle, also cannot take place. Their relativization, as it is understood here, consequently, also cannot be synonymous with their supposed convergence in the sense of a middle- or long-term mutually mixing of the decentralized market economy and the centralized planned economy.

5.2.2.2 Delimitation of the Relativization Principle of the Convergence Thesis

The preceding discussion of the question of systematic decision in the economy has led to a two-fold result:

Between the value-determining basic principles of the decentralized market economy, on the one hand, and the centrally planned economy, on the other hand, there exists a relationship of relationality. Therefore, in their difference, they are of equal value. This forbids the absolutization of both basic principles or the value-meanings established by them, which leads at the same time to their mutual relativization.

The situation is different with the contrary coordination systems of the market economy and the centrally planned economy. They mutually exclude one another. An economic order cannot simultaneously exist on both systematic foundations, and thus be mixed.[37] The systematic basis is either decentrally or centrally structured. Even Ota Šik, who actually would like to go beyond the mere opposition of the two basic economic systems, agrees with this: "I think about

[36] *Ibid.*, pp. 457-58.

[37] Hermann Sautter also emphasizes emphatically that "an unregulated juxtaposition of governmental and private-economic activity" would block "the efficiency of both a market-economic and a governmental control system" ("Die marktwirtschaftliche Idee im ordnungspolitischen Dialog mit Entwicklungsländern," in *Märkte und Mächte*, ed. Klaus Wilkens, *et al.*, Stuttgart, 1987, p. 82).

just this opposition when I say: The development of production is determined either by the market mechanism, or by directed planning that excludes the market mechanism."[38] Therefore, one must decide between the two systematic foundations. A different issue, however, is whether I am led in making this decision by the insight that the ethical basic value content of the two systems are to be understood relationally and to be taken seriously, or whether I disregard their relationality. If one does the latter, if one acknowledges in a doctrinaire-liberalistic manner only the basic values of the market economy or in a doctrinaire-Marxistic manner only those of the centrally planned economy, then the critical sense of the limits and, therefore, of the in-principle imperfection of one system or the other will be lacking.

If, on the contrary, the relationality of the opposed basic values is taken seriously as one criterion of human justice, if one sees that the individualistic market system, based on individual responsibility, can exist only as socially ordered, and that the collectivist planning system, obligating the idea of solidarity, degenerates because and insofar as the individual responsibility of the economic actors have insufficient room in it, then the two basic systems must be bound in a framework that relativizes them, which provides validity to the values and goals that they cannot validate on their own. With Šik, this reads as follow:

> There is no possibility of mixing this kind (i.e. directed-centralized) of systematic procedure and the market-oriented production decisions of firms. If, however, macroeconomic planning is understood as master planning or as macroeconomic distribution planning, by means of which different social-economic goals are combined in one way or another and are implemented with the help of economic-political instruments that conform to markets, so that the market mechanism is not only retained, but is eventually completed, there exists the possibility of a coupling of the market mechanism and macroeconomic planning.[39]

From this it follows that "coupling" can mean here neither the mere mixing of the two fundamentally different coordination systems of the economy nor their synthesis into an optimal order. The coupling or connection of "market and plan" must, instead, be achieved on the

[38] Ota Šik, *Wirtschaftssysteme*, Berlin, 1987, p. 55.
[39] *Ibid.*, pp. 55-56.

basis of one basic system or the other. The question is now posed: What possibilities exist in principle in this respect?

5.2.2.3 Fundamental Possibilities of Combining Market and Plan

When the term "market-plan combination" is used in this particular context, of course, "plan" should not be understood to mean the decentralized planning that takes place even in the market economy, which is practiced by the individual corporate units and, therefore, is micro-economically oriented and motivated by self-interest. Planning in this context means instead the macro-economically and thus overall-economically-oriented planning that has or, more cautiously, should have the goal of safeguarding the aggregate welfare of society.

The question of the market-plan combination is posed, because both in the decentralized market system and in the centrally planned system serious coordination deficits[40] appear, which suggest a correction by the order-political counter-principle. Consequently, this is about, expressed concisely, the plan-modification of the decentralized market economy, on the one hand, and the market-modification of the centrally planned economy, on the other hand.

The term "modification" already entails that the market-plan combination cannot mean anything like a relationship of equilibrium between the two contrary methods of coordination. Modification means the definite formation of a substance, in this particular case the formation or goal-directed regulation of the market by planning elements or of the plan by efficiency-increasing market elements. This is in accordance with the preceding discussion of the convergence problem, according to which the intended coupling of market and plan can be achieved in reality only on the basis of one or the other of the basic economic systems. And from that it follows that fundamentally only two possibilities of connection of this kind are conceivable. *Either the market is order-politically constitutive and the plan only regulatory or the market is only regulatory and the plan constitutive. A third possibility must be excluded.*

Evaluated by the criteria of the humanity originating from faith, hope, and love, both possibilities of market-plan combination, taken in themselves, are acceptable, because and insofar as in both the value-content specific to the basic systems are related to the other,

[40] *BEE*, Vol. II, 4.2.3 and 4.3.4.

and in this respect relativized. But, according to our ethical premises, according to which economic rationality must prove to be humanly just and human justice must prove to be economically rational,[41] it is not only about whether a market-plan combination is able to satisfy the criteria of human justice, it is also about how it is to be evaluated from the perspective of economic rationality and, connected to it, what its chances of being realized look like. This difficult question must now be taken up.

5.2.2.4 Market Modification of the Planned Economy

In accordance with the preceding restrictions, a market-modified planned economy is to be understood as an economic system that is based constitutively on the central plan, but with which market elements are given room for action, in order to raise the economic efficiency of the system, in the interest of better supplying society with the goods it needs.

In the course of efforts to improve the unsatisfactory efficiency of the communist planned economy with the help of market instruments, Yugoslavia, Hungary, and China, above all, have developed different models of reform in the last quarter century. Recently, the Soviet Union, which has traditionally shown little interest in reform, has also adopted this trend. This is not the place to analyze the reform systems that already exist or are in the process of emerging individually and to present them in their functional structure.[42] Apart from the fact that they are, for the most part, still in an experimental stage and, therefore, are also difficult to pin down, the scope of this book precludes analyzing them. Moreover, what matters in the following discussion is not a detailed picture of these concepts of reform, but only the type and consequences of their plan-market combination.

[41] *BEE*, Vol. I, 4.2. and Vol. II, 3.3.7.2.

[42] A succinct but precise overview of reform models on the basis of plan-market linking is found in Šik, *Wirtschaftssysteme*, pp. 77-108. On economic-system development (through 1975) see also *Handwörterbuch der Wirtschaftswissenschaften*, Vol. 9: Jirí Kosta, "China" (pp. 353-69); Dietrich Schönwitz, "Jugoslawien" (pp. 370-82); Günter Hedtkamp, "UdSSR" (pp. 383-99); Helmut Leipold, "Ungarn" (pp. 399-412). See also Henner Kleinewefers, *Reformen für Wirtschaft und Gesellschaft*, Frankfurt, 1985 ("Die ungarische Wirtschaftsordnung heute," pp. 141-81; "Die jugoslawische Gesellschaftsordnung heute," pp. 183-252).

As far as the reform efforts in the Eastern economy on the whole are concerned, those of the present top man in the USSR, Mikhail Gorbachev, step into the foreground, because of their enormous consequences for the entire communist world. They are authentically tangible in his bestseller, *Perestroika*.[43] At the very beginning, he launches an explosive critique of the present state of the Soviet economy,[44] which the structural afflictions cited in 4.3.3.5 largely confirm: a huge decline in the national income growth rate (p. 19); a widening of the gap with the advanced industrialized nations in the efficiency of production, quality of products, scientific and technological development, the production of advanced technologies, and the use of advanced techniques (p. 19); wasteful use of natural resources and energy relative to other developed countries (p. 20); "wage-leveling", which leads to parasitical attitudes (p. 20); inability to meet the growing requirements in housing, high-quality food, everyday consumer goods in general, as well as improving health services and education (p. 21), etc. From all of that Gorbachev draws the no less explosive conclusion:

> We can no longer run our affairs like that. The new economic mechanism must put matters right. It must become a powerful lever, a motivating force for resourceful quality performance. Every enterprise must proceed from real social demands to determine production and sales plans for itself. Those plans must be based not on numerous detailed assignments set by higher bodies, but on direct orders placed by government organizations, self-accounting enterprises and trade firms for specific products of appropriate quantity and quality. Enterprises must be put in such conditions as to encourage economic competition for the best satisfaction of consumer demands and employees' incomes must strictly depend on end production results, on profits.[45]

These are critical statements, which clearly point towards a market correction of the Soviet planned economy. This is about combining "the advantages of planning...with stimulating factors of the socialist market."[46] It is just as clear, however, that the combination of plan and market intended by Gorbachev must happen with subordination of the market to the plan: "But all this will take place within the

[43] New York, 1987. On Gorbachev's reforms, see Hans-Hermann Höhmann, "Wirtschaft und Politik in der 'Perestrojka'," *Osteuropa*, 38 (1988), pp. 537-49.

[44] pp. 17-25.

[45] pp. 85-86.

[46] p. 90.

mainstream of socialist goals and principles of management."[47] The question is whether this kind of plan-market combination can be consistent with itself and how it will interact with the overall social system of the Soviet Union.

The fact that the plan-market combination, even in subordination of the market under the plan, is difficult for the communist centrally planned system to digest can be easily ascertained. The fate of the New Economic Policy (NEP),[48] which for the first time combined market elements with central planning and which Lenin proclaimed after the break from war communism at the Tenth Party Congress in 1921, is already an important index of it. In its collapse — it was, despite considerable success, dismissed as a right-deviationist mistake in 1928 after the victory of the party leftists under Stalin — a piece of logic was revealed. This also indirectly burdens the reforms of Gorbachev, who, incidentally, appealed explicitly to Lenin and the NEP to legitimate his project ideologically.[49]

If the market modification of the centrally planned system is to become more than empty words, that has grave consequences for the overall social system in which it will take place. It means, according to the cited demands of Gorbachev, that firms must on their own orient their production and sales plans on the basis of social needs and, at the same time, convert to profit-oriented economic leadership under conditions of competition. But that can only be gotten underway if firms become autonomous, responsible corporations with power of disposal over their means of capital and production, and if they are given the opportunity to make their own investment and distribution decisions. This includes, however, regardless of whether the firms are organized according to the planning principle now followed in the Soviet Union or according to the principle of planning by the workers themselves, a decentralization of economic power, which in the long run will also have political consequences in the direction of a pluralistic society with division of power, and thus under conditions of giving up the power monopoly of the Communist Party. A fundamental conflict between the monopolistic, dominant position of the privileged party and state bureaucracy and the

[47] pp. 90-91.

[48] *BEE*, Vol. II, pp. 467-69.

[49] Höhmann labels "Perestroika" straightforwardly as the "Leninist Renaissance" ("Wirtschaft und Politik in der 'Perestrojka'," p. 540).

economic goals of Gorbachev's reform, with its latent political consequences, is consequently inevitable, unless it is defused to such an extent that it becomes rather cosmetic.

A no less fundamental conflict emerges from the combination of centralized and decentralized control processes, as Gorbachev foresees it. On the one hand, according to it individual firms should plan their own production programs at the microeconomic level according to market-economic methods; on the other hand, however, the Soviet principles of economic management, which are of a centralized, directed nature, nevertheless remain in effect at the macroeconomic level. Therefore, central plans of an imperative character will still exist as the constitutive element of the Soviet economy. But they "must not be based on numerous detailed assignments set by higher bodies."[50] They must, in other words, be restricted to the planning of large aggregates. But can this be consistently brought together in the sense that the market stimulants are able to eliminate weaknesses of economic efficiency in the central planning system, as Gorbachev and his reform tendency expect, without calling itself into question? By and large, the discipline of economics agrees in answering this question negatively. Henner Kleinewefers says bluntly in his work on the "reforms of the economy and society," which is both theoretically and empirically well-grounded: "The obligatory planning of aggregates is incompatible with the free development of its components. In such cases, a conflict of micro- and macroeconomic control processes is preprogrammed, which normally does not improve the general system characteristics."[51] And he draws from that the compelling conclusion:

> If obligatory planning is given up at the microeconomic level, it must be given up overall. With that, one enters the extremely wide spectrum of the possibilities of indicative planning and control at the macroeconomic and mesoeconomic levels, combined with market and exchange self-regulation at the microeconomic level. One finds many Western industrial states in this region today, as well as Hungary and Yugoslavia.[52]

This means, however, that the renunciation of imperative microplanning or detailed planning, if consistently carried through, must ultimately lead to a change in the system. With indicative planning,

[50] Gorbachev, *Perestroika*, p. 86.
[51] *Ibid.*, p. 435.
[52] *Ibid.*

no binding directives are imposed on factories or firms. They receive from governmental authorities, however, prognostic data concerning the presumed and also desired development of macroeconomic quantities, such as those of the population, production, consumption, and investment in the different branches of industry, etc. And from that they must then themselves draw the necessary conclusions for their own planning on the basis of the market relationships. Under such conditions, consequently, the market becomes constitutive for the economy, while the plan has only a regulatory function, which runs contrary to the principle of structure of the centrally planned economy. With that, the dilemma comes into view, before which every serious attempt at market reform of the centrally planned economy stands: It inevitably contains a potential to transform the system.

This dilemma thus consists, expressed pointedly, in the fact that the centrally planned economy in fact cannot at all be reformed in the sense of relativizing it by the market economic counter-principle: "As with every self-reforming planned economy, Gorbachev stands before the same unsolvable task; previous experience shows clearly that *market mechanisms* are not easily combined with the instruments of the planned economy and the *directives of the Politburo*, which, even if somewhat clipped, remain the same."[53] If market forces are given effective room for action in the economy, then the imperative centrally planned system, together with the state-capitalist structure of ownership, begins to totter, which necessarily has short-term or long-term destabilizing consequences for the complete structure of the communist society. If, on the other hand, the centrally planned system remains the constitutive basis of the Soviet economic order, then the market forces cannot come into play effectively and the reform impulses will fizzle out.[54] In one case, therefore, the reform strives

[53] Adam Zwass, "Gorbatschews Reform im Rahmen des Systems," *Neue Zürcher Zeitung*, No. 20, 26 January 1988, p. 39.

[54] Gorbachev's reforms are based upon three bodies of law: 1. Law concerning state companies (more independence from the centrally planning authority, more responsibility in production). 2. Law concerning individual activity (room for private initiative in small individual or family companies in the service sector). 3. Law concerning cooperative societies (since 1988), which puts cooperative ownership on equal footing with state ownership and introduces financial market incentives. The third body of law holds the strongest potential for reform, because it formally reduces the sphere of power of the centrally planning authority (Gosplan) and opens up room for competition, since its intention is that the state instructions from the central

for an order of the economy that leaves the framework of the centrally planned and directed economy; but that is already no longer merely reform, and instead a change of the basic system. In the other case, the reform denies the market forces any substantial effect, insofar as it remains with mere touchups, and thus at the surface; and that is disguised preservation of the system, but not reform. This dilemma also typically shapes the reform discussion in the Soviet Union.[55] Expressed succinctly, Gorbachev is countered, on the one hand, by critics who say that in the communist system there is fundamentally no room for the market and liberal spirit, because plan and market, direction and competition mutually exclude one another.[56] On the other hand, his reform ideas receive pointed intensification, aimed at the introduction of the market economy in the Soviet Union. According to these people, the planned system does not characterize socialism and is unproductive.[57] That is how things actually stand.

The conclusion that should be drawn from this situation, that the centrally planned economic basic system cannot really be reformed, and thus also cannot be relativized, should by no means be transferred fallaciously to socialism in general. Socialism and the centrally planned economy are not the same thing,[58] as Nikolai Shmeliov has also emphasized. If the centrally planned economy is not reformable, socialism is. Socialism[59] is compatible with a market-plan combination, with which the market constitutes the economic order and the plan only regulates. As already stated, the reforms, to begin with in Yugoslavia and Hungary, now also in Poland, and to a lesser degree in China, are headed in this direction.[60] The national economies of

authority to individual companies may contribute no more than 60% of their capacity. Actually, however, the majority of companies are still working at full capacity according to governmental instructions, so that the decentralization effect is hardly given a chance.

[55] Cf. Henning Sietz, "Lenins NEP — Gorbatschews Perestroika," *Neue Zürcher Zeitung*, No. 39, 17 February 1988, p. 5.

[56] For example, economist L. Popkova, *ibid.*

[57] For example, Nikolai Shmeliov, member of the Institute of North America in Moscow, *ibid.*

[58] Cf. *BEE*, Vol. II, 4.3.1.

[59] Socialism is understood here as a social order with dominantly public ownership of large capital.

[60] Out of the wealth of literature, only a few informative titles are named here: Yugoslavia: Gudrun Lemân, *Das jugoslawische Modell*, Frankfurt, 1976; Dragoljub

these countries still favor the socialistic common ownership of the means of production, of course no longer in a dogmatic way, since they also permit private ownership of them, in agriculture, in the commercial services sphere, in small and partially even medium industry. But they go, even though with different degrees of resolution, from imperative to indicative planning in the framework of a responsible, competition- and profit-oriented kind of economy in individual factories or firms, whereby joint ventures with Western firms are also already permitted to a considerable degree. All of that points to market-order socialism and, consequently, to a type of economic order on the foundation of the basic system of the market economy. This other way, of course, also stands open for the Soviet Union. Incidentally, it is urgently suggested by Ota Šik, when he writes that the "huge loss of effectiveness and consumption could be overcome in the USSR only with the help of really consistent and well considered reform in the direction of a socialist-market-economic system."[61] For Šik, it is more than doubtful, though not simply ruled out, that Gorbachev's reform will ultimately lead to this kind of transformation of the system.[62] The forces of resistance to changes that could

Durovic, *et al.*, *Das Gesetz über assoziierte Arbeit*, ed. Secretariat of Information of the S.F.R. Yugoslavia, Belgrade, 1977; Dennison Rusinow, *The Yugoslav Experiment 1948-74*, Berkeley, 1977; M. Sindjit, *Self-Management Planning in Yugoslavia*, Belgrade, 1981; Edvard Kardelj, *Contradictions of Social Property in a Socialist Society*, Belgrade, 1981. Hungary: Ottó Gadó, *The Economic Mechanism in Hungary*, Leyden, 1976; Gadó, "Die Strukturpolitik vom Aspekt des Mechanismus," *Marketing in Ungarn*, 1980; Gerd Biró, "Zwischenbilanz einer wirtschaftlichen Weichenstellung," *Europäische Rundschau*, Vol. 8, No. 4 (1980), pp. 75-82; Paul Marer, "Economic System," in *Südosteuropa-Handbuch*, ed. Klaus-Detlev Grothusen, Vol. V: *Ungarn*, Göttingen, 1987, pp. 276-301; Roland Schönfeld, "Außenwirtschaft," in *ibid.*, pp. 383-416. China: Xue Muqiao, *Sozialismus in China*, Hamburg, 1982; Harald Mey, *et al.*, eds., *Wirtschaftsreformen und neue Entwicklungsstrategien in der Volksrepublik China*, Frankfurt, 1986; Rolf Dubs, "Die chinesische Wirtschaftsordnung," in *Dokumentation zur Wirtschaftskunde*, ed. Society for the Development of the Swiss Economy, No. 104, Zürich, 1986, pp. 1-14; Willy Kraus, "Wirtschaftsreformen in der Volksrepublik China," in *Aus Politik und Zeitgeschichte*, ed. Federal Office for Political Education, No. B 39/85, Bonn, 28 September 1985.

[61] Šik, *Wirtschaftssysteme*, p. 91. Similar ideas are also expressed by the Polish economist Jan Winiecki, "Ein 'Marshall-Plan' für Osteuropa?" *Neue Zürcher Zeitung*, No. 277, 26/27 November 1988, p. 95.

[62] *Ibid.*, p. 86. — Gorbachev's firm statement during a meeting with journalists and artists at the beginning of July 1987 suggests as much: There have been proposals "that go beyond the borders of our system, for instance, to do away with the (central) planned economy. We have never gotten involved in that, since we have the intention of strengthening socialism, not of replacing it with another system" (cited by Sietz, "Lenins NEP — Gorbatschews Perestroika," p. 5.).

endanger the system are still strong in the Soviet Union, as elsewhere.[63] As a result of the considerations in this section, it remains that the market modification of the centrally planned economy, considered from the perspective of economic rationality, proves to be a possibility that is actually to be excluded.[64] What is true in this respect of the planned modification of the market economy? This is the next question.

5.2.2.5 The Plan-Modified Market Economy

1. If the market-modification of the centrally planned economy breaks down at its self-contradictory nature, this suggests the question whether the same thing is true of the plan-modification of the decentralized basic system of the market economy. What can be said about this?

As has become obvious, the centrally directed planning system excludes any kind of effective market-competitive coordination of the economic process, because it cannot permit independent economic subjects with autonomous decision authority, without abandoning itself. The market economy, on the other hand, does not by any means stand in an in-principle contradiction to every form of planning, but is, as was explained in 4.1.3, itself a planned economy, though of course, a decentrally planned economy. Its planners are the countless economic subjects who are motivated by self-interest and whose individual plans are coordinated through market competition. At the same time, classical market theory assumes that the individual-economic striving for success that is expressed in the diversity of individual plans also optimizes the economic aggregate welfare of everyone, without directly intending it. Now, however, the reality of the market economy shows that this happens only insufficiently, because it happens defectively, and that it thus arrives at difficult

[63] In China, in the meantime — after the great student demonstrations of June 1989 — they have at least temporarily gained the upper hand again. That will, to all appearances, also result in a turning back of the economic reform. This is according to the China specialist Armin Bohnet, "Chinas Wirtschaft im Umbruch," *Neue Zürcher Zeitung*, No. 184, 11 August 1989, p. 33.

[64] For Karl-Heinz Ruffmann, achieving the essential modernization of the Soviet economy without encroaching on the existing system of control or even altering it substantially is tantamount to squaring the circle (*Fragen an die sowjetische Geschichte*, Munich, 1987, p. 159).

coordination deficits, which have been discussed in 4.2.3. The individual economic interests always have the tendency, even disregarding the rules of competition, to be realized absolutely, without consideration of other persons. And that leads to monopolistic distortions of markets, to asocial and anti-ecological developments, in short to crass contradictions between individual interests and the aggregate interest in the economy and, therefore, to social instabilities, which call the system as such into question. If the market economy is to avoid breaking down at this point, then decentralized planning requires enlargement by a national-economic framework of order and control, and thus by an economic policy that is not necessarily governmentally monopolized, but is nevertheless comprehensive and, in this respect, centrally-guided.[65] There is, in fact, no pure, but only a decentrally-constituted market economy. All existing market economies practice, to be sure, to quite different degrees, governmental economic policy which regulates them within a framework established according to plan (economic legislation, economic policy, partial economic activity, e.g. postal and telephone services). But that amounts to a market-plan combination that is supposed to support the market economy with maintenance of economic efficiency in its function of evening out interests and defusing conflicts. Such a subsidiarily-understood modification of the market economy by a comprehensive framework of planning and control, which does not abolish individual-economic strivings for success, but is directed towards common goals, does not in itself already oppose the basic market principle. And, in this respect, the relativization of the market economy in the sense of its plan-modification cannot also be a self-contradiction.

This thesis, which I believe has been substantiated, is not true of every market-plan combination, but only of one in which the market constitutes the economic system and the plan receives a merely regulatory function. This excludes, as is evident, the combination of the market imperative-directed planning. Such an economic order, more

[65] "A distinction is usually made within economic policy between order policy and process policy. Order policy's purpose is to create or secure the order or framework for economic activity. Process policy involves intervention in the economic process; influence, direct or indirect, on economic subjects is exercised here" (Hans G. Schachtschabel, "Historische Grundformen wirtschaftspolitischer Ordnungen," *Unsere Wirtschaft — Basis, Dschungel, Dogma?*, ed. State Office for Political Education of North Rhine-Westphalia, Cologne, 1973, p. 21.

or less tied to the state but nevertheless behaving in terms of markets, would be a contradiction in itself. It would, according to its tendency, amount to a command economy and, consequently, to a break from the system. Regulatorily-understood planning of the national economy must, therefore, restrict itself essentially to indicative-oriented procedures, whereby it is necessary to estimate the future development possibilities of the national economy as well as possible on the basis of reliable statistical data and to establish the desired economic-political setting of goals. At the same time, the limits of global planning as a part of the framework within which the market-economic process should take place can be drawn narrowly or widely.

With Šik, the limits of a plan-modification of the market economy are drawn relatively widely. He proposes comprehensive "macroeconomic distribution planning,"[66] which is

> above all about the relationship between the development of the large production groups and the development of correspondingly large income groups, about the relationship between the individual and social development of consumption and investment, about the relationship between the living conditions and the environmental conditions of people and economic growth.[67]

Even with Šik, however, this extensive "regulation of the market process" has an unambiguously subsidiary character: "The macroeconomic planning of distribution should not replace the market mechanism; it should complement the market mechanism in the control of economic development."[68] And that is possible only if the prognostic, goal-directed planning is understood indicatively, not imperatively:

[66] Šik, *Ein Wirtschaftssystem der Zukunft*, Berlin, 1985, pp. 98-166. The goals of the desired macro-planning are formulated by Šik as follows: "1. Maintenance of macroeconomic equilibrium; 2. Macro-proportional regulation of the development of consumption in accordance with the desired development in the quality of life; 3. Regulation of the rate of economic growth; 4. Maintenance or alteration of individual income policy; 5. Maintenance or achievement of the desired development of work time, occupational mobility, and requalification; 6. Achievement of the desired balancing out of economic development in different nations and regions; 7. Creation of the desired, healthy environmental conditions and industrial and urban agglomerations; 8. Safeguarding of the social-medical needs of the population; 9. Securing the infrastructure and energy basis of the economy and society; 10. Achievement of the desired educational, economic, and cultural development of society" (*ibid.*, pp. 107-8). Cf. 6.2.5.1.

[67] *Ibid.*, p. 106.

[68] *Ibid.*

> This prognosis may become nothing more than a construction that is indeed meaningful, but is merely *helpful*, because it can predetermine the *exact* development neither of the demand structure nor of the possibilities for effectiveness within production with sufficient reliability. As soon as this important prognosis became a binding plan, this would mean that the market-conforming distribution planning would capsize into directed production planning, with all of its bureaucratic consequences that would kill initiative and effectiveness.[69]

From that it follows that even with plan-modification of the market economy, as is the case in Šik's "economic system of the future," the market remains the constitutive foundation. Only under this condition can a combination of market and plan be achieved that is capable of functioning and, consequently, is also economically rational.[70]

It can be said in summary, for the reasons given, that the plan-modification of the market economy, in contrast to the market-modification of the centrally planned system, is possible and, even seen from the perspective of economic rationality, represents a feasible path. After all, it has actually already been pursued for a long time, to take up that point once again, in the sense of a directed economic policy — of course in very different variations and degrees — by the existing market economies. The planning of space, energy, traffic, environmental protection, infrastructure, technology, science, education, etc. are a theme almost everywhere. In addition, there is regulation of the currency, finance, and labor markets, etc. All of these approaches to a macroeconomic structural order need not violate the market economy's ability to function, insofar as it happens in subordination to its basic system and makes use of market-conforming means of execution, as can be the case with the mere mixing of market and centrally-planning elements, which is for the most part politically-pragmatically motivated, and — one thinks, for instance, of the governmental subventions and price regulations in the agricultural sector — is also common. Certainly, the limits of merely macroeconomic planning of goals and orientations may not be overlooked. As *ex ante* coordination,[71] it is burdened with the handicap that future

[69] *Ibid.*, p. 176.

[70] Cf. *ibid.*, pp. 173-74.

[71] "*Ex ante* coordination" is the forward-looking coordination of individual plans during their development.

developments in the economy can be predicted only very approximately and, therefore, only fallibly.[72] Naive planning optimism would certainly be out of place. The question is also posed whether one can go as far as Šik does with his macroeconomic distribution planning. Despite this restriction, the actual plan modification remains in existence nonetheless, and with it the ability to relativize the market economy by an indicative master plan as a real order-political possibility,[73] which in many Western industrial nations — most distinctively in France with "*planification*," which, of course, has faded in the meantime — has more or less already become reality. For our basic thoughts directed towards finding maxims in the system question in the economy, this receives decisive importance. It includes the fact that, in the system question of the economy, the option in favor of the market-economic basic system must be exercised. That is to say, if the decentral market system and the central plan system can be received by the demand of human justice, as it originates from the humanity originating from faith, hope, and love, only in case the contrary value principles are relationally implemented, resulting in their relativization, but it proves to be the case, for objective reasons, that a system-consistent relativization by the order-political counter principle on the basis of the centrally planned economy in contrast to its market antipode hardly has a chance, then it is necessary to side with the market system as a relatively better alternative.[74]

[72] On this problematic, see Volker Nienhaus, *Kontroversen um Markt und Plan*, Darmstadt, 1984, pp. 45-52.

[73] Wilhelm Krelle, "Wirtschaftsplanung auf mittlere und lange Sicht," in *Planung ohne Planwirtschaft*, ed. Alfred Plitzko, Basel, 1964, p. 67: "The *advantages of a framework plan* would be, to my mind, first, the systematic coordination of all economic policy measures from a unified perspective.... The second advantage, which is connected to it, is the driving back of individual decisions that are isolated or associated with or driven by special interests. Third, private economic risk would be reduced in a way, insofar as more or less certain prognoses are continually provided by the state side, which the individual could make only with great difficulty, if at all. And, finally, one can expect more stable economic development."

[74] Wilhelm Korff also argues similarly: "In order to arrive at an ethical evaluation here [with the question of alternative systems], one must ask which of the two sides best allows the opportunity of a countermeasure. That is, however, true unambiguously of the former [the market economic system]" ("Orientierungslinien einer Wirtschaftsethik," in *Die Welt für morgen*, ed. Gerfried W. Hunold and Korff, Munich, 1986, p. 74).

2. This in-principle decision for the basic system of the market economy does not yet mean a decision, at least not an uncritical one, for an actually existing form of order of the market economy, not even for what is called the "social market economy" (*Soziale Marktwirtschaft*). It does not at all already equate to an undifferentiated alternative between a free, deregulated market economy that approaches the laissez-faire principle and the government-imperative, centrally planned economy. The concept of the market economy that is modified by master planning and, in that respect, is plan-coupled, and thus relativized, refuses to surrender to that kind of an "alternative radicalism." On the basis of the market-economic basic system, still other forms of organization are possible, conceivable, or already in the process of becoming, beyond the capitalistic economy conceived on deregulation and the moderately framework-oriented social market economy. Seriously intended reform efforts in the East move towards a socialistic market economy.[75] France launched the experiment of "*planification*." Sweden practices a market economy without essential governmental interventions in the sphere of production, but with strong exertion of influence on the distribution of the resulting production. Šik's reform model represents an additional example. Although Šik qualifies his economic concept as a "third way," it is nevertheless based on the plan-modified basic system of the market economy. It is an alternative to the centrally planned economy and to the existing market-economic order forms, but not to the market economy as a basic system itself. The same is true, in my opinion, of the neo-corporatist approaches, which are close to the "socially ordered economy" (*sozialgeordnete Wirtschaft*) — the term stems from Hans G. Schachtschabel[76] — and which have already been mentioned in 4.1.3. In the socially organized economy, no longer the individual business firm, but simply the economic group as an organizational amalgamation of individual firms and individual economic actors,

[75] No less an economist than Paul Samuelson says that a socialist market economy, in which the workers hold the capital and organize the production, and thus in which capitalist private ownership of the means of production does not exist, is possible in principle when he declares "that in a perfectly competitive market it really doesn't matter who hires whom: so have labor hire 'capital'." (Samuelson, *Collected Scientific Papers*, Cambridge, 1966, p. 351)

[76] Schachtschabel, "Die sozialgeordnete Wirtschaft als Grundgestalt der Gegenwart," in *Methoden und Probleme der Wirtschaftspolitik*, ed. Hans Ohm, Berlin, 1964, pp. 65-85.

are the decisive factor.[77] This means that the economy is not, as in centrally planned orders, organized primarily by the state, and also not, as in economic liberalism, primarily by the individuals, but by organizations and associations[78] — worker organizations, labor unions, cooperatives, etc. — from which a more or less strong effect on the economic life radiates,[79] primarily to the macro-sphere. To put it differently: This is about corporatist arrangements that have essential influence on the macroeconomic goals of economic policy.[80] Whether the economic organizations in their specific interest-embededness prove to be suitable bearers of a socially-organized economy remains an open question. Siegfried Katterle, whose position is close to this concept, has possibly other or still other institutions in mind: "If an undesirable governmental control monopoly is to be avoided, corporatist institutions that constitute allocation-system planning and control as the framework for the allocation-system market are advisable."[81] However that may be, it follows in any event that, here also with this order-political approach, it is a matter of a market-plan combination that has a market capable of functioning as a prerequisite. Thus Katterle explicitly maintains: "The economic-political macro-goals united in corporatist arrangements must be compatible with the institutionalized goal-system of the individual economic actors and the value orientations of their representative leadership, so that the firms contribute to achieving agreed upon macro-goals in their individual economic decisions."[82] Thus, even the corporatist, socially-ordered approach to the economy can be subsumed under the basic system of the (plan-modified) market economy. It does not establish a new basic system, according to our terminology, but it does

[77] *Ibid.*, p. 82.

[78] *Ibid.*

[79] *Ibid.*, p. 83.

[80] This includes wage agreements between social-contracting parties. In addition, there are long-term contracts of great social significance. For example, there are the agreement between the employers union and the labor unions in the Swiss clock and machine industries, which was signed in 1937 and renewed most recently in 1983, as well as the Agreement of Saltsjöbaden between the employers organizations and the trade unions in Sweden, which came into being in 1938, both of which are based on the idea of a corporatist social partnership.

[81] Siegfried Katterle, "Die institutionelle Verfassung des Systems Wirtschaft und seine theoretisch-ökonomische Beschreibung," in Katterle, *Alternativen zur neoliberalen Wende*, Bochum, 1989, p. 81.

[82] *Ibid.*, p. 85.

establish an alternative form of order to the traditionally constituted market-economic order, which wishes to establish macro-goals primarily neither in an individual-economic manner nor in a state-central manner, but by group-corporatist agreements and, in that respect, decentrally, or at least polycentrally. From all of that it emerges that the choice for the basic system of the market economy includes the option of a plurality of order forms. With that, the theme of the next chapter is intimated. But before that it is still necessary to formulate the guiding maxims of decision in the system question *expressis verbis*.

5.3 Maxims

1. There are in principle two basic economic systems: the decentral system of free, individual economic actors, oriented towards market relationships and the central system of planning the economy by imperatives established by governmental authorities — thus the market system and the centrally planned system. Whether corporativism can be considered a third fundamental coordination system is questionable. It can also be assigned to the decentralized coordination system, insofar as corporativist agreements with respect to the economic-political order of markets presuppose a poly-centric decision basis.

2. Behind both of the basic systems stand specific human values. The market economy refers back to freedom and individual responsibility, as well as to the self-interest of economic subjects. The centrally planned economy appeals, on the contrary, to social duty, solidarity, and the collective interest of persons engaged in economic activity. Both cases involve indispensable human values that can be humanly just only if they are understood relationally, and thus relativize each other and, consequently, resist all forms of absolutization. Only in such a relative sense are the contrary human values of the two basic systems acceptable ethically. This forbids ideologizing them in a liberalistic or socialist manner into ultimate values that subordinate everything else to themselves.

3. It follows from the relational understanding of the human value premises standing behind the two basic systems that both the principle of the market economy and that of the centrally planned economy are acceptable only relatively, which is to say in critical openness

to the contrary normative value. A free or self-binding economy is, from the viewpoint of the human justice that understands itself relationally, a false alternative. Liberty and commitment can never be harmonized with each other in practice without conflict, and thus free of guilt. Therefore, their relative reception also opens, in view of the claim of the absolute, order possibilities of the economy that are never already just, but that can lead to less unjust possibilities.

4. The relativization of the two basic economic systems that is to be concluded from the preceding is not only an ethical postulate; it also has strong grounds in reality. Neither an absolutely free market economy nor a pure centrally planned economy, in which everything is directed by the government, exists in the real world. Planning of the economy that is left to itself and is motivated only by decentral-individual economic decisions and the maximization of profit produces formations of market power that endanger competition, macroeconomic instabilities, social discrimination, and a serious failure to conserve the natural environment, which together call the market economy as such into question and must be met by a far-reaching planned framework-order, if necessary, also by control of processes. And a totally centrally planned, command economy that scorns the individual interests of producers and consumers leads under complex conditions, which exist most of all in industrial societies, to an inefficient economy that breaks down at the micro level and produces new social and ecological afflictions, all of which demands above all correctives of a market-economic kind. The tendency towards relativization of the two basic systems that actually exists does not lie only on the line of human justice, but also on that of economic rationality.

5. Relativization does not mean mixing, and even less does it mean synthesizing the two basic systems. Although the contrary value principles standing behind them are relational, that is not true of the coordination systems that constitute them. Economic development is determined either by the market mechanism or by directed, central planning that excludes the market. Consequently, one must choose either one or the other. And that means that the intended relativization or modification must take place on the basis of one basic system or the other. In one case, the market is order-politically constitutive and the planning or control is regulatory; in the other case the market elements brought into play are regulatory and the central plans are constitutive.

6. The choice of one basic system or the other, therefore, is not only a question of human justice, but equally one of economic rationality. That is to say, the question is posed whether in either case the corresponding modification is possible, without bringing about a breakdown of the system. And that contains a decision that is relevant to economics.

7. Maxim 5 is based on the empirically-established incompatibility of market mechanisms and directive-imperative planning that the centrally planned economy possesses. If it is to be modified in the direction of a market economy, firms must conform to responsible, profit-oriented economic guidance under conditions of competition with power of disposal over capital, together with the right to make autonomous investment decisions. Apart from the division of economic power determined by it, which also induces social pluralism, which becomes dangerous for the totalitarian political system of the centrally planned economy, this squares only with indicative master planning. With that, however, the plan has only a regulatory function, the market, on the contrary, a constitutive function. Therefore, serious market modification of the socialist centrally planned economy, as the experiences in Yugoslavia, Hungary, and China show, tends towards a socialist market economy, which amounts to a break with the coordination system of the centrally planned economy. The centrally planned economy — not the socialist economy in general — consequently, is not market-modifiable, and thus also cannot be relativized. Reforms lead either to overcoming or to restoring the system.[83]

8. In contrast to that, a goal-setting global master plan of an indicative character gets along with the market-economic coordination system, because with this kind of market-plan combination the market, with its decentrally-planning firms and households, keeps its constitutive status and restricts the global-macroeconomic planning to a subsidiary, complementary function. In this sense the market economy can be plan-modified.

9. If the humanity originating from faith, hope, and love, with its relational concept of human justice, can receive the market economy

[83] The recent contrary developments in Hungary and China substantiate that impressively.

and the centrally planned economy only relatively, but if it turns out that the centrally planned economy, in contrast to the market system, cannot really be relativized, then the order-political option can also only turn out in favor of the market economy.

10. This option does not yet amount to a decision for one of the order forms of the market economy that actual exists or is in the process of becoming. Alternative order possibilities on the basis of the market principle are to be examined. We should strive for the order form that is best able to promise a practicable answer to the main economic-ethical problem, which was examined in 3.3.

6. MAXIMS FOR EVALUATION AND DECISION-MAKING REGARDING THE QUESTION OF ORDER IN ECONOMIC SYSTEMS

6.1 Preliminary Remarks

In contrast to Chapter 5, this chapter deals with discovering evaluation- and decision-making maxims regarding the question of order in economic systems.

According to the specific definition applied to the concept,[1] the systematic discussion of economic systems deals with their fundamental system, while the question of order in the narrower sense investigates the concretely real or concretely possible forms of economic order within its fundamental systems.

Considering that regarding the question of order we basically decided on the level of maxims in favor of the market-economic system, it would be consistent to limit the new approach used during the discussion of the maxims to types of order present in the market economy.

As explained earlier, this limitation does not at all amount to a fixation on the types or forms of order factually present in the market economy, since it will always be received in relative terms. As developed in Chapter 3, based on the analyses of modern industrial society and guided by the criteria of the humanity originating from faith, hope, and love, they must face the challenges presented by the basic question concerning the ethical nature of economic systems. If they can meet the challenge, they are ethically acceptable; if they fail, however, their reception is to be disallowed. This forces us to probe beyond the existing market reality also for alternative market-like forms of order which, when compared to the status quo, can be justifiably expected to lead to more participatory, more social and more ecology-minded structures within economic systems. Therefore,

[1] *BEE*, Vol. II, 4.1.2.

limiting ourselves to market-economic types of order has nothing to do with an uncritical refusal to accept new order-political possibilities.

According to our previous discussions,[2] it stands to reason that, as is the case with existing types of market-economic systems, the market in its capacity as a competitive system of coordination must remain the constitutive foundation even when faced with alternative possibilities. Market-economic systems are essentially distinguished from one another by the various settings that incorporate the very nature of the regulatory instruments present in a market-economic system. It is therefore the setting that plays a specific role within the problem of order in the market-oriented system. No market-oriented system can do without a definitive framework of order that regulates it. At the least, it requires a legal framework that determines the basic political and social conditions that are supposed to and will underlie economic activity. Furthermore, part of this framework is the regulation of ownership relationships and especially the government's economic policy, which defines global economic goals and, in some cases, takes an active political role in the course of the economic process. Depending on the design and degree of this framework within the economic, social and ecological realm, different real or possible types of order can be differentiated with regard to the market economy. As mentioned before, the distinction between these two possibilities is not only a question of economic rationality, but is even more a question of human justice. Therein lies the reason for its need to be based on principles of assessment and decision-making that, in the sense of our terminology, take human justice and economic rationality into account, and thus relate the normative to the empirical. Therefore, to discover them presupposes at the same time sketching the specificity of several of the most significant among the real and possible forms of order within the market economy and balancing them against each other.

6.2 Categories of Order within the Market-Economy

6.2.1 *The Capitalist Market Economy*

The term "capitalism" or "capitalist," which was erroneously equated by Marxist circles to or used synonymously with the term "market

[2] See especially *BEE*, Vol. II, 5.2.2.2. and 3.

economy," are of little value to scholarly inquiry, not to mention their innate polemical and emotional subtext due to their arbitrary ambiguity.[3] However, if we adopt it here to use it attributively not with reference to the market economy as such, but as one of its definitive forms, then it will be necessary to explain the precise meaning associated with it.

As far as the history of the term "capitalist" is concerned, its use appears as early as 1805 in the works of Adam Smith's follower, Julius Graf von Soden, in his expression *"kapitalistische Produkzion"* (capitalist production). He defines capitalist production as a form of production in which capital serves not alone as the essential factor in the production process, but more so in the process where capital is produced by capital, resulting in the gain of capital.[4] Does this definition already spell out something specific?

From its very beginnings, capital belongs as an increasingly important factor of production to the most obvious characteristics of the industrial economy. The modern industrial economy is based on the progressive use of investment goods capital in the form of produced, machine-made means of production. Every industrial economy, even an economy with a socialist structure, faces the necessity of its dependency on the expenditure and utilization of capital. This is simply a result of the technologization of production typical of the industrial process that increasingly substitutes labor with capital.

However, not only the intensive use and utilization of capital rank among the real necessities of every industrially developed economy. This includes the requirement that it must be profitable. The means of production within an enterprise, its infrastructure, and its innovative research facilities wear out in the form of invested capital and must be renewed, improved and developed. In addition to fiscal burdens there will be, as a rule, increasing demands for wages and benefits by the employees as well as the recently significant expenditures for environmental protection, etc. Financing all this requires new capital obtained again from profits. No modern industrial economy can exist without the sufficient realization of profits, regardless of whether it is liberal or socialist oriented. Even Karl Marx in his 1875 "Critique of the Gotha Program" of the German Socialist Party had

[3] See Ingomar Bog, "Kapitalismus," in *Handwörterbuch der Wirtschaftswissenschaften*, Vol. 4, esp. pp. 421-26.

[4] Julius Graf von Soden, *Die Nazional-Oekonomie*, Vol. I, Leipzig, 1805, p. 149.

to take that into consideration.[5] Even the attempts at reform by the economies in the Eastern Bloc countries are largely determined by this necessity. Thus, profitability is in itself not a specific property of the "capitalist" industry, but of industrial economy as a whole.

If, therefore, the utilization or use of capital belongs to the essential characteristics of every developed industrial economy, then it cannot be specifically characteristic of that which can be described as capitalist. Yet, this term is intimately connected to it, because profitability in economic systems may have different meanings.

For instance, it may suggest that it is imperative to pay attention to interest in profitability as the very motive behind efficient economic activities. Yet, it may also indicate maximization of profits. When taken at its face value, the maximization of profits as a form of economic activity suggests that the achievement of profits assumes the highest priority within the economy and that it must take unconditional precedence over competing demands such as concerns over wages, social concerns and concerns about the environment, etc. The classical market theory affords this form of economic conduct a good conscience since, according to its principles, competition within the market economy sets up limits for the maximization of profits; indeed, it even generates its own tendency to remove profits.[6] However, in reality, there exists an antagonism between the maximization of profits within an enterprise and the limitation of profits erected by the market itself. Among other things, this leads to the formation of powerful economic positions within the market with the purpose of outmaneuvering as much as possible the competition-induced limitation of the achievement of profits. In Leipold's words, "within the market system, we must pay attention to the universal tendency to establish positions of power and in doing so reduce the processes of competition."[7] Ultimately, this reaches a point where production begins to turn into a side effect of the striving after profits when the capital achieves profits without the use of labor and the employment of the means of production, that is to achieve profits through speculative business activities. Large businesses maintain financial institutions of their own that earn massive profits in this fashion, but not through the production and the sale of

[5] Marx, "Critique of the Gotha Programme," in *Collected Works*, Vol. XXIV, p. 84.

[6] *BEE*, Vol. II, p. 444 and 4.2.2.5, fn. 46.

[7] *Wirtschafts- und Gesellschaftssysteme im Vergleich*, Stuttgart, 1980, p. 98.

investment goods, consumer goods or services. Therefore, if the striving for the profit-maximizing formation of capital dominates, be it in the production, the service, the financial or the commercial sector, then it assumes a specific structure to which one may correctly refer to as "capitalist."[8]

Thus we finally have a preliminary and important definition of how the term "capitalist" is to be understood in discussions concerning the problem of order. It describes a market-economic order, more precisely, the mode of economic activity within which the highest priority is assigned to the profit-maximizing self-interest of the capitalist, regardless of whether he or she utilizes or owns capital. Self-interest as an essentially humanly legitimate value supersedes the contrary, yet equally legitimate human values and becomes ahuman as a result of absolutization. No matter how enormous an increase of economic efficiency may be connected to this absolute nature, its primary concern is not at all a desire to better serve the human need for consumer goods and services that are vital to the preservation and promotion of the quality of life as the fundamental purpose of the economy; but rather the accumulation of capital. This becomes the true purpose of the economy. And connected to it is an additional specific aspect of the capitalist market economy.

Capital is incapable of increasing on its own. Its increase becomes possible only if, apart from speculative practices, it is used productively and creates profits in cooperation with the labor factor. Only capital invested in this sense is valuable to the capitalist: "The actual value of capital is the present value of *future* profits. If there are no profits, then practically *all* the capital is lost."[9] That is why inherent to the increase of capital is the incentive for economic growth, again only in as far as, with a lack of indispensable consumer goods and services, growth constitutes a real necessity within every economic system. However, if the increase of capital becomes an end itself and

[8] Even Oswald von Nell-Breuning defines the term "capitalism" in the same manner: "'Capitalism', this one-sided supremacy of capital and of its interest" (*Kapitalismus– kritisch betrachtet*, Freiburg, 1986, p. 70); "Capitalism, i.e. the kind of economy in which capital interests dominate" (p. 125); "As long as we have a capitalist economy, i.e. 'capital' is predominant and prominent in the economy, capital will also exert influence beyond the bounds of the individual firm and beyond the bounds of the economy" (p. 129); *et passim*.

[9] Hans Christoph Binswanger, *Money and Magic*, trans. J. E. Harrison, Chicago, 1994, p. 44.

if one attempts to infinitely increase monetary capital because of the emphasis on its acquisition — a condition known as early as Aristotle —[10] then this applies also to economic growth. It no longer matters what is produced, but that production of marketable goods exists, even if those goods were to turn out to be socially superfluous, even detrimental. In this fashion, growth-oriented industrial capitalist structures establish themselves in the market economy. These have been discussed in 2.7.2. They can turn out to be perilous to the entire ecosystem because of their equally inordinate destructive impact on the environment.[11]

Finally, there is a third specific meaning connected to the concept of "capitalist." The capitalist market economy is not only characterized by a predominance of capital interests, but also by the fact that this predominance of capital interests benefits a relatively small minority. The majority of gainfully employed people own no capital, certainly not any real capital worth mentioning. In other words, they are actually separated from the ownership of the means of production.

Certainly, the separation of the employees from the means of production with which they work is in itself no specific result of the capitalistic form of the market economy. As summarized in 2.3.4, it is primarily connected to the process of rationalization present in the developing industrial society, a process which is initially determined by modern high technology and which only permits highly well-funded individuals, enterprises or the government to acquire means of production in any significant amount. Every industrial economy, even one that is based on centrally organized state capitalism is characterized by this separation, particularly since there are no individual or private means of production present in such a system. However, what proves to be specifically capitalist is "the particular *form* this separation assumes."[12] It is based on the fact that only those who already possess sufficient amounts of capital can participate either directly or indirectly in the accumulation of capital in both production and distribution. As a rule, those who do not own such primary capital are excluded from it, except those few exceptions that merely

[10] *BEE*, Vol. II, 1.3.5, fn. 54.

[11] See the enlightening essay by Paul Erbrich, "Technik — Chance oder Verhängnis?" *Neue Züricher Zeitung*, No. 176, 30/31 July 1988, p. 17: "A definitive equilibrium ... appears to be impossible in a capitalist economy. It either grows or collapses."

[12] von Nell-Breuning, *Kapitalismus– kritisch betrachtet*, p. 149.

reinforce the rule. Already Louis Blanc pointed that out when he wrote: "*Ce que j'apellerai capitalisme, c'est-à-dire l'appropriation du capital par les uns, à l'exclusion des autres.*"[13] This kind of separation between labor and capital reveals a confrontational structure. Apart from the payment of wages, it excludes the representatives of the labor factor — including those who represent technical and administrative know-how — not only from participating in the proceeds flowing from capital gain in the economy, but also from that which weighs even more heavily when viewed from the point of view of what is humanly just, namely from the point of view of who owns the right to control the economy, a right that is connected to the power arising from owning the means of production: "Separating the worker from the means of production in the fashion typical of capitalism, signifies to most people who are able and willing to work (86% of the gainfully employed in the Federal Republic of Germany) that they are inescapably forced into the 'life-situation of dependent labor'."[14]

In as far as the capitalist market economy remains unwilling to accept any limits to its exercise of entrepreneurial capital interests other than those directly dictated by the market, it tends to identify itself with the "free" or, more correctly, the libertarian market economy, even to the point of "laissez-faire" in its most extreme form. To be sure, no truly capitalist or libertarian market economy ever existed, such as the kind that was ideologically identical with *Manchesterism;* indeed, in the long run, such a form of libertarianism could not possibly be achieved either.[15] It presupposes a kind of freedom perceived in absolute terms and emancipated from any attachment, a fact that contains the potential for its own destruction: "It was the marriage of market capitalism with state regulation that produced a hybrid politico-economic system with the necessary resilience and plasticity to survive."[16] The greater the inability of market forces was to act contrary to classical theory on their own as

[13] Louis Blanc, *Organisation du travail*, 9th Ed., Paris, 1950, p. 161. Cited by Marie-Elisabeth Hilger, "Kapital, Kapitalist, Kapitalismus," in *Geschichtliche Grundbegriffe*, ed. Otto Brunner, Werner Conze, and Reinhart Koselleck, Vol. 3, Stuttgart, 1982, p. 443.

[14] von Nell-Breuning, *Kapitalismus– kritisch betrachtet*, p. 149.

[15] Certainly, early capitalism around the middle of the nineteenth century came quite close to it and continues to exist in South America.

[16] Fred Hirsch, *Social Limits to Growth*, Cambridge, Mass., 1976, p. 118.

the so-called invisible hand and to automatically reconcile the individual economic interests of economic subjects with the common good of society, the greater was the number of monopoloid positions of power in the market that suppressed competition among individuals, even to the point of severe economic crisis and collapses, the greater was also the cry for corrective market regulation at the hand of the government. For instance, steps were taken early on in the United States (1890 Sherman-Antitrust Law, 1914 Clayton-Antitrust Law) against the formation of trusts. In 1926, the independent liberal, John Maynard Keynes came to the conclusion that "laissez-faire" practices had come to an end. [17] The catastrophic after-effects of the 1929-32 world economic crisis with its massive unemployment and the accompanying impoverishment of vast segments of the population led ultimately to the transformation of libertarian to "organized" capitalism characterized by its government-controlled market economy: "The generally accepted concept of managed capitalism runs about like this. State intervention is to set up appropriate 'rules of the game' and deliberately alter both the law and the market choices facing individuals. In addition, collective restraint in the general interest is expected from trade unions and other collective bodies."[18] Keynes, the leading and influential theorist of this transformation,[19] distanced himself from the classical theory according to which the levels of price, wages and interest balance one another under the conditions of free competition, leading automatically to full employment. In order to achieve full employment, the government must actively intervene and, in the event of a depression, it must pursue an economic policy based on demand by either assigning employment-effective government contracts, or by strengthening the purchasing power of the general public through the increase of wages and by granting tax relief out of an awareness of the fact that it will incur budget deficits during periods of economic downturn and budget surpluses during periods of economic upswing as a result of increased tax revenues. Overall, this amounted to an anti-cyclical economic policy, which was well received by the trade unions as long

[17] John Maynard Keynes, *The End of Laissez-faire*, London, 1926.

[18] Hirsch, *Social Limits to Growth*, p. 128. In his *Evangelische Wirtschaftsethik* (Tübingen, 1927, p. 478), Georg Wünsch is no longer able to refer to this type of capitalism as "pure capitalism."

[19] See especially, in addition to the aforementioned publication, Keynes, *General Theory of Employment, Interest and Money*, London, 1936.

as it involved measures of fighting depression and because it accommodated their specific social interests. Keynes was therefore frequently referred to as a "neo-socialist", a label he does not deserve. His fundamental position was liberal throughout. He basically assumed a "harmony" "between the pursuit of individual interests by individuals and the general or social environment."[20] However this harmony is no longer simply a matter of Adam Smith's 'invisible hand', but of the visible hand of the government's arsenal invoked for the purpose of regulating the market economy.

The economic policy inspired by Keynesian ideas of the type that appeared in most Western countries after World War II, has undoubtedly contributed to the strong economic growth based on a high level of employment in combination with a corresponding rise in material wealth especially during the fifties and sixties. However, as soon as the negative consequences of a Keynesianism appeared that turned out to be less refined and one-sided in the arena of practical economic policy, the response to Keynesian theory in general and government-initiated market regulation in particular was quite sobering, particularly since there was no manner in which a clear connection could be empirically ascertained between an additional purchasing power of the masses and a consumer-demand-increasing level of employment.[21] One needs to mention also the dangerously growing damage to the environment as a result of the enormous quantitative economic growth in addition to inflationary interludes that led to veritable forms of stagflation (inflation + unemployment) in various places. The most recent economic trend points, therefore, more in the direction of a deregulation of the regulated capitalistic market economy, calling for "less government." One must mention here especially Milton Friedman, the radical and prominent spokesperson for the neoclassical type of free-market economy.[22] Certainly, not even in the case of this ultra-liberal economist can one speak of a return to the libertarian market of laissez-faire capitalism. According to Friedman, government still plays a significant regulatory role within the free-market economy. In contrast to the night watchman state of classical liberalism, according to Friedman, the government is responsible for more than law and order. In addition, it is called upon to

[20] See Fred Hirsch, *Social Limits to Growth*, p. 128.
[21] See Frank Pilz, *Das System der sozialen Marktwirtschaft*, Munich, 1981, p. 31.
[22] Milton Friedman, *Capitalism and Freedom*, Chicago, 1962.

define property rights and to serve as a means whereby property rights and other rules of the economic game can be modified. Furthermore, government is called upon to adjudicate disputes about the interpretation of the rules, to enforce contracts, to promote competition, to provide a monetary framework, to engage in activities to counter technical monopolies (patents) and to remove their subsequent impact, and to supplement private charity and the private family in the care of needy relatives.[23] Incidentally, the creation of the mentioned monetary system whose duty it is to regulate the monetary supply circulating in the economy is vitally important.[24] The advocates of Keynesianism are faced with the need to steer the market because the private economy supposedly tends towards unstable business cycles due to the inconstancy typical of private demand. On the other hand, the monetarism propagated by Friedman insists on the thesis of a generally stable condition in the private sector, which is disturbed precisely by the government's interventionist, anti-cyclical economic policy. This harmful economic policy must, therefore, be replaced by a monetary supply policy subscribed to by the central banks that limits itself to consistently adapting the amount of money in circulation to the development of the production potential and simultaneously moderating the growth of the economy. Here, too, the market economy retains a government-guaranteed framework, which must be minimized however.

As to fighting inflation during upturns in the business cycle, the neo-classical monetaristic concept carries its undeniable weight. However it is doubtful whether it may serve as a suitable employment policy in times of high unemployment. As a rule, it combines with a supply-oriented economic policy that contradicts Keynesianism. The purpose of this policy is the improvement of the supply of factors (capital and labor) for the benefit of capital interests (lowering of capital and other gains taxes, incidental labor costs, etc.) in order to induce entrepreneurs to increase investment as a condition of accelerated employment-effective economic growth. However, the "postulated connection of supply-oriented structural policies between higher profits, additional investments and increased employment can be empirically confirmed."[25] If additional

[23] Friedman, *Capitalism and Freedom*, p. 34.
[24] *Ibid.*, Chap. 3.
[25] Pilz, *Das System der sozialen Marktwirtschaft*, p. 37.

investments are initially and indiscriminately used for the purpose of rationalization, economic growth will be possible accompanied by a simultaneous reduction of the size of the workforce. Whichever the case may be, this neo-classical concept that gives the appearance of genuine necessity to the minimization of government involvement in the economy as well as to the maximization of private interests in utilizing and accumulating capital, thus concealing its inherently selfish economic motivation, leads to a renewed strengthening of specifically capitalist factors when measured against the organized and tempered capitalism of the Keynesians. In fact, a free, deregulated market economy and capitalism are simply identical in the eyes of Friedman.

In conclusion, it can be stated that behind all this exists the tendency towards absolutizing the economic freedom of profit-maximizing economic subjects, that is to say the monocracy of capitalist interests. Thus the neo-classical theorist declares explicitly: "In [a free] economy, there is one and only one social responsibility of business — to use its resources and engage in activities designed to increase its profits so long as it stays within the rules of the game, which is to say, engages in open and free competition, without deception or fraud."[26] Keynes, on the other hand, did assume that the managers of capitalism are motivated by even higher goals than the mere maximization of their own interests.[27] Even the question of distribution is characterized by the specifically capitalist tendency. Therefore, the ethical basic principle of the free market economy ought to read: "'To each according to what he and the instruments he owns produces'."[28] Thus not only the profits from his own labor, but also the profits generated by the means of production belong indivisibly to the capital owner. To be sure, Friedman is not entirely happy with this "capitalist ethic": "I find it difficult to justify either accepting or rejecting it, or to justify any alternative principle."[29] However, he responds to his misgivings by not considering it as an ethical principle at all, but as the inevitable consequence of freedom, yet the kind of freedom that minimizes, if not entirely eliminates, the principle of

[26] *Ibid.*, p. 133. One ought to add that it necessarily follows from this, according to Friedman, that union leaders are to act solely on behalf of the interests of union members.

[27] See Hirsch, *Social Limits to Growth*, p. 124.

[28] Friedman, *Capitalism and Freedom*, pp. 161-62.

[29] *Ibid.*, p. 164.

solidarity in contrast to its relational understanding. Inclusive of the negative social as well as ecological consequences, all this implies a dominance of private capitalistic interests that agrees with our paraphrase of the capitalist regulatory type referred to as the market economy.

6.2.2. *The Social Market Economy* [30]

As the term suggests, the objective of the social market economy that became at least somewhat of a reality in the Federal Republic of Germany after 1945 is, in the words of the creator of the concept, Alfred Müller-Armack, to combine the "principle of freedom in the marketplace with the principle of social balance."[31] Accordingly, the fundamental principle of the market economy, that is the individual freedom of economic subjects to make economic decisions in their capacity as producers, distributors and consumers, was to be retained, however not in an absolute sense, but with regard to the opposite principle of social obligation, thus limiting in contrast to the specific tenets of the capitalist market economy the freedom of economic subjects to pursue solely their own interests. What we have here, to use our terminology, is basically the kind of relational concept demanded by human justice in the sense of a humanity originating from faith, hope, and love.

Already its fundamental relational structure reveals that the social market economy opposes two contrasting extremes: on the one hand, it opposes a centrally controlled economy that negates the principle of freedom and, on the other hand, a market economy that is left to its own devices, unregulated and characterized by the unleashing of

[30] In addition to the works of Alfred Müller-Armack cited below, the following publications should also be mentioned: Alexander Rüstow, "Wirtschaftsordnung und Staatsform," in *Magna Charta der sozialen Marktwirtschaft*, ed. Ernst Winkler, *et al.*, Heidelberg-Ziegelhausen, 1952, pp. 19-33; Ernst Winkler, "Wirtschaftsethische Probleme der Sozialen Marktwirtschaft," in *Der Christ und die Soziale Marktwirtschaft*, ed. Patrick M. Boarman, Stuttgart, 1955, pp. 53-74; Egon Tuchtfeldt, ed., *Soziale Marktwirtschaft im Wandel*, Freiburg, 1973; Frank Pilz, *Das System der Sozialen Marktwirtschaft*, Munich, 1981; Wolfgang Stützel, "Sicherung der Sozialen Marktwirtschaft durch konsequente Ordnungspolitik," in *Grundtexte zur Sozialen Marktwirtschaft*, ed. Stützel, *et al.*, Stuttgart, 1981, pp. 341-55; Siegfried Katterle, "Jenseits der sozialen Marktwirtschaft," in Katterle, *Alternativen zur neoliberalen Wende*, Bochum, 1989, pp. 32-42; Günter Brakelmann, "Wirtschaftsordnung: Eine irenische Formel," in *Moderne Zeiten — soziale Gerechtigkeit?* ed. Ulf Claußen, Bochum, 1989, pp. 74-77.

[31] Müller-Armack, *Wirtschaftsordnung und Wirtschaftspolitik*, Freiburg, 1966, p. 243.

the pursuit of private interests that effectively disregards the social principle.[32]

First of all, the social market economy proves to be primarily liberal in spite of the distance it claims to maintain from extreme liberalism. It clearly favors competition as the fundamental principle responsible for the coordination of economic processes; yet, it does so not in the manner of the old form of liberalism, but of neo-liberalism, more specifically of ordo-liberalism as one of its variants.

In contrast to the old form of liberalism, the ordo-liberalism founded by Walter Eucken[33] came to the conclusion that the principle of economic competition can only function if a clear framework assures competition with the goal of bringing the market economy closer to the ideal of complete competition, that is to say of eliminating as much as possible the formation of monopolistic as well as cartelized market forces. The government would presumably have to intervene in the economy by setting up a corresponding framework and by enforcing compliance with it. Contrary to the laissez-faire principle, this method signifies the planning of the legal framework of the market economy, but not the course taken by its economic processes.

From the beginning, the social market economy as defined by Müller-Armack adopted as its foundation the ordo-liberal principle of competition, however not without also setting itself clearly apart from it. Thus a different economic position comes to the fore. The differences are revealed by the fact that it does not consider the mechanism of competition as the sole regulating force in the economy of industrialized societies.[34] Its leading advocate states clearly: "To be sure, I have always considered the heavy emphasis on a system for regulating competition as too narrow and have, therefore, insisted on a system of market-conforming, yet socio-political measures."[35] Accordingly, contrary to the ordo-liberal position, even government regulation of economic processes is not simply excluded by the market's competitive order:

[32] The social market economy is "not a liberal market economy left to its own devices, but rather a market economy that consciously shapes its policies based on social responsibility" (*ibid.*, p. 109).

[33] Concerning ordo-liberalism, see Willi Alfred Boelcke, "Liberalismus," in *Handbuch der Wirtschaftswissenschaft*, Vol. 5, pp. 45-46, and Ernst Heuß, "Ordoliberalismus," in *Liberalismus im Kreuzfeuer*, ed. Hans G. Nutzinger, Frankfurt, 1986, pp. 25-40.

[34] Müller-Armack, *Wirtschaftsordnung und Wirtschaftspolitik*, p. 11.

[35] *Ibid.*, p. 10.

> The understanding of the technical advantages of competitive, economic exchange is easily compatible with the necessity to provide definite avenues for the economic process by providing a certain amount of planning and design in the economic realm. Even with regard to the temporal economic process, economic liberalism thought it could leave the economy to self-stabilizing forces, despite the fact that, as illustrated by the increasingly more severe economic downturns, there was no clarity at all about the ability of the market economy to neutralize universal variations. The confidence in the ability of the economy to heal itself could not be maintained during economic crises. Here, too, the liberal position is an expression of passivity that seems untenable nowadays because it is precisely this passivity that mobilized the opposing forces. In view of the passivity of the government and of the parties, the ultimately liberal economic policy designed after the First World War within the setting of the market-economic organization was in the end run over by a promotion of jobs that left the market economy in its wake.[36]

Undoubtedly, we can gather from this striking quote that Müller-Armack took a dim view of the classical neo-classical thesis of the inherent healing powers of the market-friendly structured economy during critical business cycle fluctuations and their accompanying social upheavals. Obviously, this does not mean that the coordinating efforts of the market-based economic mechanisms should be put into question at all. On the contrary, those mechanisms definitely retain their constitutive function within the order principle of the social market economy. However, they do not simply kick in automatically:

> A consciously designed market economy is not running on automatic. Holding on to this consistently dangerous image, we may compare the social market economy to a semi-automatic machine that must be operated and steered. Just as an automobile engine is an independently functioning mechanism requiring a number of external controls before its potential can be realized, the market economic exchange must be surrounded by safeguards and release mechanisms that are tailored to the specific nature of its function. Certain measures are necessary to get the market economic exchange moving, just like the starter of the car gets the engine going. The functionality of competition and the regulation of its operation needs to be continuously attended to, similar to lubricating an engine, operating the accelerator and putting on the brakes. It requires structural control not unlike the steering of a car, and,

[36] *Ibid.*, p. 107.

> finally, the market economy has certain design flaws in spite of its overall rationality that require occasional repairs, even partial modification of the design.[37]

What is striking about this passage is the instrumental understanding of the market economy. A market economy can never be an end it itself. The market economy is an instrument, a means to an end. It sees its purpose on the one hand in making possible the creation of an efficient and life-giving economy that liberates the initiative, the willingness to be innovative, and sets free the productive force of individuals participating in the economy; on the other hand, its purported objective is seen in its order which leads in turn to a balanced distribution of the produced national product which incorporates indirectly an economic policy aiming for full employment. The realization of these dual purposes require market-oriented settings in the ordo-liberal sense that guarantee a functioning competition, control powerful market monopolies, oligopolies and cartels, in other words settings that minimize restrictive practices in order to foster most effectively the kind of competition that keeps the interests of the consumer in mind, a fact that already contains a social component.[38] Yet, there is more to it:

> The concept of the social market economy is not limited...to merely making the instruments of competition socially functional. The market economic income process provides a sound foundation for social policy on which basis the government is able to redirect income for the purpose of adjusting the distribution of income in the form of welfare payments, social security payments, equalization of war burdens payments, housing subsidies, etc.[39]

In short, all this suggests that the competition-based market economy is not social in itself, even though unadulterated competition already produces results that balance various interests, especially those between producers and consumers.[40] In addition, it must be consciously shaped as a social dimension by way of regulating, targeted

[37] *Ibid.*, pp. 115-16.
[38] *Ibid.*, pp. 245-46.
[39] *Ibid.*, p. 246.
[40] Müller-Armack is able to attribute to competition an almost "solidarity-like function," despite the fact that it is "characterized as somewhat combative," as long as everyone, even those who suffer from it, "ultimately derives essential benefits from other effects of competition" (*Genealogie der Sozialen Marktwirtschaft*, Bern, 1974, p. 122.). It should also be pointed out here that the original Latin meaning of the German word for competition, "*Konkurrenz*," (= *concurrere*) is 'to run *together*.'

interventions. In other words, the market economy presupposes a government-controlled economic policy that leaves the market mechanism its constitutive function but simultaneously regulates it, mindful of social considerations, and certainly corrects and even changes it structurally at the moment defects appear in the system. This can be brought in line with what we understand by the combination of market and planning, which assigns constitutive significance to the laws of the market and regulatory importance to planning and guiding interventions.[41]

The preceding explanations elucidate that the social market economy represents a concept of the combination of market and planning according to which market laws are assigned a constitutive role, while targeted or planned interventions are to "safeguard the social purpose" without "disturbing the market mechanism."[42] They must, therefore — to repeat a key phrase mentioned earlier — "conform to the market." Thus market conformity proves to be "the regulatory principle of social intervention in the market economy."[43]

However, there are some complications in conjunction with the concept of market conformity. On the one hand, it can be interpreted in different ways. Even Müller-Armack himself admits that the definition may be "vague in borderline cases."[44] And he subsequently runs quickly into trouble with the concrete economic policy which is defined as the totality of regulatory measures in the economy. Will this policy always manage well resorting only to market-conforming interventions? Could we not imagine the kind of situation — for instance in the real-estate market with its exorbitantly speculative price haggling or when the environment is acutely endangered — when, at least in

[41] Müller-Armack himself speaks of a "dialectic" attribution of the principles of obligation (*Bindung*) and freedom (= planning and market); these would need to be "treated almost on different levels [i.e., not mixed, A. Rich] and thus made mutually compatible." — "As to the system for regulating competition, it would lead to the incorporation of competition within a general framework, within which its falsification or even the exploitation of earnings positions gained through competition would be prevented by public law, indeed, insuring that competition becomes identified with the economy as a whole" (*ibid.*, pp. 202-3). This comes close to our distinction between the constitutive and the regulatory level within the market-planning-combination, which is distinguished from the merely mechanical, mutually-paralyzing mixture of market and planning elements. See *BEE*, Vol. II, 5.2.2.2. and 5.2.2.3.

[42] Müller-Armack, *Wirtschaftsordnung und Wirtschaftspolitik*, p. 246.

[43] *Ibid.*

[44] *Ibid.*

the short term, measures not conforming to the market force themselves on the market because market-conforming measures have not taken effect, or are late in coming? The fact is, in this sense, there is no chemically pure economic policy. Therefore, its legitimate character is doubted by the purists among the advocates of the market-economy. Müller-Armack himself refuses to be a doctrinaire in this matter. Surprisingly, he meets these doubts with the unorthodox argument that experience has shown that "the market economy is capable of tolerating a substantial portion of non-conforming measures without suffering any damage to its substance." Thus "the special treatment given to agriculture or the traffic sector did not disturb the functional ability of the market economy."[45] Clearly, this means that conformity to the market must be sought as much as possible in the social market economy; however, one ought not be dogmatic about it. That is why the regulatory framework of the social market economy leaves much room for directive measures, but not just for global regulation;[46] Müller-Armack also skillfully advocated selective intervention during critical situations that exceeded or augmented global control. Exactly that happened in 1966-67, at the time of the grand coalition, when the first dangerous post-war economic crisis gripped the Federal Republic of Germany. At the time, he averred: "In addition to justifiable global control, the combination of an economic upswing with structural problems forces us to clean up at least the beginnings of widely dissimilar structural problems." He then adds five concrete postulates, such as the "constructive restoration of healthy conditions and the creation of an approximate balance in the coal-mining industry," which would make a "reduction of oil consumption, a new single mining organization, and the setting of certain safety nets during implementation" inevitable.[47] Overall, this illustrates how far the practice of the social market economy can go when it relativizes the market economic principle.

[45] *Ibid.*, p. 258.

[46] We understand "global regulation" as the influence of governmental economic policy on macro-economic magnitudes such as the money supply, the volume of investments, consumption, national income, etc., with the goal of achieving balance throughout society. See also Karl Schiller, *Preisstabilität durch globale Steuerung der Marktwirtschaft*, Tübingen, 1966.

[47] Müller-Armack, "Konjunkturelle Aussichten und konjunkturpolitische Aufgaben für das Jahr 1968," *Wirtschaftspolitische Chronik*, Issue 2/3 (1967), pp. 15-16. Regarding the overall topic, see also Katterle, "Jenseits der sozialen Marktwirtschaft," pp. 32 ff., esp. p. 37.

Nevertheless, it would not be appropriate to summarily hold Müller-Armack to the extent of these relativizing market-economic possibilities. His concept of market regulation is not that consistent and systematic. His research also includes statements that point in the opposite direction. In other words, he may view the regulatory forces of the market economy much more narrowly than previously shown, in fact, so narrowly that even global control, which he otherwise accepts as admissible and useful, falls victim to market nonconformity: "The idea that it is possible to predetermine the course of the economy by means of global control by looking ahead ten years or more, and the ideas underlying, for instance, the views expressed by French planifaction are in opposition to the style subscribed to by the social market economy."[48] In view of such a verdict by its leading proponent, one should not be surprised if the rightful and expedient support of global control within the social market economy is hotly disputed. Even its basic critics are able to refer to Müller-Armack.[49] In as much as such tendencies are more widely accepted — which is the case under the current coalition in the Federal Republic of Germany — the liberal dominates the regulatory component of the social market economy, thus leading to deregulations in the economic policy that may approximate the previous forms of pure liberalism and, therefore, also the specifically capitalist form of the market economy. Viewed in this light, the actually existing social market economy becomes dubious, erasing originally characteristic contours. Therein lies also the explanation why, using contemporary language, one can equate not only regulated capitalism but also the deregulated free-market economy with the social market economy. The latter, however, is used incorrectly and clearly contradicts the genesis of the social market economy to which Müller-Armack referred as a "constructive new creation" in 1949 that has "nothing at all to do with previous manifestations of pure liberalism."[50] There is no question that the economic development of the Federal Republic of Germany after the currency reform in 1948 is characterized by the principles of the social market economy.

[48] Müller-Armack, "Der humane Gehalt der Sozialen Marktwirtschaft," in *Soziale Marktwirtschaft im Wandel*, p. 20.

[49] For instance, Tuchtfeldt, "Soziale Marktwirtschaft und Globalsteuerung," in *Soziale Marktwirtschaft im Wandel*, pp. 159-88.

[50] Müller-Armack, *Genealogie der Sozialen Marktwirtschaft*, pp. 203-4.

Certainly, this is not to suggest, however, that its genuine fundamental concept has since become reality: "A concept always remains a design for the practice of the social market economy and must therefore not be confused with practice itself."[51] The practice of the social market economy passed through various phases during the past forty years.[52] As stated already, more and more importance was simultaneously attached to the liberal component within the regulatory framework. Whatever passes today for social market economy can be called by that name only conditionally. Nevertheless, there is no doubt that owing to its practice, the West German economy became not only strong and efficient, but that it also enabled significant social achievements. Let me just remind the reader of the subsidized housing program (1950), the passing of laws protecting workers and protecting against unlawful dismissal (1951), co-determination based on equal representation in the coal, iron, and steel industry (1951), the industrial relations act (1952), maternity laws and the protection of the severely handicapped (1953), the wage-index-linked retirement law (1957), the creation of social and industrial tribunals, etc. All these illustrate significant changes in the social realm that depart decisively from the specifically capitalist form of the market economy with its confrontational domination of capital interests.

In as much as we must appreciate and praise the economic success and social accomplishments achieved above all by the social market economy practiced during the 1950s and 1960s, we must, on the other hand, beware of viewing it as the ultimate solution. It, too, is plagued by deficiencies and weak points and, therefore, in need of new perspectives. Müller-Armack pointed that out as early as 1960 in his programmatic essay "The Second Phase of the Social Market Economy."[53] In it he demands nothing less than "its augmentation by means of a guiding principle for a new social policy." In this essay, he proposes the following cardinal points: 1. A comprehensive expansion of educational facilities on all levels all the way down to specialized vocational schools, that is to say, substantially increased investment in intellectual capital (p. 135); 2. The creation of new

[51] Tuchfeldt, "Soziale Marktwirtschaft und Globalsteuerung," p. 160.

[52] See Reinhard Blum, "Marktwirtschaft, soziale," in *Handwörterbuch der Wirtschaftswissenschaften*, Vol. 5, pp. 153-66.

[53] Müller-Armack, "Die zweite Phase der sozialen Marktwirtschaft," in *Genealogie der Sozialen Marktwirtschaft*, pp. 129-45.

independent entities by making conditions in the workplace more humane (135-36); 3. An active stabilization policy that extends beyond national borders for the purpose of assuring currency stability (136-37); 4. A universally designed environmental policy for the purpose of keeping water clean and the air pure, including the humanly just planning of cities, the countryside and traffic patterns (137 ff.). In a later publication (1969), "The Moralist and the Economist: On the Question of the Humanization of the Economy,"[54] Müller-Armack discusses additional questionable issues which necessitate a "continuation" and even a "critical evaluation" of the social market economy. This includes asymmetric formation of wealth, which it was unable to prevent. He specifically points to the "fact of increasing accumulation of business owner's assets" and the lack of participation of "large groups of people in the formation of capital" (pp. 225-26). He equally decries the disadvantages experienced by developing countries as a result of the predominant economic policy practiced by industrialized countries. If there is, therefore, substantial criticism of the social market economy from within, external criticism is even more understandable.[55]

As far as this other, external criticism is concerned, it focuses above all on three deficiencies:

- a relatively high unemployment rate with new forms of impoverishment and social instability,
- national and transnational concentrations of economic power together with their market-distorting, social and societal consequences,
- the ecological crisis which is becoming ever more severe.

Of course, we are dealing here with depressing phenomena that are not specifically tied to the social market economy as such. They are present everywhere in Western industrial society, and, in hidden form, in its Eastern counterpart, suggesting something of a common denominator. However, one needs to point out that even the social market economy was unable to prevent them and that, considering its current practices, it is hardly poised to do something about it.[56]

[54] Müller-Armack, "Der Moralist und der Ökonom," in *Genealogie der Sozialen Marktwirtschaft*, pp. 219-33.

[55] See, among others, *40 Jahre Soziale Marktwirtschaft: Bilanz und Perspektiven*, special issue of *Zeitschrift für Erwachsenenbildung*, No. 3 (May/June 1988).

[56] This is illustrated, for instance, by the merger controls that have become the central instrument of preventive control of economic power in the Federal Republic of

Together with the kind of weak points listed already by Müller-Armack, there is sufficient reason to search for possible ways of further developing it, indeed to come up with perspectives that go beyond it, without reducing the importance of the social market economy as a primary market-oriented principle of order that purposely distances itself from actual capitalism. Thus the following steps have been traced out.

6.2.3 *The Democratic Market Economy (The Swedish Model)*[57]

Similar to the social market economy of the Federal Republic of Germany, the democratic market economy, as the Swedish model can be characterized,[58] understands itself in its ideal form as a third possibility, situated "between a capitalist market economy" and the "East European planned economy."[59] Because of its importance, it would be worthwhile to discuss it in detail; however we are only able to glance at it to the extent that it will be necessary to shed light on the correspondences and differences from the form of order illustrated by the social market economy.

The Swedish model developed in three steps. It originated when political democracy broke through during pre-war Sweden. After the Social Democratic Party's rise to power, there followed an expansion of social and ultimately economic democracy in the form of so-called Workers Investment Funds.[60]

Germany since 1973. Should these controls be tightened or relaxed in view of the increasing number of economic concentrations of power? Opinions differ. Influenced by the Chicago School (Milton Friedman), the latter tendency is gaining ground. According to this view, intensive international competition will take care of limiting market power on its own. Trusting not only in the erosive forces of the market, the former tendency, however, finds itself on the defensive.

[57] Concerning the Swedish model, see Fritz Vilmar and Karl-Otto Sattler, *Wirtschaftsdemokratie und Humanisierung der Arbeit*, Cologne, 1978 (a general discussion); Rudolf Meidner, "Unsere Vorstellungen vom Dritten Weg," in *Wirtschaft und Gesellschaft*, ed. Ulrich Gärtner and Jirí Kosta, Berlin, 1979, pp. 363-87; Institute of the German Economy, ed., *Schweden*, Cologne, 1982; Meidner and Anna Hedborg, *Modell Schweden*, Frankfurt, 1984; Hans-Michael Trautwein, *Arbeitnehmerfonds in Schweden*, Frankfurt, 1986.

[58] Meidner, *Unsere Vorstellungen vom Dritten Weg*, p. 386: "It is correct, however, that the [Swedish] worker movement seeks to change the existing economic system, though not by destroying the market economy, instead by democratizing the economy."

[59] *Ibid.*, p. 382.

[60] See Trautwein, *Arbeitnehmerfonds in Schweden*, pp. 25-26.

The expansive phase of social democracy was marked by the "spirit of Saltsjöbaden." As mentioned earlier,[61] something like a corporate partnership arrangement was created there in 1938 between the association of Swedish employers (SAF) and the national organization of Swedish labor unions (LO). This arrangement granted "employers far-reaching powers in their businesses" and "unions the complete right to organization and collective bargaining." Moreover, both partners promised "to practice responsible restraint and guarantee far-reaching bargaining rights and freedom from government intervention."[62] In this way, capital and wages, that is to say, the social interests, were to check one another, a practice that reflects the fundamental principle of the social market economy.

During this developmental phase, one could refer to the Swedish economic order as a variation of the social market economy. Producers are given carte blanche in the production sector. There is essentially no government intervention in the course of the private economy. Even more so than in the social market economy of the Federal Republic of Germany, it is subject to the market's self-regulation. On the other hand, the ability to influence the distribution of the products of production is much greater. The primary instruments for the purpose of achieving this distribution are both a solidarity-minded wage policy and the government's fiscal policy, which both share the declared goal of achieving as high a degree as possible of social equality among all members of society.

The solidarist wage policy[63] proceeds from the socialist idea that the distribution of the national product of the economy must not be left primarily to market forces. Labor is not a commodity, but a human act, and wages are not the price paid for a commodity, but the act of honoring a socially produced human performance. In other words, the human dimension of labor is taken seriously here. That is why the decisive factor regarding wage structures should be the type of labor and not, as is the case in a pure, autonomous market economy, the bottom line of the enterprise and any accompanying fluctuations in the demand present in the labor market.[64] Certainly, this

[61] *BEE*, Vol. II, 5.2.2.5, fn. 80.

[62] Meidner, *Unsere Vorstellungen vom Dritten Weg*, p. 366.

[63] See Meidner and Hedborg, *Modell Schweden*, pp. 66-78; Meidner, *Unsere Vorstellungen vom Dritten Weg*, pp. 370 ff.

[64] *Ibid.*, p. 370.

will lead to differences in the amount of pay, depending on the type of labor, but it will mean equal pay for equal work in all the various branches of industry.[65] The consistent practice of this principle leads to a great equalization of pay differences among the branches of industry, between skilled and unskilled workers, men and women, population centers and the provinces, etc. "In less than fifteen years, the discrepancies in pay (measured against the average wages paid in the approximately 130 bargaining areas) was reduced by half."[66] The equalizing effect of a solidarity-based wage policy is thus quite obvious.

Government fiscal policy also serves the principle of equality motivated in a socialistic manner. Its purpose is essentially twofold: First, to provide the government with the means needed for the purpose of financing its universally conceived and expensively affluent society and, secondly, in order to be able to distribute the wealth in the country equally.

The condition for procuring the means for paying for the ever-increasing social expenditures is an efficient, growth-oriented and profitable industrial economy. In other words, a market economy that is profit-oriented and favorably disposed towards the creation of capital in conjunction with the formation of income. This means from a fiscal-political point of view that in Sweden the profits of corporations are taxed relatively moderately, in order to spur their desire to invest.

On the other hand, the distribution of income is influenced by the egalitarian-socialist tendency. To be sure, there are differences in pay depending on the type of work, however this is supposed to simultaneously create a market-economic incentive to perform. Yet, the pay differences in the presence of a very high taxation level when compared internationally are subsequently equalized by a most aggressive progressive system; that is to say, income is largely redistributed by the government. Thus the highest possible tax bracket in 1981 for an income of 25,000 krona was 31.5%, for an income of 75,000 krona it was 58.5%, while for 200,000 krona or more it was 85%.[67] In turn, the Swedish welfare state assumes basic responsibility for "employment opportunities and the existence of a comprehensive social security system for everybody [benefiting even wealthy

[65] Meidner and Hedborg, *Modell Schweden*, p. 67.
[66] Meidner, *Unsere Vorstellungen vom Dritten Weg*, pp. 371-72.
[67] Institute of the German Economy, ed., *Schweden*, p. 25.

citizens; A. Rich] offering financial compensation in the event of illness, for college education, childcare and retirement."[68]

If the Swedish model can, therefore, be understood from the point of view of social democracy as a variation of the social market economy that differs from the German model primarily because of the greater emphasis placed on the egalitarian component in an effort to solve the distribution of wealth, this looks essentially different on the level of economic democracy. Economic democracy not only aims to democratize society in the social realm by means of an egalitarian policy of distribution, but it follows such a policy also in the productive market-economically oriented sector. The reasons for this are, however, rooted already in certain real constraints present in social democracy according to the Swedish model.

As mentioned, the centerpiece of Sweden's social democracy is formed by the government's socially oriented fiscal policy, together with a solidarist wage policy that relies on intervention in the market's mechanisms by means of distributing the national product. This causes a chain reaction throughout the entire structure of the economic order, which, according to Meidner/Hedborg,[69] two influential co-framers of the Swedish model, leads to the following consequences:

1. Generally speaking, the solidarity-based wage policy brings on an increase in the cost of wages and of labor. Providing conditions of free competition, enterprises are able to head that off by economizing productive, administrative and distributive activities through rationalization. In the event of insufficient competition, cost increases can be offset also by compensatory price increases.
2. If weak companies with low profits are forced to pay wages that are determined in accordance with the solidarist principle based on the average profits earned by all businesses and if the funds mentioned under (1) become exhausted, this may lead to reductions of plant activities or even closing down, hence to a loss of jobs.
3. On the other hand, profitable businesses can achieve "excessive profits" because their wages are equally based on guidelines supplied by the average profit picture of the productive economy.

These consequences have two possible effects that frequently occur simultaneously.

[68] Meidner and Hedborg, *Modell Schweden*, p. 61.
[69] *Ibid.*, p. 75.

On the one hand, they stimulate a drifting of local wages leading to a conflict with the solidarity-based wage policy. On the other hand, they strengthen the tendency of concentrating capital among potent businesses that is typical of the capitalist accumulation process. Together, all this means that the solidarity-based wage policy harbors a tendency to generate unemployment, local pay differences, capital or economic concentrations of power and possibly inflationary price pressure. Those are the danger points one cannot simply ignore.

The Swedish unions headed off these danger points by making it their goal as early as 1971 to come up with a method to soften the mentioned dilemmas caused by the solidarity-based wage policy, especially in an effort to defend against the concentration of assets in private hands resulting from increased self-financing by businesses benefiting from those "excessive profits" and, finally, to grant workers the ability to influence the course of the economy by way of their co-ownership of the means of production.[70] From these efforts stems the concept of the Workers' Investment Funds that was proposed for the first time to the National Trade Unions Congress in 1976.

There is no need to go into the technical details of the concept of the Workers' Investment Funds. In this context, only the basic features are relevant. According to Rudolf Meidner they can be summarized as follows:[71] A portion of the profits earned by large companies are to be handed over annually as so-called "workers' stocks" to a number of representatives of the workers, more specifically the accounts administered by the unions. There are no individual, only collective shares in these stocks. Moreover, they are non-negotiable and the capital remains therefore in the companies. By virtue of their right to vote at the stockholders meeting, the funds are able to elect representatives chosen by them to the supervisory boards. In the interest of a decentralization of power, the funds must transfer a substantial portion of their voting right to the employees of enterprises where profits are allotted to the funds in the form of stocks.

From this follows already that these workers' funds are expected to meet a great number of objectives. Above all, the investment potential of the entire economy, particularly of the large profitable

[70] Meidner, *Unsere Vorstellungen vom Dritten Weg*, p. 381.
[71] *Ibid.*

companies is supposed to be preserved. That would not be the case if the excess profits were to be divided up into individual profit shares for workers who are privileged due to the high productivity of their companies, that is to say, they would be transformed into purchasing power. Moreover, apart from the inherent inflationary potential, this would contradict the principle of the solidarity-based wage policy. Furthermore, capital power should be divided and the workers should be granted a collective right to co-determination in company decisions regarding the means of production. Also, to insure the preservation of existing jobs or the creation of new ones, opportunities should be created to deliver capital means at favorable conditions to businesses that are weaker, but have the potential for development; indeed, a structural, employment-effective labor market policy should be pursued by controlled investments.[72] Finally, the earnings accruing from the workers' stocks could be used for the additional alimentation of the social security system; this would then be equal to indirect profit sharing. In sum, the purpose of this model is a democratization even of the economic sphere of society.

Now, a comparison between the later Swedish concept of the democratic with the social market economy of the Federal Republic of Germany results essentially in the following.

Both forms of order intend to socially engage and transform the capitalist market economy without abandoning the market-based system of coordination that makes up the economy. That is why both want to do as much as possible without government intervention in economic processes, yet they want to provide to workers influence on company decisions and company affairs by way of institutions affording them co-determination, especially in matters concerning the humane design of the workplace. As to regulating the market economy, apart from the social net, the social market economy advocates actively, at least in theory, the kind of ordered competition that harnesses economic power, whereas, intent on the egalitarian distribution of the national product, the democratic market economy emphasizes a solidarity-based wage and fiscal policy together with a social security system that is based on it.

Connected indirectly to this policy is precisely the most significant difference between the democratic and the social market economy.

[72] Concerning the labor market policy of the Swedish model, see Meidner and Hedborg, *Modell Schweden*, pp. 104-12.

As was pointed out, it minimizes in the area of distribution the mechanisms of the market economy. The resulting negative consequences cause corrective action in the form of the concept of the Workers' Investment Funds, which leads simultaneously to the reorganization of ownership rights and to the right to participate in company decisions making. It is here that the Swedish model goes decidedly beyond that of the Federal Republic of Germany.[73]

This raises the question if such an incisive reshuffling or socialization of the ownership of the means of production in the hands of the workers would have to lead not only to a departure from the specifically capitalist form of the market economy, but if it would undermine it despite the protestations by the unions to the contrary.[74]

We must beware of a hastily affirmative or negative response to this question.

First of all, it must be pointed out that the partial socialization of productive real capital held by the workers as required by the Swedish funds concept must not need to be incompatible with the market-economy-based principle. Paul A. Samuelson, a decided advocate of the market-economy-based fundamental system even states that "in a perfectly competitive market it really doesn't matter who hires whom: so have labor hire 'capital'."[75] The fact is that, under the conditions of functioning competition, even "labor" as a capital factor will have to employ resources in a manner conforming to the market in order to generate sufficient profits, if it wants to avoid suffering losses and endangering the existence of businesses.[76] In other words, this means that, in their role as responsible guardians of the workers' funds, the unions must thus take care not only of the legitimate social needs of the people active in the economy, but also of the indispensable capital interests of the companies, that is to say,

[73] During the 1960s, even the Federal Republic of Germany underwent extensive discussion of ownership rights, which benefited the unions and the Social Democratic Party in Sweden, although the results were different. Regarding the ownership discussions in Germany, see Wilhelm Krelle, *et al.*, *Überbetriebliche Ertragsbeteiligung der Arbeitnehmer*, Vol. I, Tübingen, 1968, and Trautwein, *Arbeitnehmerfonds in Schweden*, pp. 37-41.

[74] See 6.2.3, fn. 58.

[75] Paul A. Samuelson, *Collected Scientific Papers*, Vol. I, Cambridge, 1966, p. 351.

[76] Thus, Rudolf Meidner emphasizes also that, in an economy influenced by the workers, the maximization of profits will no longer be the goal of investors and management but "a restriction which is necessary for the existence of the company and which must not be compromised" (cited by Trautwein, *Arbeitnehmerfonds in Schweden*, fn. 30).

they must play a double role fraught with conflict. What remains is the question if they are able to assume this role by relying on their traditional responsibilities, or if they will allow themselves or are forced into being guided one-sidedly by the short-term social interests of their members during their capital involvement and the accompanying entrepreneurial decisions. The latter will be less the case if the workers' funds do not gain excessive capital weight. Any excessive concentration of capital, no matter whether it happens in the hands of private owners of capital, consortia or corporations, of the government, or even of the unions and, therefore, any form of a monocracy of interests, be it capitalistic or labor-based, is a bad situation that can hardly be reconciled with the principle of a socially shaped and yet efficiently functioning market economy.

The actual realization of the Workers' Investment Funds in Sweden[77] — they were enacted at the beginning of 1984 — did not proceed without significant modifications of the original concept. For one, the annual profit sharing tax to which corporations, co-operatives, banks and insurance companies were subject, as well as the workers' funds that were spread over five regional entities, was limited to 20% of real profits. Furthermore, in what amounted to the most serious restriction, each one of these individual funds was not to receive more than 8% of the voting rights at the meeting of a given company, so that the five funds were merely able to acquire only up to 40% of the voting holders' capital.[78] Finally, the Social Democratic government declared that after 1990 the development of workers' investment funds was to be considered complete.[79] In this fashion and in accordance with the practices of the Swedish model, collective participation of the workers in the capital stock with its voting rights, as well as indirect participation in the eventual dividends via the allocation to the general pension funds, are supposed to be guaranteed without causing an excessive concentration of capital power in the hands of the unions. Thus, in addition to the politically motivated distribution component, the goal is a kind of division, that does not always exist, of the legal control over capital in the companies. On the one hand, their

[77] For more details, see *ibid.*, pp. 89-105.

[78] *Ibid.*, p. 93 and 95-96. If the voting rights of the General Pension Fund are added, then a maximum share of 49.95% may be possible (*ibid.*, p. 93).

[79] *Ibid.*, p. 97.

social and democratic controllability is to be made possible; on the other hand, a barrier is to be erected against company mergers or company takeovers that run counter to the interests of the employees. Even in the presence of such a restriction, the system of the workers' investment funds entails in contrast to the social market economy a change in the traditional structure of the ownership of the means of production in the companies as well as in the voting rights that are attached to them.

Although the currently practiced form of the system of workers' investment funds appears to be tenable also from the point of view of a market economy — the general situation of Sweden's economy attests to that fact — it remains as debatable as ever, even among union representatives.[80] Nevertheless, the principal opponents are the employers' associations. One important reason for their opposition lies in the uncertainty of future development. If the current government considers the creation of the workers' investment funds complete as of 1990, then the Swedish Association of Unions (LO) merely considers it a first step towards economic democracy.[81] Will there be any additional steps and what will be their objectives? The employers' groups are afraid that it might lead to a centrally controlled economy in which the market loses its constitutive function. If workers' investment funds were indeed to achieve excessive capital power within companies under the auspices of a democratization of the economy and, contrary to the interplay of market forces, aiming at forcing the favoring of social interests, then a switch towards central control of the economy via the workers' investment funds bureaucracy all the way to the micro-economic areas of companies and plants would not be entirely out of the question.[82] Considering these facts, one could speak of the potential for an economic centralism in view of the type of order prevalent in Sweden's democratic market economy.

[80] *Ibid.*, p. 100.

[81] *Ibid.*, p. 97.

[82] Furthermore, the public sector in Sweden, with its approximately 60% share of the GDP, predominates in the economy, a fact that in itself contains a regimenting effect and has led most recently to heated controversies, even in the inner circles of the Social Democratic Party of Sweden. For more about this, see Robert F. Lamberg, "'Rosenkrieg' in Schweden," *Neue Zürcher Zeitung*, No. 44, 22 February 1989, p. 37.

6.2.4 *The Socialist Market Economy*

Even the socialist market economy seeks to live up to its fundamental tendency by "taking a path on the opposite side of bureaucratic capitalism and the Soviet-type centrally planned economy."[83] Although it primarily characterizes today's radically understood economic reform efforts in the communist ruled countries, the concept is rooted in the West. To my knowledge, Alfred Weber was the first scholar to use the term.[84] Subsequently, Kurt Nemitz systematically clarified it, using it to define the order-political concept of German Social Democracy as documented in the Godesberg Program of 1959.[85] We are therefore dealing with two variations of the Socialist Market Economy, a Western one, conceived by democratic or liberal socialism, and an Eastern version that is supposed to be purposely setting itself apart from the centrally controlled economic system without "restoring" capitalism. It will be expedient to offer separate views of the two variations.

6.2.4.1 The Western Type of the Socialist Market Economy

As portrayed explicitly by Nemitz, the socialist market economy did not manage to go beyond its programmatic stage; it must be understood as the order-political example of democratic socialism. This variation of socialism is, therefore, characterized as liberal because of its determination to be firmly rooted in the liberal state founded on the rule of law and because of its advocacy of a fundamentally market-oriented economy. It is socialist to the extent that it subjects individual economic interests to the interests of the public and because, rather than leaving it to itself, it seeks though a regulatory device to order the market economy in social terms and to promote simultaneously businesses characterized by collective ownership. This coincides in many ways with the goals of the social as well as the Swedish-type democratic market economy. However, the collective component gains greater weight and planned modification of the market economy is felt more during the implementation of the regulatory element. Let us begin by discussing the latter point.

[83] Zsuzsa Szabó-Raducziner, *Pläne, Märkte und laufende Prozeßpolitik in Ungarn*, Bern, 1988, p. 11.

[84] Alfred Weber, "Sozialistische Marktwirtschaft," *Gewerkschaftliche Monatshefte*, 1 (1950), pp. 393 ff.

[85] Kurt Nemitz, *Sozialistische Marktwirtschaft*, Frankfurt, 1960.

All concepts of the socialist market economy agree in their rejection of the so-called "irreconcilability theory" regarding market and planning, as established by Walter Eucken and vigorously defended by Friedrich A. von Hayek.[86] According to this theory, mixed orders lack stability and tend towards a pure market or a pure centrally planned economy. Beyond that, Hayek envisions only a one-way street. Accordingly, even sporadic government intervention in the market economy leads to ever-greater intervention, ending inevitably in a totally planned economy. Any combination of market and planning is thus out of the question. According to our earlier reflections,[87] the irreconcilability theory might prove to be correct, in so far as, in practice, a merely mechanical mixing of contrary systems of coordination of the market and the centrally planned economy is bound to founder on its own internal contraction. To repeat, a combination of market and planning must not necessarily be characterized by such a mix. It may occur also in such a way that, during the course of economic events, a constitutive function is attributed to the market, while a regulatory function is attributed to the plan.[88] In this case, the plan presents itself as a framework, laying down global data, that is to say, it determines the fundamental objectives of economic policy. In other words, the plan plays a subsidiary role that does not supersede the market economy, rather one that qualifies and supports it. What, then, is the nature of the combination of market and planning within the concept of the socialist market economy of democratic socialism?

To begin with, it must be pointed out that Nemitz's representative portrayal frequently depicts the socialist market economy as a "mixed system" or a "mixed economic order."[89] That suggests that one ought to view the combination of market and planning merely in terms of a cumulatively mechanical combination of the two principally different systems of coordination. However, that is hardly the case. The meaning of this combination is more differentiated.

For one, it must be stated that in the case of this type of socialist market economy "the optimum functional conditions for planning

[86] See *ibid.*, pp. 81-82. See also Béla Csikós-Nagy, *Sozialistische Marktwirtschaft*, Vienna, 1988, pp. 103 ff.; Zsuzsa Szabó-Raducziner, *Pläne, Märkte und laufende Prozeßpolitik in Ungarn*, p. 11.

[87] See especially *BEE*, Vol. II, 5.2.2.2. and 3.

[88] *Ibid.*, p. 241.

[89] Nemitz, *Sozialistische Marktwirtschaft*, pp. 82, 86, 89, 127, etc.

are rooted in the macro-economic realm, while the conditions for competition lie in the micro-economic relationships of economic subject."[90] At the same time, both the macro-economic as well as the micro-economic level are understood to be complementary. Together they represent a whole without mixing arbitrarily. Similarly, the relationship between competitive and planning elements is complementary, meaning that, according to the mentioned concept, "the desired system" can "be achieved neither by a mechanical installation of market elements into a planned economy, nor by isolated interventions in a 'free' economy." "Rather, isolated inventions should be particularly avoided due to the fact that both elements are *a priori* viewed as components of the economic order system."[91] This represents a rejection of both the mere market-economic veneer of the centrally planned system as well as of government interventionism in the sense of the mixed systems marked by Western and Eastern characteristics.

This complementary perception of market and planning poses another issue. The macro-economic planning, the purpose of which is to set socio-political goals and to bring into harmony legitimate individual as well as collective economic interests, should not displace the market-economical coordination on the micro-economic level, but is rather to support it as much as necessary: "The coordination tied to planning in a socialist market economy does not come to the fore...until an equilibrium that corresponds to the goals of the economic policy is no longer guaranteed by competition."[92] Therefore, it serves basically in a subsidiary role; at the same time, the economico-political objectives must serve the state as a guide and thus be dominant in this respect.

Finally, the subsidiary function of plan-based coordination is further underscored by the fact that proof of its necessity must be in the hands of "the enforcing government authority, and not in the hands of those who wish to preserve their freedom of disposition" and that, in those cases where it imposes itself, the method deserves "preference that will entail the least invasive intervention in the market structure."[93] From this results the "principle of minimal planning."[94]

[90] *Ibid.*, p. 83.
[91] *Ibid.*, p. 105.
[92] *Ibid.*
[93] *Ibid.*
[94] *Ibid.*

Nemitz describes the meaning of minimal planning in great detail.[95] Its core appears in the form of long-range framework planning on the basis of national economic calculations by means of which fundamental data must be established for a national budget during the upcoming year, which are then to pave the way for the economy, based on macro-economic principles. We are dealing here primarily with the large-scale aspects of investment policy and the distribution of income: "Thus, according to liberal socialist thought, framework planning can and should not deal with the implementation of individual interventions; its task is rather to render intervention *superfluous* by providing suitable precautionary measures and suggestions within the realm of the aggregate economy."[96] Neither should it act coercively. On the one hand, framework planning must be understood in the indicative sense; on the other hand, the economic subjects must be involved extensively in its establishment, because they will then be more likely to be prepared to abide by it.[97] Also included in the framework planning of the economy is a government policy that aims for full employment as well as control of economic power by decentralizing the distribution of power in the interest of functioning competition. As to the latter, there are significant parallels to the corresponding postulates of the social market economy.

We may thus summarize by insisting that, at least in a programmatic sense, the Western-style socialist market economy rests on a combination of market and planning according to which the market functions constitutively, while planning serves in regulatory capacity. This fact agrees also with the genuine ideas of the earlier social market economy. What differs, however, is the weight placed on the social, more precisely, the collective (*gemeinwirtschaftliche*) component the regulation of the market.

The socialist market economy rejets not only the irreconcilability theory regarding market and planning, but also the irreconcilability of private and collective ownership.[98] Even on the level of the ownership of the means of production, the one does not exclude the other. Therein lies the rejection of the classical-Marxist as well as of the classical liberal perception of ownership.

95 *Ibid.*, pp. 104-41.
96 *Ibid.*, p. 121.
97 *Ibid.*
98 *Ibid.*, pp. 141-42.

This dual rejection manifests itself, on the one hand, by affirming in principle the right to private ownership even of the means of production, as long as it does not impede the creation of a just social order. Above all, this is true of middle and smaller ownership that is said to be entitled to protection and promotion, particularly since "*these* ownership categories are primarily suitable to contribute to the maintenance of a healthy order of competition."[99] On the other hand, the social obligation of ownership is effectively accentuated. It does not constitute an absolute right, but one must constantly question it in an effort to determine where its power is being abused and whenever it causes damage to society. Should this happen, its socialization suggests itself, which is, however, not viewed as a dogma by the advocates of the socialist market economy but, instead, amounts to a question about its expediency and necessity: "Changing over to collective ownership is viewed as a legitimate form of public control that no modern state may forego. However, it is supposed to be applied only to limited areas of big business, and even then, only if other means of order or control fail."[100]

Moreover, from the viewpoint of the socialist market economy, socialization in the sense of a transfer of the ownership of the means of production to collective ownership[101] must not be equated with estabilishing state ownership. On the contrary, nationalization — the earlier core of forms of socialization — is viewed rather negatively. In the modern society, it supposedly leads to control over the economy by government administrative agencies and not to a genuine collective economy.[102] Rather, public, freely collective and cooperative forms of enterprises are favored; they are expected to compete with the traditional forms of enterprises:

> The material differences to earlier calls for socialization are most clearly illustrated by the efforts put forth by liberal socialists to maintain competition, especially in those areas where the transfer of an enterprise into collective ownership proves to be necessary. Whereas the specific function of socialization was to abolish the market in earlier days, it is today viewed as one of the tools used to "decapitalize" this market and to make it functional in a socialist sense. This is primarily reminiscent of those forms of socialization that, as

[99] *Ibid.*, pp. 145-46.
[100] *Ibid.*, pp. 145-46.
[101] See Wilhelm Reuß, "Zum Begriff 'Gemeineigentum'," in *Die Sozialgemeinschaften*, ed. Harald Koch, Hamburg, 1948, pp. 6-9.
[102] Nemitz, *Sozialistische Marktwirtschaft*, p. 161.

Alfred Weber emphasizes, "remove the power of capital, but retain the socialized sections outside the bureaucratic apparatus within the sphere of economic activity based on unfettered spontaneity."[103]

6.2.4.2 The Eastern Version of the Socialist Market Economy

Whereas the Western form of the socialist market economy has essentially remained merely an inspiring program, its Eastern counterpart finds itself in the midst of experimental realization. Its separation from the centrally controlled economy originated in the reform-minded communistic countries under its auspices. At the same time, the budding Hungarian economic order played an ever-greater role. It certainly does not represent

> the only, already practically functioning alternative to bureaucratic Communism and to the centrally controlled economy in developed industrial societies. However, it represents today's most imitated departure from the centrally controlled economy. The attempts at reform in countries such as Poland, Bulgaria, China and, above all, the perestroika under Mikhail Gorbachev, to name only the most important ones, all point, although with different intensity, to the socialist market economy modeled by Hungary.[104]

It therefore goes without saying that this model is representative of this type of market economy.

Up until now, Hungary's economic reform aiming at a socialist market economy has taken three successive steps.[105]

At the beginning there is the reform of 1957. It already marks a conscious turn away from the pure form of a centrally controlled economy practiced during the Stalinist era. No longer is there preference given to heavy industry, but agriculture, light industry and services came to the fore. In the industrial sector, a reduction of plan projections

[103] *Ibid.*, pp. 157-58.

[104] Szabó-Raducziner, *Pläne, Märkte und laufende Prozeßpolitik in Ungarn*, p. 11; see also Henner Kleinewefers, "Pläne, Märkte und Prozeßpolitik in Ungarn," *Neue Zürcher Zeitung*, No. 189, 16 August 1988, p. 33: "What is being discussed and done in the *U.S.S.R.* today and has been discussed and done for a long time in *all of Eastern Europe* in the area of economic reform is unambiguously oriented towards the *Hungarian example*, while the *Yugoslavian model*, for political reasons that are well known, was always considered from a great distance and in the meantime has also lost attraction in broad intellectual circles."

[105] For a detailed analysis, see Kleinewefers, *Reformen für Wirtschaft und Gesellschaft*, Frankfurt, 1985, pp. 144-81.

took place together with economic incentives for managers and workers for the purpose of assuring their implementation. Above all, this step towards reform introduced a new constitution for agricultural co-operatives, granting them more room for individual initiatives. The government purchase prices for agricultural goods were increased and the co-operatives were granted private acreage for the purpose of independent cultivation and marketing. The results were spectacular: "In contrast to the earlier days and to other communist countries, the agricultural sector became a producer of surpluses and an exporter."[106] The living standard and the quality of life of Hungarian farmers improved substantially, leading to renewed attractiveness of working and living in the countryside.

Although the 1957 reform produced the expected results in the agricultural sector,[107] this was not at all the case in the industrial sector. The reason being that, although the parameters set up for the economic conduct of the managers of the enterprises as well as the workers had widened, the production continued to greatly exceed need, because there was no market demanding pricing determined by scarcity:

> This was the reason for the economic reform of 1968, whose fundamental goals were the independence of enterprises made possible by abolishing imperative micro-planning, the introduction of pricing dictated by scarcity, and, because of that, the rationalization of the economy, that is an increase in labor productivity and the assurance of further growth.[108]

This stage moved along only hesitatingly, however, because of a lack of consistency during the implementation of the concept. It was not until the reform resolutions of 1980 that "a great step forward took place."[109] According to Henner Kleinewefers, they essentially generated the following changes:[110] — Numerous exceptions employed to regulate the economy fell by the wayside, amounting to an approximation of a macro-economic control of the economy. — Price formation was exposed as directly as possible to foreign competition and

[106] *Ibid.*, p. 145.

[107] For more detailed information on this subject, see K.-E. Wädekin, "Ungarns Landwirtschaft," *Neue Zürcher Zeitung*, No. 285, 12 July 1982, p. 23 and No. 286, 12 December 1982, p. 23.

[108] Kleinewefers, *Reformen für Wirtschaft und Gesellschaft*, p. 146.

[109] *Ibid.*

[110] *Ibid.*, pp. 179 ff.

the range of free pricing was further expanded. This increased the influence of global events on the Hungarian economy, particularly since enterprises could now increasingly engage directly in export transactions. — There was supposed to be a tendency to decentralize large businesses, trusts and associations, perhaps even to disentangle them in order to promote the beginnings of an internal policy of competition within the industrial sector. — Small private businesses were granted more elbowroom, which brought relief to central planning and control, increased competition and improved supply. — Even the market-economic performance principle was given more room through increased differentiation of personal income. On the one hand, the differences in the qualification of workers was supposed to be reflected more noticeably in the amount of pay and, on the other hand, the income margins for similar work were supposed to be increased in different enterprises.

Certainly, all these renovations, or expansions had already been inserted into the fundamental reform of 1968. However, they also signified a decisive step towards their intended goal: the construction of a functional, efficient socialist market economy. At the same time, one must keep in mind that the Hungarian economic order remained nevertheless tied to the socialist system in the traditional Marxist-Leninist sense. This applied above all to the existing ownership structures. As late as 1985, Kleinewefers still surmised that "there will be no restoration of private ownership of the means of production beyond the presently tolerated small businesses."[111] Furthermore, apart from membership in the Warsaw Pact, this also involved the interconnection between the Hungarian national economy and COMECON, together with all the accompanying planning duties. Finally, the single-party system and, therefore, the monopoly of power enjoyed by the Communists even in matters of basic economic decisions continued as a political framework, albeit in less stringent form. All this entailed that, although the central planning system became severely restricted, it did not simply disappear in Hungary in spite of far-reaching modifications in the market economy. In fact, this established a combination of planning and market, that is to say, economic control that was dubious at its core and thus, in a bad sense, a compromise. This was reflected even by the theoretical underpinnings of the new Hungarian economic order. At any rate, it seems to be present in Béla Csikós-Nagy's book.

[111] *Ibid.*, pp. 180-81.

Like all defenders of the socialist market economy, this prominent economist presumes that there cannot be purposeful economic development without a planned national economy and planned control, nor can there be a rational economic order without a functioning market mechanism and its control function.[112] Eucken's and Hayek's irreconcilability theory is thus clearly rejected. It is replaced, however, by the synthetisization theory. "Practically speaking, there is [supposedly] always talk about the *synthetisization between the plan and the market*, but not a word about a market economy without planning or a planned economy without a market."[113]

In this context, the synthesis of market and planning signifies that the contrary systems of coordination must be on the same level. Csikós-Nagy speaks explicitly of a "coordination" of market and planning, whose meaning clearly intends a combination of the two fundamental systems on the same level. The contradiction innate in this kind of combination between planning and market has been discussed earlier.[114] Both market and planning cannot simply be combined in a manner that creates a synthetic whole with equal weight. There will always be imbalances in the sense that the one system of coordination will be constitutive during the coupling, while the other will be regulatory. Even Csikós-Nagy does not ultimately deny these facts. According to his theory, the market possesses essentially a regulatory function, that is to say, a function subject to planning: "The real problem of the socialist economic control system is the manner in which planning and market are coordinated. The variations of the control system model depend on it for their formation. The *peculiarities of the market mechanism* create the possibilities for it. The market is capable of functioning as a comprehensive regulatory or partially regulatory entity."[115]

Because the market played merely a regulatory role in the Hungarian economic system, there were some consequences. This showed up particularly in the pricing system as probably the most significant market element of this socialist reform. According to Kleinewefers' view, it was "solely an expedient measure to assure the efficiency of

112 Csikós-Nagy, *Sozialistische Marktwirtschaft*, p. 103.
113 *Ibid.*
114 *BEE*, Vol. II, pp. 505-506.
115 Csikós-Nagy, *Sozialistische Marktwirtschaft*, p. 105.

particular allocations, however it must not determine the general direction of the development. The economy is controlled by politics in accordance with the goals of the plan."[116] What this means is that the market mechanism must replace the imperative planning on the micro-economic level, but that the plan is to continue determining the macro-, and partially also the meso-economic level. One can hardly overlook the fact that such a duality of planning and market still conceals a good amount of dogmatic faith in planning. Thus we read in Csikós-Nagy: "If the welfare optimum cannot be achieved in a free market economy because of imperfect market conditions, neither will it not be possible in the classical model of the socialist planned economy because the bureaucracy is imperfect."[117] The actual cause of the failure of the centrally planned economy, therefore, does not lie in the state planning system, more precisely in the factual impossibility of a perfectly comprehensive economic plan, but in the imperfect nature of the planning bureaucrats. Certainly, since the planning bureaucracy belongs essentially to the system of the centrally controlled economy, its apparently deep-rooted imperfection must affect it and render it factually incapable of improvement. This practically favors the market economy, a consequence not lost on Csikós-Nagy when he finally admits that one could "agree with those who believe that, for all practical purposes, the imperfect market represents a better alternative when compared to the imperfect bureaucracy."[118] However, this does not bode well for a merely regulatory function of the market in matters of economic planning, a fact that once again reveals the mentioned inherent conflict.

Connected to this conflict (dominance of planning on the macro-level, market dominance on the micro-level) is the fact that the Hungarian economic reform encountered ever greater difficulties, despite the fact that it counted in fact on the market as the better alternative and that it achieved even economically more efficient results than the non-reformed planned economies. Although the importance of planning had already dwindled significantly by that time, the passion of the planning bureaucrats active in the macro-economic sphere to intervene had not. It was "essentially replaced *not* by functioning

[116] Kleinewefers, *Reformen für Wirtschaft und Gesellschaft*, p. 181.
[117] Csikós-Nagy, *Sozialistische Marktwirtschaft*, p. 390.
[118] *Ibid.*

markets but by excessive interventionism through economic policies."[119] Similarly, Zsuzsa Szabó-Raducziner opines:

> The increasing deterioration of the systematic characteristics of the Hungarian economic order is the fault of the inconsistent, overly differentiated, small-minded bureaucratic process policy. The greatest mistake of the past twenty years is presumably the fact that the structure of the institutions of economic control was not fundamentally changed after 1968. People falsely assumed that the ministerial bureaucracy was going to surrender its power to the enterprises without a fight.[120]

As a matter of fact, this grave insufficiency triggered most recently a new, radical push for reform. The imperative planning institutions are abandoned nowadays, even on the macro-economic level, thus depriving them of direct, forceful interference in economic processes. This leads to an economic order in which the market is assigned a constitutive role and market planning a regulatory one, a fact that, on the whole, amounts to an extensive approximation of the types of market economic order models sketched out in 6.2.2, 6.2.3, and 6.2.4.1. The socialist component of this variant of the market economy is marked by the ownership order according to which government ownership, at least of land, retains a significant position, while individual private ownership is increasingly permissible without becoming hardly dominant. If the socialist reform also aims at an increased substitution of government ownership by collective ownership, subsuming not only co-operatives and businesses run by workers, but also corporations and related capital enterprises[121] in the manner currently advocated even by Soviet economic reformers, then the distance from the Western forms of order present in the market economy will be reduced even further, amounting to an actual break with the system.

[119] Kleinewefers, *Grundzüge einer verallgemeinerten Wirtschaftsordnungstheorie*, p. 33.

[120] Szabó-Raducziner, *Pläne, Märkte und laufende Prozeßpolitik in Ungarn*, p. 208.

[121] The new Hungarian company law, which was enacted on 1 January 1989, permits, in addition to stock corporations, also general partnerships, limited partnerships, and limited liability companies. Establishment of a stock company requires at least five stockholders. The capital stock must remain above 10 million forint. All of these private businesses must not employ more than 500 persons (except in the case of foreign majority ownership). Thus, the key positions of the economy remain in governmental hands (*Neue Zürcher Zeitung*, No. 295, 17/18 December 1988, p. 37).

Overall, the Hungarian reform movement is undergoing a complete transition to a form of order patterned specifically after the market economy, but by retaining ownership conditions following largely socialist lines, however, similar to the situation in Poland, with an already pluralistic and democratically impregnated political constitution striving for a multi-party system. The transition itself is fraught with difficulties and dangers. The aftermath of past economic mismanagement — one may wish to recall the high amounts of foreign debt — weigh heavily. Moreover, large segments of the population live in abject poverty. The increase in the efficiency of the economy, hoped for as a result of consistently pursued reform as a real condition of a general rise in the social standard will materialize, if at all, only in the long run and hardly without strong Western assistance and above all participative and cooperative structures (such as favorable investment credits, ease of trade) that transcend the Eastern Bloc.[122] In the short run, many citizens may even experience a deterioration of their current situation, because previous job security, as well prices for basic necessities that had been kept artificially low, will disappear and the income gap between the various economic subjects will widen. The resulting tensions could easily lead, and not only in Hungary, to a serious endangerment of a reform movement that is principally oriented towards a social market economy, especially since the means of establishing a corresponding social net are for the time being non-existent.

6.2.5 *Humanly Reformed Market Economy (Ota Šik's Human Economic Democracy)*

At first glance, one may be surprised to learn that Ota Šik's model, to which he himself refers as "Human Economic Democracy,"[123] is simply listed here among the order types of the basic market-oriented economic system. After all, this economist, who started as a Marxist and was the leading spokesperson for the socialist reform movement of the Prague Spring, desires to propose nothing less than "an economic system for the future," which also happens to be the

[122] Similarly, Theodor Strohm, "Die EG — 'Gemeinschaftscharta der sozialen Grundrechte' — eine Chance 'systemöffnender Kooperation'?" *Zeitschrift für Evangelische Ethik*, 33 (1989), p. 248.

[123] Ota Šik, *Wirtschaftssysteme*, Berlin, 1987, p. 56.

title of one of his recently published works,[124] and is understood as "the third way," to quote from the title of an earlier, yet ever so seminal publication.[125] As mentioned already in 5.2.2.2 and 5.2.2.5, however, the "third way" between the basic systems proves on closer inspection to be a concept of "proposals for reforming market-oriented economic systems."[126] After all, we are dealing here with a humanly reformed market economy in the sense of Šik that resides as a form of order beyond the reach of the communist planned economy as well as the capitalist market economy. It has no intention to replace the market with a different system of coordination; rather, it aims at regulating it by modifying the plan, that is to say, by augmenting it. Central to this concept of reform is a reform of the market regulation by establishing a macro-economic plan of distribution to be determined by a democratic decision-making process and a property reform originating from the comprehensive participation of all employees in the capital stock of medium and large-scale businesses. We will have to return to this in greater detail and examine especially Šik's two most recent works mentioned in the previous two footnotes.

6.2.5.1 Macro-Economic Plan of Distribution

Ota Šik's macro-economic plan of distribution is shown as a separate type of global framework planning of the market economy introduced in many a Western economy. Above all, one ought to mention the attempts at economic planning by political entities following World War II, for instance in Great Britain under the Labour governments, the indicative French planification, but also the concerted efforts under Karl Schiller in the Federal Republic of Germany.

According to Šik, "the planning of the economy concerns itself with goals for a country's entire economic development, as well as with the allocation of means with which a systematic course for all important economic processes is to be accomplished."[127] It includes more than just a prognosis, because it aims at securing the goals

[124] Šik, *Ein Wirtschaftssystem der Zukunft*, Berlin, 1985.
[125] Šik, *Der dritte Weg*, Hamburg, 1972.
[126] Šik, *Wirtschaftssystem*, p. 203.
[127] *Ibid.*, pp. 59-60.

set down by the plan by influencing the course of the economic processes.

Moreover, one must differentiate between the planning of the economy and economic policy. While the latter seeks merely to influence selectively certain economic processes, the former is concerned with the complexities of primarily anticipating all essential economic processes together with all their reciprocal connections. Both can be combined in the sense that the economic policy serves the planning of the economy during its implementation, a fact that was expressly emphasized by Šik.

As a type of economic planning, Šik's concept of planning goes beyond a merely selective economic policy. Like all global framework planning, its objective is to prevent, if possible, macro-imbalances in the economy and to ascertain on the whole the priority of common interests over special interests. Therefore, its purpose is to strive by means of targeted regulation built into market events for a condition that will occur eventually on its own, at least in the long term, according to both the classical and the neo-classical theory; however, this remained merely an expectation that failed to come to pass or, if it did, only incompletely. In this sense, it is concerned with supporting and not at all with supplanting the market economy. Now, the difference between Šik and the traditional plan modification of the market economy lies in its special design: "Western, indicative planning efforts attempt primarily to determine the investive allocation and the structural development of production."[128] Šik, on the other hand, concentrates on what he refers to as "macro-economic distribution planning."

Basic to this type of planning is the functional distribution of income: "The functional distribution of income is that distribution of the national income from which issues a certain relationship between consumption and investment. Especially the spreading of income over wages and profits determines decisively the relationship between consumption and investment."[129] It is especially the disproportional relationship that is typical of the distribution of the national income between investment and consumption that Šik blames for economic crises and mass unemployment in most existing market economies. In order to countervail that problem, "one must therefore

[128] *Ibid.*, p. 183.
[129] *Ibid.*, p. 176.

achieve a balance between the development of consumption and investment that will be suitable to the long-term development of capital productivity."[130] This requires, he states, a "planned regulation of the functional distribution of income."[131] That is all. Direct planning of investment or even production is out of the question for Šik:

> If the market mechanism is to continue to function fully, planning must not extend to production and investment activity. Companies must themselves continue to determine the development of their production and investment. The goals accepted in the plan can be realized by means of certain processes of distribution, that is to say, by distributing the gross or national income among certain income groups; this development of distribution can in turn be achieved by an appropriate economic policy. The realization of planned goals is to be effected by means of indirect regulatory instruments, that is to say, essentially by means of an economic policy of the government tailored to the projected economic goals. The instruments needed for achieving the planned objectives, therefore, do not consist of a regimentation of production that would obstruct market-oriented autonomy and responsibility of the companies, but rather an economic policy that conforms to the market, guiding the development of production and investments towards the planned objectives.[132]

6.2.5.2 Democratic Planning Decisions

The passage just quoted clarifies that macro-planning of the economy, according to Šik, distinguishes two aspects: On the one hand, there are the plan objectives that need to be aspired to and, on the other hand, the instruments by means of which the objectives are to be achieved. Šik himself is in a position to speak of two "sides" to planning.[133] What he has in mind is its "teleological" or goal-setting, and its "genetic" side, "which needs to be examined by means of scientific, analytical methods in order to determine whether the goals to be set can be attained under the given economic conditions."[134]

The teleological aspect of planning thus refers to the setting of economico-social goals. Contrary to Hayek, the goals of the economy,

130 *Ibid.*
131 *Ibid.*
132 Šik, *Ein Wirtschaftssystem der Zukunft*, p. 108.
133 *Ibid.*, p. 107.
134 *Ibid.*, p. 109.

according to Šik, do not issue from merely spontaneous development. They are set externally, more specifically, by people. If this task is not supposed to remain a matter attended to by powerful groups with special interests of their own, but is, instead, a manifestation of the common weal, then these goals must be established in a manner that enables the participation of all segments of the population in the decision-making process. In other words, it must be accomplished in democratic fashion: "The democratic organization of the macro-planning is therefore important."[135] This, however, marks only one of the two aspects.

The other aspect, referred to as the "genetic" aspect of macro-planning, is inseparably interwoven with the "teleological" one. To prevent the development aspired to by the plan from turning into a mere conglomerate of purely wishful thinking, Šik suggests that the realization of the democratically set goals be based on the recognized possibilities of the development of production: "In this sense, on the one hand, planning will therefore always be composed of an analysis of available productive forces as well as real possibilities for their development during the plan's duration, and, on the other hand, of the needs and interests that enter into the plan's design and determine the concrete goals of future economic development."[136] Expressed in our terminology, this means that the postulates of that which is humanly just and that which is economically rational must be mutually related, that is to say, they must not be pursued independently of one another. Šik's macro-planning, therefore, deals with a dialectical process that synthesizes usually contrary concerns of an economy whose goals are human-oriented and whose course is efficient. In Šik's own words:

> Planning must be organized in such a way that scientifically based analytical methods can be combined with democratically achieved objectives while the planning is still going on. Clear ideas regarding the needed distribution processes must arise from scientifically predicted macro-proportions of the future production and democratically set macro-proportions of the needs. Resorting to instruments of economic policy, the kind of demand that corresponds to the planned objectives must be created.... The market will then be controlled indirectly via the processes of distribution. In this way, a desired development of production is achieved without having

[135] *Ibid.*, p. 108.
[136] *Ibid.*

> weakened or even undermined the market interest and the market responsibility of the enterprises.[137]

A macro-economic plan of distribution that is democratically organized in this fashion places high demands on the population base of a society. Not only is this plan expected to agree on the desired setting of human-oriented economic goals, such as the elimination of mass unemployment, a development of consumption that adapts itself to the requirements of environmental protection and the responsible handling of natural resources, to the humanization of labor, and, on the whole, on a general improvement of the quality of life. During the macro-distribution of the national income among wages and profits, this plan of distribution is also expected to accommodate the legitimate wage interests of the workers as well as the legitimate profit interests of the capitalists, in order to reach a balanced development between consumption and investments with the objective of forestalling economic crises and their anti-human effects. The latter will happen only if the traditional alienation of the workers from the profit or capital interests and, together with it, the confrontational battle of distribution can be overcome. This cannot be expected to happen as long as the confrontational distribution of capital stock,[138] which is characteristic of the capitalist order,[139] remains in existence. According to Šik, the condition for a successful plan of distribution amounts, therefore, to a reform of ownership with regard to capital stock that is capable of abolishing the contradiction between profit and wage interests.[140]

6.2.5.3 Šik's Ownership Reform (Collaborative Companies)

As mentioned, the objective of the reform of ownership in question is to reduce the alienation of the workers from the companies and their capital interests decisively.[141] This does not simply happen by replacing capitalist private ownership of the means of production with collective state ownership. According to Šik, this kind of alienation is typical of both the capitalist and the communist system. Nor

137 *Ibid.*, p. 109.
138 *BEE*, Vol. II, pp. 405-06.
139 *BEE*, Vol. II, pp. 527-28.
140 Šik, *Wirtschaftssysteme*, pp. 183 ff.
141 Šik, *Ein Wirtschaftssystem der Zukunft*, p. 64.

will it suffice to augment the assets of those who are in dependent working relationships by creating individual employee's stocks or by forming collective employees' funds. The abolition of alienation is instead a matter of an

> altered attitude of the wage earners with respect to the economic activity and the goals of the production set for the companies. What is at stake here is the abolition of the social contradictions between the wage and profit interests, because the struggle over the distribution of income and, therefore, also the macro-economic disturbances with all their consequences cannot otherwise be eliminated.[142]

In Šik's eyes, the proper means for abolition is the so-called "neutralization of capital ownership." What does that mean?

> What we understand by neutralization of capital ownership is the design of a form of ownership according to which the ownership of capital can no longer be distributed among individual persons. Entitled to the ownership is the pertinent production collective of an existing or newly founded company. The collective, which is called an asset administration company, is not entitled to distribute the capital among its employees. It merely forms the basis of interest for a legally (statutory) determined administration of the capital by an elected body. The asset administration company administers the assets in a fiduciary capacity and leaves its effective and productive use to the management company for effective and productive utilization. The control of individuals over the capital, as well as the individual accumulation of capital and the corresponding influences, can no longer develop. Companies that function based on such neutralized capital are referred to as collaborative companies.[143]

Thus, the neutralization of capital ownership is realized in these collaborative companies.[144] They differ fundamentally from communist enterprises, from Western corporations, and also from free co-operatives. They are distinguished from communist enterprises, because they own the means of production, determine corporate policy autonomously, and because they are decidedly controlled by demand or by the market. They are distinguished from co-operatives, because

[142] *Ibid.*
[143] *Ibid.*, p. 69.
[144] For more detail, see *ibid.*, pp. 64-97.

the shared capital cannot be distributed among the individual shareholders. They are also distinguished from capitalist enterprises, because capital stock ceases to be privately owned, be it by individuals, families, or a multitude of stockholders. Legally speaking, the collaborative company resembles most closely a foundation, a fact Šik himself occasionally points out.

If there are, therefore, no individually distributable ownership rights in the collaborative companies, individual co-workers still share the profits: "The greater the profits realized by the collaborative company, the greater also the profit shares of individual co-workers. Hence the interest of all members in an as effective as possible use of capital, production, and development of capital."[145] Thus profit interests are in accord with wage interests and also lead to greater distributive fairness in the economy. In this fashion, the combination of indivisible collective ownership and the individual right to profits should make it possible to abolish the alienation between the two fundamental interests existing in enterprises and to avoid distributive disadvantages existing in the capitalist order of private ownership without giving up the advantages of its efficiency.[146]

Co-determination is inseparably tied to profit sharing in collaborative companies: "Profit alienation cannot be overcome progressively until the distribution of profits in the companies can be controlled directly by the co-workers by means of elected representatives and until a set percentage of profits is allotted to them directly."[147] For only a distribution of profits that is assured in this way by co-determination and takes effect directly can make exercising the right to profits into an individual, personal experience for the wage earners and change their attitude towards economic activity and the companies' production goals. Without co-determination, the profit interest of the companies would remain a fundamentally alien matter to the co-workers, a fact that would have to unfortunately allow profit alienation to persist. On the other hand, in Šik's view, co-determination without an interest by the co-determiners in the profits would be equally fatal. If the demand for co-determination were not tied to the attempt to alter the economic position as well as the interests of the wage recipients, then

[145] *Ibid.*, p. 70.
[146] Cf. Kleinewefers, *Reformen für Wirtschaft und Gesellschaft*, p. 268.
[147] Šik, *Wirtschaftssysteme*, p. 184.

the latter would only pursue "their one-sided interest in wage increases and the preservation of jobs" and thus frequently obstruct "necessary technological and structural changes."[148] Co-determination and sharing in profits or losses must, therefore, be viewed as one. Only together are they socially and economically in order.

The aforementioned observations reveal that Šik's reform of ownership does not at all originate, like Marxist socialism, from the principal discrimination against private ownership of the means of production. The fundamental concern to neutralize capital ownership is not aimed at the doctrinaire removal of this form of ownership; it instead strives to overcome the confrontational dualism of wage and profit interests as a precondition for the possibility of successfully planning distribution. It should, therefore, be accomplished only in a sector of the economy where the mentioned dualism is most relevant, namely in the sector of the large corporations.

In his model for human-oriented economic democracy, Šik relies on the "continued existence of three economic sectors":[149] the sectors of the small, the medium-sized, and the large companies operating as stockholding corporations. Because the capital owner is both entrepreneur and laborer in the first sector, private capital remains fully in place. In the second sector, too, where the capital owner assumes the role of the entrepreneur who is personally responsible for the capital functions, private capital is to be preserved and permitted to grow; however, co-workers are to share simultaneously both capital and profits.

> Only in the third sector, today's corporations, in which the separation of capital ownership from the capital function took place a long time ago — with a few exceptions — and the supervisory function was turned over to paid managers, are collaborative companies expected to originate. However, the complete removal of private stock ownership is not necessarily proposed even here, but rather the achievement of a majority representing the neutralized capital and the conquest of large, concentrated stock ownership in the hands of a few large stockholders.[150]

[148] *Ibid.*, p. 189.
[149] *Ibid.*, p. 198.
[150] *Ibid.*

Collaborative companies, as Šik understands the concept, therefore, have a specific place in big business. As to their formal decisional structure, they are similar to stockholding companies, however with the fundamental difference that the co-workers assume the position of stockholders. As already mentioned, collaborative companies are divided into an asset management and a plant management company. As co-workers, the employees own both companies. In the plant management company, they elect and control the supervisory board that in turn appoints the directors; and in the asset management company they control the board of asset managers. As for the rest, the separation between these two bodies is not entirely clearly defined in Šik's work. However, "it appears to agree essentially with the common concept of the operating company that takes care of daily operations, and the holding company that owns the plant management company(ies), takes care of paying dividends and disposes over the profits held back for the purpose of a continuous development of the plant management company(ies)."[151] The purpose of this structure is to make possible, within the framework of co-determination by the employees as a precondition of a human-oriented order of the workplace, management with separate space for maneuvering and exercising responsibility, management acting in its own as well as in the co-workers' perceived profit interests and thus able to operate efficiently. In this sense, the decisional structure of the collaborative companies also differs from that of traditional co-operative companies:

> The direct election of the director from the ranks of associates, as well as the direct decision by the associates concerning technical and structural innovations have placed the old co-operatives at a disadvantage vis-a-vis capitalist competition. In collaborative companies, the position of management would be entirely different and approximate far more closely the selection of managers and the activity of managers in corporations than in traditional co-operatives.[152]

On the whole, it can be said that Šik's ownership reform amounts to a fundamental change of the human, social, and economic status of the wage earner. He is no longer supposed to be a labor unit whose only job it is to execute the production plan; in the collaborative company workers are instead supposed to be involved as co-owners in

[151] Kleinewefers, *Reformen für Wirtschaft und Gesellschaft*, pp. 268-69.
[152] Šik, *Wirtschaftssysteme*, p. 201.

the entrepreneurial responsibility and to share directly in the economic success or failure by way of their share in both profits and losses. Wage and profit interest, job security, and efficient company management are thus no longer pure contradictions. And that is precisely the condition for objectifying the functional distribution of income as an instrument of macro-economic distribution planning as understood by Šik.

6.2.5.4 Problems

Although Šik's concept of the human-oriented economic democracy is attractive because of its internal consistency and compactness, it nevertheless poses a number of serious questions:

First, there is the prognosis issue. Macro-economic planning of distribution is primarily proactive (*ex ante*) planning. All such planning is in need of a prognosis; in this particular case, it is in need of a prognosis regarding the growth of the future national income that is to be distributed among wages and profits. Neo-classical economists question the possibility of such a sufficiently reliable prognosis. Even Šik is aware of this difficulty: "There are no absolutely reliable prognoses."[153] Yet he insists that the degree of their reliability can be improved. This is evidence of a certain planning optimism that would have to be further justified. Certainly, he views this optimism in clearly relative terms in the sense that he himself subjects short-term prognoses to constant correction: "Of course, a substantial improvement of prognostication signifies no absolute reliability of the prognosis. A planned income distribution for between four to five years must therefore be always subjected to annual concretization and correction."[154] Naturally, we could ask ourselves if that would amount to a viable foundation for long-term planning and if planning in view of the mentioned uncertainties can be deemed meaningful, even if the uncertainties are not understood imperatively, but are undertaken with methods that conform to the market. Of course, one can also ask if foregoing macro-economic planning entirely would not lead to even greater uncertainties. Šik decidedly believes the latter: "At any rate, a systematic distribution of income in the presence of expected short-term goal corrections would afford both

[153] *Ibid.*, p. 182.
[154] *Ibid.*, p. 183.

the economy and the population greater assurances and more reliable perspectives than completely unplanned and unforeseeable battles over distribution."[155] No doubt, this is open to debate. Neither the problematic nature of planning optimism in view of the problems in conjunction with prognoses nor the danger of increases in the bureaucracy justify being absolutely pessimistic about planning and certainly not about a plainly deregulated market economy that is left on its own. If there is a chance of only a reduction of festering problems such as the questions about ownership and distribution, fluctuations in the development with their crisis-prone collapses of business cycles, the self-destruction of competition, the destruction of the environment, etc., then a macro-economically designed, more or less plan-supported regulatory economic policy will be essential. At the same time, there will be the question about how deeply one can become involved in planning without abandoning its market compatibility and without finally permitting it to deteriorate into mere regulation of the economy. Yet this must be decided sensibly and pragmatically, while simultaneously respecting that which is humanly just and economically rational, that is to say without any ideological bias, just as Šik had intended.

An additional problem area is introduced by the postulate of economic democracy that subjects the concretization of distribution to direct popular vote.

We noted earlier that the fundamental planning objectives, according to Šik's concept, must be determined democratically. Yet that is not all. Based on the planning objectives feasible plan alternatives must be worked out by plan commissions composed of representatives from the economic sector, from research institutes, science, and interest groups. Again referenda will have to decide which developmental alternative is supposed to be selected.[156] Therefore, not only the determination of macro-economic planning objectives is subject to democratic decision, but also the decision concerning the question of which plan alternative deserves under the circumstances priority as factually more correct in view of the set plan objectives. And here begin the difficulties.

The first difficulty lies in finding a sustainable majority not only in favor of a better, but essentially in favor of one of the proposed plan alternatives. If a majority decision faces an almost equally large

[155] *Ibid.*
[156] Šik, *Ein Wirtschaftssystem der Zukunft*, pp. 113 ff.

minority — a fact that is not all that uncommon in democratic referenda — then the result will be a stalemate which can lead to blocking and may fatally affect economic development.

A second complication arises as a result of the uncertainty of the prognoses on which all planning relies. If the prognoses are faulty, so will be planning. Thus, plans must be correctable in case they prove to be faulty, and in the short term, if the economy is not to suffer severely. As shown above, Šik, too, shares this view. Yet, are plans that were approved by a referendum immediately correctable? Certainly not if the correction must again be obtained by a referendum. As desirable as the economic democracy may be, because of the highest possible participation in the mapping of the course of the economy by the citizenry, it must have its limits. In my opinion, these limits are not apparent in Šik's work.

Ultimately, even Šik's reform of ownership reveals problems within the confines of the basic market economic system. The principal problem is the question of the compatibility of neutralized capital with the market economy. The task of capital to engage labor, i.e. the rise and fall of the market economy together with private ownership in the means of production is a *unité de doctrine* so to speak in the eyes of advocates of the classical or neo-classical market economy. This applies undoubtedly to the capitalist order form of the market economy. Yet, will it also apply generally to the market economy that is not identical to capitalism according to one of our basic theses? Competition is a constitutive element of the market economy, and so is price formation that is controlled by the interplay between supply and demand. Competition forces the producer to manage efficiently in order to be able to offer the goods he produces at a price that makes them marketable. The conditions of ownership under which they were produced are irrelevant, regardless of whether those who own the capital, or those who utilize it are responsible for them, or if the labor sector is responsible for them. This was mentioned earlier in connection with the discussion of the prominent American economist Paul Samuelson, who specifically insisted that the question of who engages whom was irrelevant to a completely competitive market, if capital engages the labor force, or if labor engages the capital.[157] Only in the second scenario, the representatives of the labor

[157] *BEE*, Vol. II, p. 518.

factor who are also responsible for the entrepreneurial function must observe the competitive efficiency principle and permit the necessary elbowroom to the capital or the profit interests. Because, according to Šik's concept, the neutralized capital must bring into accord especially the wage interest with the capital interests that are absolutely indispensable to the market economy, there is no reason why this ownership reform should be incompatible with the market economy, especially since it is limited to large corporations which are already characterized by the separation of private capital ownership from the exercise of the entrepreneurial function.

Thus, Šik's ownership reform, which contradicts both private capitalism and state socialism, proves to be compatible not only with the market economy, but also contains the additional potential to protect and promote the market economy. Indeed, the functioning of the market economy is not only imperiled by the state's directive intervention that does not conform to the market, but also, even more so, by the actions of powerful monopolies in the economic process whose goal is to oust competition from the marketplace and take control of price formation, a scenario that must lead to the self-destruction of the market economy. As is commonly known, the essential purpose of competition in the market economy is by no means the suppression of competitors, but the process of overhauling by means of better and more flexible performance.[158] The prerequisite for the formation of monopolies and their destructively repressive competition is excessive capital accumulation combined with the latter's expansionist tendencies that are inherent to the capitalist principle of maximization of profits and independent of the imperative survival of the company. Because of the structural form of ownership present in collaborative companies, according to which both profit and wage interests are relationally tied to each other, restrain one another, and suppress the maximization of both profits and wages, the mechanism that balances the interests in the market economy would be institutionally strengthened. That would be a definite boon with respect to its social as well as its economic and, ultimately, ecological ability to function.

[158] See Šik, *Ein Wirtschaftssystem der Zukunft*, p. 178.

6.2.6 *The Ecologically Regulated Market Economy*

6.2.6.1 The Fundamental Problem

The forms of order of the market economy discussed thus far raise primarily questions about an as efficient and as humanly just as possible coordination of the "capital" and "labor" factors in the production processes or in the creation of wealth in the industrial society. Can and should this coordination be exclusively effected by the market's mechanisms, or is it to be controlled on a subsidiary level by plan-containing regulations in the form of setting goals and devising appropriate instruments? What should be its extent and modality if the question is answered as yes? The third factor of production, land as the embodiment of the environment, together with all its natural resources, remains largely bracketed out. In addition to the order political importance of an economically and ethically justifiable balance between the requisite labor and capital interests, as a matter of fact that characterizes the still prevailing economic theory, regardless of whether it is neo-classical or Keynesian, the production factors are reduced to capital and labor.[159] Production is supposedly essentially the result of capital and labor. Since natural resources would exist in abundance and, therefore, be considered as quasi-free commodities, only the expenditures of labor and the cost of investment would be considered for production during their extraction. However, this view is unrealistic. It seemingly relies on a creation out of nothing. Indeed, the basis of the entire economic activity, together with its obvious use of capital and labor, is the consumption of natural resources. Hans Christoph Binswanger states precisely that when he insists that production and consumption are in reality a mere transformation, "namely the transformation of raw materials into consumable goods, and the transformation of consumable goods into waste."[160] The modern growth-oriented economy needs, therefore, not only an ever-growing increase in capital and labor. At the same time, labor can be increasingly substituted by capital by means of electronically

[159] See *BEE*, Vol. II, 2.4.2.1, fn. 91.

[160] Binswanger, *Ökologisch orientierte Wirtschaftswissenschaft* (manuscript), St. Gallen Research Group for Macroeconomics (Working Paper No. 36), St. Gallen, 1984, p. 2. See also Binswanger, "Ökopolitik — eine Ergänzung," in *Die Zukunftstauglichkeit der schweizerischen Entscheidungsstrukturen*, ed. Andreas Blum, Gerhard Kocher, and Walter Wittmann, Diessenhofen, 1982, pp. 53-54.

supported rationalization. Capital is acquired by an ever-increasing utilization of and encumbrance on the land/nature factor, which cannot be substituted. In other words, the productive creation of wealth by capital and labor runs parallel to a counter-productive devaluation of land and nature, because it consumes, on the one hand, irreplaceable raw materials, fossil fuel energy, utilizable land reserves, etc., and, on the other hand, increasingly stresses the environment with the waste and toxins it generates all the way to its possible destruction. An economic system that brackets out these hard facts is a monstrosity, because it violates its most rudimentary foundation.

The exclusion of the land/nature factor from the process of production and consumption makes the destabilization of the environment as the foundation of everything, even the economy, unavoidable. In fact, land and nature have been instituted by the Creator and are, in principle, finite, because of their pre-ordination. The factor's utilization and carrying capacity has irremovable, objective limits. By contrast, neither capital nor labor, in as far as the latter can be substituted by capital, possess any natural limitations. As a produced means of production, capital can be arbitrarily increased. The greater the production, the greater the possibilities for capital formation, and the greater the accumulation of capital, the greater the possibility for expanding production. The economic growth that is invested in it, quantitative by nature and measured against the national product, occurs inevitably at the expense of the third factor. The non-renewable, natural resources are ruthlessly exploited and the entire environment suffers from the increasing mountains of waste on the ground and especially from noxious emission into the water, the air, even the stratosphere, in a manner that is progressively ushering in a lower quality of life; indeed, it could even lead to the endangerment of the survival of the human race. The entire ecosystem that formed over the course of millions of years breaks down under the pressure of such an economic expansion of instability. Clearly, this urgently calls for a fundamental reversal in order to prevent an irreversible destruction of nature that will destroy also the foundations of the economic system.

It goes without saying that the intended turnaround cannot simply consist in belatedly correcting or at least alleviating, even at a high cost, the already existing damage to the environment, which is a strategy still pursued by environmental policies. The issue is not to tackle the consequences, but to begin with the causes of the diagnosed destabilization of the environment. Undoubtedly, the causes can be traced to the traditional underestimation of the significance of the land/nature factor for production. As discussed earlier, this factor, apart from the extreme scarcity of land for real estate development in urban areas, was and still is considered as a negligible quantity. The fact that raw materials will become ever more scarce in the long term, because of accelerated consumption in an exponentially growing economy, is reflected only insufficiently by actual price formation in the market economy, because the supply is at the moment still more or less plentiful. And the extraneous effects that impact or even destroy the environment continue to be largely ignored, at least in business circles, and if removal or other costs are incurred, they are extrapolated, that is to say passed on to the public. The integration of the fundamental ecological requirements into economic growth could not and cannot take place under these circumstances. Both neoclassical and the Keynesian-inspired economic policies "lack sensibility regarding environmental problems."[161] What will be necessary are fundamental changes in the setting of economic policy goals. In this sense, Binswanger demands that, in addition to full employment and price stability, environmental stability must be one of the indispensable goals of today's economy.[162] However, this includes the concept of an ecologically oriented economy that breaks with the traditional reduction of the economic production to capital and labor.

6.2.6.2 The Ecology-Oriented Economy

The term "ecologically oriented economy" signifies, therefore, an economy concerned with stabilizing the environment. Its goal is to take fully into account the fundamental importance of the land/nature factor during the processes of production and consumption. In other words, economic needs must be confronted by those of the environment.[163]

[161] Udo Ernst Simonis, "Ökologische Wirtschaft und Wirtschaftspolitik," in Simonis, *Ökologische Orientierungen*, Berlin, 1988, p. 42.

[162] *BEE*, Vol. II, pp. 425-26.

[163] The following discussion is based on Binswanger's "Umrisse einer umweltkonformen Wirtschaftsordnung," in *Neue Ziele für das Wachstum*, ed. Johannes Schlemmer, Munich, 1973, pp. 118 ff.

Economic necessity is defined as the need for consumer and investment goods. Their sum total represents the national product of the economy. Only things that cost money are included in the national product. As long as an increase in the national product remains the declared goal of the economy — a goal shared by both Western and Eastern economic systems — economic growth is generated to which all that matters is quantitative production that costs labor and capital and is translated into consumption.

It is contrasted by the needs of the environment that are concerned with environmental or natural goods. Binswanger divides them into three groups:

1. The aesthetic need for a humanly appropriate, beautiful, diversified living space in the cities and in the countryside,
2. The ecological need for a clean and sound environment, for clean and healthy air and water, for natural living space, for poison-free food, etc., and
3. The need to provide for the frugal use and consumption of natural resources in the future and, thus, for the guarantee of survival not only for us, but for generations to come.

The consumption or lessening of environmental resources that meets the needs of industrial production and a consumption-oriented society has no place in the calculation of the national product, because their very utilization does not require a price tag. Thus the door is wide open to wasting the mentioned goods. Considering this fact, is there any way that we can put a halt to the excessive use of the environment? According to Binswanger, the representative advocate of an ecologically oriented economic system, this is only possible if we institute a drastic reform of traditional economic activity:

> Considering the fact that we have succeeded in doing at least partial justice to the aesthetic needs by establishing national monuments and protecting nature, if emissions can be restricted to a degree by establishing emission standards and measures for cleaning up the water and the air without having to subject our economic order to a fundamental revision, we will still need to do more to preserve the foundations of life and to defend against the exploitation of nature. What will be needed is a reform of the economic order itself, beyond emission and environmental protection legislation and legislation establishing national monuments and protecting nature.

> What is needed, and I would like to emphasize that, is a reform of both the capitalist and the socialist economic systems.[164]

For in the East, as well as in the West, "the national product increases at the expense of the consumption of the environment and progress increases at the expense of its violation."[165]

This statement illustrates clearly that Binswanger's call to a reform of the economic order does not amount to a fundamental rejection of the market economy, or even to a call for its replacement by a central planning system:

> On the contrary, proceeding from today's conditions, we are dealing here with continued economic development by including meaningfully market-economic as well as interventionist elements in a manner that will take ecological conditions increasingly into account. Should there be a need to propose elements of an "originally ecological" nature, then we will be dealing with additional measures and not merely alternatives to the existing order.[166]

This may be interpreted in the sense that the market-oriented economic system serves as a constitutive foundation for the ecologically oriented and correspondingly reformed economic order, albeit augmented by a regulatory element that does not simply exclude interventionist acts and whose purpose is an approach to the economy that erects barriers against the excessive consumption of natural goods. In other words, quantitative economic growth that rests on the mere increase of the gross national product and the exploitation of natural resources is to be replaced within a solid market-oriented system by qualitative[167] economic growth that is measured against the increase in the quality of the social life "that is to be achieved with lesser, or at least not increasing use of non-multipliable or non-renewable resources, as well as decreasing or at least non-increasing negative impact on the environment."[168]

This raises the question of the elements of such a regulatory system that modifies the market economy with ecology in mind.

[164] *Ibid.*, p. 120.
[165] *Ibid.*, p. 123.
[166] Binswanger, "Ökopolitik — eine Ergänzung," p. 53.
[167] *BEE*, Vol. II, 2.7.3.
[168] Expertenkommission des Eidgenössischen Volkswirtschaftsdepartement, "Qualitatives Wachstum," Bern, 1985, p. 15.

6.2.6.3 Elements of an Ecology-Oriented Regulatory System of the Market Economy

The previous explanations illustrate that the elements of an ecology-oriented regulatory system of the market economy must aim at an economic order that conforms to the environment, instead of one whose intentions are to extricate from the land/nature factor as much as possible, because only "extrication" augments the national product but not "conservation."

According to Binswanger, "an environmentally impoper concept of ownership, especially ownership of the land and its resources,"[169] is at the root of today's exploitation of natural resources. He distinguishes two kinds of ownership,[170] "*dominium*" and "*patrimonium*." The legal structure of the concept of *dominium* dates back to Roman law that defines ownership as a "domineering relationship." According to this definition, in the interest of maximizing profits, the owner possesses the right to arbitrarily exploit a thing he owns both commercially and financially. It is truly an ownership that entitles to exploitation and utilization and is, as such, fundamental primarily to the market economy's capitalist form of order. However, it is not only typical of the market economy, but also of the centrally administered economy: "In the East, the government usurped this 'dominium', but far from abolishing it, it merely replaced commercial utilization with the fulfillment of quotas."[171] In both cases, the legal owners, be they private citizens or the government, are entitled to absolute control over the property and thus to an unlimited right of use.

Patrimonium, on the other hand, describes "ownership rights in the continuance or preservation of the property,"[172] a kind of fiefdom that was inherited from one's forebears and is passed on to one's offspring. It creates merely a relative ownership right insofar as the present owner can neither freely sell nor utilize it, because the heirs are entitled to it, also. According to Binswanger, the residents of a community or a region could be the owners of a patrimonially constituted ownership right; they could form an association of owners and establish rules regarding utilization:

[169] Binswanger, "Umrisse einer umweltkonformen Wirtschaftsordnung," p. 123.
[170] *Ibid.*, pp. 124-28.
[171] *Ibid.*, p. 125.
[172] *Ibid.*, p. 127.

> The state must not itself be the owner, however, because nationalization would merely reinforce the 'dominium' by the 'imperium.' A state that is as interested in economic utilization as private producers and, as experience has shown, often squanders resources more than anybody else, should be permitted to enjoy just like private owners the utilization of the land and the environment in the form of a lease. The size of the lease payment should be determined by the degree of permitted utilization, making competition among the beneficiaries a possibility.[173]

If we see the root of economic exploitation of natural resources in the dominium-based ownership right to exploitation and utilization, we will quickly recognize that the prerequisite of an economic order that genuinely conforms to the environment is a reform of ownership that relativizes the absolute control of the owner over the land and its resources with a view to a patrimonial understanding of the ownership right.[174] Just as the ownership of the means of production involves social responsibility in both the socialist and social market economy, ownership of natural resources ought to be accompanied in the ecologically regulated market economy by responsibility for the environment: "This means that a portion of the national product must be returned to 'nature,' whose resources had been taken. Therefore, in addition to income from labor and capital, there must also be 'income' benefiting the environment, lest we jeopardize the basis of our existence."[175] The consumption of natural resources would thus be liable to be paid in addition to the cost of extraction. It would thus be slowed down automatically and all economic activities would be redirected towards a qualitative growth of the economy. This would be even more the case based on Binswanger's proposed ownership reform that aims for the preservation of natural resources for the benefit of our offspring. According to this reform, the scarcity of resources is not only to be evaluated in terms of current market supply, but in terms of long-term utilization (the precautionary principle), and, because, if subject to payment, the growing scarcity of environmental goods — air, water, land, etc. — due to waste and destruction must be included in the data on which the market-economic price system is based (the polluter pays principle).[176]

173 *Ibid.*, pp. 127 ff.
174 Binswanger, *Eigentum und Eigentumspolitik*, Zürich, 1978, esp. pp. 96-113.
175 Binswanger, "Ökopolitik — eine Ergänzung," p. 57.
176 *Ibid.*, p. 58.

Order-political reforms serving a market economy taking environmental issues more seriously need to be changed even on the level of macro-economical process policy before they will be able to be effective: "As long as the macro-economical *process policy* aims solely at an increase of the national product, any long-term order-political reform will prove to be fruitless. Any increase in the national product must be qualified in the sense that it is to be sought under conditions of no additional or only minimally additional consumption of natural resources."[177] This includes a substantial revision of the definition of what is the national product. In a similar context, Udo Ernst Simonis talks about the "eco-national product cost calculation,"[178] distinguishing it from traditional methods of calculating the national product. According to Simonis, the expenditures for environmental damage or the cost of environmental protection must be figured into the total, because the quantitatively growing production is connected to a quantitatively growing consumption of natural resources, that is to say, a decrease of real natural capital faces the increase of the monetary income generated by growth. From this would then follow that the size of the national product could be maintained only, or even raised, by the optimum protection and, wherever possible, by reconstructing natural capital and, therefore, by a transition from quantitative to qualitative economic growth; this would bring an increased transformation of labor-reducing investments to investments that spare both resources and the environment, that is to say a new form of rationalization. That, in fact, would mean that the national product generated by the economy would be allotted not only to, or almost exclusively, to the capital and labor factors, but also to the land/nature factor. A corresponding modification of the macro-economical policy of distribution and process belongs, therefore, together with the reform of ownership rights, to the regulatory measures in an economy that conforms to the environment. According to Binswanger, the market-economic price signals which function as coordinators of individual economic and ecological interests, and which are corrected in accordance with the precautionary principle and the polluter pays principle, must, therefore, be given priority over interventionist measures of the kind practiced by the planned economy because of their

177 *Ibid.*
178 Simonis, "Ökologische Wirtschaft und Wirtschaftspolitik," p. 40.

presumed greater effectiveness.[179] To sum up, his concept represents clearly an ecologically regulated market economy that has people pay for the utilization of environmental goods, owing to the reform of ownership rights; it refocuses the macro-economic process policy on qualitative growth of the economy[180] thanks to the inclusion of environmental damages in the calculation of the national product, that is by accounting for the cost of protecting the environment; and it directly forces both producers and consumers to utilize all natural goods most sparingly on account of the shifting of the cost to the market prices.

6.2.6.4 Unanswered Questions

Even if effective market regulation were possible by being mindful of ecological issues, there would still be some questions left.

1. First of all, one needs to mention that even an economic order that is ecologically appropriate will not be able to bring about a stabilization of the environment as long as the growth of the world's population fails to stabilize.[181] The rapid increase in population typical of many developing countries will necessarily lead to an analogous increase in the demand for consumer goods. It remains doubtful if sufficient qualitative economic growth, that is to say, growth without increased demand for non-renewable resources and without increased stress on the environment, can be achieved in order to meet the enormously increasing demand caused by population policies. However, the problem of effectively slowing down the exponential increase of the world's population in a humane manner remains as yet unsolved.

2. Furthermore, one can also ask whether any qualitative growth of the economy — in fact, there is need for economic growth in view of

[179] Binswanger, "Ökopolitik — eine Ergänzung," p. 58. See also Alfred Nydegger, who makes noteworthy suggestions concerning the energy problem ("Mehr Weitblick und mehr Markt in der Energiepolitik," *Neue Zürcher Zeitung*, No. 199, 29 August 1989, p. 21).

[180] According to recent reports — *Tages-Anzeiger* (Zürich), 16 May 1989, p. 31 — the ideas of Simonis and Binswanger appear to have consequences. According to a spokesman of the Federal Statistical Office, the Federal Republic of German intends to calculate, in addition to Gross National Product, an "Ecological National Product," for the control of economic growth.

[181] See *BEE*, Vol. II, 3.3.6.1.

the existing shortages in the Third World — does not also remain tied to an increased consumption of non-renewable resources and an increased negative, though less intrusive, impact on the environment. Ultimately, any form of production entails the transformation of raw materials and energies into consumable goods and of consumable goods into waste, no matter how slight its impact on the environment. This means, however, that there are limits even to qualitative economic growth, and that a renunciation of material goods in favor of greater spiritual values and a more ascetic life style are still a far cry from becoming reality primarily in developed industrial societies.

3. This gives rise to another question, namely, limited economic growth represents a serious problem to employment policies, particularly since the productivity of labor is enhanced due to the rationalization of labor. Will that not lead to higher unemployment? The transition to qualitative economic growth also contains a positive aspect from an employment political point of view, because it is accompanied by a new concept of rationalization, namely fewer labor-saving investments in favor of investments that have less of an impact on natural resources and the environment. Still, the first category of investments will be unable to disappear. Even in the future, jobs will be eliminated as a result of labor-saving measures of rationalization. A reduction of the number of working hours at full pay — today's preferred strategy — is not a long-term solution. For the cost of labor will increase, thus fuelling even more labor-saving rationalization at the expense of a rationalization that minimizes the impact on natural resources and the environment, or forces economic growth at all cost for the purpose of creating new jobs. On the other hand, is a reduction of the number of working hours combined with reduced pay socially tolerable, or are there ways to compensate for wage loss without having to lower the quality of life, but enhance it instead? Once again, these are questions awaiting answers.

In this context, one suggestion by Binswanger is highly noteworthy. He is pleading for supplementing the monetary economic realm with one that is proprietary and/or barter based.[182] In other words, the working hours gained by reducing working time in an economic system based on the division of labor should be utilized by

[182] See Binswanger, Holger Bonus, and Manfred Timmermann, *Wirtschaft und Umwelt*, Stuttgart, 1981, pp. 77-83.

supplying reciprocally commodities one can produce on one's own, in do-it-yourself fashion, and services for others that one can perform oneself. This would lead to a lowering of the cost of living, which would in turn largely compensate for the loss of income due to the reduction in working hours without full pay. According to Binswanger:

> The possibilities for such a cost reduction are substantially increased if people create internal specialties in the apartment complex they live in, within their immediate or more distant neighborhood, perhaps even within a geographic region in the form of so-called "mini-networks." The objective here is to improve the efficiency of individual production or of social services, without any monetary compensation for mutually provided goods and services, thus creating a stronger counterbalance to the cost explosion in the industrial and particularly also in the services and health sectors. Three objectives will be accomplished by shifting working time in the monetary economy based on the division of labor to working time for the benefit of direct, individual need or the "mini-networks": the shift enables all workers to find jobs in an economy based on the division of labor despite rationalizations; it raises the material standard of living; and it enhances even the quality of life by reducing the environmental impact and, possibly, because life styles will be established within the 'mini-networks' which will lead people out of an isolation that is perceived to be problematical and blamed on today's work and housing patterns.[183]

Following this overview of real and possible forms of the market-economic order, we must now zero in on fundamental ideas for the purpose of finding maxims about the issue of order.

6.3 Some Basic Ideas about Finding Maxims Regarding the Problem of Order in the Economy

Even the search for maxims regarding the problem of order in the economy calls for two kinds of basic reflection: those dealing with the economically rational and those dealing with the humanly just, that is to say the kind of human justice that includes the quality of

[183] *Ibid.*, p. 79.

life and, therefore, also environmental justice. The primary issues discussed in Chapter I (The Question of Meaning in the Economy) and Chapter III (An Analysis of the Principal Problems in Business and Economic Ethics) against the background of a humanity originating from faith, hope, and love must serve as our normative stimuli.

It is appropriate to begin with a discussion of the principle of economic rationality.

6.3.1 *Some Basic Thoughts on the Aspect of Economic Rationality*

In 1.3.1, the fundamental purpose of the economy was defined as an activity that serves life. The economy's primary task should be to enable human beings to enjoy as good a quality of life as possible through the production of vital or life-enriching commodities. The more efficiently the economy performs, the better its position to accomplish this task, that is to say, it will achieve as high a benefit as possible given a certain commitment of resources that conforms to the ecological conditions. The need for an efficient economy is, therefore, already inherent to its purpose. Thus an economically rational economy is always also an efficient economy.

From the perspective of microeconomics, the classic measure of efficient economic activity within a market economy is the profit realized by individual companies or groups of companies; in macro-economic terms, it is the national product that evolves from the production and marketing of goods and services. The higher the individual economic profits and the higher the entire economy's national product, the better the shape the economy is supposedly in, and the greater its ability to comprehensively realize its fundamental life-serving purpose. Does this not imply, however, that the economically rational coincides with the maximization of individual economic profits and the entire economy's gross national product?

One can rightfully speak of an efficient economy only if output surpasses input. Profits that are realized in this manner are undoubtedly a criterion of efficiency. Nevertheless, as mentioned in an earlier context,[184] it would be fallacious and thus economically irrational to equate profit-oriented efficiency with the life-serving purpose of the economy. Individual economic profits are frequently obtained at the

[184] *BEE*, Vol. II, 3.3.2.

expense of national economic losses. If a company cuts jobs ruthlessly in an effort to rationalize in the interest of maximizing its profits, or of maximizing its economic efficiency, if it neglects for the same reason to design job conditions in a humanly appropriate manner, and if it puts as great a downward pressure as possible on the wages and social contributions of its work force as well as on the expenses for environmental protection, then unemployment and physical and psychological damages will result among the workers; the economically weakest will suffer deprivation, serious environmental damages will ensue, etc., all in all, negative effects with accompanying external cost that must be paid for by society and that can most severely burden a national economy. Individual economic profits — whose level, as a rule, correlates to the size of the national product — are thus confronted by losses throughout the economy. This insight must be taken into account when one determines the efficiency even an economy ordered in market economic terms. It will stand the test of economic rationality only if the minimization of external costs, too, will be accepted as proof of efficient economic activity. Individual economic profit orientation can, therefore, claim efficiency only to the extent that it finds a way of avoiding negative external effects and thus remains unlinked to a lessening of the current or future quality of life. At best, this can be called optimization of profits, but not maximization of profits.

Such reflections on the concept of efficiency in the economy are mandatory in order to forestall misjudgments. If one were to consider economic efficiency as a criterion of an appropriately ordered economic system only or primarily under the premise of the prosperity of individual companies or groups of companies, then one might be tempted to claim the capitalist form of the market economy, as defined in 6.2.1, as the most economically rational form of order. Indeed, the capitalist market economy, with its dominance of capitalist interests devoted chiefly to the principle of profit maximization, testifies to an efficiency of production that obviously impressed even Marx and Engels[185] and continues to impress greatly today's reformers in socialist countries with their hardly efficient centralized planned economy. This generally generates wealth-increasing effects, although not for every segment of the population. The more companies could

[185] Marx and Engels, "Manifesto of the Communist Party," in *Collected Works*, Vol. VI, New York, 1976, pp. 487-89.

operate based on capitalist principles and the less they would be subject to governmental or corporate regulation, the more efficient and, therefore, wealth-increasing the market economy would become; in short, its superior life-serving ability would be proved. And that, its advocates insist, reveals the capitalist form of the market economy as the most economically rational among its possible forms of order. Yet, is that really true?

Probably the most impressive contemporary example of a capitalist form of a market economy is illustrated by the economic reforms in Great Britain under the leadership of Margaret Thatcher, summarily referred to as "Thatcherism." Genetically speaking, "Thatcherism" is a neo-liberal reaction to the economic concept adopted by the Labour governments during the period after the Second World War. Apart from expanding the social net, it was characterized by the extensive nationalization of key industries, subsidizing unprofitable companies, as well as conserving outdated, labor-intensive production methods in the interest of an artificial preservation of existing jobs and primarily by a controlling, interventionist economic policy. This all leads to a deterioration of efficiency and, therefore, to a decline of the entire British economy. By contrast to such regimented government and bureaucratic control, which reduced individual responsibility and initiatives and paralyzed competition in the market place, "Thatcherism" bets on the liberal values supported by individual economic interests, that is to say, on an economy that was relieved as much as possible of governmental and corporate strictures (trade unions) and regulated by the free play of market forces. Although it did not simply glorify "laissez-faire", particularly since it, too, utilized a macro-economic control instrument in the form of the monetary regulation of the money supply by the central bank, "Thatcherism" still comes very close to what we refer to as a libertarian market economy.[186] At any rate, it effectively shifted the economic weight from the government to the individual intent on maximizing his or her own profits. Against union opposition, nationalized companies were re-privatized and subsidies of non-profitable businesses were stopped. This eliminated thousands of badly-run plants, but increased unemployment at least temporarily. At the same time, a supply-side economy enhanced the opportunity to maximize profits and hence the willingness to invest of initiative-driven and innovative entrepreneurs.

[186] *BEE*, Vol. II, p. 529.

For this reason, the steep progression of the income tax was taken back, because it impeded the private accumulation of wealth and, therefore, the desire to take private initiatives. Step by step, the highest rate of 83% was reduced to 40% and the minimum rate of 33% was reduced to 25%, while at the same time increasing to 15% the value-added tax that affected all levels of the population equally.[187] These measures, as well as additional ones benefiting capital interests, significantly boosted the British economy. Small businesses in particular mushroomed, though mostly in the already economically thriving southeastern part of the country. Thatcher's business-friendly administration clearly promoted economic efficiency in the private sector, as well as an increase in the individual wealth of many people. However, this is only one aspect of the capitalist renaissance experienced by the British economy.

Even the London correspondent of the *Neue Zürcher Zeitung*, who is a proponent of a clear liberal position and who took a generally favorable view of Thatcher's economic reform could not get around talking about the "other side of the coin":

> Without a doubt, *prosperity increased* during her administration. But, the discrepancy between the rich and the poor and the number of *needy people* increased as well. In 1979, 2.8 million people had an income at or below the minimum level determined by Parliament; now the number stands at 4.5 million. Moreover, the number of homeless people is increasing parallel to a rapidly growing number of homeowners that increased from 50% to 68% under Thatcher.[188]

Moreover, the number of unemployed did not decrease in the northern parts of the country, the training of unemployed youth in skills currently in high demand in the economy is in sad shape, and the restrictions as well as the expenditures for environmental protection are entirely inadequate. From all this follow presently and especially

[187] According to Andreas Uhlig, "Die unvollendete Revolution des 'Thatcherismus'," *Neue Zürcher Zeitung*, No. 103, 6/7 May 1989, p. 33. This does not include any disavowal of the value-added tax as such. It does have definite advantages. Above all, it falsifies competition much less. One should ask, therefore, whether the value-added tax, as envisioned by the European Community, ought not to apply two rates: a lower one for essential goods and a substantially higher one for non-essential commodities. I owe this suggestion to Hans-Erich Roth, President of the Administrative Council of Mühlebach AG (Switzerland).

[188] Roger Bernheim, "Zehn-Jahr-Amtsjubiläum Frau Thatchers," *Neue Zürcher Zeitung*, No. 101, 3 May 1989, p. 5.

in the years to come enormous social, human-related, and ecological costs that must be shouldered by society and that substantially relativize the overall economic efficiency in spite of individual economic gains. Based on the argument of efficiency, any attempt at presenting "capitalism" as the most economically rational form of the market economy is, therefore, fallacious. The other real or possible order forms of the market economy we have examined may possess smaller individual economic profit quota and may, therefore, be tied to less economic efficiency of the private sector. Yet, what matters in assessing the life-serving aspect and thus the economic rationality of the economy is its total efficiency. An essential part of it results from human, social, and ecological accomplishments which minimize the external costs that must otherwise be paid for by society and supported by the entire economy. In short, what matters is the proliferation of general welfare by raising the quality of life. This illustrates in a different way that nothing can be truly economically rational unless it is also humanly just.

Thus we are already touching on the other point of view that must mark the road to our discovery of principles inherent to the question of order in the economy.

6.3.2 *Some Basic Reflections on What Is Humanly Just*

6.3.2.1 Principal Issues

Our previous discussion of economic rationality illustrated that the economy can live up to its fundamental mission of providing human beings with commodities that are essential and also enhance the quality of life, only if their production and marketing proceed efficiently. Thus efficiency in the above sense proves to be an indispensable maxim of economically rational activity.

Our reflections also revealed that efficiency, as an optimal lessening of the economic scarcity restrictions, serves the principle of economic rationality, only if it is understood totally in an economic sense. In other words, in order to be truly efficient, individually efficient economic production and marketing of scarce commodities requires an equally efficient minimization of negative external effects that charge the entire economy with human, social, and ecological costs. However, this suggests that efficiency can be valid as an order-political maxim for an appropriate design of the economy only in as far as it is viewed as comprehensive and as long as it rates the human, social, and ecological meaning or purpose of the economy no less than its fundamental purpose. Already purely from the point of view of economic rationality, considerations of human justice cannot be suppressed. In light of our theologically based theory of business and economic ethics, this means that the recourse to fellow-humanness, participation, fellow-creatureliness, and relationality as fundamental criteria of the humanity originating from faith, hope, and love is indispensable to the establishment of maxims regarding economic order policy.

Sections 3.3.4-7 discuss and categorize in detail from the point of view of the aspect of the mentioned criteria the principal problems facing economic ethics in the industrial society, including the resulting fundamental requirements. It will serve our continued discussions well to recall the result, briefly summarizing it.

1. The criterion of fellow-humanness poses the problem of the ability of human beings to be persons in all areas of life. Economic processes, too, are to respect human beings as persons. Particularly in their concrete labor relationships, human beings should never have to play the role of merely efficiently positioned and perhaps well-paid means of production, but rather be called upon to act as responsible subjects who enjoy a realm of their own for self-determination, without which labor must turn into alienating servitude and thus lose its human dimension. Rational organizations of production and distribution must not, therefore, lead to the loss of a person's individual role as a subject within the labor process.

2. Participation, as a Christian criterion of what is humanly just, reflects what is understood to mean "feelings for our fellow human beings," i.e. fellow-humanness, on the level of economic-social institutions or structures. Accordingly, the order-political structures of the economy can be humanly just only as long as the cooperation of various economic subjects, which is indispensable in industrial society, does not establish a one-sided dependency that leads to confrontation, as long as all those willing and able to work are entitled to a job and to those educational and training opportunities that enable them to meet the labor qualifications demanded today, as long as all members of society are able to share in the national product according to their performance *and* based on their needs, as long as productive capital ownership does not remain a power factor in the hands of some few capital owners, and as long as possibilities for co-determination are

available to all concerned, in companies and plants as well as in critical macroeconomic decision-making processes. Thus, participation is the fundamental and comprehensive criterion underlying the question of an ethically responsible, structural order of the economy.

3. The criterion of fellow-creatureliness concerns itself with the issue of elementary relationships of human beings to the natural environment. Just as we are fellow human beings in the social environment, we are fellow creatures in the natural environment. And just as human beings have a right to participate in the economic and cultural goods produced by society as their social environment, human beings also have a right to participate in the natural goods that creation offers to them as their ecological environment and which they need for their productive activities in their effort to satisfy their essential material and cultural needs. However, this right to partake is limited. Within the social environment, the needs of our fellow human beings determine the limits and, in the ecological realm, restrictions on the use of and the impact on nature set the limits. In other words, apart from the capitalist interest of maximizing profits, this means that if nature is to be preserved as a stable foundation for the lives of subsequent generations of human beings and non-human fellow creatures, the size of economic production must not be oriented solely towards the extent of human needs, but equally towards the limitations to the use and carrying capacity of nature. Thus, the postulate of stabilizing the environment, which contains within itself the stabilization of world population growth, as well as a stabilization of human needs, derives necessarily from fellow-creatureliness as a criterion for what is humanly just.

4. The criterion of relationality is concerned with the clarification of humanly just employment of the fundamental values, that is to say, the fundamental interests that are connected to them. Clearly, every fundamental value, no matter how high its ethical rank, and every fundamental interest, no matter how legitimate, becomes non-human if the relationship to its opposite value or interest is disregarded and it is rendered absolute in its extremeness, leading to total confrontation. It will, thus, be necessary to simultaneously uphold the value of individual responsibility and the individual self-interest allied with it, and the value of solidarity, as well as the collective general interest, its corollary. This, however, does not signify, certainly not in principle, but pragmatically, that one or the other may take precedence in given

situations. Among other things, this means that if an economic order is to approximate the demands of the humanly just, it must lay out its structures in such a way that their objective will be to reduce the traditional clash between individual and general interests, that is the interest of the entrepreneurs in profitable economic activities and the interest of the workers in good pay, that is to say, in social conditions that guarantee workers financial security, and an understanding between the two. Naturally, a similar understanding applies to the ecological interests and the interests of society in an economically and socially efficient economy.

5. The principal problems of economic ethics posed by today's industrial society in view of the criteria of fellow-humanness, participation, fellow-creatureliness, and relationality, and the fundamental demands resulting from this examination point the way to the following considerations that serve the justification of maxims for critical examination and decision-making. The issue is which order structures in the economy, i.e. in the market economy, most likely meet the demands of the humanly just, marking the fundamental criteria of humanity originating from faith, hope, and love, without disregarding the demands of economic rationality. Just as no basic economic system, even in its ideal form, can prevail in the face of the absolute requirement of the Christian criteria of humanity; neither can a market-economic order form, not one that really exists, nor one that represents a desirable alternative. They are all constructs of penultimate, historical time that comes and goes. And whenever they pretend to be something like the ultimate, the humanly just in the sense of humanity originating from faith, hope, and love calls for an uncompromising, critical distance all the way to their absolute rejection. To be sure, the criterion of relative reception also belongs to the critical distance as a criterion representative of what is humanly just. In spite of its critical distance, faith-based humanity cannot and must not be indifferent to whether in the penultimate an economic system or economic order aims relatively more or relatively less for what the humanly just requires. We must search our consciences and balance our priorities, expressing the results in the form of binding maxims. Yet these maxims deal with norms of conditional and not unconditional obligation. They are typical directional markers in need of constant examination and not apodictic rules that are valid forever. Neither do they stipulate a certain order-political economic model.

They permit different possibilities of order, but indicate the normative markings within which a market-economic form of order must operate if it is to be received by the humanly just evaluated by the criteria of humanity originating from faith, hope, and love, striving simultaneously for economic rationality.

6.3.2.2 Weighing the Options

If it comes to considering carefully which order structures can be appropriated by the market economy based on the criteria of the humanly just and which order structures will be unacceptable, that is to say, which structures deserve priority when compared normatively, then we must return to the overview presented in 6.2, discussing several of their real or possible order structures.

1. During the course of these considerations it will be necessary to decide first what the maxims of critical examination and decision-making are with regard to the system question in the economy. Accordingly, the humanity originating from faith, hope, and love must opt for the basic market-economic system. The reason is that, aside from the unalterable human values that also support it, it is more efficient and therefore, in view of the fundamental purpose of the economy, also more rational than the centrally planned economy. The decision in favor of the market-economic system is particularly appropriate, because it can be relativized by its opposite and its equally unalterable human values using regulatory means containing planning and control elements without losing its function. The option favors, therefore, a regulated market economy.

The classical theory is based on a market economy that is left on its own in the sense of the concept of "laissez-faire." Libertarian capitalism that does not believe in market regulation originated on the basis of this concept.

Libertarian capitalism affords entrepreneurs free reign in their pursuit of specific individual, that is capital-oriented interests aiming at the maximization of profits. On the one hand, this occurs at the expense of the wage or social interests of employees and, indeed, also of the common interests of society, as long as the other side does not know how defend itself by forming unions. On the other hand, it leads to war in the marketplace of everyone against everyone else, because the interests of competitors aiming at maximizing profits clash and mutually hinder one another. The consequences are serious social conflicts, a descent into a competition aiming solely at the elimination of competitors and characterized by the formation of monopolies that both dominate and restrict the market. And in all, this leads to confrontational disparities that, in extreme cases, led to catastrophic crises that rocked the entire economy. Thus the capitalist form of the market economy harbors the potential for self-destruction.

Based on these experiences, Keynes critically evaluated the classical theory. He postulated the government's need for regulating, that is to say, controlling the capitalist market economy if it was to survive. Since the 1930s, Keynesian economics was widely embraced, especially in public economic policies. This led to a transformation to regulated or organized capitalism.

On the other hand, the stagflationary crisis during the 1970s revealed the weaknesses of the Keynesian economic theory. That led again to a paradigm shift in economics. The neo-classical theory gained the upper hand over the theoretical approaches developed by Keynes.[189] Once again, economists are betting on the automatic self-healing powers of the economy and demand in principle its deregulation. This led to a renewed strengthening of libertarian capitalism, accentuated particularly by "Reaganomics" and "Thatcherism," both based on their characteristic supply-side economics that favored capital interests. Certainly, attempts at deregulation in the market economy are justified in as much as they deal with the dismantling of regimentation instituted by the government bureaucracy, that is to say, interventionist individual interference with the course of macro-economic processes that make the functioning of the market more difficult, or even impossible. However, regimentation is not the same as regulation. On the one hand, market regulation means bringing order into competition, in the sense that the market honors as much as possible better and more flexible performance, but not greater power, that is to say, it saves competition from degenerating solely into eliminating competitors, a trend that would ultimately have to end in self-destruction. On the other hand, it signifies the ordering of process policies in a manner that determines within the framework of a global concept that is oriented on everyone's interests the desired macro-economic goals, such as full employment, social balance, and

[189] See Katterle, *Alternativen zur neoliberalen Wende*, p. 11.

stability of the environment. All of these were to be achieved by applying measures conforming to the market as much as possible. Regulation of the market economy in this sense is, therefore, not aimed at an interventionist, regimented process policy, but, on the contrary, aims to make it superfluous.

Now, if no distinctions are made between regulating and regimenting the market economy and if there is a tendency to question regulation at all, then, to the extent that this occurs, the market economy becomes a victim of confrontational disorder. It turns into something like an econo-Darwinistic playground, where the stronger push the weaker aside, where capital and labor, the economy and the environment forcibly clash, where the weight of the ownership of the means of production is divided disproportionately and one-sidedly, where most of the employed are denied any participation in economic decisions that affect them directly and where the masses of the gainfully employed are forced into a life of dependency that is determined by other people and characterized by work threatened by increasing uncertainty, in short, where profit and capital interests of the companies do fight against the population's wage, social, and ecological interests by denying the existence of any sort of relational existence. All of this contradicts the commandment of the humanly just as well as the economically rational. The humanity that originates from faith, hope, and love and lives up to the criteria of the humanly just in real, economic contexts, is in no position to accept a deregulated type of capitalism. To be sure, it is obligated to retain its basis, but it must search with all its might for a form of order that is as humane and as environmentally appropriate as possible, and that encompasses both regulation and de-capitalization of the market.

2. The order form of the social market economy, at least in its original form, first described by Alfred Müller-Armack, must be distinguished from the concept of libertarian or deregulated capitalism.

As described in 6.2.2, even the social market economy purposely advocates the principle of the freedom of the marketplace. But the freedom of the marketplace does not signify libertarian freedom that excludes government intervention into market events. It rather needs a binding regulatory component in order to protect competition from deteriorating into predatory competition that, in its extreme form, would necessarily cause its own termination. On the other hand, it needs to create an institutionalized base of government-sponsored social institutions in order to promote the social balance that the laws of the marketplace are unable to establish independently between those with high and those with low incomes, between the haves and the have-nots. Basically, it is a question of a concept that allows itself to be guided in its economic policy by the relational nature of the individual interests of the economic subjects that compete with one another in the marketplace, and by the collective interests of society; through the building of a social network, it strives also to improve the opportunities to participate in the national product for the weaker among the population or, mindful of the principle of solidarity, to rectify the distribution of income based on the performance principle. The co-determination of workers in the workplace and in companies, as guaranteed in various ways by the social market economy of the Federal Republic of Germany, by the Miners' Co-determination Act, and by the Business Organization Act, also increases the opportunities for a majority of employees to influence operational and partly also corporate policy decisions. This can provide some autonomy to employees in merely executive positions within the factory and business processes, and, above all, it may also increase the opportunity for humanizing concrete working relationships, a fact that once again is in line with fellow-humanness as personal criterion of what is humanly just.

Considering all of the above, it might become obvious that the reasons arguing from the point of view of economic ethics against a reception of its specifically capitalist form largely disappear in the case of the original form of the social market economy. To be sure, the latter is not simply congruent with the claims resulting from the criteria of humanity originating from faith, hope, and love; yet, there is a convergence with them, especially in as far as participation and the relational character are concerned. At any rate, because its regulatory component is critical of capitalism, it comes close to a humane order form of the market economy. That is why it is fundamentally acceptable to us. Yet some caution is in order.

The first reservation concerns the practice of the present-day social market economy. As already pointed out, its actual form diverges from the original concept, and there is a tendency today to suppress its regulatory component with liberal, deregulatory measures. These amount to a return to specifically capitalist practices, making us think primarily of a situation that favors an extreme form of supply side economics. The greater the degree to which this applies, the lesser the social market economy's acceptance of the humanity originating from faith, hope, and love. The other reservation deals with efforts to turn the social market economy into something final. At least in its actually existing form, it does not represent an order-political optimum. On the contrary, the basic design of its concept will survive only if it undergoes continued development. Indeed, Müller-Armack pointed this out rather emphatically.[190] He speaks of a second phase of the social market economy that would have to generate, among other things, increased investment in spiritual capital, a new measure of autonomy resulting from a greater humanization of the conditions in the workplace, a universally designed environmental policy for the purpose of keeping the water clean and the air pure within the framework of humanly just city, landscape, and traffic planning, as well as the participation of large segments of the population in the formation of capital. Thus, the social market economy must continually develop; it will be acceptable only under these conditions. This does not include only a corresponding expansion, but also the clarification of the nature of its regulatory control function, which, as pointed out already, contains some contradictions in Müller-Armack' concept. On the one hand, he does not welcome "a liberal market economy that is left to its own devices," but wishes "to have purposeful control, that is to say, a socially controlled market economy."[191] On the other hand, he becomes sceptical later in his life to the point of rejecting global control or macro-planning serving social considerations.[192] One will have to look beyond contradictions that cause confusion within the concept of a social market economy. This, however, does not suggest at all that one would have to be against it;[193] but that one has to

[190] *BEE*, Vol. II, p. 543.

[191] *BEE*, Vol. II, 6.2.2, fn. 32.

[192] *BEE*, Vol. II, p. 542.

[193] Katterle argues for a position "beyond the social market economy" (*Alternativen zur neoliberalen Wende*, pp. 32-42). This might give the impression that one would have to part with the market economy. This, however, is not what Katterle means. "A new 'qualitative' model of prosperity characterized by a 'new urgency' assigned to achievements and damages not adequately rated by the market, and growth controlled in accordance with socially agreeable priorities are calling for a reconstruction of the economic control system that makes it possible to formulate far-reaching social goals with new priorities and to implement them together with appropriate measures of control in the production system. To assure the social compatibility and applicability of these priorities, a politico-economic system of social planning and control ('economy-wide co-determination') must be institutionalized parallel to the market

reconsider the combination of market and planning and continue to develop the economy in the suggested areas and welcome new possibilities. The question is: which way to go?

3. Sections 6.2.3-6 contain other outlines of market order forms in addition to the social market economy that, in its original concept, purposely distinguishes itself from specific capitalism. Pointing beyond, these order forms are already partially and gradually realized, or exist only in the form of innovative drafts. They can be summarily characterized in the sense that, when compared to the social market economy, they go much further with respect to the de-capitalization of the market by fundamentally changing relationships of ownership with regard to large-scale ownership of capital goods and the means of production that are relevant to distribution, taking on a clearer position regarding the regulatory augmentation of the market's system of coordination through macro-economic planning and control elements. Although their basic concepts differ, they represent different market-principle-based order possibilities that can also be critical to the continued development of the social market economy. How are they to be rated in light of the critical aspects of the humanly just in a Christian sense, particularly in light of participation, relationality and fellow-creatureliness? Let us begin with those order possibilities that deal with the question of ownership, or the problem of distribution.

a) Without a doubt, the issue of distribution is crucially significant in today's industrial society.[194] Opinions vary widely, especially on the question of how large-scale business ownership can or should be handled.

Things are different regarding smaller or medium-sized business ownership. Because they are so widely scattered, these forms of

system and interlaced with it" (p. 40). Thus, even Katterle is calling for a combination of market and planning. Yet, I believe that the question of the actual constitutive factor remains unresolved: will it be the market or the economic system composed of planning and control? According to our approuch, the latter is part of the regulatory component that needs to take effect, not 'in addition to' but subsidiary to the market economy. The social market economy offers steps towards such a combination of market and planning, making it, on the other hand, humanly and ecologically possible to attain order forms that are more just with respect to continued development. These inherent possibilities for continued development are also emphasized by Brakelmann, "Eine irenische Formel," p. 77.

[194] See Kleinewefers, *Reformen für Wirtschaft und Gesellschaft*, p. 466.

ownership have no significant impact on the market; their role is rather to maintain healthy and orderly competition. Contrary to orthodox Marxism-Leninism, which disallows any capital or business ownership in private hands, the representatives, critical of capitalistic order forms of the market economy, agree that the nationalization of the means of production is incapable of offering a humanly just or economically rational solution to the problem of distribution; they also agree that smaller and even medium-sized capital ownership in private companies is not only permissible but that it should be protected and promoted. On the other hand, there remain controversies that significantly affect distribution with regard to ordering large-scale business ownership.

In addition to the promotion of small-scale and the reduction of large-scale business ownership, the solution in the social market economy, or more precisely, the de-emphasis of the problem of distribution, is seen in the broader casting of productive capital. Share capital should also be accumulated by workers. As the smallest stockholders, workers thus share individually, albeit very modestly, in the profits accruing to the capital; still, nothing changes regarding the relationships of power that safeguard the existence of large-scale business ownership. The entrepreneurial and, therefore, the economic power to make decisions remains undivided in the hands of the majority stockholders and, even more so in the hands of managers who not own the productive capital but de facto control it and essentially make decisions affecting company policy. The small stockholders do not participate in this process at all, and the social status of the worker stockholders in a company remains unchanged. They are in no position to modify the confrontational relationship existing between capital and labor on the company level.

The situation is different in the case of the Swedish model of the democratic market economy. According to this model, those who depend on wages participate quite heavily, through workers investment funds, in the capital stock of the large manufacturing and service-sector companies. That is why they do not only share substantially in the operating profits, but also influence company policy, albeit not as individuals and not directly, but collectively and indirectly because the unions administer the workers investment funds and because the profits derived from the equity participation are diverted to social security. The advantage of this system lies in the fact that both private concentration of capital and formation of power are limited, that the economy has also at its disposal the necessary means of investment, that the general prosperity level of the population is raised and that workers are able to influence employment policy. The disadvantage of this system, however, is that the participation works only collectively and indirectly, that is to say it is incapable of entering the immediate personal sphere of the individual worker and of abolishing his or her alienation from the company and its specific interests. The relationship between capital and labor remains confrontational, as in the social market economy, while the relationship between wage or social interests and the interest of companies in efficiently employing the capital means does not become any more transparent to the workers.

Even in the concept of the Western-type socialist market economy smaller and medium, private business ownership remains untouched. Yet, private business ownership does not give rise to an absolute right of disposition; it is rather subsumed under social duty that includes a participatory order of the labor relationships in the sense of co-determination, as well as a participatory policy of distribution. Whenever private business ownership neglects its social obligations, causing harm to society, it should be socialized in a form that is primarily socio-economical and cooperative, pointing in a direction that the criteria of the humanity originating from faith, hope, and love follow. This applies particularly to the cooperative system. Because of their shares, the members of the cooperative are the direct owners of capital stock; they decide independently how the shares are to be used, they assume personal responsibility for business policy and the organization of labor as well as the allocation of profits to the necessary investments and to adequate wages or to expenditures for social security. To be sure, they must also absorb any losses. This system permits high-grade participation and brings the criterion of relationality to bear on the relationship between capital and profits and between wages and social interests. On the other hand, it must be pointed out that the application of the co-operative model has some serious limitations, as is the case, to some extent, with the worker-administrated business illustrated by the Yugoslavian model. According to past experience, it is fitting in the manufacturing sector merely in the case of small, homogeneous, and stable groups. As a rule, large-scale production cooperatives suffer from a lack of operational and managerial efficiency. However, whenever they succeeded for a change, they did so by adapting to the structure of anonymous corporations.

Thus, they hold relatively little promise for an economically rational handling of the problem of distribution in the case of large earned income.

In view of this conclusion, Šik's ownership reform deserves even greater recognition. As illustrated in 6.2.5.3, it is tailor-made particularly for the kind of large, business ownership, that is, since it constitutes neutralized capital, neither private nor government-owned, but rather an inalienable good belonging to the worker-owned company (*Mitarbeitergesellschaft*). As Henner Kleinewefers points out, "it contains the advantages and avoids the disadvantages of the co-operative model."[195] Since every co-worker participates in the same way in the neutralized capital stock, the differences in the relative ownership of the means of production are balanced, rendering the problem of distribution moot: "The differences in ownership are largely reduced to the workers' incomes."[196] Because there are no individually distributable ownership rights, but, instead, co-workers participate individually in profits and losses while exercising far-reaching operational and entrepreneurial co-determination, there exists a direct connection between the decisions of the co-workers and the ensuing consequences. In their co-determinative decisions that also include the appointment of capable managers, co-workers are forced to take the indispensable capital interests of the companies into account, because they would also be suffering the consequences themselves if they were to disregard them. Thus the individual economic incentive function of ownership that is essential to the structure of the market economy is assured. We can, therefore, insist that this reform of large-scale business ownership affords co-workers not only a high degree of participation in the business income of the capital and in the co-determinative rights which derive from it, but this reform might also contribute a great deal to the relational rather than the confrontational regulation of the relationship between profit and wage interests, indeed between capital and social interests.[197] In this way it would have the potential to noticeably change the status of the workers in the companies and to reduce the notorious alienation from which they suffer.

[195] *Ibid*, p. 471.

[196] *Ibid.*

[197] To be sure, this applies only to large-scale earned ownership in co-operative companies. At the medium ownership level, the participation of workers is reduced to their participation in the profits. In the case of the smallest owner, who is identical to the worker, the participation problem becomes moot.

Šik's ownership reform would certainly have to be expanded to include a reform of business ownership of the land as well as the natural resources. There exists not only a problem of distribution between capital and labor, but, according to the criteria of creatureliness, a similar problem exists between capital and labor on the one hand, and nature on the other. Capital and labor must not be permitted to exploit natural resources for the purpose of maximizing their specific interests. Business land ownership must, therefore, be ordered in such a way that institutionalized exploitation is held in check, that the utilization of natural resources proceeds as environmentally safe as possible, and that an amount of money sufficient to pay for the minimization of inevitable damage is set aside.

This still leaves us with the question about the presumed effects of Šik's proposed ownership reform and its ecological dimension on the economic efficiency of enterprises. Kleinewefers, who is well known for being a highly critical economist responds as follows:

> It is ... possible that the concept could lead to a lack of economic efficiency in two areas. On the one hand, the elimination of the (bigger) individual entrepreneur may in some cases curtail managerial performance. On the other hand, it is conceivable that accumulation will be less under the conditions of neutralized capital than in the case of private business ownership. However, these possible losses in efficiency must be weighed against the gains in efficiency resulting from the removal of the fights over distribution and power and the corresponding rise in the quality of the political, administrative and legal system. Moreover, a reduction of capital accumulation can be viewed positively even with regard to ecological considerations.[198]

The accompanying reduction of individual economic efficiency due to this reform would thus likely be paralleled also by a gain in economy-wide efficiency.

All of these considerations urge us to conclude that we must continue to develop today's economic system, including the social market economy, with regard to the order of business ownership of productive capital and of the natural resources, in a direction similar to the one indicated by Šik and Binswanger. This could and

[198] Kleinewefers, *Reformen für Wirtschaft und Gesellschaft*, p. 471.

would have to take place gradually. The idea of a sudden transformation of corporations into worker-owned companies (*Mitarbeitergesellschaften*) would be unrealistic. A gradually increasing number of such companies within the framework of the market economy is, however, conceivable. Private stock capital must not necessarily disappear according to Šik. It suffices to have a majority favoring neutralized capital, or the elimination of the stock ownership that is concentrated in the hands of a few and is difficult to control.

Binswanger's proposal of a patrimonial reform of the right to land ownership is similar. Private land ownership that is based on the concept of *dominium*, as well as its largely unrestricted right of usufruct is, historically speaking, rather recent, that is to say, it is rooted in nineteenth-century liberalism.[199] Prior to that, ownership was, particularly in Switzerland, largely in the hands of communes, co-operatives using the commons (*Allmendgenossenschaften*) and comparable church-owned or secular corporations, some of which are still in existence. Why should it not be possible to revive this type of socialization in timely fashion and combine it with an ecologically appropriate regulation of the private enjoyment of the rights of usufruct within the realm of market-economy-based competition?

b) The other sizeable problem of a regulated market economy raises the question of the extent to which it can and should be controlled by planning in order to maintain the priority of general interests over special interests, without abandoning the constitutive system of coordination expressed by competition and by the price formation that is tied to it. Here, too, the answers vary among the advocates of an in principle regulated market economy.

The question remains largely undecided in today's social market economy. Tendencies to regulate and to deregulate contradict one another, and the possibility or the feasibility of combining market and planning is controversial. By contrast, the concept of the socialist market economy as well as Šik's and the Swedish model's derive clearly from the necessity and compatibility of the combination between market and planning. Yet the attempts at planning vary (production, investment, distribution planning, etc.). However, all

[199] Gottfried W. Locher, *Der Eigentumsbegriff als Problem der evangelischen Theologie*, Zürich, 1962, pp. 59-73.

three seem to be agreed on restricting planning to the macro-economic realm and to keeping regulation and intervention at a minimum. To be sure, we are dealing here with macro-economic global planning, the purpose of which is not to replace the market's system of coordination, but to support and augment it in a manner that will prevent any unrestricted assertion of private special interests (for instance the chaotic conditions in the [Swiss] real estate market), but to promote, instead, an increase in general welfare. Plan-oriented coordination, therefore, plays a clearly subsidiary role. The humanity originating from faith, hope, and love is thus unable to determine which regulatory types of planning will take effect and where the limits of subtle global planning should be: decisions such as these are best left to economic experts. On the other hand, because it is rooted in the specific criteria of the humanly just, it readily tackles the issue of global planning objectives that are to be achieved, as well as of the economic-political measures it wishes to promote.

Generally speaking, the fundamental purpose of global planning may be seen in the effort to prevent as much as possible the imbalance that may arise in the market economy as a result of the domination of special interests over general interests, or to reduce them wherever they are discovered. These forms of imbalance manifest themselves above all in the gross disparity of distribution, in mass unemployment, inflation and, last but not least, in the excessive and destructive demands made on the environment. We have already discussed the possibilities of changing the existing structures of distribution under the auspices of a participatory reform of earned ownership. There still remains the question of how to stabilize employment in the sense of creating jobs for all those who are willing to work, as well as how to stabilize the value of money and the state of the environment. There is probably widespread agreement on the desirability, indeed the necessity of these particular objectives. Aside from insisting on its fundamental relationality, the humanity originating from faith, hope, and love has, therefore, nothing special to contribute.

The situation is different in the case of measures dealing with economic policy whose purpose is the achievement of the goals set by the plan. They must be examined prior to determining whether they are acceptable in view to the humanitarian criteria of participation, fellow-creatureliness, and relationality. Thus, for instance, the humanity rooted in faith, hope, and love must oppose a job creation policy that simply divides the number of existing jobs among more people by shortening the amount of working hours at full pay. This procedure unilaterally provides those who have a job with the usufruct of the improvement in productivity;[200] moreover, it raises the cost of labor, a fact that promotes particularly the labor-saving measures of rationalization and further worsens the conditions for those who are out of a job and who are no longer capable of adjusting to the new qualification requirements. Certainly, this situation is far removed from a participatory handling of the employment problem under the conditions of increased unemployment.

Similarly, the humanity originating from faith, hope, and love must object to an environmental policy that merely confines itself to reducing the worst kinds of environmental damage only after they have occurred, instead of developing effective regulations whose implementation could protect nature and its resources from the destructive exploitation by capital and labor, production and consumerism. This derives necessarily from the criterion of creatureliness.

And finally, the humanity originating from faith, hope, and love cannot agree with a market-regulating economic policy that is based on the disregard of relationality among different planning objectives. A balanced distribution of earned income, as high a degree of stability of employment as possible, the stability of the value of money, and the stability of the environment are global goals that must not be traded off against one another. Any form of extreme treatment in either direction will lead to the monocracy of an essentially justified fundamental interest, but it will simultaneously cause injustice and prove to be contradictory to what is humanly just. At best, only constructive, viable and sensible compromises among the planned objectives can be achieved here.

For all of these reasons, humanity originating from faith, hope, and love will be able to accept only macro-economic attempts at planning and regulating whose economic-political arsenal also takes into account the relational nature of the various global objectives in addition to the concerns of participation and creatureliness; it has no intention to regulate the market using strict control, but, instead, desires to regulate it in a way that supports or augments those mechanisms that balance its interests and thus conform to the market. Moreover, the coordination of the various planning

200 Productivity = gross national product divided by the number of working hours.

objectives and the establishment of elementary instrumental measures used to implement them would have to be democratically legitimized either by way of parliamentary decrees or, if possible, by cooperative agreements between the social opponents and various other influential social forces. It appears that the market-economic proposals of Ota Šik and Hans Christoph Binswanger approximate most closely these planning objectives. Once again this points in the direction of possible and desirable continued development of today's market economy, a fact that might also erect bridges to order forms that have recently been arising in the East.

4. According to the above considerations, the economic-ethical option of a regulated market economy does not at all include a decision in favor of a certain type of its possibilities of order. It is an option favoring an open, self-critical market economy in need of constant development, permitting, therefore, a reception of different regulatory measures that determine the concrete form of the economic order. Which of these possible forms of order are acceptable and which are not, and in which direction they could and should be developed further in view of existing principal economic-ethical problems in today's industrial society is clearly a matter of fundamental and careful concern that must be guided by the viewpoints of human justice *and* economic rationality. They are summarized by certain maxims that are characterized, on the one hand, by being evaluative and, on the other hand, by being decisive. Since these maxims must essentially meet the demands of what is humanly just as well as what is economically rational, their claim to validity can only be conditional, because what is truly humanly just or economically rational in a given situation cannot be determined *a priori* but rather a posteriori, based on the experience gained. Among the maxims, therefore, those that are described as decisive must certainly be subjected to constant scrutiny in accordance with the "trial and error" principle. If they prove to be unsuitable to a (more) humanly just or functional form of market-economic order and thus erroneous, they must then be revised or abandoned.

The validity of the following maxims that are explicitly included in the following fundamental and careful considerations of the market-economic order question is subject to this specific reservation.

6.4. Maxims

1. As a mechanism of economic coordination, the market economy is not a "natural" system, but a man-mandated system for whose anthropological and social as well ecological consequences, manifesting themselves in all its possible forms of order, we are responsible.

2. The entire market economy is based on the interests of individuals and the individual responsibility of the various economic subjects. These are obligated to utilize as much as possible their investments for the purpose of production as well as consumption. That favors an optimum allocation of the factors of production, as well as a price formation oriented towards demand and, therefore, also efficient economic activity.

3. The profit interest of the entrepreneurs or the producers is limited by competition as the central element of market-economic coordination. In a pure market economy with perfect competition there is even a tendency to remove profits, a fact that benefits consumers. Yet even the interests of consumers are limited by competition, because commodities whose price does not generate any profits are no longer produced. Thus competition possesses a mechanism that tends to balancing the interests of economic subjects and promoting the general welfare if economic efficiency is high. This speaks decidedly in favor of the market economy.

4. The market-economic and competition-oriented mechanisms must, however, not be viewed as some kinds of natural laws whose impact would be necessary, even automatic, that is to say, independent of the will of the economic subjects and their individual interests. The economic subjects are instead capable of willfully interfering with competition, either by restricting or by completely abolishing it. The tendency for such a manipulation of competition becomes all the more powerful, the more the economic subjects seek to unscrupulously maximize their own self-interests and by doing so experience competition as an obstacle. Complete freedom to pursue their self-interests leads to cartel-like or monopolistic formations of power in the marketplace, with the objective of driving out inconvenient competition, likely leading in extreme cases to the replacement of market prices by prices that are entirely dictated by power,

and to the de facto abandonment of meaningful competition spurring better performance.[201] Thus there is no point in talking about the promotion of general welfare interests solely by resorting to market-economic mechanisms.

5. Real competition that balances the individual interests of the various economic subjects and, therefore, serves indirectly the general interests is not possible if it is based on a market economy that is left on its own in the sense of "laissez-faire." It requires for this purpose an institutionalized regulatory device that is structured in such a way that legitimate individual interests are permitted the necessary amount of free play that benefits economic efficiency, yet by regulating them in a manner that primarily emphasizes general interests.

6. As long as the market economy, together with its mechanisms, shows a tendency to balance the individual interests of the various economic subjects for the benefit of society, such a regulation will not contradict the very nature of the market economy. It rather supports and augments it by erecting institutional barriers against maximizing or rendering individual interests absolute, and, in doing so, it counteracts through the process of competition the formation of market power with its private, market-destructing possibilities to intervene. At the same time, this signifies that both the market and its mechanisms of coordination must play a constitutive role. On the other hand, regulation that is tied to a certain measure of planning must restrict itself to the regulatory and, therefore, subsidiary function.

7. The general welfare interests of society converge largely with the fundamental, the human, the social, and the ecological purposes of the economy on the battlefield of the relative and the absolute.[202] They thus combine with the socio-ethical demands contained in creatureliness, fellow-humanness, participation, fellow-creatureliness,

[201] This does not at all mean that cartels are not distinguished from monopolies. Monopolies represent pure formations of power in the marketplace, while cartel-like agreements can also intend to save the competition from economic-Darwinistic and, therefore, self-destructive repression, without simultaneously abolishing competition. In the latter case, cartel-like arrangements function as market regulators. However, this does not apply to cartels that aim at dominating the market in order to keep unwelcome competition at bay.

[202] *BEE*, Vol. II, 1.3.6.

and relationality, all fundamental criteria of the humanly just anchored in the humanity originating from faith, hope, and love. This humanity will only be able to agree with a regulated market economy whose subsidiary regulatory system orients itself towards the aforementioned criteria of the humanly just and the meaningful purposes of the economy converging with them.

8. A set of regulatory measures that is oriented towards the criteria of the humanly just must establish certain goals for the market economy that serve life in the broadest sense of the word "life-serving" and to which the market economy must be committed. They focus essentially on the following objectives:

a) The minimization of instabilities in the business cycles and in the structures, particularly for the purpose of defending against unemployment;
b) Adaptation of economic growth and economic activity to what is ecologically sustainable;
c) Keeping inflation at an optimum low in order to preserve purchasing power;
d) Highly efficient production and distribution of consumer goods and services under humane working conditions and under conditions of environmentally just utilization of nature;
e) The creation of a social net for the purpose of safeguarding the livelihood of all social groups;
f) The participation of workers in business ownership and in corporate and plant decisions of concern to them;
g) Co-workers sharing profits and losses for the purpose of allowing them to participate in the success of the company and in order to do justice to the relationality of capital interest and wages or profit interests;

9. In order to assure their effective implementation, the purposeful selection of objectives must be supported by economic macro-planning, at least as far as objectives (a), (b), and (c) are concerned. The intricacies of business cycles and structural as well as environmental stability factors in the market economy can hardly be approached without a foresighted, mutually attuned, and equitable distribution of the national income among consumption, investments in production and education dictated particularly by today's technological advancements,

and investments necessitated by a change of the economy from quantitative to qualitative growth. This suggests a focused macro-economical planning of distribution. In order to get a handle on inflation and to assure as high a degree of price stabilization as possible, there will be the need for a prospectively planned adjustment of the money in circulation to the anticipated development of the production potential as already practiced more or less by many market economies.

Overall, economic macro-planning in its market-subsidiary function must not interfere on the micro-economic level with the production and investment activities of companies; nor should it touch their responsibility for them. Furthermore, it must apply indirect, market-conforming control elements during the implementation of its planned objectives. This will probably include a largely indicative regulation, but not an imperative regimentation of the economy at the hands of government bureaucrats. In order to fend off the possible danger of a bureaucratic handling of the regulation and a deterioration into interventionist regimentation, macro-planning should be democratically legitimized and economic-political measures should not be shouldered solely by the government, but, as much as possible, by cooperative agreements between trade associations and ecologically motivated circles of interest.

10. The fourth objective (d) can be approached only under the conditions of a concept of efficiency that does not remain limited to the individual economic efficiency of the companies, but that it is broadened in a total economic sense. This calls for the minimization of negative external human, social, and environmental effects by incorporating their high social cost in the market-economic price formation employing the precautionary principle and the polluter pays principle. This broader concept of efficiency, therefore, provides space for the humanization of concrete working conditions, as well as for ecologically responsible utilization of natural resources.

11. The objective of creating a social net for the purpose of assuring the livelihood of all social groups is indispensable to a socially regulated market economy.

In the pure market economy, the national product is distributed among the gainfully employed based only on performance, despite the fact that it is socially produced in the industrial sector with its highly differentiated division of labor, and that it is impossible to measure individual performance. The market price of a certain amount of labor, therefore, must not necessarily reflect the effective output. This leads to unjust wages, if performance is only rewarded by the marketplace. Furthermore, in every society there are people who are not yet or are no longer gainfully employed, and people who, because of physical, mental, and even society-caused handicaps, are not very productive, if at all. However, as human beings they have a right to an adequate livelihood. Thus the performance principle can be affirmed only in relationship to the principle of solidarity, and vice versa. In a regulated market economy, the socially oriented state should assume the function of accentuating next to the performance principle the solidarity principle, that is of raising to a dignified level the living conditions of the economically weakest and weaker segments of the population by fiscally redistributing earned and capital income in accordance with the humanity originating from faith, hope, and love.

12. In order to address the goals mapped out in (f) and (g), a reform of the capitalist ownership structures that prevail in the traditional market economy is imperative. What must be overcome is their typical separation of potential business ownership, with its right to determine company and plant policy legitimized by it, from the large majority of workers and the accompanying, solely confrontational relationship between capital and social interests, and between profit and wage interests. Both contradict a participatory distribution of capital stock with its rights to determine company and plant policy; both impede a relational structuring of profit-wage relationships and they lower employees to the status of merely dependent labor. While the same holds true also of the mere nationalization of ownership of the means of production, it contradicts the requirements of the humanly just. Indeed, it also has a socially destabilizing effect, because the workers are notoriously alienated from the legitimate vital individual interests that are indispensable to doing business; in turn, this can easily turn into an incentive to make excessive and, therefore, intolerable wage, social, and job-security demands. Based on all these reasons, an ordering of large-scale business ownership must be sought that makes participatory distribution possible within the framework of the market economy, that, while letting them share both profits and losses, allows workers an effective right to co-determination in matters of company and plant policy and forces them also to pursue not only their special social interests but also the indispensable entrepreneurial interests in a relational manner.

13. Maxim No. 12 illustrates already that the specifically capitalist form of the market economy[203] is not acceptable to the humanity originating from faith, hope, and love. This is the case not only because its reception contradicts the manner in which earned income and co-determination rights are distributed in companies and plants, as well as the confrontational, non-relational relationship between capital and social interests. In the capitalist market economy, the unleashed capital interests dominate all other interests. The economic success of a company takes precedence over the overall welfare of society, the rationalization of production that maximizes profits eclipses concerns about humanizing the workplace, and continued economic growth pushes aside the demands of an ecologically just environmental policy, etc. All of this fundamentally contradicts the demands of human justice, despite the fact that the capitalist structure of the market economy raised massively the level of material affluence for broad segments of the population — but not the overall quality of life.

14. The situation is different in the case of the social market economy. It is acceptable to the humanity originating from faith, hope, and love. According to its original purpose, it contradicts the one-sided hegemony of capital and its interests. Competition is not to be manipulated by the formation of market power favoring it. That is why it requires the regulation of competition, in contrast to the capitalist or "free" market economy, for the purpose of supporting its inherent, yet not automatically effective mechanisms that balance the interests of the various economic subjects, and of combining economic and social efficiency. It also enabled the implementation of institutionally backed co-determination rights in all sizeable and large-scale companies all the way to co-determinational parity in the big mining companies in the Federal Republic of Germany. The social safety nets — a great achievement — were expanded significantly, thereby sending signals to the entire Western world. The criteria of human justice in the sense presented here are rated entirely differently in it than in the specifically capitalist market economy.

Aside from being weakened by the tendencies of deregulation that exclusively favors capital interests, in practice, the social market economy reveals structural deficits that remind us not to stop here. Even moderate macro-planning is controversial. The measures that prevent

[203] *BEE*, Vol. II, 6.2.1.

market power take hold only slowly or even weakly,[204] not least because the social market economy shies away from an ownership reform of large-scale businesses. Also the ecological crisis causes much trouble. For all these reasons, the social market economy is in need of continued development.

15. Regarding the continuous, on-going development of the social market economy, we must be mindful of the aforementioned maxims and pay attention to the impulses that arise from the model of a market economy that is humanly reformed and ecologically regulated.[205] It could offer the tools to move several crucial problems closer to human justice: the problem of connecting market and planning in the interest of minimizing the business-cycle-induced, structural and ecological instabilities; the problem of concentration of economic power; the problem of labor's participation in business, especially large-scale business ownership; and the environmental problem.

16. The mentioned maxims contain no specific model for an order of the market economy. They rather draw the lines within which the options are to take effect in light of the humanly just and the economically rational. There are several such options. There are good although not cogent reasons why the nod goes in the direction indicated in the maxim 15 favoring the continued development of a social market economy that stands the test of economic rationality. Should this option not live up to this test and show that it condemns the market economy to inefficiency or even paralyzes it, then it must be abandoned. For what is not economically rational cannot also serve humanity in the broadest sense of the word.

[204] This was recently illustrated by the gigantic merger plans of Daimler-Benz AG with the Messerschmitt-Bölkow-Blohm (MBB) corporation. The German Federal Cartel Office vetoed the proposed merger, while the Commission on Monopolies recommended it, albeit with considerable restrictions. In the meantime (8 September 1989), the Federal Secretary of Commerce issued a special approval of the merger, including conditions that were milder than even those imposed by the Commission on Monopolies. The latter was therefore disappointed, stating: "The conditions are not sufficient since Daimler/MBB would dominate in important markets" (*Neue Zürcher Zeitung*, No. 209, 9/10 September 1989, p. 35).

[205] *BEE*, Vol. II, 6.2.5 and 6.2.6.

7. THE GLOBAL ECONOMIC OUTLOOK

7.1 Preliminary Remarks

In the preceding chapters, the problem of the market-oriented order of the economy was discussed merely within the context of national economies. Global aspects were mentioned only marginally (2.6.3 and 3.3.5.3). The truth is, however, that the global economy plays a central role. The future of the market economy will be decided primarily by its ability to establish an economic order on a global scale that is not only functionally capable, but also justifiable in view of the humanly just that is inseparable from what is socially and ecologically just. Yet the market economy as such never by itself becomes humanly just. As should have become evident by now, it requires a certain framework capable of regulating the market processes in such a way that they will not run counter to the needs of the commonweal.[1] On the national level, it is primarily the duty of the government in addition to corporative agreements to provide regulations based on business and economic ethics and to create a culture of compliance. The international arena, on the other hand, lacks a corresponding authority possessing the necessary degree of authority to enact and enforce laws. Can there be a market economical order of the global economy that could serve the welfare and, therefore, the legitimate interests of all national economies and strata of population? Such is essentially the global economy's real challenge to the basic market economic system. This new set of problems, the treatment of which would require writing a separate monograph, can be considered only to the extent that they have been broached before and that a discussion of them will, therefore, be necessary in the interest of completeness.

[1] See also Otto Schlecht, "Soziale Weltwirtschaft," *Wirtschaftswoche*, No. 38, 16 September 1988, pp. 92-93.

7.2 Global Challenges for the Market Economy

The challenges presented by the global economy to the system of the market economy are decidedly connected to the removal of borders between national markets and subsequent expansion to a worldwide market of global interdependencies. Interdependence means mutual dependency. Nowadays, national economies have become highly dependent on one another. Such global reciprocity necessitates an international cooperation no country will be able to avoid in the long term.[2] Even countries with centrally controlled economies are increasingly becoming aware of the need to enter exchange relationships with market-oriented industrialized countries for the simple reason that they wish to benefit from their advanced technical know-how. This applies even more to developing countries. They can gather economic strength only if they are able both to participate in the financial and technological resources of the First World and to satisfy the needs existing in its markets. Conversely, the industrial countries recognize their dependency on Third World countries as suppliers of raw materials, as buyers of their industrial products, and as purveyors of services. Economic crises in developing countries, therefore, have repercussions on industrialized countries, just as crises in industrialized countries affect developing countries. It would, therefore, benefit both worlds to work towards a form of international cooperation that would serve the welfare of all participants. Is there a way to accomplish such cooperation?

Ever since Adam Smith and David Ricardo, both classical and neo-classical economic theory have firmly believed that under conditions of free world trade an automatic balancing of the interests of economic partners at higher levels of utility takes place. The laws of the marketplace will take care of that. That is why there exists a preference for the "laissez-faire" concept. Despite the fact that there are many reasons favoring free trade, this extreme market optimism remains problematic. Reality contradicts the doctrine of the automatic harmony of interests in the market economy. Even such an avid advocate of the basic market economic system as Walter Eucken is unable to hide what Siegfried Katterle rightfully points out,[3] namely that there will be serious disparities in the

[2] This is the decisive objection to the dissociative or auto-centric development strategy. See *BEE*, Vol. II, pp. 417-18 and p. 420.

[3] Siegfried Katterle, *Alternativen zur neoliberalen Wende*, Bochum, 1989, p. 233.

competitive market form, requiring corrective intervention if left on its own:

> Considerable differences in the distribution of purchasing power will arise, resulting in the redirection of production, so that it will satisfy relatively insignificant needs, while the pressing needs of other income earners remain unsatisfied. The disparity of income leads to a situation where the production of luxury goods takes place despite the existence of urgent needs in households with low incomes.[4]

In other words, this means that if market competition simply follows the principle of "laissez faire", a discrepancy of power will originate that brings structural advantages to those who are economically stronger and disadvantages to those who are economically weaker. This applies not only to nationally limited economies, but even more so to the global economy with its borders removed. If there is a need to resort to "spears of unequal length" in international competition, then one will be unable to avoid having undeserved winners and losers. Thus the market economy develops a confrontational structure that makes already stronger competitors even stronger and weaker ones still weaker. This results in a one-sided and exploitative dependence of the weak on the strong in the global economic cooperation. It would be an illusion to assume under these circumstances that market-economic processes would automatically lead to a balance of interests that promotes everyone's welfare among the national economies vying with one another. Precisely the opposite happens to be the case. Generally speaking, the extremely conflict-ridden polarity between economically potent industrialized countries and economically less potent or impotent developing countries must be viewed extremely negatively as probably the most festering problem in the contemporary global economy.

The confrontational character of market reality in today's global economy has been mentioned now and then during our previous discussions.[5] It manifests itself especially in the international debt crisis, in the growing protectionism practiced by industrialized nations, and even in the business practices of large multinational corporations.

[4] Walter Eucken, *Grundsätze der Wirtschaftspolitik,* ed. Edith Eucken and K. Paul Hensel, Bern, 1952, p. 300.

[5] Especially 2.6.3 and 3.3.5.3.

The international debt crisis is particularly significant. One must, however, beware of unilaterally blaming the causes of this as yet unsolved calamity on the industrialized countries. The developing countries share some responsibility, too.[6]

Thus, many Third World countries yielded to the temptation of borrowing large amounts of money when large amounts of petrodollars flooded the international financial markets and credit became available at favorable interest rates. Instead of investing in productive securities, the money was used to finance prestigious projects, armaments,[7] or even subsidies for the purpose of artificially reducing the price of some basic foods. The resulting enormous rise in government expenditures was solved by printing more money, contributing substantially to high inflation rates[8] and to the flight of domestic capital to hard currency countries. This is accompanied by an extremely disparate distribution of the national product.[9] Taken all in all, this signifies a poor national economic policy.

In as much as we must not hide these facts, we must also realize that the principal reasons for the astronomical amount of foreign debt in developing countries[10] must be sought in external factors.[11] Included is the dramatic rise of the price of oil in the 1970s, the global

[6] A variety of things actually lie hidden behind the cliché-like concept of the "developing countries." Apart from the poorest developing countries, such as those found primarily in sub-Saharan Africa and to some extent also in Central and South America, there are typical exporters of agrarian products, such as Argentina and Malawi, oil-exporting countries, like Venezuela and Mexico, and countries whose currency earnings depend upon the markets for a few mineral resources, such as Niger and Zambia. In addition, there are countries that already offer an assortment of exports, such as India, and others that specialize in the export of industrial goods, for instance South Korea, Singapore, and Hong Kong. See Arthur Dunkel, *Was müssen die Entwicklungsländer tun?* St. Gallen, 1988, pp. 6-7.

[7] The ratio of arms imports and development of arms-related industries to total foreign debt is estimated at 1/5. See German Conference of Bishops, ed., *Die internationale Schuldenkrise*, Bonn, 1988, p. 17.

[8] This applies particularly to Latin American countries, where the average inflation rate in 1985 was 164%, while it was 21% in Africa (1984) and a mere 7% in Asia (source: IMF Survey of 11 August 1986, p. 1).

[9] In Brazil, for instance, the top 10% of all incomes claim fully 46.2% of all salaries (*Neue Zürcher Zeitung*, No. 30, 6 February 1987, p. 19).

[10] In 1986, the international debt of all developing countries totaled $1,054 billion (Richard Gerster, *Aus Fehlern lernen?* Zürich, 1987, p. 34). The World Bank estimates an increase of indebtedness to $1,245 billion (*World Debt Tables, 1987-88*, Washington, 1988).

[11] Cf. Klaus Lefringhausen, "Marktwirtschaft und Entwicklungspolitik," in *Märkte und Mächte*, ed. Klaus Wilkens, *et al.*, Stuttgart, 1987, p. 120.

recession at the beginning of the 1980s, the rapid collapse of the prices for raw materials during the past three decades,[12] the unexpectedly rapid rise in interest payments, especially in the case of variable interest credits caused by high budget deficits in the U.S.A., the financing of which necessitated importing expensive capital, driving up the interest rate level to dangerous heights in areas dominated by the U.S. dollar; this is, aside from fears of inflation, the primary reason for the flight of capital from developing countries. In this context one must also mention the abrupt transition from careless to overly careful lending of credit by private commercial banks, the increasing protectionism practiced by industrialized countries, especially with regard to agricultural products from developing countries, and, last but not least, the profit-taking practices of multinational companies in the Third World countries, which is aggravating their notorious lack of capital even more.[13] All this has led to gigantic foreign indebtedness and subsequently to an ever more stringent debt service that has now become simply intolerable (see Table 4).[14]

This catastrophic development has now reversed the flow of money between industrialized countries and developing countries:[15]

> Whereas in 1980 the net amount of money going to Third World countries was still $15 billion, the net return flow in 1981 was $8 billion, $20 billion in 1982, $15 billion in 1983, $35 billion in 1984, $34 billion in 1985, and $28 billion in 1986 (OECD, 1986, p. 80). According to these official estimates, commercial banks in the industrialized countries earned $140 billion more in 1981-1986 than the amount of capital they had lent the Third World during the same period of time.[16]

This trend illustrates a growing power disparity in the flow of capital, putting the developing countries at a disadvantage and, therefore, underscoring the confrontational structure of global economic cooperation.

[12] Cf. Gerster, *Aus Fehlern lernen?* pp. 17 ff. In comparison, the purchasing power index for raw materials (1980 = 100) still stood at 152 in 1950; by 1986, it had sunk to 76 (*ibid.*, p. 20).

[13] According to estimates by Gerster (*ibid.*, p. 142), the earnings of Nestlé, the largest Swiss multinational company, in the Third World amounted to SF 525 million. This is more than Switzerland's entire bi-lateral foreign aid during the year in question.

[14] *BEE*, Vol. II, 3.3.5.3, p. 417.

[15] *Ibid.*

[16] Gerster, *Aus Fehlern lernen?* pp. 36 and 38.

The exchange of commodities between the First and the Third World follows a similar pattern. As a result of collapsing prices for raw materials, the principal export items in developing countries, the terms of trade in these countries, that is the relationship between the indices for export prices and those for import prices, have severely deteriorated. Today, they are able to import less and less with the earnings from the same amount of exports. Here, too, Third World countries that export raw materials have less leverage and are thus tremendously handicapped with respect to their options for development. Additionally, the protectionist tendencies practiced by the economic policies of many industrialized countries compound the issue, affecting especially agricultural products, but also industrial products in threshold countries. A particularly dramatic example is the international sugar market. For instance, Switzerland heavily promoted the cultivation of sugar beets using price subsidies in order to raise the income of Switzerland's own sugar growers. Today, Switzerland imports over 50,000 tons less than only 25 years ago.[17] The sugar beet policy of the European Community (EC) has an even greater impact. It not only reached a self-sufficiency level of 100%, but currently produces one third more sugar than it consumes,[18] thus flooding the international sugar market at dumping rates. Whereas the net production cost per kilogram of refined sugar in the Federal Republic of Germany in 1985 was CHF 1.09, Switzerland exported sugar at a cost of CHF 0.36 per kilogram (at a domestic price of CHF 1.17), including freight charges to the border. By comparison, the production cost for sugar in the Philippines was CHF 0.45, despite starvation wages.[19] Clearly, under these conditions the producers of raw sugar in the developing countries do not stand a chance in the global marketplace. Theirs is a losing proposition from the very beginning. For instance, the World Bank calculated that Third World sugar exporters had to accept nearly $7.3 billion in losses in 1983, caused by the protectionist trade restrictions imposed by industrialized countries.[20] The madness hidden beneath these extremely confrontational competitive conditions dictated by market power is obvious. How will developing countries ever be in a position to service their exorbitant debts if

[17] *Ibid.*, p. 148.
[18] *Ibid.*
[19] *Ibid.*, p. 149.
[20] World Bank, *World Development Report*, Washington, 1985, p. 47.

— in addition to the collapse of raw materials prices — a more or less protectionist trade policy practiced by the industrialized countries deprives them of the possibility, or severely hampers their ability to take advantage of their location or their cost-effective production of agricultural and industrial goods for the purpose of acquiring the hard currencies needed for servicing their debts. As long as these confrontational conditions persist, global economic cooperation based on the market economy turns into a trap for the economically weak. Confrontational cooperation must, therefore, be replaced by participative cooperation, allowing the Third World to partake fairly in the opportunities available in the market-oriented order of the global economy. In other words, the global market economy must adapt itself to the parameters of participation and cooperation in the global economic marketplace. The challenges facing the global market economy in this time and age are, therefore, more clearly defined.

7.3 Basic Conditions for Participative Cooperation in the Global Economy

We already discussed the "participative global economy" in general terms in 3.3.5.3. The general idea was that the humanity originating from faith, hope, and love was pushing towards a participative order of the global economy. Now will be the time to shed more light on the economic-ethically relevant fundamental conditions for such an order, particularly in view of the relationship between the industrialized world and the developing world. The basic tenet is this: The sizes of the weapons used in global market competition and in the exchange process must be more equal and the relationships shaped by economic power and market forces must be more balanced. Once again, the issue here is — primarily — the question of indebtedness of the developing countries and the problematic character of protectionism in the industrialized countries.

7.3.1 *Participative Debt Redemption*

Clearly, the process of Third World indebtedness[21] has assumed proportions today that are economically and socially intolerable for the

[21] For a detailed discussion, see Alfred Jäger, "Die internationale Kreditkrise 1982/83 und ihre wirtschaftsethischen Konsequenzen," in *Tu deinen Mund auf für die*

people affected by it. The economic intolerability results from the average size of the debt service rate, that is the relationship between a country's debt and its earnings from exports. According to research published by the Commission on Global Tasks of the German Conference of Bishops, the average rate rose from 34% in 1985 to 37% in 1986.[22] Significant differences appear when these average figures are broken down according to continents. For instance, the rate for Latin America stood at 46%, for Africa at 30%, and for Asia at approximately 13%. Debt service rates of 30% or more create an excessive economic burden on a national economy. The rates are reflected by reduced growth rates of an average of 3% during the period of 1983-1987.[23] The results are simply ruinous.

The economic component of the indebtedness is accompanied by a social component:

> The debt crisis creates a kind of a vicious circle: In order to be able to pay back their debts, ever larger segments of the domestic resources that are actually needed for consumption and investment in one's own country must be deeded over to foreign countries. People are forced to work, produce and export more and more, just to earn the interest for the credits they hardly benefited from. The consequences are an ever-worsening supply situation as well as growing impoverishment and misery among those large segments of the population who are least able to fight against this development.[24]

Thus, two components play a role in the problem of debt redemption: a financial and a social one. The requirements for scheduling participative debt redemption, that is when both debtors and creditors share mutually obligations and sacrifices, is possible only if both components are duly taken into consideration.

Thus far, only the financial component has been emphasized. When the Mexican Secretary of Commerce, Jesus Silva Herzog, announced a three-month moratorium for debt repayments by his country in the summer of 1982, at the time the second-highest debtor nation, the banks in large financial centers panicked. If interest payments and scheduled loan repayments by the debtor countries

Stummen, ed. Frank-Matthias Hofmann and Eberhard Mechels, Gütersloh, 1986, pp. 115-28.

[22] German Conference of Bishops, ed., *Die internationale Schuldenkrise*, p. 11.

[23] *Ibid.*, pp. 11-12.

[24] *Ibid.*, p. 13.

become overdue, the entire international financial system would be in danger of coming unraveled. The danger was averted when billions of dollars were released by the United States and the International Monetary Fund (IMF) for the purpose of rescheduling debts.[25] Essentially, the purpose of the transaction was to grant new loans in order to put insolvent developing countries in a position to continue to be able to meet their debt redemption obligations. However, the new loans were tied to adaptation conditions stipulated by the IMF that were bound to have largely devastating consequences. (This is not the place to summarily condemn the IMF). Thus, at the expense of meeting domestic demands they were urged to turn towards exports and an economic policy intent on spurring growth, a fact that strikes one as fairly cynical in view of the protectionist tendencies prevalent in many industrialized countries. Moreover, government expenditures by the borrowing countries were supposed to be drastically reduced in order to head off rampant inflation. The hardest hit were above all the poorest segments of the population, because the governments were free to determine the areas where government expenditures were to be cut. The path of least resistance was reducing, or even canceling, subsidies for basic foods, because that would end up being the least burdensome to the ruling elites. Even if there is a silver lining in this, namely fewer people leaving the countryside, on the whole, it signifies the exact opposite of a participative handling of the debt problem. On the one hand, the debt problem burdens exclusively the impoverished masses, while it permits on the other hand an increase of the mountains of debt instead of reducing them, thus merely postponing the eventual collapse.

The primary condition for participative debt redemption is, therefore, a poverty-oriented economic development policy pursued by both creditor and debtor nations.[26] The debt redemption burden would have to be divided up in such way that the accompanying social cost would not be shifted exclusively to the poor. Meanwhile, even the World Bank with its close ties to the IMF has acknowledged that "hitherto existing adaptation programs have negative

[25] Markus Mugglin, "Alternativen sind unausweichlich," in "...*in euren Häusern liegt das geraubte Gut der Armen*", ed. Kuno Füssel, *et al.*, Fribourg, 1989, pp. 45-46.

[26] This is also the position of the Council of the German Lutheran Church in charge of the Church's Third World Relief Services. See Church Office of the Evangelical Church in Germany, ed., *Bewältigung der Schuldenkrise*, Hanover, 1988, pp. 8 ff.

consequences for the poorest segments of the population. Moreover, reviving only growth will not suffice for the protection of the interests of poor people; instead, special programs are required."[27] In other words, what this means is that new loans underwritten or initiated by the IMF must take the social component into account as much as the financial one, so far as they are materially justified and, therefore, also economically legitimate.[28]

In the meantime, the developing countries will not be in a position to establish a poverty-oriented debt redemption policy until a genuine and sizeable reduction of the debt burden has been achieved.

It has been pointed out that rescheduling debts does not offer any long-term help. It is, indeed, capable of bridging a momentary repayment squeeze; however, as long as it is not tied to an increase in economic performance, it will lead to even higher indebtedness and, on the whole, will serve more the consolidation of the international financial system.

On the other hand, even a general and total cancellation of foreign debt offers no real solution to the crisis, especially if it is based on unilateral acts by the debtor countries. For one, the complex causes of indebtedness would be far from solved, leading merely to a treatment of its symptoms and not its causes. On the other hand, severe sanctions against the developing countries would likely follow (seizure of the foreign assets of debtor nations, imports only after prepayment, no new public or private loan assistance,[29] etc.). Instead of general debt cancellations, the fact is that only selective, that is to say, only targeted debt relief is taken into consideration.

[27] Mugglin, "Alternativen sind unausweichlich," p. 68.

[28] No doubt, one of the legitimate financial components is the fact that the IMF assigns the highest priority to monetary stability as a fundamental prerequisite of a healthy economy and that it combines its loan allocations to developing countries with high inflation rates with proportionate conditions. Every effective anti-inflationary policy demands sacrifices by the population. It acts non-socially only if the socially weak groups carry the heaviest burden, as in today's Third World. Until now, this undoubtedly applied to the IMF's existing concept of development.

[29] In contrast to private loans and debts from foreign banks, public credits in the form of developmental aid are owed to foreign governments by the developing countries. According to the World Bank's *Debt Tables* from 1988, the long-term debt of developing countries owed to foreign governments amounted to $405 billion, and to private sources $575 billion.

At any rate, partial or complete debt relief is desirable in the case of the least developed countries (LDC).[30] This is the strategy already followed to a limited extent today, at least in the case of loans underwritten by foreign governments. For instance, since 1978 the Federal Republic of Germany has released twenty-four such countries from loans provided by government development aid in the amount of $4.2 billion.[31] France is prepared to proceed similarly, however it favors the cancellation of one third of the rescheduled debt of the poorest African states. Great Britain, on the other hand, supports a lowering of the interest rate to 3.5%, or cutting in half previous interest rates as long as these are below 7%.[32] Although all these efforts seem to be rather modest, they are nevertheless steps in the right direction.[33]

A course of action similar to that pursued in the case of the LDC countries could be applied also to significantly more developed, yet highly indebted countries, such as Mexico, Brazil, and Argentina. They, too, could be granted partial remission of debts owed to foreign governments, of course in combination with certain conditions. Most noteworthy in this context are proposals suggesting depositing the monetary interest and amortization obligations accruing from the remaining debt in a national development fund. That fund would have to be converted to the local currency and administered democratically, that is by including representatives of the vital interests of the poor; the fund would then have to grant new loans, primarily for the purpose of financing poverty-oriented development projects.[34]

[30] According to a UN Nations committee, the "Least Developed Countries" are those with a per capita annual income below $355, where the industrial sector takes up only 10% of the Gross National Product, and where the literacy rate of the population under fifteen years of age is less than 20%. Currently, the LDC list includes forty-one developing countries, most of them located in Sub-Saharan Africa (German Conference of Bishops, ed., *Die internationale Schuldenkrise*, p. 29).

[31] *Ibid.*

[32] Mugglin, "Alternativen sind unausweichlich," p. 70.

[33] This also applies to the World Bank's new credit policy of "extending the free years prior to the amortization of its normal loans (until now, three to five years) and also extending the repayment terms (until now, fifteen to twenty years). For those debtors who benefit from it, this amounts to a reduction of the amount of indebtedness; at the same time, the World Bank raises its net capital flow to the debtor countries by the amount of the extended repayment terms" (Daniel Hofmann, "Die neue Rolle von Weltbank und Währungsfonds, *Neue Zürcher Zeitung*, No. 88, 16/17 April 1988, p. 35).

[34] "Creative reimbursement," proposed by Susan George in *A Fate Worse than Debt* (New York, 1988, pp. 236 ff.), is worth mentioning in this context.

This way, the claim for the redemption of the debts would stand, albeit in local currency. In other words, providing a low rate of inflation, the debtor country could not simply shirk its obligations; yet, it would no longer be forced to orient its economic potential exclusively towards exports generating foreign currency. On the other hand, the creditor countries would have to make sacrifices in their budgets, ultimately deferring the burden to their taxpayers. That would correspond precisely to a participative debt redemption policy and, therefore, a humanly just development policy particularly with a view to the poorest among the population.

Of course, such a participative structure of the debt redemption policy remains limited primarily to loans made by foreign governments. However, the situation differs in the case of loans from private sources, such as large banks or banking consortia that provide the majority of all the loans.[35] Indeed, in countries based on market-economic principles, the government cannot force banks to agree to a partial remission of the debts of developing countries. Most bankers do not want to have anything to do with concessions made to large debtor nations. In their opinion, they would significantly reduce the credit rating of the debtors, creating severe disadvantages not only for the creditor banks, but especially for the debtor nations themselves. There is a possibility, however, that people will eventually change their minds.

At any rate, a group of North American bankers under the leadership of Anthony Solomon, former President of the Federal Reserve Bank of New York, insists that the reduction of debt service, in addition to granting new credits, ought be an integral part of any future debt strategy. The spokesperson of Deutsche Bank, Alfred Herrhausen, made a similar plea during the 1988 annual meeting of the IMF and the World Bank. Comparing the situation to that of an insolvent business,[36] he proposed to reach a settlement with the debtor nations instead of continuing to increase their debt burden by simply rescheduling the loans. Of course, the banks would have to forego a majority of their outstanding debts.[37] On the other hand, the debtor nations

[35] See 7.3.1, fn. 29.

[36] According to Mugglin, "Alternativen sind unausweichlich," p. 71.

[37] This solution might be acceptable to the international banking system. This is corroborated by the fact that the banks have already written off some of their claims against highly indebted developing countries and that they are selling debt certificates in financial markets at prices substantially below their nominal value. Of course, this continues to place the same amount of financial burden on the debtor nations.

would have to provide guarantees for their willingness to stand by their greatly reduced redemption obligations. This, too, would be in accord with a participation-oriented solution to the indebtedness problem of the Third World. It would demand sacrifices from the international banking community with which it could cope and, because of the remaining obligations, it would simultaneously force debtor nations to use new credits efficiently, both economically and socially, promising a climate favoring investments for the purpose of revitalizing the economy. Such participative behavior, instead of behaviour that is confrontational, would ultimately benefit both sides.

7.3.2 *Participative Market Order*

The second fundamental prerequisite of global cooperation worthy of its name is a participative structure of the order of the international markets. This includes a clear rejection of the kind of protectionist trade policy practiced in certain markets by some industrialized countries. As already mentioned, a drastic illustration is the protectionism of the EC countries and Switzerland against sugar-exporting developing countries.[38] It would be quite easy to cite additional examples, especially from the agricultural markets. For instance, export-promoting subsidies of corn by the United States severely affect countries such as Argentina. Furthermore, competing industrialized countries continue to erect protectionist barriers against industrial products from emerging economies in order to protect domestic production in endangered branches of industry. All this amounts to confrontational, self-asserting, and therefore contradictory "cooperation," with severe consequences for developing countries. Aside from their repayment obligations, how are these countries supposed to develop economically if their access to the markets in the industrialized countries is made difficult or even denied? The declaration published by the Commission on Global Tasks for the Church by the German Conference of Bishops (May 16, 1988) holds true:

> The developing countries depend on earnings from their exports in order to be able to finance much needed imports and to be able to service their debts. Various protective measures by the industrialized countries obstruct trade with the developing countries. Also,

[38] *BEE*, Vol. II, pp. 624-25.

> promoting the exporting ability in developing countries with investments and loans, and then turning around and denying access to our markets to products that are intended for export is against all economic logic. We consider it an absolute necessity to continue reducing trade barriers denying access to markets in the industrialized countries.[39]

A participative international market order, allowing developing countries' competitive agricultural and industrial products free access to the markets in the First World can become possible only if protectionist trade impediments by the industrialized countries are reduced, indeed are progressively reduced. Therein lies the sacrifice that these countries must make. At times, the sacrifices could be substantial, because it will bring about partial changes in the economy of the industrialized countries, especially in the area of agriculture and the production of simple industrial goods. Indeed, this will imply a structural adaptation process that will be very painful for the economic branches affected by it. "Thus, much persuasiveness will be required to convince entrepreneurs and workers of the necessity of this adaptation."[40] This cannot be accomplished without a long-range structural policy aiming at creating new jobs that offers the means necessary for the innovative development of branches of production with the potential of impacting the future, instead of subsidies for the purpose of retaining traditional jobs. At the same time, there will undoubtedly be a need for protective measures to absorb the inevitable social burden for segments of the population directly affected by the structural adaptation process. Taken all in all, this means that the regulatory measures of the market economy need to be expanded proportionately.

If the structural adaptation process in the industrialized countries that favors a participative market order of the global economy combines, therefore, at least for the short term, with more or less incisive sacrifices, the long term effect will no doubt be also positive for these countries.

Fair access to their markets strengthens the economy of the developing countries. As a result, their markets will become receptive to

[39] German Conference of Bishops, ed., *Die internationale Schuldenkrise*, p. 35. Could not the European Community industrial norm restrictions also be considered barriers of this type?

[40] Schlecht, "Soziale Weltwirtschaft," p. 96.

imports, a fact that will benefit the export needs of the industrialized countries. Indeed, a participative market order is identical with a free and reciprocal exchange of goods. Of course, one must beware of turning this into an absolute principle. As long as developing countries are still not, or cannot be the economic equals of the industrial countries, protective tariffs for their still budding industrial branches might not be entirely out of the question. In fact, during their development in the nineteenth century, even the industrialized countries on the European continent did not entirely put their trust in the free-trade market philosophy during their efforts to catch up with England, then the leading industrial power. An international participative market order in the above sense can never be realized overnight; neither will it be possible to implement it completely. It will require time and patience.

7.3.3. *Requirements for Developing Countries*

The aforementioned explanations illustrate already that an international participative market order will also place high demands on the developing countries. It will be effective only to the degree that the market partners become sufficiently equal. However, developing countries do not attain sufficient equality merely by being massively or completely relieved of their debt repayment obligations, or by experiencing greatly increased export opportunities as a result of fair access to the markets in the industrialized countries. This will not be possible until they simultaneously contribute actively to raising their economies economically and socially to a level that becomes moderately comparable to that in the First World.

7.3.3.1 Requirements with Regard to the Economic Efficiency of an Economic System

As illustrated in chapters 4 and 5, the economic efficiency of an economy is decisively connected to the economic system it chooses. This also applies particularly to the Third World. One can hardly deny

> that developing countries oriented towards a *market economy* and the global market have achieved higher average growth rates in their economy-wide production, their production of agricultural goods, their exports and their per-capita income than countries leaning more towards a planned economy...and that the diversification of the exports in the first group of countries is more advanced than in

> the second. Moreover, there are some indications that the efficiency of the utilization of resources in countries oriented towards a market economy is higher than in countries characterized by governmental intervention.[41]

This permits us to conclude that the developing countries — if this has not already occurred — will need to opt in their domestic market for the basic market economic system in order to be able to reach a degree of economic efficiency that approaches that of the Western industrialized countries. Therein lies the first requirement.

7.3.3.2 Requirements in View of the Social Efficiency of an Economic System

The second requirement refers to the social efficiency of the economic-societal system. There is no doubt that this type of efficiency is closely connected to the economic one. There cannot be any social efficiency without economic efficiency. Conversely, social ills are equally capable of minimizing the economic efficiency of an economic system. For instance, this is illustrated by the grossly unequal distribution of land in many developing countries. Especially in Latin America, farmland is mostly owned by a small group of feudal landowners. The large masses of those who cultivate the soil, however, own no land. According to information provided by the FAO (Food and Agriculture Organization of the United Nations), small farmers in Brazil harvested 40%, in India up to 80% more per hectare than large farms with more than 20 hectares.[42] A redistribution of land ownership favoring those who cultivate it — the core of any land reform — corresponds, therefore, not only to the dictates of the humanly just, but also to those of economic reason. It would be an effective remedy against hunger and misery, as well as a foundation for an agricultural and industrial economy capable of exporting its goods. "This is illustrated...by the history of the development of Korea and Taiwan. In the beginning of their successful industrialization there were sweeping land reforms that took seriously the principle 'Land for those who farm it'."[43] At the same time, the land

[41] Hermann Sautter, "Die marktwirtschaftliche Idee im ordnungspolitischen Dialog mit Entwicklungsländern," in *Märkte und Mächte*, ed. Klaus Wilkens, *et al.*, p. 57.
[42] Gerster, *Aus Fehlern lernen?* p. 203.
[43] *Ibid.*

could also be formally socialized property, if the farmers had only hereditary, albeit government-regulated control over it. Furthermore, free access to education is also necessary to enhanced social efficiency. This is also illustrated by South Korea and Taiwan. Not only do both countries "share high growth rates but also a remarkably equitable distribution of the national income,"[44] an indicator of the economic as well as the social efficiency of an economic order.[45]

7.3.3.3 Requirements in View of the Ecological Efficiency of an Economic System

The ecological problem calls for a third requirement. The more the economy in developing countries grows and the more their effectiveness in international competition approximates that of the industrialized countries, the greater their need for energy, the use of natural resources, and therefore the negative impact on the environment. If raising the economic and social level is intended not only for the short term, these countries are also forced to adopt an environmentally sensitive strategy throughout their economic development, in addition to reigning in their high population growth rates. Unfortunately, even the legal basis for this is in a bad way in these countries: "In most Third World countries, there are only sporadic provisions for the protection of the environment, and even compliance with these is rarely enforced. Legal loopholes, an administration susceptive to corruption, and businesspersons who act shortsightedly, all contribute to ecological damages that are frequently hardly irreversible."[46] Developing countries must, therefore, be urged to try to improve as much as possible not only the economical and social, but particularly also the ecological efficiency of their economies. This is undoubtedly a task they will find difficult to live up to, not only in a legal sense, but above all also in economic terms, "because in the short term the environmentally sensitive strategy causes additional expenditures for these countries and threatens a slowdown of their

[44] See footnotes in Sautter, "Die marktwirtschaftliche Idee im ordnungspolitischen Dialog mit Entwicklungsländern," p. 72.

[45] See Ernst Dürr, "Die Übertragbarkeit der Sozialen Marktwirtschaft auf Entwicklungs- und Schwellenländer," in *Weltwirtschaft im Wandel*, ed. Dürr and Hugo Sieber, Bern, 1988, pp. 647-64.

[46] Sautter, "Die marktwirtschaftliche Idee im ordnungspolitischen Dialog mit Entwicklungsländern," p. 64.

economic growth."[47] They are, therefore, facing conflicting goals, a dilemma with which industrialized countries are also familiar, which, however, seems to be much more difficult to handle for developing countries. In many cases, minimizing the ecological impact would amount to having to forego temporarily material improvement of broad segments of the population, which would lead to an increase in the already existing social and political instability. If there exists, as in most cases, an understandable preponderance of short-term national popular interests, then environmental protection will suffer, despite the fact that it would be economically beneficial in the long term. Without substantial financial aid provided by the industrialized countries, the majority of developing countries will, therefore, not be in a position to meet the ecological challenges facing them. The nature of their environmental problem is not only national, but has even more international aspects.[48]

The international repercussions also result from the fact that the increasing negative impact on the environment in the Third World also endangers the industrialized countries to a degree that can hardly be overestimated. For instance, Hermann Sautter points to the enormous significance of the rain forest in the Amazon Basin for the stabilization of the global climate and for the regeneration of oxygen in the entire biosphere. It is a "treasure shared by all people."[49] Because of that, other countries could contribute financially to Brazil as the country mainly responsible for its preservation. By the way, this is a cogent paradigm for the need for participative economic cooperation on an international scale.

7.3.3.4 Order-Political Requirements

Any compelling reason for believing that the economic, social, and political demands placed on developing countries could best be mastered on a market-economic foundation, would not simply suggest that these countries would have to rely on Western-type market-economic order forms that developed into actual realities or future concepts. The system of the market economy tolerates a plurality of

[47] Alfred Nydegger, "Mehr Weitblick und mehr Markt in der Energiepolitik," *Neue Zürcher Zeitung*, No. 199, 29 August 1989, p. 21.

[48] Sautter, "Die marktwirtschaftliche Idee im ordnungspolitischen Dialog mit Entwicklungsländern," pp. 65-66.

[49] *Ibid.*, p. 65.

order forms, depending on the regulatory measures it prescribes for itself. Precisely this flexibility is also one of its decisive strengths. Developing countries must independently discover market order forms suitable to them. As in South Korea and Taiwan, the relationships between the state and the economy will likely be tighter and the regulatory structure will, therefore, place greater emphasis on the state than most market economies patterned after the Western system. Order-political dogmatism would be out of place here. One must only caution against an unregulated co-existence of market and planning. Such a contradictory order would be instantly condemned to inefficiency. The developing countries will also have to realize that the market economy harmonizes with government control, only if the market is assigned a constitutive role and planning elements merely a regulatory function.

7.4 Global Economic Market Regulation: A Problem in Need of Solution

Hopefully, the previous explanations have sufficiently demonstrated that experience has taught us about the obsoleteness of the thesis that a market economy left on its own in the sense of the laissez-fair system would automatically reach a balance between the antagonistic economic interests and the economic forces, as old liberal contentions of harmony would have us believe. Even capitalism, claiming to represent a "free" market economy, cannot function without a certain degree of government regulation. At any rate, an extreme form of a de-regulated market economy proves to be an impossible alternative. In order to remain functional, and in order not to fall prey to self-destructive economic Darwinism, the economy needs at least a framework of order safeguarded by the government that obligates people to maintain the rules of fair competition, to restrain developing market powers, and to provide adequate pay for every type of work, even in the presence of significant wage differences, as well as a minimum of social security for everybody. In principle, this applies to the national as well as the global market economy. Yet this brings us face to face with a thorny problem.

As mentioned above, the problem is rooted mainly in the fact that within nationally limited markets there is a government that is in a position to regulate them because of its economic-political jurisdiction, whereas there is a lack of a comparable institutional power in the borderless, international marketplace. Can we, therefore, continue thinking of a reciprocal, socially, and ecologically relevant developmental policy and regulatory system as a condition for a participative structure of a market-oriented global economic order?

Attempts at economic integration on an international scale are already in full swing.[50] The most important and most successful of these efforts is the Europe-wide 'domestic' market of the EC (European Community) which is to take full effect in 1992. Yet, we are dealing here not with a global, but merely a regional, albeit large-scale integration that will lead to the combination of twelve separate national markets into one market with 322 million people and a gross national product of $ 3.3 trillion.[51] Moreover, this process of integration can rely on supra-national institutions: 1. an assembly (European Parliament) with consultative and control functions, 2. the European Council (cabinet) with decision-making powers, and 3. the EC Commission, whose duty is to oversee the implementation of the decisions reached by the European Council, and to submit proposals and drafts, recommendations and opinions to the European Council in accordance with the statutory objectives outlined by the Treaty of Rome of 1957. The European Community has at its disposal supra-national bodies able to issue binding rules and regulations for the common market.

The beginnings of such a set of regulatory measures already exist in the EC. This clearly follows from the concluding observations at the session of the European Council in Madrid on June 26-27, 1989. Two particularly important points discussed at the meeting are especially pertinent to our present discussion.

The first point concerns the social dimension of the impending economic integration within the framework of the European Community:[52] "It is the opinion of the European Council that the same amount of importance must be attached to the social aspects within the frame of the integrated European market as to the economic

[50] See *BEE*, Vol. II, 2.6.2.

[51] By way of comparison, the economic area of the United States counts 242 million people and a gross national product of $4.2 trillion. Japan's comparable figures are 122 million people and a gross national product of $2.0 trillion.

[52] For more details, see Theodor Strohm, "Die EG–'Gemeinschaftscharta der sozialen Grundrechte' — eine Chance 'systemöffnender Kooperation'?" *Zeitschrift für Evangelische Ethik*, 33 (1989), pp. 242-48.

aspects; they must be further developed in harmony with one another."[53] The European Council refers to the draft of a social charter by the EC Commission. It determines the basic social rights that will apply within the EC (free choice of residence, fair pay, social protection, the right to occupational and educational training, equal treatment of men and women, health care, protection of children and young persons, the right of the handicapped to gainful employment). The Council simultaneously stated expressly that the realization of the indicated rights must not lead to treatment that is less than what already exists in individual member countries.

The second point is aiming at the problem of the environment:

> Aware of its responsibility in view of the threats to the entire planet (climate changes, deforestation, desertification, etc.), the European Council takes the view that the European Community must play a decisive role in the protection of the environment by enacting internal laws and by actively contributing to the initiatives adopted on the international level. Within the framework of a global environmental policy that includes the fight against desertification, erosion, and deforestation, the European Council asks the European Commission to submit a program protecting the environment in areas in the EC suffering from these problems.[54]

In the European Community, the creation of regulatory measures for its supra-regional domestic market is accomplished by supranational organs that seize some of the sovereign rights of the individual member states. There are no comparable institutions in the global realm of the world economy. Certainly, there are international organizations, such as the Conference on Trade and Development (UNCTAD), the Food and Agriculture Organization (FAO), the World Bank (IBRD) and the General Agreement on Tariffs and Trade (GATT). However, they have no supranational character with corresponding jurisdiction. The achievement of international cooperation among national economies within the framework of a global market-economical order guided by the principle of participation will be possible under the current conditions, only if the countries involved in this enterprise will be able to come to a binding agreement on appropriate regulatory measures that can be institutionalized. The success

[53] Commission of the European Communities, "EG Informationen," *EGmagazin*, No. 7/8 (1989), p. iv.

[54] *Ibid.*, p. v.

of this undertaking is absolutely vital to the future of a market economy that encompasses the entire world.[55]

It is not the task of business and economic ethics to introduce detailed, reciprocally tuned, functional, and enforceable proposals for such regulatory measures. This belongs to the jurisdiction of expert economists, ecologists, politicians, and, of course, also of legitimate representatives of the various economic and social groups whose fundamental interests very often clash with one another. Yet, one must also emphasize which fundamental objectives are to be singled out by the regulatory measures, given that these measures are to serve the realization of a global economic order with a participative structure equipped particularly to help disadvantaged nations and population groups attain better living conditions.

The critical issues have already been addressed in 7.3. The conclusions reached there have normative meaning in this context.

It ought to go without saying that, if participative global regulatory measures are to obtain the required and also institutionally backed commitment, they can be agreed upon only by engaging a genuine, open, and constructive dialog between the industrialized countries and the developing countries on an equal footing. At the same time, the already existing international organizations could offer valuable services by contributing their knowledge and experience. This will presume, one all sides, the breaking down of confrontational attitudes characterized by one-sided, non-relational insistence on one's own interests and the willingness to realistically overcome existing economic and political contradictions.[56] If this fails to come to pass, constructive results will fail to materialize, and if things continue in familiar ways, then the imbalances in the global economy tending to cause

[55] In this respect, the postulates of a "new economic world order" that have been kept on the backburner have retained their validity. For a similar view, see Jäger, "Die internationale Kreditkrise 1982/83 und ihre wirtschaftsethischen Konsequenzen," p. 128. Similar questions are raised in view of the most recent system-unlocking changes in the Second World.

[56] Similarly, Helmut Hesse, "Internationale Wirtschaftsbeziehungen als Gegenstand der Wirtschaftsethik," in *Wirtschaftswissenschaft und Ethik*, ed. Hesse, Berlin, 1988, p. 200: "The fundamental moral norm underlying the formation of international economic relations, the mutual acknowledgment that we are all different, is reflected in international agreements that make it possible, on the one hand, to limit and control rising conflicts of interests and, on the other hand, to promote partnership and cooperation for mutual benefit. Every international economic order should be rooted in these two principles, i.e. the avoidance of conflict and cooperation."

chaos and disorder will become more severe and make a disastrous conflict between North and South inevitable. A business and economic ethics committed to faith, hope, and love will have to turn decisively against such a fatalistic "laissez-faire."

We are still left with the task of highlighting the evaluation and decision maxims that result from this global economic outlook, or that are already implied in it.

7.5 Maxims

1. The global economy with its removal of borders from national markets forms a global web of complex interdependencies that makes international cooperation among individual national economies indispensable. Interdependent cooperation is compatible with the demands of the humanly just to the extent that it rests on mutual, i.e. equitable dependencies.

2. Experience has shown that economic imbalances that lead to one-sided dependencies do not automatically balance one another in a market economy that is left on its own and simulates the laissez-faire system. On the contrary, they become more severe and permit the rise of exchange structures characterized by a confrontational design, according to which the stronger market force decides the competition and the weaker economic partners are necessarily left behind. This applies to international market relationships no less than to national markets.

3. The economically unfortunate, if not catastrophic conditions of the majority of developing countries is conditioned largely, although with some shared responsibility by the latter, by the confrontational structure of international cooperation, with consequences that put these countries at a gross disadvantage in global competition.

4. A new ordering of economic cooperation between "North and South," in the sense of a participative structure, will be necessary if we are to avert the intolerable disadvantages incurred by developing countries in market exchange relationships, conditions that run counter to what is humanly just and also endanger the long-term survival of the potent industrialized world.

5. A participative structuring of the global economy means essentially the creation of general conditions that will enable developing countries to eventually catch up with the competition from their industrialized counterparts. Under today's conditions, this implies primarily:

- Massive, selective, differentiated, and targeted debt relief for developing countries.
- Raw material prices dictated primarily by future, not present, scarcity.
- Industrialized countries are to forego protectionist trade barriers that make access to the markets difficult or even impossible for competitive products from the Third World.
- An environmental policy that is characterized by solidarity on the part of the wealthy nations, whose financial and technological subsidies make it possible for developing countries to attack effectively ecological problems relevant world-wide.
- The willingness of industrialized nations to tolerate a lowering of their excessive prosperity levels if these postulates necessitate it.

6. On the other hand, participative structuring requires that the developing countries do everything in their power to attain a higher economic and social standard. The establishment of effective incentives would be a way of holding them to this. Thus, those among them who are committed to order their economy according to criteria of efficiency, who try to stem inflation, who initiate social reform for the benefit of the poorest segments of society, and who wish to stabilize population growth as well as ecological impact, should be given long-lasting preferential credit treatment by the World Bank, International Monetary Fund, or individual industrialized nations. This could also cause a reversal of capital flight in favor of these countries and thus alleviate the scarcity of available capital.

7. Cooperation with a participative structure based on a global market economy is possible only if it can be properly regulated, that is, if it is not left to laissez-faire. For instance, it probably should not be entirely up to transnational companies to determine if and how much of the profits realized in the Third World ought to be reinvested locally and how much they wish to transfer to their own countries. Because of a lack of international institutions to oversee and enforce any regulation, regulatory measures can be realized only on the basis of binding agreements between highly different cooperating entities.

8. Agreements are binding to the contracting parties only to the degree that they are based on common decisions that were not dominated by either party. There are definite consequences issuing from regulatory measures based on a participative structure and intended to guide the market-based global economy along paths that lead to the removal of scandalous disparities in the global distribution of prosperity. Such measures can be implemented only under the condition that industrialized countries as well as developing countries act as political equals. The industrialized countries would, therefore, have to quit taking political advantage of their economic or capital-based superiority, and the developing countries would have to forego taking political advantage of their numerical majority.

9. If they do not rely on equitable, participative regulation, the contracting partners on the global economic stage will miss their self-obligation to avert the intolerable economic and social disparities between "North" and "South". The result will be a global market "order" characterized by a confrontational, capitalist structure that will make a life of hunger permanent for hundreds of millions of people, creating a challenge to the market system that it can hardly survive.

10. Humanity originating from faith, hope, and love that is sustained by the encouragement and lives up to the demands of the impending Kingdom of God and his justice, inspired by the peculiar criteria of what is humanly just without neglecting what is economically rational, must take on the role of an advocate for the living rights of the poorest of the poor. In our time and age, these are the powerless masses of people living in the Third, more precisely, in the Fourth World. This humanity can accept the market-based economic system in the global economy only to the extent that it is in the process of adopting new order forms. In analogy to national market economies that are becoming increasingly ordered socially and aware of their ecological responsibility and mindful of the mandate of participation, these order forms tend to distribute prosperity among all nations in a participatory manner to take up the legitimate interests of individual national economies with relationality in mind, and to keep the negative impact on the environment from production, trade, and traffic as low as possible. An order form of the basic market-based system with opposite tendencies in the global economy is entirely unacceptable to business and economic ethics based on the humanity

originating from faith, hope, and love. This applies also to the economies of the Second World, in as much as they become receptive to a system-changing process that is inspired by market-economical principles.

8. EPILOGUE

At the end of the second volume of this work on business and economic ethics, it might be useful to highlight once again the salient points of the theological context in which it was written and which unites the two volumes.

1. We must begin with our specific conception of business and economic ethics (*Wirtschaftsethik*). According to this conception, business and economics ethics is concerned with how human beings, social groups, and social organizations conduct themselves within and towards the economic structures within which they reside. As a result, it is characterized by two aspects.

In as far as we are dealing with the mutual conduct of human beings as individuals, as groups, as corporate bodies, etc., within the existing structures, business and economic ethis is interpersonal ethics. How do I ought to conduct myself, if my conduct has to be justified in light of the demand of the humanly just? What does it mean in this context to act responsibly as a manager, a union leader, or some other guardian of interests within the economic and sociopolitical realm? It is here that we ought to locate an ethics of management and of business of organizations.

Nevertheless, such questions are meaningless if the economic-social order structures prevent an actual acknowledgement of responsibility defined in these terms. For instance, motivated by their interpersonal sense of responsibility, entrepreneurs may go all out in their efforts to preserve jobs for their fellow workers and to keep wages at as high a level as possible. If they are confronted by an economic-Darwinistic competitive structure, all good intentions will come to naught. He or she will be caught in a situation that leaves essentially only two options: either howl with the wolves and pursue in the interest of competitiveness an extremely cost-saving corporate policy that will make life difficult for the workers, or throw in the towel and quit. One speaks here of indispensable factual constraint in the face of which every ethical demand would have to fall silent.

There are indeed factual necessities in the economy that are similar to natural laws; they must be accepted by any kind of ethics not oblivious to reality. Among these are facts such as the following:

- An economy, regardless of the form of its system or its order, cannot distribute more than it produces.
- The possibilities for growth are objectively limited in every economic system by the limited availability of resources, particularly the availability of energy, but especially the limited degree to which the ecosystem can be impacted.
- In view of the unlimited growth of the human population and its demands for prosperity, available goods are becoming scarce.
- The scarcity of goods cannot be alleviated or even solved by increasing the purchasing power of the population. That would lead only to inflation.
- Inefficient economic activity, that is a relatively high consumption of resources under conditions of relatively low productivity, increases scarcity and renders the economy absurd.

One must distinguish these necessities or laws from factual constraints inherent in the structural characteristics of the forms of systems or orders in the economy.

To the extent that the distribution of income is unequal, scarce goods in the market economy follow the lure of the greater purchasing power, instead of where there is greater need for them. Or, if extremely unequal distribution of capital resources occurs among companies or conglomerates, market-like structures will come into existence, because what matters is no longer better market performance but greater market power, that is selective performance competition turns into pure predatory competition. Yet these are not constraints, comparable to natural laws; they are rather constraints that are rooted in a structural order of the market economy that was created by those engaged in economic activity, and who are, therefore, also responsible for it. In other words, they are not unalterable, but instead they can be removed by appropriately regulating the market-economical mechanisms.

There is thus not only an ethical responsibility of economic subjects within the historically existing order structures, but also a responsibility with regard to the social and societal consequences of these structures.[1] This is the meaning behind what business and economic ethics refers to as socio-societal responsibility, in contrast to interpersonal responsibility. Clearly, business and economic ethics that has as its special subject the economic order problem must put the aspect of social structure at the center. Of course, this has nothing to do with disregarding the interpersonal aspect. We are dealing here with two aspects that are inseparable. Without economic structures that create room for the exercise of interpersonal responsibility of those engaged in the economy and their interest groups, this particular aspect of responsibility has no ground. And without the willingness of economic subjects to take advantage of the space they created and to truly exercise interpersonal responsibility, even the best structures would be useless. We must beware here of false alternatives.

2. If the social, societal, and ecological effects caused by economic or political structures are of the kind that opposes the demands of the humanly just, then one may speak justifiably of something that is structurally evil.[2] This evil is inherent in these structures. Of course, one could object that evil can emanate only from the human person, but never from impersonal structures and that these order structures are ethically neutral. What matters is what human beings do with them.

It is correct to argue, especially if the issue is approached from a theological perspective, that the source of evil lies in the personhood of the human being. Just as in the story of the temptation in Genesis 3:1 ff., the creature possesses the personal will to emancipate himself from the creator, to build his existence on himself, to determine for himself what is good and what is bad, and to make himself the measure of all things. This manifests itself in economic terms when self-interest is made absolute, as the truly fundamental motive of all economic activity. Self-interest in its relative legitimacy is not pursued in accordance with the will of God relative to the equally legitimate interests of others; rather, it is monocratically enforced. Ultimately, this leads to economic order structures of a confrontational nature that establish themselves in powerful positions and gain

[1] Georg Wünsch saw these facts quite clearly: "The assumption that the order of the economy is of no concern to [Christian ethics], and that all that matters is the attitude one assumes when obeying the order, is impossible and superficial and cannot be opposed too strongly" (*Evangelische Wirtschaftsethik*, Tübingen, 1927, pp. 477-78).

[2] For a detailed discussion, see Arthur Rich, "Sachzwänge und strukturell Böses in der Wirtschaft," *Zeitschrift für Evangelische Ethik*, 26 (1982), pp. 62-82.

power over human beings, even over those who oppose them with their personal ethics. This tough realization reiterates what the teachings of the Christian Church mean by "original sin," a term that is rather unfortunate. We are born into a world in which structural evil is effective, enmeshing us, whether we like or not, in events and activities that make us also personally guilty.

3. The reality of structural evil in the existing world has, to put it bluntly, led to two opposite fundamental positions.

One of these fundamental positions can be characterized as resigned adaptation. One simply adapts oneself to the existing confrontational structures, comes to an arrangement with them, and yields to the desire to "get ahead," rising to those levels of society that take advantage of the confrontational relationships in life. Moral scruples, if one has any at all, are dismissed by arguing that one is dealing with necessities that are inherent in the nature of our living world. Ultimately, one would have to decide whether one wishes to be above or below, to be a hammer or a nail. Constraints originating from the structural evil in the form of social objectifications of human activities are simply identified with factual necessities existing beyond good and evil. This applies even to those who, turning things around, resort to class struggle in a desire to change from nails to hammers.

The other fundamental position opposes the first one with utopian denial. One simply refuses to deal with the existing world and its structural evil. What matters is the utopian situation characterized by a society that is under nobody's rule, is classless and unrestricted, in which the imperfect must make way for the perfect. The present world with all its vicissitudes is simply left behind and the futuristic dream of a transcendental world freed from all evil is declared to be the true reality that will abolish the current necessity-driven realities, including all factual necessities. It is towards this futuristic reality one has to orient oneself already in the here and now. The consequences, should one succeed in implementing this reality, can supposedly be only a strict negation of all historically existing, or still developing relationships of order, because there will be no single reality that will satisfy the utopian claims to perfection.

4. The humanity originating from faith, hope, and love exists on the other side and not between these two extremely contrary fundamental positions. It neither arranges itself with the structural evil in the

existing world, nor does it turn a blind eye to it by indulging in dreams about the utopian leap out of the realm of necessity into the realm of freedom that provides liberation from all constraints. It is sustained by the hope-based faith of love in the coming of the Kingdom of God.[3]

It is true, however, that it has become fashionable in theological circles to view the Kingdom of God as a utopia: as the most comprehensive and most radical of all utopias. Yet this stems from a misleading confusion.

Utopias take on the form of human visions. They originate from man's desire to transcend himself in a world that is characterized by structural evil. People place their bets on a future world that will evolve from the present and its apparent difficulties, but promises to put them behind in one miraculous, qualitative leap.

By comparison, the message of the Kingdom of God as presented in the Bible does not deal at all with the possibilities of a utopian transcendence of the self and of approaching a divine and perfect world. On the contrary, it deals with the reality of the self-transcendence of God through the incarnate Jesus Christ in the present world, initiating the beginning of the redemption of all evil, both personal and structural.

Similarly, the Kingdom of God also represents the future for a humanity originating from faith, hope, and love. This is not a futuristic kind of future, however, originating from the present and propelled by man's desire for self-transcendence; on the contrary, it is a coming, an impending coming initiated by God and permeating a world that is characterized by its personal and structural evil. In short, the future we are talking about is an advent-like future, a future beyond man's making, a future we can only await actively, one that commits us to assume responsibility for what is yet to come in the here and now.

The humanity originating from faith, hope, and love dwells, therefore, neither in a heavenly beyond nor, in secular terms, in a utopian future. Aesop's "Hic Rhodus, hic salta" applies. In the here and now it must bring to bear its criteria of the humanly just by stating unequivocally what God wants in his coming Kingdom. It is, of course, forbidden to adapt itself opportunistically to the order structures of this world that cannot be reconciled with the humanly just.

[3] See Martin Honecker's enlightening study *Technischer und gesellschaftlicher Fortschritt aus christlicher Sicht*, Kassel, 1981, pp. 4-5.

On the other hand, it is also forbidden to simply withdraw from this world and to reach for the unreachable stars in an attempt to establish a utopia. The humanity rooted in faith, hope, and love must turn rather deliberately and decidedly to the world with its pressing issues, instead of chasing unattainable visions; it must strive for the reachable, exploring its most extreme possibilities. It is in this way that it demonstrates its intention to go after the ultimate in the penultimate and the absolute in that which is relative, fully aware that the penultimate offers only "next to last" and the relative only relative "solutions," because the absolute, the ultimate, that is the Kingdom of God, is identical with the reality emanating from God beyond all human capability. There are clear consequences for business and economic ethics growing out of this humanity and its criteria of the humanly just.

5. Clearly, the fundamental consequence is to be circumscribed as follows: Business and economic ethics must rest in the penultimate and, therefore, in the relative. If it deals with the economic order problem, as it does here, then it neither can be nor may be its task to cultivate visions of an absolutely just economic order and subsequently to deem all real or really possible order forms of the economy as ultimately not acceptable, because the ideal will never be reached. This also entails that economic-ethical reflections must occur in the real world. In the event that a quintessentially just order of the economy existing in the penultimate should prove to be impossible, then business and economic ethics conscious of reality must concentrate on establishing economically rational and normative conditions comparably capable of leading to less unjust or, what amounts to the same, relatively better order forms. That is, indeed, an arduous task that will not be completed during the historical time of the penultimate.

Two unalterable premises must characterize the relationship of business and economic ethics to reality:

For one, there is a complete respect for real economic necessities. Clearly, we must uphold imperturbably that nothing can be truly humanly just unless it is also simultaneously economically rational.

This, however, definitely includes the responsibility that business and economic ethics must distinguish precisely between economic "contraints" based on real necessities and others that are rooted in order structures established by people, making them subject to alteration or at least to influence with a view to the humanly just. With regard to the second type of constraints, business and economic ethics must unambiguously assert that nothing can be really economically rational unless it is also humanly just.

Both of these inseparable premises reveal a problem of mediation that is as demanding as it is difficult. Mediation cannot be simply defined as steering a middle course. One cannot skimp any less on the side of the economically rational than on the side of what is humanly just. Any compromise along these lines would be both ethically and economically intolerable. On the contrary, both the economically rational and the humanly just must be taken entirely seriously, yet in a relational way, in order to prevent the one from displacing the other. This requires that any arguments on the humanly just level must also consider the economic dimension, while any economic argument must also be receptive to the demands of the humanly just, which includes the environmentally just.

The problem of relational mediation appears not only in the relationship between the economically rational and the humanly just, but also in the relationship between fundamental human values and the fundamental interests connected to them. Individual responsibility and self-interest, solidarity and collective interest, are particularly economically relevant. Both fundamental values or interests are indispensable to economic activity oriented towards the humanly just. Economic systems or orders become unjust as soon as they absolutize one of these fundamental values, thus pretending to represent the human per se and, in doing so, excluding any of the remaining fundamental values. A complete synthesis between self-interest and solidarity is impossible, because it could only be love, love as the form of existence in the Kingdom of God where everyone loves everyone else as oneself. And, similar to the Kingdom of God, this love cannot be realized as a structural foundation of the economy in the penultimate, because it is impossible to impose it on society. Again, what is left is the possibility of relational mediation in a manner that maintains individually conflicting fundamental values and the fundamental interests inherent to them. What this means is that their mutual claim to validity is preserved in its entirety.

For all the reasons mentioned above, such attempts at mediation will not come to fruition during the penultimate. They remain caught in the irreversible and conflict-ridden polarity between the relative and the absolute and, depending on the situational changes in economic events, must be ventured upon time and again. They must be guided along this path by the question of which order-political structures will most likely enable the establishment of an economic form that will take on the role of mediator in this sense, that is an economic form that can be justified in light of the demands of the humanly just as well as the economically rational. The pertinent maxims at the end of chapters 5, 6, and 7, together with the discussions preceding them, are attempts at such relative mediations. Their success, or lack thereof, must be decided by the critical readers themselves. Yet the author can and may claim that he made an honest effort to set in motion this difficult form of mediation, which is averse to every form of pseudo-radicalism.

BIBLIOGRAPHY

Abbing, P. J. Roscam, *Ethiek van de inkomensverdeling*, Deventer: Kluwer Academic Publishers, 1973.

Albers, Willi, *et al.*, ed., *Handwörterbuch der Wirtschaftswissenschaften*, 9 vols., Stuttgart and New York: Gustav Fischer Verlag; Tübingen: J.C.B. Mohr (Paul Siebeck); Göttingen and Zürich: Vandenhoeck & Ruprecht, 1977-82.

Appelrath, Hans-Jürgen and Jirí Kriz, "Wissensbasierte Expertensysteme," *Neue Zürcher Zeitung*, No. 251, 29 October 1986, pp. 91-92.

Aristotle, *Politics*, trans. Carnes Lord, Chicago: University of Chicago Press, 1984.

Bänziger, Andreas, *Die Saat der Dürre: Afrika in den achtziger Jahren*, Bornheim-Merten: Lamuv Verlag, 1986.

Balkhausen, Dieter, *Die dritte industrielle Revolution*, Düsseldorf: Econ Verlag, 1978.

Batel, W. and H. Hesse, "Möglichkeiten der Automation bei der landwirtschaftlichen Produktion," *VDI-Zeitschrift, Fortschritt Berichte*, Ser. 14, No. 2, Düsseldorf: Verlag VDI, 1966.

Bazard, Saint-Amand, *Doctrine de Saint-Simon: Exposition* (1829), ed. Célestin Bouglé and Elie Halévy, Paris: Librairie des Sciences Politiques et Sociales Marcel Rivière, 1924.

von Beckerath, Erwin, *et al.*, eds., *Handwörterbuch der Sozialwissenschaften*, 12 vols., Stuttgart: Gustav Fischer Verlag; Tübingen: J.C.B. Mohr (Paul Siebeck); Göttingen: Vandenhoeck & Ruprecht, 1956-65.

Behrman, Jack N., "Können nationale Regierungen die multinationalen Unternehmen unter Kontrolle bringen?" in *Multinationale Unternehmen: Anfang oder Ende der Weltwirtschaft?* ed. Dietrich Kebschull and Otto G. Mayer, Frankfurt am Main: Athenäum Fischer Taschenbuch Verlag, 1974, pp. 203-18.

Berg, Curt and Barbo Mazurczak, "Autonome Arbeitsgruppen als neue Form der Arbeitsorganisation — ein Bericht über die Erfahrungen eines schwedischen Unternehmens," *Wirtschaftswissenschaftliches Studium*, 4 (1975), pp. 190-94.

Bergier, Jean-François, *Die Wirtschaftsgeschichte der Schweiz: Von den Anfängen bis zur Gegenwart*, Zürich and Cologne: Benziger Verlag, 1983.

Bernheim, Roger, "Zehn-Jahr-Amtsjubiläum Frau Thatchers: Bedeutende Leistungen — nachteilige Nebenwirkungen," *Neue Zürcher Zeitung*, No. 101, 3 May 1989, p. 5.

Beyeler-von Burg, Hélène, *Schweizer ohne Namen: Die Heimatlosen von heute*, Pierrelaye: Verlag Science et Service, 1985.

Biedenkopf, Kurt H., "Auf dem Weg zu einer freien Weltwirtschaftsordnung," in *Multinationale im Nord-Süd-Konflikt, Brennpunkte*, ed. Gottlieb Duttweiler-Institut, Zürich: Verlag Ex Libris, 1976, pp. 11-32.

Binswanger, Hans Christoph, *Eigentum und Eigentumspolitik: Ein Beitrag zur Totalrevision der Schweizerischen Bundesverfassung*, Zürich: Schulthess Polygraphischer Verlag, 1978.

—, *Money and Magic: A Critique of the Modern Economy in the Light of Goethe's* Faust, trans. J. E. Harrison, Chicago: University of Chicago Press, 1994.

—, *Ökologisch orientierte Wirtschaftswissenschaft* (manuscript), St. Gallen Research Group for Macroeconomics (Working Paper No. 36), St. Gallen, 1984.

—, "Ökopolitik — eine Ergänzung," in *Die Zukunftstauglichkeit der schweizerischen Entscheidungsstrukturen*, ed. Andreas Blum, Gerhard Kocher, and Walter Wittmann, Diessenhofen: Verlag Rüegger, 1982, pp. 53-60.

—, "Umrisse einer umweltkonformen Wirtschaftsordnung," in *Neue Ziele für das Wachstum*, ed. Johannes Schlemmer, Munich: R. Piper & Co. Verlag, 1973, pp. 118-29.

—, "Eine umweltkonforme Wirtschaftsordnung," in *Umweltschutz und Wirtschaftswachstum: Referate und Seminarergebnisse des ersten Symposiums für wirtschaftliche und rechtliche Fragen des Umweltschutzes an der Hochschule St. Gallen vom 19. bis 21. Oktober 1971*, ed. Martin P. von Walterskirchen, Frauenfeld and Stuttgart: Verlag Huber, 1972, pp. 127-41.

Binswanger, Hans Christoph, Holger Bonus, and Manfred Timmermann, *Wirtschaft und Umwelt: Möglichkeiten einer ökologieverträglichen Wirtschaftspolitik*, Stuttgart, Berlin, Cologne, and Mainz: Verlag W. Kohlhammer, 1981.

Binswanger, Hans Christoph, H. Frisch, H. G. Nutzinger, B. Schefold, G. Scherhorn, U. E. Simonis, and B. Strümpel, *Arbeit ohne Umweltzerstörung: Strategien einer neuen Wirtschaftspolitik*, a publication of the "Bund für Umwelt und Naturschutz Deutschland e.V." (BUND), 3rd Ed., Frankfurt am Main: S. Fischer, 1983.

Binswanger, Hans Christoph, Werner Geissberger, and Theo Ginsburg, eds., The NAWU Report: *Wege aus der Wohlstandsfalle: Strategien gegen Arbeitslosigkeit und Umweltkrise*, Frankfurt am Main: S. Fischer, 1978.

Binswanger, Hans Christoph and Alfred Jäger, "Ökonomie und Ökologie," in *Zwischen Wachstum und Lebensqualität: Wirtschaftsethische*

Fragen angesichts der Krisen wirtschaftlichen Wachstums, ed. Sozialwissenschaftliches Institut der EKD, Munich: Chr. Kaiser Verlag, 1980, pp. 70-115.

Biró, Gerd, "Zwischenbilanz einer wirtschaftlichen Weichenstellung," *Europäische Rundschau*, Vol. 8, No. 4 (1980), pp. 75-82.

Blaich, Fritz, "Merkantilismus," in *Handwörterbuch der Wirtschaftswissenschaften*, Vol. 5, pp. 240-51.

Blanc, Louis, *Organisation du travail*, 9th Ed., Paris: Au Bureau du Nouveau Monde, 1850.

Blum, Reinhard, "Marktwirtschaft, soziale," in *Handwörterbuch der Wirtschaftswissenschaften*, Vol. 5, pp. 153-66.

Bodmer, Walter, ed., *Automatisierung in der Industrie*, Vol. 40, No. 5, Zürich: Society for the Development of the Swiss Economy, May 1984.

Boelcke, Willi Alfred, "Liberalismus," in *Handbuch der Wirtschaftswissenschaft*, Vol. 5, pp. 32-47.

Bog, Ingomar, "Kapitalismus," in *Handwörterbuch der Wirtschaftswissenschaften*, Vol. 4, pp. 418-32.

Bohnet, Armin, "Chinas Wirtschaft im Umbruch: Konsequenzen der Juni-Ereignisse für das China-Geschäft," *Neue Zürcher Zeitung*, No. 184, 11 August 1989, p. 33.

Bonhoeffer, Dietrich, *Ethics*, trans. Neville Horton Smith, New York: Macmillan, 1955.

Borner, Silvio, *Einführung in die Volkswirtschaftslehre*, 2nd Ed., Diessenhofen: Verlag Rüegger, 1980.

Bornschier, Volker, *Wachstum, Konzentration und Multinationalisierung von Industrieunternehmen*, Frauenfeld and Stuttgart: Huber, 1976.

Brakelmann, Günter, "Arbeit," in *Christlicher Glaube in moderner Gesellschaft*, Vol. 8, ed. Franz Böckle, Franz-Xaver Kaufmann, Karl Rahner, and Bernhard Welte, Freiburg im Breisgau, Basel, and Vienna: HerderVerlag, 1980, pp. 99-135.

—, "Wirtschaftsordnung: Eine irenische Formel: Ordnungspolitische Fundamente der Sozialen Marktwirtschaft," in *Moderne Zeiten — soziale Gerechtigkeit? 20 Jahre Sozialwissenschaftliches Institut der Evangelischen Kirche in Deutschland*, ed. Ulf Claußen, Bochum: SWI-Verlag, 1989, pp. 74-77.

Brentano, Lujo, *Ethik und Volkswirtschaft in der Geschichte*, Munich: Verlagsbuchhandlung Ernst Reinhardt, 1902.

Brödner, Peter, Detlef Krüger, and Bernd Senf, *Der programmierte Kopf: Eine Sozialgeschichte der Datenverarbeitung*, Berlin: Verlag Klaus Wagenbach, 1981.

Brunner, Emil, *The Divine Imperative: A Study in Christian Ethics*, trans. Olive Wyon, Philadelphia: Westminster Press, 1947.

Buckley, Peter J. and Patrick F. R. Artisien, *Die Multinationalen Unternehmen und der Arbeitsmarkt*. Frankfurt/New York: Campus Verlag

1986. (IRM-Dossiers, hg. vom Forschungs- und Informationsinstitut Multinationale Konzerne, Genf).

Burr, Manfred, "Computer Aided Design (CAD) — Auswirkungen des Rechnereinsatzes in der Konstruktion," *Die Mitbestimmung*, Vol. 30, No. 2 (1984), pp. 91-96.

Carell, Erich, "Arbeit," in *Handwörterbuch der Sozialwissenschaften*, Vol. 1, pp. 229-34.

—, "Boden," in *Handwörterbuch der Sozialwissenschaften*, Vol. 2, pp. 316-21.

Claußen, Ulf, ed., *Die im Dunkeln sieht man nicht: Massen- und Langzeitarbeitslosigkeit, die neue soziale Frage*, Bochum: SWI Verlag, 1985.

Church Office of the Evangelical Church in Germany, ed., *Bewältigung der Schuldenkrise — Prüfstein der Nord-Süd-Beziehungen: Eine Stellungnahme der Kammer der EKD für kirchlichen Entwicklungsdienst*, Hanover: Kirchenamt der Evangelischen Kirche in Deutschland, 1988.

Commission of the European Communities, "EG Informationen," *EGmagazin*, No. 7/8 (1989).

Conze, Werner, "Arbeit" and "Beruf," in *Geschichtliche Grundbegriffe: Historisches Lexikon zur politisch-sozialen Sprache in Deutschland*, ed. Otto Brunner, Werner Conze, and Reinhart Koselleck, Vol. 1, Stuttgart: Verlag Klett-Cotta, 1974, pp. 174-81 and 490-507.

Csikós-Nagy, Béla, *Sozialistische Marktwirtschaft*, Vienna and Zürich: Europaverlag, 1988.

Dopfer, Kurt, *Ost-West-Konvergenz: Werden sich die östlichen und westlichen Wirtschaftsordnungen annähern?* Zürich and St. Gallen: Polygraphischer Verlag, 1970.

Drechsler, Wolfgang and Martin Wansleben, *Mitarbeiter-Beteiligung in Unternehmen: Was der Praktiker wissen muß. Wie Unternehmen des deutschen Maschinen- und Anlagenbaus sie praktizieren*, ed. Verband Deutscher Maschinen- und Anlagenbau, Frankfurt am Main: Maschinenbau-Verlag, 1986.

Dreyfus, Hubert L. and Stuart E. Dreyfus, *Mind over Machine: The Power of Human Intuition and Expertise in the Era of the Computer*, New York: Free Press, 1986.

Drucker, Peter F., *The New Society: The Anatomy of Industrial Order*, New York: Harper & Brothers, 1950.

Dubs, Rolf, "Die chinesische Wirtschaftsordnung," in *Dokumentation zur Wirtschaftskunde*, No. 104, ed. Society for the Development of the Swiss Economy, Zürich: Wirtschaftsförderung, 1986, pp. 1-14.

Dunkel, Arthur, *Was müssen die Entwicklungsländer tun?* St. Gallen: Hochschule St. Gallen für Wirtschafts- und Sozialwissenschaften, 1988.

Durovic, Dragoljub, *et al.*, *Das Gesetz über assoziierte Arbeit*, ed. Secretariat of Information of the S.F.R. Yugoslavia, Belgrade: Dopisna Delavska Univerza, 1977.

Dürr, Ernst, "Die Übertragbarkeit der Sozialen Marktwirtschaft auf Entwicklungs- und Schwellenländer," in *Weltwirtschaft im Wandel: Festgabe für Egon Tuchtfeldt zum 65. Geburtstag*, ed. Dürr and Hugo Sieber, Bern and Stuttgart: Verlag Paul Haupt, 1988, pp. 647-64.

Eggebrecht, Arne, Jens Flemming, Gert Meyer, Achatz v. Müller, Alfred Oppolzer, Akos Paulinyi, and Helmuth Schneider, *Geschichte der Arbeit: Vom Alten Ägypten bis zur Gegenwart*, Zürich: Buchclub Ex Libris, 1982.

Egner, Erich, "Konsumentenschutz," in *Handwörterbuch der Sozialwissenschaften*, Vol. 6, pp. 149-54.

Enderle, Georges, ed., *Ethik und Wirtschaftswissenschaft*, Berlin, Duncker & Humblot, 1985.

—, *Ein Leitbild für die Sicherung des Existenzminimums in der Schweiz*, St. Gallen: Forschungsstelle für Wirtschaftsethik, 1986.

—, *Sicherung des Existenzminimums im nationalen und internationalen Kontext: Eine wirtschaftsethische Studie*, Bern and Stuttgart: Verlag Paul Haupt, 1987.

Enderle, Georges and Ambros Lüthi, "Ökonomische Abhängigkeit und Dissoziation," *Concilium*, 16 (1980), p. 700-707.

Erbrich, Paul, "Technik — Chance oder Verhängnis?" *Neue Zürcher Zeitung*, No. 176, 30/31 July 1988, p. 17.

Eucken, Walter, *Grundsätze der Wirtschaftspolitik*, ed. Edith Eucken and K. Paul Hensel, Bern: A. Francke Verlag and Tübingen, J.C.B. Mohr (Paul Siebeck) 1952; Abr. Ed., ed. Edith Eucken-Erdsiek and K. Paul Hensel, Hamburg: Rowohlt Taschenbuch Verlag, 1959.

Expertenkommission des Eidgenössischen Volkswirtschaftsdepartement, "Qualitatives Wachstum," (Bundesamt für Konjunkturfragen, Study No. 9), Bern: Eidgenössisches Volkswirtschaftsdepartement, 1985.

Federal Minister for Research and Technology, ed., *Technischer Fortschritt: Auswirkungen auf Wirtschaft und Arbeitsmarkt*, 2nd Ed., Düsseldorf and Vienna: Econ Verlag, 1981.

Feigenbaum, Edward A., "SHZ-Interview," *Schweizerische Handelszeitung*, 5 December 1985, p. 53.

Frey, Bruno S., "Licht auf die Schattenwirtschaft," in a Bulletin edited by Credit-Suisse Holding, Vol. 93, 1 February 1987, pp. 6-8.

—, *Theorie demokratischer Wirtschaftspolitik*, Munich: Verlag Franz Vahlen, 1981.

Frey, René L., *Wirtschaft, Staat und Wohlfahrt: Eine Einführung in die Nationalökonomie*, 4th Ed., Basel and Frankfurt am Main: Verlag Helbling & Lichtenhahn, 1985.

Friebe, K., "Mikroelektronik — Perspektiven der industriellen Revolution," in *Mikroelektronik — Chancen und Probleme*, Berlin: VDI-Technologiezentrum, 1983.

Friedman, Milton, *Capitalism and Freedom*, Chicago: University of Chicago Press, 1962.

Friedmann, Georges, *Grenzen der Arbeitsteilung*, Frankfurt am Main: Europäische Verlagsanstalt, 1959.

—, *Der Mensch in der mechanisierten Produktion*, Cologne: Bund-Verlag, 1952.

Friedrich, Jürgen, Friedrich Wicke, and Walter Wicke, *Computereinsatz: Auswirkungen auf die Arbeit*, Reinbek bei Hamburg: Rowohlt Taschenbuch Verlag, 1982.

Friedrichs, Günter and Adam Scheff, eds., *Auf Gedeih und Verderb: Mikroelektronik und Gesellschaft: Bericht an den Club of Rome*, Vienna, Munich, and Zürich: Europaverlag, 1982.

Fritsch, Bruno, *Wachstumsbegrenzung als Machtinstrument*, Stuttgart: Deutsche Verlags-Anstalt, 1974.

Fürer, Arthur, "Die Multinationalen in einer Welt des Umbruchs," *Neue Zürcher Zeitung*, No. 52, 3/4 March 1979, p. 37.

Furger, Alex R. and Fanny Hartmann, *Vor 5000 Jahren... So lebten unsere Vorfahren in der Jungsteinzeit*, Bern and Stuttgart: Verlag Paul Haupt, 1983.

Gadó, Ottó, *The Economic Mechanism in Hungary — How it works in 1976*, Leyden: A.W. Sijthoff and Budapest: Akadémiai Kiadó, 1976.

—, "Die Strukturpolitik vom Aspekt des Mechanismus," *Marketing in Ungarn*, 1980.

Galbraith, John Kenneth, *The Affluent Society*, Boston: Houghton Mifflin, 1958, Rev. Ed., 1985.

—, *Economics and the Public Purpose*, Boston: Houghton Mifflin, 1973.

—, *The New Industrial State*, 2nd Ed., Boston: Houghton Mifflin, 1971.

Gasser, Christian, "Das Mitbestimmungspostulat aus der Sicht der Unternehmung," in *Mitbestimmung in der Unternehmung*, ed. Charles Lattmann and Vera Ganz-Keppeler, Bern and Stuttgart: Verlag Paul Haupt, 1972, pp. 111-20.

Gasser, Thomas P. and Jacques A. Rossier, "Multinationale Expansion — neue Chancen für mittelgroße Unternehmen," *Neue Zürcher Zeitung*, No. 460, 4 October 1973, p. 21.

Geißler, Heiner, *Die Neue Soziale Frage: Analysen und Dokumente*, Freiburg im Breisgau and Basel: Herder Verlag, 1976.

George, Susan, *A Fate Worse than Debt*, New York: Grove Press, 1988.

German Conference of Bishops, ed., *Die internationale Schuldenkrise — eine ethische Herausforderung*, Bonn: Sekretariat der Deutschen Bischofskonferenz, 1988.

German Federal Cartel Office, *Bericht des Bundeskartellamtes über seine Tätigkeit im Jahre 1972 sowie über die Lage und Entwicklung auf seinem Aufgabenbereich*, Bundestags-Drucksache 7/3574, Bonn, 1972.

Gerster, Richard, *Aus Fehlern lernen? Die Schweiz und die Dritte Welt*, Zürich: Buchclub Ex Libris, 1987.

Gimpel, Jean, *La révolution industrielle du Moyen Age*, Paris: Editions Seuil, 1975.

Gorbachev, Mikhail, *Perestroika: New Thinking for Our Country and the World*, New York: Harper & Row, 1987.

Graf, Gerhard, "Beschäftigungstheorie," in *Handwörterbuch der Wirtschaftswissenschaften*, Vol. 1, pp. 513-43.

Gröner, Helmut, "Deregulierungsansätze im Energiesektor: Die Berücksichtigung zukünftiger Knappheit durch den Markt," *Neue Zürcher Zeitung*, No. 237, 13 October 1987, p. 37.

Groskurth, Peter, ed., *Arbeit und Persönlichkeit: berufliche Sozialisation in der arbeitsteiligen Gesellschaft: Ergebnisse der Arbeitswissenschaft für Bildung, psychosoziale und gewerkschaftliche Praxis*, Reinbek bei Hamburg: Rowohlt Taschenbuchverlag, 1979.

Gutenberg, Erich, *Grundlagen der Betriebswirtschaftslehre*, Vol. I: *Die Production*, 12th Ed., Berlin, Göttingen, and Heidelberg: Springer-Verlag, 1966.

Hafner, Pius, Ernst Meili, Hans Ruh, Peter Siber, Christoph Stückelberger, Lukas Vischer, and Eugen Wirth, *Mensch sein im Ganzen der Schöpfung: Ein ökologisches Memorandum im Auftrag und zuhanden der Arbeitsgemeinschaft Christlicher Kirchen in der Schweiz*, Zürich: Institut für Erwachsenenbildung, 1985.

von Hayek, Friedrich A., *Die Theorie komplexer Phänomene*, Tübingen: J.C.B. Mohr (Paul Siebeck), 1972.

Hedtkamp, Günter, "UdSSR," in *Handwörterbuch der Wirtschaftswissenschaften*, Vol. 9, pp. 383-99.

Heiner, Volker, "Nur keine Insellösungen... Computer-Integrated-Manufacturing (CIM) als Chance und Herausforderung," *Schweizerische Handelszeitung*, No. 45, 10 November 1988, pp. 85-86.

Heinrich, Walter, *Wirtschaftspolitik*, Vol. 1, 2nd Ed., Berlin: Duncker & Humblot, 1964.

Henrichsmeyer, Wilhelm, Oskar Gans, and Ingo Evers, *Einführung in die Volkswirtschaftslehre*, 7th Ed., Stuttgart: Verlag Eugen Ulmer, 1986.

Hensel, K. Paul, *Grundformen der Wirtschaftsordnung: Marktwirtschaft — Zentralverwaltungswirtschaft*, 3rd Ed., Munich: Verlag C. H. Beck, 1978.

—, "Planwirtschaft," in *Handwörterbuch der Sozialwissenschaften*, Vol. 8, pp. 325-38.

—, *Systemvergleich als Aufgabe: Aufsätze und Vorträge*, ed. Hannelore Hamel, Stuttgart: Gustav Fischer Verlag, 1977.

Herzberg, Frederick, Bernard Mausner, and Barbara Bloch Snyderman, *The Motivation to Work*, 2nd Ed., New York, London, and Sydney: John Wiley & Sons, 1967.

Hesse, Helmut, "Internationale Wirtschaftsbeziehungen als Gegenstand der Wirtschaftsethik," in *Wirtschaftswissenschaft und Ethik*, ed. Hesse, Berlin: Duncker & Humblot, 1988, pp. 195-214.

Heuß, Ernst, "Ordoliberalismus," in *Liberalismus im Kreuzfeuer: Thesen und Gegenthesen zu den Grundlagen der Wirtschaftspolitik*, ed. Hans G. Nutzinger, Frankfurt am Main: Verlag Josef Knecht, 1986, pp. 25-40.

Hilger, Dietrich and Lucian Hölscher, "Industrie, Gewerbe," in *Geschichtliche Grundbegriffe: Historisches Lexikon zur politisch-sozialen Sprache in Deutschland*, ed. Otto Brunner, Werner Conze, and Reinhart Koselleck, Vol. 3, Stuttgart: Verlag Klett-Cotta, 1982, pp. 237-304.

Hilger, Marie-Elisabeth and Lucian Hölscher, "Kapital, Kapitalist, Kapitalismus," in *Geschichtliche Grundbegriffe: Historisches Lexikon zur politisch-sozialen Sprache in Deutschland*, ed. Otto Brunner, Werner Conze, and Reinhart Koselleck, Vol. 3, Stuttgart: Verlag Klett-Cotta, 1982, pp. 399-454.

Hirsch, Fred, *Social Limits to Growth*, Cambridge, Mass.: Harvard University Press, 1976.

Hobbes, Thomas, *The Elements of Law, Natural and Politic*, ed. Ferdinand Tönnies, London: Cambridge University Press, 1889.

Hoffmann, Lutz and Hermann Sanders, "Entwicklungspolitik," I: "Strategien," in *Handwörterbuch der Wirtschaftswissenschaften*, Vol. 2, pp. 393-407.

Hoffmann, Walther, *Stadien and Typen der Industrialisierung: Ein Beitrag zur quantitativen Analyse historischer Wirtschaftsprozesse*, Jena: Gustav Fischer Verlag, 1931.

Hofmann, Daniel, "Die neue Rolle von Weltbank und Währungsfonds, *Neue Zürcher Zeitung*, No. 88, 16/17 April 1988, p. 35.

Höhmann, Hans-Hermann, "Wirtschaft und Politik in der 'Perestrojka,'" *Osteuropa*, 38 (1988), pp. 537-49.

Holler, Manfred J. and Claus J. Tully, *Arbeit und Mensch: Vom reduzierten Maß der Humanität in der Arbeit*, Munich: Verlag N. Leudemann, 1981.

Honecker, Martin, *Technischer und gesellschaftlicher Fortschritt aus christlicher Sicht — Ökumenische Verantwortung für die Zukunft der Welt*, Kassel: Pressestelle der Arbeitgeber- und Wirtschaftsverbände in Nordhessen, 1981.

—, "Verantwortung für die Umwelt als Auftrag des Menschen," in *Vorsorge für die Umwelt: Neun Vorträge*, ed. G. Hosemann and E. Finckh, Erlangen: Universitätsbibliothek, 1984, pp. 9-22.

Hörmann, Otto, *Von Breschnew zu Gorbatschow: Als Reporter in Moskau*, Graz, Vienna, and Cologne: Verlag Styria, 1987.

Huber, Joseph, *Die zwei Gesichter der Arbeit: Ungenutzte Möglichkeiten der Dualwirtschaft*, Frankfurt am Main: S. Fischer Verlag, 1984.

Institute of the German Economy, ed., *Schweden: Modell in der Krise*, Cologne: Institut der deutschen Wirtschaft, 1982.

Jäger, Alfred, "Die internationale Kreditkrise 1982/83 und ihre wirtschaftsethischen Konsequenzen," in *Tu deinen Mund auf für die Stummen: Beiträge zu einer solidarischen Praxis der christlichen Gemeinde:*

Festschrift für Wolfgang Schweitzer zum 70. Geburtstag, ed. Frank-Matthias Hofmann and Eberhard Mechels, Gütersloh: Gütersloher Verlagshaus Gerd Mohn, 1986, pp. 115-28.

Jöhr, Walter Adolf, *Galbraith und die Marktwirtschaft: Mit einem Anhang über Gäfgens Kritik des Galbraithschen Ansatzes*, Tübingen: J.C.B. Mohr (Paul Siebeck), 1975.

—, "Das Problem der Wirtschaftsordnung," in *Individuum und Gemeinschaft: Festschrift zur Fünfzigjahrfeier der Handels-Hochschule St. Gallen*, St. Gallen: Verlag der Fehr'schen Buchhandlung, 1949, pp. 231-62.

—, "Wirtschaft und Politik," in *Handwörterbuch der Wirtschaftswissenschaften*, Vol. 9, pp. 1-33.

—, *Zur Arbeitslosigkeit der Gegenwart: Wie ist langdaurnde allgemeine Massenarbeitslosigkeit bei vorwiegend marktwirtschaftlicher Ordnung möglich?* Tübingen: J.C.B. Mohr (Paul Siebeck), 1986.

Kaiser, Helmut, "Ansatzpunkte für eine normative Erweiterung der ökonomischen Rationalität — 'Humanisierung' der ökonomischen Theorie als Aufgabe einer sich als ethische Ökonomie verstehenden Wirtschaftsethik," *Zeitschrift für Evangelische Ethik*, 28 (1984), pp. 285-320.

Kant, Immanuel, *Groundwork for the Metaphysics of Morals*, ed. and trans. Allen W. Wood, New Haven, 2002.

Kapp, K. William, *The Social Costs of Private Enterprise*, Cambridge, Mass.: Harvard University Press, 1950.

Kardelj, Edvard, *Contradictions of Social Property in a Socialist Society*, Belgrade: Socialist Thought and Practice, 1981.

Kaser, Michael, *Wirtschaftspolitik der Sowjetunion: Ideologie und Praxis*, Munich: Kindler Verlag, 1970.

Katterle, Siegfried, *Die Alternativen zur neoliberalen Wende: Wirtschaftspolitik in der sozialstaatlichen Demokratie*, Bochum: SWI-Verlag, 1989.

Kaufmann, Franz-Xaver, "Solidarität als Steuerungsform — Erklärungsansätze bei Adam Smith," in *Markt, Staat und Solidarität bei Adam Smith*, ed. Kaufmann and Hans-Günter Krüsselberg, eds., Frankfurt am Main and New York: Campus Verlag, 1984, pp. 158-84.

Keynes, John Maynard, *The End of Laissez-Faire*, London: Hogarth, 1926.

—, *The General Theory of Employment, Interest, and Money*, London: Macmillan, 1936.

Kleinewefers, Henner, *Grundzüge einer verallgemeinerten Wirtschaftsordnungstheorie*, Tübingen: J.C.B. Mohr (Paul Siebeck), 1988.

—, "Pläne, Märkte und Prozeßpolitik in Ungarn," *Neue Zürcher Zeitung*, No. 189, 16 August 1988, p. 33.

—, *Reformen für Wirtschaft und Gesellschaft: Utopien, Konzepte, Realitäten*, Frankfurt am Main and New York: Campus Verlag, 1985.

—, "Theorie der Wirtschaftspolitik" VI: "Wirtschaftsordnungstheorie," unpublished lecture notes, 1986.

Kleinewefers, Henner and Regula Pfister, *Die schweizerische Volkswirtschaft: Eine problemorientierte Einführung in die Volkswirtschaftslehre,* Frauenfeld: Verlag Huber, 1977.

Kliemt, Hartmut, "Der Homo Oeconomicus zwischen Ethik und Biologie — Aspekte seiner Geschichte und Wirkungsgeschichte," in *Homo Oeconomicus I,* ed. Manfred J. Holler, ed., Munich: Verlag N. Leudemann, 1983, pp. 9-20.

Klotz, Ulrich, "'Künstliche Intelligenz' und Expertensysteme — Mythos oder Realität?" *Die Mitbestimmung,* Vol. 32, No. 11 (1986), pp. 562-67.

Kohn, Melvin Lester, *Persönlichkeit, Beruf und soziale Schichtung,* ed. Kurt Lüscher, Stuttgart: Verlag Klett-Cotta, 1981.

Komarov, Boris (pseudonym), *Das große Sterben am Baikalsee: Der geheime Bericht eines hohen Funktionärs über die Umweltkrise der Sowjetunion,* Reinbek bei Hamburg: Rowohlt Verlag, 1979.

Koopmann, Georg, "Warum gibt es multinationale Unternehmen?" in *Multinationale Unternehmen: Anfang oder Ende der Weltwirtschaft?* ed. Dietrich Kebschull and Otto G. Mayer, Frankfurt am Main: Athenäum Fischer Taschenbuch Verlag, 1974, pp. 36-50.

Korff, Wilhelm, "Orientierungslinien einer Wirtschaftsethik," in *Die Welt für morgen: Ethische Herausforderungen im Anspruch der Zukunft,* ed. Gerfried W. Hunold and Korff, Munich: Kösel-Verlag, 1986, pp. 67-80.

Koslowski, Peter, *Evolution und Gesellschaft: Eine Auseinandersetzung mit der Soziobiologie,* Tübingen: J.C.B. Mohr (Paul Siebeck), 1984.

Kosta, Jirí, "China," in *Handwörterbuch der Wirtschaftswissenschaften,* Vol. 9, pp. 353-69.

Koubek, Norbert, "Neue Entwicklungen in der Unternehmens- und Konzernorganisation," *Die Mitbestimmung,* Vol. 32, No. 1 (1986), pp. 5-8.

Kraft, Ueli, Kurt Häfeli, and Urs Schallberger, *"...natürlich hat mich meine Lehre verändert." Ein Bericht über Zusammenhänge zwischen Berufsausbildung und Persönlichkeitsentwicklung,* Zürich, Schweizerischer Verband für Berufsberatung, 1985.

Kraus, Willy, "Wirtschaftsreformen in der Volksrepublik China," in *Aus Politik und Zeitgeschichte: Beilage zur Wochenzeitung Das Parlament,* ed. Federal Office for Political Education, No. B 39/85, Bonn, 28 September 1985.

Krelle, Wilhelm, "Wirtschaftsplanung auf mittlere und lange Sicht," in *Planung ohne Planwirtschaft: Frankfurter Gespräch der List Gesellschaft,* ed. Alfred Plitzko, Basel: Kyklos-Verlag and Tübingen: J.C.B. Mohr (Paul Siebeck), 1964, pp. 62-69.

Krelle, Wilhelm, Johann Schunck, and Jürgen Siebke, *Überbetriebliche Ertragsbeteiligung der Arbeitnehmer: Mit einer Untersuchung über die Vermögensstruktur der Bundesrepublik Deutschland,* Vol. I, Tübingen: J.C.B. Mohr (Paul Siebeck), 1968.

Krupp, Hans-Jürgen, "Lohnpolitik und Vermögensbildung — Wege aus der verteilungs- und beschäftigungspolitischen Sackgasse?" in *Wirtschaftspolitik in den 80er Jahren,* ed. Alex Möller, Bonn: Verlag Neue Gesellschaft, 1984, pp. 145-61.

Külp, Bernhard, with H. Drost, D. Leuschner, V. Schiffer, and K. Wiedemann, *Grundfragen der Wirtschaft: Eine Einführung in die Sozialökonomie,* Cologne: Verlag J. P. Bachem, 1967.

Küng, Emil, "Die Qualität des Lebens als Ziel der Wirtschafts- und Gesellschaftspolitik," *Schweizer Monatshefte,* 54 (1974), pp. 21-32.

—, *Wirtschaft und Gerechtigkeit: Sozialethische Probleme im Lichte der Volkswirtschaftslehre,* Tübingen: J.C.B. Mohr (Paul Siebeck), 1967.

Küng, Emil and Erwin Bielinski, in *Die Zukunft der Industrie in Europa, Brennpunkte,* ed. Gottlieb Duttweiler Institute, Zürich: Verlag Ex Libris, 1976.

Lafontaine, Oskar, *Der andere Fortschritt: Verantwortung statt Verweigerung,* Hamburg: Hoffmann und Campe, 1985.

Lamberg, Robert F., "'Rosenkrieg' in Schweden: Unwillen über liberale Vorstöße des Finanzministers," *Neue Zürcher Zeitung,* No. 44, 22 February 1989, p. 37.

Landmann, Michael, "Ökologische und anthropologische Verantwortung — eine neue Dimension der Ethik," in *Gerechtigkeit: Themen der Sozialethik,* ed. Armin Wildermuth and Alfred Jäger, Tübingen: J.C.B. Mohr (Paul Siebeck), 1981, pp. 157-78.

de Lange, Harry M., "Die Kirchen und die Einheit Europas," *Zeitschrift für Evangelische Ethik,* 27 (1983), pp. 41-49.

Langer, Gerd, "Können multinationale Unternehmen international kontrolliert werden?" in *Multinationale Unternehmen: Anfang oder Ende der Weltwirtschaft?* ed. Dietrich Kebschull and Otto G. Mayer, Frankfurt am Main: Athenäum Fischer Taschenbuch Verlag, 1974, pp. 219-44.

Lattmann, Charles, "Arbeit als Selbstentfaltung des Menschen," in *Arbeit und Humanität,* ed. Arthur Rich and Eberhard Ulich, Königstein: Athenäum Verlag, 1978, pp. 33-46.

—, *Die verhaltenswissenschaftlichen Grundlagen der Führung des Mitarbeiters,* Bern and Stuttgart: Verlag Paul Haupt, 1982.

Lefringhausen, Klaus, "Marktwirtschaft und Entwicklungspolitik — Erfahrungen aus Gesprächen zwischen Vertretern von Kirche und Unternehmen," in *Märkte und Mächte,* ed. Klaus Wilkens, Hermann Sautter, Klaus Lefringhausen, and Christian Uhlig, Stuttgart: Verlag Dienste in Übersee, 1987, pp. 93-123.

Leipold, Helmut, "Ungarn," in *Handwörterbuch der Wirtschaftswissenschaften,* Vol. 9, pp 399-412.

—, *Wirtschafts- und Gesellschaftssystem im Vergleich: Grundzüge einer Theorie der Wirtschaftssysteme,* 2nd Ed., Stuttgart: Gustav Fischer Verlag, 1980.

Lemân, Gudrun, *Das jugoslawische Modell: Wege zur Demokratisierung*, Frankfurt am Main and Cologne: Europäische Verlagsanstalt, 1976.

Lenin, V. I., *Collected Works*, Vol. 27, London: Lawrence and Wishart; Moscow: Progress Publishers, 1965.

Leontief, Wassily, "Den technologischen Schock dämpfen," Interview in *IAO-Nachrichten* [*International Labour Organization News*], Vol. 19, No. 4, 1983.

Leu, Robert E., "Bedürftigkeit und Armut als relative Begriffe," *Neue Zürcher Zeitung*, No. 193, 22 August 1989, p. 33.

Leu, Robert E. and René L. Frey, "Mehr Umweltschutz mit geringeren Kosten: Marktwirtschaftlich orientierte Umweltpolitik," *Neue Zürcher Zeitung*, No. 230, 4/5 October 1986, pp. 17-18.

Locher, Gottfried W., *Der Eigentumsbegriff als Problem der evangelischen Theologie*, 2nd Ed., Zürich and Stuttgart: Zwingli Verlag, 1962.

Løgstrup, Knud E., *Norm und Spontaneität: Ethik und Politik zwischen Technik und Dilettantokratie*, trans. Rosemarie Løgstrup, Tübingen: J.C.B. Mohr (Paul Siebeck), 1989.

Ludewig, Jochen, "Software Engineering: Computerprogramme als technische Produkte," *Neue Zürcher Zeitung*, No. 209, 10 September 1986, p. 113.

Mann, Fritz Karl, "Physiokratie," in *Handwörterbuch der Sozialwissenschaften*, Vol. 8, pp. 296-302.

Männer, Leonhard, "Kapital," I: "Theorie, volkswirtschaftliche," in *Handwörterbuch der Wirtschaftswissenschaften*, Vol. 4, pp. 346-59.

Marer, Paul "Economic System," in *Südosteuropa-Handbuch*, ed. Klaus-Detlev Grothusen, Vol. V: *Ungarn*, Göttingen: Vandenhoeck & Ruprecht, 1987, pp. 276-301.

Markl, Hubert, *Natur als Kulturaufgabe: Über die Beziehung des Menschen zur lebendigen Natur*, Stuttgart: Deutsche Verlags-Anstalt, 1986.

Marx, Karl and Frederick Engels, *Collected Works*, 50 vols., New York: International Publishers, 1975-1998.

Meadows, Donella H., Dennis L. Meadows, Jørgen Randers, and William W. Behrens III, *The Limits to Growth: A Report for the Club of Rome's Project on the Predicament of Mankind*, New York: Universe Books, 1972; 2nd Ed., 1974.

Meidner, Rudolf, "Unsere Vorstellungen vom Dritten Weg: Einige Bemerkungen zum gesellschaftspolitischen Konzept der schwedischen Arbeiterbewegung," in *Wirtschaft und Gesellschaft: Kritik und Alternativen: Festgabe für Ota Šik zum 60. Geburtstag*, ed. Ulrich Gärtner and Jirí Kosta, Berlin: Duncker & Humblot, 1979, pp. 363-87.

Meidner, Rudolf and Anna Hedborg, *Modell Schweden: Erfahrungen einer Wohlstandsgesellschaft*, Frankfurt am Main and New York: Campus Verlag, 1984.

Mey, Hansjürg, "Auch Japaner kochen nur mit Wasser," *Schweizerische Handelszeitung*, No. 22, 29 May 1987, pp. 73 & 80.

—, *Mikroelektronik: Grundlagen der Informatik im betrieblichen Einsatz*, Bern: Schweizerische Volksbank, 1985.

—, *Mikroelektronik — Möglichkeiten, Gefahren und Grenzen*, 2nd. Ed., Zürich: Zürcher Kantonalbank, 1982.

Mey, Harald, Reinhard Roericht, and Manfred F. Romich, eds., *Wirtschaftsreformen und neue Entwicklungsstrategien in der Volksrepublik China*, Frankfurt am Main, Bern, and New York: Verlag Peter Lang, 1986.

Meyer-Abich, Klaus Michael, "Die ökologische Grenze des herkömmlichen Wirtschaftswachstums," in *Die Zukunft des Wachstums: Kritische Antworten zum "Bericht des Club of Rome,"* ed. Henrich von Nussbaum, Düsseldorf: Bertelsmann Universitätsverlag, 1973, pp. 163-86.

Meyer-Abich, Klaus Michael and Bertram Schefold, *Wie möchten wir in Zukunft leben: Der 'harte' und der 'sanfte' Weg*, Munich: Verlag C. H. Beck, 1981.

Michalet, Charles-Albert, *Multinationale Unternehmen und die Wirtschaftskrise*, Frankfurt am Main and New York: Campus Verlag, 1986.

Mieth, Dietmar, *Arbeit und Menschenwürde*, Freiburg im Breisgau, Basel, and Vienna: Herder Verlag, 1985.

Mittelstraß, Jürgen, "Wirtschaftsethik als wissenschaftliche Disziplin?" in *Ethik und Wirtschaftswissenschaft*, ed. Georges Enderle, Berlin: Duncker & Humblot, 1985, pp. 17-32.

Mollat, Michel, *Die Armen im Mittelalter*, Munich: Verlag C. H. Beck, 1984.

More, Thomas, *Utopia*, 1516.

Mugglin, Markus, "Alternativen sind unausweichlich," in *"...in euren Häusern liegt das geraubte Gut der Armen": Ökonomisch-theologische Beiträge zur Verschuldungskrise*, ed. Kuno Füssel, Franz Hinkelammert, Mugglin, and Raúl Vidales, Fribourg, Edition Exodus, 1989, pp. 45-77.

Müller-Armack, Alfred, *Genealogie der Sozialen Marktwirtschaft: Frühschriften und weiterführende Konzepte*, Bern and Stuttgart: Verlag Paul Haupt, 1974.

—, "Der humane Gehalt der Sozialen Marktwirtschaft," in *Soziale Marktwirtschaft im Wandel*, ed. Egon Tuchtfeldt, Freiburg im Breisgau: Verlag Rombach, 1973, pp. 15-26.

—, "Konjunkturelle Aussichten und konjunkturpolitische Aufgaben für das Jahr 1968," *Wirtschaftspolitische Chronik (Beiträge zur Wirtschafts- und Sozialpolitik: Festgabe für Fritz W. Meyer, Institut für Wirtschaftspolitik an der Universität zu Köln)*, Issue 2/3 (1967), pp. 13-21.

—, *Wirtschaftsordnung und Wirtschaftspolitik: Studien und Konzepte zur Sozialen Marktwirtschaft und zur Europäischen Integration*, Freiburg im Breisgau: Verlag Rombach, 1966.

Müller-Jentsch, Walther, "Industrielle Beziehungen im Umbruch," *Die Mitbestimmung*, Vol. 32, Nos. 8 & 9 (1986), pp. 440-43.

Muqiao, Xue, *Sozialismus in China: Erfolge, Fehlschläge, Reformperspektiven*, Hamburg: Verlag Weltarchiv, 1982.

National Conference of Catholic Bishops, *Economic Justice for All: Pastoral Letter on Catholic Social Teaching and the U. S. Economy*, Washington: United States Catholic Conference, 1986.

Negt, Oskar, *Lebendige Arbeit, enteignete Zeit: Politische und kulturelle Dimensionen des Kampfes um die Arbeitskraft*, Frankfurt am Main and New York: Campus Verlag, 1984.

von Nell-Breuning, Oswald, "Die Arbeitswertlehre in der scholastischen Theologie, in der katholischen Soziallehre und nach Karl Marx," in *Christliche Wirtschaftsethik vor neuen Aufgaben: Festgabe für Arthur Rich zum 70. Geburtstag*, ed. Theodor Strohm, Zürich: Theologischer Verlag, 1980, pp. 57-74.

—, *Kapitalismus — kritisch betrachtet: Zur Auseinandersetzung um das bessere 'System'*, Freiburg im Breisgau: Herder Verlag, 1986.

Nemitz, Kurt, *Sozialistische Marktwirtschaft: Die wirtschaftspolitische Konzeption der deutschen Sozialdemokratie*, Frankfurt am Main: Europäische Verlagsanstalt, 1960.

Nienhaus, Volker, *Kontroversen um Markt und Plan: Sozialistische Wirtschaftsrechnung, indikative Planung, Konvergenzthese, überbetriebliche Investitionsplanung*, Darmstadt: Wissenschaftliche Buchgesellschaft, 1984.

Nutzinger, Hans G., "Marktliberalismus und Produktionsorganisation," in *Liberalismus im Kreuzfeuer: Thesen und Gegenthesen zu den Grundlagen der Wirtschaftspolitik*, ed. Hans G. Nutzinger, Frankfurt am Main: Verlag Josef Knecht, 1986, pp. 103-28.

Nydegger, Alfred, "Mehr Weitblick und mehr Markt in der Energiepolitik," *Neue Zürcher Zeitung*, No. 199, 29 August 1989, p. 21.

Oplatka, Andreas, "Der Comecon im Banne des Jahres 2000: Abkommen über wissenschaftlich-technologischen Fortschritt," *Neue Zürcher Zeitung*, No. 295, 19 December 1985, pp. 15-16.

Ott, Alfred Eugen, "Marktformen," in *Handwörterbuch der Wirtschaftswissenschaften*, Vol. 5, pp. 104-13.

Pascal, Blaise, *Pensées*, trans. A. J. Krailsheimer, Harmondsworth: Penguin Books, 1966.

Pechan, Hermann, *Louis Blanc als Wegbereiter des modernen Sozialismus*, Jena: Verlag von Gustav Fischer, 1929.

Peters, Hans-Rudolf, "Ordnungstheoretische Ansätze zur Typisierung unvollkommener Wirtschaftsordnungen," in *Hamburger Jahrbuch für Wirtschafts- und Gesellschaftspolitik*, ed. Heinz-Dietrich Ortlieb, Bruno Molitor, and Werner Krone, Vol. 18, Tübingen: J.C.B. Mohr (Paul Siebeck), 1973, pp. 47-77.

Peters and Robert H. Waterman, Jr., *In Search of Excellence: Lessons from America's Best-Run Companies*, New York: Harper & Row, 1982.
Pilz, Frank, *Das System der Sozialen Marktwirtschaft: Politisch-ökonomische Grundlegung der Konzepte, Prinzipien und Strategien*, 2nd Ed., Munich: Ernst Reinhardt Verlag, 1981.
Preiser, Erich, *Nationalökonomie heute: Eine Einführung in die Volkswirtschaftslehre*, 4th Ed., Munich: Verlag C. H. Beck, 1963.
Prosi, Gerhard and Jörn Biel, "Unternehmen, multinationale," I: "Volkswirtschaftliche Probleme," in *Handwörterbuch der Wirtschaftswissenschaften*, Vol. 8, pp. 84-95.
Pross, Helge, "Kapitalismus in der demokratischen Gesellschaft," in *Meyers Enzyklopädisches Lexikon*, 9th Ed., Vol. 13, Mannheim, Vienna, and Zürich: Bibliographisches Institut, 1975, pp. 423-27.
Radig, Bernd, "SHZ-Interview," *Schweizerische Handelszeitung*, No. 16, 16 April 1987, p. 61.
Ramm, Thilo, ed., *Der Frühsozialismus: Ausgewählte Quellentexte*, Stuttgart: Alfred Kröner Verlag, 1956.
Rathenau, Walther, *Die neue Wirtschaft*, Berlin: S. Fischer Verlag, 1918.
Rawls, John, *A Theory of Justice*, Cambridge, Mass.: Harvard University Press, 1971.
Recktenwald, Horst Claus, "Ethik, Selbstinteresse und *bonum commune*: Eine Analyse der klassischen Ordnungstheorie Adam Smiths," in *Ethik und Wirtschaftswissenschaft*, ed. Georges Enderle, Berlin: Duncker & Humblot, 1985, pp. 143-61.
—, "Ökonomische und christliche Ethik: Mißverständnisse trotz zahlreicher Gemeinsamkeiten," *Neue Zürcher Zeitung*, No. 48, 27/28 February 1988, p. 95.
Reuß, Wilhelm, "Zum Begriff 'Gemeineigentum'," in *Die Sozialgemeinschaften: Entwurf des Hessischen Sozialisierungsgesetzes*, ed. Harald Koch, Hamburg: Rechts- und Staatswissenschaftlicher Verlag, 1948, pp. 6-9.
Rich, Arthur, *Christliche Existenz in der industriellen Welt: Eine Einführung in die sozialethischen Grundfragen der industriellen Arbeitswelt*, 2nd Ed., Zürich and Stuttgart, Zwingli Verlag, 1964.
—, *Mitbestimmung in der Industrie: Probleme — Modelle — Kritische Beurteilung: Eine sozialethische Orientierung*, Zürich: Flamberg Verlag, 1973.
—, "Sachzwänge und strukturell Böses in der Wirtschaft," *Zeitschrift für Evangelische Ethik*, 26 (1982), pp. 62-82.
Rich, Georg, "Ist die schweizerische Geldpolitik wirklich monetaristisch?" in *Geld, Währung, Konjunktur*, ed. Swiss National Bank, Vol. 2, No. 3 (September 1984), pp. 53-60.
Riklin, Alois, *Verantwortung des Akademikers*, St. Gallen: VGS Verlagsgemeinschaft, 1987.

Rothschild, Kurt W., "Kritik marktwirtschaftlicher Ordnungen als Realtypus," in *Zur Theorie marktwirtschaftlicher Ordnungen*, ed. Erich Streißler and Christian Watrin, Tübingen: J.C.B. Mohr (Paul Siebeck), 1980, pp. 13-37.

Ruffmann Karl-Heinz, *Fragen an die sowjetische Geschichte: Von Lenin bis Gorbatschow*, Munich: Deutscher Taschenbuch Verlag, 1987.

Ruh, Hans, "Gerechtigkeitstheorien," in *Gerechtigkeit: Themen der Sozialethik*, ed. Armin Wildermuth and Alfred Jäger, Tübingen, J.C.B. Mohr (Paul Siebeck), 1981, pp. 55-69.

Rumpf, Max, *Deutsches Handwerkerleben und der Aufstieg der Stadt*, Stuttgart: Verlag W. Kohlhammer, 1955.

Rusinow, Dennison, *The Yugoslav Experiment 1948-74*, Berkeley: University of California Press, 1977.

Rüstow, Alexander, "Wirtschaftsethische Probleme der Sozialen Marktwirtschaft," in *Der Christ und die Soziale Marktwirtschaft*, ed. Patrick M. Boarman, Stuttgart and Cologne, Verlag W. Kohlhammer, 1955, pp. 53-74.

—, "Wirtschaftsordnung und Staatsform," in *Magna Charta der sozialen Marktwirtschaft*, ed. Ernst Winkler, Rüstow, Werner Schmid, and Otto Lautenbach, Heidelberg-Ziegelhausen: Vita-Verlag, 1952, pp. 19-33.

Samuelson, Paul A., *Macroeconomics*, 7th Ed., New York: McGraw-Hill, 1967.

—, *The Collected Scientific Papers of Paul A. Samuelson*, Vol. I, edited by J. Stiglitz, Cambridge: MIT Press, 1966.

Sautter, Hermann, "Die marktwirtschaftliche Idee im ordnungspolitischen Dialog mit Entwicklungsländern," in *Märkte und Mächte*, ed. Klaus Wilkens, Sautter, Klaus Lefringhausen, and Christian Uhlig, Stuttgart: Verlag Dienste in Übersee, 1987, pp. 27-92.

—, "Wie moralisch ist der Markt? Mit Adam Smith gegen angebotsorientiertes Wirtschaften," *Evangelische Kommentare*, 16 (1983), pp. 602-5.

Schachtschabel, Hans G., "Historische Grundformen wirtschaftspolitischer Ordnungen: Merkantilismus, Liberalismus, Sozialismus," in *Unsere Wirtschaft — Basis, Dschungel, Dogma? Marktwirtschaft in der gegenwärtigen Auseinandersetzung*, ed. State Office for Political Education of North Rhine-Westphalia, Cologne: Verlag Wissenschaft und Politik, 1973, pp. 20-34.

—, "Die sozialgeordnete Wirtschaft als Grundgestalt der Gegenwart," in *Methoden und Probleme der Wirtschaftspolitik: Gedächtnisschrift für Hans-Jürgen Seraphim*, ed. Hans Ohm, Berlin: Duncker & Humblot, 1964, pp. 65-85.

Schelhammer, Carlo, *Internationale Wirtschaftsorganisationen*, 2nd Ed., Zürich: Zürcher Kantonalbank, 1982.

Schiller, Karl, *Preisstabilität durch globale Steuerung der Marktwirtschaft*, Tübingen: J.C.B. Mohr (Paul Siebeck), 1966.

Schlecht, Otto, *Ethische Betrachtungen zur sozialen Marktwirtschaft*, Tübingen: J.C.B. Mohr (Paul Siebeck), 1983.
—, "Ethische und ökonomischen Ziele im Konflikt," in *BMWI Dokumentation*, ed. Federal Minister of Economics, No. 266, Bonn: Bundesministerium für Wirtschaft, 1985.
—, "Soziale Weltwirtschaft," *Wirtschaftswoche*, No. 38, 16 September 1988, pp. 92-96.
Schlögel, Karl, *Der renitente Held: Arbeiterprotest in der Sowjetunion 1953-1983*, Hamburg: Junius, 1984.
Schneider, Helmut, "Preise," I: "Konkurrenzpreisbildung," in *Handwörterbuch der Wirtschaftswissenschaften*, Vol. 6, pp. 173-88.
Schönfeld, Roland, "Außenwirtschaft," in *Südosteuropa-Handbuch*, ed. Klaus-Detlev Grothusen, Vol. V: *Ungarn*, Göttingen: Vandenhoeck & Ruprecht, 1987, pp. 383-416.
Schönwitz, Dietrich, "Jugoslawien," in *Handwörterbuch der Wirtschaftswissenschaften*, Vol. 9, pp. 370-82.
Schumpeter, Joseph A., *Capitalism, Socialism and Democracy*, 3rd Ed., New York: Harper & Row, 1950.
Schwamm, H., "Verhaltenskodex: Auf jeden kommt es an!" *Schweizerische Handelszeitung*, No. 23, 4 June 1981, p. 2.
Schwarz, Peter, *Management in Nonprofit-Organisationen: Öffentliche Verwaltungen und Betriebe, Verbände, Vereine, Parteien, Kirchen, Sozialwerke*, Bern: Schweizerische Volksbank, 1986.
Seiwert, Lothar, "Moderne Formen der Arbeitsorganisation (II): Autonome Arbeitsgruppen und Beurteilung der Verfahren," *Wirtschaftswissenschaftliches Studium*, 8 (1979), pp. 185-87.
Sellien, R. and H., eds., *Dr. Gablers Wirtschaftslexikon*, 9th Ed., Vol. 2, Wiesbaden: Betriebswirtschaftlicher Verlag Dr. Th. Gabler, 1976.
Sietz, Henning, "Lenins NEP — Gorbatschews Perestroika: Zu einer Diskussion in der sowjetischen Presse," *Neue Zürcher Zeitung*, No. 39, 17 February 1988, p. 5.
Šik, Ota, *Der dritte Weg: Die marxistisch-leninistische Theorie und die moderne Industriegesellschaft*, Hamburg: Hoffmann und Campe Verlag, 1972.
—, *Das kommunistische Machtsystem*, Hamburg: Hoffman und Campe Verlag, 1976.
—, *Ein Wirtschaftssystem der Zukunft*, Berlin, Heidelberg, New York, and Tokyo: Springer-Verlag, 1985.
—, *Wirtschaftssysteme: Vergleiche — Theorie — Kritik*, Berlin, Heidelberg, and New York: Springer-Verlag, 1987.
Simonis, Udo Ernst, *Ökologische Orientierungen: Vorträge zur Strukturanpassung von Wirtschaft, Technik und Wissenschaft*, Berlin: Ed. Sigma, 1988.
Sindjit, M., *Self-Management Planning in Yugoslavia*, Belgrade, 1981.

Smith, Adam, *An Inquiry into the Nature and Causes of the Wealth of Nations*, London: W. Strahan and T. Cadell, 1776; ed. R. H. Campbell and A. S. Skinner, Oxford: Clarendon Press, 1976.

—, *The Theory of Moral Sentiments*, London: A. Millar, 1759; ed. D. D. Raphael and A. L. Macfie, Oxford: Clarendon Press, 1976.

Society for the Development of the Swiss Economy, ed., *Notizen zur Wirtschaft*, No. 4, Zürich, 1986.

Socioeconomic Institute of the Evangelical Church in Germany (ed.), *Zwischen Wachstum und Lebensqualität. Wirtschaftsethische Fragen angesichts der Krisen wirtschftlichen Wachstums*, Forum Kirche und Gesellschaft Nr. 1, Munich: Chr. Kaiser Verlag, 1980.

Soden, Julius Graf von, *Die Nazional-Oekonomie: Ein philosophischer Versuch, über die Quellen des Nazional-Reichthums, und über die Mittel zu dessen Beförderung*, Vol. I, Leipzig: Johann Ambrosius Barth, 1805.

Sonderegger, Alfons, "Die existentiellen Risiken des Arbeitnehmers," in *Christliche Wirtschaftsethik vor neuen Aufgaben: Festgabe für Arthur Rich zum 70. Geburtstag*, ed. Theodor Strohm, Zürich: Theologischer Verlag, 1980, pp. 323-48.

Steiger, Alois, *Sozialprodukt oder Wohlfahrt? Kritik am Sozialproduktkonzept: Die Sozialen Kosten der Umweltzerstörung*, Diessenhofen: Verlag Rüegger, 1979.

Steinmüller, Wilhelm, "Die zweite Phase der Industrialisierung," *Neue Zürcher Zeitung*, No. 98, 29 April 1987, p. 69.

Stolz, Peter, "Arbeit, Umwelt, qualitatives Wachstum — ökonomische und wirtschaftsethische Perspektiven," *Zeitschrift für Evangelische Ethik*, 30 (1986), pp. 191-210.

Strohm, Theodor, "Die EG — 'Gemeinschaftscharta der sozialen Grundrechte' — eine Chance 'systemöffnender Kooperation'?" *Zeitschrift für Evangelische Ethik*, 33 (1989), pp. 242-48.

Stückelberger, Christoph, *Aufbruch zu einem menschengerechten Wachstum: Sozialethische Ansätze zu einem neuen Lebensstil*, Zürich: Theologischer Verlag, 1979.

Stützel, Wolfgang, "Sicherung der Sozialen Marktwirtschaft durch konsequente Ordnungspolitik," in *Grundtexte zur Sozialen Marktwirtschaft: Zeugnisse aus zweihumdert Jahren ordnungspolitischer Diskussion*, ed. Stützel, Christian Watrin, Hans Willgerodt, and Karl Hohmann, eds., Stuttgart and New York: Gustav Fischer Verlag, 1981, pp. 341-55.

Swiss Federal Statistical Office, ed., *Öffentliche Finanzen der Schweiz, December 1985, wf-Dokumentation zur Wirtschaftskunde*, Zürich: Wirtschaftsförderung, 1985.

Szabó-Raducziner, Zsuzsa, *Pläne, Märkte und laufende Prozeßpolitik in Ungarn*, Bern, Frankfurt am Main, and New York: Verlag Peter Lang, 1988.

Thurow, Lester C., "Das aktuelle Interview," *Schweizerische Handelszeitung*, No. 10, 5 March 1987, p. 7.

Tinbergen, Jan, "Kommt es zu einer Annäherung zwischen den kommunistischen und den freiheitlichen Wirtschaftsordnungen?" *Hamburger Jahrbuch für Wirtschafts- und Gesellschaftspolitik,* Vol. 8, Tübingen: J.C.B. Mohr (Paul Siebeck), 1963, pp. 11-20.

—, "Die Rolle der Planungstechniken bei einer Annäherung der Strukturen in Ost und West," in *Wirtschaftsplanung im Ostblock: Beginn einer Liberalisierung?* ed. Erik Boettcher, Stuttgart and Berlin: Verlag W. Kohlhammer, 1966, pp. 35-53.

Todenhöfer, Jürgen Gerhard, *Wachstum für alle: Plädoyer für eine Internationale Soziale Marktwirtschaft,* Stuttgart: Seewald Verlag, 1976.

Tödt, Heinz Eduard, "Die Ambivalenz des technischen Fortschritts als Thema christlicher Ethik," *Zeitschrift für Evangelische Ethik,* 25 (1981), pp. 18-29.

Trautwein, Hans-Michael, *Arbeitnehmerfonds in Schweden — der dritte Weg? Entwicklung und Kritik eines aktuellen Modells zur Demokratisierung der Wirtschaft,* Frankfurt am Main, Bern, and New York: Verlag Peter Lang, 1986.

Troy, Norbert, "Computergerechte oder menschengerechte Lösungen: Psychologische Probleme der Büroautomation," *Technologie und Kultur, psychosozial 18,* Vol. 6, Reinbek bei Hamburg: Rowohlt Taschenbuch Verlag, June 1983, pp. 51-69.

Tuchtfeldt, Egon, ed., *Soziale Marktwirtschaft im Wandel,* Freiburg im Breisgau: Verlag Rombach, 1973.

—, "Wirtschaftspolitik," in *Handwörterbuch der Wirtschaftswissenschaften,* Vol. 9, pp. 178-206.

—, "Wirtschaftssysteme," in *Handwörterbuch der Wirtschaftswissenschaften,* Vol. 9, pp. 326-53.

Tugendhat, Christopher, *The Multinationals,* London: Eyre & Spottiswoode, 1971.

Turner, Louis, "The Multinational Company: Some Social and Political Implications," *Journal of Business Policy,* 2 (1971), pp. 49-55.

Uhlig, Andreas, "Die unvollendete Revolution des 'Thatcherismus': Eine Bilanz nach zehn Jahren," *Neue Zürcher Zeitung,* No. 103, 6/7 May 1989, p. 33.

Ulich, Eberhard, "Alternative Arbeitsstrukturen — dargestellt am Beispiel der Automobilindustrie," *Psychologie und Praxis: Zeitschrift für Arbeits- und Organisationspsychologie,* 27 (1983), pp. 70-78.

—, "Arbeitspsychologische Konzepte und neue Technologien," in *Personalwirtschaftliche Aspekte neuer Technologien,* ed. Klaus J. Zink, Berlin: Erich Schmidt Verlag, 1985, pp. 135-59.

—, "Industrieroboter: Chance oder Gefahr für die Humanisierung der Arbeit?" in *Technologie und Kultur, psychosozial 18,* Vol. 6, Reinbek bei Hamburg: Rowohlt Taschenbuch Verlag, June 1983, pp. 109-24.

—, "Präventive Intervention im Betrieb: Vorgehensweisen zur Veränderung der Arbeitssituation," in *Präventive Intervention im Betrieb, psychosocial 20,* Vol. 6, Reinbek bei Hamburg: Rowohlt Taschenbuch Verlag, December 1983, pp. 48-70.

Ullrich, Otto, *Weltniveau: In der Sackgasse des Industriesystems,* Berlin: Rotbuch Verlag, 1979.

Ulrich, Hans Jürgen, "Automation ist nicht alles," *Schweizerische Handelszeitung,* No. 36, 5 September 1985, p. 69.

Ulrich, Peter, "Die sprachpragmatische Wendung der ökonomischen Rationalitätskonzeption als Grundlegung einer Ethik der Unternehmung," unpublished manuscript.

—, *Transformation der ökonomischen Vernunft: Fortschrittsperspektiven der modernen Industriegesellschaft,* Bern and Stuttgart: Verlag Paul Haupt, 1986.

Ulrich, Werner, "Zum Stand der schweizerischen Armutsforschung," *Neue Zürcher Zeitung,* No. 168, 22/23 July 1989, p. 21.

van der Ven, Frans, *Sozialgeschichte der Arbeit,* Vol. I, *Antike and Frühmittelalter,* Munich: Deutscher Taschenbuch Verlag, 1972.

Vilmar, Fritz and Karl-Otto Sattler, *Wirtschaftsdemokratie und Humanisierung der Arbeit: Systematische Integration der wichtigsten Konzepte,* Cologne and Frankfurt am Main: Europäische Verlagsanstalt, 1978.

Volpert, Walter, "Denkmaschinen und Maschinendenken: Computer programmieren Menschen," in *Technologie und Kultur, psychosozial 18,* Vol. 6, Reinbek bei Hamburg: Rowohlt Taschenbuch Verlag, June 1983, pp. 10-29.

Wädekin, K.-E., "Ungarns Landwirtschaft — ein Sonderfall in Osteuropa," *Neue Zürcher Zeitung,* No. 285, 7 December 1982, p. 23 and No. 286, 8 December 1982, p. 23.

Walter, Helmut, "Technischer Fortschritt, I: in der Volkswirtschaft," in *Handwörterbuch der Wirtschaftswissenschaften,* Vol. 7, pp. 569-83.

Weber, Alfred, "Sozialistische Marktwirtschaft," *Gewerkschaftliche Monatshefte,* 1 (1950), pp. 393-401.

Weber, Max, *The Protestant Ethic and the Spirit of Capitalism,* trans. Talcott Parsons, London: Harper Collins, 1930.

Weck-Hannemann, Hannelore, Werner W. Pommerehne, and Bruno S. Frey, *Die heimliche Wirtschaft: Struktur und Entwicklung der Schattenwirtschaft in der Schweiz,* Bern and Stuttgart: Verlag Paul Haupt, 1986.

Weinberger, Otto, "Kapital, I: Geschichte der Kapitaltheorie," in *Handwörterbuch der Sozialwissenschaften,* Vol. 5, pp. 480-88.

Weis, Josef, *Wirtschaftsunternehmen und Demokratie,* Cologne: Bund Verlag, 1970.

Weisser, Gerhard, *Beiträge zur Gesellschaftspolitik,* ed. Siegfried Katterle, Wolfgang Mudra, and Lothar F. Neumann, Göttingen: Verlag Otto Schwartz, 1978.

Wenke, Karl Ernst, ed., *Ökonomie und Ethik: Die Herausforderung der Arbeitslosigkeit*, Frankfurt am Main: Haag + Herchen Verlag, 1984.

Werner, Josua, "Beziehungen zwischen Beschäftigungspolitik und Arbeitslosigkeit," *Das Wirtschaftsstudium*, 5 (1985), pp. 255-59.

—, "Qualitatives Wachstum — was is das?" *Neue Zürcher Zeitung*, No. 13, 17/18 January 1987, pp. 17-18.

Willeke, Rainer J., "Marktformen," in *Handwörterbuch der Sozialwissenschaften*, Vol. 7, pp. 136-47.

Winiecki, Jan, "Ein 'Marshall-Plan' für Osteuropa?" *Neue Zürcher Zeitung*, No. 277, 26/27 November 1988, p. 95.

Woll, Artur, *Allgemeine Volkswirtschaftslehre*, 7th Ed., Munich: Verlag Franz Vahlen, 1981.

World Bank, *World Development Report, 1981*, Washington, 1981.

—, *World Development Report, 1985*, Washington, 1985.

—, *World Debt Tables, 1987-88*, Washington, 1988.

Wünsch, Georg, *Evangelische Wirtschaftsethik*, Tübingen: J.C.B. Mohr (Paul Siebeck), 1927.

Zinn, Karl Georg, with Norbert Wieczorek, *Wirtschaftszusammenhänge verständlich lehren*, Munich, Berlin, and Vienna: Urban und Schwarzenberg, 1976.

Zwass, Adam, "Gorbatschews Reform im Rahmen des Systems," *Neue Zürcher Zeitung*, No. 20, 26 January 1988, p. 39.

INDEX OF NAME

Abbing, P. J. Roscam, 411
Adorno, 81
Albert, Hans, 84-85, 88, 90, 95, 429
Althaus, Paul, 138
Antonin of Florence, 337
Apel, Karl-Otto, 429
Appelrath, Hans-Jürgen, 322
Aristotle, 11, 20, 45, 200, 237, 293, 530
Artisien, Patrick F. R., 367

Balkhausen, Dieter, 304
Bänziger, Andreas, 419
Barth, Karl, 133-139, 144-159, 161f., 164
Barz, Helmut, 54
Basaglia, Franco, 46
Batel, W., 303
Bayer Oswald, 173
Behrman, Jack N., 370
Bellegarrigue, A., 215
Bentham, Jeremy, 208
Berdyayev, Nikolai, 41, 60, 173
Berg, Curt, 313
Bergier, Jean-François, 302
Bernardin of Siena, 337
Bernheim, Roger, 593
Beyeler-von Burg, Hélène, 284
Biedenkopf, Kurt H., 365
Biel, Jörn, 363, 366f.
Bielinski, Erwin, 361
Binswanger, Hans Christoph, 74, 292, 333, 376f., 380-383, 405, 407, 417, 424-425, 429, 529, 579-587, 588, 607, 611
Bloch, Ernst, 100, 178
Biró, Gerd, 512
Blaich, Fritz, 351
Blanc, Louis, 284, 531
Bloch Snyderman, Barbara, 311
Blum, Reinhard, 543
Blumhardt, Christoph, 129
Bodmer, Walter, 318, 320
Bock, Martin, 162
Boelcke, Willi Alfred, 537
Bog, Ingomar, 527
Bohnet, Armin, 513
Bonhoeffer, Dietrich, 57, 171, 274
Bonus, Holger, 383, 425, 588
Borner, Silvio, 299, 349
Bornschier, Volker, 364-365, 367
Bowman, John Wick, 127
Brakelmann, Günter, 128, 281, 536
Brentano, Lujo, 270-271
Breschnev, L.W., 486
Brödner, Peter, 326
Brouwer, L. E. J., 367
Brunner, Emil, 27, 107, 118, 139, 141-148, 152f., 155, 160, 199-201, 277
Brunstäd, Friedrich, 138
Buber Martin, 39, 140
Buckley, Peter J., 367
Bultmann, Rudolf, 113, 165
Burckhardt, Jacob, 214

Callies, Rolf-Peter, 60
Camus, Albert, 100, 175
Carell, Erich, 332f.
Carey, Henry Charles, 332
Clark, John Bates, 332
Claussen, Ulf, 284

Conze, Werner, 279, 287, 306
Conzelmann, Hans, 113
Csikós-Nagy, Béla, 555, 562

Daheim Hansjürgen, 51
Dannemann, Ulrich, 130, 137
Delling, Gerhard, 165
Descartes, 44
Dopfer, Kurt, 469
Dostoyevski, 179
Drucker, Peter F., 68
Drechsler, Wolfgang, 409
Dreyfus, Hubert L., 322f.
Dreyfus, Stuart E., 322f.
Drucker, Peter F., 311
Dubs, Rolf, 512
Dürr, Ernst, 635
Dunkel, Arthur, 622
Durovic, Dragoljub, 511-512

Ebel, Marianne, 188
Ebeling, Gerhard, 87, 94, 103, 109, 242
Ebner, Ferdinand, 39, 141
Eggebrecht, Arne, 277
Egner, Erich, 350
Einstein, Albert, 227
Eltert, Werner, 138
Elizabeth of Thuringia, 18
Enderle, Georges, 284, 395, 413f., 416, 430
Engels, Friedrich, 18, 51, 111, 274, 279, 302, 337, 464-467, 472, 591
Erbrich, Paul, 530
Eucken, Walter, 437f., 537, 555, 562, 621
Eugster-Züst, Howard, 129
Evers, Ingo, 453
Expertenkommission des Eidgenössischen Volkswirtschaftsdepartements, 583

Feigenbaum, Edward A., 321f.
Feyerabend, Paul, 88
Fiala, Pierre, 188
Fichte, Johann Gottlieb, 12
Fletcher, Joseph, 29f.
Frankena, William K., 21
Francis of Assisi, 18
Frey, Bruno S., 368, 415
Frey, Christofer, 33, 166, 200
Frey, René L., 353, 379, 426, 436, 444, 458f.
Friedrich, Gerhard, 182, 235
Fries, Friedrich, 90
Fritsch, Bruno, 69
Fritzsche, H.-G., 235
Friebe, K., 318
Friedmann, Georges, 309-311
Friedman, Milton, 456, 533-535
Friedrich, Jürgen, 326
Friedrichs, Günter, 326
Fritsch, Bruno, 374
Fromm, Erich, 54, 58, 104
Fürer, Arthur, 366
Fürstenberg, Friedrich, 51
Furger, Alex R., 306

Gadó, O., 512
Galbraith, John Kenneth, 336, 347, 369, 498-502
Gans, Oskar, 453
Gardawsky, 120
Gasser, Christian, 347
Gasser, Thomas P., 365
Gauderon, E., 325
Geiger, Max, 130
Geissberger, Werner, 74
Geissler, Heiner, 413
George, Susan, 629
Giersch, Herbert, 68
Gimpel, Jean, 303
Ginsburg, Theo, 74
Goethe, Johann Wolfgang, 102
Gogol, Nikolay, 14
Gorz, André, 72, 112
Grosser, Alfred, 187
Gerster, Richard, 622f., 634

Gorbatchev, Mikhail, 485, 507-512, 559
Graf, Gerhard, 391
Gröner, Helmut, 446
Groskurth, Peter, 279
Gutenberg, Erich, 330

Habermas, Jürgen, 82f.
Häfeli, Kurt, 279
Hafner, Pius, 289
Hamann, J. G., 173
Häring, Bernhard, 26
Hartmann, Fanny, 306
von Hayek, Friedrich A., 485, 555, 562, 568
Hedborg, Anna, 545, 546f., 550
Hedtkamp, Günter, 506
Hegel, Georg Wilhelm Friedrich, 80-81, 111
Heiner, Volker, 320
Heinrich, Walter, 474
Hempel, Johannes, 198
Henrichsmeyer, Wilhelm, 453, 457
Hensel, K. Paul, 72, 353, 436-439, 442, 454, 456, 458f., 475f., 478f.
Herder, 102
Herrhausen, Alfred, 630
Herzberg, Friedrich, 311
Herzog, Jesus Silva, 626
Hesse, Helmut, 208, 303, 640
Heuss, Ernst, 449, 456, 537
Hilger, Dietrich, 301f.
Hilger, Marie-Elisabeth, 337-340, 531
Hirsch, Fred, 531f., 535
Hitler, Adolf, 152
Hobbes, Thomas, 272
Hofmann, Daniel, 629
Hoffmann, Lutz, 416-418
Hoffmann, Walther, 303
Höffe, Otfried, 35, 193, 197, 204, 209f., 218, 223
Höhn, Rudolf, 106
Hofmann, Rudolf, 240
Höhmann, Hans-Hermann, 507f.
Holler, Manfred, 401
Hölscher, Lucian, 301
Holz, Hans Heinz, 138
Honecker, Martin, 71, 122, 126, 129, 167f., 274, 421, 649
Horkheimer, 81
Hörmann, Otto, 482
Horst, Friedrich, 172
Huber, Gerhard, 117, 122
Huber, Joseph, 385
Huber, Wolfgang, 59f., 126, 184f., 185

Jäger, Alfred, 417, 424f., 429, 625, 640
Jöhr, Walter Adolf, 277, 405, 438, 446, 501
Jonas, Hans, 33, 58f. 126
Jung, C. G., 54

Käsemann, Ernst, 105, 128, 165, 179
Kaiser, Helmut, 71, 399, 431
Kant, Immanuel, 12, 20, 24, 30f., 36, 55, 102, 165, 205, 222, 400
Kapp, K. William 399
Kardeli, Edvard, 512
Karrenberg, Friedrich, 71, 74
Kaser, Michael, 481, 484
Katterle, Siegfried, 68, 88, 91, 126-128, 519f., 536, 541, 599, 602f., 620
Kaufmann Franz-Xaver, 493
Keynes, John Maynard, 391, 438, 532f., 535, 599
Kierkegaard, 39, 138
Kinsey, Alfred C., 22
Kittel, Gerhard, 120
Kleinewefers, Henner, 22, 356f., 437f., 441, 448, 449, 453, 456, 484, 506, 509, 559-561, 563f., 572, 574, 603, 606f.
Kliemt, Hartmut, 271

Klotz, Ulrich, 322
Kluge, Friedrich, 43, 118
Kolakowski, Leszek, 163, 175
Koller, Peter, 213
Kohn, Melvin Lester, 279
Komarov, Boris, 483
Koopmann, Georg, 367
Korff, Wilhelm, 517
Koslowski, Peter, 269
Kosta, Jirí, 506
Koubek, Norbert, 317
Kraft, Ueli, 279
Kraus, Willy, 512
Kreck, Walter, 164
Krelle, Wilhelm, 517, 551
Kriton, 13f
Kriz, Jirí, 322
Krüger, Detlef, 326
Krupp, Hans-Jürgen, 404
Kubicek, H., 326
Kümmel, Werner Georg, 127
Küng, Guido, 205
Küng, Hans, 114
Künneth, Walter, 138
Kutter, Hermann, 130-134, 137, 139
Külp, Bernhard, 333, 339, 355
Küng, Emil, 273, 285, 361, 381

Lafontaine, Oskar, 287
Lamberg, Robert F., 553
de Lange, Harry M., 218, 384
Landmann, Michael, 287, 290
Langer, Gerd, 370
Lassalle, Ferdinand, 75
Lattmann, Charles, 51, 279, 311
Lefringhausen, Klaus, 622
Leibniz, 301
Leipold, Helmut, 437f., 461, 469, 473-476, 479f., 506, 528
Lemân, Gudrun, 511
Lenin, 467-469, 473, 485f., 508
Leontjef, Wassiliy, 318, 500
Leu, Robert E., 395, 426
Levinas, Emmanuel, 39
Lindt, Andreas, 130
Link, Christian, 223
Locher, Gottfried W., 235, 608
Lochman, Jan Milič, 80, 175
Löwith, Karl, 83
Løgstrup, Knud E., 138, 495
Lorenz, Konrad, 11
Ludewig, Jochen, 383
Luther, Martin, 145, 154, 184, 236f
Lüthi, Ambros, 416
Lutz, Friedrich A., 69

Machoveč, 120
Männer, Leonhard, 337
Malthus, 391
Mandeville, Bernard, 496
Mann, Fritz Karl, 331
Marcuse, Herbert, 82, 178
Marer, Paul, 512
Markl, Hubert, 421, 423
Marquardt, Friedrich-Wilhelm, 130
Marx, Karl, 18, 46, 51, 53f., 75, 82, 107f., 110-112, 173-175, 184, 274f., 279, 283, 295, 334, 339f., 345f., 378f., 402f., 409f., 439, 458, 463-467, 472, 528, 591
Matthias, E., 320
Mattmüller, Markus, 130
Mausner, Bernard, 311
Maximov, Vladimir, 116
Mazurczak, Barbo, 313
Meadows, Dennis, 58, 287, 372
Meidner, Rudolf, 545-551
Mesarovic, Mihailo, 58
Mey, Hansjürg, 314f., 328
Mey, Harald, 512
Meyer-Abich, Klaus Michael, 379, 385
Michalet, Charles-Albert, 366, 367, 371
Mieth, Dietmar, 280

Mill, John Stuart, 208, 429, 431
Mittelstrass, Jürgen, 269, 430, 433
Mollat, Michel, 413
Moltmann, Jürgen, 118, 159f.
Moore, George Edward, 23
More, Thomas, 284
Morelly, 284
Mostert, Walter, 106, 121
Mounier, Emanuel, 60
Müller-Armack, Alfred, 536-545, 602
Müller-Jentsch, Walther, 321
Mugglin, Markus, 627-630
Muqiao, Xue, 411, 512
Myrdal, Gunnar, 429

National Conference of Catholic Bishops, 285
Negt, Oskar, 404
von Nell-Breuning, Oswald, 238, 407, 529, 530
Nemitz, Kurt, 554-557, 558
Niebuhr, Reinhold, 65
Nietzsche, Friedrich, 175
Nienhaus, Volker, 436, 517
Noth, Martin, 233
Nutzinger, Hans G., 482
Nydegger, Alfred, 587, 636

Oldham, Joseph H., 222-223
Oplatka, Andreas, 320
von Oppen, Dietrich, 60
Orwell, George, 196
Ott, Alfred Eugen, 356
Ott, Walter, 211
van Oyen, Hendrik, 234

Pankow, Wladimir, 486
Pascal, 316, 491, 497
Pascal, Blaise, 12, 31, 80, 87, 173, 188
Pechan, Hermann, 284
Pedersen, Jørgen, 495
Pelagius, Alvarus, 239
Pestalozzi, Heinrich, 18, 120, 141
Pestel, Eduard, 58
Peter, Hans-Balz, 106
Peters, Hans-Rudolf, 273
Peters, Thomas J., 311
Pfeiffer, Arnold, 131
Pfister, Regula, 356
Pfürtner, Stephan, H., 60
Pirenne, Henri, 237
Pius XII., 26
Pilz, Frank, 533f., 536
Plato, 13, 131
Plessner, Helmuth, 39
Pöhlmann, Horst Georg, 29, 150
Popper, Karl R., 67, 91
Portmann, Adolf, 139
Pommerehne, Werner W., 415
Popkowa, L., 511
Preiser, Erich, 341
Prosi, Gerhard, 363, 366f.
Pross, Helge, 440

Quesnay, François, 331, 338

von Rad, Gerhard, 176, 190, 192
Radig, Bernd, 322
Ragaz, Christine, 130
Ragaz, Leonhard, 130-133, 139, 146, 153, 159
Rahner, Karl, 118
Ramm, Thilo, 287
Ramp, Ernst, 228, 229, 237
Rathenau, Walther, 466
Rawls, John, 93, 204-217, 415
Recktenwald, Horst Claus, 492f., 496
Rendtorff, Trutz, 34, 184
Rengstorf, Karl Heinrich, 183
Reuss, Wilhelm, 558
Ricardo, David, 269, 334, 340, 407, 620,
Rich, Arthur, 270, 279, 399f., 647
Rich, Georg, 457
Riesman, David, 41

Riklin, Alois, 496
Roloff, Jürgen, 195
Rother, Siegfried, 228
Rousseau, Jean-Jacques, 205
Rossier, Jacques A., 365
Roth, Hans-Erich, 593
Rothschild, Kurt W., 440
Ruffmann, Karl-Heinz, 513
Ruh, Hans, 106, 212, 415
Rumpf, Max, 307
Rusinow, Dennison, 512
Russell, Bertrand, 227
Rüstow, Alexander, 182, 536

Saint-Simon, 284, 287
Samuelson, Paul A., 300, 354f., 389, 447, 518, 551, 577
Sanders, Hermann, 416-418
Sartre, Jean-Paul, 28
Sattler, Karl-Otto, 545
Sautter, Hermann, 492, 495, 503, 634-636
Say, Jean Baptiste, 330, 391
Schachtschabel, Hans G., 439, 514, 518
Schaff, Adam, 326
Schallberger, Urs, 279
Schefold, Bertram, 385
Schelhammer, Carlo, 360
Schillebeeckx, Edward, 39, 46, 199
Schiller, Karl, 541, 566
Schlecht, Otto, 460, 619, 632
Schlier, Heinrich, 183
Schlögel, Karl, 481
Schmauch, Werner, 162
Schmeljov, Nikolai, 511
Schmid, Heinrich, 228
Schneider, Helmut, 299
Schneider, Johannes, 177
Schönfeld, Roland, 512
Schönwitz, Dietrich, 506
Schrage, Wolfgang, 195
Schulz, Walter, 222
Schulze, Hans, 44f., 61, 167, 236
Schulze, Thea, 44, 237, 61
Schumacher, E. F., 74
Schumpeter, Joseph A., 339, 346, 429, 465
Schwamm, H., 370
Schwarz, Peter, 392
Schweitzer, Albert, 126f., 139
Schweizer, Eduard, 115, 195
Seiwert, Lothar, 313
Sellien, R. and H., 208
Senf, Bernd, 326
Shaull, Richard, 156-159
Sietz, Hennig, 511
Šik, Ota, 409, 436, 450, 463f., 466-468, 472, 475-480, 484f., 504, 506, 512, 515-517, 518, 565-578, 606-608, 611
Simonis, Udo Ernst, 581, 586
Sindjit, M., 512
Smith, Adam, 269f., 278f., 283f., 334, 338f., 340, 348, 352, 359, 366, 382, 429f., 445-447, 453, 492-496, 533, 620
Socrates, 11, 13
von Soden, Julius Graf, 527
Sohmen, Egon, 209
Sölle, Dorothee, 109
Solomon, Anthony, 630
Sonderegger, Alfons, 406
Specker, Louis, 129
Stachanov, A. G., 478
Stalin, 468, 473, 486, 508
Stamm, Johann Jakob, 233
Steck, Odil Hannes, 191f.
Steiger, Alois, 380
Steinmüller, Wilhelm, 304
Stolz, Peter, 288, 397
Storm, Theodor, 32
Strohm, Theodor, 406, 638
Stückelberger, Christoph, 371
Stützel, Wolfgang, 536
Sydow, H., 321

Szabó-Raduczíner, Zsuzsa, 554f., 559, 564

Thatcher, Margaret, 593f.
Theunissen, Michael, 83
Thielicke, Helmut, 232
Tillich, Paul, 120, 166
Timmermann, Manfred, 383, 425, 588
Timpe, K.-P., 321
Tinbergen, Jan, 498-502
Tinguely, 323
Todenhöfer, Jürgen Gerhard, 396f.
Tödt, Heinz Eduard, 222f., 290
Toynbee, Arnold, 302
Trautwein, Hans-Michael, 545f., 551
Troy, Norbert, 323-325
Tuchtfeld, Egon, 383, 436, 440f., 445, 500, 502, 536, 542
Tugendhat, Christopher, 362-364, 367-369
Tugendhat, Ernst, 205
Tully, Claus J., 401
Turner, Louis, 363

Uhlig, Andreas, 593
Ulich, Eberhard, 51, 310, 311-313, 320f., 322-325
Ullrich, Otto, 301
Ulrich, Hans Jürgen, 324
Ulrich, Peter, 399, 429-434
Ulrich, Werner, 395

van der Ven, Frans, 281
Vilmar, Fritz, 545
Visser't Hooft, Willem A., 223
de Vogue, Arnaud, 368
Volpert, Walter, 326
Voslensky, Michael, 108

Wädekin, H.-E., 560
Walter, Helmut, 330
Walther, Christian, 130, 188
Wansleben, Martin, 409
Waterman, Robert H., 311
Watrin, Christian, 205
Weber, Alfred, 554f.
Weber, Hartmut, 231
Weber, Max, 32f., 67f., 89, 292
Weck-Hannemann, Hannelore, 415
Weinberger, Otto, 337
Weinstock, Heinrich, 175
Weis, Josef, 333
Weiss, Konrad, 165
Weisser, Gerhard, 69, 88-94, 167, 204, 211, 216-221, 269, 282, 429
Wendland, Heinz-Dietrich, 61, 166, 194f.
Wenke, Karl Ernst, 407
Werner, Josua, 381, 404
Westmüller, Horst, 127
Wettstein, Harri, 214f.
Wicke, Friedrich, 326
Wicke, Walter, 326
Wildberger, Hans, 170f.
Willeke, Rainer J., 355
Wilken, Folkert, 68
Winiecki, Jan, 512
Winter, Gibson, 67
Wogaman, John Philip, 76
Wolf, Erik, 228
Wolf, Ernst, 162
Woll, Arthur, 331, 339
Wünsch, Georg, 31, 532, 647

Yiming, Guo, 418

Zinn, Karl Georg, 334
Zwass, Adam, 483, 510
Zwingli, Huldrych, 14, 137, 145, 228f., 241

INDEX OF SUBJECT

Abbreviations:

H	Humanity originating from faith, hope, love
E	Economy
ME	Market economy
CPE	Centrally planned economy
CME	Capitalistic market economy
SME	Social market economy
DME	Democratic market economy
SstME	Socialist market economy
HRME	Humanly reformed market economy
ERME	Ecologically regulated market economy

absolutizing values, 291f.
by capital interests, 293, 530, 598
liberal values, 461f.
socialist values, 486f.
account balances of macroeconomic planning, 437
methodology, 475f.
adaptation, resigned, 648
allocation, 369, 389, 392, 436f., 443f., 455, 612
altruism, altruist, 24, 56, 190, 447, 490, 493, 496
analogy according to Barth (concept), 148
analogia entis, relationis, fidei, 149
anarchism, 45f., 49
artificial intelligence, 321 (esp. n. 64)
automatic system, 314; *see also* division of labor
"autonomy" of the economy, 75
basic relationships
I-Self, 38
I-Thou, 39ff.
I/We-It, 41, 44
basic values
liberal 294, 296; 462 and 496 (absolutized)
socialist, 294, 296; 462 and 486f. (absolutized)
relationality of, 428
business and economic ethics, 61f., 224
concept, 645

CAD (computer aided design), 319
CAM (computer aided manufacturing), 319
CAP (computer aided planning), 319
capital, 337-340
as investment, 338f.
as materialized labor, 340
as means of production, 338f., 393, 471, 527
as production relationship, 340
human, 340-405
neutralized, 571-573; compatible with ME, 577
physical, 338
capital flight, 622, 642
capitalism, 68, 73, 178, 292, 526-536
industrial, 377- 379, 381; involves force to growth, 529
organized (Keynesianism), 532
deregulated, 599; not acceptable by H, 600
capitalist(s), 345, 346
centrally planned economy (CPE), 178, 203, 463-487

basic principle, 469f.
conceptual clarifications (not equal to socialism), 463f.
coordination system: basic principle, 469f.; dilemma, 476
in Marxism-Leninism, 463-468
in Stalinism (USSR/GDR-System), 468ff., 469 n. 90
limitations, 483-486
market modification, 505-513
relativization, 521f.
unable to be reformed, 510f., 522
CIM (computer integrated manufacturing), 320
CNC (computerized numerical control)-machines, 278, 319f., 324
code of conduct (for multinational corporations), 370
co-determination, 196, 198, 543, 572, 601
cognitivism (naturalist and intuitionist), 20, 36
collective ownership
cooperative, 471
state, 470
collectivism, 41f.
combining market and plan
according to Šik, 565
neither mere mixing nor synthesis, 504, 521
SME, 540
SstME/east, 562f.
SstME/west, 555
two possibilities, 505
COMECON (Council for Mutual Economic Assistance), 361, 365, 561
common good, 25, 208
communal life of the early-Christian parish, 195
communism, 110f.
community of property, early-Christian, 195
competition, 72ff.
economic-darwinistic, 645
imperfect, definition, 447
monopolistic, 358, 449
of performance, 646
perfect, 349f., 357, 442f.; definition 447 n. 128
predatory, 577f., 646
concerted efforts, 566
conformism, 162, 178
conscience, 12, 15, 30, 31, 122
consumer loans, 235
convergence (theory)
according to Galbraith, 500
according to Tinbergen, 502
demarcation from the principle of relativity, 503ff.
of the basic economic systems, 498-503
cooperation
basic assumption of the industrial economy, 402
confrontational, 402f.; in the international market order, 631
participative, 402; in the international market order, 631
cooperative companies, 574, 471, 571, 574, 605f.
in USSR, 486 n. 133
cooperatives/collaborative business organizations, 572- 574
corporativism, 438, 519f., 615
creation faith, 171, 173
creatureliness, 189, 191-193
criteria
absolute orientation point of all social-ethical judgment-formation and decision-making, 167
of prescriptive character, 96

principal determination of human justice, 96
second level of social-ethical argumentation, 103
voluntary, prescriptive "ought" propositions, 223
criteria of humanity
creatureliness, 275, 280f., 607, 610
critical distance, 296f., 597
fellow-creatureliness, 289, 420, 423f., 596f.
fellow-humanness, 285, 400, 595
participation, 285, 402-420, 595, 610
relative reception, 297, 462, 597
relationality, 427-429; of basic values, 461, 596; of the basic principles of ME and CPE, 503; of the humanly just and the social-scientifically correct, 429-434; of social and capital interests, 605
critical rationalism, 83-88, 94
critical theory, 80-83, 94
critique, absolute, 179
culture/cultivation, 43ff., 47
customs, habits, legality, 17, 18

Decalogue, 233, 234, 236, 236f., 237
decision, 28, 32, 225, 225
decisionism, 28f., 35
demand
absolute, 12, 14, 24, 26, 27
merely limited, 12, 97
developing countries (Third World), 368, 369, 396, 423f., 619-640, 641-643
development strategies
dissociative, 417f., 419
associative-export-oriented, 418f., 419
deregulation (of ME), 355, 533, 542
justified, 599
diastase of economics and ethics 430
distribution of income, 224
distribution of wealth, 224
distribution problem (of fundamental importance), 603
in the ME, 458ff.
in the CPE, 478-482
in the SME, 604
in the DME, 604f.
in the HRME, 605f.
confrontational (of the productive capital), 408f.
participative: of income, 408-413; of labor, 404-407; of productive capital, 408f.
distributive justice, 282, 397, 459
division of labor, 278f., 306-317
product-oriented, 305, 306-308
production-oriented, 305, 314-317, 326
mechanically-aided, 308-310
electronically-aided, 314-317
location-oriented305, 359f.
international, 359, 416
DNC (distributed numerical control), 319
dogmatism
epistemological, 84, 90
ethical, 34, 91, 93
religious, 87

EC (European Community), European internal market, 360, 638ff.
economic theory, 429
(neo)classical, 376, 429f., 442, 538, 567, 577ff., 581, 599
(post-)Keynesian, 376, 579, 581, 599

(neo-)Marxist, 376
economism/economistic, 269, 280, 430
eco-national product cost calculation, 586
economic growth, 284
as purpose of the economy, 376
exponential, 74
qualitative, 47f., 380-384, 424; concept, 382 n. 202
quantitative, 380-384; concept, 380
speeded up, 218
stimuli, 371-377
economic order, as distinct from economic system, 435f.
economic policy (of government), 455, 540
both neoclassical and Keynesian lack sensibility regarding environmental problems, 581
definition, 514 n. 65
demand-oriented, 532f.
supply-oriented, 534, 599
economic subjects, 342-355, 212f.
consumers, 348-351
producers, 342-348
state, 351-355
economic system, as distinct from economic order, 435f.
"economism", 218
economy (E), 277f.;
definition, 299
theories of economic systems, 436-439
ecosystem
instable, 581
vulnerable, 393
effects, external, 399, 445, 456, 591
efficiency, economic, 278, 300; definition, 392n. 4, 394
condition of the economy's service to life, 398f., 399
aspect of economic rationality, 399, 590
of the entire economy as distinct from maximization of individual economic profits, 590f.
higher in ME than in countries characterized by governmental intervention, 634
egoism, 54, 56, 190, 491, 492f., 535
entrepreneur
in collaborative companies, 574
manager, 328, 346f., 347
owner, 327, 345f., 347
environment, 42, 44, 57f.
environmental destruction, 47, 74
equality, 187, 199ff,
eschatology, 83, 125-129, 126f.
ethics, 11f, 32, 36, 134, 240
analytical, meta, 19f., 67
business and economic, 61f., 224, 645
casuistic, 25ff.
Christian, 240f.
deontological, 24
descriptive, 17f.
empiricist, 21f.
environmental, 57f.
individual, 53f.
norm or principle, 23ff.
normative, 19f.
of conviction, 30f.
of responsibility, 31ff.
personal, 55f.
situation, 27ff.
social, *see* social ethics
utilitarian, 24
ethical skepticism/relativism, 94, 227
ethology, 17
ethos, 11, 13

evil, 102-109, 111
  dialectic of personal and structural evil, 109, 177
  fundamental, 109
  identical with monological existence, 177
  personal, 105f., 146f., 647
  radical, 102, 109
  structural, 105, 106ff., 145f, 177, 647f.
  see also sin
existence
  dialogical, 56, 101
  monological/monocratic, 56, 176
experience-certitude, 92, 94, 99, 101, 121, 122, 167, 221, 225
exploitation
  of humans by humans, 287, 348
  of nature by humans, 287f.
extremism/extremization, 185, 187; *see also* radicalness

factors of production
  capital, 333-337, 579
  entrepreneurial performance (depending upon "know how"), 327f., 336
  generally, 307, 329f.
  labor, 333-337, 579
  land/nature, 331-333, 580
factual constraints, 22, 46, 71, 73, 399, 646f.
factual/objective necessity in the economy, 400, 646f.
FAO (Food and Agriculture Organization), 360, 639
FAS (flexible assembling system), 319f.
faith, 99f., 113, 115, 169
fellow-creatureliness, 191-193f.
fellow-humanness, 189f., 211
FFS/FMS (flexible manufacturing system), 319
force, use of, 138
free trade, 360, 620, 633
freedom, 18, 202, 213
  absolute, 184, 213
  Christian, 184
  economic, 214
  existentialist, 28
  independence and emancipating self-realization, 184
freedom, economic, 461, 486, 490
  according to Friedman, 535
  according to Marx, 464
  according to Smith (not absolute), 495
future in the sense of "adventus" and "futurum", 118, 157, 177

GATT (General Agreement on Tariffs and Trade), 360, 639
global economy, 416-420, 619-641
  confrontational, 416
  participative, 420f., 625-633, 641
good, radical, 109
goods
  free, 299, 380
  scarce, 299, 380
  natural (environmental), 393f., 583, 585
  material, 393
government expenditure ration
  definition, 354 n. 137
Gross Domestic Product (GDP)
  definition, 364

homo conservator, 191
homo faber, 191, 197
homo oeconomicus, 22, 271, 430, 447, 497
hope, 100, 117
human justice, the humanly just ("menschengerecht")
  aiming into the subject matter, 274

as formal and material category, 77
based in humanity, 400
based on certitude of conviction, 80
basis of, 169
guiding principle of social ethics, 67
impossible to ground it in universally-valid rationality, 93
includes the environmentally just, 393, 421, 651
its relationship to economic rationality, 70, 75
relational to the social-scientifically correct, 313, 393, 433f., 506
which obligates everyone, 128
see also humanity
human relations, 310
human rights, 77f., 79, 94
humanism, absolute, 174
humanity originating from faith, hope, love (H), 55, 99f., 116-121, 149, 275, 294, 387, 397
accepts value-basis of ME only relatively, 462f., 520
accepts value-basis of CPE only relatively, 486, 520
cannot accept deregulated CME, 600f.
opts for regulated ME, 599
sides with the poorest, 643

IBRD (World Bank), 360, 639
IMF (International Monetary Fund), 360, 639
imperative, categorical, 11
in Kant, 55
in Marx, 108
in Paul, 121
of love, 181
in the image of God, 171, 199
individualism, 41, 191
individuality, 38, 40
indebtedness / debt service (of developing countries), 418f.
creative reimbursement, 629 n. 34
financial component, 626f.
problems of debt relief, 627-631
unbearable, 621ff.,625
industry / industrialization, 301-304, 372,
double face, 384-387
presupposed collaboration, 402
industrial robots, 318f., 321
input-output-analysis, 500
institution / institutionalization, 45, 45f., 48, 49
effect of, 46-52
institutions of creation
according to E. Brunner, 140-146
of nature, 45
interdependence,
globally, 641f.
in national economies, 620f.
interest(s)
profit-: motivates to doing business efficiently, 527
individual (self-): according to Smith, 492; optimizes general interest, 441, 490; relational to collective interest, 601
collective (general): optimizes individual interest, 470, 490; relational to individual interest, 601
interests of capital formation, 403
indispensable for economy, 547, 578
interim ethics, 139, 144
intuitionism, 20, 67; *see also* cognitivism
invisible hand, 492, 494, 533

irreconcilability theory regarding
market and planning, 555, 562

Jesus/Christ, 101, 113, 169, 175, 181, 190f.
joint ventures, 418, 512
justice
commutative, 200
distributive, 200
divine (absolute), 129, 228, 236
needs, 459
performance, 459
social, 111, 163, 198-204, 228, 229

Keynesianism, 456, 533f., 599
kingdom of God (eschaton, ultimate), 114, 128, 130, 163, 297, 432; *see also* eschatology
not futuristic-utopian but advent-like future, 649
the whole of humanity, 497

labor
as means of production, 336, 393
as necessity, 280f.
as subject of production, 333
as uplifting work, 280f.
obligation to work, 235, 239
precedence over capital, 341
rationalization of, 51
right to work, 240
see also work
labor market, 358, 367, 458f.
labor productivity, 278, 375
labor theory of value 334; 407 n. 39
laissez-faire (principle), 352, 531, 637
laws of nature (invariable), 70f.
law of the Bible, 140
legality/lawfulness, 12
civic, 14
ethical, 24, 231
liberalism, liberal 272, 537, 542
economic, 519
libertarian, 531, 533, 592, 600
Manchester, 496
neo, 537
old form of, 537
Ordo, 537
value based, 296, 486
love, 29, 100, 119f., 122, 164, 165f., 166, 194f., 199, 200f., 214, 215, 240
compassionate pity, 119
erotic devotion, 40, 119
friendly affection, 119
quintessence of human justice, 433
the whole of humanity, 294
see also humanity

magic triangle, 425f., 508
new (Binswanger), 425
old, 425
mammon, 293
management (technostructure), 328, 346f., 499f.
according to Šik, 574
marginal costs, 444f.
marginal utility (theory), 431
market/markets, 355-359;
black in USSR, 486
concept, 355
differentiations, 358
forms, 356f.
market domination, 354, 366, 451
market economy (ME), 202, 216, 439-461, 520-523
general:
basic principle, 441f., 461, 469, 490
concept, 440 (not equal to capitalism)

deregulated, 637
limitations, 445ff., 455-461
plan-modified, 513-520; ME is no principal opposite to planning, 513
pure, 444; utopia, 461
real, 446-451
regulated, 598f., 611, 613
relativization, 461f.
system of coordination: competition, 441-446; dilemma, 452-455, 476
order forms:
capitalistic (CME), 225, 528-536, 590-594; not acceptable by H, 600
democratic (DME), 545-553; solidarity-based pay policy, 546; egalitarian fiscal policy, 547f.; worker funds, 549-553
ecologically regulated (ERM), 579-589; combination of market and planning, 583; ownership reform, 584; eco-national product cost calculation, 586
humanly reformed (HRME), 565-578; combination of market and planning, 566; macroeconomic planning of distribution, 566; reform of ownership, 570-575
social (SME), 225, 536-545; concept/basic structure, 536; ME instrumental, 539; social achievements and deficiencies, 543; acceptable by H, 600, 617; need for further development, 602, 618
socialist (SstME), 217, 439, 512, 518
western, 554-559; combination of market and planning, 555; minimal planning, 556f.; conception of ownership, 557 f.
eastern (Hungary), 559-565; reforms, 559; contradictory combination of market and planning, 562f.; most recent reform drive, 564f.
market system (according to Galbraith), 498
maximalism
moralistic, 129
social-political, 163
utopian, 178
maxims, 298, 434, 523f., 597f., 611
concept, 489
conceptual differentiation of the maxim concept of Kant and Walter Schulz, and the "middle axioms" of J. H. Oldham, 222
distinction between general and tentative-pragmatic, 230
in the Bible, 233-240
of prescriptive and explicative structure, 66, 95, 197
regarding the global order of the economy, 641-644
regarding the question of the economic order, 612-618
regarding the question of the economic system, 520-523
relative, yet related to the absolute, 227f.
their relativity includes claim to validity, 227
they must be humanly just and social-scientifically correct, 226f.
third level of social-ethical argumentation, 168f.
volitionally and cognitively oriented, 221f.
maximization
of economic growth and increase of well-being, 287

of national product, 285, 377
of profit, 292, 377; limitations, 445, 451, 528
of wage and social demands,409, 578
special characteristic of capitalism, 529, 578
Meadows report (Club of Rome), 287
means of production
non-produced (land / labor), 340
produced (capital), 341, 377
mercantilism, 351f.
metaethics, 19; *see also* ethics
monetarism, 456, 534, 592
monopoly(ies), 357f., 366, 447-451, 451f.
macro-, 450f.
micro-, 449
moral, 28, 28, 31
moral statistics, 22
morality, 12
multinational corporations, 361-371
definition, 361 n. 151

natural law, idea of natural law, 78ff., 81
naturalistic fallacy, 20, 23
national product, 369, 375
definition, 353 n. 135
distribution, 407ff.
need, needs, 349f., 390, 475
individual, 390
collective, 390, 444
of the environment, 581f.
neoliberalism, *see* liberalism
New Economic Policy (NEP), 467, 508
networks
small, 589
social, 412, 565
nihilism, social-political, 129, 176
noncognitivism, 20, 36
normativeness of the factual, 22
norms
absolutely (unconditionally) valid, 23, 34
problem of justifiability, 35
relatively (conditionally) valid, 34

occupation(s) as professionally-conducted means of earning a living, 306
new structure of qualification, 405f.
primary, 306f.
specialized, 306
occupational splitting, 306
OECD (Organization for Economic Cooperation and Development), 360
ontological difference, 171
order of international markets, to be structured in a participative manner, 631-633
overall control (planning) of the entire process, 608; in SMEs, 460, 541f.; in SstME / west, 556; according to Šik, 566
ownership of means of production:
cooperative, 471; in USSR, 486 n. 133
freely collective, cooperative, 558, 564
neutralized, 571-573
of natural resources, 585-588
private, 440, 512; in SstME / west, 557
state, in USSR, 209f.; in SstME / east, 564
workers' investment funds, 549-553, 571
ownership reform

ecology-oriented according to Binswanger, 584f., 607f.
humanly oriented according to Šik, 570-574, 605f.

Pareto principle, 208f.
participation, 193-198
person, 41, 60
personalism, 60, 105, 140
participation,
in the distribution of work, 404-407
in the global cooperation, 416-421
in the industrial cooperation, 402ff.
of the productive capital, 408
of the national product, 407-412
structural category, 402
Perestroika, 507ff.
personality, 40f.
physiocrats, 331, 334, 351
planification, 517f., 566
planning/planned economy, 72f.
centralized, see CPE
characteristic of the economy in general, 436
decentralized (ME), 441ff.
macroeconomic (global), 515f., 541, 556f., 566f., 609, 614
microeconomic, 476 and 484 (impossible in CPE), 560
of the framework or overall control, 460, 502, 522, 537, 555, 567
planning system (according to Galbraith), 499f.
politics of development, 105
polluter pays principle, 585
population explosion, 373f.
positivism/positivist, 18, 20
positivist resignation, 86, 90
power, economic, 364f., 370, 448, 451, 522, 544, 613
abuse of, 214
concentration, 544, 608; of multinational corporations, 365
control, 365, 564 n. 56,
monopoly of the Communist Party, 472f., 508
pragmatism, pragmatic, 24, 230f.
precautionary principle, 585
price stability, 425, 456, 615
principle of efficiency, 71, 225
principle of falsifiability, 84
principle of foundation, 83, 90f., 93
process of emancipation, 82, 155
productivity, 278, 405
definition, 278 n. 21
profit maximization, 68, 74; *see also* maximization
profit optimization, 591
profit principle, 68, 75, 444f., 477f., 527f.
according to Šik, 572 f.
from non-performance, 453
from performance, 453
in CPE, 448
profit sharing, 408, 550, 572
progress, 117
prohibition of interest, 234, 237f.
proletariat, 110f.
protectionism, 360, 623, 631, 642
purposes of the economy
ecological, 286-290
fundamental, 275-277, 282, 397f., 590f.
humane, 277-282, 282
relationality of, 290-295
social, 282-286

quality of life, 398, 424
question of money, 292

radicalness (as opposite to extremism), 188f.

rationality, economic, 22, 71, 72, 429-434; *see* also social-scientific correctness
rationalization
  generally, 277, 301, 405
  location-oriented, 305, 359
  product-oriented, 305, 306-308
  production-oriented, 305, 308-317
  sparing resources and the environment, 586
Reaganomics, 599
reason, 122, 204
reconciliation, 139, 188
reduction of working hours, 375f., 406, 588
regulatory (as planning or controlling instrument of ME), 505, 514, 521, 526
  goal-oriented, 614f., 639
  in the EC, 639
  in the global economy, 640
regulation (of the ME), 496
  not equal to reglementation, 599
related to knowledge of the subject as practical expertise or scientifically established, discipline-related knowledge ("Sachbezug"), 65
relationality, 181-189, 212
relativism/relativistic, 26f., 231
  ethical, 34f., 92, 94
  normative of situation ethics, 29
  pragmatist, 129
relativity, 29, 227
responsibility, 53, 54, 126, 141, 172
  individual, 51, 185
  for the environment, based on ownership of natural resources, 585
resurrection faith, 115f., 116f.
revolution/revolutionary, 131, 156
  industrial of the Middle Ages, 303
  industrial of the modern era, 303f., 315
  neolithic, 305
  theology of, 155
right of ownership, 180

Say's theorem, 391
scarcity (rules), 390, 395, 426, 436
self-alienation, 51, 60, 76,
  as fundamentally evil, 104
  of the proletariat according to Marx, 110f.
self-governance, 196
self-realization, 38, 41, 54, 55
shadow economy, 415
  USSR, 486 n. 133
sin
  as personal and structural evil, 105
  existence of unbelief, 109, 176
  see also evil
situation, 27f, 230, 237ff.
slavery, 80, 195
social ethics, 53, 59-61, 65, 67, 95
  Christological approach, 146-154, 161
  creation-theological approach, 138-147, 160
  existential-eschatological approach, 159-166
  historical-theological approach, 154-159, 160
  transcendental-eschatological approach, 130-138, 156, 160
  see also business and economic ethics; ethics
social obligation (of ownership), 558
socialism
  democratic-liberal, 217, 554

not equal to CPE, 463f., 511
really-existent, 108, 178
religious, 130-133, 137
value based, 296
social-scientific correctness, economic rationality ("Sachgemässheit"), social-scientifically correct, economically rational ("sachgemäss"), 66f, 70ff.
relational to the humanly just, 313, 394, 433, 506
society (conception of), 110, 202
solidarity (participative), 413-415
sovereignty of consumers, 351f.
stabilization of demands, 423f., 587
stabilization of population, 421f., 587, 636
stabilization of the environment, 424-427, 457,
indispensable purpose of the economy, 581
stabilization of the fluctuations of business cycles, 457, 614
state (different conceptions of K. Barth and E. Brunner), 152
subjectivism, 44, 91
subsistence economy, 419
super-ego, 19
system of coordination
of ME (= competition), 442-446, 452-455; dilemma, 476
of CPE (= central planning), 469- 483; dilemma, 476
system of order, economic, 177f.,
liberal market economy, 208
Rawls' option for a liberal market economy without excluding a socialist market economy, 217

Taylorism (assembly line), 310f., 312, 316, 323, 325, 401
technology, 43, 192
as an instrument of domination or service, 289
terms of trade (to the detriment of developing countries), 417
Thatcherism, 592-594, 599
Third Way (between capitalistic ME and communist CPE)
democratic (Swedish) ME, 545
humanly reformed ME, 565
social ME, 536
socialist ME, 554

UNCTAD (United Nations Conference on Trade and Development), 360, 639
unemployment, 375, 404-407
Universal Declarations of Human Rights, 79f.
UNO, 360
utilitarianism, 208f.
utility, economic, 22, 68
utility maximization, 47
utopia/utopian, 128, 177, 178, 232

value convictions
according to Albert, 85
according to Rawls, 210
according to Weisser, 91
value freeness or value neutrality of economics, 67, 430
value judgments, 85, 88f

wage
need 411f., 460f
performance, 411f., 459f.
war communism, 467
weighing of goods, 26
wealth, 282, 293, 384f., 594, 617
concept, 382 n. 201
welfare, 290, 384f.
concept, 382 n. 201
welfare economics, 68, 208f, 218

welfare state, 412-415
work, *see* labor
work humanization, 311ff., 323, 329, 401, 601
  job enlargement, 311, 324
  job enrichment, 312, 324
  job rotation, 324
  semi-autonomous work groups, 312, 325
work motivation
  intrinsic, 308, 309f., 329
workers' funds, 549-553, 571

PRINTED ON PERMANENT PAPER • IMPRIME SUR PAPIER PERMANENT • GEDRUKT OP DUURZAAM PAPIER - ISO 9706

N.V. PEETERS S.A., WAROTSTRAAT 50, B-3020 HERENT